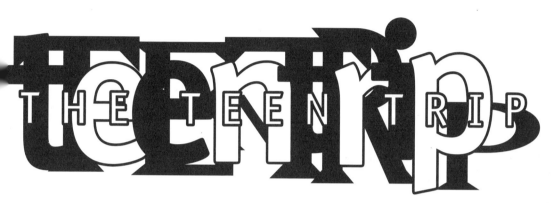

THE TEEN TRIP

The Complete Resource Guide

Gayle Kimball and
1,500 young authors

Other Books by Gayle Kimball
How to Survive Your Parents' Divorce:
Kids' Advice to Kids
Everything You Need to Know to Succeed After
College, ed.
50/50 Parenting
50/50 Marriage

Cover Design and Original Interior Concept Design
by Kevin Tamura-Murphy
Prepress by Hannah Sitzer, Blynda Barnett,
and Jacob Early Design

The Teen Trip:
The Complete Resource Guide
Copyright © 1997 by Gayle Kimball.
All rights reserved. Printed on recycled paper in the United States of America. For permission to reprint excerpts other than brief quotations in articles and reviews, or to send your comments, write to Equality Press, 42 Ranchita Way, Suite 5, Chico, CA 95928.
Cover art © 1996 by Kevin Tamura-Murphy. All rights reserved.

Teenagers—Life Skills Guides
Includes bibliographical references and index
ISBN 0-938795-26-0   p. cm.
Library of Congress Catalog Card Number 96-083772
HQ796.K56 1997

The Teen Trip

The Complete Resource Guide

Table of Contents

Dedication

Dedicated to my son Jed, voted the most outrageous and funny in his class, who teaches me about teenagers today, and Kelly Lynn Baylor, a contributing expert. Kelly dedicated her adult life to help countless teens realize their potential. Many call her "mom" because of her abundant unconditional love for them. In this book she shares the wisdom gained from years of welcoming teens into her home, "her family of the heart."

Acknowledgements

Thanks to the youth authors who shared their experiences and to my college students who distributed surveys, especially Liz Fellows, Corey Hirsch, Joe Horgan, and Kyle Clark.

Various teachers and youth leaders gave the survey questions to their students or youth organization, including: Judy Bordin, Julie Boyd, Kay Cohen, Ms. Filzen, Eric Geary, Susan Groves, Paul Galioni, Faye Hays, Leslie Howard, Janis Kartman, Leslie Mahan, Stephanie Marshall, John McKeown, Cindie Myers, Diane Roberts, Emily Robin, Marissa Sarabando, David Sepe, Cynthia Sharp Monteiro, Jane Reed, and Cheryl Schuler. Thanks to the English students of Zack Kincheloe and Charlie Helbling for their comments and additions. High school art teachers Paul Stephens, Mike Simpson, and Reta Rickmers linked me with their art students to draw the illustrations. Communications professor Bobbi Long introduced me to her students Kevin Murphy and Hannah Sitzer.

Outside of classroom assignments, teens Emma Jesse and Danisha Jefferson commented on the entire manuscript, and Brandon Blizman, Joey Gall, Jed Kimball-Hait, Kelley Klein, Jennifer Peterson, and Jason Ropp critiqued chapters. These adult experts critiqued various chapters: Peter Castle, M.A., Deanna Figueira, Dido Hasper, Dr. Roland Lamarine, Debbie Powers, R.N., and Carolyn Van Derpool. I'm appreciative of the insights shared by the over 30 experts who wrote sections of the book.

Thanks to copyeditor Phyllis Mannion, pre-press work—Hannah Sitzer, Jake Early and Blynda Barnett; typists Michele Emerson, Jeff Camozzi, and Jennifer Crumrine; cover copyeditor Dolores Blalock; and library assistant Jan Camozzi.

Comments from Readers

Parents and people who care about young people wish we could make growing up easy and painless. No one has all the answers, but *The Teen Trip* has most of them. It's a fun, interesting book that is guaranteed to make growing up easier. The book combines the wisdom of young people with Dr. Kimball's research for a useful and important resource. This book will be read, reread, underlined, marked, and loved by every young person who reads it. It is a vital resource that will make growing pains easier and growing up more fun.

—*Teen Voices* magazine editor Alison Amoroso and the teen board

The Teen Trip is a candid and thorough look at the potentially daunting issues faced by today's teenagers, refreshingly presented through the voices and stories of the teenagers themselves.

—Sylvia Ann Hewlett, Ph.D., author and President of the National Parenting Association

Not only does it provide provocative and useful information to teens but parents also stand to gain from the book. *The Teen Trip* succeeds at debunking many inaccurate and unfair stereotypes about today's youth with a multitude of candid opinions by those who know firsthand of the painful pressures and opportunities that face their generation. I think a lot of adults who are trying to figure out how to collaborate with youth will be eager to read this book.

—Wendy Schaetzel Lesko, director of the national Activism 2000 Project and author of *No Kidding Around! America's Young Activists Are Changing Our World & You Can Too*

The Teen Trip provides a peer support group for teens, and any one of the sections can spark in-depth discussion between youth and adults who care about them. Adults who work with teens, or parent them, will gain new insights, new information, and a wealth of comprehensive resources to explore with young people.

—Charlie Helbling, teacher, Whitfield School, St. Louis

This book offers valuable knowledge from across the generations: Personal stories from teens and research from the author (a professor and mother of a teenager) combine to provide down-to-earth and practical advice any teen can relate to. Not only a reference tool, this book serves teens by providing them a unique forum to discuss their issues and common experiences. Without preaching or judgment, it tackles private problems in a straightforward and honest way.

—Paula Kamen, author of *Feminist Fatale: Voices from the 'twenty-something generation'*...

High School Students' Comments from California and Missouri

It's time someone wrote a book that teens can actually use and get help from.
—Ashley

The book has a two-sided feel which neither encourages or discourages teens to do whatever. It's a good book.
—Aimery

Readers will find out that it includes a lot of things that teenagers want to know about, like colleges or getting a job.
—Tyler

I'd read this book any time I had trouble with my feelings and I am not saying that to get a good grade.
—John

One heck of a book.
—Ryan

We like the stories the teenagers told. They were fun to read and exciting; you could almost picture them in real life.
—Erica, Jeff, and Pearl

This is great. Teens these days need someone they can talk to, but if they don't, this book will help.
—Janna

The book lets us know that feelings are real and not just some dumb word and will help us respond better in certain situations.
—Ryan, Josh, Tyler, and Kent

This book could definitely help many teenagers and give them many solutions to the problems we all have to deal with at some time or another.
—Betsy, Fernando, Nathan, and Andrew

Very insightful into the innermost feelings of teenagers. It helped us realize that maybe other people have problems just like ours. We could really relate to the kids who spoke about the different topics. We thought the information given to us about how to deal with the problems helped a great deal.
—Whitfield School students

Becoming an adult and leaving childhood is not the easiest thing to do. You try to be an adult but you're not mature enough or don't have the experience to know what to do. You may act like a child, but you find it not as fun and really immature. As a teen you do a lot of experimenting. You may get into trouble, but how are you supposed to learn if you don't make mistakes? Along the way to adulthood you have people to help you, but you do most of the work and you are your own best teacher. Find someone with a similar situation and share your feelings so you know that you are not the only one going through this.
—Anita, 18, Wisconsin

[I guarantee you'll find situations similar to yours in this book; if not, please write to me.]

Introduction

Whew! You experience pressure to do well in school, prepare for a career, decide on your own values in the face of strong peer pressure, establish your place in a circle of friends, begin romantic relationships, explore sexual feelings, cope with adult stereotypes of teens as troublemakers, establish a new balance of power with your parents, learn independence, perhaps compete in sports and perform in the arts, and earn money.

At a time when teen drug use, sexual activity, STDs (sexually transmitted diseases), and violence are on the increase, parents are away from home more often than in earlier generations. Long work hours, the need for both parents to work, and the high divorce rate take them out of the home. These facts indicate that it's especially challenging to make the journey from childhood to adulthood today.

Clif, 16, California, explains:

> *Teens are faced with an odd situation. They must make the transition from being a child to being a responsible adult. With no official initiation which addresses all aspects of adulthood clearly, teens are forced to initiate themselves and each other. They do this blindly in most instances, with no clear idea of what they intend or how to go about it.*

To assist in your trip to adulthood, I asked young people (mostly in the U.S.) to describe their main issues and how they cope, and then compiled all the information I could find to respond to their concerns. I see this book as a "juicy" encyclopedia, full of facts and resources, but also intriguing to read about your peers' actual experiences. You'll see that you're not alone in your feelings and see what works.

Brian, a survey respondent from Wisconsin, states the goal of the book well:

> *Information should cover issues that teens have to deal with, but many times don't have the resources to answer their questions. Kids are normally bombarded with information about not smoking or taking drugs, deciding on a career, etc. Kids need to know where they can get information about sexuality, physical challenges, depression, poor self-image, families, what to do if someone they know has a drinking or drug problem, etc. I have seen little information that is not extremely biased one way or another.*
>
> *Kids need to find out where they can find out FACTS so that they can make decisions on their own. Kids are not as dumb as many adults make them out to be. If given information, they are very capable of making smart decisions.*

How This Book Works

Each chapter explores a topic, such as your body, and is divided into sections organized alphabetically—Acne to Wellness. Each section usually includes three parts: information, quotes from youth, and resources for further exploration. Resources are listed in this order: telephone helplines, organizations, books, and Internet sources. The type style changes to indicate *student voices*, my information, or **adult experts**.

I envision that you will use the book over time to look up a particular topic as it becomes important to you, rather than read an entire chapter at a time. For example, if you want to find out about how to deal with the breakup of a relationship, look under "B" in the peers chapter, or look in the index in the back to find the location of a topic, or at the table of contents at the beginning of each chapter.

Students suggest you write your reactions to what you read, set goals, and formulate questions to explore in a journal. You might want to use a beat-up old notebook or a hiding place so you don't have to worry about someone else reading your private thoughts. Your journal should be a safe place where you don't have to censor your feelings, drawings, and souvenirs. The act of writing and rereading later will help you learn about yourself, clear out your feelings, and clarify your thinking. You might want to continue your dialogue with a friend or family member.

In the resource lists, if an 800 toll-free number is not current, call the 800 information number at 1-800-555-1212 and give the operator the name of the organization. To find books listed in the resource sections, see your librarian, or a book store may be able to order the book if it's not on the shelves. (A listing of a resource doesn't mean I recommend it.) Regarding several style details readers commented on, I spelled out numbers under 10 only, so that's why you may see numerals and words in the same sentence. When you see et al. in the resources, it stands for additional authors not listed.

I would like to hear from you about information, experiences, and insights you'd like to add to a later edition of this book. Please write to: Gayle Kimball, Sociology Dept. 445, CSUC, Chico, CA 95929 or e-mail gkimball@oavax.csuchico.edu.

The Authors

The books I've written reflect my life stages: high school teacher, college professor, partner, and parent. My son Jed is now a teenager and, as I learned about the issues he and his friends face, I realized the need to provide teens with a one-stop guidebook. I couldn't find an inclusive book for teens of both sexes, ranging from how to get good grades, to sex education, to drugs, so I wrote *The Teen Trip*. I learned a lot in the process and I've taught many different subjects since I was 21, so I expect you'll learn new information too. Between the well over 1,500 contributors to this book, I trust we've provided useful information to assist you on your journey to adulthood.

The heart of *The Teen Trip* is the youth authors. I contacted over 1,500 people in their teens and 20s, from 1994 to 1996. My sources were international Internet discussion groups; students at California State University, Chico, where I teach; and high school teachers and youth group leaders around the country (California, Colorado, Connecticut, Illinois, Louisiana, Missouri, North and South Dakotas, Massachusetts, New York, Ohio, Tennessee, Texas, Virginia, Washington, and Wisconsin). I also interviewed youth activists in various states, usually on the telephone, and include their last names.

Youth answered these survey questions:

1) What is the most difficult challenge you've faced as a teen?

2) What helped you to cope with this challenge? What advice would you offer to someone younger who is facing the same problem?

3) What other issues should be included in a resource book for teens? (You might start your journaling now by answering these questions and comparing your responses with theirs.)

I edited students' responses for spelling and punctuation and deleted parts. I also gave a longer survey to my students, their friends, and Internet respondents. See the Appendix for a more detailed profile of the youth and their issues. The main messages in the survey responses are (1) be true to yourself, do what you think is right, and resist peer pressure; (2) if you have a problem, tell someone you trust about it. Don't try to ignore it.

High school students in English classes at the Whitfield School in St. Louis, Missouri, (Charlie Helbling, teacher), and Chico High West students in California (Zack Kincheloe), critiqued a draft of *The Teen Trip*, as did other teens listed in the acknowledgments. I responded to their questions and added some of their comments to the book, where they're referred to as "readers." High school students also drew the illustrations. Over 30 adult experts added information to some of the sections and others critiqued various chapters.

Teens Today

Youth Power! UNICEF estimates that the year 2000 marks the first time when kids under 18 comprise one half of the world's population! In 1992, 24 million teenagers lived in the U.S. (nine percent of the population). A record high of 52 million students were enrolled in U.S. schools in 1996 and the number of teens will increase in the next decade.

Our social environment makes this is an especially challenging time to grow up. About half of young people will live in single parent families before they reach age 18. It's difficult to find a well-paid job. The U.S. has the highest teen pregnancy and birth rates of all the industrial nations. STDs, including AIDS, are spreading fast among young people. Drugs and alcohol are easily available. Adolescent crime is increasing and more teens die from murder and suicide than natural causes. Too many schools are unsafe places.

The Children's Defense Fund (an advocacy organization in Washington, DC) reports that every day in the U.S.:

- 6 children or youth commit suicide

- 15 children are killed by firearms

- 165 youth are arrested for drug offenses

- 322 youth are arrested for drinking or drunk driving

- 342 youth are arrested for violent crimes

- 1,234 children run away from home

- 2,660 children are born into poverty

- 2,781 teenagers get pregnant and 1,407 give birth

- 2,833 students drop out of school

- 2,860 children experience their parents' divorce

- 8,493 children are reported abused or neglected

- 13,076 youth are suspended from school

- 135,000 children bring guns to school.

To insure a brighter future, we need to spend as much thought, energy, and money developing programs for youth as we do building prisons, roads, and weaponry. Healthy, well-educated youth are the real defense system that keeps a country strong. I encourage you to become an activist in your community, using the skills described in Chapter 11.

Two Teens and Their Issues

The book is built around short quotes from many young people, so here is one section that focuses more fully on two of the authors. I named the issues they raise in brackets and invite you respond in your journal to the concerns you currently share.

—Jeremy, 15, Saskatchewan, Canada

[Pressure] *The most difficult thing to overcome in life is all of the pressures. Some can just put them on the back burner and cruise through life, but most can't. I haven't had the best life, regardless of what I have been given and what I have taken. My family is financially secure, with no problems within. What has challenged me so far is basic pressure.*

[Establishing your individual identity] *I am expected to get good grades, told not to have sex, told not to smoke, told not to drink, told this and that. I do not want to live up to my parents' and teachers' expectations, I want to live my life the way I want to. I do not want to be protected from making mistakes; if I don't, I will never learn. Another big problem is facing those who pressure me. I have always been too shy or afraid to tell my parents how I feel about issues.*

[Prejudice] *I have lived in many different cities, but the most difficult part of my life was when I lived in Chicago when I was about 10. I spent the two longest years of my life there. The second I entered my new school, I was branded a loser. The people there were all completely prejudiced against Canadians. I had nothing in common with anyone; I never fit in. When I moved back to Canada, I was once again a part of a group. I grew taller (over six feet), which helped my game of basketball, and I once again had things in common with my friends.*

[Popularity] *Now, I am considered to be very popular (not trying to sound conceited). Although, as some of my friendships progressed, many relationships fell apart.* [Dating] *I am very interested in one girl, but she is taken and I don't have the heart to interrupt their relationship—not while she's happy. I wondered about how people would react if I told them how I feel, so a while ago, I did tell my girlfriend how I felt; she said that she cared but she turned out to be a fake. She couldn't have cared less about it all.*

[Real friends] *My family doesn't understand (I would tell my parents, but they are such a trivial pair, they can't relate, and they have natural power over me). I have basically one friend I can talk to—Linn. We're always there for each other, we can trust each other, and she's always understanding and knows the right thing to say, and I love her for it.*

Her boyfriend just dumped her and he isn't exactly a caring guy. He used her, he's continuing to use her, he makes her feel guilty for being friends with me (I went out with her for a short time, he lied to her, and convinced her to go out with him), and he basically treats her like shit. I can't remember the last time I've gone a full day without hearing her cry because she was upset over him. It kills me to see him do this to her and not be able to do anything about it. This guy also hit on my last girlfriend and caused us to break up in spite. He's ruining my friendships, and if I do anything to retaliate or defend myself, at least one person sees me as the bad guy. I can't win.

[Drugs] *I have begun to drink and smoke also. It makes me feel good when I do it; I do like it, but deep down I feel that I have let people down by doing so. I know I shouldn't feel this way but I can't help it.*

[Sports] *I have had many other problems also, not being able to trust people whom I had considered friends, not succeeding in basketball the way I would like, no matter how hard I tried. I no longer play much; I missed a three-pointer for the championship which crushed me. My parents tell me that whatever hobby I take up, I must stick with (golf, hockey cards), even if I would only like to participate at a leisurely pace.*

[Self-esteem] *I really have low self-esteem; I have no will-power (I keep trying to lift weights regularly but I just can't), even* though people tell me otherwise. I did quit smoking; it just didn't appeal to me anymore. One good step forward I guess. I am also trying to play basketball regularly again; I figure if I try hard enough I can make senior boys' next year. I am trying to keep myself busy; the more stuff I have to occupy my thoughts, the less I worry, I guess.

[Suicide] I have thought about suicide a few times, but what has kept me going is the beautiful music of Pearl Jam. [Music] Eddie Vedder is my idol. He came from a much worse environment than me and look at him—a superstar (although it isn't exactly the life he wishes to have). The lyrics are deep and meaningful, the sound is amazing, and the intensity with which they play with is unbelievable. "Jeremy" was the first song I heard and I was hooked. It is a great song but it meant even more to me when I found out about Jeremy Wade Delle, the real teen who killed himself. From the moment I heard that, I listened and paid more attention to the lyrics and looked for a deeper meaning. What I found was amazing—rape, repression, suicide—all real issues that ended up facing me at one time or another.

This may sound a little weird, but it's true. I know that my problems are very minimal and that others have it MUCH worse than me, but it's not always the problems that push people to the edge, it's their inability to deal with them. As for what should be put in the book, just the truth and what people have told you worked. [Values] They should pick a role model, whether it be a parent, a sports star, a musician—whatever, but someone who means something to them. Live life the way you want to, not the way you are told to. Don't be afraid to make mistakes, you learn from them. Remember that a kick in the rear is a step forward, and live life to the fullest; don't waste it just to please someone. One more thing that helped me is quotes. I have several pages of quotes by people I am interested in.

All that's sacred comes from youth.
—Eddie Vedder

I don't care what they say, I'm still gonna make it.
— Arthur Agee, "Hoop Dreams"

You know what the Mexicans say about the Pacific? They say it has no memory. That's where I want to live the rest of my life, a warm place with no memory.
— Andrew Defreine, "The Shawshank Redemption"

As for Jennifer's story, I've read it many times. Sometimes it feels really good to know that I'm not the only one. Everyday it seems like everyone around me is happy and I'm the only one with problems, but I guess some of those smiles are facades.

—Jennifer, 16, Texas

[Prejudice] I am a teenager, incomprehensible, mysterious, troubled, dangerous, stereotyped unfairly in an unjust and biased *world.* [Parents] *I must deal with my parents, who do not understand me anymore, but still pretend that I am the child I once was, free and innocent, without adultish complexities. I must deal with my need for peace, solitude, and thoughts that the rest of the screaming, roaring highway of the world cannot accept.*

[Adult world] *I must deal with the media and its tilted, slanted portrayals of life. I must deal with the painful reality dawning on me that I do not understand the workings of the world: taxes, real estate, credit cards, and crime prevention. I must deal with my sister, poor child, who will enter high school next year in the midst of the mess of changes.* [Racism] *And I must deal with the racial tension imposed upon me every day, all day, at school.* [Grades] *Is it no wonder my grades are falling?*

[Irritation with adults] *I don't understand why I am so quickly frustrated with my elders. I used to love them all and join family activities enthusiastically, but now I would just as soon stay home. My cousin was like that. He became a rumor, a ghost. He turned vegetarian, shaved his hair, and wore a ponytail. I avoid my family now, whenever possible, and am happy to retreat to my room with my thoughts and my books, in peace and quiet. I think I understand him now. To me, the adults just seem so old and slow. I can see the same ideas starting to appear in my sister's mind. She gets angry with Mom very easily. She wants to do what she wants to do, but Mom has other ideas.*

[Establishing independence] *I know my limits now and the extent of my own powers. I don't try to break laws and I don't try to hurt people. I am learning to be independent and to make choices for myself. I think most teens do this, at one point or another. My mom still tries to control my sister and me. She reads the backs of movies we rent and books we read, but there's not much she can do about it. She won't let me learn to drive, but Dad helped me get a learner's permit and he's teaching me. He seems to understand I've grown wings, and he's helping me fly, carefully, so I don't kill myself.*

The major issues raised by the over 1,500 other young people I surveyed were similar to Jennifer's and Jeremy's, and perhaps to yours. The top vote getters were peer pressure around drugs and sex, getting along with peers and parents, and school success. Please write to me about your concerns.

Directionless Lately

—Phoebe Ambrosia, 16

I think of all the things
I could have done
and could have said
if I had enrolled in
ballet or soccer when I was three.
Then maybe now
I would be a star.
It's strange to wonder who you are
and wonder
if you'll ever be good at who you want to be.

.

But now I find
I'm wandering
in the middle
somewhere
between innocence and sexiness
ignorance and light
between arrogance and meekness.
And all I feel
right now
is that—

.

No one really knows
me.
In a room full of my 'friends'
they only recognize my face.
And, when pressed,
they know my name.
But how can I criticize
when I am unsure of my own place?

Chapter 1

Vashti O'Donnell

Body

A t a time when your body is rapidly changing, people's responses to you change as well. The media tell you, above all else, to be attractive and conform to their definitions of sexy. No wonder eating disorders and sports injuries are so common among teenagers trying to live up to someone else's standards of femininity or masculinity. This chapter provides some suggestions about how to be healthy and promote vibrant wellness, especially important in an era when U.S. child health measures score a pitiful D minus.

Acne

I had extremely bad spots on my face for a LONG time, and nothing was working towards getting rid of them. I finally went to the doctor with my Mum, and she prescribed some antibiotics that I had to take for about a year or more to help my skin calm down. She said that they weren't caused by eating too much chocolate or sweets and that it wasn't that I hadn't kept my skin clean; it was just something to do with my hormones. [Fatty foods don't cause acne but can make it worse.]

Well, the medicine didn't have much effect at first, but after a while, the redness slowly went away and then, slowly but surely, the spots just disappeared. I am very glad I went to the doctor and I would advise anyone in the same situation to do the same. Now I have OK skin and it's getting better by the day!

—Adrienne, 14, England

Most teenagers (80 percent) have to deal with acne at some point, more boys than girls because of male hormones. Acne begins when ducts of the oil glands plug with dead skin cells, sebum (a fatty lubricant secreted by skin glands), and bacteria. A pimple forms when white blood cells create pus, an inflamed condition. A non-inflamed condition occurs when a whitehead covers the blocked duct and it turns into a blackhead when oxidized (combined with oxygen). The duct continues to produce oils that push against the whitehead, causing a break in the duct walls. This attracts white blood cells as the fluids escape into the surrounding tissue. If the duct walls rupture in deeper skin layers, a cyst may form. The larger the pustule, the more chance of scarring, so see a dermatologist.

To treat acne, wash your face several times a day with a mild water-soluble cleaner followed by an oil-free moisturizer, and shampoo often. Don't squeeze pimples as this can cause scarring. Keep your blood circulating well by exercising and drinking lots of water. A healthy diet helps, as does sleeping eight to ten hours a night (see the section on wellness), reducing stress, and avoiding foods high in iodines (processed foods, salty snacks, etc.). Girls who use make-up should use water-based rather than oil-based make-up; girls taking birth control pills should consult with their doctors about acne and proper pill dosage. Excessive antibiotic use can cause excessive yeast in the digestive system and acne.

Medications commonly contain keratolytics which increase the shedding of oils and remove the top layers of skin to help prevent the formation of whiteheads and blackheads. This can be irritating for sensitive skin. Nonprescription medications should contain at least 2.5 percent benzoyl peroxide which increases the growth rate of cells by irritating them. Never treat your skin more than twice a day and use moisturizer such as aloe vera gel to prevent more oil production: Facials with glycolic acid and alphahydroxy acis are gentle exfoliators. Avoid granular scrubs, scrubbing the skin, harsh astringents, and heat as irritating to the skin. The mineral zinc is healing but is often lacking in diets of teens with acne.

Nutrition specialist Donald Payne reports a high success rate with taking a red clover combination of herbs as a blood cleanser—taking a bottle of capsules every three months or so, followed by an herbal skin formula of root herbs such as burdock and dandelion to neutralize the acids in the blood. He recommends not eating chocolate, sugar, soft drinks, or red meat, and eating five to seven servings of vegetable a day.

—Joey, 15, California

Acne has always played a major part in my self-confidence while growing up. Ever since puberty, I've been self-conscious about zits and pimples, especially when swimming around girls, because I'd get them on my face and back. Taking care of your body contributes a lot to fighting the acne war and boosts your confidence also. I didn't have much self-confidence for years, because I just didn't like myself, so I didn't take care of myself. Once I started taking care of myself, which was just showering everyday and washing my face twice every day, I noticed the acne going down. Of course, I still have pimples, I'm 15, but they don't phase my confidence and they shouldn't phase yours either.

—Tim, 21, California

The biggest problem I had as a teen was a bad acne problem. To me, I felt I was unattractive. I coped by taking myself out of the high school dating pool, then going through a variety of acne drugs and ending with the powerful Accutane. Have confidence in yourself.

Body Image

Boys' body image problems are when I'm in PE and I can't lift as much weight, or do a pull-up, or changing in front of everyone when I don't like my body.

—David, 15, Missouri

It's hard trying to fit in with the crowd, have the coolest most popular friends, and stay skinny and pretty so the guys will like you.

—Alice, 15, California

Forty percent of high school girls have a negative body image, compared to 15 percent of boys. Millions of children know the story of "The Little Mermaid" who painfully changes her body in order to please a man, just as 78 percent of high school girls are unhappy with their bodies by age 18. Many underweight women think they are too fat and dieting is big business. Estimates are that Americans spent $33 billion on diets and diet-related services in 1990, plus over $one million on cosmetic surgery. Cosmetics are a $20 billion industry worldwide. The amount spent on cosmetics every year in the U.S. could buy three times the amount of day care offered by the U.S. government, 2,000 women's health clinics, or 33,000 battered women's shelters.

A survey of 8th grade girls in Boston found that only 16 percent were not self-conscious about their bodies and over one-quarter believed that others considered them unattractive. This feeling was linked to low self-esteem (Sumru Erkut and Fern Marx, "Raising Competent Girls," Wellesley Center for Research on Women, 1995).

Young men tend to want to be bigger and young women tend to want to be smaller. What does this say about our sense of ourselves? Female fashion models weigh almost one-fourth less than the average woman. The emphasis on thinness has increased over time; Marilyn Monroe would be told she was much too fat if she walked into a modeling agency today. As a result, two-thirds of teen girls are trying to lose weight.

Studies consistently show that girls' self-esteem drops during puberty when they start to gain weight and curves. Looking at European American girls, 55 percent of elementary school girls report, "I'm happy the way I am," but only 29 percent feel the same in junior high, and 22 percent in high school. For Latinas, the figures are 68 percent in elementary school, 54 percent in junior high, and 30 percent in high school. African American girls have higher self-esteem as 58 percent are happy with themselves in high school. Researchers believe it's because they don't try to fit into the white beauty standard (The American Association of University Women report "How Schools Shortchange Girls"). However, Danisha comments from Seattle,

I think this is only true of body figure, but as far as everything else goes (i.e., hair, eyes, features), I disagree. African American female teenagers are getting their hair straightened every other week, getting blue or green colored contacts, bleaching their skin, and trying to do anything else in their power to alter their characteristics.

The image of ideal female beauty changes in order to sell new clothes and accessories and keep women in their place. In the mid 19th century, the hourglass figure was created with corsets, hoop skirts, and bustles, which prevented much movement. Being on a pedestal is confining. The opposite look characterized the boyish flapper era of the 20s when breasts were bound to look flat, and waists were hidden by dresses sashed at the hips. During World War II, when women went to work in factories, masculine shoulder pads, suits, and hats were in. In reaction, the 50s were a decade of curvy women like Marilyn Monroe in low-cut dresses, followed by starved-looking Twiggy in the 60s, and the 90s alternated between athletic, busty models and the anorexic waif. Why try to keep up with a standard that is always changing, especially when it's an illusion created by photographers, make-up artists, and computer-generated changes? In real life, even the models don't look like their pictures.

Authors Naomi Wolf and Susan Faludi maintain that the intent is to keep women powerless through self-doubt and to make them concentrate on appearance rather than action. Think about this point—it has deep implications. The ideal is to create your own look, appreciate your unique body, and nurture it with exercise, regular sleep, positive thinking, and natural foods (see the wellness section).

Very little is written about how young men feel about looking attractive, but a *GQ* magazine survey of men under the age of 25 reported they average 53 minutes a day arranging their hair and clothes. In this book the boys comment about their sports performance and injuries more than body image. Do you agree guys get more pressure to perform athletically and be buff? Steroid use suggests some boys also try to alter their bodies to fit an unrealistic standard.

Body image has more impact than apparent at first thought. Take time to define your attitude toward your appearance and its affect on your confidence. I'd like to hear from guys about this issue, since most of the research is about young women's body images.

—Amanda, 14, Virginia

I think one of the hardest challenges for young people is accepting your own self and not comparing yourself to or striving to be like others. I just came back from a ballet festival where I was really intimidated by the many beautiful dancers with collar bones so defined, protruding from their bodies.

My mom, with her amazing maternal instincts, talked to me beforehand and told me that you do not have to have every bone sticking out to be a good dancer. She also said that often the longing to be skinny only leads to a big heap of trouble.

Try to avoid, at all costs, comparing yourself to others. I think weight is a big thing on people's minds today. You shouldn't let your weight take control, where it becomes the main focus and you want to be skinnier. Then when you achieve that weight, you want to be more thin and the ultimate destruction is immense.

—Joey, 15, California

You can't be completely satisfied with your body and the way you dress until you know yourself and like yourself. I struggled with an identity problem for about a year. I didn't know how I should dress or act, so I tried different things, such as becoming a skater (didn't work) and dressing Gothic (all in black; didn't like that too much either). It wasn't until my sophomore year that I just became myself and that was perfect.

—Jennifer, 15, California

I always buy fashion magazines to keep up with trends, but by the time I get a new magazine, the trends have changed. I can't keep up. I'm only trying to be cool like everyone else, although I know if I don't have a pair of Guess jeans, somebody will talk to me, be friends with me—maybe.

—Jed, 16, California

I've always been skinny. I like being skinny. For some people this would be a reason for insecurity, and I'll admit for a while it was for me, too. But I realized I only get one body, so I should accept it and love it.

I figure if someone is willing to disregard you as a friend because of the way you look, they aren't worth it. The only standards I should meet are my own. An exercise is to try and look at yourself in the mirror, tell your reflection you love it, and smile while you are saying it. I know it sounds dumb, but it works.

I've always been good at sports and very coordinated, so I have no reason to be insecure. Sure, there are those people who feel they are doing you a favor by telling you how skinny you are, as if I didn't know, but I just say thank you. The good thing about bodies is they are changeable, and if you aren't happy about the way you look or how your body is, then change it. Work out, eat right, exercise, and make the change happen. It will if you work hard enough.

—Elena, 18, Illinois

Here's some body image activities that I did in the eating disorders program at the hospital, with my ideas added.

1. Make a list of 55 positive things about yourself.

2. Make a list of 50 ways to take care of yourself. They should be things that you enjoy and that make you feel good, including getting at least eight hours of sleep a night and eating a balanced, sufficient diet that includes foods you enjoy. Other ideas are coloring with crayons, taking a walk, whatever.

3. Keep a journal of your thoughts and feelings, insights, moods, dreams, and life events.

4. Build a strong support system that consists of people who empathize with you, can be trusted, affirm your individuality and strengths, play with you, are open-minded, and accept your ups and downs without being judgmental.

5. Replace body hate with body love: Speak out against media images of the body, be in touch with how your body feels and meet its needs, don't weigh yourself or obsess about your weight, focus on parts of your body that you like, enjoy the way your body can move, tell yourself how beautiful you are, and hang around with people who foster a good body image.

6. Write a love poem or letter about the part(s) of your body you hate most. You don't have to believe it, but tell the world how beautiful this part of your body is. Hang this poem on your mirror or someplace where you'll read it a lot.

7. Picture your naked body in your head without judgment. Imagine that the different parts have feelings. Imagine how they feel after all the abuse you've put them through. Write a dialogue of what this part would say to you if it could talk. Then do something loving for this part of the body every day of the week.

8. Think of a part of your body that you like (it can be anything, even your pinkie finger), then think of a part of your body you hate. Write why you feel the way you do about these parts, their advantages and disadvantages. Then write a dialogue between the two about how they feel about how they're treated, about you, and about their purposes. Focus on the positive purposes of each body part and remember them.

9. Write five negative thoughts you have about your body, your weight, and food. For each of these thoughts, write an affirmation to tell yourself the next time you have these thoughts.

10. Identify three situations each that make you sad, angry, left out/lonely, and something else you feel a lot. Then think of an emotional outlet for each of these situations that doesn't hurt you or anyone else.

—Anne, 19, Ohio

I'm overweight and anything but a knockout. I've spent most of my time trying to avoid all situations where my looks would be critiqued. I've developed a sort of selective hearing so I don't have to acknowledge the hurtful comments of others. You know, like when your mom says ignore them and they'll stop. This has been hard to control even as I have become more comfortable with my self-image. Most of the time, I find myself pretending not to hear what people are saying to me so I can assess the comment before having to reply.

My advice to someone younger who has yet to go through the teen years is being proud and confident of one's self can go a long way in convincing others of your worth. Don't forget to remind younger girls of their value even without a boyfriend. I've seen a lot of my girlfriends from high school beat themselves up for not having one. It shouldn't be the only thing that makes a girl special.

—Lisa, 19, Washington

Feeling good about yourself and your body? I don't think there's an easy answer. The best I can come up with is avoiding "meat-market" type situations where you're looked over by a group of the opposite sex. If you look for a partner who likes and respects you, rather than someone who finds you attractive from across the room, you'll probably spend less time worrying about your appearance to the exclusion of all else. Also, dressing up, however you do it, is supposed to be fun, not something you do because you have to. Any attention you pay to clothing, hair, whatever, is something you are doing for yourself, because it makes YOU feel good. The attention it gets you is a bonus, not the goal. If it feels like a job, it's time to tone it down or change it.

—Ralph, 21, California

Being too small to play sports like football and basketball was my most difficult challenge as a teen. I tried steroids but I didn't like how it made me feel. It's not worth it. I wasn't able to get on the teams, but I still played after school with my friends.

—Jennifer, 21, California

When I'm around other women, I find myself thinking, how does my body compare to hers? Is her skin clearer than mine? Am I thinner than her? My friend noticed how she and her high school basketball teammates' legs jiggled when running down the court. When she stopped eating, her legs began to slim and jiggle less. She got compliments which reinforced her behavior. Not only did her overall muscle mass decrease, even as an athlete, but she experienced hair loss, and her naturally dark skin turned a yellowish hue because she ate only oranges.

—Melissa, 22, California

Remember that girls in magazines are air-brushed. No one is perfect and there are more bodies like yours than perfect ones. [Who defines what's perfect? This unrealistic image does not equate with a healthy body.] Don't ever forget that you're a good, worthwhile person who deserves the best.

—Jennifer, 25, Texas

I find that exercise makes me feel a lot better about my body, not to lose weight or make myself perfect, but to experience my body as part of me that's capable of doing things, not just being looked at and judged.

Most importantly, always keep in mind that you ultimately control your body, your mind, and your life. Take care of yourself emotionally and physically, and don't worry too much about what other people think you should be.

—Lisa, 25, California

Surround yourself with positive influences. Reinforce positive ideas. Be proud of your uniqueness. Celebrate it. If you are not happy with your body, it is possible you are not happy emotionally. Examine those feelings and get some form of assistance in resolving them. If you still aren't happy with your body, respond with positive healthy actions, such as consulting a physician for a proper plan for changing your daily diet. Exercise regularly as the brain chemicals produced, called endorphins, cause a positive, energetic feeling.

—Rebecca, 25, California

Your body is YOUR BODY, unique in its shape and beauty and that's good. Julia Roberts' character in Pretty Woman says the simplest, most profound thing when talking about her self-esteem: "It's easier to believe the bad stuff." It seems no matter how many times your mom or your best friend tells you you're BEAUTIFUL, some one can make a crack about your nose and that's it: You're the most repulsive thing to ever walk down main hall. I'm not trivializing this: I still live with the "bad stuff" that's been said to me. Somehow we've got to learn to trust the trustworthy people and make the opinions of the right people matter.

—Stephanie, 26, Oregon

The media image of sexy, THIN women had a great impact on me (and still does) and also the double standard for women (in every area). I've had problems with self-esteem and self-confidence and dealt with it by being a loner instead of being competitive and assertive (even though I was also very independent and mature).

It has taken me years to deal with all the ideas about women that I was indoctrinated with as a teen. I think the most devastating issue is concerning our bodies. I had a perfectly fine body, but was always feeling too fat, too this, too that. I never just enjoyed being myself and loving my body. Looking back at photos, I wonder what I was thinking! I had some tendencies to eating disorders, but because I always wanted to be mature and in control of my life, I wouldn't let an eating disorder take control of me (interestingly enough, just this past year I have become addicted to food and have developed a serious, compulsive eating habit).

Looking back I would advise any teenager to look for the answers they are seeking instead of being quiet. Ask people, read books, talk to friends—even if it is embarrassing or you feel stupid. Education is so important, especially when it comes to personal issues. We live in a society in which teens are not educated about sex even though it's so important.

Girls especially need to be aware of their own sexual desires and not just be sexual to get attention from boys. Girls need to have ways to feel good about their bodies in other ways than just their looks. They should be complimented on achievements and not how their hair looks or how their dress fits. I think it's important for girls to challenge what they learn in school and how they are treated by males (and females).

Body Image Books

Kathy Bowen-Woodward. *Coping with a Negative Body Image*. NY: Rosen Publishing Group, 1989.

Susan Douglas. *Where the Girls Are: Growing Up Female with the Mass Media*. NY: Random House, 1996.

Susan Faludi. *Backlash: The Undeclared War Against Women*. NY: Dial/Doubleday Press, 1991. (An author in her 20s, she includes chapters on the beauty industry and media's impact on women's power.)

Rita Freedman. *Beauty Bound*. Lexington, MA: D.C. Heath, 1986. *BodyLove: Learning to Like Our Looks and Ourselves*. NY: Harper Collins, 1990.

Barbara McFarland and T. Baker-Baumann. *Shame and Body Image, Culture and the Compulsive Eater*. Deerfield Beach, FL: Health Communications, 1990.

Naomi Wolf. *The Beauty Myth: How Images of Beauty Are Used Against Women*. NY: Anchor Press, 1992. (A powerful book written by a woman in her 20s, it shows how body image oppresses women.)

Dieting

One of the most difficult challenges I've faced as a teen is when people look at you just because there is a flaw in your appearance. As a younger teenager I was overweight and fat. The only way I coped with this challenge was with moral support from my parents and seeing the results of exercising which made me want to keep losing the weight. The advice I would give to someone facing the same challenge is to keep exercising, cut down on your fat intake, and don't let the problem lower your self-esteem.

—Duane, 16, Illinois

A whopping 61 percent of teenage girls say they have dieted, compared to 28 percent of boys. The number one wish for girls ages 11 to 17 is to be thinner, rather than get A's or be the lead in the school play! Seventy percent of normal weight women want to be thinner and almost one-quarter of underweight women think they are overweight.

Female dieters should remember that the average model's weight is at least 20 percent less than the recommended pounds for her height, so trying to match her skinniness is both unrealistic and perhaps unhealthy. Most diets fail in the long run since weight loss requires practicing a new lifestyle rather than just eating grapefruit for two weeks.

—Judith Eberhart, counselor

The average woman goes on one and one-half diets per year. Severely restricted calorie intake and diets which are not nutritionally balanced deny the body nutrients and change its chemical composition. A study at the Mayo Clinic observed a group of emotionally healthy young women who had no need to lose weight but volunteered to live together in a clinic under supervision and eat a restricted diet for an extended period of time. Before three months had passed, the women's personalities underwent startling changes. They began to quarrel endlessly with one another. They experienced unprovoked feelings of anxiety, persecution, and hostility. Some suffered nightmares; others felt extreme panic at times. These reactions were due to a lack of carbohydrates which provide energy, and a low intake of vitamins and minerals which maintain the ability of the body to handle stress, fight disease, and function normally.

—Debbie Powers, R.N.

The more times one cycles through yo-yo dieting, the easier it becomes to put weight on and it becomes increasingly difficult to take it off. Fat cells prefer the larger size and resist shrinking when weight loss is attempted. Yo-yo dieting also increases the risk of developing a cardiovascular disease.

Losing one or two pounds a week is probably safe, but talk with a health practitioner or dietitian about what is healthy for you. Slow weight loss allows the body to lose fat rather than water and muscle, especially if combined with exercise. All of us should eat lots of vegetables, fruits, and whole grains and avoid high fat, sugary, or salty foods. Yet the average American's diet is 35 to 40 percent fat!

To lose weight we need calories to fuel our metabolism. This is why fasting doesn't work; we need calories to burn calories. Also, having enough sleep cuts down inclination to eat extra calories. We lose weight when calorie intake is less than the calories used in exercise and body functioning. It takes a deficit of 3,500 calories to lose one pound. Exercise not only uses up calories but suppresses the appetite and changes body metabolism. Toned muscles burn more calories than slack ones. People who exercise regularly keep weight off, while people who rely just on dieting usually gain their weight back.

To lose weight, keep a journal of your eating and exercise habits. Do you eat when you are frustrated or depressed, rather than just when you're hungry? When you see the problem areas, brainstorm solutions, such as eliminating unhealthy snacks in your home or taking a walk instead of eating when you're frustrated. Set a specific goal and then evaluate how your plan worked at the end of month.

How to Lose Weight

◎ Work with a plan such as Overeater's Anonymous, Weight Watcher's, or Diet Workshop.

◎ Only buy food you should eat and get rid of food that may tempt you. Remove food from rooms other than the kitchen.

◎ Eat in only one location, eat slowly, and never eat out of the container. Put just the amount you want to eat on a plate. Make your plate fuller by including a pile of vegetables and a filling starch like rice or baked potatoes. Stop eating when you're full.

◎ Make a list of activities that you can substitute for eating. Read the list when you feel like eating.

- Stock up on low calorie foods to snack on such as celery and unbuttered popcorn. Eat high-fiber foods like whole grains and fresh fruits as they take up a lot of space in your stomach and tell the body to store less fat. Also, drink lots of water, herb tea, and juices to feel full.

- Repeat affirmations such as, "I eat only what's healthy." Before you enter the kitchen, visualize yourself doing what you have to do and not eating, or eating a small amount.

- Joint a weight-loss support group or have a buddy to call when you feel like overeating.

- Think about other ways to bring nurturance and sweetness into your life, which could be as simple as reading novels or dancing.

Nutrition specialist Donald Payne suggests eliminating sugar, eating seven servings of vegetables a day, and using herbs which block the absorption of the fat in the digestive system. Citrimax is the brand name for the herb garcinia cambogia which converts fats into glycogen. When there is plenty of glycogen in the liver, we feel full. He recommends about two grams about one-half hour before each meal. It takes about 20 days before it kicks in. Also, the mineral chromimun increases the body's metabolism. Overall, focus on exercise and healthy food rather than dieting.

—Bryan, 26, Wisconsin

My weight has been a problem since I was about three or four. I could be a couch potato because I did not have anyone to play with. I also lived in a family that liked to cook and bake. Put these together and you have a 4th grader who weighed 140. I finally got a handle on the weight problem when I was a high school junior. I knew I was overweight and hated it. I was very active in the FFA [Future Farmers of America] *and the beginning of my junior year, my FFA advisor asked me if I wanted to go to a national leadership workshop in Washington D.C. The conference was the motivation I needed to lose some weight. It was by luck that our high school offered racquetball as a physical education class. For some reason, that was one sport that I had an interest in. By the time the trip came around I had lost 40 pounds. I still have to closely watch my weight.*

Understanding Overeating

National Association to Advance Fat Acceptance
P.O. Box 188620
Sacramento, CA 95818

Overeaters Anonymous
P.O. Box 44020
Rio Rancho, NM 87194

Rebecca Ruggles Radcliffe. *Enlightened Eating.* Minneapolis, MN: EASE, 1995. (P.O. Box 8032, Minneapolis, MN, 55408) (Chapters include: why we eat, finding joy, rage response, surviving the holidays, etc. Also provides a newsletter.)

Suzie Orbach. *Fat Is a Feminist Issue.* NY: Berkeley Books, 1994.

Eating Disorders

I was bulimic and basically avoided contact with others and allowed the pressure to eat away at me [interesting word choice]. *I was extremely self-destructive, hated myself, and thus attempted suicide, undetected, several times. I finally had the courage to speak to people about my problems. I learned to trust others, then finally understood that I wasn't alone anymore; actually I never was.*

All my life I have been a perfectionist trying to escape negative feedback. Finally able to trust others, I now believe that I no longer have to be all that everyone expects me to be and, if I make a mistake, it is because I'm human and humans often err.
[Mistakes teach us where we need to grow. Perfectionism is typical of people with eating disorders.]

—Melissa, 19,
New York

About 90 percent of the anorexics and bulimics are females, who usually begin their unhealthy eating habits between the ages of 16 and 20. Between six to 10 percent die as a result of their illness. Eating disorders may stem from negative effects of dieting, sexual abuse, stressful changes such as divorce or puberty, depression, perfectionism, low self-esteem, feeling powerless and having a need for control, and brain chemical imbalances in serotonin.

Anorexia Nervosa is self-starvation to achieve thinness and control. The disorder often begins after an extended loss of weight from a diet. Anorexics have both a fear of food and an obsessive interest in it. They often practice compulsive food rituals such as cutting food into small pieces. They may obsess over buying and preparing food, lose ability to concentrate, and avoid contact with people. Starvation causes menstrual periods to stop, growth of soft body hair, intolerance to cold, constipation, slow pulse rate, low blood pressure, anemia, and brittle hair and nails. About 40 percent of anorexics also have bulimic tendencies.

The strict clinical definition of anorexia is an intense fear of becoming fat, a belief that one is fat, weight at least 15 percent below normal, and missing one's period for at least three months in a row due to low body fat. About one percent of teens fit this strict definition, but many more practice harmful anorexic behaviors. Girls with anorexia or bulimia sometimes are also compulsive exercisers who feel irrationally anxious and worried about gaining weight if they aren't exercising.

Suzie Orbach, author of *Fat Is a Feminist Issue*, believes that anorexia can be both a rebellion against developing into a curvy woman and a desire to fit the feminine beauty ideal of thinness. (She suggests that compulsive eaters may become large to avoid feminine stereotypes of being passive and small.) Ms. Orbach suggests that both anorexics and compulsive overeaters share a reaction to the feminine role and a desire not to be noticed as women, although there are many different causes.

Bulimia Nervosa is bingeing and purging by inducing vomiting (the body retains 25 percent of the calories consumed), taking laxatives intended to correct constipation, or taking diuretics intended to eliminate water from the body through urination. The last two methods eliminate fewer than 10 percent of the calories consumed. Bulimics may binge to relieve stress. The clinical definition of bulimia is purging at least two times a week for three months. One to three percent of adolescents fit this strict definition.

Bulimics may have puffy cheeks, tooth decay, and an ongoing sore throat. Frequent vomiting results in injury to the esophagus leading from the mouth to the stomach, kidney and heart problems caused by lack of water and low potassium levels, hemorrhages in the blood vessels in the eyes, erosion of tooth enamel, and inflammation of the stomach lining (gastritis). Laxatives and diuretics can cause ulcers (due to injury to the intestines), dehydration, and mineral imbalance. With time, heart irregularities may develop, along with severe dental and digestive problems.

Compulsive Eating Disorder or binge-eating, like bulimia, is periodic dieting followed by bingeing but without purging. It is the most common clinically treated eating disorder. As weight increases, overeaters may suffer from high blood pressure, joint problems, and shortness of breath. Severe obesity can cause diabetes and heart and gall bladder diseases.

If you have a friend with an eating disorder, be direct in letting her know your concern, even though she might react with anger or denial. Ask if she is willing to let you assist in getting help. Don't pretend the problem does not exist or will go away on its own. Eating disorders are like loaded guns; someone needs to be told. Most people can't stop on their own. Eating disorders require the assistance of trained professionals as they may stem from an untreated problem such as sexual abuse. Some teens find a peer support group led by a counselor trained in the treatment of eating disorders to be most helpful. Sometimes drug treatment by a physician is effective in decreasing the urge to binge or in treating depression that may trigger eating disorders.

The media tells females both to be thin and to make people happy by baking cakes. Food is mentioned an average 4.8 times per half hour of commercial TV— mostly fattening goods served by thin actors, according to researchers at the University of Minnesota School of Public Health. Despite these conflicting messages, what do you think is the best weight for your body type? Some people use food to cope with their emotions, or protect themselves from intimacy with others, or to feel in control over their lives by not eating. List the first thoughts that come to your mind when you hear the word "food."

Signs of a Compulsive Eating Problem

Estimates are that one in four college-aged women suffer from an eating disorder. About eight million Americans have an eating disorder, according to the National Association of Anorexia.

- ✪ preoccupation and obsession with food and weight
- ✪ counting calories obsessively
- ✪ skipping meals daily
- ✪ fad dieting or long-term dieting
- ✪ getting on the scales frequently
- ✪ eating food without enjoying it
- ✪ not wanting to eat with other people
- ✪ eating when you have a problem
- ✪ eating when you're not hungry
- ✪ rigid rituals about eating, including frequently skipping other activities to follow an eating or exercise schedule
- ✪ feeling powerless over food
- ✪ mood swings or depression caused by not eating enough nutrients
- ✪ compulsive over-exercise

—Megan, 21, California

When I was in high school I didn't know anyone else did what I did. I had never heard the terms bulimia or anorexia. I didn't know what an eating disorder was. Bulimia was my way of coping with body image and perfectionism. Bulimia seemed to be the perfect solution; I could eat anything I wanted and not have it count. Now I know it did count. I did a lot of destructive things to my body in the attempt to take care of my emotions. I now know that I used food to fill my emptiness, to cure my frustration, and vent my anger.

Women need to talk to other women. We need to know that what one of us suffers, many suffer. We need to empower each other and ourselves. We need to notify the world; our voices need to be heard. If we stay silent, our sisters and daughters will continue to hurt. So talk to someone—a friend, a parent, a counselor. I remember being very surprised, relieved, and supported when I found out that other people binge on food and then purge themselves as a method to control a situation. After that, I began to understand and accept myself.

—Susan, 22, Wisconsin

I lost about 20 pounds within about two months. I looked great because I joined the varsity soccer team and got lots of exercise, but when I came home from practice I would eat a whole bunch and throw it up. That was all that I would eat all day. Every day I purged myself.

To be honest, I never really felt that there was a problem with what I was doing until one day, when I was puking in the bathroom sink, my brother walked in on me and looked at me with a horrified look. He said, "What are you doing? That is so gross." He just stood there and stared at me, for what seemed like an hour but was only like 20 seconds, and there I sat with a pile of vomit in the sink and my fingers covered. That incident made me realize what I was doing and I stopped. I gained the weight back but I was never fat.

—Patrick, 23, California

The pressure of wrestling competition was so great that it forced me into three years of bulimia. Then once I injured my knee, I had no clue of what to do, because I was playing on a full scholarship. Being number one is not worth destroying your body. Enjoy the sport and the competition, but at the same time stay healthy.

—Michele, 28, California

Just because you binge but don't use laxatives, or exercise to an extreme, or use diet pills, or vomit after a meal does not mean you don't have an eating disorder. Compulsive overeaters binge and then emotionally beat themselves up about it. They have many of the same personality characteristics that anorexics and bulimics do. They have low self-esteem, are usually perfectionists, and tend to excel in other areas of their lives. They too use food as an emotional crutch.

For me the only thing I felt I had control over was food. I would be faced with some kind of stress from an outside pressure, such as a deadline for a paper, test, or speech and it would trigger a binge. Usually I just wanted something sweet, a whole bag of Oreos, whatever was available. I would binge and then I would feel miserable, depressed, and sick to my stomach. I felt like I needed to cut off the fat around my middle, and hated my body. This of course would trigger another binge. I descended into this vicious circle of hating and hurting my body. I did not enter therapy until I was 25. My compulsive overeating started when I was a sophomore in high school, so for 10 years I did not acknowledge I had a problem.

I wish someone had told me how to take care of myself. Learning to care for your own emotional well—being is incredibly important. You can't depend on other people to give you happiness or fulfill your needs. I knew how to take care of everyone around me, but had no idea how to take care of myself without involving food. High school is incredibly hard emotionally. You are increasingly expected to make adult decisions without any backup experience. I never learned that it was OK to feel confused, or OK to not know what you are going to do with the rest of your life. The best thing you can do is acknowledge those feelings and try to deal with them.

Another tool is learning to treat yourself well. Sometimes this means giving yourself a treat. I treat myself with flowers, a long walk in the park, new earrings. A pedicure, manicure, and massage are all fabulous things you can do to make yourself feel good. A really great book can be a wonderful way to pick yourself up. Other times it means allowing yourself time to catch up, to physically rest. Setting limits can help in allowing yourself time to see to your needs. If you can't learn to say no, then outside forces limit the time that you need to take care of yourself.

The most important thing you can do is first admit your problem to yourself and then get help. If you have an eating disorder, talk to a professional counselor, someone who can help you create tools in your life to deal with stress. Probably people come to you to unload their problems. You need that same kind of support. I attended group therapy and it was the best move I have ever made. You often feel isolated when you have an *eating disorder. It was such a relief to know that other people faced the same problems every day. A counselor and a group can give you the ideas that break you free of the binge cycle. Learning to take care of yourself is not easy, but incredibly life saving.*

Books that helped Michelle

Geneen Roth: *When Food is Love: Exploring the Relationship Between Eating And Intimacy* and *Breaking Free From Compulsive Eating* (both Plume), and *Why Weight? A Guide to Ending Compulsive Eating* (New American Library).

Barbara McFarland and T. Baker-Baumann. *Feeding the Empty Heart: Adult Children and Compulsive Eating* (NAL-Dutton).

Susan Kano. *Making Peace with Food: Freeing yourself from the Diet/Weight* (Perennial).

Eating Disorder Organizations

Bulimia/Anorexia Self–Help Hotline
1-800-227-4785

Eating Disorder Hotline
1-800-382-2832 (1-212-222-2832 in New York)

Food Addiction Hotline
1-800-USA-0088

American Anorexia/Bulimia Association
418 E. 76th St., Suite 3B
New York, NY 10021

Anorexics/Bulimics Anonymous
4500 E. Pacific Coast Hwy., Suite 330
Long Beach, CA 90804

Anorexia Nervosa and Related Eating Disorders
P.O. Box 5102
Eugene, OR 97405

Eating Disorders Awareness and Prevention
P.O. Box 14469, Dept. P
Seattle, WA 98114

F.E.E.D. (Foundation for Education About Eating Disorders)
P.O. Box 34
Boring, MD 21020
National Association of Anorexia Nervosa and Associated Disorders
Hotline 1-708-831-3438
P.O. Box 271
Highland Park, IL 60035

National Eating Disorders Organization
The Ashlawn Building on the Harding Hospital Campus
445 E. Granville Rd.
Worthington, OH 43085

Overeaters Anonymous
4025 Spencer St., Suite 203
Torrance, CA 90503

National Institute of Mental Health Consumer Information Center, Dept. 38
Pueblo, CO 81009 Eating Disorders (free booklet)

Catherine Baker, *The Perfection Trap: College-Age Women and Eating Disorders.* (This booklet may be ordered from Health Education, Box 3886, DUMC, Durham, NC 27710.)

Michael Maloney. *Straight Talk About Eating Disorders.* NY: Dell, 1993.

Terence Sandbek. *The Deadly Diet: Recovering from Anorexia and Bulimia.* Oakland, CA: New Harbinger, 1993.

Kitty Scott. *My Fight for Life: I Am a Teenage Anorexic.* NY: Vantage, 1991.

Disabilities
**(useful information about coping
with any problem you might face)**

I am blind. I can't see except for some large, fuzzy shapes and
a kind of blotching of light and dark. I majored in child development
and graduated from community college with an AA in child development. Then I tried to open a child care center. The state would not
allow me to do that because I am blind. I could own a center, but they
would require me to have at least two employees to watch the children.
Then the insurance companies said that they would NEVER insure me.

Obviously, it wasn't the right thing to do. No matter how hard I
tried, it just would not work out. Now I run a 163,000-acre ranch with
3,000 head of range cattle. I have more men after me than flies on a
peach pie in August and I tell them all to take a number and wait.

There is a voice inside of you that will tell you what is right
and what is wrong. If you listen to that voice you will seldom be
wrong. I believe in God in a very nondenominational way [doesn't follow the teachings of one particular religion] and teens should be told
that it is an option. I did not learn this until I was out of high school
and in college. God is part of that voice inside you.

[A reader asked how we can hear this voice. The conscious mind
needs to be calmed to hear the deeper voice of intuition, the knowledge

stored in the unconscious mind, divine guidance, or whatever you believe is a higher source of wisdom. Meditation, prayer, taking time to be still—perhaps relaxing in a bathtub, asking a question before you go to sleep, paying attention to your dreams, journal writing, and exercise are ways to quiet the mind and tune in to your deeper intuition. See the happiness and stress management sections in Chapter 2.]

You have to be strong and believe that you can succeed. When I got a job as a waitress, people said I was crazy: How could a blind person be a waitress? I could barely see the table, let alone forks, knives, etc. How could I put food down? How could I clean up if I could not see dirt? But for most of that winter I made more in tips and outlasted all the other high school students who were working there. I did it because I knew I could. The boss said that if he did not know, he would not believe I was blind.

How could a fat, ugly girl ever be happy? Well, I just knew I could. And I am. Right now I am back in college for a couple of hours a week learning how to use a new program with a voice that will read the computer screen to me to help me run the ranch. And I get to meet more guys. When I was 15, I would never have believed that an ugly duckling would grow up a swan. I am not a swan, but I don't sit home on Friday nights either.

—Sarah, 24, Nevada

—Kitty, 25, California

I was born with only one hand; I had to work out a lot of things my whole life. People stared at me a lot when I was in school. Even in high school people would make fun of me because I could not do things they could do, or because I was different, and it hurt a lot. I had to learn how to do things by myself. Even when I quit using drugs I had to do that by myself. People can help you a little, but you are the one who has to do things. I had to learn on my own. I know it sounds crazy but 12-step programs have some good advice for solving most problems. They helped me a lot when I needed to make decisions in my life.

—Jay, 25, California

A common question is, "How did you deal with the loss of your sight so well?" The number one force in my recovery was the love and support of friends and family. When I lost my sight I thought that I had changed in some way. I had not yet discovered that the loss I experienced did not change who I was inside. My friends and family seemed to recognize this early in my recovery.

The small things changed in some ways, but the major ones did not. I still enjoy going to movies, dancing, waterskiing, and many of the activities I had before. This is not to say that some of them are not difficult, but I found that if I want to do something badly enough, it is usually quite possible. I enjoy skydiving, snow skiing, and some other activities that I never had the opportunity to enjoy before I went blind.

The best thing that happened to me was that my friends and family did not allow me to sit at home and feel sorry for myself. I found that the people around me still expected me to participate in as many activities as I had before. This kept me busy, and therefore I did not really have time to feel sorry for myself. This is not to say that there were not bad days, but on the whole, I had very little time to be depressed. Just when I would start to feel down, my friends would show up on the doorstep and say, "Come on, let's get moving," and we would be off to enjoy ourselves. This positive support is very vital in reestablishing a healthy self-image.

I also had to be strong on a daily basis. Sometimes it was all that I could do to get out of bed, but that was enough. Just the fact that I would get out of bed and face a new day kept me going. Each day I found it a little easier to get moving and involved in the activities that I love. Slowly but surely, the confidence that I was still the same person began to return. I feel that every day is still a challenge, but each day was always a challenge before I went blind. Has anything really changed?

Resources for Disabled Persons

(One in five Americans have a disability.)

National Information Clearinghouse
1-800-922-9234
(information and referrals for families
with children with disabilities)

**National Information Center for
Children and Youth with Disabilities**
1-800-695-0285 1-703-893-8614
(TDD)

U. S. Department of Justice
1-202-514-0301
Americans with Disabilities Act
Information Line
(This act outlaws discrimination
against people with disabilities, in
employment, services, public accom-
modations, and telecommunications.)

**Association for Persons with Severe
Handicaps**
11201 Greenwood Ave.
Seattle, WA 98133

ATP Services for Handicapped Students
CN6400
Princeton, NJ 08541-6400

**Disability Rights Education
and Defense Fund**
2212 Sixth St.
Berkeley, CA 94710

**Federation for Children
with Special Needs**
95 Berkeley St., Suite 104
Boston, MA 02116

Foundation for Technology Access
1128 Solano Ave.
Albany, CA 94706-1638
(helps disabled people get access to
computers and other technologies)

Resources for Rehabilitation
33 Bedford St., Suite 19A
Lexington, MA 02173
(distributes books and pamphlets on
topics such as living with vision loss
or diabetes)

*How to Choose a College: Guide for the
Student with a Disability.* The
American Council on Education, Health
Resource Center. (One DuPont Circle,
Suite 800, Washington, D.C. 20036)

Jill Krementz. *How It Feels to Live
with a Physical Disability,*
NY: Simon and Schuster, 1992.

Charles Mangrum and S. Strichart.
*Peterson's Guide to Colleges with
Disability Programs.* Princeton, NJ:
Peterson's Guides, 1994.

An Internet site for hearing impaired
and chronically ill teens:
http://www.netzone.com/marion/yak.
html

DO-IT resources for disabled teens:
http://weber.u.washington.edu/~doit/
press/press.html

National Information Center for
Children and Youth with Disabilities:
http://www.aed.org/NICHCY or:
gopher_aed.org.

Driving Safely

I am a very active member of our SADD club [Students Against Drunk Driving], *because my life has been affected quite a bit by the effects of drunk driving. I've had two very dear friends, Noelle and Steve, die at the hands of a drunk driver, and I think that people just don't realize how horrible it is.*

—Dena, 15, California

Motor vehicle crashes are the leading cause of death for young Americans (followed by homicide and suicide). Drunk drivers cause almost 15 times as many deaths as guns! Over half of all fatal accidents involve a driver or pedestrian who has been drinking. Every 23 minutes someone dies because of a drunk driver. A 1993 study found that 18 percent of high school students had driven a car while drunk in the previous year and 72 percent didn't wear a seat belt (Centers for Disease Control, 1992; Josephson Institute of Ethics, 1993). People ages 21 to 34 cause about one half of all such fatal crashes.

♦ Each day 39 young people ages 15 to 24 are killed in motor vehicle accidents.

♦ Over 3,000 youths die in alcohol-related car accidents each year, and 65 percent of traffic accidents involving 20 to 24-year-olds are alcohol related, according to the National Commission Against Drunk Driving.

♦ Drivers under the age of 21 killed 2,200 people in car accidents in 1994 (National Center for Health Statistics).

If friends have been drinking and plan to drive, you can save a life: call them a taxi, drive them home, call their parents, or invite them to spend the night on the couch. Better to be angry at you than dead. Driving safely is also an issue for sober drivers looking for cheap thrills, as guys relate in their stories. Think of a car as a lethal weapon.

—Matt, 18, Vermont

The main issue facing teens in my area is driving and alcohol; accidents take many lives. I know that commercials have an impact because I've heard friends quote beer slogans at parties where people are drinking. I used to feel stupid when I didn't join in with my twin brother and his friends, but now I feel OK being able to stand alone.

As well as being president of the student body last year, I was active in our SADD chapter. I love to be on the go, to help people, and make changes. I wanted to be known as someone who made a difference for my school.

Our SADD group met every week. We did a Ghost Out where we represented people who died in the U.S. that day in alcohol-related deaths. We wore black, painted our faces white, and didn't speak. At the end of school, we sat holding candles. People would ask why I was dressed that way, but since I represented someone who had passed on, I couldn't say anything. Other students would explain.

We did a red ribbon campaign at Christmas time, where we gave students a red ribbon attached to a green paper giving information on drunk driving. People put the ribbon on their car antennas as a reminder to drive sober. After the Christmas break we tied them on the school Christmas tree as another reminder. We also did seatbelt surveys four times a year as students drove into the parking lot. This increased the number of people using their belts from 49 percent last year to 73 percent this year.

What makes a difference with my friends is real life experiences. When a best friend who abuses drugs and alcohol got in a car accident, we were all more careful about using seat belts. A speaker at the high school gave us facts about marijuana use: That made an impact for a while because people hadn't known pot had an impact on driving.

–John, 19, California

I destroyed my mom's car while trying to see how fast it would go. I lied and said that I swerved to miss hitting a dog. I should have told the truth.

—Ben, 20, California

When I was 14 and 15 it was a common weekend event to stay at my buddy Paul's house, steal his mom's car, and drive around in the early hours of the morning. The problem was I never had the guts not to go. I hated the idea of going on a car excursion. We got caught by the cops at 4:30 a.m. one Sunday morning, 45 minutes away from home. It was the worst experience ever to happen to me.

—Gary, 20, West Virginia

With the ability to travel by car without your parents, the ability to pay for your own items because of a job, and the increased social life, there is a tendency for teenagers to gain an over-independent feeling. This feeling leads to thoughts of invincibility whereby teens take great risks. Luckily, I was able to survive this time period, but not without consequence. Three years and three car accidents later, I'm beginning to realize that my parents were right most of the time, contrary to what I believed at that time. My parents were strict at first. I think that this caused a rebellion-type attitude *that caused me to take a few too many risks (thus the accidents). But I finally asked my parents to respect a few of my decisions and allow me to make my own responsible decisions. We agreed upon this and as more and more of the responsibility was placed on me, I began to make better decisions.*

—Jim, 21, California

My most difficult challenge in my teen years was driving safely. Not that I didn't know how or understand the importance of safe driving, but it was just so much fun to drive like a maniac. I got in three minor accidents that were big wake-up calls. The advice I would give to someone younger is that even sober drivers need to be careful.

—Brian, 22, California

In my senior year, on my way back to campus from lunch, I hit and killed a pedestrian. I had to deal with the fact that I had taken someone's life and the pain I caused their family. It was an accident but if I had been more careful, it wouldn't have happened. Fortunately, I didn't go to jail, but I had to do a lot of community service. I had a clean record before this, so that helped.

To cope with this situation, I went to a counselor for a while. Rather than pretend it didn't happen, I faced the problem and dealt with it. I completed all my community service as soon as possible and tried to move on.

—Kyle, 22, California

Dealing with a DUI at the age of 18 was my most difficult experience as a teenager. I worked my rear off to pay for the fines and bills. My advice would be NOT to drink and drive.

Organizations to Stop Drunk Driving

Mothers Against Drunk Drivers (MADD)
511 E. John Carpenter Frwy.
Irving, TX 75062

National Commission on Drunk Driving
1140 Connecticut Ave., NW #804
Washington, DC 20036

Students Against Drunk Driving (SADD)
Box 800
Marlboro, MA 01752
(SADD will provide information to help you organize a chapter in your school.)

Illness & Injuries

I had to go through chemotherapy for my leukemia. The thing that helped me cope with the challenge was having a positive attitude. That is the one thing that is a sure cure. Without it, you're letting the leukemia get to you. You'll beat it at its own game with a positive attitude.
—Danielle, 18, California

Allergies

Nutrition specialist Donald Payne recommends not eating sugar, milk products, beer or wine; using a homeopathic remedy available in a health food store; and taking freeze dried nettles three times a day. An herb called quercetin, combined with vitamin C, helps stop the allergic response, he reports. Blue green algae helps some people with hay fever.

Colds and Flu

Americans suffer about one billion colds each year. Colds are spread mainly through hand-to-hand contact (this includes hard surfaces such as a telephone or doorknob, if an infected person recently touched it) and then touching your eyes or nose. Therefore, the best prevention is washing your hands and not touching your face. An overheated room dries out mucus membranes in the nose which allows the cold virus to take hold, one reason people get more colds in the fall and winter.

Colds and flu are caused by a virus and thus can't be treated with antibiotics which only work against bacterial infections. Americans spend more than $550 million a year on cold remedies but most of the money is wasted. Drugs which suppress cold and flu symptoms may do more harm than good; a fever, for example, slows down the spread of a virus, and drugs like antihistamines have side effects. Children and teens should not take aspirin for the flu because of the danger of bringing on a dangerous illness called Reye's syndrome.

Effective treatments include drinking plenty of warm liquids to relieve nasal congestion, gargling with salt water to reduce throat swelling, inhaling warm/moist air, and resting. Some people think vitamin C helps, as well as herbs such as goldenseal, echinacea, and garlic capsules to boost the immune system.

Mononucleosis

Mono, the "kissing disease," spreads through saliva. Someone can be infected with the virus without becoming ill and unknowingly pass it on. It is not caught through casual contact, unlike a cold. Symptoms include fatigue, swollen glands, fever, muscle aches, and sore throat. The Epstein-Barr virus causes more than 95 percent of the cases among both teens and adults. Most people who get mono can resume most normal activities after about two weeks. Once infected, the person is usually immune from getting mono again, although the virus stays in the body forever. As viruses can't be treated with antibiotics, no cure exists other than rest.

—Kieran, 23, Maryland

Check out alternatives to treatment; do you REALLY need that surgery or drug? Is there a more natural, less invasive way to solve your problem? Buy a book on naturopathic medicine [Cummings and Ullman, *Everybody's Guide to Homeopathic Medicines*, or Panos and Heimlich *Homeopathic Medicine at Home*, both J.P. Tarcher], *or go by an herb shop/health food store. Don't assume that the doctor is all knowing. If you have a chronic condition, buy some books on it, join a support network, check the Internet, and be aware of all of your options!!!*

Read up on whatever your problem is—newspaper articles, magazine articles, etc. Try out several different doctors before you settle on one (try three in your health plan). Ask LOTS of questions, no matter how dumb you think they are; educating you is part of their job. If they claim they don't have time, ask if there is a nurse or PA [physician's assistant] *who does. Be as demanding as you would be in any other service situation. I know tons of people who let their doctors get away with things they'd never let a waiter or dry cleaner get away with, and it's the same thing. You're paying for a service. And if it's a clinic or something and you're not paying, rest assured SOMEONE is—the government, whoever, that DOCTOR is getting paid! The medical industry has a lot of mythology built up around them and we give it more respect and mysticism than they deserve.*

Sport Injuries

Each year injuries kill about 10,000 children under age 15, more than deaths from diseases. Sports injuries are a topic where gender differences show up; guys wrote about sports problems and driving, while young women were more likely to write about body image. (Guys who are overweight or have acne worried about this as much as females, though.) Over 300,000 young men are injured every year in high school and college football, with over 15,000 requiring surgery.

To treat a sprained muscle, ice the injury, using crushed ice or frozen vegetables in a plastic bag. Leave the ice on 20 minutes and off 10 minutes. You can elastic wrap the injured area to limit swelling. Keep the injury elevated during the first 48-hours to minimize bleeding and swelling. The initial stage of healing usually takes two to three weeks. When you're ready, do some stretching of the injured area. Always warm up and stretch before exercise to prevent re-injury.

—E.J., 17, Wisconsin

After only playing four football games my first year, I broke my collarbone. I then took off two years because of a car wreck I was in. Now as a senior, I am not getting to play because I'm really a pretty rotten player. I cope with this by just not letting it bother me. My friends also cheer me up. My advice for teens is not to put too much emphasis on sports because you usually just end up with a bad knee or arthritis.

—Chris, 21, California

I dislocated my shoulder several times in sports and I found out my sophomore year that I had to have surgery and that I was going to be slightly handicapped. I made myself join the swim team, basically to prove to myself that I wasn't a failure, that I could work my arm out. It was a really good way to cope. It was really frightening to know how much motion I was going to lose. Don't give up and at the same time don't push it too far. I was able to take something that was really disturbing to me and turn it into something positive.

—Jeff, 25, California

It was my best baseball season ever. I was a freshman in high school, the year of my hitting pinnacle. I had a .536 batting average midway through the season, by far my best year of nine years of playing organized baseball. Besides playing baseball, I was also captain of the football team in off-season preparation for the upcoming year. This was the year we hoped to win the league championship. This was a great time in my life, or so I thought.

During off-season workouts I had recurring knee aches and pains that had started earlier that year. Sometimes they were so painful I would have to use my arms to help myself stand up. "It's growing pains," everyone kept telling me, including my family doctor. Finally the pain became so excruciating my coach referred me to an orthopedic specialist. Since I was putting a lot of pressure on my legs from the intense workouts and from playing baseball, I expected the doctor to either tell me to relax my workouts or that it is just "growing pains."

The doctor returned to my room, x-rays in hand, with a serious look on his face. I knew I was not going to like the news I was about to hear. He said I had calcium deposits on both knees the size of marbles that would require surgery to remove immediately, or my knees could lock up at any time. He said it may have been caused by my nine years as a baseball catcher. I was frightened, angry, and determined at this news. I was afraid I would have pains in my legs the rest of my life and could never play sports again. I was angry because I had to quit one of my best baseball seasons and my upcoming championship season was in jeopardy. I was determined to not let this get me down.

The surgery lasted seven hours as the doctors removed the deposits from both knees. The five days in the hospital were frustrating ones as I knew my baseball teammates were playing without me and my football teammates were preparing for the season without me. I could not do anything since I had what felt like two-ton braces around my legs. This immobility was killing me and I was even more determined to get stronger and be prepared for the upcoming season that started in four months.

After I was able to stand and move with crutches, the doctors allowed me to go home. With determination, I slowly regained full flexibility in my legs within two months. I was walking with a slight limp and my strength still was not back. I was frustrated at the time because the healing was not moving as fast as I would like, with the season just a short two months away. I received the OK from my doctor to start light weight training, as well as do some slow jogging. The team trainer put me on a program and with the support of my coaches, family, and teammates, I was recovering nicely but also painfully.

Within weeks my strength and flexibility were back to normal and I was again working out with my teammates. With perseverance and determination in the face of adversity, I was able to overcome this obstacle and enjoyed a championship season with my team.

Bike Injuries

About 400,000 kids age 14 and under are treated in hospital emergency rooms each year for injuries suffered while riding their bikes; about a third are head injuries. Wear a helmet while riding your bike, as it reduces the risk of head injury by 85 percent and reduces brain injury by almost 90 percent.

Lifting

To prevent injuries to your back while lifting heavy objects:

⊙ Bend at the knees, not the waist.

⊙ Squat to reach low objects.

⊙ Keep the object close to your body to distribute the weight evenly.

⊙ Avoid twisting motions and never lift a heavy object higher than your waist.

Fire

Make sure your smoke alarms work and learn the location of fire extinguishers and how to use them. Too many electrical cords plugged into an outlet can overload the circuit. If a fire occurs:

★ Call 9-1-1 immediately.

★ Never use an elevator.

★ Stay beneath the smoke by crawling.

★ Don't open a door if it is warm.

★ If you are trapped in a room, open the windows and shout for help.

★ Don't jump if the room is over two stories high.

Body · 27

Men's Health

The Men's Health Network suggests that teen boys get examined by a doctor for testicular masses (cancer, varicose veins, etc.), undescended testicles (they increase the risk of testicular cancer), abnormal penis development (when the urethra is in the wrong place), and for chlamydia and gonorrhea if sexually active.

The most common cancer for young men ages 20 to 35 is testicular cancer so it is smart to do self-exam, especially if your testicles have not descended or did so after age six. Once a month, after a warm shower when the scrotum is relaxed, examine each testicle by rolling it between your thumb and fingers for a small lump about the size of a pea.

The Men's Health Network reminds us that men die seven years earlier than women, on the average, although 50 years ago the difference was only one year. Men develop prostate cancer (a gland near the urethra) at about the same rate that women get breast cancer, and heart disease affects men 15 years earlier than it affects women. One in every five men has a heart attack before age 65. Cholesterol and lack of exercise is part of the problem, so get in the habit of eating healthy low-fat food and daily exercise now. To prevent prostate cancer later in life—the most common cancer for men—nutritionist Donald Payne suggests taking at least 15 milligrams of zinc a day, or 25 milligrams if active in sports.

He reports the most frequent question boys ask him is about body building. He recommends adequate protein intake, and a supplement called Metabalo 2, which contains essential proteins, vitamins, and amino acids. He advises against sugar and soft drinks because he thinks sugar disrupts the digestion of protein, and both sugar and soft drinks leach minerals out of the joints, ligaments, and bones—increasing the chance of injuries.

Chris Wahlberg, M.D., points out that the growth hormone is stimulated by exercise and sleep, and requires adequate nutrition. He recommends that you eat lots of fresh vegetables and fruit, and avoid junk food and caffeine. He's a vegetarian who finds that this low-fat diet maintains a proper weight and can provide essential nutrients.

Hazards of the Male Role

The pressures of the male role to compete, perform, be cool and tough, and not seek help, can be very punishing to boys' physical and mental health. Boys need to talk about their feelings and ask for help when needed.

- Between the ages of 10 to 18, boys are four to five more likely to commit suicide than girls (see the section on sex roles in Chapter 6 and suicide in Chapter 2) and are over 60 percent of the high school dropouts.

- Steroid use is mainly confined to teen guys, with harmful affects.

- More boys die from homicide than natural causes. Accidents (mainly motor vehicles) and gunfire are the two leading causes of death among Americans ages 10 to 19.

Eighty percent of the people with serious drug addictions are men and men are more likely to be in accidents. Men are most of the employees in dangerous occupations and suffer most of the fatal accidents at work. Men are 43 times more likely to be admitted to psychiatric hospitals; they're about 66 percent of the patients admitted to emergency rooms, and nearly 80 percent of the homicide victims. The Men's Health Network maintains that the men's health crisis can be prevented by changes in lifestyle and wellness efforts, although there is a "tragic lack of health care information for men."

Men's Health

Men's Healthline
1-888-636-2636 (information about men's diseases and a special service for teen boys)
Mensnet@capaccess.org
(See the puberty section in Chapter 3 for books about boys' bodies)

Violence Prevention

(see school violence in Chapter 7 and
neighborhood organizing section in Chapter 11)

> *Out of a high school graduating class of 94 people, 11 are*
> *dead from drugs, guns, drinking, and auto crashes. Four*
> *were in jail the last I heard of them. I truly thought some*
> *would be more than a statistic.* [In light of the men's
> health section, a good guess is most of these statistics
> were men.]
>
> -Lon, 35, Colorado

Youth Victims of Violence

✪ Among seven-to-10-year-olds, 63 percent report they are afraid they might die young, and 70 percent are afraid of getting shot or stabbed at home or in school, or worried about being hit by an adult (a 1995 study by Kaiser Permanente and Children Now, including a telephone poll of 1,000 youth).

✪ Nine out of 10 murders of youth worldwide take place in the U.S. The homicide rate for people 15 to 24 is five times that of the second most dangerous country, Canada (1993 report from the United Nations Children's Fund).

✪ A child is killed by a gun every 92 minutes—5,751 children in 1993 (including suicides).

✪ From 1979 to 1991, 40,000 teenagers and 10,000 younger children were killed by firearms.

✪ Each day 5,703 teenagers are victims of violent crimes.

✪ One in four youth ages 10 to 16 (surveyed in 1993) reported being assaulted or abused the previous year, triple the assault rate reported by the National Crime Survey in 1991. One in 10 said they had been sexually abused or assaulted. A third of 8th and 10th graders who were sexually abused thought about suicide the previous year. (Michelle Wilson and Alain Joffe, *Journal of the American Medical Association*, June, 1995)

Increasingly, youth perpetrate violence against other kids, although a national survey suggests that 83 percent of all serious crimes committed by youth are carried out by just five percent of them. Arrest rates for juveniles accused of violent crimes increased rapidly between 1982 and 1991 (the murder rate increased 93 percent), up nearly 60 percent over the seven-year period, then fell in 1995.

A "National Program on Girls and Violence" was launched by the Center for Women Policy Studies in 1995 because other programs focus on boys, although girls' arrest rate for violent crimes is increasing faster. Arrest rates increased 125 percent for girls (1985 to 1994), compared to 67 percent for boys. Many of these girls have been abused and some are addicted to crack cocaine. Almost one-fourth of girls reported being in at least one violent conflict during the previous year, according to the National Adolescent Health Survey.

One explanation for the increase in juvenile crime is the increasing number of children living in poverty. The U.S. child poverty rate, double that of any other major industrial nation, has gotten worse. The breakdown of traditional supports given to young people by families and neighborhoods contributes to the problem. Older people report that when they were young they could not get away with much because neighbors kept an eye on them. Drug addiction aggravates violence and is also connected to poverty. A fourth cause of increasing youth violence is the over 250,000 U.S. gun dealers interested in promoting gun sales.

People are increasingly concerned about the effect of violence in the media on copycat crimes. An American child will see 8,000 murders and 100,000 acts of violence on television before he or she leaves elementary school. Over 65 percent of major TV characters are involved in violence each week.

A $1.5 million study of television programming (excluding sports and news) found that 57 percent of programs contained some violence, the perpetrators of violence usually go unpunished, and only 16 percent showed any long-term problem for the victims. Only four percent of the programs discussed nonviolent alternatives to solving problems (a 1996 study by researchers at the University of California at Santa Barbara). Newspaper columnist Ellen Goodman reported that a review of 3,000 studies proves that violence on TV causes aggressiveness, fearfulness, and insensitivity in children. Readers often don't believe this, as it may not have an impact on you, but it does on more vulnerable and angry youth.

In response, good schools develop conflict resolution, peer mediation, and other prevention programs (see Chapter 7). For example, "Squash It" is an anti-violence program created by the Harvard School of Public Health. When a confrontation arises, youths say "Squash It" and make a time-out hand gesture placing a flat hand onto a vertical clenched fist.

The first local implementation of "Squash It" began in Kansas City, Missouri, in 1994, organized by the Partnership for Children. Their solutions to end violence are to keep schools open and active after school as a place to hang out, teach conflict management, provide employment as an alternative to hanging out, and provide adult mentors. As a Kansas City youth explains, "Kids need someone who's in their face, looking out for them."

Kansas City also hosts perhaps the most extensive mentoring program in the U.S., called YouthFriends, organized by the school districts and the YMCA. Youth participate in two conflict resolution trainings. They learn about their personal conflict styles (avoidance, control, accommodation, compromise, and collaboration), how to de-escalate conflict, active listening, assertive communication, I-messages, and problem-solving. (See the communication and conflict resolution sections in Chapter 2.) You might want to investigate what your community is doing to prevent violence and propose the Kansas City model.

Violence Prevention Efforts

Crime Prevention Coalition and the U.S. Department of Justice. 1-800-WE PREVENT (how to prevent violence and drug sales in your neighborhood)

National Neighborhood Watch Program 1-800-424-7827

National Organization for Victim Assistance 1-800-879-6682

Coalition to Stop Gun Violence 100 Maryland Ave., NE Washington, DC 20002

Handgun Control, Inc. 1225 Eye St., NW #100 Washington, DC 20005

Hands Without Guns 294 Washington St., Room 749 Boston, MA 02108

Kids Against Crime P.O. Box 22004 San Bernardino, CA 92406

Kidpower/Teenpower 1-800-467-6997 KIDPOWER1@AOL.COM http://pub-web.acns.nwu.edu/~bnm784/KIDPOW-ER.html (self-defense program that teaches violence and abuse prevention)

Los Angeles Police Department 10250 Etiwanda Ave., Dept. P Northridge, CA 91352 (how to organize a Neighborhood Watch)

Mad Dads, Inc. 2221 W. 24th St. Omaha, NE 68110

National Crime Prevention Council's
"Youth as Resources" Program
NCD, 1700 K St., NW, 2nd Floor
Washington, DC 20006-3817

National Mental Health Association
1021 Prince St.
Alexandria, VA 22314-2971
(*Voices vs. Violence* describes community programs to prevent violence)

National Program on Girls and
Violence/Center for Women Policy
2000 P St., NW
Washington, DC 20036

National Institute for Dispute
Resolution
1726 M St., NW, Suite 500
Washington, DC 20036-4502

National McGruff House Network
1879 S. Main St., Suite 180
Salt Lake City, UT 84115
(helps organize neighborhood safe
houses for latchkey kids)

National Sheriffs' Association
1450 Duke St.
Alexandria, VA 22314-3490
(Neighbors watch out for each other
and work with the police to establish
"safe houses" where latchkey
children can go for help, and develop
escort services.)

Neighborhood Anti-Crime Center
305 Seventh Ave., 15th Floor, Dept. P
New York, NY 10001

Partnership for Children
1055 Broadway, Suite 170
Kansas City, MO 64105

Resolving Conflict Creatively
163 Third Ave., #239
New York, NY 10003

Act Against Violence Guide (a booklet
about community violence prevention
programs)
Dept. P, P.O. Box 245
Little Falls, NJ 07424-0245

*The Prevention of Youth Violence: A
Framework for Community Action.*
Atlanta, GA: Centers for Disease
Control, 1993.

*You Can Raise Violence-Free Kids
National Crime Prevention Council*
1-800-NCPC-911
(a book about strategies communities
and families can use)

Geoffrey Canada. F*ist Stick Knife Gun*.
Boston: Beacon, 1995

Allan Creighton and P. Kivel. *Helping
Teens Stop Violence*. Alameda, CA:
Hunter House, 1990.
*Young Men's Work: Building Skills to
Stop the Violence and Making the
Peace.*
(curricula) 1-800-328-9000

Jane Goldman. *Streetsmarts: A
Teenager's Safety Guide.*
Hauppauge, NY: Barron's Educational
Series, 1996.

Myriam Miedzian. *Boys Will Be Boys:
Breaking the Link Between Masculinity
and Violence*. NY: Anchor, 1992

Fiona MacBeth and Nic Fine. *Playing
with Fire: Creative Conflict
Resolution for Young Adults.*
Philadelphia: New Society
Publishers, 1995.

Deborah Prothrow-Stith, M.D. *Deadly
Consequences: How Violence is
Destroying Our Teenage Population
and a Plan to Begin Solving the
Problem*. NY: HarperCollins, 1991

Internet violence prevention resources

gopher://pavenet.esusda.gov:70/11/
violence
http://education.indiana.edu/cas/
adol/adol.html

Wellness

Although the U.S. is one of the wealthiest nations in
world, and spent $949 billion on health care in 1994
($3,510 for each person in the U.S.), too many young peo-
ple are on the road to poor health. The American Health
Foundation report card rated the health of American children
as D minus in 1995, down from C minus the previous year. The
poor grade was based on the increase in high school seniors
who smoke (to 19 percent), the use of marijuana by 31 percent
of seniors, the obesity of 21 percent of youth ages 12 to 17, and
the unfortunate fact that only 34 percent of high school students get daily exercise at school. At least 40 percent of 12- to-
13-year–olds have a risk factor such as smoking, obesity, or
poor exercise recovery ability. Studies of young adults show a
decline in cardiovascular health since the mid 1980s. As a consequence, the Federal Office of Technology Assessment found
that about one of five of adolescents ages 10 through 18 has at
least one serious health problem. The same percentage have a
"diagnosable mental disorder," while one in seven lacks health
insurance (*American Psychologist,* February, 1993).

The World Health Organization defines health
as "a state of physical, social, and emotional well-being and
not merely the absence of disease." Our health depends on
genetic inheritance from our parents, environment (air and
water pollution, pesticides in food), and the life style we create for ourselves. Over 80 percent of major illnesses in the
U.S. are related to life style factors we can control, including
high-fat food, smoking, drinking, STDs, lack of exercise, and
accidents. Actions we can take to stay healthy follow.

Exercise

Lack of exercise, too much time in front of the television, and junk food take their toll on our health. In a large survey of high school students, only one-quarter of the girls and half the boys said they regularly engaged in strenuous exercise (the 1990 Youth Risk Behavior Survey looked at 11,631 students). Half of teenage boys and three-fourths of teen girls cannot walk up and down stairs for longer than six minutes without straining their cardiovascular system. Children average only 15 minutes of exercise a day. As a result, childhood obesity increased over a third in the last 20 years.

Get your heart rate up through exercise for at least 30 minutes a day; make it a habit like brushing your teeth. Moderate, extended exercise is best, such as walking, cycling, jogging, aerobics, dancing, or swimming. Sustained physical activity not only keeps your cardiovascular system healthy, it also increases production of endorphins, the brain chemicals that increase positive feelings and reduce anxiety.

Suggestions

📖 Warm up before vigorous exercise and cool down afterwards with stretches or walking to prevent injury and soreness.

📖 Develop an exercise schedule as one of the regular events on your calendar. Start with what is easily available, such as walking, jogging, or stair-climbing.

📖 Get support from an exercise buddy, a regular aerobics class, or as part of a team where you have to work out.

📖 List your favorite excuses for not exercising and how to respond with positive self-talk when you think of the excuse.

—Judith Eberhart, M.A.

As a counselor, when I talk with people with stress-related health problems, I ask, "Do you exercise?" Often they respond "No, I'm too busy." Yet they must find time to go to the doctor for muscle relaxants for their back spasms or to treat stress-related headaches and other ailments. Not all illness is related to lack of exercise, of course, but regular aerobic exercise is one of the best ways to:

- ⊙ reduce the stress hormones in our bodies
- ⊙ decrease intramuscular fat and increase lean muscle
- ⊙ improve circulation
- ⊙ lower the heart rate
- ⊙ improve absorption and utilization of food
- ⊙ increase energy and stamina
- ⊙ encourage restful sleep and release muscle tension
- ⊙ decrease nervous tension and depression.

Regular, continuous (30 minutes) aerobic exercise is time well-spent. An exercise hour could look like this: walk at lunch with a friend instead of sitting and eating, ride your exercycle or jump on your mini-trampoline for 20 minutes before your day starts, or dance with an exercise video. Continuous, aerobic exercise makes your heart rate increase and generally makes you sweat. Generally, if your heart rate is between 20 and 30 beats for a 10-second count and you can continue to talk to a friend while you exercise, then you are exercising aerobically.

It is important to stretch out before and after exercise, and you will also want to do some basic toning for the major body parts, using hand weights for the upper body and leg lifts for the lower body. Having a healthy cardiovascular system is not enough when your back is hunched over or your arms are flabby.

Positive Thinking

Emotions and thoughts impact our health, as TV reporter Bill Moyers explores in his book *Healing and the Mind*. Scientists discovered that our thoughts influence chemical messengers (neurotransmitters or neuropeptides) that hook up to receptors on the surface of our cells. The mind is literally spread throughout every cell in our bodies, so we aren't only what we eat, but also what we feel. Negative thoughts can suppress the immune system, allowing a virus easier access to cell receptors, whereas positive ones—such as love and faith, stimulate the immune system.

A study of 200 business executives whose companies were undergoing a stressful time found that the executives who handled stress well were much less likely to get severely sick. Rather than feel defeated, the executives who stayed healthy approached problems as a challenge, took action and stayed in control, exercised, and had support from their families. (S.R. Maddi and S.C. Kobasa. *The Hardy Executive*, Dow-Jones-Irwin.) To cope with tension and worries, use relaxation techniques (see *The Relaxation Response* by Herbert Benson, M.D., Wings Books), meditation, exercise, writing in a journal, reading humorous books or watching comedies, and talking with supportive friends and family members.

Healthy Food

In a week an average teenager consumes 9.8 soft drinks, 3.6 salty snacks, 2.7 fast-food purchases, and 2.3 candy bars (survey by Teenage Research Unlimited, 1993). In another nutritional survey only 15 percent of teens had eaten the recommended amount of fruit and vegetables the day before (the survey of 12,000 teenagers was conducted in 1993 by the Division of Adolescent and School Health of the federal Centers for Disease Control and Prevention).

Americans would be healthier if they reduced the amount of fat, sugar, salt, refined foods, and calories they consume. Only 25 percent consume a really healthy diet. These foods are associated with high blood pressure, heart disease, high cholesterol, and colon cancer. Fat is linked to heart disease and certain cancers; 25 percent or less of your daily calories should be provided by fat, although the average American consumes 35 to 40 percent of calories in the form of fat.

The U.S. Department of Agriculture recommends that you eat daily from these food groups:

        cereals, grains, and breads: 6 servings
        vegetables: 5 servings
        fruits: 2 to 4 servings
        milk products: 2 to 3 servings
        protein sources: 2 to 3 servings (fish, chicken, eggs, beans, etc.)
        fats, oils: small amounts

A 1995 survey by the U.S. Department of Agriculture shows that only one in eight Americans comes close to the department's dietary guidelines. Only 25 percent eat a healthy diet according to a large survey published in the September 9, 1996 *New England Journal of Medicine*. Their 1993 study found that school meals exceeded guidelines for fat by more than 25 percent, saturated fat by 50 percent, and salt by nearly 100 percent. Almost none of the 545 schools inspected followed the USDA's Dietary Guidelines (see school services section in Chapter 7 and check out your cafeteria).

Keep track of what you eat during a day and see how you compare with the recommended diet. Aim for at least 20 to 30 grams of fiber a day (the average American only eats 10 to 12 grams). Proteins help build new cells and repair injured ones, but most Americans eat more protein than they need. Remember that carbohydrates such as whole wheat bread or brown rice are the main source of energy and a good source of fiber. Fats carry fat-soluble vitamins (A, D, E, and K) and provide essential fatty acids and energy. Water is required for all cell functions, so drink at least eight glasses a day.

The American Institute of Cancer Research reports that as much as 40 to 60 percent of cancer is caused by our diet. Some families of vegetables help fight cancer, including the crucifers (broccoli, cabbage, cauliflower, etc.). High fiber/low fat diet is linked to lower rates of colon and breast cancers. Most fresh vegetables and fruit contain vitamin C which helps knock out free radicals (unstable oxygen molecules) that are thought to damage the DNA in our cells and make them more vulnerable to cancer.

Healthy Foods to Include in Our Diets

🔸 Flower-like vegetables such as broccoli and cauliflower, and soy bean products such as tofu, help fight some cancers.

🔸 Eat fish several times a week.

🔸 Avoid fried foods, preservatives, and soft drinks with caffeine and sugar. Processed foods are not only more expensive, but often very high in fat and salt. Buy fresh fruits and vegetables, or frozen, rather than canned ones.

🔸 Season food with herbs rather than salt.

🔸 Use olive or canola oil rather than hydrogenated oil and animal fat; substitute lowfat snacks such as ricecakes and homemade frozen juice popsicles for high fat snacks.

🔸 Eat whole grain breads and cereals; avoid white bread and white rice, as the nutritious hulls have been removed. To reduce fat intake, drink low fat milk or rice or soy milk, eat yogurt instead of ice cream, and reduce meat consumption.

🐟 Drink eight glasses of water daily.

🐟 Eat breakfast every day—pastries do not count.

Be aware of good and bad fats (liquid fats are called oils). Over one-third of young people have an unhealthy blood cholesterol level, so heart disease begins in childhood. Examinations of the bodies of young soldiers killed in wars showed that many already had advanced plaque deposits in the arteries to their hearts. In China, where the average diet includes about 14 percent fat, the heart disease rate is one-tenth of ours, and the breast cancer rate is one-sixth.

The body needs some cholesterol to keep cell membranes strong, but too much of it clogs the arteries with deposits on the inner layer of the arteries. Atherosclerosis can lead to heart disease. Saturated fat and partially hydrogenated oil raises blood cholesterol levels. These fats come from animal products, such as meat and dairy products, or are made by running hydrogen through unsaturated vegetable oils to increase their level of saturation—like turning a plant fat into an animal fat.

If you cook meat, cut off all visible fat and remove the skin from poultry before cooking. Chill soups, gravies, and stews so you can easily remove the hardened fat that rises to the surface. Palm oil and coconut oil are the most saturated fats of all, and are frequently used in commercial baking. Some plant oils reduce cholesterol levels, such as olive oil, peanut oil, and canola oil. Polyunsaturated fat lowers both the good (HDL) and bad (LDL) cholesterol levels and is made from seeds and grains such as safflower or corn.

Food labels must list total fat, saturated fat, cholesterol, sodium, carbohydrate, fiber, sugars, protein, Vitamins A and C, and the minerals calcium and iron. Some labels list content by servings rather than the total, so watch for this.

Avoid food poisoning by handling raw meat, poultry, seafood, and eggs as if they were contaminated with disease-causing bacteria. These bacteria include E. coli, listeria, campylobacter, and salmonella—the most dangerous. Undercooked beef can easily be contaminated, so always overcook hamburgers. When preparing meat, clean up with paper towels and throw them away, rather than spreading germs around with sponges.

Never eat raw shellfish. Marinate raw meat, fish, and poultry in the refrigerator rather than on the counter. Stuff a turkey just before cooking it, or cook the stuffing separately. Cook eggs until the whites are firm. It's worth learning about nutrition and diet to maintain your health and vitality.

Additional Wellness Checklist

◎ Have your teeth cleaned by a dentist twice a year.

◎ Get regular health checkups.

◎ When in the sun, use sunscreen and wear a hat to prevent skin cancer and premature aging of the skin. This may not seem important now, but it will when wrinkles start showing up.

◎ Have a consistent sleep schedule.

If you have trouble sleeping, ways to prevent insomnia include: Stick to a schedule of going to bed about the same time every night. Exercise early in the day, rather than in the evening. Don't take naps. Don't eat heavy, spicy meals or drink lots of liquids before bedtime. Avoid caffeine (in many soft drinks as well as coffee) and nicotine.

Since many illnesses can be prevented, start learning know about wellness techniques and apply them daily to remain energetic as you age.

Wellness Resources

American Dietetic Association
Nutrition Hotline
1-800-366-1655

Nutrition hotline and information from the American Institute for Cancer Research
1-800-843-8114

U.S. Food and Drug Administration, Office of Consumer Affairs
5600 Fishers Ln., Room 16-85 Rockville, MD 20857 (health pamphlets for teens)

James Balch and P. Balch. *Prescription for Nutritional Healing*. Avery Publishing Group, 1990. (practical A-Z reference to remedies using vitamins, minerals, herbs, and food supplements)

Susan Lark, M.D. *Self Help Nutritional Guide and Cookbook*. Berkeley, CA: Celestial Arts, 1995.

Lynn Lawson. *Staying Well in a Toxic World*. Chicago, IL: Noble, 1993. (how to fight to reduce pollutants and toxins in our environment, which damage our food, water, and air).

Louise Hay. *You Can Heal Your Life*. Carson, CA: Hay House, 1984.

James Marti. *The Alternative Health & Medicine Encyclopedia: The Authoritative Guide to Holistic and Nontraditional Health Practices*. NY: Gale Research, 1995.

Kathy McCoy and Charles Wibbelsman. *The New Teenage Body Book*. Berkeley Publications, 1992.

Bill Moyers. *Healing and the Mind*. NY: Doubleday, 1993.

Tom Robbins. *Diet for a New America*. Walpole, NH: Stillpoint, 1987.

Gail Slap and Martha Jablow. T*eenage Health Care*. NY: Pocket Books, 1994.

Women's Health

Note: girls should eat enough calcium-rich foods or take at least 1,000 mg of calcium a day to build bone mass and prevent brittle bones later in life. Folic acid should be taken well before child-bearing.

Women are often not included in medical studies, such as how to prevent heart disease, because researchers don't want to factor in changing hormones. As a result, a common problem like PMS was ignored as a medical problem until recently. In the early 1980s a federal Food and Drug Administration representative said the existence of PMS was as likely as the existence of aliens, so it didn't deserve study!

Premenstrual Syndrome (PMS)

About 40 percent of women experience PMS—about 10 percent have severe symptoms. A hormonal disorder, it occurs before a woman's period and stops when her period starts. More than 150 symptoms have been connected to PMS; it can include breast tenderness, moodiness, irritability, tension, depression, anxiety, hostility, back pain, acne, nausea, headaches, bloating, food cravings, weight gain, and fatigue. Some suggested causes are low blood sugar, fluid retention, stress, chronic yeast infections, vitamin-mineral deficiency, and hormone imbalance.

Some women find that avoiding salt, caffeine, alcohol, and sugar helps with PMS and cramps, as does taking calcium and magnesium pills, vitamins E, B-6 and other B vitamins, and vitamin C a week before menstruation. Women may crave sugar and chocolate before their period, but sugar can intensify PMS during the blood sugar low that follows the sugar high. If you crave sugar, try eating fruit. Eat complex carbohydrates, six small meals daily—including fruits, vegetable, grains and legumes, for a slower release of sugar into the bloodstream. Some herbalists recommend taking the herb chasteberry.

Regular exercise is one of the best treatments because it releases tension and produces endorphins that relieve pain.

One cause of PMS is an imbalance in estrogen levels. High blood levels of estrogen can be increased by eating too much animal fat and by a lack of nutrients needed by the liver to break down surplus estrogen. These nutrients include vitamin B complex, vitamin C, vitamin E, and the minerals selenium and magnesium. Estrogen-like compounds formed from isoflavones (a plant phytoestrogen found in soybeans and other legumes such as beans, lentils, and peanuts) can help normalize estrogen levels. An easy way to include soy in your diet is to drink a glass of soy milk every day. Isoflavones may also protect against breast cancer, as shown by women in Asian countries who eat soy products and have lower cancer rates.

Nutrition specialist Donald Payne explains that PMS is connected with excesses in estrogen. He suggests taking evening primrose oil capsules, available in a health food store, to balance the estrogens. He has also found it very helpful to cut out caffeine, saturated fats, sugar, marijuana and other drugs. On the subject of estrogen, he adds that the body produces three kinds: estrone (has an anti-cancer effect), estridol, and estriol. Birth control Pills contain only estriol, thereby loosing the cancer protection offered by estrone. He suggests that girls taking the pill should nourish their liver by taking the herbs dandelion root and milk thistle extract. Self-help books include Dr. Michelle Harrison's *Self—Help for Premenstrual Syndrome* (Random House) and Dr. Susan Lark's *Menstrual Cramps and Premenstrual Syndrome Self-Help Book* (Celestial Arts).

Vaginal Yeast Infections

Yeast is a normal part of the flora that live in the vagina. An infection occurs when the yeast takes over from the other bacteria that normally keep it in balance. The vagina is naturally slightly acidic. If this chemistry is changed, yeast and bacteria grow and cause an infection. It may cause itching, a burning feeling, and abnormal discharge from the vagina. Causes of the imbalance can be transferring yeast from the bowel to the vagina by wiping toilet paper from back to front, eating too much sugar, antibiotics which kill off the normal bacteria in the vagina, frequent intercourse (semen is very alkaline), stress, or inserting oils or other non-water based lubricants in the vagina. Some women are likely to get a yeast infection before their period when the hormone progesterone is increasing. Birth control pills increase the chance of yeast infections for some users.

To prevent yeast infections, some women eat acidophilus (the useful flora found in unsweetened plain yogurt) or take acidophilus capsules. Some women insert plain live culture sugarless yogurt in the vagina (with a spermicide dispenser sold in drug stores) to reestablish the healthy balance of bacteria. Others use a vinegar douche with one tablespoon of vinegar to a quart of warm water. Avoid eating sugar as it feeds yeast growth by changing the normal pH chemistry of the vagina. Avoid pantyhose, nylon underpants (wear cotton pants that aren't tight fitting), and deodorant tampons. If the infection persists, see a health practitioner.

Urinary Tract Infections (UTI)

The symptoms of UTIs are painful and frequent urination and feeling tired. This infection can spread to the bladder or kidney so it needs to be treated quickly by a doctor. To prevent infections, some women drink concentrated cranberry juice without the sugar which makes bacteria grow. You can find this juice (or extract in capsules) in a health food store if it's not in your grocery store. Some women take 1,000 milligrams of vitamin C several hours before sexual intercourse. The herb uva ursi can be taken as a tea or in capsules to prevent urinary tract infections for some women.

How to Lower the Risks for Breast Cancer

(One out of eight women will get it if they live to be 80, so start prevention early):

★ Keep your weight normal as too many extra pounds increase the risk of breast cancer, partly because fat stores estrogen.

★ Get regular exercise. Women who are active have a much lower rate of breast cancer than inactive women. Some think that exercise keeps estrogen levels at a lower rate, which reduces the chance of breast cancers that are stimulated by estrogen. This is connected to the fact that women who got their period early and started menopause late are slightly more likely to get breast cancer.

★ Don't smoke or drink alcohol, as several studies found that women who smoke and drink two drinks or more a day have a higher rate of breast cancer.

★ If you have a baby, breast feed him or her for at least six months.

★ Do regular breast self-exams about 10 days after your period when you reach 20 or 25.

Women's Health Resources

PMS Access/Women's Health America
1-800-222-4767

Federation of Feminist Women's
Health Centers
633 E. 11th Ave.
Eugene, OR 97401

National Women's Health Network
514 10th St., NW, Suite 400
Washington, DC 20004 (pamphlets
for teens)

Boston Women's Health Book
Collective
240 Elm St.
Somerville, MA 02144
The New Our Bodies, Ourselves. NY: Simon and Schuster, most recent edition.
http://www.healthgate.com
info@healthgate.com

Lynda Madaras with Area Madaras. *My Body, My Self: The What's Happening Workbook for Girls.* New Market Press, 1993.

Christiane Northrup, M.D. *Women's Bodies, Women's Wisdom.* NY: Bantam, 1994.

Since your health and feelings are intertwined, an important part of wellness is positive management of your feelings—the subject of the next chapter.

Chapter 2

Aaron Needham

Topics

Feelings

T he transition to adulthood isn't easy. In addition to changing hormones, you feel increasing pressures to do well in school, earn money, date, and define your own identity and future goals. Carefree childhood days aren't possible when you have piles of homework, a job after school, and sports practice. Our society doesn't do a very good job of teaching people the skills to manage and communicate anger, depression, guilt, grief, love, and other normal human emotions. As a consequence, teens' self-esteem suffers. This chapter describes how to express feelings and deepen our understanding of them.

—David, 16, California

The most difficult thing I face as a teen is the strong emotions that overcome me, because of the imbalance of hormones running through my body. I feel sudden mood swings, feeling depressed, then suddenly something makes me happy. The thing that has helped me the most with this challenge is knowing the part of my life that is the hardest is the shortest—adolescence.

Anger

I had, and still have, a lot of anger inside of me. Most of this anger was towards my mom, and I don't know why. She says it was me dumping on her, but it wasn't that. I was just angry. She said she thought it made me feel big and powerful, and I guess in a way it did, but it also made me feel weaker and more insecure because I thought my mom hated me. I didn't know how to control my anger, and I think this is one of my lessons in life I have to learn.

I'm getting better at controlling my anger through meditation, and the knowledge that I am in control of my body, my feelings, my emotions, and most importantly, my anger. When I'm stressed out or angry, I meditate, and everything seems to work itself out. Feelings are controllable. You have to decide what, how, and why you are feeling the way you are. If you want to change it, then start acting the opposite of how you're feeling. It's OK if you just pretend; it will still work.

—Derren, 16, California

Anger is useful when it propels us to take action to achieve our goals or prevents us from being hurt. It's harmful when we stuff it or express it unwisely. If you're the kind of person who ignores her or his anger, or has been told it's not polite to express it, you may not allow yourself to really feel your anger. Over time this can cause health problems because buried anger causes depression and undermines the body's immune system. Get in the habit of saying hello to all your feelings, bringing them into the light, then deciding the wisest way to express them—which may be just to write in your journal.

Frustration, hurt, disappointment, abuse, unfairness, and irritation can cause anger. People usually explode after a series of frustrations or hurts, like gradually fueling a rocket launch. Defuel your anger before it reaches the explosive point by taking positive action and by talking about it.

To manage anger, the secret is not to suppress it but to learn to express anger appropriately. As the body gets ready for action, the blood pressure rises and the muscles tense. A simple technique to calm down is to concentrate on counting backwards from 10 to one. Useful ways to vent your anger include: write a nasty letter (which you tear up), write in your journal, kick cardboard boxes, pound pillows, yell and scream in the shower or while riding your bike, take a walk, jog, lift weights, and talk to a trusted friend or family member. Danisha mentioned it's not realistic to scream around other people; maybe you could warn your family members if you like the shower idea. I mentioned the bike because that worked for me when I had a difficult boss. I'd yell, growl, and make faces at him while cycling to school so I could be centered when I saw him in person.

If you are angry with someone, use the communication techniques described in this chapter. Try the techniques described in the conflict resolution section, which suggests offering a specific solution for negotiation. Keep summarizing what you think the other person is saying to make sure your assumptions and perceptions are accurate.

Sometimes understanding each other isn't enough, and we must establish consequences. For example, your sibling keeps coming in your room and borrowing your things without asking. An "I message" is "I feel angry you took my shirt without asking me," while a "you message" is "You're an inconsiderate brat to take my stuff." It may be true, but it blocks communication. Moving in the direction of conflict resolution, you might ask, "I'd like to hear why you did that and your suggestion for how to solve this problem." If unsatisfied with the explanation or solution, provide a clear outcome, such as "I'm going to lock up my shirts. I won't lend anything to you for a month if you come in here again without my permission."

If someone is angry with you, listen, and repeat the point in your own words so he or she feels you've understood the message, even if you don't agree. Include a summary of the message and the feelings that go with it. If you think you made a mistake, apologize, ask what you can do to correct it, and learn from it to deepen the trust you feel in each other. If you think the angry person is an irrational bully and dumps bad feelings on you just because you're close at hand, say so and leave. No one ever has a right to inflict emotional or physical harm on you. If this happens, tell someone who can do something about it, such as a parent or school counselor.

Author Leona Eggert explains that people deal with emotional upsets in different ways, including depression, anger, worry, feeling worthless, considering suicide, using drugs, or giving up. She believes that all emotions are the result of our thinking habits and we can choose to change our thinking and our response (called cognitive therapy). She says, "We feel the way we think." That is, do I think of my glass as half full or half empty? If I think about what's missing, I feel cheated and angry. If I think about what I've got, I feel blessed and appreciative. If I look at a challenge as an opportunity to grow rather than a burden, I feel on top of the situation rather than victimized. Personally, I look at every difficulty as a lesson, a message that I need to grow.

Dr. Eggert observes that anger is "a combination of discomfort, tenseness, resentment, and frustration." Improper expression of anger ranges from rage to striking out at others, to physical violence and verbal abuse, to sarcasm and the "silent treatment." Proper expression of anger can lead to assertive behavior, as when I get angry I know it will propel me to take necessary action.

Keep a diary where you record when you get angry, how you respond, and the effect. When you become aware of what triggers your anger, such as when someone criticizes you or doesn't follow through on a promise, you can develop a plan to put in practice when you start to feel angry.

Practice "self-talk" to repeat when a trigger arises. Instead of egging yourself on by thinking about what a jerk the other person is, focus on relaxation techniques and positive self-talk. Dr. Eggert suggests directions to repeat to yourself as soon as a trigger happens: "This is going to be upsetting, but I can handle it," or "Stop! Stay calm. Think!," or "As long as I keep my cool, I'm in control."

She also suggests that we stop our usual response by substituting a long, deep breath from the abdominal area and counting to 10 while we exhale. (This Quieting Response is a common technique of stress management.) Taking time to cool off allows us to think about a plan rather than blowing up. The first 10 seconds are critical to gaining control, she says, so get in the habit of taking a deep breath as soon as you start feeling angry. (Emma says pausing makes the other person even more angry at you because you are not saying anything. This may seem like you are ignoring them, so explain you need a minute to think.)

It takes practice to change old habits, so if you slip back into an old anger response, let the person you attacked know that you slipped but are working on changing your behavior. If there is one person whom you usually dump on, talk with that person about triggers. Brainstorm how you can communicate your anger constructively, as by writing notes rather than speaking, or by taking turns to really listen to each other. Anger can be positive if expressed constructively.

—Jason, 16, California

To deal with my anger or other people's, I picture a rose between the other person and me, absorbing all the negative feelings. Then I imagine blowing up the rose to get rid of the feelings I don't want. If you become aware of your breath, you stay calm and can get through almost anything. I try to get a good view of the whole situation by trying to see all the different viewpoints, separating myself from what's going on. I recommend Louise Hay's book Heal Your Body (Hay House), which explains the effect of emotions on our health.

—Brandon, 20, California

We must all spend some time learning how to vent our anger. Whether we do journal writing or play sports, suppressed anger can lead to harmful behaviors. Anger is a healthy human emotion when we learn to recognize anger in ourselves and in others and understand the real reason for our anger. Physical outlets for anger are:

1. vigorous exercise

2. screaming or yelling from the solar plexus

3. punching bag or pillows

4. beating the ground with a knotted rope

5. making and kneading bread

6. writing a letter to the person, and not sending it

7. role playing, role reversal

8. sports

9. talking about it with a person who's not involved, support groups

10. playing music

11. singing.

—Greg, 21, California

Dealing with anger was the most difficult experience I faced as a teen. I saw various counselors, fell for a girl, and listened to reggae music to help me cope.

Leona Eggert. *Anger Management for Youth: Stemming Aggression and Violence.* Bloomington, IN: National Education Service, 1994.

Ron Potter-Efron. *Letting Go of Anger.* Oakland, CA: New Harbinger, 1995.

Assertiveness

Being assertive in my family is very frustrating for me. Living up to my parents' standards was always difficult. I've learned that liking myself and being confident helps me to be assertive. So finding hobbies you're good at and like will help you become confident and assertive.

—Joey, 15, California

Assertive communication is expressing your rights and feelings without being an aggressive bully or a manipulative person who only indirectly expresses his/her needs. Unassertive people are afraid to disagree for fear of being unliked. They remain quiet when something upsets them, find it hard to receive or give criticism, and have a hard time asking for help. At the other extreme, aggressive people demand rather than ask, are verbally abusive, get angry when criticized, and think of compromise as losing.

A bully might yell, "You fool, I'll punch your lights out," while a manipulative person might give you the cold shoulder. If you ask what is wrong, he or she might lie and say, "Nothing."

Assertive people can say No when it's appropriate, without feeling guilty, apologetic, or fearful of disapproval. They can express their viewpoints directly and disagree without being nasty and defend what's fair. Examples of assertive behavior include not allowing yourself to be interrupted ("I'd like to finish my thought"), asking someone not to smoke near you, or telling someone you do not want advice or insults. Sometimes being assertive simply requires firmly repeating your request until you get a response, such as "I'd like to return these shoes because the sole came off the first time I wore them." If the person does not respond, ask to speak to the supervisor, and repeat your request. Body language is important, including eye contact and erect posture.

You can be both assertive and understanding by adding your recognition of the other person's feelings, such as telling a friend you realize he is giving you advice because he cares about you, but you want to make your own decision. Effective communication is the secret of being assertive, using "I" statements rather than "you" statements (see the next section). When you need help, be direct and specific, rather than just hinting. Give the person time to think about your request. If someone gives you a compliment, accept it with thanks, rather than putting yourself down.

To say No, be direct so the person doesn't have to guess at your intention. You may be able to offer a compromise or substitution to the request, as by saying, "I can work for two hours on the project, but not four." You don't have to give specific explanations; saying "I'm sorry, I already have plans for Friday," is adequate.

Emma is one of those people who can't say No without feeling guilty and wonders why. It's often harder for females because of the expectation to be especially nice, ladylike, helpful, kind, and not come on too strong. Girls need to be kind to themselves and be aware of the unassertiveness built into "women's language." Women tend to avoid making a declarative statement such as "It's hot in here." Instead, they add tag questions such as "Don't you think?" or "OK?" or make a statement sound like a question by using a questioning inflection in their voice. They are also more likely to apologize for a statement or ask for attention, such as, "I may be wrong, but..." or "Listen to this...." They are more likely to allow themselves to be interrupted, touched, and patted, to smile, nod their head in agreement, tilt their head to the side, and drop their gaze rather than look at someone directly. These are the behaviors of subordinates, such as children in relation to adults or an office worker in relation to the boss. Females also talk less in mixed sex groups and ask more leading questions, while males answer at length.

To check on these scientific observations by linguists, observe next time you are in a classroom or at a party to see who talks the longest, who gets interrupted, who uses a questioning inflection, and who encourages the other person to continue speaking with comments such as "Then what happened?" or "Wow!" (See books by Deborah Tannen for more examples.)

How effective are you in making your wishes known and saying No to unreasonable demands? What would you do if a friend asked you to do something that was unfair or unreasonable?

—Anna, 16, California

School poses many frustrations. I'm very assertive and opinionated and because of it have been called a bitch. Whenever any of my strong girlfriends or I take control of an activity or asserts our beliefs, other classmates—including other young women—snicker. Yet, any guys who assert themselves are looked on as smart and powerful, living up to their full potential. It's a demeaning double standard.

Stay strong. There are strong women just like you out there. High school is a long trial on your strength, with teachers, administrators, and "friends" trying to dictate your personality. Although the real world reflects some of these pressures, there is more room for individual pursuit and more people who sympathize. Hold your head high, and realize that you have just as much right to an opinion as anyone else, and just as much right to assert it and follow it.

—Nili, 17, California

The most difficult challenge as a teen is not being treated as an equal. Many adults try to take advantage of teens, and even more adults think that teens don't know what they're talking about. My advice is to always speak your mind. If more teens speak up, then one day soon those adults will see what you can do.

I think it's important for teens to know how to deal with their emotions because too many teens are killing themselves just because they don't know how to deal with what they're feeling. The other thing that is important is that teens should know that whatever they're going though there are other people around the world who feel the same as they do. If I knew that when I was younger, it would have made me more confident.

—Beth, 21, California

Don't let anyone bring you down. It's tough; people are mean, fake, and untrustworthy. Stand your ground and be assertive and self-confident. Trying hard to be popular and fit in never got me anywhere. It's when I decided to be myself that I found really lasting friends.

—Ellie, 29, California

I wish someone had told me as I entered high school that I could be in control, if I wanted to be. I spent high school either waiting for things to happen or letting them happen to me. I didn't know until the very end that I could be in charge.

Communication Skills

My experience in peer counseling at school has been wonderful. With two years of this training, I feel confident I could walk into a problem and help the person out. But not many guys come in for peer counseling. I've noticed guys tend to keep things bottled up inside until they get so bad that the only thing you can do is come out with it, because it's eating you up. Masculinity has a big part in it because we think that if we open up and become sensitive, it's showing that we're weak.

Boys aren't interested in relationships like girls are, because honestly we don't care about them as much. Guys are interested in sports because guys need to feel macho and show off just because it makes us feel special. Sometimes it's easier for guys to talk on the phone.

—Martin, 14, California

[Observations of babies and little children reveal that parents talk more with girls about emotions and by age three girls engage in more detailed discussion of feelings. Part of the explanation is that girl babies are born more developed, make more eye contact, and do more "vocalizing," so parents find it easier to talk to them. Also, the toys we give girls stimulate more talking about feelings and interaction, such as dolls, while action toys usually evoke noises rather than words from boys. The way a child communicates defines the child in many ways.]

—James Sniechowski, Ph.D., Director, The Menswork Center in Santa Monica, California, gives an explanation for Martin's observations of boys.

In the work I do with young men around the country, I help them question the "warrior culture" they've been raised to believe in. The warrior culture teaches that the only way to be "manly" and "masculine" is to act tough and never reveal tender emotions. Ever hear of "Big boys don't cry"? In Tom Cruise's movie *Mission Impossible*, warrior masculinity is implicit in the title. It's a mission and it's impossible—just the job for a warrior hero.

Defense is a reality and someone must do the defending. But masculinity and defense are defined as equivalent and that leaves a lot of males out of the loop. Warriors are necessary but limited; unfortunately, their experience of life has been elevated to be the symbolic experience of being a man. That's the problem.

The warrior culture demands that boys and men give their lives to a belief in cut-throat competition and that, because females are not tough, males are superior. But, what do you think of a society that promotes the raising of young girls so that they are not supposed to be tough and then ranks them in second place to boys and men?

Our unrealistic, inhumane ideas of what makes a man a "man" lead to feelings of isolation, loneliness, brutal violence, and depression. If you were comfortable with your masculinity would you would you feel compelled to "prove your manhood" all the time? No! That's what insecure males have to do.

I suggest you consider that the real test of manhood—the only one that will give you internal confidence and comfort, is your ability to respect and express your own feelings, whether fear, sadness, anger or love, admiration and joy. The full range of emotions that make you human are what can set you free to be a fully developed, truly powerful man.

You hear a lot about the need for effective communication but not much about how to do it. When I interview couples and survey students, they usually pick good communication as the key to a successful relationship. These skills are useful in your family, with your friends, sweethearts, in the classroom, in team sports, and at work. When I ask my students to practice a skill like active listening, they think it's easy, but usually can't do it on the first try. Practice the following essential techniques.

1. **Be direct**, clear, and honest rather than sarcastic, manipulative, or withholding. Manipulators blame, sulk, use sarcasm, threats, criticism, interrupting, and one-upmanship instead of stating their needs clearly. If you feel hurt say, "I feel angry and hurt because you ignored me at the party last night," rather than pouting. Saving up resentments in the name of politeness, called "gunnysacking," only leads to dumping bad feelings later. For example, if you don't say anything about your irritation over the wet towels left on the bathroom floor, after the thousandth towel, you blow up and the person thinks you're overreacting to one wet towel.

   Sometimes people don't discuss their feelings because they are afraid to hurt the other person or fear rejection. But the feelings won't go away. They'll seep out and muddy the waters, so it's better to clean them out as they come up. Working through conflicts, hurts, misunderstandings, and power struggles is how we grow as individuals and as a couple or family. As we learn to trust our friends' commitment to honesty and growth, our love and respect deepen.

2. **Comment on the person's behavior** or action rather than on the person. Instead of saying, "You're a selfish creep to ignore me at the party," stick to your feelings and suggest a solution: "I felt hurt when you ignored me at the party. In the future I'd like us to check in with each other from time to time. How do you feel about doing that?"

3. **Speak for yourself** rather than judge the other person. "I feel you're selfish" is simply a disguised "you" message. Sticking to your own feelings is a very powerful technique because it encourages the other person to sympathize with you, rather than shut you out or attack you in a defensive reaction to your blame. (Emma discussed these techniques in class and the "general feeling was they were stupid and don't work." That's because they weren't actually trying to work through being jealous, hurt, or angry with a boy/girlfriend.) You don't have to repeat these exact words, but focus on how the problem affects you rather than criticizing the other person and cutting off dialogue. I guarantee effective communication can work wonders in your relationships.

4. **Active listening** is a very effective communication technique which draws people to you. This involves letting the speaker know you understand what she is saying, how she feels, and why, as in "You're angry because the grade your English teacher gave you is really unfair." You paraphrase (summarize in your words) what you think the person said, perhaps starting with a phrase such as "What I hear you saying is _____," "In other words _____," or "Do you mean _____?"

You may need to clarify by asking questions or asking for specific examples. Aim for open-ended questions such as "How did you feel about that?" instead of "Did that make you feel angry?" This lets the speaker know you truly care about understanding her. Watch out for "noise" that distracts you from concentrating, such as thinking about your own issues or whether you're hungry or bored, or what you'll say next. Most people speak about 200 words a minute, but the mind thinks twice as fast; your job is to keep your mind focused on the speaker's words and feelings.

Sixty-five to 80 percent of communication is nonverbal, so notice what the speaker's body language is saying. If it contradicts what you hear, ask about the seeming contradiction. For example, if someone says he's not upset but you observe his foot is jiggling, his body is tense, and his voice gets louder, you might say, "It looks like you're upset about this. Would you like to tell me about it?" Your own body language should convey your concentration by maintaining eye contact, leaning slightly forward, nodding, and avoiding distractions such as playing with your hair or looking away. Erica, a reader, adds, "It really makes me mad when I'm talking to friends and they don't make eye contact, because it makes me feel they aren't paying attention."

Much good follows from attentive listening. Paraphrasing helps you really listen to your partner and creates opportunities to clear up misunderstandings. Many times we think we understand but don't. Arguments often occur because people feel misunderstood and try to make their point more forcefully. Feeling you're understood cools down the frustration that leads to arguments. You may need to paraphrase and incorporate corrections several times before you get it right. Practice this by having a friend tell you about an important event in her life and you repeat back what she said, along with her feelings.

Your focus on the speaker is a marvelous gift of your attention and concern, which makes her feel cared for and important. Your attention also encourages the speaker to solve the problem by working through the feelings enough to think rationally about options. This means you must not interrupt to tell about your own experiences or try to offer solutions. Wait until the speaker has cleared up his feelings and can think logically before you brainstorm what to do. Keep your focus strictly on the speaker, rather than on your thoughts and feelings.

When you move to the problem-solving stage, it's more useful to share information and options with the person than your advice about the best solution, which may not be right for her or him. Most of us like the freedom to make our own decisions.

5. Make sure each person gets her share of time to talk. Sometimes it works to **take turns**, each person talking and the other doing active listening, for a half hour each—or whatever you have time for. Some people exert their power by unfairly doing most of the talking and interrupting.

Communication reminders

from Linda Frazee (Positive Imagery, Inc., Laurel, Maryland)

1. If you don't ask, the answer is always No.

2. Tell the truth faster.

3. Remember to appreciate and bless differences.

—Paula, 16, California

Most people really don't let the person who has the problem let it all out before trying to solve the problem for them. Thus the problem stays. We need to know how to listen.

—Ben Jones, 18, Texas

I have a real concern for other people. My dad told me to put other people ahead of myself, and he did that for me. My high school offered a class called PAL, "Peer Assistance and Leadership." The first half of the semester we learned how to practice active listening and to ask open-ended questions (How does that make you feel?) instead of giving advice.

We learned about backing up words with body language, using the SOFTEN techniques. This stands for: smile, be open, lean forward, touch (as in patting the person on the back) [use your judgment, as some people don't like to be touched by someone they don't know well], *keep eye contact, and nod. I found that people open up if they know you really care. Some of my friends get tired of me asking how they're feeling, but girls say, "Ben, nobody has ever cared before about how I think and feel."*

The second half of the course we put what we'd learned into action as peer mediators/counselors. We have six "Lifesaver" boxes around the school where people can ask for help, or they can contact a counselor, a principal, or our advisor. We handled about 60 disputes last year—all resolved. Most of the problems were about boy-to-boy or girl-to-girl miscommunication, and about rumors like "I heard you called me a loser." [Interpersonal conflicts are the main cause of killings at or near schools!]

During the mediation sessions, I explained the program and the rule that they could only talk to me, not to each other. I summarized what the first person said and asked the second how he or she felt about it, and repeated the process for the second person. Then I'd ask, "John, what do you see as the solution?" Then I'd ask Tim. If they couldn't agree we'd go through the first process again to see if there was another underlying problem. [Try applying these techniques the next time you face a conflict.]

—John, 21, Colorado

If you want to go anywhere in this world you need to know how to treat others. I think that it is very important to learn manners. Parents are not teaching manners and teachers are not trying to gain their students' respect in the right ways. (Teachers need to learn how to talk to their students on the level of their students.)

I think that all manners are centered around respect. If you respect others then you are more likely to do nice things for them such as open doors. And you are not going to talk with your mouth full because that would be disrespectful to the other person. Manners basically come down to the golden rule: Do unto others as you would want them to do unto you. You need to respect others even though they are not like you. If someone has problems learning, for example, you should respect that and maybe offer your help.

It is natural for the younger generation to rebel against the older but this rebellion should be done respectfully. You need to understand society before you can change it, and you certainly can't understand society if you don't respect it. Rebellious kids today are lacking in respect for themselves and others. This lack of respect is what I think contributes to their lack of manners.

I have benefited greatly from being well-mannered. I know how to speak to people so they can listen and understand. I feel that my manners are key to portraying my knowledge and opinions. You can be smarter than anyone but if you don't talk to others respectfully and politely, nobody will listen. You can't get anywhere in this day and age if people won't listen to you.

—Suzy, 24, Nevada

The basic good manners are thank you notes, birthday cards, letters to friends who have experienced the death of a loved one, congratulations to graduates and for births, marriages, and engagements. Manners have not only helped me react properly to important events in life, but have also given me feelings of repayment. For example, when someone goes out of their way for my benefit, I feel that I need to return the favor and create a balance in the friendship. This, in return, has applied positively in the way I make, keep, and search for friendships.

Children's and Youth's Emotions
Anonymous
P. O. Box 4245
St. Paul, MN 55104
(program for young people to
develop healthy emotions using
the 12-step program)

National Self-Help Clearinghouse
25 W. 43rd St.
New York, NY 10036

Conflict Resolution

U ntie "knots" of disharmony with people as soon as you're aware of them. Stick to how you feel, why, and suggest a solution: I feel _____ when you _____ because _____ and would like _____.

Techniques to Solve Conflicts

◎ Tell your side of the story, the facts as you see them. Stick to this one topic, rather than throwing in past grievances. Paraphrase the other person's grievance even though you may not agree with it: "What I heard you say was I'm trying to get your best friend (Chris) away from you."

◎ Add the emotional dimension as in, "This makes you feel you can't trust me and you're angry with me."

◎ If you need clarification, ask for more information: "Give me an example of something I did to take Chris away from you."

◎ Suggest a specific solution: "I won't talk about you with Chris." See if you can find an area where you agree or have a common concern.

◎ Agree in advance that if one or both of you starts feeling your anger is getting out of control, it's OK to take a quick walk or other time out to calm down.

◎ Switch roles so the other person explains her side. Often just the process of active listening and letting her know you understand her point of view solves the conflict. If not, try to negotiate a compromise.

Go through these steps the next time you have a disagreement with a friend or family member and notice at what point you get stuck. Are you really listening to each other and paraphrasing feelings, even if you don't agree? You may need to include a neutral third person to help you really listen to each other and suggest a fair compromise.

Depression

The rate of depression for Americans is increasing, with an even higher increase among teens. Depression affects 17.6 million Americans each year, according to the National Institute of Mental Health. People born after 1955 are three times more likely than their grandparents to suffer from deep depression; six percent are depressed by age 24, according to a 1992 article in the *Journal of the American Medical Association.* The gap between males and females is narrowing, with boys catching up.

Depression is a natural withdrawal from stress and feeling powerless. When it is ongoing, professional help is necessary. Causes include loss (such as a divorce), feeling unable to cope and overwhelmed, learning disabilities, drugs, and illness—loneliness is the theme in the stories you'll read next. Self-critical, perfectionist people who don't feel in charge of their lives and dependent people are more likely to be depressed. For some people, depression stems from imbalances in their brain chemicals, which may be a genetic inheritance (see the mental illness section). Depression can lead to suicide so treatment should occur before it reaches this dangerous stage.

In a survey of nearly 43,000 Minnesota high school students in 1986, 39 percent suffered mild to severe depression; of these, nine percent were severely depressed, and six percent reported suicide attempts in the previous six months. The most common causes of their depression were conflict and loss (including breaking up with a boy or girl-friend), family arguments, divorce, and serious illness or injury of a family member.

Signs of depression are sadness, inability to enjoy favorite activities, feeling hopeless and empty, restlessness, pessimism, headaches and stomachaches, low self-esteem, poor concentration, loss of energy, and change in eating or sleeping patterns. Depressed people may withdraw from others, lose ability to concentrate, be irritable, cry a lot, feel sad, lonely, and hopeless, or try to self-medicate with alcohol and other drugs.

To cope with mild depression, reach out and find a supportive, good listener and learn problem-solving skills (read the stress management section). Make yourself get out of your room: Exercise to relax and sleep better, try an enjoyable new activity, and get help from a mental health professional. Students say to reach out for support, as other people have the same feelings. Severe and ongoing depression requires the help of a mental health professional who may prescribe medication as well as therapy.

Cognitive psychologists (who emphasize the importance of self-talk) teach their clients that they can change their thinking patterns to change their feelings and behaviors. For example, pessimistic/negative thinking leads to depression, illness, and less productivity, says Martin Seligman (*Learned Optimism*, Pocket Books). When we have a depressing thought, such as "I can't do math," we can substitute, "With the right help, I can do math" and seek out help from the teacher, a tutor, or a friend.

Kelly Lynn Baylor suggests keeping a good news journal where you make yourself write in your journal before going to bed; you can't write the bad stuff in this journal, only good things that happened during the day. It may not be easy at first, but you can include items like a stranger smiled at you. If you do this faithfully, it starts keying your mind to look for the positive almost in spite of yourself. Ms. Baylor reports she has seen suicidal people get better after just two weeks of doing the good news journal.

If you have a depressed friend: Listen to him, don't deny his pain, let him know your concern, and especially if he appears suicidal, get help from a professional such as a counselor or religious leader, or call a crisis line.

—Lauren, 17, New York

The most difficult challenge has been dealing with depression and loneliness. Writing down my feelings, and doing a zine [a handmade, xeroxed magazine] has helped tremendously, although I still haven't gotten over everything, and am still working on it. If others face the same problem, I would tell them to use their emotions creatively, to do something for themselves. Writing down what you're feeling, all your anger and pain, can be a big help.

—Thomas, 17, Iowa

Crisis is a two-way street. Either you can let it overwhelm you and let it destroy you, or you can use it to be a stronger person. I've had two friends try to commit suicide in the last two years (they've probably attempted it more times than I'm aware of). The sad thing is one of them achieved her desperate goal with a shotgun blast to the chest. That's reality.

I spend a lot of time alone in my thoughts. I learned how to cope with depression mainly by realizing that there are probably many other people out there who feel the same way I do—alone, ignored, and downright low. After I came to that conclusion, depression just seemed to fade. It's like this: You feel alone, but when you realize that out of the five billion people living on this rock, there's got to be at least ONE other person out there who feels the same way. Even though you may never meet or know that person, you can't really say you're all alone. It's a bonding of sorts.

—Robert, 18, Minneapolis

I "smoked out" and got high any way I could. I fell in with the wrong crowd, but they were the ones who kept me alive. I went through shrinks like crazy and even had one commit suicide—quite the role model. My grades got worse and worse (I ended up failing the 9th grade), but I was "having fun" while hiding behind a mask of self-pity and fear. I was afraid that people hated me and I knew my family did (I "knew" a lot back then). My friends, my computer, and my music were my escape. I even began withdrawing from my friends and all I had left was my computer work and my songs. I wrote like mad. I even began a novel but stopped after 115 pages. It was getting too long and not really going anywhere, but it was my fantasy, my escape.

I ran away and squatted for a while before I was found half-dead with various drugs in my stomach. I was sent to a mental health center for three months where I learned how to deal with things better and how to cope with reality. It was there that I found the connection between loneliness and computers. It seems to me that kids who can't find friends make their own friends online.

I was given anti-depressants and put on a monitoring system where I had to report to certain people throughout the day. Soon I was able to go home, but that didn't last. I fell back into my old ways and within three days was back in the hospital for more treatment. It went on like this for a while, getting help and finding new ways to cope. I haven't been in the hospital or a center for four years and I haven't drank for four years. I see things differently when I am sober and clean. It's amazing that in a large family and large community I can still feel lonely. But I cope.

—Jennifer, 25, Texas

I learned to ask for help when I needed it. I was depressed a lot and sort of romanticized and wallowed in it. I used to think about suicide a lot. Then one of my friends attempted suicide and was hospitalized for most of her junior year, and another friend got so sick from anxiety-related illnesses that she couldn't even go to graduation. I had no idea that either of them was in bad shape, and hearing our other friends and myself wondering, "Why didn't she talk to us about this?" made me realize that I was keeping a lot of stuff inside, too, and that scared me.

Coping with Depression

**Depression Awareness Recognition
and
Treatment Center
1-800-421-4211
(free brochure)**

**Focus on Recovery
1-800-888-9383
(referral to self-help groups)**

**Humanistic Mental Health Hotline
1-800-333-4444
(information about depression, suicide
prevention, and drugs and alcohol)**

Susan Newman. *Don't be S.A.D.: A Teenage Guide to Handling Stress, Anxiety and Depression.* Englewood Cliffs, NJ: Julian Messner, 1991

Howard Rosenthal. *Help Yourself to Positive Mental Health,* (Taylor and Francis) suggests the amino acid L-tyrosine, the hormone melatonin, the herb St. John's wort, the mineral magnesium, and chamomile tea to counter depression.

Grief

By far the most difficult thing I had to face in high school was my mother's death a month before graduation. She had been sick with inoperable lung cancer, and that in itself put stress on me. Her death threw me into a serious battle with depression that I'm still coping with. Thinking about all the things I have from her (personality, physical characteristics, lessons learned, etc.) has helped me to deal with the loss. Working hard to better my family relations has helped to fill some of the void I feel. Also, I take full advantage of my university's counseling center through personal and group counseling. [See the death section in Chapter 5.]

—Michelle, 19, Georgia

Grief and joy are both parts of human development. Grief is a natural response to losing a pet or a friend, breaking up with a sweetheart, parents' divorce, giving up on a desired but unattainable goal, leaving one secure place (such as leaving high school for college), or the death of a loved one. Try to process the feelings rather than ignore or repress them—they will not go away. Guys I surveyed often report they deal with their pain by ignoring it, playing sports, or doing some other activity. However, repression just puts off processing our feelings. Unconscious feelings influence our decisions and behavior even if we're not aware of them, such as whom we pick for close relationships.

It's healing to talk about your loss with a trusted person. Grief work involves accepting the loss and the feelings it generates. It's more painful in the short-run but better than pretending nothing happened. It helps to find a purpose for your grief work, such as becoming a stronger and more understanding person, one who knows how to work through painful feelings and understands how others feel when they are grieving.

Grief causes emotional and physical reactions: not wanting to eat, tears, sighing, dry mouth, feeling exhausted, restlessness, and inability to concentrate. Don't hold back tears because they release toxins (body wastes) associated with depression, although tears caused by peeling an onion do not.

People go through emotional stages after a loss, just as you probably do after even a minor event like getting woken up from a sound sleep by an alarm clock. You start with denial, "It's not really time to get up," and move through the other four stages before you get out of bed. All the stages are necessary and some may occur at the same time, or we may repeat an earlier stage later. The grieving process and time is different for everyone. Dr. Elisabeth Kübler-Ross, a well-known researcher on death and dying, defined these stages.

Grief Recovery

1. **Denial**: "It isn't true. "This temporary reaction of numbness gives us time to cope with overwhelming shock and sorrow.

2. **Anger**: "I don't deserve this." Vent this feeling by ripping up and throwing newspapers, writing letters and tearing them up, etc. Emotional release, including crying, is common.

3. **Bargaining**: "If I do _____ maybe this will go away." Sometimes people blame themselves and feel guilty, thinking about what they might have done to prevent the loss. A young person might think "If I'd behaved better, my parents wouldn't have separated, so I'll act like an angel now."

4. **Depression**: "There's no hope." Feelings of sadness, helplessness, and lack of energy are common. Acknowledge them as part of the healing process rather than trying to ignore them.

5. **Acceptance**: "What's next?" After talking out feelings and reliving memories, the person is ready to get on with his or her life.

Journal writing can help us be aware of the stages as we go through them. If you have a grieving friend, the best thing you can do is listen with your full attention and offer hugs. Don't say to get over it or not to cry, to be strong, or other statements that shut down their feelings. You may be more likely to encourage girls to cry, so be aware of sexism; it's unfair to boys to keep them from the healthy clearing out of their grief. A counselor or grief support group can help.

—Greg, 22, California

My most difficult experience was carrying my best friend's coffin and dealing with his death. I had help from my father. My advice is to have a good relationship with your parents because they have gone through everything.

How to Survive Grief and Loss

Grief Recovery Program
1-800-852-2188

Association of Death Education and
Counseling
638 Prospect Ave.
Hartford, CT 06105

Melaba Colgrove, et al. *How to Survive the Loss of a Love*. Boston: GK Hall, 1992.

Hope Edelman. *Motherless Daughters: The Legacy of Loss*. NY: Delta, Dell, 1995.

Virginia Lynn Fry. *Part of Me Died, Too: Stories of Creative Survival Among Bereaved Children and Teenagers*. NY: Dutton, 1995.

Marilyn Gootman. *When a Friend Dies: A Book For Teens About Grieving and Healing*. Minneapolis: Free Spirit Publishing, 1994.

Karen Gravelle and Charles Haskins. *Teenagers Face to Face with Bereavement*. Englewood Cliffs, NJ: Julian Messner, 1989.

Earl Grollman. *Straight Talk About Death for Teenagers: How to Cope with Losing Someone You Love*. Boston: Beacon Press, 1993.

Elisabeth Kübler-Ross. *On Death and Dying*. NY: Macmillan, 1993. *On Life After Death*, 1991. *On Children and Death*, 1993, both Celestial Arts.

Elyce Wakerman. *Father Loss: Women Discuss the Man That Got Away*. NY: Holt, 1987. (She found that the loss of their father was the most significant event of their lives. However, 82 percent of the women were not encouraged to express their feelings at the time of his death.)

Happiness

My students and I asked hundreds of people of various ages what makes them happy. At the top of the list were families, friends, sweethearts—the people we love. Other popular responses were achieving a personal goal and engaging in enjoyable leisure activities such as sports or being in nature.

Instead of waiting for someone else to make us happy, we can take charge of our own attitudes. The secret is to approach difficulty as an opportunity to get stronger and count one's blessings. For example, if I run for school office and lose, I can be unhappy and blame myself or I can be happy about my courageous act and what I learned from campaigning. Make a list of what makes you enjoy life and structure in time for these healthy activities.

Since happiness stems from feeling good about ourselves, I asked Karen Joiner, director of the Chico Psychic Institute, how to take control of your own feelings. She teaches meditation skills and is writing books about her techniques.

How to Control Your Emotional Space

1. Find a comfortable, **quiet space** where you won't be interrupted. Turn off the phone. Have a glass of water to drink and a pad of paper nearby in case a thought comes up that you want to remember. Sit in a comfortable chair with your feet on the ground to help ground you.

2. Take a slow **deep breath** to become aware of your body. Notice how you're feeling. Engage all your senses, listen to any sounds in the room, notice how it smells, see what colors stand out, become aware of your body in the seat and your feet on the floor. A lot of athletes know how to be comfortable in their bodies which helps them feel sure of themselves. Here's another way to gain that comfort.

3. Once you're focused on your body, rather than thinking about your homework or a friend, put your attention on the base of your spine. Feel it, imagine what it looks like. Then visualize the molten core of the center of the earth. Picture connecting a hollow tube from the base of your spine to the center of the earth and anchoring it in with the force of gravity. You can imagine this **grounding cord** as a tree with long roots, a waterfall, a chain with an anchor on it, a rope, or lightning, or anything that will release stuff you don't want in your space.

4. Let gravity suck whatever doesn't belong down your grounding cord. This could be someone else's problem that you're carrying around, anxiety, fear, anger, self-doubt, confusion, stress, or excess nervous energy. You don't have to name what you want to be released, it will happen by itself. Imagine **pulling the plug** in your bathtub or a sink filled with water. Or imagine dumping out a bag of marbles, so just the bag remains. Say to yourself, "My feet are releasing," "My ankles are releasing," and work on up your body, including your organs and all the cells in your body. Visualize your body safe, grounded, centered, and amused (amusement is healing).

5. It's very important to replace the negative energy you've released down your grounding cord with positive energy, or else similar yucky stuff will fill in again. Imagine creating a **big, gold sun** about a foot and a half above your head. If you have trouble imagining this at first, go stand outside in the sunlight and allow the sun's rays to warm and fill your space. Once you've created the gold sun, imagine it tipping over so it goes into every nook and cranny of you, like a pat of butter melting into an English muffin. Or you can imagine creating a hole in the sun to release the gold light, or standing under a golden waterfall or shower washing through every part of you. Say to yourself the gold sun is filling up my head, my shoulders—and on down your body. After doing this exercise for a month or so, people do start to feel more grounded, clear, and at peace with themselves. You'll be able to hear your own answers.

Note: When you're out and about and get in an unpleasant or unsafe situation, you can imagine yourself inside an electric-blue bubble or protected by a field of flowers to absorb any negative energy before it gets to you.

I recommend *The Aura Coloring Book* by Levanah Shell Bdolak (Voyant Press in Beverly Hills), which illustrates some of these exercises, even though it's been a while since you've used a coloring book. Hey, it's still fun.

How to be Happy

1. **Emphasize the positive** rather than the negative. Positive thinking becomes a habit when you interrupt and cancel out self-defeating thoughts, such as "No one likes me," "I look terrible," "I can't do science," or "Nothing goes right for me." Refuse to

accept negative labels from others or yourself, such as "I'm lazy." Stop negative "what ifs," such as "What if I blow it on my first date with Devon?" Choose a symbol, such as a stop sign or red light, to imagine when you start negative thinking or "awfulizing." Substitute visualizing your goal, such as having fun with Devon.

The Campus Wellness Center at CSUC where I teach recommends these books for positive support: Gerald Jampolsky, *Love is Letting Go of Fear*; Shirley MacLaine, *Dancing in the Light*; Shakti Gawain, *Creative Visualization*; Barbara Sher, *Wishcraft*; Bernard Gunther, *Energy Ecstasy*; Gay Hendricks, *Learning to Love Yourself*; Hugh Prather, *Spiritual Book of Games*; Spencer Johnson, *One Minute Manager*; and Sondra Ray, *I Deserve Love*.

2. Remind yourself that **you are in charge of your life**. You can take action, get help, practice positive self-talk, make changes, develop your talents, and refuse to listen to irrational criticism.

3. **Avoid "catastrophizing."** When therapists use this term they mean making a mountain out of a molehill. A "D" on a test may seem like a disaster at the time, but in the long run it does not mean you won't get into college. Some things just are not that important or urgent. There is gray between white and black, maybe between yes and no, and something between all or nothing. Ask yourself, "Will this matter a year from now?"

4. **Avoid perfectionism.** Perfectionism is "a set of self-defeating thoughts and behaviors aimed at reaching excessively high and unrealistic goals." It is impossible, self-defeating, and a waste of energy. You can't please everyone, so don't waste time trying. If you disappoint yourself, look for the lesson. Instead of thinking about winning or losing, think about the opportunities to learn.

Unrealistically high expectations lead to disappointment. If you know a friend is a gossip, for example, don't expect her to change. Simply don't share anything you don't want spread around and you won't be disappointed.

5. **Just because you fear something doesn't mean it will happen.** You may feel scared about giving an oral presentation and making an embarrassing mistake (I did have my half-slip fall off while teaching class one day, just picked it up, and didn't give it any attention). However, with preparation and positive self-talk, focusing on your audience rather than yourself, you can give an effective speech without embarrassment. (See the oral reports section in Chapter 8, since this is something many people fear.)

6. **Nurture yourself** by recharging your batteries with quiet time to reflect and get centered. Nurture your relationships with communication skills.

7. **Appreciate your successes and talents.** Be as kind to yourself as you are to others. Tell others what you appreciate about them every day, and do the same for yourself. Accept compliments with appreciation rather than contradict them. For example, if someone says, "You look great today," say, "Thanks," rather than, "Are you kidding? I look terrible."

8. **Accept the challenge** of learning a new skill, meeting new people, or changing an old habit, even if it stretches you and seems difficult. Take reasonable risks.

9. **Think about the "should" messages** in your life and evaluate which are rational for you. For example, "Everyone should go to college to get a good job;" but there may be a better career path for you. Follow realistic goals that are important to you rather than to others. Listen to your own inner/highest guidance. Schedule regular time for fun.

10. Practice techniques to **achieve your goals**, including clarifying your priorities, time management skills (see Chapter 8), and taking action every day to move toward your goal. Follow this procedure:

  a. Write your goal in your journal
  b. List the barriers or problems you may have to tackle
  c. List the actions you will take
  d. Decide how you will reward yourself for your success.

Your Identity

There is always a need to fit into a certain crowd, the cool crowd, the ones who are always the talk of the school and in fashion. [Emma comments, "The cool crowd is only cool to themselves. They think so much of themselves there is no room for anyone else."]

The friends I have now helped me to learn that you do not need to change yourself to fit into a certain crowd. They taught me the wisdom that if you have to change to fit in then you must not belong in that crowd. I have also learned that there is no need to be someone you are not just because of a boy. If they end up liking you for what you are not, then they are liking a fake. Just BE YOURSELF!

—Carinna, 14, California

To consciously shape your identity, observe role-models such as parents and teachers to see what to apply or avoid. However, a survey of 10- to 14-year-olds discovered that 43 percent have no one they want to be like, because no one is special enough (a 1995 survey by KidsPeace). Of the 57 percent who said they have a hero, a family member was the most popular choice. In a 1996 Horatio Alger survey, 19 percent of girls and 13 percent of boys cite a parent as their hero. You might interview people you admire, and ask how they got where they are.

Our identity is influenced by at least three forces. Your genetic heredity from your parents gives you talents such as musical skill or high-level math ability. Fascinating studies of identical twins separated at birth (the University of Minnesota) reveal that our genes strongly influence some of our personality traits, including whether we're shy or outgoing, thrill seeking or conservative, worriers or calm, etc. Your cultural background influences your identity through the beliefs, language, customs, religion, and values passed on to you by your relatives. Your environment—your school, your neighborhood, your friends, and the media, is a third factor in your development. You might list the two main influences for you in each of the three categories. Knowing yourself allows you to build on your talents and change some aspects you don't feel work well for you. (If you aren't happy with your present setting, you can create a new one by becoming a lady or lord in the medieval Society for Creative Anachronism (1-408-263-9305)!)

Here are some questions to answer in your journal to spark your thinking about your identity. You might want to share responses with a close friend or family member.

Who Am I?

1. Who are you most similar to in your family? Most different from?

2. Are there patterns in the kinds of friends you pick?

3. Are there patterns in the kinds of people you're attracted to romantically? Make a list, including people you haven't met in person, such as a singer or actor. Sometimes we're attracted to people who express traits we haven't developed (i.e., strength or emotional expressiveness) or to people similar to, or the opposite of, a parent.

4. If, at the end of your life, a tombstone is engraved with your most important life accomplishment, what do you hope will be written on it?

5. If you could be an animal for a week, which would you be? Why?

6. Name five things you like about yourself. Name five things you like about your body.

7. Name two things you would like to change about yourself and can (i.e., you might like to be five inches taller but have no control over this).

8. What was your favorite possession as a child? Your favorite holiday? Your most exciting moments?

9. What is your favorite movie? What character would you most like to be?

10. If you were going to make a film about your life, what high points and low points would you include? What actor would you pick to portray you?

11. What is your favorite book? What books have most influenced your beliefs? What book do you want to read next?

12. What was your most embarrassing moment?

13. How would you be different if you woke up tomorrow as the other sex, besides the obvious physical changes?

14. What is your first memory?

15. How would you describe yourself in a single's personal ad in the newspaper?

16. What talents were you born with? What skills have you learned that didn't come easy? What really interests you?

17. Are you an introvert (you need time alone to recharge your personal batteries, have a few very good friends, and may not be comfortable in large groups) or an extrovert (a people-person, you feel energized by being with groups of people and enjoy having lots of friends)? Many people are introverts at some times and extroverts at others.

18. Is your first reaction to a problem to think it over or feel intuitively what to do?

19. At what times of day are you most energetic?

20. Do you like structure and planning or open options and spontaneity in your life?

21. Do you learn best by seeing, hearing, doing, touching, or a combination?

22. Where is your favorite place to be?

23. What do you believe about God, the afterlife, and the purpose of life?

24. What values are most important to you?

25. What is your most important goal now? For the next month? For the next year?

One of the best ways to understand your whole self is to record your dreams as they are the most direct route to learning about the activities of your unconscious mind. If the conscious mind is like the visible tip of an iceberg, the unconscious mind is the largest part of the iceberg and propels it. It's smart to be aware of the whole iceberg so you are aware of where you're headed and why. Dreams deliver their messages in symbols and drama. Books by Ann Faraday and others explain how to interpret your dreams.

Write down your dreams every morning if you can. Get in the habit of asking yourself what you dreamed even before you open your eyes. Make your mind like a blank TV screen and see if a dream will appear. Dreams won't make any sense at first, because their language is symbolic rather than verbal. Patterns will emerge as you read over your dream journal and the messages of the dreams will become clearer as you learn your personal symbols.

I'll give you some examples so you can see how dreams work. I had a series of dreams about having to teach math, something I'm not prepared to do. Finally in the last of five dreams over time, I said No, and the principal agreed. My unconscious was practicing becoming more assertive. My friend Jake dreamed his girlfriend was trying to take his towel off rather than going swimming as they'd agreed. This is a visual picture of his feeling she's trying to expose his inner self when he's not ready to do so. Many dreams are about releasing anxiety, as when we dream about being chased or not knowing any test answers. Some dreams are wish fulfillment, such as dreaming about eating or sex.

Personality inventories/questionnaires help us understand our personality types. The most frequently used is the Myers-Briggs, as explained in Keirsey and Bates' *Please Understand Me* (Prometheus Nemesis Books). The book includes the personality survey and explanation of the eight types. This understanding is a valuable tool for self-awareness and for getting along with others. Instead of judging people who are different from me, now I see that they simply have a different style that is not better or worse. Defining your style, values, goals, and interests is one of the major tasks of adolescence. Do it consciously and actively rather than reacting to pressures from others.

—John, 14, California

It's taken me years to get into a status where I feel somewhat accepted and comfortable. I have made myself into 100 personalities at once. I talk differently with friends, other students, jocks, druggies, and other expressionists. I know the goal is to be yourself and express yourself how you feel comfortable.

—Amy, 15, California

All teens have to go through changes to become mature enough to cope with grown-up responsibilities. My parents don't always approve of my decisions and our relationship has changed a lot because I am becoming my own person. Tell your parents you would like to be treated as an individual and as a young adult.

—Linnea, 15, California

Figuring out who I am has taken time because I can't analyze myself. I am able to see other people's feelings better than mine and unable to see myself well. I'm trying to let my emotions show and not get sidetracked by anyone. [To help understand your hidden feelings, one way is to write down your dreams, then read them at the end of each month to see what your unconscious mind is working on. A counselor can help you make sense of the dreams, too. Other ways to contact your deeper self are to write in your journal, draw, daydream, meditate and talk with someone you trust who is a good listener.]

—Jake, 17, Pennsylvania

Teens face decisions about where they want to go with their lives, whom they identify themselves with—basically how they should act. A lot of people never discover the answer to these questions (e.g., mid-life crisis). Being an "adult" and dealing with those responsibilities is hard.

Well, drugs are NOT the answer. I did that for awhile and it just messed me up. It helped me cope for a little while, but in the long run it caused more problems than it fixed. (Actually, it never fixed any problems, but that's another story.) What helped me cope with being a teen is the same thing that makes me get up every morning: I do what I love, I'm true to myself, and true to others. The only way to live is by doing what you love, 'cause if you don't want to get up in the morning, you won't.

For me, that "love" is for music and writing. In turn, I run two zines, am in a band, and run a record label. I keep myself busy. That keeps me from focusing too much on the problems in my life. Coping for me is about looking at the better part of life. To me, that's music and literature, to others it may be something else. As long as it warms their heart when they do/think/listen/play with it, then it's worth more than all the gold in the world. Every time I hear someone walking around humming a song by my band, my heart feels like it's going to explode.

—Shana, 17, Wisconsin

I keep a journal and write all my thoughts in times of crisis. Then I look back later and see my errors. To relate with your peers you first need to relate to yourself. Accept yourself so you can accept others.

—Seth, 20, Oregon

Take the time to develop your own sense of identity. Realize that this is your life and you have the right to do with it as you please. Live with integrity and every-thing else follows.

—Kathleen, 21, Missouri

I felt pulled in so many directions by others that I really didn't know what I wanted or what I wanted to become. Talking with parents, teachers, and friends helped me to cope with this, also just experiencing things in high school and learning along the way. My advice would be to seek out help from others, talk to others, experience new things—but the ultimate decision on who you want to be should be your own. It takes time to figure it out.

—Jason, 21, California

In all my four years of high school I never truly acted like myself. I was always worried about what other people thought of me, so I never really let my guard down (except around close friends). Most teens are worried that if they act like themselves, other people will not like them. But, the more I grew up, the more I acted like an indi-vidual and I cared less about what my peers thought of me.

Self Awareness Tools

Renee Baron and Elizabeth Wagele. *Are You My Type, Am I Yours?* **NY: Harper Collins, 1995. (explains the "enneagram," which defines nine personality types: perfectionist, helper, achiever, romantic, observer, questioner, adventurer, asserter, and peacemaker)**

Robert Fisher. *The Knight in Rusty Armor.* **No. Hollywood, CA: Wilshire Book, 1990. (a humor-ous novel about finding identity)**

Mindy Bingham, et al. *A Teen Woman's Journal for Self-Awareness and Personal Planning. A Young Man's Journal for Self-Awareness and Personal Planning.* **Santa Barbara, CA: Advocacy Press, 1993.**

Andrea Johnston. *Girls Speak Out.* **NY: Scholastic Press, 1997.**

Nancy Rubin. *Ask Me If I Care: Voices from an American High School.* **Berkeley, CA: Tricycle Press, 1995. (a high school teacher of "Social Living" includes excerpts from her students' journals)**

Mental Illness

I never really knew what depression was until I found myself ready to kill myself. I was having an extremely difficult time dealing with the breakup of a three-year relationship with a girl. I went straight to drugs as an escape. I ran from myself, my family, and my friends. After taking several hits of acid, kidnapping my ex-girlfriend, and waking up the next morning holding a shotgun in my mouth, I decided to check myself into a mental hospital. It was extremely difficult dealing with only being allowed out of the hospital until midnight on graduation night. I wanted to kill myself even more than ever when I knew I had to go back to the mental hospital while all of my peers were having a great time partying.

I eventually got out of the hospital to supposedly enjoy my graduation present which was a bicycle tour through Europe. In Europe some days were better than others. There were days that I remember standing on several different church towers and thinking about jumping off to my death. When I got back to the States I was happy to be back around some of my old friends.

Then the whole college thing came up. I enrolled the last minute in the local university, feeling overwhelmingly lost, and more down than ever. I was completely catatonic, sleeping and staying in my bed for 16 to 22 hours at a time. One night after an argument with my girlfriend, I drove up into the mountains and, in an attempt to kill myself, I crashed my car. Much to my own disgust, I was still alive. A passer-by drove me to the fire station where my parents came and got me. To this day I can't quite figure out why I didn't die that night, I surely wanted to.

Then they tried to put me on anti-depressants but they didn't go over well with me. I could go on about many other attempted suicides but I think my point is conveyed. Just an overwhelming feeling of hopelessness had engulfed me and I wasn't going to let anything let me be happy. I was extremely distant from everyone; I straight up wanted to die. Why was I so depressed, you may be wondering? I felt Earth Mother crying in pain over the destruction we humans had done to it. When I looked around all I saw was death and destruction and raping and ravishing of the planet we all share. I saw poor lost souls wandering around sending horrible messages of self-destruction. I basically saw only the negative in anything and everything that came my way.

A book by the name of *As You Think* by James Allen (Whatever Publishing) really helped me learn to focus my thoughts and pull out of my negative depression cycle. We make that choice at every instant we think. Some good words of advice about positive thought may be gained from any of Depok Chopra's writings, including *The Way of the Wizard* (Harmony Books), *The Seven Spiritual Laws of Success* (Amber-Allen), or *Perfect Health* (Harmony). The focus on breath alone has many healing properties. Bringing the power of nature into my body in the form of eating healthy foods and meditating has helped me considerably. Using the combination of counseling, self-hypnosis, and holistic herbal supplements (mahung and valerian) has helped me achieve balance in my life.

—Barry, 20, California

The Institute of Medicine estimates that as many as 12 percent of kids age 18 and younger suffer from a psychological illness caused by a chemical imbalance in the brain. These disorders may be genetic and thus inherited from our parents. They can be treated with medication and therapy. The following common mental illnesses involve loss of touch with reality.

Anxiety Disorders

✪ Anxiety disorder—an unreasonable fear, such as fear of going outside your home. The most common severe mental illness, it affects about 10 to 15 percent of the adult population.

✪ Panic disorder/panic attack—an anxiety disorder with unpredictable periods of intense fear. Some symptoms are a racing heartbeat, dizziness, feeling short of breath or smothered, shaking, sweating, smothering sensations, trembling, faintness, and a fear of dying or going crazy. Phobias are irrational fears of ordinary things (such as crowds or spiders) and cause panic attacks. At least half the people with panic disorder and phobias also experience depression.

- Obsessive-compulsive disorder—feels compelled to do repetitive actions such as constant hand washing to fight germs, even though he or she knows it's unreasonable. Compulsions are repetitive actions such as constantly arranging things.

- Post traumatic stress disorder—feelings of depression, low self-esteem, and changes in eating and sleeping patterns, caused by a painfully violent experience such as rape, abuse, or a car accident.

Depressive Disorders

- **Bipolar mood disorder/manic-depression**—mood swings from deep depression to intense irrational hyperactivity, delusions, and excitement.

- **Severe depression**—feel sad and restless, loss of energy, life seems meaningless, may be suicidal. About 10 million Americans face clinical depression, as compared to the temporary down times we all feel.

- **Schizophrenia**—this brain disorder can cause hallucinations, hearing voices, delusions (such as believing you can control other people's thinking), confusion, paranoia (irrational fear), repetitive movements like rocking, or withdrawing—not moving for hours.

Some Other Disorders

- **Seasonal Affective Disorder (S.A.D)**—depression during certain months of the year, usually during the winter. Bright lights can help.

- **Multiple personality disorder**—usually caused by a desire to escape child abuse, the person develops distinct identities, with their own names and personalities, who are not aware of each other.

In the past, most mentally ill people were placed in mental institutions. Now, with new medications, up to 80 percent can live normal lives. Since the 1960s, the number of Americans in mental institutions fell by 85 percent. A problem for some mentally ill people is they try to self-medicate with illegal drugs that don't correct the problem. Mental illness can be treated by a professional similarly to diabetes or any other chemical imbalance in the body.

Hartgrove Hospital Program
1-800-DONT-CUT
(referrals to treat self-abuse and
self-mutilation)

KidsPeace 1-800-KID-SAVE (mental
health referrals)

National Alliance for the Mentally Ill
1-800-950-6264

National Clearinghouse on Family
Support and Children's Mental Health
1-800-628-1696

National Depressive and Manic
Depressive Association
1-800-826-3632

National Foundation for Depressive
Illness
1-800-248-4344

National Institute of Mental Health
Panic Campaign
1-800-64-PANIC

National Mental Health Association
1-800-969-6977
(provides information, referrals, and
advocacy)

Anxiety Disorders Association of
America
6100 Executive Blvd., Suite 200
Rockville, MD 20852

B.E.A.M. (Being Energetic About
Multiplicity) Newsletter
P.O. Box 20428
Louisville, KY 40250-0428

Federation of Families for Children's
Mental Health
1021 Prince St.
Alexandria, VA 22314-2971
(parent-run organization for children
with mental health problems)

Obsessive-Compulsive Anonymous
P. O. Box 215
New Hyde Park, NY 11040

U.S. Dept. of Health—Alcohol, Drug
Abuse and Mental Health Division
5600 Fishers Ln.
Rockville, MD 20857

Jack Gorman. *The Essential Guide to
Psychiatric Drugs.*
Enid and Richard Peschel, et al., eds.
*Neurobiological Disorders in Children
and Adolescents.* These and other
informative books can be ordered
from NAMI, 200 N. Glebe Rd., Suite
1015, Arlington, VA 22203-3745.

Internet psychology self-help
resources:

http://www.gasou.edu/psychweb/reso
urce/selfhelp.html

support group:
ftp://rtfm.mit.edu/pub/usenet/alt.su
pport.anxiety-panic/psychology-%26-
support

Self-Esteem

My most difficult challenge has been finding confidence within myself. Friends, sports, and achieving recognition for my efforts have helped. Being accepted by kind people helps too. Look inside yourself for confidence. Try to forget what society has crammed into your delicate head about appearances and images. Life means much more than that.

—Alexandra, 15, California

Self-esteem is how you feel about yourself. People with healthy self-esteem have a realistic view of their strengths and weaknesses, take pride in their accomplishments, act on what they think is morally right, and accept and learn from their mistakes. With high self-esteem you feel worthy of being valued and successful. It becomes a self-fulfilling prophecy. If I expect to do well, I'll do a lot better than if I think of myself as a failure. Positive thoughts build high self-esteem and help us take charge of our lives.

People with low self-esteem tend to feel passive, powerless, negative, and victims of bad luck. Michele Borba reports in her book *Esteem Builder's Resources* (Jalmar Press), that students' self-esteem has tragically dropped because "a breakdown is occurring in a number of support networks [married parents, neighbors, extended family] that used to enhance students' self-esteem." She quotes a study that self-esteem is often more important to school success than intelligence scores.

Because self-esteem is the foundation for success, I asked three experts to give their suggestions for how to build esteem.

—Claudia King, a teacher and an author of a book on self-esteem, would like you to think about your life as a process for your growth.

So-called mistakes and failures are really ways to tell you to try it differently. They are the universe's attempt to perfect you and make you stronger than the circumstances you are attempting to master. Learn your own process. Learn the sorts of problems that happen to you repeatedly. Try to figure out why they are your problems. What is it about how you look at the world or go about doing things that brings these problems to you? Notice that when you get closer to mastering some aspect of your life the problems will get harder and what appear to be mistakes may seem more difficult. Understand that your life is a process in which you are becoming more and more the person you're intended to be.

—Peter Hill, an author who works with youth in Arizona observes that:

Self-esteem rises from feeling good about ourselves. Developing skills on any level—whether athletic, social, academic, religious, community service, hobbies—will help to do this. Unfortunately, teenagers face a crushing disillusionment that sometimes they cannot voice; it is the realization that they are moving from being loved unconditionally for the most part when they were younger, to being "loved" for how they look, dress, talk, what they drive, what they have, and what they do. So they begin to feel used and manipulated—not loved. That also makes them highly susceptible to people who appear to love them unconditionally for whatever they are or do. As educators/parents/friends of teenagers, we must love them unconditionally and teach them responsibility for their actions and words.

—A former superintendent of schools, Robert Reasoner developed a five-step self-esteem building process for students and educators, with remarkable changes in the schools that apply these principles.

How to Develop Self-Esteem

1. Realize you can't make everyone happy. Make choices about your own goals and behaviors. Feel in control of your life by getting organized.

2. Identify your strengths and weaknesses. Draw on what makes you feel secure and strengthen it, such as your religious beliefs or your family.

3. Build a support group of people who value you.

4. Develop your sense of purpose and intention. Set goals. Without purpose, depression results. Establish dreams and a positive outlook about your future.

5. Strengthen your sense of competence by moving toward your goals. List the resources available to help achieve goals and get feedback from knowledgeable people.

(Materials for educators are available from Reasoner's Self-Esteem Resources, 234 Montgomery Ln., Port Ludlow, WA 98365.)

Many studies show that esteem is a gender issue because, when girls enter puberty, their self-confidence drops. A survey of 33,000 Canadian students in 5th, 7th, and 10th grades found 96 percent of boys, but only 56 percent of girls, had confidence in themselves. Fifty-three percent of girls wished they were someone else, compared to 39 percent of boys (The Canadian Health Attitude and Behavior Survey, conducted in the 1980s).

Peggy Orenstein reports in her book *School Girls: Young Women, Self-Esteem, and the Confidence Gap* (Doubleday) that a girl's entry into adolescence is "marked by a loss of confidence in herself and her abilities, especially in math and science. It is marked by a scathingly critical attitude toward her body and a blossoming sense of personal inadequacy." As a result, girls are much more likely than boys to have eating disorders like bulimia, to try to commit suicide, to be diagnosed with depression, and not to prepare for science and math careers.

The AAUW (American Association of University Women) study on *Shortchanging Girls, Shortchanging America* reports on a survey of 3,000 youth:

Girls	Boys	agree:
29%	46%	"I'm happy the way I am."
15%	28%	"I argue with my teachers when I think I'm right."
23%	42%	"I'm good at a lot of things."
61%	72%	"I like math."

They also found girls with high self-esteem are more likely to take math and science courses than girls with low self-esteem. Girls who are active in sports have higher than average levels of self-esteem and have less depression than other girls.

Eighth grade girls surveyed by Wellesley College researchers defined a girl who likes herself as having feelings of confidence and pride and a strong sense of her own individuality. They observed that sources of high self-esteem are having supportive and respectful parents, good friends, a positive role model, and someone to listen to and understand them (Sumru Erkut and Fern Marx conducted the study of Boston girls).

Studies confirm that having the support of at least one competent adult builds self-esteem. Having several encouraging teachers, low levels of family stress, and spiritual connectedness are other factors that increase teens' self-esteem (Michael Resnick, University of Minnesota Adolescent Health Program).

To summarize, techniques to increase your self-esteem include: Take good care of your body, be aware that advertisers often want us to feel badly about ourselves so we feel we need to buy their products, do nice things for yourself, accept what you can't change and change what you can, concentrate on the positive, imagine yourself achieving your goals and take some action every day, look at mistakes as opportunities to learn, develop skills, and help others. Finally, get inspired by inspirational books, sermons, audio tapes, the stars in the night sky, or whatever connects you to the highest part of yourself!

—Jackie, 17, Colorado

The main thing that helps me cope with too-high expectations is being involved in a variety of activities. Being involved has helped me realize who I really am, what I'm interested in, and what is good for me. It helps raise my self-esteem and reminds me that I am allowed to be my best and not what someone else believes is best.

—Sara, 18, California

My most difficult challenge as a teen was feeling that my life was too good. I felt that everyone had these great problems that they got attention for and my life was boring. I coped with my challenge by making things up. I suggest that people find the truth and power within themselves to be confident with who they are. Everyone is beautiful and divine in their individuality—that's what makes us special, not boring.

—Teresa, 18, Michigan

The most difficult challenge I faced as a teen was learning to rely on and believe in myself. I had a group of very close friends who were always there for me, to support me and help me through my problems. They tried to show me that I was a good person, but I had a hard time believing it. It took me a long time to figure out that they were telling the truth. One of the things that really changed my mind was having a close friend who was a lot like me. He had very low self-esteem and didn't believe us when we told him that he was a wonderful person. As I got to know him better, and tried to convince him, I realized that the reason I got so frustrated with him was because he was so much like me. I realized that, just like him, I was a good person who had a lot to offer to my friends and to the world.

Another thing that helped me was getting involved in clubs and activities at school, because I was able to use my talents to help others. I became a leader in one of these groups, and the responsibility that I took on also taught me that I was an important person. You are the one person you are going to have to spend the rest of your life with, so believing in yourself is the most important belief to have.

—Elena, 19, Illinois

I had a really rough time as a teen. I had a lot of anger at my family that was bottled up; I was constantly battling depression, and occasionally thought of suicide. I had some really destructive relationships, both friend and boyfriend type, that played a huge part in putting me where I am today. I think that everything goes back to self-esteem, of which I have none. I have always been awkward, pretty different from everyone else. I always wanted to be popular and never was. I was always much more mature than everyone else, and subsequently felt very isolated and alone sometimes.

I always had a boyfriend, often for long periods of time. I hit an age, around 13, when I judged my worth as a person by my boyfriend. I always depended on others to tell me I was good enough and smart enough and pretty enough, but they never did. I hated myself a lot, thought I was stupid and fat and ugly and a complete social reject. I tried so hard to be the nicest, best person I could be, but no matter how hard I tried, people didn't pay attention to me or they criticized me.

I coped with my depression, lack of self-esteem, and self-hatred in a lot of very destructive ways. I tried to commit suicide, mostly to scream for help. It didn't come, so I got into drinking too much. I lashed out at my family and blamed them for everything when I hit high school. I worked hard to make others happy, and sacrificed myself for that cause. I dabbled in self-mutilation, mostly carving with a razor. I began to diet, which rapidly turned into bulimia and then anorexia. That landed me in a psychiatric hospital last year, and I'm still in therapy.

On a positive note, there were a few positive coping mechanisms I had. I kept a diary/journal (and still do) that I told EVERYTHING to. It was like talking to a best friend, but that best friend was me. I kind of projected myself into my stuffed elephant and this diary, and served as my own best friend. I also came to value my uniqueness, and turned it into an attribute. I got really involved in volunteer work and political causes, which helped surround me with people who appreciated me.

When people make fun of you, it's because they're jealous, and because you're doing something right. Popularity isn't anything; it dies in high school or college. You are not alone, as there is a sea of others in the same boat as you. Don't keep things bottled up, talk to people—friends, teachers, parents, whomever. They'll probably have a lot of wisdom. Plus, talking helps. Write a journal. If your thoughts are on paper, you can delete them from your head and think about other things. Don't listen to what society tells you about how you should look, it's not human, and it's oppressive. Appreciate the beauty of nature, your body (no matter what it looks like), and other people. Take a second look at your family, as they're probably cooler than you think.

—Navy, 19, Maryland

If you have low self-esteem, bring it into the open, so your parents, teachers, and friends can help you and encourage you. If it's severe, get professional help. You will always have times when you'll be put down. Remember, though, what's important is how you feel about yourself, not what somebody else says. It's important to have a healthy body more than an attractive body. But if you don't like the way you look, do something about it. Again, not because somebody else tells you that you look bad, but because you feel that way.

—Captain, 20, California

Sports and a job made me feel better. I think it was the responsibility that helped.

—Kerryn, 20, Australia

God wouldn't have made you if She didn't think you were worthwhile, so trust Her opinion.

—Megan, 20, Michigan

Unlike some of my friends, I had a wonderful time as a teen. I was one of the lucky ones who had close friends I could trust and turn to whenever I needed them. They had very few expectations of me and I didn't have to face much negative peer pressure. I have been involved in a group called Youth-to-Youth, an international teen-led organization that supports and promotes the lifestyle of "My Choice, Drug-Free." It is not a drug treatment program, but prevention and education. It made a great difference in my life and gave me the support that every teen needs.

I've realized that the single greatest problem facing teens is self-esteem. Somewhere along the line, someone tells all teens that they are not good enough, that they are not smart enough, and who they are is wrong, so they must try to be something else. And many teens believe it. Starting somewhere around middle school for me, earlier for some, later for others, there is a desperate search to be something. No one really knows what. You have to try be whatever "the crowd" is being. All too often the crowd is doing something stupid.

Whether it's cigarettes, cheating on tests, mouthing off to teachers, or diet pills, to fit in you feel like you should be doing those things too.

Peer pressure is not what most adults seem to think it is or what I expected it to be. It's not scary looking people in dark corners telling you to smoke a joint to be cool like everyone else. It's far more subtle than that. It's the girls in the locker room talking about how much fun they had Friday night and what a blast it was to be totally smashed. If you're the girl in the corner who was lonely Friday night, suddenly alcohol doesn't seem like such a bad idea after all. Peer pressure to me was always an internal feeling of wanting to be liked and wanting to have fun, and wondering if maybe those girls had figured out a way to have fun and maybe if I got drunk, I wouldn't feel so lonely, so ugly, so geekish. Luckily I didn't listen to those nagging feelings.

I found friends who thought I was a good person. It's taken years, but I now feel I have the self-confidence to accept who I am. Many of the people around me in college don't have that self-confidence. A group I was in was asked who thought they were nice looking. Out of 14, four of us said we did. That surprised me. Even in college, many people still are not comfortable with who they are and what they look like.

There are innumerable challenges and issues facing today's teens. It's amazing that any of us comes out sane! However, if teens had more self-confidence; if they were told more often that they are worthwhile human beings, and that if they are trying their best, we are proud of them; if they could somehow be taught to love themselves and respect their own bodies, they could deal with the other problems facing them with greater confidence and success.

—Vincent, 22, California

If you do something bad or regrettable, learn from that mistake. Don't worry too much, there are plenty of others who have made the same mistake you have. Listen to those who care about you and love you. Don't turn them off. Listening can do a lot to help you find your way through life.

—Chuck, 23, California

I found that surfing got me through. My love of the sport and the ocean kept me focused and realizing my place on the planet. Find something that is positive and focus your energy into it.

—Matt, 24, California

I think one of the most difficult challenges I faced as a teen was having low self-esteem. The confidence that I lacked came from having a reserved personality. I could never just let myself go. Sports really helped me in this area. I made many friends through playing various sports and it helped to build some confidence in myself.

Suggestions to Develop Self-sufficiency

—Stuart, 29, Washington

➜ Get involved with a hobby that takes only one person (e.g., building models, computer ray tracing).

➜ Read about, and practice, wilderness survival.

→ *If funds permit, take lessons in something that is generally assumed to be for people beyond their teens (e.g., flying).*

→ *Try to write a full-length novel (I had two written before I graduated from high school.)*

→ *Do personal interviews at a rest home to research a certain facet of the past (e.g. war veterans).*

→ *Volunteer for a political campaign or a non-profit organization.*

→ *Specialize in babysitting children with physical or developmental disabilities.*

The key is to find activities done alone (or with people outside the same age group) that force you to rely on yourself and your intuition and resourcefulness.

How to Build Self Esteem

Doc Lew Childre. *The How To Book of Teen Self-Discovery,* 1995. *Heart Smarts: Teenage Guide for the Puzzle of Life,* 1992. Boulder Creek, CA: Planetary Publications.

Jean Isley Clarke. *Self-Esteem: A Family Affair.* Minneapolis: Winston, 1978.

B. Friedmann and C. Brooks. *On Base! The Step-by-Step Self-Esteem Program for Children from Birth to 18.* Kansas City, MO: Westport, 1990.

Robert Fulghum. *All I Really Need to Know I Learned in Kindergarten: Uncommon Thoughts on Common Things.* NY: Columbine Fawcett, 1988. (inspirational and humorous essays)

Claudia King. *Life Mastery: A Self-Esteem Handbook for Adults and Children.* Orland, CA: Light Paths Communications, 1994. (P.O. Box 3576, Chico, CA 95927)

Janina Malecka. *Valuing Yourself: 22 Ways to Develop Self-Esteem.* Portland, ME: J. Weston Walch, 1992. (for students grades six to 10)

Matthew McKay and Patrick Fanning. *Self-Esteem.* Oakland, CA: New Harbinger, 1992.

Pat Palmer. *Teen Esteem: A Self-Direction Manual for Young Adults.* (written with the help of teens, includes how to be assertive and refusal skills) San Luis Obispo, CA: Impact Publishers, 1989.

Shyness

Shyness is a personality trait we're born with. A shy person probably feels most comfortable with a few good friends rather than a large circle of acquaintances, which is perfectly fine. But, like Katie, shy people can stretch their boundaries and learn to enjoy an activity as public as cheerleading. If you feel self-conscious, focus on getting to know other people so you forget to judge how you're doing. Shy people often report greater ease with people as they move into their 20s.

—Eric, 19, Michigan

I'm not comfortable among large groups of people I don't know unless I have a tight knot of friends around me. But among friends, among people I'm comfortable with, I've had a couple people be surprised when I told them I thought I was shy. I'm not real fond of parties, unless I know a significant fraction of the people there. Or alternatively, if I know no one there, and no one else knows each other either. I've always been able to be outgoing if I put aside my worries and expend a lot of effort to keep myself smiling, listening, and not worrying about being self-conscious. As time goes on, the effort required lessens.

—Lauren, 19, California

The most difficult challenge I faced as a teen was shyness in large groups, and overall being too quiet! Also the fears of being judged. Really good friends who made me feel comfortable helped me cope. My best advice is to just be yourself!

—Katie, 20, California

When I was in high school, one of my biggest problems was my shyness and insecurities. In my freshman year I was so insecure about myself and afraid of everybody. I hated the way I looked and I was constantly embarrassed about myself when I was around other people. All of my other friends were pretty and popular. They had outgoing personalities and were well-liked by the majority of people. It made me hate high school. I was like the "ugly-duckling" who tagged along with a fun, outgoing group of girls.

I was so shy that I don't think I ever held my head up high. I always walked with my head down and never stood up for myself. I was an easy target for bullies to pick on. If it weren't for my other friends who always stood up for me, I'm sure I would have been harassed a lot more.

It wasn't until my sophomore year that I finally gained some confidence in myself and my self-esteem rose a bit. I tried out for cheerleading. Our school was really small so my chances were pretty good. Tryouts were probably the hardest thing for me to do. But once those were done, life started changing for me.

Cheerleading was a very fun time for me. The girls were my support group and we were always there for each other. It got me involved in school spirit, I got to meet new guys, and I had more respect and self-confidence. I was constantly in front of a large crowd dancing and cheering, which made me more outgoing and more outspoken. I enjoyed the physical part of cheering and knew that I was good at it, which gave me something to be proud of.

People knew who I was and I made more and more friends. There were always some people who still didn't like me (jealousy), but as long as I had my friends to support me it didn't matter. I felt good about myself and I was happy. By my senior year I had, as my mother put it, "blossomed" into a beautiful young woman. I definitely believed her. I'm still growing and learning to be more assertive and overcome my shyness.

—Andrea, 20, California

One thing I wanted to change was my shyness. I did not have the courage to be outgoing since I didn't feel I was good enough to make friends. Once I gained some confidence, I felt I was worthy of friends, but I was still fairly shy. I got "unshy" in steps. First, I smiled at people I recognized, then started asking, "Hi, how are you?" Then, I was able to carry on conversations with those who spoke to me first (rather than stunting conversation by answering questions with a brief Yes or No). Now I can sometimes instigate conversations.

Stress Management

There are things that can cause stress in school, like teachers, other kids, and grades. To deal with stress maybe go to your basement and scream. Another would be to write a story or something. The last would be to prove the math teacher, or whoever, was wrong about you.

—Missy, 14, Michigan

Over one-third of teens report high stress levels. A Gallup poll found that 46 percent of girls and 37 percent of boys reported high stress in their lives. In another nationwide survey, 17 percent of girls and 10 percent of boys said the strain in the past month was "almost more than I could take," and in a survey by Barna Research Group, 20 percent of younger teens and 30 percent of older ones felt stressed. In a school survey in my town of Chico, well over one-third of the students are often "stressed out" and about 15 percent feel lonely. The pressure comes from trying to balance expectations from parents, teachers, and friends, while trying to determine your own identity.

Stress is your physical, emotional, and mental response to any situation that's new, exciting, or threatening. The stressor is usually not as important as how we react to it, as one person can react to a hardship by becoming more determined to achieve while another person in the same situation gives up. Some stress is a natural part of life, presenting us with challenges and preventing boredom. The adrenaline our body produces gives us more energy and improves muscle strength. Like a rubber band, we need some stretch to use our strengths and generate energy, although too much can break us. Good stress is called *eustress*.

Distress occurs when our bodies overreact to frustrations such as waiting in line, being late, being blamed, not knowing test answers, and running out of time. Stressors can be family disagreements, changes, having to make a difficult decision, being sick, or going to a crowded school. Stress comes from the Latin word meaning "to draw tight." This tension results in increased heart rate, higher blood pressure, and muscle tension. Overreacting is punishing to the body over time. Chronic distress can lead to: inability to concentrate, anxiety attacks, depression, irritability, nightmares, headaches, backaches, indigestion, diarrhea, frequent colds, frequent injuries, becoming accident prone, problems with eating or sleeping, and fatigue. Studies indicate that distress affects your immune and nervous systems, heart function, metabolism, and hormone levels.

The Project Teen Canada Survey found the most stressful problems for students, in order of frequency, were figuring out what to do after high school graduation, money, school, time management, looks, wondering about the purpose of life, boredom, and height or weight. (The survey of 3,600 teens was conduced by Professor Reginald Bibby, University of Lethbridge, Alberta.)

Three types of stress management are (1) cognitive (thinking) as in changing your "self-talk," (2) behavioral, as in using time management skills, and (3) physical, as in getting enough exercise and laughter. Studies of "Type C" people who cope best with stress reveal that they manifest "hardiness," a cluster of healthy personality traits: a sense of being in control of their lives, an ability to view difficulty as a positive challenge to be won, and a commitment to living well. This "Type C" behavior is contrasted with the hurry sickness and angry irritability of the "Type A" behavior linked to heart attacks. Hardiness leads to reduced chances of severe illness as well as increased happiness.

A Conference Board (respected business research organization in New York City) seminar on peak performance teaches that highly successful people "prepare themselves not only in the traditional skills of their business, but also by mastering the mental components of performance: positive/effective thinking, goal setting, attention skills, stress management, and imagery and visualization." You can apply these techniques in your own life without taking an expensive seminar.

How to Destress

—Kelly Lynn Baylor

1. Ideally, sit where your head and whole body are supported, but you can also do this in class or wherever you feel you need some peace—after you've practiced it.

2. Starting with your toes, work up to your head. Tighten your toes as tight as you can, then relax your toes, blowing out any tension. Then move on to your ankles, calves....

3. With your eyes closed, imagine a flight of 20 descending stairs. Walk down five, then pause on the landing, taking time to relax. With each step, imagine more stress releasing from your body. Then walk down five more, pause, until you reach the bottom step.

4. Visualize your own private place of beauty, such as a beach or a Japanese garden, which is my place. I've visited this place for over 20 years, so I see the seasons change, flowers bloom, and see koy fish being born in the pond. When I visit, I listen to the stream, feel the earth, rake the gravel into a pattern I like, create new additions or change existing parts of the garden. I don't choose to have other people there, but you might. This is totally your place of serenity.

—Nick, 15, California

The biggest challenge I face as a teen is trying to put things in perspective. I can't allow myself to be taken in by all of this b.s. that high school truly is. When you think about it, the things we teenagers argue about are pretty pointless. I don't have too many people to help me solve this problem. My friends all have their heads in the clouds. The thing that helps me put things in perspective is being alone and thinking. Often, the greatest release I have can be sitting in my room and thinking about life. I can usually find solutions if I just think about a certain problem. I also find that the greatest release for me is to play music really loud on headphones. For some reason, that really calms me down. [It can also cause hearing damage!]

—Emma, 15, California

I've always been a procrastinator. Most of my big projects and papers have been done late at night a few days before they were due. I would stress out a lot. I learned that if you're in the middle of a project and it seems too big and impossible, step back and take a break for a while. Just calm down, get something to drink, and relax for a few minutes. When you get back to what you were working on, it won't seem so bad.

Also, everyone expects me to do outstanding work and thinks the best of me, so I strive for perfection in everything I do. I push myself over the limit. I often get stressed over small assignments like an overnight essay. I would be up until 2:00 or 3:00 a.m. finishing all my work after an out-of-town athletic event, then get up at 5:00 for a 6:00 a.m. practice. My friends and family kept telling me, "You just have to let some things not get done." I couldn't though. I finally realized that it was insane to work like this. I had to prioritize my life and schedule my time better.

—Jed, 16, California

When I'm feeling stressed out, I just skateboard and it takes my mind off the stress and relaxes me. The feeling you get when you've skated for hours and you get home and relax is great.

—Aliah, 16, California

The most difficult challenge I've faced is keeping my grades up, while trying to deal with the pressures of my family and friends. There is always so much to do in one day that sometimes I can't deal with it. I just plan my days in advance and prioritize my time. Kids should try to do well in school, get involved, make great friendships, and have some fun to ease the stress. Talk to your parents and tell them about your problems—they will try to understand.

—Abby, 17, Wisconsin

I believe that drugs and alcohol play a big factor in teenagers' lives. Young people today believe that these will solve their problems and relieve their stress. In coping with this challenge, I stuck to my beliefs and decisions about not using drugs and alcohol.

Positive Self-Talk

Deborah repeats the following phrases in stressful times because, "As tacky and cliché as these are, they help me put the right perspective on situations."

❖ Stop and smell the roses along the way.

❖ Tomorrow is another day.

❖ And this too shall pass.

❖ Life is only as good as you make it.

❖ Look on the bright side: Every cloud has a silver lining.

Barbara (my mom) put these phrases on her refrigerator:

❖ Honest praise is pure gold: It works magic.

❖ Dance to the music of the spheres.

❖ Look for the little joys of life; savor the sunshine smile of a baby.

❖ Look for the good in all things, even adversity. It can be your teacher.

❖ Forgive and you go free. Forgiveness opens the door to love.

❖ You don't have to be perfect to start loving yourself.

"The disasters of life are often the genius of the unconscious, forcing our egos into a new experience of the self" is the quote I have on my refrigerator is (Robert Johnson, *We*). Studies reveal though that changing one's attitude is not as effective, as changing behavior, like sharing work equally rather than trying to be positive about doing most of the work.

Stress Management Techniques

1. Take frequent mini-breaks to **stretch and relax**. Tense emotions usually lead to tense muscles. Imagine the most peaceful place for you, such as a tropical beach. Breathe deeply into your abdominal area, hold it, and exhale slowly. Count your breaths in and out.

    Progressively tense and relax each muscle, starting with your toes up to your scalp. "Progressive relaxation" instructs the muscles to release their tension. It involves making a tight fist, raising your eyebrows as high as you can, wrinkling your nose, clenching your teeth, shrugging your shoulders, sucking in your stomach, etc. As you tense and release, you can think "My feet feel heavy, warm, and relaxed," and move on up your body, then stretch.

Repeat positive affirmations (a positive goal) such as "I am relaxed." One of my favorites is "I have all the time in the world." Laughter is one of the best relaxation tools, so rent funny videos, tell jokes, and read funny books!

2. **Set realistic goals and expectations** that are yours, not someone else's. Accept that there are some things you can't change, such as a friend who is consistently late. Just factor this fact into your plans. When you have a long list of things to do, prioritize, don't do the least important ones, see which ones can be done by someone else, or ask for an extension on a due date. Also, it's not important to win each time you compete or to have the last word.

3. **Look at the big picture** to get perspective. Humor can help relieve an overly dramatic reaction to a problem. Is this your problem or is it someone else's? If it's your problem and it matters, take action, such as confronting a friend and you'll feel back in control of your life.

4. **Practice organizational skills.** Plan your day, week, and month. Schedule daily time for exercise, quiet reflective time, play time, and keep current on school assignments. Carry a planner in your backpack, check your list of things to do, and add events and assignments to your calendar. Do the top priority items first.

5. **Avoid procrastination** because a major cause of stress is putting things off. Break a large task into small parts and do one part each day. Reward yourself for achieving your goals. Simple rewards I've used are to cross tasks off my list, eat dessert, or post the result where I can see it and be proud.

6. **Exercise regularly** as it is an effective stress reliever. It helps to have an exercise partner or to take regular classes in aerobics, dancing, martial arts, etc.

7. **Take time each day to get centered.** For me, this requires exercise and meditation. Students also mentioned music, journal writing, taking time to be alone, a hot bath, and reading. How to meditate? Author Barbara Brennan suggests in *Hands of Light* (Bantam) that you first define your learning style (see Chapter 8).

   a. If you are a kinesthetic type, close your eyes and concentrate on your breath as it flows in and out of your body, following it all the way to your center.

   b. If you're a visual type, imagine a golden tube in your spine. Then visualize a golden ball above your head, sinking through the tube into the central part of your body. You can imagine the ball of light expanding and then bringing it back into your center. Or you can focus on an actual flower or candle flame, or on an imaginary light in the center of your head.

   c. If you are an auditory type, repeat a sound, such as *Om*, or "Be still and know that I am God," or a musical note.

      Ms. Brennan recommends *Voluntary Controls* by Jack Schwarz (Dutton) for additional centering exercises.

8. **Practice wellness techniques** of a regular sleep pattern, eating unprocessed foods, and avoiding sugar, caffeine, nicotine, and other drugs (see the wellness section in Chapter 1).

9. **Cultivate support networks** of friends you can talk with and who care about you. The wise thing to do is get emotional help when you need it from a counselor, religious leader, family member, or friend. Get academic help from a tutor before you get behind in school. Identify exactly what causes you to feel stress and research possible solutions.

10. **"Pace, not race."** Plan for more time than you think you'll need between appointments so that you don't have to hurry. Do one thing at a time and don't expect to solve a major problem in a flash.

11. **Practice positive thinking.** Stop self-defeating messages such as "I can't _____" and "I never _____" as soon as they surface. Take charge of your feelings.

12. **Plan for stressful events** by practicing how you will handle them, what you will say, and visualizing yourself staying centered and calm. For example, if you have an important job interview, role-play it by practicing your answers and imagine how well you'll do.

Tension—causes and solutions

—Judith Eberhart, M.A. counselor

The ability to adjust to stress is not so much the problems faced, but rather how we perceive these problems. Psychologist Dr. Murray Banks tells of two women he counseled. Both had recently lost their boyfriends. The similarities in their situation were striking, but their adjustments to the same problem were radically different. Ultimately, one woman committed suicide while the other simply found a new boyfriend!

Stress can be reduced or magnified by our **personal habits:**

Too much fat: Not only is fat high in calories, creating obesity that stresses the heart, but it is also hard to digest and contributes to intestinal discomfort. Fat reduces the oxygen-carrying abilities of the red blood cells by globbing onto them, and reduces the body's energy level by actually suffocating the cells.

Too much caffeine: Caffeine increases the heart rate, blood pressure, and oxygen demand upon the heart. The average cup of coffee contains about 108 milligrams of caffeine. Caffeine consumption of more than 250 milligrams per day is considered excessive and has an adverse effect upon the body. Caffeine is also found in tea, cola drinks, and chocolate.

Too much sugar: Sugar depletes vitamin B in the body and causes fatigue. The process works like this: Sugar enters the blood stream, the pancreas is alerted and dumps insulin in the blood system, the insulin metabolizes the sugar, causing low blood sugar, which causes fatigue and perhaps depression. A second harmful effect is that initially the sugar gives energy, but because there are no vitamins in sugar, the body borrows vitamin B from other sources to metabolize the sugar. This causes a vitamin debt and the person may feel irritable, anxious, and generally nervous. Try an experiment where you cut down on your sugar consumption and notice how much better you feel!

Dieting (see Chapter 1) and **not enough sleep**: A person can function on a few nights' sleep deficit. After that, clarity of thinking, reaction time, poor judgment, and irritability ultimately reduce the body's ability to protect itself from disease.

Negative thinking: Worry, guilt, anxiety, and negative thinking create stress. When a person is connected to a biofeedback machine or to a lie detector (polygraph), the machine immediately reflects a negative thought (such as a lie) even though the person may say something to the contrary. This is the same way the body responds to a physical stress. The response may not be visible to someone else, but the body registers a reaction. Think about people you know who are always complaining, who worry about everything, and who have a negative outlook on life. Do they have lots of colds, bodily complaints, or some kind of illness? They may seem healthy now, but something is brewing for their future!

Change your thoughts and you change your world.
—Norman Vincent Peale

Meditation—researchers have found that meditation lowers metabolic rate, respiratory rate, pulse rate, oxygen consumption, and blood pressure. This state is the opposite of the physiological condition that occurs in reaction to stress. Dr. Herbert Benson, a Harvard heart specialist, suggests that a similar technique is just as effective in creating the relaxation response, and involves the following steps:

☆ Sit quietly in a comfortable position.

☆ Close your eyes.

☆ Deeply relax all your muscles.

☆ Breathe through your nose and say the word "one" each time you breathe out.

☆ Do this for 20 minutes maintaining a passive attitude; that is, don't strain to be relaxed. If a thought comes up, acknowledge it, and go back to counting your breath.

While handling a maximum amount of stress, if you add one more activity, something has to give. So don't start a diet when you are moving, ending a relationship, or undergoing some other emotional or physical trauma. Reducing stress in your life allows your mind to focus on a new pattern and adjust to it. It is like letting a pot that has food cooked hard on the bottom soak overnight. The next morning the food is easily scrubbed off. Becoming more relaxed allows the new thought patterns to "soak" in and replace old ones.

Quick Tension Reducers

☆ drink herbal teas such as chamomile or mint

☆ take a hot shower or a warm bubble bath

☆ rest with your eyes closed for 10 minutes (research shows that often this is as good as a nap)

☆ take five deep breaths from your abdominal area (try that now!)

☆ stretch

☆ do something different for 10 minutes

☆ listen to relaxing music

☆ get a massage

☆ have a good hearty laugh

☆ change your expectations by riding the horse in the direction that it is going.

"I didn't get the job." "My sweetheart doesn't want to commit to me." "I didn't get the grade I wanted." " I can't change that, but I can learn from this and move on." Yes, there will be disappointment and pain, but what is, is. The sooner you grieve the loss and move on, the faster you move through the pain. Steven Covey in *The 7 Habits of Highly Successful People* (Simon and Schuster) lists a "win/win" attitude as a key habit, the belief that there is enough to go around so that everyone can win. Remind yourself you do not have to do everything, be everything, save everyone, experience everything, and get straight A's.

Stress Management Guides

National Mental Health Association
1-800-969-6642
(brochures on surviving stress, self-esteem, etc.)

Susan Hart. *Entering Adulthood. Balancing Stress for Success: A Curriculum for Grades 9-12.* Santa Cruz, CA: Network Publications, 1990.

Earl Hipp. *Fighting Invisible Tigers: A Stress Management Guide for Teens.* Minneapolis: Free Spirit, 1985.

Steven Selzer. *Life's Little Relaxation Book: Over 300 Ways to R-E-L-A-X.* NY: Crown, 1995.

Bettie Youngs. *A Stress Management Guide for Young People.* Del Mar, CA: Bilicki Publications, 1986.

Thomas Thiss. *The How-to-Be Book: A Fable with Exercises to Take the Stress Out of Your Life.* Minneapolis: Fairview Press, 1995.

Suicide Prevention

I had a very close friend commit suicide. She was always happy and she joked around with us constantly; she was a really great person. We didn't know she was unhappy, and it made us feel like it was our fault that we didn't see it coming, or that we didn't pay enough attention to her. The big question we asked was Why?

I cope with it by remembering all the good times we had, or by talking about her with my friends. My friends and I made ribbons for her, and we had everyone who was close to her sign a poster for her family. I think that people facing the same problem should open up to their family and their friends; I know that's what got me through it. Be sure not to bottle everything up inside, because you'll pay for it later. Remember it's OK to cry; no one expects you not to.

—Annie, 15, California

One in three teens has thought about committing suicide and the suicide rate has tripled in the past 30 years. Every 78 seconds an American teenager attempts suicide, according to the National Center for Health Statistics, and every 90 minutes, someone succeeds. One in every 12 high school students has attempted suicide; out of 500,000 attempts there are 6,000 teen suicides a year.

The American Health Foundation reports that 18 percent of girls and 11 percent of boys have attempted suicide. Increases are especially alarming among 10- to 14-year-olds (up 120 percent in 10 years) and African American males ages 15 to 19, whose rate quadrupled. One reason for the growing number of suicides is teens are now more likely to use guns. Many suicides are the result of untreated depression or other mental illness.

In a survey of over 3,000 high-achiever high school students in 1995, 29 percent of the females and 18 percent of the males had thought about committing suicide. The main causes were depression, school pressure, fights with parents and other family problems, and the breakup of a relationship. Their main coping technique was to work through it themselves.

Suicidal people tend to be socially isolated, and suicide most often occurs in times of major change in their lives. Family problems associated with suicide attempts are history of depression and/or suicide, alcoholism and drug addiction, abuse, long-lasting illness, death, mental illness, divorce, and family conflict. The piling up of stressful events such as death or divorce, social rejection, failure to achieve goals, changing schools, conflict, financial problems, or an unplanned pregnancy also contributes to the profile of a person likely to think about suicide.

About 70 percent of people who commit suicide give some clue about their problem before they make the attempt to end their lives. Eight out of 10 people who commit suicide tell someone they're thinking about it before they take action.

Warning signs of suicide include: serious depression, risky behavior such as reckless driving and increased use of drugs, a major change in behavior such as poor school performance, giving away favorite possessions, emotional withdrawal, depression, frequent fatigue, talking about death or suicide, decreased appetite, changes in sleep patterns, and unusual calmness caused by making the decision to die. Examples of warning statements to take seriously are "It's no use," "I won't be a problem to you much longer," or "I won't see you again."

If you know friends in crisis, let them know they are not alone, and that even terrible pain is bearable with help. Take their threats seriously and discuss your concern frankly. Call a suicide hotline, local crisis line, or hospital emergency room to get help. Look for a peer support group or call an 800 number to get referral information.

—Danny, 15, Colorado

The repeated suicide attempts of a friend, whether to get her to someone who could really help, has been my main challenge. She was someone I looked to whenever I was lost; to lose her to death would have been like losing my compass. But to tell a professional was to make her lose her home and get shipped to some mental institute. That's the hardest decision I ever made.

When people tell you of a suicide attempt, whether they know it or not, they're crying for attention, for help. If they die, like so many of the people in the endless nationwide statistics, it will be forever. No one will blame you for their death, you'll go on happily. But you'll always know inside that your friend could still be alive. No matter what, you've got to tell a wiser person. It broke my heart, and my friend and I have never spoken since, but she's alive, taking care of her sister, her friends. Sometimes I'll see her lying in the grass, dancing on a street corner, and I know I was right.

—Brandie, 16, Illinois

Teens need to know that all their problems and feelings are normal—they are not alone. In this year of high school, I have lost five friends due to car accidents and suicide. They don't think about the people left behind or how in a few years all those problems they were thinking of will seem funny, and maybe even stupid.

Every time I started thinking about suicide, I thought about how much I had going for me, and how a lot of people always said I'd end up with a nervous breakdown due to the pressure I put on myself. Thinking about giving them the satisfaction of watching me commit suicide made me mad enough that I usually didn't get much farther than just thinking about it. After my friend's dad died, I thought about how well she was coping and how hard it would be for her.

Talking about how I'm feeling and letting myself cry have been the saving factors in my life. My mom and I used to argue a lot, but we're getting closer now, and I tell her a lot. Not everything, but when I'm having a hard time with purely platonic friendships, I talk to her. I still have a hard time talking to her about love/sexual relationships, I guess because she still thinks of me as her little girl.

I hate to cry in front of people, but I do a lot of sobbing into my pillow. I write down whatever comes to mind, and read it over when things start to look bad, and think, "I made it through that, so I can make it through this." I have one friend who knows pretty much everything about my life and he can usually help me through my down moods, just by listening and letting me bounce my feelings around, and occasionally interjecting a bit of advice. The one other thing that has helped me is that I am so intensely competitive that I hate the idea, if there truly is an afterlife, of watching my friends I'm competing with for valedictorian of my high school class, making it to graduation and getting to stand up there and give the speech without me.

—Kathy, 19, West Virginia

As cliché as this may sound, I had a hard time accepting myself in high school for who I really was. I kept comparing myself with other people. I compared grades, friends, everything, to see if I could come out on top anywhere. I was always worried about not having any friends and the friends I did have were not the ones I wanted. It was as if they were the leftovers and if I became friends with them, that meant that I was also part of the leftovers.

To be honest, I really contemplated suicide a lot because I didn't feel as if I really had any place at all. I knew that it was only a phase. I was smart enough to go on, but I feel as if I had an extraordinary pride factor that would not let high school get the better of me. Many other students may not have such a factor to keep them going. I didn't do the same thing because I just kicked myself in the rear really hard all the time and told myself to cope. That's not exactly the best method, huh?

—Stuart, 29, Washington

I didn't cope very well with getting past the grief of my older brother's suicide and working out my own suicidal feelings. In retrospect, I'd say that I should have allowed myself to grieve, rather than letting people tell me to "be strong for mother." As for my own suicidal feelings, I finally realized that I could "kill myself" without dying. If life ever got so bad that I wanted to give up, I could just change everything about my life. For better or worse, the "old me" would be dead but I'd still be alive. Suicide and running away are essentially the same thing, but running away lets you go on to live a new day, and maybe someday return.

It also helps to realize that life is not, and never will be, fair. The more people say to themselves, "This just isn't fair," the more they delude themselves into believing *they're getting something worse than what everyone else is getting. The approach, "OK, it's not fair, but let's see how we can make it better," is much better for solving problems.*

Suicide Prevention

American Suicide Foundation
1-800-531-4477
(survivor support groups for families and friends of a suicide)

Boys Town National Hotline
1-800-448-3000
(crisis intervention, information, and referrals for youth and their families)

Kid Helpline 1-800-334-4KID
(listens to problems and makes referrals to helpful agencies)

National Adolescent Suicide Hotline
1-800-621-4000

Suicide and Rape Hotline
1-800-333-4444

Youth Crisis Line
1-800-HIT-HOME

American Association of Suicidology
4201 Connecticut Ave., NW, Suite 310
Washington, DC 20008
(booklets, *Surviving Suicide* newsletter, guides to school suicide prevention programs)

National Committee on Youth Suicide
Prevention
65 Essex Rd.
Chestnut Hill, MA 02167

National Mental Health Association
1021 Prince St.
Alexandria, VA 22314-2971

Youth Suicide National Center
445 Virginia Ave.
San Mateo, CA 94402

Youth Suicide Prevention Programs: A Resource Guide
CDC National Center for Injury Prevention
MS K60, 4770 Buford Hwy., NE
Atlanta, GA 30341-3724

Susan Kuklin. *After a Suicide: Young People Speak Out.* NY: G.P. Putnam's Sons, 1994.

Richard Nelson and Judith Galas. *The Power to Prevent Suicide: A Guide For Teens Helping Teens.* Minneapolis: Free Spirit Publishing, 1994.

Chapter 3

Kylee Johnson

Sexuality

Abortion

Teen sexuality is a controversial topic, with some groups for sex education and health clinics in schools, and others strongly against them. Teen magazines tell girls to turn boys on but say No, and *Playboy* tells boys, Yes, go for it. The majority of teens have sex before they graduate from high school, but almost as many decide to wait. This is not a decision to make in the heat of the moment in the back seat of a car. Think through your values, the depth of your relationship, the consequences of getting pregnant, and the possibility of contracting an incurable sexually transmitted disease (STD). This chapter will provide information to assist you in making knowledgeable decisions.

Look at the back of the chapter for a definition of terms used.

About 60 percent of all pregnancies in the U.S. are unplanned (teens make up 21 percent). About half of the pregnancies end in abortion, according to the National Institute of Medicine. Nearly 20 percent of American women have had an abortion at some time in their lives (*The Social Organization of Sexuality.* Edward Laumann, et al., University of Chicago Press).

Teen Abortions

◎ Every 31 seconds an adolescent becomes pregnant. About a million teens become pregnant each year and about half give birth.

◎ Every day 1,336 babies are born to teen mothers and about 1,140 teens have abortions.

◎ Four in 10 teen pregnancies end in abortion.

◎ Among pregnant teens, girls whose parents have more education and higher incomes are more likely to get abortions than girls in low-income families.

Most induced abortions occur in the first three months of pregnancy with vacuum aspiration, performed in about 10 minutes in a doctor's office, either under local anesthesia or just with a tranquilizer. The cervix is gently opened, a small plastic tube is inserted into the uterus, and a vacuum suctions out the embryo, placenta, and lining of the uterus. The woman may experience bleeding and cramping for several days after the abortion. If a pregnant woman delays until the second trimester (the fourth through sixth months), a similar procedure is used with additional dilation of the cervix one to three days before the abortion.

Another early term method is for the woman to take pills that cause an abortion. RU-486 (mifepristone) is a drug used in Europe but political pressure from anti-choice groups slowed its use in the U.S., despite its other medical uses. A new method uses a combination of two drugs already on the market to induce early term abortions with a 96 percent success rate. The drugs are Methotrexate, used in cancer treatment, and Misoprostol, an ulcer medication. The first drug disrupts the uterine lining and the second triggers uterine contractions to remove the fetus.

As you know, people have strong feelings about abortion, although their passion for life may diminish once a baby is born to a poor family without health coverage or money for preschool education. The main Supreme Court decision, Roe v. Wade, in 1973, was based on the constitutional right to privacy. An abortion before the fetus could survive outside the womb (about 24 weeks) is the private business of a woman and her doctor—not the government, or even the father of the fetus. States can prohibit an abortion of a viable fetus (could live outside the uterus) unless the woman's life or health is at risk. The decision has been upheld over the years despite many state challenges to the Supreme Court. Before Roe v. Wade, about 10,000 women died each year in the U.S. from illegal abortions and half were women of color. Women with money can travel to get a legal and safe abortion, unlike poor women. However, only 48 percent of teens surveyed in 1996 think abortion should remain legal and 40 percent believe that premarital sex is OK (Horatio Alger Association).

In 1992 the Supreme Court voted that states can't put an "undue burden" on a woman who seeks an abortion, although currently at least 36 states restrict teen abortion rights by requiring minors to notify a parent or judge before an abortion. In 16 states consent of one or two parents is required as well, even if the parents are divorced. Sixty-one percent of minors have abortions with their parents' knowledge and 45 percent of these parents are informed by their daughters. In some states, teens have a right to state-funded abortions for low-income women. In most states, minors may legally put their baby up for adoption without their parents' consent.

—Barbara, 16, California

I was going out with this guy, Tony; I had been with him for three years. He got locked up, so again I was on my own. I went out with a friend one night and we ran into some people we knew, so we went with them to this get-together thing. Well, everyone got wasted pretty much. I ended up falling asleep but I woke up later to find this guy on top of me, and he wouldn't get off. About eight weeks later I find out I'm pregnant. I personally don't believe in abortion and I can't give away my baby even though it's a totally awesome thing to do.

For the longest time I let everyone believe I was pregnant with Tony's baby. I just let the rape sit in the back of my mind until I decided to break up with Tony. I told my foster parents what had really happened. They wanted me to give my baby up, so I wouldn't be stuck with a reminder of the rape forever. I just couldn't do that; this baby is a part of me no matter how she came about and I would love her no matter what the situation was. It's really hard to handle when people ask about her dad but all I have to say is I don't want to talk about it and that pretty much works. I think the worst thing I did in this situation was not telling anyone. If I could do it all over again, besides not going out that night, I would tell someone immediately. Don't let something like this sit in the back of your mind.

—Nicki, 22, California

I've had two abortions and they weren't as easy as I thought they would be. I experienced some pain and went through emotionally hard times because of my decision. But, it was my decision and I survived with the support of close friends and the knowledge my decision was OK and was right for me and my situation. I would never want anyone to dictate to me what I can and cannot do with my body, nor would I tell others what to do with theirs.

Abortion Groups: Pro-Choice and Anti-Abortion

Abortion Hotline
1-800-772-9100

Alternatives to Abortion: Florence Crittendon Association
1-212-254-7410 (referral)

Birthright 1-800-848-5683
(information for pregnant girls, including shelters and adoption referrals)

National Abortion Federation
1-800-424-2280 or
1-800-772-9100

Planned Parenthood
1-800-230-PLAN
(will refer to local clinic)

Pregnancy Hotline
1-800-238-4269

Right-to-Life/Birthright
1-800-230-PLAN
(pregnancy counseling)

Catholics for a Free Choice (CFFC)
1436 U St., NW, Suite 301
Washington, DC 20009-3916

National Abortion Rights Action League
1156 15th St., NW
Washington, DC 20005
(provides a newsletter and information guide to companies that are pro-choice, i.e., Levi Strauss and Esprit, and anti-abortion i.e., Domino's Pizza)

The Fight for Reproductive Freedom:
A Newsletter for Student Activists
**Civil Liberties and Public Policy
Program
Hampshire College
Amherst, MA 01002
http://hamp.hampshire.edu/~clpp/ind
ex.html**

**Abortion Clinics on-line:
http://www.realpages.com/abortion**

Anatomy/Puberty

Female Anatomy

> *Mentally my mind was very mature, but not yet my body. But then my body started developing the form of a young woman. I felt like I should hide myself, like it wasn't right, and you feel so self-conscious. But it's part of nature to grow like a tree which blossoms in spring. And now with my hourglass shape and my fullness, I believe life can get better. The feelings you have inside aren't of a child but the feelings of a goddess on her journey into the vast* _____ *world.*

—Sumer, 15,
California

Girls experience changes as the hormone estrogen kicks in between ages nine and 19. The average age of menstruation is about 11, but some girls start at nine and others at 18. Most girls start their growth spurt soon after menstruation and continue growing rapidly for about two years, about two years ahead of boys.

Breasts get bigger (first the area around the nipples gets thicker and darker and the nipples grow larger), body hair grows thicker, the vulva develops pubic hair, height increases, the girl gets taller, her hips get wider, the uterus and vagina grow, mature eggs are released by an ovary each month as menstruation begins, skin gets oilier and may cause pimples, sweat glands develop, and sexual feelings increase.

Inside the breasts, the mammary glands include alveolae to produce milk and ducts through which the milk travels to the nipple to nurse a baby. The amount of fatty tissue determines breast size, an inherited trait.

Sometimes breast tenderness occurs before menstruation, along with water retention in the tissues (eating lots of salt can increase water retention). Some women experience normal secretions from their nipples, but pus or blood could indicate an infection and the need for a medical examination. Some women have inverted nipples which turn in towards the body instead of out. This does not interfere with breast feeding or sex play.

Since one of eight women will get breast cancer if she lives to be 80, it is important to start doing self-exams around age 25 to be familiar with your body. Brochures showing how to do breast self-exams are available at hospitals and health clinics. (Read the breast cancer prevention section in Chapter 1 and start now on a wellness program.)

Another area for self-exam is the vagina. If you do a self-exam using a clear plastic speculum (a device to hold the vaginal walls apart) to see inside with a mirror and flashlight, the following describes what you will see. You can ask a doctor to give you a mirror to use during your pelvic exam. (A male reader commented, "Gross," but it's informative to see your own body and know what's normal for you.)

The outer lips and inner lips are pads of skin that protect the clitoris. This is a small organ found under the top of the inner lips. The clitoris, like the penis, has many nerves that make it the center of sexual sensations. The clitoris is the only human organ designed solely for sexual pleasure! Like the penis, the clitoris has a head (glans), which is the most sensitive part, and a shaft with spongy tissue that becomes engorged with blood during sexual excitement. The clitoris gets bigger and the area around it swells too, becoming even more sensitive, leading to orgasm when rubbed. Because it's so sensitive, it can hurt to rub the clitoris without a lubricant such as K-Y jelly, saliva, or vaginal secretions.

Down from the clitoris, also protected by the inner lips, is the urethra through which urine passes. This tube is about 1-1/2 inches long. Below the urethra is the opening into the vagina. The outer third of the vagina is most sensitive. Some women are aware of the "G-spot," a small oval spot in the vagina which swells when stimulated and may lead to orgasm. Some girls have an intact hymen in the vagina, skin that partly blocks it and may tear during first intercourse and bleed. Many girls unknowingly stretch the hymen during physical activities and don't notice it even the first time they have sex. The vaginal walls make mucus to keep the proper chemical balance in the vagina to prevent infections, and to produce lubrication when sexually aroused.

Kegel exercises (named after the doctor who suggested their usefulness) help to develop strong pelvic muscles. Some women and their sexual partners find it sexually stimulating for both to contract these muscles during intercourse. Men can use this technique to stop ejaculation to prolong intercourse. The way to be aware of these muscles is to urinate, and stop the flow of urine. Squeeze and release these muscles; some people do these exercises when they are sitting in a car or at a desk. Pregnant women are especially advised to do these exercises to stay in shape after childbirth.

At the end of the vagina is the cervix, the lower part of the uterus. The small opening into the uterus, the os, is where sperm enter and menstrual blood or babies exit the uterus. The uterus is about the size of your fist. The uterus is connected to the ovaries by the Fallopian tubes, about four inches long but only as wide as a needle. If an infection caused by an STD leaves scar tissue, infertility can result, as the eggs can't pass into the uterus. The ovaries are about the size and shape of an almond and contain eggs stored in follicles.

Each month an ovary releases one of about 400,000 eggs a baby girl is born with. Ovaries also produce the hormones estrogen and progesterone. Some women feel a twinge when the egg breaks out of its follicle and know they are ovulating. At this time the vaginal mucus looks like egg white, whereas later in the cycle it becomes thicker and opaque to block the ovaries. A girl can sometimes feel this sticky clear liquid when she wipes after urination and discover her fertile time.

As an egg leaves the ovary, it is caught by the moving fringy ends of the fallopian tube, and moves down the tube and into the uterus. Fertilization by a sperm usually occurs inside the fallopian tube at the end closest to the ovary, then the egg moves down to implant in the uterine wall. The most fertile time is probably the six days before ovulation.

Girls usually start their period about a year after pubic hair develops. Menstruation discharges the lining of the uterus, composed of tissue, mucus, and blood. The monthly cycle is counted from the first day of a woman's flow. Some women have a regular 28-day cycle but many women have longer or shorter cycles and are frequently irregular, making rhythm methods of birth control difficult.

Cramps occur when the uterine muscles push the lining out. Some techniques to relieve cramps are massaging your belly or back, using a heating pad, relaxing, deep slow breathing, taking a mild pain reliever, and doing regular exercise.

Girls can choose between sanitary pads, a tampon, a diaphragm, or a sponge to collect the menstrual flow. Those who use tampons should not leave them in all night because of the risk of toxic shock syndrome (TSS is probably caused by bacterium which produce poisons that move into the blood stream to cause a high fever, drop in blood pressure, and vomiting). TSS is most likely to affect young menstruating women who use a highly absorbent tampon and leave it in too long. Also, perfumed deodorant tampons should be avoided because they may irritate the vagina.

The third opening, below the vagina, is the anus where bowel movements leave the rectum. Since the anus is close to the vagina, always wipe from front to back to prevent bacterial infection.

Male Anatomy

The most difficult challenge I've faced as a teen is the idea that all teens have "hormonal imbalance" and that we should all take Prozac.

—Justin, 16, California

During puberty, hormones produced by the brain's pituitary gland cause secondary sex changes. Boys grow taller, the penis and testicles get bigger and start to produce sperm and to ejaculate, sexual feelings get more intense, pubic hair grows, other body hair gets thicker, facial hair starts to grow, voice lowers around age 14 or 15, skin becomes oilier (which may cause pimples), sweat glands are more active, and muscle strength increases. About the time pubic hair develops, testicles begin making sperm. About two-thirds of boys experience some degree of "gynecomastia" or short-term breast growth that disappears in a year or so.

Many boys reach their adult height between 16 and 19. The first ejaculation often occurs around 12 or 13, during a "wet dream" (nocturnal emission) when he is asleep, or during masturbation when he stimulates his penis with his hand. This means sperm have grown in the testes and that the boy can father a baby. During this time the penis and the testes grow larger until growth stops around age 17. Some boys worry about the size of their penis, but the size of a flaccid or limp one does not predict the size of an erect penis. Size is not what makes a good lover anyway as the vagina expands to fit the penis: A female reader pointed out that, "It's not the size of the ship, it's the motion in the ocean."

The penis has two parts. The glans is the head and the most sensitive part. If a boy wasn't circumcised as a baby, the glans is covered by the foreskin (circumcision removes the foreskin). The shaft is the part that gets hard during an erection as the spongy canals fill with blood. The testicles are glands that hang in the scrotum; one usually hangs lower than the other. The testicles pull closer to the body when it's cold or in times of danger as protection from harm.

Inside the testicles, tubes called the *vas deferens* carry sperm to the seminal vesicles for storage. (These tubes are cut and tied in a vasectomy, the most common form of birth control used by married men.) The seminal vesicles and the prostate gland make semen, a fluid ejaculated with the sperm during an orgasm. A tube in the penis, the urethra, carries urine from the bladder released during urination. The urethra is also the path for semen during ejaculation when a valve closes off the bladder to prevent urine and semen from mixing. About 400 million sperm are released during ejaculation, and some swim in the fluid released before ejaculation. This is one of the reasons withdrawal is a risky form of birth control.

Erections are caused by fantasies, touch, sounds, visual turn-ons, or are spontaneous due to the high level of the hormone testosterone in adolescent males. Blood rushes into the blood vessels and spongy tissue in the penis. The muscles at the base of the penis tighten to keep the blood in, so the penis becomes larger and darker. Boys have erections as babies, so they are not new at puberty. Many males wake up in the morning with an erection and spontaneously have them off and on during sleep and during the day, as testosterone levels rise.

—Chad, 18, California

I was 5'2" from 6th grade till around 10th. I didn't think I was ever going to grow. Now I'm 6'1" and going strong. I prayed to the growing god. Let nature take its course.

—Eric, 19, Michigan

Basically, I'm a late bloomer. My first bike ride, my first inclination towards any kind of sports activity, my first kiss, my first date, etc., all happened significantly later than my peers. What I'm finally beginning to appreciate is that in no way does this mean that I'm deficient or that I'm unlikely to have these experiences. I just have to be a little more patient. These past two terms of college contained experiences that I've been seeing in others for years, experiences both positive and negative. Thus there is a caution in this as well as a hope. I'd like to tell others that their time will come, so be prepared for it.

—Joe

I thought I had a real problem because I would get hard-ons about 15 or 20 times a day, for no reason at all. I'd be sitting at my desk, and maybe my mind would be wandering and all of a sudden, ZAP! there it would be. I used to put a book down in my lap and read it from there [cited in *Changing Bodies, Changing Lives*].

Books About Puberty and Sexuality

Sex Information and Education
Council
130 W. 42nd St., Suite 2500
New York, NY 10036

Journeyworks Publishing
P.O. Box 8466
Santa Cruz, CA 95061-8466
(publishes inexpensive pamphlets
about health, including STDs, birth
control, and smoking cessation)

Cythnia Akagi. *Dear Larissa:
Sexuality Education for Girls Ages 11-
17*. Littleton, CO: Gylantic
Publishing Co., 1994. (a series of
letters from a mother to her teen
daughter)

Ruth Bell, et al. *Changing Bodies,
Changing Lives*. NY: Vintage Books,
1988.

Mary Calderone and E. Johnson.
The Family Book About Sexuality. NY:
Harper Collins, 1990.

Robie Harris. *It's Perfectly Normal:
Changing Bodies, Growing Up, Sex and
Sexual Health*. Cambridge, MA:
Candlewick Press, 1994.
(topics include puberty, reproduction, ways to avoid sexually transmitted diseases and sexual abuse)

Lynda Madaras and Area Madaras. *My
Body, My Self for Boys*. NY: New
Market, 1995. *What's Happening to
My Body Book for Girls,* 1987. *My
Feelings, My Self,* 1993.

Kathy McCoy and C. Wibblesman. *The
New Teenage Body Book*. Los Angeles:
The Body Press, Perigee, 1992.

Carol Weston. *Girltalk: All The Stuff
Your Sister Never Told You*. NY:
Penguin, 1993.

Double Standard

I hate the double standard people have toward sex. If a guy is sexually active, he is cool and looked up to. If a girl has sex, she is easy, a slut, and looked down upon. For every "cool" guy who has sex, he must have a girl to have it with. Why does she become the hussy?

—Emma, 15, California

The average teen television viewer sees between 1,900 to 2,400 sexual messages a year. These images shape our attitudes towards sexuality and birth control, by focusing on sexual passion but ignoring birth control, and STDs and pregnancy. By 9th grade, almost 50 percent of the boys and 37 percent of the girls surveyed said they'd had intercourse, according to the Centers for Disease Control in 1992. A telephone survey of 503 high school students found that 62 percent of sexually active girls and 48 percent of the boys said they wished they'd waited until they were older. Also, 81 percent of the boys—but only 59 percent of the girls—said sex was a pleasurable experience (Siecus, 1994)!

A national survey reported that over half of the sexually active girls, compared to over one third of the sexually active boys, didn't want to have sex again or didn't care if they did (*Journal of Adolescent Health*, 1994, V. 15, No. 5). In a survey of over 3,000 high-achiever high school students in 1995, 47 percent of the females and 33 percent of the males wished they had stayed virgins. Do these three survey findings suggest boys and girls have different attitudes about sex and different experiences?

We're raised with fairy tales in which the heroine is so passive she appears dead (*Snow

White, Sleeping Beauty) or she just waits for the prince to take all the action (*Cinderella, Rapunzel*). Widely read romance novels are called "bodice rippers" because the hero shows his passion by ripping off the heroine's blouse against her will, which somehow turns her on. In my surveys, boys report pressure to lose their virginity, while girls feel pressure to keep it. Girls and boys agree that a girl's reputation is hurt when students find out she's had sex, while this is not true for boys. (This 1996 *USA Weekend* magazine survey reports 87 percent of girls and 70 percent of boys think sex hurts a girl's reputation; while 22 percent of boys and 15 percent of girls think it hurts a boy's reputation.)

Another way to analyze the sexual messages we get is to think about the words used for sex and sex organs. I asked my students in a Sociology of Sex course to survey their acquaintances about the words they used. Most were mechanical ("getting laid," "screwing"), sports-style competition ("scoring," "getting to home base"), or violent (the "f" word, "slamming"). The only positive phrase was "making love." We insult someone by telling them to have sex, when it should be a positive statement. The terms seem mostly to come from the male culture and are not romantic—perhaps part of the double standard of sexuality which may inhibit women.

Our attitudes are manipulated by the popular culture and therefore change with time. The 17th century colonial era viewed both men and women as sexual beings and discussed sex openly. For example, the first published American poet, Anne Bradstreet, wrote in a poem about her children as the fruit of her and her husband's "heat" without shocking her readers. But the 19th century Victorian era concocted a new image of middle-class women as ladylike, angelic, and not sexual. Sex was a wifely duty rather than a womanly pleasure and no lady would dream of writing publicly about her "heat."

The Victorians created a double standard of sexuality, with men viewed as more sexual than women. The culture divided Victorian women into two groups, good women and bad women. We still refer to some sexually active girls as sluts, while we view the same behavior in boys as natural and studly. We still blame women for tantalizing men's uncontrollable sexual appetites, as in accusing women of causing rape by wearing sexy clothes, or being a tease in a dating situation. This view unfairly patronizes men as being unable to control of their actions and faults women for being sexual.

This double standard carried over into adulthood; a *Sports Illustrated* American Male '91 survey asked men and women what subjects interested them most. Men's list in this order was money (86%), family (75%), sex (73%), and sports (69%). Women's list was family (81%), money (80%), health (71%), and reading (68%)—sex didn't make the list.

Because of the double standard, it may take longer for females to learn about their sexuality, express their likes and dislikes, and be able to relax and enjoy sex enough to have orgasms. Because sex education is so minimal, many teens don't learn that the clitoris is the center of female sexual excitement and orgasms. It isn't as obvious as a penis that has spontaneous erections and is touched every time a boy urinates. This is part of the reason sexologists often say males are at their sexual peak in their late teens and women peak in their thirties. It takes time to undo the passive good girl messages and become an equally active sexual partner, tuned into her own sexuality.

Sexuality and Gender
—Sociology professor Don Sabo, Ph.D.

Our inner sense of "maleness" or "femaleness" influences the ways we see ourselves as sexual beings. Traditional male scripts that emphasize competition, winning, aggression, domination, and goal attainment, shape men's love-making behavior. Taught to be "achievement machines," many males organize their lives around a performance ethic that spills over into sexual relations. Contemporary women seem to be telling men to pay less attention to actual intercourse and orgasm, and to get into the overall process. Put another way, making love isn't like running a 50-yard dash, but rather, a delightful jog in the park.

When intercourse becomes the chief goal of sex, it increases men's performance pressures and limits their ability to enjoy other aspects of sexual experiences. It can also create problems for both men and their partners. Since coitus requires an erection, men are under pressure to get and maintain erections. If erections do not occur, or men ejaculate "too quickly," their self-esteem as lovers and men can be impaired. Sex therapists tell us that men's concentration on and anxieties about erection, penis size, and performance can cause the very sexual dysfunction they fear.

Two books I recommend to friends who want to better understand men's changing sexual needs, fantasies, and experiences are Bernie Zilbergeld, *Male Sexuality* (Bantam Books) and Michael Castleman, *Sexual Solutions: A Guide for Men and the Women Who Love Them* (Touchstone Books).

In the past, men's views of women's sexuality and love-making were distorted by myths and misinformation. Nineteenth century medical opinion, for example, held that women were "naturally" passive and did not enjoy sex. This belief meant that, for many couples, the sex act got defined as a progression from male erection, to penetration, to ejaculation, with very little sensitivity to women's sensual needs or orgasmic response. These false attitudes toward female sexuality spilled over into the 20th century. Indeed, it was not until the mid-1960s that sex researchers William Masters and Virginia Johnson established that most women achieve orgasm primarily through clitoral stimulation rather than from stimulation within the vagina.

Cultural myths about female sexuality flourished, in part, because women's opinions on sexual matters were seldom heard. Male "experts" discussed and defined "human" sexuality. Sigmund Freud went so far as to say that women who experienced clitoral orgasms were immature and frigid [non-orgasmic]. Such notions placed expectations on men to prolong erection to stimulate orgasm without touching the clitoris. In the past, most males learned about women's sexuality from these "experts" or from other males. Boys gleaned "how-to" information from older boys or male peers who, in turn, got their insights from other males, the media, or pornography. "Real" men are portrayed as being interested in having sex all the time, always ready for action. Penis size is also likely to be exaggerated, as is the role of penis in love-making.

In more recent decades, women have been more outspoken about their sexual preferences and desires. The publication of *The Hite Report* on female sexuality in 1976 created controversy because it asked new questions about male sexual performance. Shere Hite's study of female sexuality was unique in that women, rather than male experts, defined their own sexuality. Public and educational discussion of female sexuality became more common during the 1980s and many males began to listen to women's voices. Whereas Sigmund Freud had misguided earlier generations of males through the corridors of female sexuality, authors Shere Hite, Lonnie Barbach, Nancy Friday, and "Dr. Ruth" Westheimer helped younger generations to better understand women's sexual makeup, fantasies, and needs.

Both females and males have much to gain from restructuring sexual relationships along egalitarian [equal] lines. The psychologist Abraham Maslow found that self-fulfilled persons made no distinctions between the roles of the two sexes in sex play, hence providing evidence for a positive interplay between gender equality and sexual adjustment. Egalitarianism fosters greater communication between women and men that may facilitate better understanding of one another's sensual desires and needs.

—Pete, 16, California

I think so much bad communication goes on between guys and girls just because everyone expects the guy to move first. He's supposed to call up for a date, he's supposed to initiate all the sex, and he's supposed to know what to do. That's such a drag. Like I'm not into coming on too strong, that's just not my style. I don't believe in pressuring people into things, and I don't want to pressure my girlfriend. But she doesn't think the girl's supposed to be aggressive, especially not in sex, so she's always waiting for me to make all the moves. And since I don't want to pressure her, I usually hold back. I would feel a whole lot better if she'd let me know what SHE wants some of the time.

      [Shere Hite's *Hite Report on Male Sexuality* (Alfred Knopf) also reports that adult men would like women to take more sexual initiative and to inform them about what turns them on.]

—Sheri, 17, New England

*   The first time I had intercourse I was lying there thinking, "You mean this is IT? Am I supposed to be thrilled by this?" It wasn't that it hurt me or anything, because it didn't. It just didn't feel like anything to me. I figured there must be something wrong with me, so I didn't say a word to him.*
Quoted in Ruth Bell, et al. *Changing Bodies, Changing Lives.*

      [A female reader added, "This is so true. You can't stress this enough." Another girl asked, "What happened, can you not get excited when you're having sex?" Remember the brain and the heart are the main sexual organs. A girl may have sex for the wrong reasons, such as giving in to pressure or to keep her boyfriend. If a woman is not into it or doesn't tell her partner what she needs, it's possible he may hurry into intercourse without enough foreplay. He may not know the importance of the clitoris. If she's not ready, the vagina won't lubricate enough for enjoyable intercourse.]

—Andy, 18, California

*   Society says to young men it doesn't matter who you have sex with, it only matters that you have it at a young age. I regretfully failed at my attempt to abstain. I am now suffering for actions that I wish I could take back. Don't abstain for yourself, but for the one girl you'll want to spend the rest of your life with.*

—Lisa, 19, Washington

*   We girls need to realize that wanting sex doesn't make us bad people. Often times, we can get so wrapped up in the notion that only boys should want sex that we let them control us sexually. Saying Yes to anything can make us "bad girls" in our own minds, and bad girls don't have a right to say No when they're uncomfortable. We need to understand that we have a right to say No AND a right to say Yes. Our comfort level, our religion, and our family background are going to determine when and how we exercise those rights, but we don't ever lose them. Understanding that will not only make it easier to say No when we need to; it will also make it easier to demand safe sex and a respect for our own needs when and if we choose to say Yes.*

*   Find out about sex and sexuality. The more you know and the more confident you feel, the less likely you are to allow yourself to be pressured into something you don't want to do. The real self-confidence booster for me was getting educated about sexual assault and self-defense. The notion that no one should be able to push me around sexually was a pretty powerful one and it carried over into my dating life.*

—Kevin, 21, Iowa

*   I felt bad about being a virgin when I was in high school, when of course you're not a "real man" until you've "done it." Did I really think less of myself for not having had sex? Not really. After all, I didn't really feel responsible enough in high school to deal with a sexual relationship and everything that goes with it. What I really feared was that people would find out I was a virgin and think less of me for that. But that was silly. Most of my good friends I knew well enough to know that they wouldn't really*

think any less of me if they found out.

Traditional masculinity and sexism keep us from enjoying sex to its fullest. We are so engrossed with the "pornographic culture" that we don't see physical intimacy as what it should be—a beautiful exchange of love between two people. Instead we see it as a "game" or even a "sporting event" where, instead of focusing on our feelings and our sense of togetherness, we keep trying to "score" or to see "how far we can get." We are so engrossed with living up to stereotypes of what the "real man" is like (having sex all the time), that we almost become unable to enjoy physical intimacy the way it should be enjoyed. We feel that unless we have "gone all the way," what we do doesn't really count.

We feel that unless the person we are with lives up to the unrealistic body type of a Playboy bunny, we couldn't possibly enjoy physical intimacy with her. We are taught that sex itself is primarily a visual experience, and that the only sex organs are the penis and the vagina, when in fact, the sex organs are in reality (in my opinion) the skin and the heart.

—Pedro, 22, California

I tried to smooth talk women into my bed. Or I attempted to have a relationship in which I was dominant and the woman should try to satisfy the male's needs.

—Tracy, 24, Arizona

My mother's attitudes toward sex gave me a guilt trip. I'm the oldest child in my family and my parents were both very sheltered, so they were unprepared for my body's changes just as much as I was. My mother was afraid of me becoming sexual because, in her view of the world, sex gets women into trouble. She reacted by trying to convince me that I shouldn't acknowledge my new sexuality and scolding me for "having too much of it." So as a very young woman trying to figure out the world, this is what I got from my mother: sex=scolding=guilt.

Feminism helped me get a very needed attitude adjustment about sex. I took a sociology course on women and I think that started the ball rolling. Then I happened to get a roommate who was a feminist and she had all these wonderful books that I devoured. At the same time, I was in a relationship with a man who was less than desirable. I started to realize that all this stuff I was reading about in the books really did apply to me and my life in very real ways. After that I started to seek out anything feminist I could find.

Lots of feminism addresses sexuality and body image and stuff like that. This was the kind of stuff that really helped me get over my guilt. I started to believe that I was meant to be sexual, just like everyone else, and it wasn't a punishment or an unfortunate accident and there wasn't anything wrong with me. I could really be me and celebrate who I am, including the sexual parts.

—Sam, 24, California

Fitting in with the cool crowd was my issue. Drugs were a big problem, and sex—trying to get laid to be cool. I did all of it. I learned to be yourself, as people will like you for who you are.

—Curval, 26, California

I spent three years desperately trying to make it with any girl who seemed interested. Getting that over with was quite a relief.

Birth Control

Teens ages 16 and under shouldn't be having sex, but, if you have sex, get birth control and use a condom. You should listen to someone who knows and who cares about what you're going through. This one-night stand can turn out to be an all-day, all-your-life baby.

The most difficult challenge I've faced as a teen is being pregnant. It all happened on a Friday night when I went out with my friends; of course they were bad, but it isn't their fault that I am pregnant. Now I have a baby and I need to finish school. It is pretty hard having to wake up, get myself and my baby dressed. Sometimes I'm tired but it's my problem. As my baby gets older it will be easier for me to do things faster.

—Simitria, 15, California

Our bodies are designed for reproduction of the species and young people are especially fertile.

Teen Pregnancy

✪ One million teens, 12 percent of girls ages 15 to 19, become pregnant each year. About half of the pregnancies end in birth, about a third in abortion, and 14 percent in miscarriage.

✪ Eighty-five percent of teen pregnancies are unplanned.

✪ Six in 10 teen pregnancies occur among 18 to 19-year-olds. Studies report that over half of the fathers of babies born to teenagers are over age 20.

✪ The U.S. pregnancy rate is higher than in other developed nations, nine times as high as in the Netherlands or Japan.

✪ The majority of sexually active teens regularly use a contraceptive, as condom use doubled in the 1980s. Higher income teens are more likely to use birth control.

Compared to 20 years ago, more youths are sexually active earlier, but have lower pregnancy rates. Pregnancy rates for sexually active teens fell 19 percent between 1972 and 1990. About 70 percent use contraception sometimes, compared to 50 percent surveyed 10 years previously (Alan Guttmacher Institute). However, one in four sexually active teens does not use contraception. Half of teen pregnancies occur within six months of first sexual intercourse because of not using birth control.

Despite the risk of getting AIDS and other STDs, only 53 percent of 16,000 high school students surveyed in 1993 used condoms the last time they had intercourse. The survey by the federal Centers for Disease Control and Prevention found that 54 percent had engaged in intercourse at least once, and 19 percent had at least four different sexual partners. They also found that 18 percent of girls used birth control pills. Eleven percent used alcohol or drugs before their last experience of sexual intercourse.

The founding director of a health clinic, Dido Hasper points out, "One of the problems young people have with birth control is that in order to get it, you have to admit to yourself that you are planning to be sexually active. Going to a clinic to get prescription birth control is one more barrier, so is having to ask for condoms at a drug store." But, think about the consequences of not using birth control.

More than one million teenagers received birth control in Title X clinics each year it was funded. This legislation, part of the Public Health Services Act, authorized funding for family planning to "all persons desiring such services" regardless of their age and without requiring parental notification. The Supreme Court ruled in 1967 that, "Constitutional rights do not mature and come into being magically only when one attains the state-defined age of majority." Later decisions confirmed that minors have a constitutional right to privacy, although this principle isn't applied to abortion in many states. Despite the need, total public dollars spent for contraceptive services fell by one-third between 1980 and 1990.

Birth Control Methods

Chemical contraceptive methods kill sperm, barrier methods block the opening to the uterus or capture sperm, and hormonal methods prevent a woman from ovulating or prevent the implantation of a fertilized egg. Only condoms and spermicides protect against STDs, and they're not 100 percent effective.

Effectiveness of Various Forms of Birth Control

Percentage of Women Who Get Pregnant in the First Year of Average Use (rather than perfect use)

No method	85.0	Diaphragm	18.0
Spermicides	30.0	Condom	16.0
Sponge	24.0	Pill	6.0
Withdrawal	24.0	IUD	4.0
Rhythm	19.0	Depo-Provera	0.4
Cervical Cap	18.0	Norplant	0.005

(Alan Guttmacher Institute)

High Risk Methods to Avoid

Some couples use the rhythm method by avoiding intercourse during ovulation. But sperm can live in the uterus as long as five to seven days after ejaculation and women can ovulate unexpectedly due to stress or illness. A woman is usually most fertile at midcycle when she ovulates, usually around two weeks before menstruation. Some women use a basal thermometer (designed for healthy women without a fever) to chart their fertility because a woman's temperature drops before ovulation and rises afterwards. Some women feel a slight pain in their ovary when they ovulate and, for many, their sexual desire increases. Although ovulation can be tracked, the problem is that women can spontaneously ovulate and both eggs and sperm can last for days in the fallopian tubes.

Withdrawal does not work because sperm can leak out with the fluids released before ejaculation and men may ejaculate sooner than they expect, in a "sneaker." Douching or washing out the vagina after intercourse just pushes sperm towards the uterus.

Yes, a woman can get pregnant the first time she has intercourse, before she has her first menstrual period (if her hormones have just started releasing an egg to be fertilized), and any time during the month when she ovulates.

Other unreliable methods are taking a bath, urinating after intercourse, using vaginal suppositories, the woman not having an orgasm, using plastic wrap on the penis, and certain positions for intercourse such as standing up. None of these stop 400,000 sperm.

Hormones

Oral Contraceptives, **the Pill**, have been available since the early 1960s. The Pill contains the synthetic (manufactured) hormones estrogen and progesterone to prevent ovulation. The hormones also thicken the mucus plug in the os to block the entry of sperm. If fertilization of an egg does occur, the hormones prevent the implantation of the egg in the uterine wall. Most failures are due to human mistakes such as forgetting to take a pill. Because of the low dose of pills today, it's important to take one every day at the same time.

A woman begins a monthly cycle by taking a pill on the fifth day after menstruation begins. She continues taking a pill about the same time each day for 20 more days. Then her period starts two to five days later. If a woman forgets to take a pill for two days in a row she must use another method of birth control such as a condom for the rest of the month, to protect against pregnancy.

The Pill causes side effects in about 25 percent of users; some effects are correctable by changing the amount of hormones. Other women continue to experience nausea, breast tenderness, water retention, weight gain, migraine headaches, mood changes, and yeast infections. Some studies link estrogen pills with slightly increased chances of developing breast cancer later in life (and other studies don't), especially for women with a mother or sister who developed breast cancer before menopause (the time when women stop menstruating, around age 50).

Norplant was approved by the Food and Drug Administration in 1990. A doctor implants six silicone rubber capsules under the skin of a woman's upper arm. They can be felt but not seen. The capsules gradually release the hormone progestin for up to five years. Side effects can include long menstrual periods or no periods, breast tenderness, weight gain, and spotting between periods. Some women report very unpleasant side effects, including depression, and that it can be difficult to surgically remove the implants.

—Dido Hasper, health clinic director, reports they do more Norplant removal than insertions in the Chico Feminist Women's Health Center. She is concerned that,

Norplant and Depo have not been tested on young women. This raises concerns about future fertility, and other effects it can have on women who have not matured physically. The other concern with long-acting contraceptives is their lack of immediate reversibility. If you take the Pill and experience side effects, you can stop. With Norplant, you have to have them removed, which is expensive and also difficult at times. With Depo, you have to live with whatever side effects you have.

Depo-Provera was approved by the Food and Drug Administration in 1992. The hormone progesterone is injected into the woman's buttocks every three months to stop ovulation. Most women who use this method of birth control stop menstruating after a year; some gain weight and experience mood swings. Another brand, Noristerat, lasts for two months, and Cyclofem and Mesigyna are injected every month, combining estrogen with progestin.

Few **IUDs** are available today, but they include the copper-T IUD and Progestasert, a devise inserted in the uterus to release small amounts of the hormone progestin. IUDs can cause infections which can affect future fertility so they are rarely used by young women. The infamous Dalkon Shield IUD was finally taken off the market because it caused sterility in too many of its users, evidence that better birth control testing is needed. Norplant may be another case of needing a longer test period before experimenting on women consumers.

The "Morning After Pill" is a one-time, high-dosage birth control pill taken up to 72 hours after unprotected sex. It is 75 percent effective in ending a pregnancy and must be prescribed by a doctor. Side effects may include nausea and vomiting. To find out more about emergency contraception, call 1-800-584-9911 or look on the Internet at http://opr.princeton.edu/EC/ec.html.

Barrier Methods

Hollowed out lemon halves were used in Europe as early as 1600 to cover the cervix. The **diaphragm** used today is a dome-shaped rubber cup folded in half and inserted into the vagina to cover the cervix. It must contain spermicidal cream or jelly to be effective, as sperm can travel around the diaphragm. A diaphragm requires a nurse practitioner or a doctor's examination and a prescription. If a woman loses or gains much weight, she should be refitted for a new diaphragm.

The diaphragm can be placed in the vagina up to two hours before intercourse and must be left in place for at least six hours. If the couple has intercourse again, spermicidal cream should be inserted in the vagina using a plastic applicator sold with the spermicide. There are few side effects, although some women are allergic to the spermicidal cream or to the rubber and get bladder infections.

The **cervical cap** is similar to the diaphragm in that it is placed over the os, but is smaller and less flexible. It was approved by the FDA in 1988 but is not widely used. Some women find it more difficult to insert and some report that it comes off during intercourse. Dido Hasper reports that their clinic users have similar failure rates for the cervical cap and the diaphragm, "but both methods require a familiarity with your body and comfort in use. The most important aspect is learning how to put in the diaphragm or cap."

Sperm-killing chemical **spermicides** are mixed in foams, creams, jellies, and tablets bought without a prescription. They are much more effective when used with a diaphragm, cervical cap, or condom. They must be reinserted in the vagina if the couple have intercourse again. Some users report they cause irritation of the vagina or penis.

In ancient Roman times men used a **condom** made of animal intestine. A latex rubber condom was available in the U.S. by 1876. Condoms are a barrier to most, but not all, STDs. For example, herpes, warts, and crabs can be transmitted through skin-to-skin contact around (but not beneath) a condom.

Condoms cover the erect penis and collect the sperm ejaculated during orgasm. A condom should be put on as soon as the penis is erect, before insertion into the vagina, and used with a spermicide. The failure rate is over 10 percent, as condoms can break or slip off.

The female condom first appeared on the market in France and Switzerland in 1992. The inner ring of the seven-inch-long pouch is put over the cervix and the outer ring is placed outside the vaginal opening. It is less likely to tear than the male condom although it's thinner. However, it's more expensive.

Some men may resist using condoms: 75 percent of men ages 20 to 39 told interviewers that condoms reduced sensation (a study by the Battelle Human Affairs Research Center in Seattle). Only 30 percent of teen males surveyed say they use condoms every time they have sex and almost 20 percent say they never use them, according to researcher Dr. Joseph Pleck. If a man always uses a condom while having intercourse, however, he gets used to it, and it may prolong his erection.

The condom should be latex/rubber as animal membranes (lambskin) are less dense and therefore can be penetrated by a bacteria or virus. Don't save money on condom purchase as one of the inexpensive brands has a failure rate of 20 percent, about the same chance of getting pregnant without birth control. Keep condoms away from sunlight, never in your wallet or glove compartment of the car. Check to make sure it's not brittle, yellowed, old, or damaged. Never use petroleum jelly, hand cream, or oil with a condom as oils can make it break and are not healthy for the vagina.

Also, never use a condom if the woman is using yeast infection cream or other medications that can break down latex (including a latex diaphragm). Use only water-based lubricants such as K-Y jelly. Some condoms include a water-based lubricant that makes them easier to apply and some are coated inside and out with spermicide. (Unlubricated condoms are used for oral sex on a man.)

Some people practice by putting a condom on a cucumber or squash. Hold the condom by the last half-inch at the tip. Squeeze out any air. Place the condom on the tip of the penis. If uncircumcised, pull back the foreskin. Unroll rather than pull the condom to the base of the penis, smoothing out any extra air. If the condom doesn't have a reservoir tip at the end to catch semen, leave one-half inch of space at the end when putting on the condom. After ejaculation, hold the condom ring in place and withdraw slowly while the penis is still erect. Roll it off away from the vaginal area. Do not flush down the toilet as condoms can clog plumbing.

How to Reply to a Partner
Who Is Reluctant to Use a Condom

—Alan Grieceo

✳ *"They interfere with spontaneity and romance"* or *"I'll lose my erection."*
Include putting them on as part of foreplay, something you both do.

✳ *"They interfere with sensation; they feel like taking a shower in a raincoat."*
Even if you lose some feeling, you'll have plenty left. You can get used to them and they're better than an incurable STD.

✳ *"I'm on the Pill."* Only latex condoms can prevent contact with STD germs. We may have infections we don't know about.

✳ *"Do I look like I have an STD? I haven't had sex for months."*
People can have an STD and not know it.

✳ *"I'm a virgin."* I'm not, so this way we'll both be protected.

✳ *"None of my other friends use a condom."* Please don't compare me to them. If we care about each other, we will protect each other from disease.

✳ *"Just this once."* Once is all it takes to get pregnant or contract an STD.

✳ *"I don't have a condom with me."* Then let's wait or take a trip to the drug store.

✳ *"You carry a condom around with you?"* I care about my health and yours.

✳ *"I won't have sex with you if you insist on using a condom."* Let's wait until we can agree or let's enjoy each other without intercourse.

A reader asks, "How can you get your partner to agree with you?" You may not be able to. It's simple and doesn't take lengthy discussion; if he doesn't put it on, he doesn't put it in. Or, she can use the female condom. Your life is at stake, because people lie about their sexual history or may not know they are HIV positive. Read the AIDS section carefully. Also, a reminder that STDs can cause sterility and some are incurable.

Researchers are working on newer forms of birth control, including stronger and more sensitive condom materials, vaginal rings that release a contraceptive hormone in the vagina, a vaccine, a pill to induce menstruation, and an injectable male hormone. Our current methods aren't perfect, but if you're sexually active and care about your health, a condom is a must.

—Sophia, 16, Washington

There's pressure to have sex, but it's rare to have a teen health center that's free and confidential. There's a lack of sex education, you don't know where to go. A lot of people get drunk and then have sex. We need support groups in school for relationships, sex, and drugs.

—April, 19, California

Be safe. I've known so many girls who have had to put their lives on hold because they accidentally got pregnant. Learn about birth control and abortions, and know where you stand on them. This is difficult because they don't teach you in high school. Ask a doctor for birth control information when you go in for a checkup.

—Joyce, 20, California

The most difficult challenge I faced as a teen was trying to get birth control without my parents finding out. I checked with clinics, but they were very costly for an unemployed high school student. Fortunately, my mom came to me and told me to make an appointment with the doctor to talk about birth control. I would advise someone in my position to go to her mother and talk to her. It ended up a lot cheaper for me to get the right kind of birth control through my own doctor.

—Jennifer, 21, California

One of my most difficult challenges in high school was when I thought I was pregnant. Many fears came along with this: 1) raising a child at 16, 2) disappointing and shaming my family, and 3) being kicked out of school. My high school kicked out young women who became pregnant, but even when the male was known, he was always allowed to stay.

I had to decide if I should tell my family, keep the baby, abort the baby, or put the baby up for adoption. Do I tell my boyfriend before I am sure? I had long talks with friends about what I could do. Friends said they would help, but this is very unrealistic. How can friends help? Babysit? What about loss of sleep, neglect of studies, cost of raising a child [the average cost is $145,320 to age 18], morals to teach the child, how to raise and provide for the child?

Luckily I was not pregnant. All of this could have been avoided if I had used a condom (for HIV as well as pregnancy), and other forms of birth control (condoms are not 100 percent effective). Society makes it seem wrong to have sex and makes some people feel ashamed or embarrassed to buy the condoms. Make birth control available as it is better to be safe than sorry. This is the attitude my parents had (about three months after my scare), although I never told them about it.

—Christopher, 22, California

The most difficult experience I faced as a teen was when my girlfriend missed her period and she thought she was pregnant. We stressed for about a week and a half.

In the end, she wasn't pregnant but it put a strain on our relationship. I was stressed out. My advice is to take responsibility for your actions and try and have some fore-sight as to the consequences of your actions.

—Gena, 22, Tennessee

In high school we got information from someone who had overheard something from people older and misinterpreted it to become a fountain of misinformation. I had a friend in school who had been given a single birth control pill that she carried in her purse "just in case." For her, that "just in case" wasn't in case she forgot to take hers that morning because she wasn't on oral contraceptives: It was her "safeguard" if she was to have sex. Teens can get information from their local heath department or family planning center about STDs and viable methods of birth control.

—Andrew, 24, Oklahoma

Use a condom. Get information about how to use it before. Use another form of birth control for the female. Be smart. Know why you want to do it, i.e., pleasure, love, etc.

—Richard, 24, California

I got a girl pregnant when I was 17 and still had a year of high school left. I ended up marrying her, having the baby (being the father), and getting my GED. Then I went into the Marines. I'm divorced now, but I still see my daughter. If I had it all to do over again, I wish I knew how easy it was to get a girl pregnant. I would use a con-dom EVERY TIME I had sex.

Birth Control Information

Birth Control Information
1-800-INTENDS

Planned Parenthood
1-800-829-PPFA

Males Preventing Pregnancy, Inc.
P.O. Box 8435
Portland, ME 04104
(multimedia campaign targets teen males and provides workshops and training sessions)

Joy Dryfoos. *Putting the Boys in the Picture: A Review of Programs to Promote Sexual Responsibility Among Young Males.* **Santa Cruz, CA: Network Publications, 1988.**

Alan Grieceo,"Cutting the Risk for STDs," *Medical Aspects of Sexuality,* **March, 1987.**

Education about Sex

Sex education is a controversial topic even though the facts are clear. Studies show most parents do not adequately inform their children about sex, masturbation, STDs, and pregnancy. Almost a third of teens report no discussion of sex or birth control with their parents (a 1988 Louis Harris poll). Mothers are more likely to discuss these issues than fathers, and mothers are more likely to share information with their daughters than sons, so boys get left out. We need to remind school boards that over half of teenagers are sexually active, a million girls get pregnant each year, STDs are common, and AIDS is spreading fastest among teens.

Adoption of health textbooks still causes a fuss, as when the health textbook director for the California Department of Education reported in 1995, "There is still a lot of tension about sex education and health. With all our enlightenment and education, we still have a hard time talking about sex and AIDS. There was a general recognition that students needed a lot of information, yet many people didn't want it taught in their communities."

Polls report that 89 percent of Americans favor sex education in schools. When parents have the choice to remove their children from these programs, fewer than five percent accept the option. Public schools, however, average only two hours a year providing information about contraception and prevention of pregnancy!

By 1996 the AIDS crisis propelled 39 states to require STD/HIV and sex education. An overview (as of 1995) shows that 22 states require both types of programs, 15 states require only STD/HIV education, and 13 states don't require either program. Twenty-six states require abstinence instruction; only 14 of these states require information about birth control, pregnancy, and STDs. Five states prohibit or restrict discussion of abortion and eight states require or recommend teaching that homosexuality is not acceptable and/or is a criminal offense under state law. More and more states are considering legislation to restrict comprehensive sex education because they think it should be provided by parents. You might want to investigate the laws in your state.

A variety of right-wing organizations aim to influence public schools, by running for school board, attacking sex education and parent education programs, censoring texts, and accusing schools of promoting immorality. (Examples of these groups are Focus on the Family, The Family Research Council, Education Research Analysts, and the Traditional Values Coalition.) We will not see the development of more family life education courses if they have their way. One of these groups, Citizens for Excellence in Education, reports that people who oppose sex education in schools control about one-fifth of the nation's school boards.

Anti-sex education organizations campaign for abstinence education and prohibiting information about contraception, sexuality, and reproduction. They maintain that sex education classes are recruiting grounds for homosexuals or encourage teens to have sex. Some of their curriculums are "Sex Respect," "Choosing the Best," "Postponing Sexual Involvement," and "Teen Aid." False information is included (i.e., you can get AIDS by deep kissing), as well as their particular values (i.e., a double standard of male and female sexuality, homophobia, and that "after one has aborted a child, an individual loses instinctual control over rage" and will abuse future children). In contrast, a curriculum such as "Values and Choices" recognizes that some teens are sexually active.

Studies consistently show that comprehensive sex education programs cause students to wait longer before having intercourse, reduce pregnancy rates, or don't affect rates of sexual activity. The main finding is sex education does not lead to increased rates of sexuality (a World Health Organization review of more than 35 studies). Advocates for Youth (a research organization) cites studies proving that availability of contraceptives does not increase teen sexual activity either. An analysis of five teen pregnancy prevention programs finds they succeed by providing information on contraception along with emphasizing postponing sexual activity. The programs also teach decision-making and negotiation skills (the journal *Family Planning Perspectives*). You might want to investigate the curriculum used in your school—if any.

Of the 84,000 public schools in the U.S., only 700 provide health services, while 19 states prohibit schools from providing contraceptive services and/or abortion referrals. (*NARAL, Sexuality Education in America: A State-By-State Review*, 1995. 1156-15th St., NW, Washington, DC 20005.) This number is up from 31 school clinics in 1984 and 162 clinics in 1990. About two-thirds of the clinics provide condoms or prescriptions for birth control pills. Many students have no other source of health care and no health insurance. Some clinics train peer sex educators to do outreach to sexually active students, offer counseling with a nurse, and provide group counseling sessions about sex. For example, Central High School, in Little Rock, Arkansas had a 12 percent drop in pregnancy in 1994. They believe the decline occurred because the school clinic provided these services, including birth control.

—Ben, 18, Texas

We were forced to hold back from starting an effective campaign to prevent teen pregnancy in our high school because it was a long process for the school board to approve any literature we wanted to hand out. I ran for school board and did a lot of one-on-one communication, but I got killed in the election. This is a conservative county which didn't like the idea of an 18-year-old board member, despite the essential perspective.

—Sarah, 21, California

I was raised in a home where little information was given to me. I believe my parents were quite embarrassed when their young innocent baby girl started to ask questions about the "birds and the bees." I still remember when I asked that question, and I was met with smiles and chuckles of deflections from my parents. For a child like I was, this just caused me to seek information wherever I could. Growing up I heard many myths about how not to get pregnant and not a thing about how to avoid getting a sexually transmitted disease. By the time high school came around, most of my friends were sexually active and did not use any form of birth control.

Sex Education Sources

Planned Parenthood
1-800-539-2378
(distributes publications such as *Teensex* and *How to Talk with Your Child about Sexuality: A Parent's Guide*)

Advocates for Youth
1025 Vermont Ave., NW, Suite 200
Washington, DC 20005

Alan Guttmacher Institute
1120 Connecticut Ave., NW, Suite 460
Washington, DC 20036

Association of Sex Educators, Counselors, and Sex Therapists
435 N. Michigan Ave., Suite 1717
Chicago, IL 60611

Coalition for Positive Sexuality
3712 N. Broadway #191
Chicago, IL 60613
(*Just Say Yes* and other sex ed. booklets. Also has an Internet site and e-mail: talk-back@positive.org)

Sex Information and Education Council of the U.S.
The National Coalition to Support Sexuality Education
Dept. MM, 130 W. 42nd St., Suite 2500
New York, NY 10036-7901
(For a catalog, enclose a self-addressed, stamped envelope.)

Videotape, "Sex, Teens and Public Schools," an October 23, 1995, PBS documentary.
1-800-343-4727

Judy Drolet and Kay Clark, eds. *The Sexuality Education Challenge: Promoting Healthy Sexuality in Young People. Prevention Skills for Youth: Focus on Sexuality.* ETR Associates, 1-800-321-4407

Post Writers Group. *Issues in Adolescent Sexuality: Readings from the Washington Post.* Boston, MA: Allyn and Bacon, 1996.

Search Institute. *Human Sexuality: Values and Choices.* (for middle school students)
1-800-888-7828

Andrea Warren and Jay Wiedenkeller. *Everybody's Doing It! How to Survive Your Teenager's Sex Life and Help Them Survive It, Too.* NY: Viking, 1993.

Lois Ann Wodarski. *Adolescent Sexuality: A Comprehensive Peer/Parent Curriculum.* Springfield, Ill: C.C. Thomas, 1995 (for parents and schools).

Masturbation

Masturbation is common, although most people don't talk about it. Sexual tension builds in the genital organs and causes a desire for release. Self-stimulation does not have any negative physical effects, contrary to myths about causing acne, warts, hairy palms, blindness, or mental illness. Some babies do it, and it is common among kids ages three to six, as well as after puberty. Some studies show that 90 percent of men masturbate and 35 to 65 percent of women—depending on the survey.

Masturbation is touching one's sex organs to create pleasurable sexual feelings, often associated with orgasm. Some people imagine sexual fantasies as they masturbate, and some like to look at erotic pictures. Most women rub their clitoris and some insert objects in their vagina. They may use a water-based lubricant such as K–Y jelly, as oils should not be put in a vagina where they can cause infection. Also, the object should be clean.

Dr. Ruth Westheimer, a well-known sex educator, suggests that sexually active teen couples practice mutual masturbation rather than risk intercourse. Sex therapists often advise sexually active women who do not experience orgasms to masturbate to learn about their sexuality.

Teen Parenting

I think the two most difficult things I've had to deal with are becoming a parent and a wife. Pregnancy had many small challenges, as does marriage. Both experiences were difficult, yet educational. One thing that helped me deal with the challenge of being pregnant was talking to other people in similar situations. It was nice to know that I wasn't the only one who had made that mistake.

Another thing that I did was sign up for some county government programs. Some of these programs helped me deal with problems such as Medi-Cal and they listened when I had personal problems. I also signed up for WIC [a federal government food program for mothers of young children] *which took a lot of the guilt burden off me. I really wanted to help pay for groceries but a paycheck from McDonald's doesn't buy much food when you're trying to pay bills and save money to buy baby furniture.*

—Melinda, 18, California

The teen pregnancy rate declined in the 1980s, but started to climb again in the 1990s. However, birth rates for teens were lower in the 1990s than in the 1950s. The average time between when a teen first has sex and starts using birth control is about a year and this lag has stayed about the same since the early 1970s. As a result, over half of teen pregnancies occur within six months of first having intercourse. Television plays a part in this gap between intercourse and birth control, by portraying an average of 27 sexual scenes each hour with almost no reference to birth control or sex education (according to a Louis Harris study for Planned Parenthood).

Teen Moms

◎ By age 19, one in seven white women and one in four black women are mothers.

◎ Twelve percent of all births, and 30 percent of births to unmarried mothers, are to teens. In 1993, 71 percent of teen mothers were unmarried.

◎ Teen pregnancy costs federal taxpayers over $25 billion a year in welfare and other services, although only eight percent of welfare mothers are teens and payments average only $367 a month.

◎ Over 70 percent of teen mothers complete high school, but they are less likely to go to college than other girls.

◎ A quarter of teen mothers have a second baby within two years of their first.

(Alan Guttmacher Institute)

Early signs of pregnancy include: a missed period, nausea, vomiting, breast tenderness, unusual fatigue, more frequent urination, and increased vaginal discharge. However, some women may not experience or notice these signs. A home pregnancy urine test may not catch early pregnancy, but a blood test in a doctor's office can determine it as early as 14 days after conception. Urine pregnancy tests can result in a false negative if the pregnant woman used drugs such as marijuana before the test, soap is left in the urine container, or the urine is not concentrated enough (it's most concentrated when you first wake up).

The girls most likely to get pregnant are those who don't see other options for achievement, are poor and don't do well in school. Studies indicate that a significant number of pregnant teens were sexually or physically abused as children. Two-thirds of the girls interviewed by researchers Debra Boyer and David Fine (for a 1992 study of pregnant teens) had been raped or sexually abused, usually by fathers, stepfathers, or other relatives.

Teen mothers are a major social and economic issue because more than half of the approximately five million women on welfare started receiving aid as unmarried teen mothers. However, studies show that most poor women don't get pregnant to get welfare payments. (Note that welfare spending amounted to about one percent of the federal budget in 1994.)

Although most teen mothers are unmarried, 70 percent of births to unmarried women in 1993 were to women older than 20, and 60 percent of the mothers were white. To deal with the problem of teen parents, in 1996 President Bill Clinton permitted states to deny welfare payments to teen mothers who drop out of high school, permitted states to pay a bonus to moms who stay in school, and require unmarried teen mothers to live with a legal guardian. Welfare reform legislation later that year made these penalties a requirement not an option.

In almost half of all births to teens, the mother does not get early prenatal care, possibly resulting in expensive medical costs for the baby. Their babies are more likely to have health problems. (At least one in 10 of all the babies born in the U.S. has been exposed to illegal drugs used during pregnancy.)

Government Aid Programs for Low-Income Parents

✦ WIC (Women, Infants and Children) gives food coupons to pregnant women and mothers of young children.

✦ AFDC (Aid to Families with Dependent Children) provides a monthly check and/or food stamps to parents below the poverty level.

✦ Head Start is a successful preschool program for low-income children ages three to five years, which includes parent education.

✦ JOBS (Job Opportunities and Basic Skills Training) targets teen parents who have not finished school by offering funding for child care, transportation to school, etc. However, many states delayed the start-up of this teen parent program. (Welfare reform in 1996 cut funding for many of these programs and requires a mother to go to work or school when her baby is 12 weeks old.)

In discussions about how to prevent teen pregnancy or care for young mothers and their children, we have been strangely silent about the other half of the equation—fathers. The first national study of teenage fathers didn't occur until 1985, when a Ford Foundation study talked with nearly 400 young dads, participants in teen parenting programs. Most of them (82 percent) had daily contact with their children; however, generally studies show that as many as 70 percent of teen fathers are not involved with their children and about one-third of teen mothers receive welfare.

Some studies show that over half of fathers of the babies born to teen mothers are age 20 or older, not teens. In response, states are dusting off statutory rape laws (prohibiting sex between an adult and a minor), increasing prison sentences for statutory rape, and pressing these adults for child support. California, for example, set aside $8.4 million in 1996 to prosecute men who have sex with underage girls. The laws vary as to the age of consent, from 14 in states such as Pennsylvania, to 18 in many other states.

Outreach to both males and females through realistic sex education and making condoms available are two proven ways to reduce the high teen pregnancy rate, but the real solution is a hopeful future for young people.

—Andrea, 17, California

I was given the most difficult challenge a 15-year-old could handle—I got pregnant. I was so scared I tried to forget all about it. Rae, my boyfriend, kept pushing me to go to the doctor and to tell my parents. I couldn't do it. I was so afraid and I didn't know what to do or what I would say.

Three months went by. It was a week before my 16th birthday and I was still trying to think how I was going to tell my family. I finally had to tell my parents. First I told my mom. I sat her down on the couch and I pulled out some papers and handed them to her and then I said to her, "Mom, I'm pregnant." Those two words I bet just rang in her ears over and over. My mom then asked why I kept it from her and why I didn't tell her earlier. I guess she took it pretty good. She didn't say much.

Later on that day I had to tell my dad. I was kind of scared. Then my mom said she wanted to tell him. Later on that night, my parents came in and wanted to talk to me. We had a good talk. They told me they were 100 percent behind whatever I chose, and I was really lucky for that.

It was hard being a pregnant teen. Some people looked at me like I was trash, others questioned me about my whole life. "How old are you? Are you keeping it? Are you still with the father?" At times it seemed I should just walk around with a note on me saying, "16, Yes, Yes."

Rae and I had a pretty good time with me being pregnant, but we also had our bad times. He would get all stressed out and confused about what we needed for the baby being born. I guess he was finally realizing that this was his baby too, and that they were not cheap. Rae was really different through the whole pregnancy. He would gain weight when I did, he would get all kinds of cravings for weird foods, and he would have moods—bad, good, and great. A lot of times Rae would stress because we didn't have our own place to have our own family. Instead we lived with a group of roommates.

At times I would worry and hope we were doing the right thing in keeping the baby but I knew I would not be able to give him up to anyone else. We knew what we had done and we were going to live up to our responsibility. On October 2, I had a nine-pound baby boy. Rae was so happy, and I was so scared and happy at the same time because I knew that I had to be responsible for this little person. This was my most difficult challenge and it was just beginning and it was never going to end until the day I die.

I can't say I have overcome this challenge or fear of being a teen parent, but I have gotten more familiar with my challenge with the help of a teen parent program. I go to a parenting class at school with almost all the other teen moms in my town. It has helped me in a lot of decisions I have to make, and I don't think I could be where I am today if I didn't have that program. It's hard being a teen parent, like when I need to study and my son is crying because he wants me to hold him, or when I want to go out and he is sick, or I can't find anyone to babysit because everyone else is out at parties on the weekends. Then I just have to stay home and play blocks.

So I would say to anyone who gets into this same kind of challenge to find some type of support group, a good friend, family member or someone. I think that anyone in this situation needs someone to lean on; it's really important.

—Robert, 18, Minnesota

It was tough finding out I was going to be a dad for many reasons. My wife has been pregnant before with me and she miscarried during the fourth month. I never shared that with anyone, not even my parents. No one knows but us. We were scared it would happen again, but in a way we prayed it might. We knew what we were losing. Sally had just entered college and I was in my senior year of high school. The greatest years of our lives were ahead of us and we found ourselves looking down a narrow tunnel filled with pain, fear, and despair. We were scared of how our parents would react and that something would go wrong.

Neither of us had jobs. I want to be a musician. I had just released my first CD (local) and things were starting to go well for us (we were already engaged). Sally was unsure of where she wanted to go, so this was a center for her to focus on and work towards. It has been very good for her (the birth). I was scared, but at the same time very excited. I knew I was mature enough to handle a child and I was thinking like a dad already. I wondered where we would get the money and tried to find ways to budget ourselves so that we wouldn't be left out in the cold. We don't do many expensive things. We stay up and watch movies on TV while drinking Kool-Aid—cheap fun. We don't eat fast food and have lots of noodles.

Caring for the baby is easy—now. Carrie is only three weeks old and has few needs beyond clean diapers and nourishment. It was very scary at first. Though I come from a large family and had handled babies all my life, it was different when it was mine. I had to be serious and do the right thing. I couldn't waste time or money on things. It has not been easy.

Being a husband is easy (sort of); being a dad means I don't sleep as much anymore. I get up around 5:00 a.m. everyday so that I can take care of Carrie and get ready for work. When I get home (between 5:00 and 6:00 p.m.), I help make dinner and give Sally a break from work. I end up working a lot. Advice? Don't have sex. Be sure to express how wonderful the teen years can be. I have lost mine and I miss them. Being young is not something we should take for granted. I have a little girl and I can't enjoy my youth.

—Lenny, 23, California

We had been going out for almost two years when my girlfriend got pregnant. She wanted to keep the baby and I wanted her to get an abortion. After the baby was born, we were always fighting so I broke up with her. Some of our mutual friends hated me after that. My advice to other teens is to always practice safe sex. Do what you have to do for you, but still take care of your responsibilities.

—Ellie, 29, California

Your child is a person, not a possession. Don't use the baby as a bargaining tool in your relationship. A baby needs his or her father's involvement as much or more than you need his money or time. This doesn't mean he shouldn't pay support, but even if he can't, he can contribute time and attention.

If you were planning on college before, talk to family and schools, and find a way to follow through on your plans. College is hard when you have a child, but a life of poverty is harder.

Teen Parenting

Bright Beginnings
1-800-641-4546
(answers questions)

Parents Anonymous
1-800-421-0353

Adolescent Pregnancy Program
U.S. Department of Health and Human Services
200 Independence Ave., SW, #736E
Washington, DC 20201

MELD for Young Moms & Dads
123 N. Third St., Suite 507
Minneapolis, MN 55401 (referrals)

National Organization of Adolescent Pregnancy and Parenting
4421A East-West Hwy.
Bethesda, MD 20814(provides referrals for pregnant teens)

J.W. Lindsay. *Teen Parenting: Your Baby's First Year: A How-to-Parent Book Especially for Teenage Parents* (2 vols). Buena Park, CA: Morning Glory Press, 1991.

Karol Maybury. *Teen Father Handbook for Teen Fathers and Teen Fathers-To-Be: Straight Talk for Young Fathers.* 1991, 27 pages. (answers frequently asked questions and describes the YWCA Teen Father's Program, ED 334 334 Eric Clearinghouse on Urban Education)

Models of educational programs for teen parents and legal information are available from the NOW Legal Defense and Education Fund (99 Hudson St., New York, NY 10013-2815)

Rape

(See also sexual harassment in chapters 7 and 10 and child abuse section in Chapter 5)

I have some important advice for young females. If you try to be cute, or friendly, or polite, many men might take that to mean that you are inviting sexual advances. Many men see such invitations as justifications for rape, and many judges believe them. So, if a stranger asks you for the time, or for directions, or what your name is—especially if someone wants to follow you home, have no inhibitions about brushing him off, or assertively rejecting him. Trust your gut feelings about a person; if he makes you nervous, stay away.

—Anna, 15, New Jersey

Some people think of rape as a sexual act, but mostly it is about asserting power over another person, using sex as a weapon to humiliate and control the victim. Sexual violence is unwanted sexual contact forced upon a person, most often by a person known to the victim. About one in 10 high school students has been the victim of physical violence in a dating situation. Rape is the most rapidly growing violent crime in the U.S. and the rape rate is higher in the U.S. than in other industrial nations. The chances of being a victim of sexual assault in your lifetime are one in four for females and one in 10 for males.

Rape Facts

* Every 15 seconds a woman is battered and every 45 seconds a woman is sexually assaulted in the U.S.

* Every three minutes a woman is raped. Rape victims are nine times more likely than nonvictims to attempt suicide.

* Three-quarters of sexual assaults are committed by an acquaintance or family member.

* The FBI estimates that there are about 300 rapes reported each day in the U.S; however, few rapes (16 percent) are actually reported to the police and few rapists are ever convicted (some estimate only two percent). Most young women don't report date rape because they mistakenly think of a rapist as a stranger.

* Sixty-one percent of female rape victims are under the age of 18. The risk of rape is four times higher for women 16 to 24 than any other age group. One out of three or four women will be attacked in her lifetime and more than half of these attacks will occur before the women are 18. The younger a girl, the more likely she knows the rapist.

* In a survey of over 3,000 high-achiever high school students in 1995, 11 percent of the females had been sexually assaulted, usually by someone they knew. Over one-quarter knew a girl who was a victim of date rape. When the male students were asked when they thought a female who says No really means Yes to more sexual activity, 42 percent replied it's when she continues to be affectionate.

Myths about Rape

* "A woman deserves to be raped if she wears sexy clothes." No one deserves to be assaulted. The victim often blames herself for being in the wrong place at the wrong time, but like a robbery, sometimes you can't prevent the crime.

* "Rapists can't help themselves." Most rapes are planned.

* "Women say No but mean Yes." No means No.

* "Men of color rape white women." Over 90 percent of rapes happen between people of the same race.

Women are the most frequent victims, but rape happens to men too, as in prisons. Estimates are seven to 10 percent of all rape victims are adult men, but they are less likely than women to report the crime. Only five percent of reported sexual assaults have male victims. There were over 10,000 reports of rapes of males in 1990, according to the Bureau of Justice statistics.

Date Rape

Date rape can be seen as the extreme of sex roles teaching men to be aggressive and dominant and teaching women to be passive, subordinate, and self-blaming, making the victim think it was her fault. Young women often say No too indirectly because they don't want to hurt a guy's feelings.

Official reports of date rape have risen steadily since the 1980s. It is more common than left-handedness or alcoholism. Some studies report that as many as a quarter of high school girls have been victims of date rape or other forms of sexual and physical violence.

The highest rate of acquaintance rape is among college freshmen. In one survey of college students, a quarter of the women had been the victims of rape or attempted rape, and 84 percent of the attackers were acquaintances. In the same survey, a quarter of college men admitted to using sexual aggression with women. In acquaintance rape, the majority of both men and women had been drinking or taking drugs before the attack.

College men and women often have different perceptions of acquaintance rape. Rapists report the victim physically struggled 12 percent of the time, while 70 percent of raped women report they struggled. Men report the victim tried to reason with them 36 percent of the time, while 84 percent of the women said they tried to reason with their attacker, as reported in Robin Warshaw's *I Never Called It Rape*. Girls must be firm in saying No and boys must honor that. The bottom line is if it is against your will, it is against the law.

An influence on male sexuality is pornography; the combined circulation of *Playboy* and *Penthouse* is greater than *Time* and *Newsweek*. The average boy first sees porn magazines by age 11. One in five women has been sexually abused by a man as a result of this use of pornography, according to the response of 6,000 readers to a 1986 *Woman's Day* questionnaire. This pattern is similar to copycat crimes duplicating crimes, the perpetrator saw on TV. (Jed, a reader, commented, "We are in charge of our own actions. A magazine can't make us rape someone." True, but it can suggest it or make it seem like women enjoy it.)

To avoid date rape: Don't go out alone with boys who make you uncomfortable, drink a lot, don't respect what you say, grab you, and are controlling. Be clear about setting limits. Always let someone know where you are going, with whom, and when you intend to be back. Plan a way to get home on your own, such as having enough money for a taxi. Men never have the right to force someone even if you paid for the date, she is dressed in sexy clothes, she agrees and then changes her mind, or if you have had sex with her before.

Preventing Rape

Some people suggest attacking the rapist's eyes, Adam's apple, or crotch. You can also attack with words to turn him off and cool him down. Some suggest trying to do something gross like urinating or vomiting, or telling him you have herpes. If you're in danger, yell "fire" as people respond to that more than to shouting "help."

In her book *Defending Ourselves*, Rosalind Wiseman quotes Mary, a raped woman, who said almost every victim of rape she talked with had a premonition something bad was going to happen. Mary asks, "When are we going to start listening to ourselves? Listening to that inner voice was one of the positive things I learned from the rape."

To guard against rape, Ms. Wiseman reminds us that rapists attack to assert their power and control, so they do not pick confident, assertive victims. If attacked, she suggests women use verbal self-defense, face the attacker, look him in the eyes, and command him in a firm voice to stop. Ms. Wiseman advises practicing screaming No at the top of your lungs.

She suggests that if you jog alone don't wear headsets, so you can hear someone behind you, and borrow a dog if you don't have one. If you hear someone break into your house, call 9-1-1 right away. She suggests carrying pepper gas in a canister with a recessed button, which prevents it from going off accidentally, and one without a safety latch which takes too long to adjust. She does not believe in having a handgun but recommends learning a martial art.

◎   Avoid isolated places such as garages and elevators.

◎   If someone is following you on the street, cross the street. If the person is in a car, turn and walk in the opposite direction. If the person continues to follow you, go into a store and call the police. Carry a whistle and blow it. Walk confidently.

◎   If you have car trouble, raise the hood, put on emergency flashers, lock the doors, stay inside the car and ask someone who stops to call the highway patrol.

If either you or a friend is raped, immediately call your local rape crisis center, crisis intervention center, or the police, and ask them to meet you at the hospital emergency room. Do not shower or change clothes so medical staff can collect evidence about the rapist, such as a semen sample or pubic hair.

About one-third of rape victims suffer from trauma syndrome including depression, thoughts of suicide, or drug/alcohol abuse. Some victims experience a delayed reaction called post traumatic stress disorder, similar to experiences of war veterans or disaster survivors. The trauma of a violent act like rape stays with the victim for a long time, so counseling is useful in learning how to cope with feelings of anger, fear, shame, loss of trust, powerlessness, depression, and self-blame. The common theme in the experiences you'll read about is to tell someone you trust right away.

—Jennifer, 16, Colorado

The most difficult thing that I've ever faced as a teen was that I was sexually assaulted at age 12. One of my best friends tried to force me to have sex and it hurt me very badly. I was destroyed inside but wasn't brave enough to tell anyone what had happened. It took four years for me to tell my own mother with whom I had a very special relationship.

What helped me cope with this challenge was the fact that I knew it wasn't my fault and that I could've been in a worse position, like dead. My advice to anyone who has had this same experience is to tell someone, no matter how hard it is, because it helps to talk about your feelings and to go on with your life.

—Lisa, 22, California

My most traumatic experience in high school was when I lost my virginity. I was 15 and had planned on keeping my virginity until I was married. During the summer, I met this guy and we went on a date. During the date we fooled around but I specifically told him that I didn't want to have sex. Several days later he came over to my friend's house to hang out. My friends and I had all been drinking, and I had about four wine coolers and was drunk. After being there for awhile, he asked me if I wanted to go to a room with him. I said Yes, being completely naive.

We ended up climbing up on bunk beds and getting together. One thing led to another and we had sex. I didn't really want to but it's hard to jump off bunk beds when he is not listening to your No.

After this happened, I didn't have much confidence in the field of men. I thought that men wanted sex and that was how you got them to like you. As for my first, I worked with him and I can't remember somebody treating me so horribly. I then went on a guy spree, thinking that it was the thing to do. Two years later I decided that sex was not the right answer. At this point in time I haven't had sex for a year and a half.

Even after seven years I am still emotionally irritated because of sex. I believe that my first would not recognize me or remember what he did to me. To this day, I can't have sex. I think that I have a fear of sex. It's hard to believe that one thing can change one's life so much. My advice is don't have sex until you're ready. Sex is not a way for guys to like you. Have respect for yourself and others will have respect for you.

—Taylor, 23, California

My most traumatic event in high school was the night I disobeyed my parents on my whereabouts. I said I was going to a high school play but I went out with another couple and I was set up with a senior. We went up to the top of a famous local mountain to hang out. We listened to music and drank beer. Then my friends (the other couple) started to go off and make out. Well, of course, this gave the dirt bag I was with the idea that we should make out. At first I felt OK then he started to get a little out of hand. I said No and "Let's stop," but being a male, older, and hormones flying, he ignored my pleas of No. I unfortunately had no way to stop him and I had to give in.

When my dad came to school to pick me up I felt so bad. I felt awful that I had lied to my parents who do so much to protect me. I had been put in a situation that I had no control over. **[The lesson is not to go to an unsafe place to start with and to scream for help.]**

I had my friends and myself to cope with this traumatic situation. I've never told my parents because I had disobeyed them and I had an awful thing happen that I felt very guilty about it. I put up a huge wall around me and became somewhat afraid of men, but then I took an attitude of getting back at them. I didn't realize this until I came out to my friends about what happened and how I handled it. I would have sex with men and either stop them in the middle of it, tease men, or have sex and never talk to them again.

I should have told some people in my family or have gotten psychological help. My advice is to talk to people, someone whom you trust and can confide in. Talking to people at rape prevention or rape clinics is great. Writing out your feelings will help you a great deal too. Now I'm a very healthy person and have cleared up my feelings on the subject of rape!

One thing I'd like to really express is please try to obey your parents! They know what goes on and they are only trying to protect you. They will never intentionally do anything to hurt you! I know the classic statement is, "I've got to experience it for myself," but really look at the situation and think about it.

—Charlie, 24, California

Date rape situations can happen to anyone. You hear it all the time. This is something I don't think I will ever fully recover from. I have yet to have another sexual experience since then, and I don't know if I will. I haven't been in a long-lasting relationship because when guys try to get close to me, I have major anxiety attacks and push them away. Despite all warnings, the reality is that once it happens you can't go back and it really screws up your life. I don't think I'll ever be able to trust anyone ever.

You can take precautions though: 1) If you have to drink, drink responsibly. 2) You can never know someone too well. If you feel uncomfortable get away fast. 3) Make your intentions and feelings known early on and loud and clear. Be firm. 4) Secluded places aren't good places to be if he has other ideas than you do.

—Janet, 25, Illinois

The most difficult challenge I faced as a teenager was date rape. It may be hard to believe, but less than a decade ago, this type of rape was ignored. Teenage girls were made to feel as if they brought it on themselves.

Many years of counseling helped me to let go of the self-blame. I shut out others for a very long time. Additionally, a wonderful and trusted loved one became my confidant and friend. With his shoulder and wisdom, I could begin to let go of the shame.

The advice I would give to another teen, is simply this: "It is not your fault." If it feels wrong, it is wrong, and you do not deserve to have your body taken advantage of. Additionally, find someone you can trust and let go of the emotion and the shame. By sharing your experience, you can begin to let go of the destructiveness of the event. If you keep it all inside, it will reemerge.

Rape Prevention

Coalition Against Rape
1-800-692-7445

Rape and Suicide hotline
1-800-333-4444

The Empower Program
7300 Pearl St., Suite 220
Bethesda, MD 20814
(an educational organization which offers seminars mainly for schools and youth organizations)

The American Woman's Self-Defense Association
713 N. Wellwood Ave.
Lindenhurst, NY 11757 (referrals)

Preventing Teen Dating Violence: A Three-Session Curriculum for Teaching Adolescents. Dating Violence Intervention Project.
(P.O. Box 530, Harvard Square Station, Cambridge, MA 02238)

Deollo Johnson. *The Anti-Rape Manual: Self-Defense Techniques of Mind and Body.* (P.O. Box 5668, Duke Station, Durham, NC 27706)

Gayle Stringer, et al. *So What's It to Me? Sexual Assault Information for Guys,* and *Top Secret: Sexual Assault Information for Teenagers Only.* King Co. Sexual Assault Prevention (P.O. Box 300, Renton, WA 98057)

Rosalind Wiseman. *Defending Ourselves: A Guide to Prevention, Self-Defense, and Recovery From Rape.* NY: Farrar, Strauss and Giroux, 1994.

Feminists Against Violence Network:
mdubin@ix.netcom.com
(mention can-yfn) (The founder is an attorney for the federal Violence Against Women office but the list is his personal one.)

Sexual Response Cycle

My first sexual experience didn't work out the way I wanted it to. Because I was nervous and inexperienced, I didn't/couldn't get an erection. I thought I had a big problem; I didn't know what was wrong. I knew I could get an erection, but I didn't know why I didn't for my first time. Throughout high school this occurred several times because I was always afraid that it would happen. I was always very nervous and couldn't get an erection.

After I got older, I matured and just didn't worry any more. I knew I could get an erection and I did. I just don't worry any more because there is nothing to be scared or nervous about. It's like it never happened and I'm not embarrassed to talk about this because I'm normal and can get an erection.
—Brandon, 20, California

William Masters and Virginia Johnson are famous for their observations of couples having sexual intercourse in the laboratory. (They married and divorced in the process of their research, in case you're wondering.) After years of study, they found there are four physiological stages of sexual response similar for males and females.

Excitement Phase: The body responds to sexual stimuli which can include touches, thoughts, sights, and sounds. Erogenous zones such as the mouth or genitals are especially sensitive to touch. In response, the genitals become swollen with blood and muscle tension increases. The blood pressure rate and heart rate increase. In women, the vagina secretes fluids to lubricate the vaginal walls, the clitoris swells as it engorges with blood, and the uterus expands and pulls up the cervix and upper end of the vagina. Nipples may become hard and erect. In males, the penis gets erect as it fills with blood, the scrotum lifts up, and the testicles get bigger.

Plateau Phase: The heart rate and blood pressure rate continue to increase. In women, the vagina continues to secrete lubrication and the diameter of the vagina contracts by almost one-half. In men, the head of the penis gets larger and the abdominal and buttocks muscles tighten.

Orgasmic Phase: With continued stimulation, orgasm occurs as rhythmic contractions in the genitals release engorged blood and muscle tension. Males ejaculate seminal fluid. Some people can have more than one orgasm in a row if stimulation continues, especially females. Heartrate and blood pressure may double, breathing may become faster, facial muscles may contract, and brain-wave patterns change.

Masters and Johnson observed that the clitoris is like the penis in having the most sensation and acting as the main organ of orgasmic response. Most women need direct clitoral stimulation to have an orgasm, just as men need direct penile stimulation. The euphoric enjoyment of orgasm is usually followed by relaxation and contentment.

—Pat Hanson, Ph.D., sex educator

Most women have a series of nerve endings on the front, upper, inner wall of their vagina called the urethral sponge or the G-spot. When stimulated, either by a finger or a penis in the right position, the nerve endings of this G-spot, which are actually connected to the clitoris, can produce an intense sensation sometimes feeling like a pressure to urinate, and can lead to orgasm. A few women release fluid from their urethra when they have an orgasm produced by stimulation of the G-spot. This is called female ejaculation.

There are three female magic spots: the breasts, the clitoris, and the G-spot that, when consistently stimulated, either separately or simultaneously, can produce an orgasm in a woman who is psychologically ready and willing to allow one. The secret lies in that last word, readiness. For many women that state of mind depends on many factors: the kind of day they've had, how they feel about their partner, where they are in their monthly hormonal cycle, and how able they are to surrender to a particular sexual moment. Many women choose to enhance their sexual arousal with fantasies, either by reading, viewing or sharing their erotic visual images with their partner, or keeping them to themselves.

Some girls are not sure what an orgasm is, but once they've had one, the uncertainty clears up. Some reasons a woman doesn't have an orgasm are not enough kissing and touching to become sexually aroused, being anxious because she doesn't feel comfortable with her partner or the environment, fear of getting pregnant or catching an STD, her clitoris isn't touched enough or is rubbed too hard without lubrication, or she's judging how she's responding or how her body looks, instead of feeling. If she's worrying about having an orgasm, it probably won't happen. Having a sexual fantasy and focusing on her partner and her sensations are much more likely to lead to orgasm than anxiety. Another reason to not rush into having intercourse is it takes time for a couple to relax with each other, to learn about their likes and dislikes, and to trust each other's caring and commitment.

Young men may ejaculate quickly after their penis enters the vagina, before they learn to make erections last longer. Some couples start foreplay again as the guy is likely to maintain an erection longer the second time. Some sex therapists recommend the squeeze technique to prolong erection, where one of the partners squeezes the base of the penis with a hand. Or the man can do Kegel exercises (see female anatomy section) to stop himself from ejaculating. Some guys use the old technique of thinking about something else (like baseball scores) when they feel they're about to ejaculate. Some guys stop moving, slow down, rub her clitoris, or change position to keep from having an orgasm before they're ready.

Guys, too, can be anxious about sex, especially if they feel the pressure to be leaders who are supposed to know exactly how to be good lovers. Problems with getting an erection or maintaining it can occur when they feel anxious, when they're not in the mood for sex, or if they don't know their partner well enough to feel comfortable with her. Alcohol and some drugs can keep men from getting an erection as well.

Resolution Phase: Blood pressure, heart rate, breathing, and muscle tension return to normal. The vagina and penis decrease in size.

STDs
(Sexually Transmitted Diseases)

When I was 16 I made the mistake of having unprotected sex and I contracted an STD which I am forced to deal with for the rest of my life. I was so concerned with having sex I did not hear the warnings in school to be safe. I've seen a doctor and suppressed a lot of my feelings because I am uncomfortable talking about my STD with other people. I am very responsible about it. I make sure the people I am involved with know about it and I am always protected.

—Jim, 21, California

STDs include a wide variety of bacteria, viruses, protozoans, and yeast infections passed on by sexual contact. Twelve million Americans—three million of them are teens—get an STD each year, one of the highest rates in the industrialized world. More than one in five Americans has an incurable viral STD, not including AIDS. A quarter of sexually active teens become infected with an STD each year, or about one in eight teens. By age 21, about half of sexually active youth have had an STD, according to the Centers for Disease Control.

STDs are transmitted through vaginal, oral, or anal sexual intercourse. Bacteria or viruses are carried in semen, vaginal fluid, an blood, and can enter through breaks in the skin. Bacterial STDs may not lead to visible symptoms but, if untreated, can lead to infertility and increased cancer risk. To avoid these diseases, abstain from intercourse, or if sexually active, use a latex condom with spermicide containing the chemical Nonoxynol-9, and remain monogamous.

Some STDs have symptoms such as blisters, warts, sores, itching, and discharge and pain when urinating. Others have no symptoms or may be too small to be seen without a medical examination. Herpes and genital warts increase the risk of cervical cancer for women. Chlamydia (the most common) and gonorrhea can jeopardize female fertility by developing into pelvic inflammatory disease.

STDs without a cure are herpes, AIDS, and hepatitis B. Those which can be treated medically include syphilis, gonorrhea, genital warts, and chlamydia. Pubic lice and scabies mites are also transmitted during sexual contact and are treatable.

If you are sexually active, regularly get checked for STDs because many people have no early symptoms. Eighty percent don't know they're infected. Women are more susceptible to infection, less likely to experience symptoms, and more likely to become infertile than men. Your doctor, Planned Parenthood, and health clinics can provide these tests. A blood test is used for syphilis and HIV, and a tissue culture tests for gonorrhea, herpes, and chlamydia.

Bacterial STDs

About one-quarter of sexually active teenage women have **chlamydia**, according to the Centers for Disease Control. Chlamydia can cause irritation during urination and a clear discharge, although many people don't have these symptoms. This infection can lead to sterility in both sexes. Up to 150,000 American women become infertile each year as a result of Pelvic Inflammatory Disease, most often caused by an untreated infection from chlamydia or gonorrhea. PID is the most common complication of STDs in women; teen girls have the highest rate of hospitalization for severe PID. The infection may cause pain in the lower abdomen, fever, chills, irregular bleeding, and tiredness. Women with PID are more likely to have a dangerous ectopic (tubal) pregnancy. This occurs when a fertilized egg can't pass through scarred fallopian tubes and instead implants itself and grows in the tube. As many as four million people were infected in 1995.

Gonorrhea can affect the eyes and mouth as well as the genital organs. Over 800,000 Americans contract gonorrhea each year and most are teens. It can be contacted through fellatio as well as intercourse. Symptoms include yellowish green discharge, pain and burning during urination, abnormal periods, and fever. In the early stages many people do not have these symptoms. If left untreated, it can cause sterility, blindness, arthritis, and heart disease. It can be cured with antibiotics.

Syphilis, up to a month after infection, causes a hard, painless oval-shaped sore on the genitals, about the size of a dime. When this sore is no longer visible, the second phase sets in as the bacterium enters the bloodstream. The person may have red patches around the genitals that weep a clear liquid. The person may also have fever, headaches, and weight and hair loss. These symptoms may go away and reappear. If untreated, syphilis can cause blindness, heart disease, insanity, and paralysis. Penicillin can treat the disease at any of the three stages, although the bacterium may be becoming resistant to penicillin. About 43,000 cases were reported in 1995.

Trichomoniasis in women is a heavy, bad-smelling discharge caused by a one-celled protozoan, passed on through sex or contact with a wet toilet seat or towel, as it can live in urine and water for days. About three million women were infected in 1995. It can lead to sterility but can be treated. In men it can cause inflammation of the penis.

Viral STDs

Genital warts are the most common viral STD, caused by the human papilloma virus (HPV). As many as 15 percent of sexually active girls are thought to be infected with HPV. Contact between a wart and a cut in the skin spreads this STD. The warts appear on a man's penis or anus and a woman's vagina, vulva, cervix, anus, or urethra. Venereal warts are grayish white warts with a cauliflower-like texture; some are so small you can't see them. If untreated, they increase the chance of cervical cancer in women and penile cancer in men. About 95 percent of cervical cancers are linked to HPV (cervical cancer kills nearly 5,000 women each year). They can be removed by a doctor with liquid nitrogen, podophyllin ointment, laser surgery, or interferon.

As many as 500,000 new cases of genital **herpes** are reported each year. About 31 million Americans have herpes. The virus causes outbreaks of cold-sore-like blisters on the genitals. Cold sores on the mouth are also caused by a herpes virus and can be transmitted to the genital area during oral sex, just as genital sores can be transferred to the mouth. Before the blister appears, the infected person is usually warned by itching at the place where the blister will appear. Some people feel burning during urination or experience a discharge, fever, weakness, and fatigue. The virus can be spread to the eyes by touching them with infected fingers; herpes is the main cause of infectious blindness. The first outbreak is usually the most painful and the attacks diminish with time.

Studies suggest a small percentage of people can pass on the virus even with no outbreak of blisters. The virus can be transmitted when an outbreak starts, even before the blisters form. In women, genital herpes increases risk of cervical cancer and may be passed on to their babies during childbirth. Outbreaks can be triggered by stress, the hormonal changes before a menstrual period, too much sun, and foods high in argenine.

There is no treatment, but the drug Acyclovir (taken orally or applied as an ointment) speeds the healing process for some people. People who use natural remedies take the amino acid lysine in capsule form (and eat potatoes, fish, eggs, and other foods high in lysine) and avoid another amino acid, argenine, which is found in foods such as chocolate, peanuts, and cola. Some have success with large doses of kyolic garlic, taking 12 capsules at first sign of an outbreak, then three capsules every two waking hours. Vaccines are being developed.

One of the fastest-spreading STDs is **hepatitis B** which can be transmitted by contact with saliva while kissing, or by blood, semen, and vaginal secretions. Hepatitis B is a viral infection of the liver. About 50,000 Americans get it each year and about 6,000 die, although it can be prevented by a vaccine. Ten percent of those who get hepatitis B are infected for life and have a high risk of developing serious liver diseases. About half of those infected with the hepatitis B virus never develop symptoms, but they can become permanent carriers of the virus. Symptoms can range from indigestion, to diarrhea and vomiting, to jaundiced skin and eyes (yellowed by the liver problem). Hepatitis B increases the risk of liver cancer.

Hepatitis C is similar and infects about 3.5 million Americans. About half the people infected with hepatitis C develop chronic liver disease, which can be spread by contact with semen, vaginal secretions, and saliva. Many of these STDs can be prevented by faithful use of condoms and spermicide.

—Pete, 21, Washington

There are now about 50 different STDs and also HIV, not to mention getting pregnant for heterosexual kids. Sex is usually considerably better when you love the person as well. I know of very few high school romances that turn into TRUE love anyway. Be prepared for the emotional consequences such as a likely broken heart, too.

—Beth, 27, Maryland

My most traumatic experience as far as a blow to my self-esteem was contracting genital herpes. I was 14 and had been sexually active for two years with the same man. He was four years older and sleeping with lots of other women. I was devastated and it was the only time in my life that I thought about suicide. I felt dirty and that no one would want to marry me, but it has not been a big problem for me other than in my mind. I take lysine (an amino acid) and I never have outbreaks.

STD Phone Information	Herpes Resource Center

STD Phone Information

**American Social Health Association
1-800-982-5883**

Herpes Hotline 1-415-328-7710 (San Francisco)

**Herpes Resource Center
1-800-230-6039**

**The National STD Hotline
1-800-227-8922
(makes referrals to clinics and hospitals for testing and provides information)**

AIDS

—Tina, 15, California

My uncle had AIDS and towards the end of his life he was so miserable, he had to be hooked up to a machine 15-hours a day and he never had any energy. He was an outside, energetic person and I hated seeing him like that. He passed away last year. I miss him so much. I wish there was no such thing as AIDS.

When kids ages 10 to 13 were asked their main concerns about health, safety, and lifestyle, AIDS was at the top of the list, with 40 percent very concerned. (Next on the list were fear of death, being kidnapped, being abused physically or sexually, and taking drugs.) HIV stands for the human immunodeficiency virus which causes AIDS—Acquired Immunodeficiency Syndrome. AIDS is not a single disease, but occurs as the virus disarms the immune system's ability to fight off infections and diseases.

Every hour another teen contracts the AIDS virus. Between 40,000 and 80,000 Americans are infected with AIDS each year, and 25 percent are under 20. About one million Americans have the HIV virus although many are unaware of it. You can't tell if someone is HIV positive because it can take up to 10 years to develop AIDS (the average length is about eight years). Most people with HIV will develop AIDS and about 40,000 Americans die each year from AIDS.

Who Gets AIDS

- The HIV infection rate is rising faster among teens than any other group in the U.S. Half of the new infections occur in people younger than 25; one-fourth are teenagers. Part of the reason for the high rate is that most teens don't use birth control when they first become sexually active.

- AIDS is the leading killer of Americans ages 25 to 44. Two hundred people get AIDS every day.

- Over one-third of teens with AIDS are female, although women were only 13 percent of all people diagnosed with AIDS in the U.S. through 1994. HIV infection is spreading fastest among women, intravenous drug users, and people of color.

One of every 92 young men (ages 27 to 39) may have AIDS; remember that it takes years to break down the immune system, so many of these victims contracted the virus as teens. Gay and bisexual men were a minority of new cases (43 percent) in 1994. However, recent interviews with 1,781 homosexual young men found that more than a third of them had not used a condom in the past six months (Dr. Linda Valleroy, Centers for Disease Control and Prevention).

The AIDS virus is spread by body fluids (blood, semen, vaginal secretions, and breast milk) exchanged through sex, shared needles, or from mother to fetus. Between 10,000 and 20,000 American children are HIV positive. Most are infected as fetuses by their mothers or through sexual intercourse as teens.

In oral sex, the preejaculation fluid, as well as the semen, can contain the HIV virus which can enter the mouth through small cuts. There are about 15 known cases of transmission through oral sex, but no known cases through French kissing, although it could happen if the infected person has a bleeding cut or tooth. HIV is not transmitted by saliva, sweat, urine, coughs, sneezes, food, or other casual contact with an infected person; body fluids must be exchanged.

HIV invades the white blood cells where it binds to the DNA in the T-cell (an immune cell called CD4). Eventually it kills the T-cell and creates new viruses that invade other T-cells. The most effective anti-viral treatment of AIDS is a combination of drugs called AZT, 3TC, and Norvir that attack an enzyme which the AIDS virus needs to reproduce itself. New drugs are continually being developed to be more effective in fighting HIV, aided by the discovery of the protein needed by the virus to replicate. Drugs can now greatly diminish the amount of HIV in the blood cells, if treatment begins early.

Symptoms include fevers and night sweats, diarrhea, swollen glands, fatigue, skin rashes, weight loss, dry cough, and bruises, as portrayed by Tom Hanks in the film "Philadelphia." About half of AIDS patients suffer brain damage and some develop infections such as pneumonia, skin cancer, and lymphoma.

Current tests for HIV are almost 100 percent accurate, although it may take up to six months for a recently infected person to develop the antibodies detected in the blood test. To take the test, contact your doctor, public health department, or Red Cross chapter, or purchase a home test such as Orasure (uses a tissue sample from your mouth).

Some health experts suggest that all pregnant women take the AIDS test because there is a 30 to 50 percent chance the baby of an HIV positive mother will be infected during pregnancy or delivery. If a pregnant HIV positive woman uses the drug

AZT (zidovudine) during her pregnancy, and the drug is given to the baby after birth, the rate of transmission falls to eight percent.

How can you escape AIDS? Really safe sex means avoiding intercourse, either abstaining or reaching orgasm through other stimulation of the genitals. The next safest step is using a latex condom and spermicidal jelly (it should contain Nonoxynol-9 which can kill viruses) and knowing your partner's history. Some people insist on an AIDS test before having intercourse, but remember it can take six months for the virus to show up. Avoid IV (intravenous) drug users: By 1994, more than 110,000 AIDS cases had been reported among IV drug users and at least 30 percent of U.S. AIDS victims had injected drugs.

Any open sore can provide entry to the bloodstream by the virus. Latex squares (called dental dams) are recommended for oral sex on women, to prevent exchange of blood or vaginal secretions. The square is placed over the vaginal opening and held in place with the fingers during oral sex. Your local AIDS hotline can tell you where to purchase latex squares. Nonlubricated (perhaps mint-flavored) condoms are used for oral sex for men. Don't risk becoming a teen statistic by not practicing safe sex or sharing infected needles.

—Michael, 18, Washington, DC

[A sexually active teen who used drugs and had sex with both boys and girls, at age 15 he had a blood test before surgery to correct a broken nose and was diagnosed with the virus.] *I just wanted to have fun and never gave a moment's thought to consequences. I never thought it would happen to me. But from that day on my life changed. I want you always to remember that having sex without a condom could kill you months or years later. I want to get the message across so people understand that HIV is a permanent situation— you can't correct it. Having HIV is like having a rain cloud over my head 24 hours a day.*

(Quoted from *Straight Talk: A Magazine for Teens*. The magazine is part of a series about teen health and lifestyle issues available from The Learning Partnership, P.O. Box 199, Pleasantville, NY 10570-0199.)

—Louis, 20, Colorado

Sex is best with someone who matters to you emotionally. Practice safe sex or die.

—Mary, 20, New York

As a person who is HIV positive, I just live day by day, and hopefully there'll be some kind of cure. I was perfectly clear what the disease was about and what I had to do to prevent it. I understood, and like any other teenager, I didn't listen. Well, I asked my partner to use a condom. He said No, and I said OK. It's just the same as telling a teenager to use birth control. They say OK and they don't and they get pregnant.

—Barbara, 21, New York

The reason that I was so sexually promiscuous [and got AIDS] goes back to not having anyone to talk to. You meet a guy, you fall in love, and it comes off as love and attention. If he asks a little thing like don't wear a condom, you're going to say OK, at least he loves me, and you're going to do whatever you can for this guy.

(*Mary and Barbara quoted from National Public Radio, "All Things Considered," August 23, 1993.*)

AIDS Information

AIDS Action Hotline
1-800-235-2331

AIDS Drug Information, National
Institute of Allergies and Infectious
Diseases
1-800-874-2572

AIDS Hotline 1-800-227-8922

CDC National AIDS Clearinghouse 1-
800-458-5231

Latino AIDS Line
1-800-637-3776

IYG Gay/Lesbian Youth Hotline 1-
800-347-TEEN

The National AIDS Hotline
1-800-342-AIDS
1-800-344-SIDA (Spanish)
1-800-AIDS-TTY (hearing impaired)
(provides referrals to HIV/AIDS counseling and testing in your area, and
provides information and materials)

Project Inform HIV/AIDS Treatment
Hotline
1-800-822-7422

Teens TAP (Teens Teaching AIDS
Prevention) 1-800-234-TEEN

Youth Only AIDS Hotline
1-800-788-1234

AIDS Action Council
2033 M St., NW #802
Washington, DC 20036

Citizens Commission on AIDS
121 Sixth Ave., 6th Floor
New York, NY 10013

National Association of People with
AIDS
1413 K St., NW, 7th Floor
Washington, DC 20005

Project AHEAD (Alliance for the
Health of Adolescents)
375 Woodside Ave.
San Francisco, CA 94127

Women and AIDS Resource
Network
30 Third Ave., Suite 512
Brooklyn, NY 11217

Earvin "Magic" Johnson. *What You
Can Do to Avoid AIDS*. NY: Times
Books/Random House, 1992.

When to Make Love?

The Alan Guttmacher Institute reports in "Sex and America's Teenagers" that about half of the girls and three-fourths of the boys have sexual intercourse by the time they are 18. The average age is about 16. The rates are up, as 20 years ago about one-third of the girls and half the boys had sex by age 18. Sexual activity of white females rose in the 1980s, while that of Latina and black girls leveled off. Most young teens have not had intercourse. The large majority (about 70 percent) of girls under 15 who have had sex were forced to, often by a much older male. Teens who engage in other risky behaviors, such as using drugs, are more likely to have sex at younger ages.

Six in 10 teens don't approve of premarital sex, although 61 percent believe condoms should be available in schools and 78 percent believe schools should provide sex education, according to a survey for the Horatio Alger Association.

In a survey of over 3,000 high-achiever high school students in 1995 (72 percent female, mostly 16 and 17), 22 percent had engaged in sexual intercourse. The main reason virgins gave for abstaining was to wait for marriage. The main reasons to have sex were they were in love, curious, or "swept away by passion." Forty-seven percent of the females and 33 percent of the males wished they had stayed virgins. The most common places to have sex were at home or in a parked car. Few had more than two sexual partners. Only 56 percent said they always used birth control.

A survey of 2,000 never-married males ages 15 to 19 (in 1988) found that they were having sex at earlier ages but not with many partners. Forty percent to 50 percent of the boys said they had only one sexual partner in the last year. Only 10 percent had sex with two different partners in the same month, and only five percent had five or more partners in the last year, reported professor Joseph Pleck. Among sexually active girls ages 15 to 17, 55 percent have had two or more partners and 13 percent have had at least six lovers.

I asked a group of teen guys if they used lines to get a girl to have sex. About half did and these are their standard lines: "I really care about you." "This is right." "I only want you. You're my only woman. She didn't mean anything to me." "I love your ears." Regarding the last line, Jeff's thinking was that girls are used to hearing about their beautiful eyes so it's better to pick something different. "What if you think she has ugly ears?" I asked. "Doesn't matter," he said.

We did an anonymous survey of 33 of my students in an upper division sociology college course—mostly in their early 20s. If you're curious about their sexual history: three were virgins, 17 had sex for the first time between ages 17 and 18, while six had sex when they were between 12 and 14, 10 when they were 18 to 20, and one after age 21. Thirteen had between one and three sexual partners, and 10 had between four and seven. Fifteen had lived with a sexual partner. Eight had contracted STDs and five had an abortion (or their partner did). Seven women had been raped and 18 had experienced sexual harassment at work or school. Their main forms of birth control were the Pill and the condom or both; in the last year, 14 had engaged in unprotected sex. One was gay, two bisexual, and the rest heterosexual.

Making Love Versus Sex

—Kelly Lynn Baylor has been a mother, foster mother, and counseling graduate student.

Media messages are about sex, not about making love, and there is a considerable difference between the two. Any animal can have sex and it is a biological urge that exists in all of us. Only humans make love. Making love is the most incredible experience that happens between two people who love each other. All boundaries are lost and the two people meld into one being, the highest of all highs.

It doesn't take a genius to have sex, or even a commitment to the other person. You can have sex anywhere, anytime, and in only a few minutes. It does take time and a loving, caring commitment to make love. It requires an almost total focus on wanting your partner to feel the extent of your love and have the most incredible experience of their life. When you make love, time doesn't exist, and a look or a touch from your partner can reach all the way to your soul.

The decision whether to have sex or not, and when, is a moral one. A lot of things enter into making this decision, including your religious beliefs, your parents' wishes, and whether your friends are doing it. Ultimately this is a decision that you and you alone must make. It is not a decision to be made by group consensus and it is not something to be used as a weapon to hurt your parents. You will live with the results of this decision the rest of your life.

I hope that you will delay making this decision until you are older and have a deeply committed relationship. I have seen far too many teenagers spoil their first experience by having quick sex, usually in an awful setting that does not lend itself to a memorable experience. Wait until you are truly ready to make LOVE and it will be a memory that will stay with you for a lifetime.

Questions to Ask Yourself and Your Partner About Sex

1. What are my moral and religious values about premarital sex?

2. Am I doing this mainly to please or keep my partner?

3. Do I feel pressured to have sex by my friends?

4. Have I thoroughly talked this issue over with my partner?

5. What do I know about birth control methods?

6. What do I know about sexually transmitted diseases?

7. What would I do if I or my partner got pregnant?

8. How would my parents feel about my having sex?

9. What are the alternatives to intercourse?

10. Is there a really valid reason not to wait to have sex?

11. How well do we really know each other? For how long? How long do you think the relationship will last?

Sex is a divine way to express love and be intimate, but can also be dangerous and be abused. Take time to get informed and think through your values and what's right for you.

—Sarah, 14, Nebraska

You want to abstain from sex but there is so much pressure. Then if you do you're a slut and if you don't you're a tease; it is very hard. Peer pressure is hard too; if you do it, you're awful; if you don't, you're lame. Teens are very hypocritical.

There is pressure from both sides. Say you go out with someone. OK, naturally he is hormone crazed [double standard?]. *He wants you to sleep with him, he tells his friends, who tell their girlfriends, who are your friends, who tell you to do it and bother you about it. So the guy is pressuring you and so are the girls. If you finally do, the guys all think you are easy and the girls accuse you of being a slut. If you don't (in my experience) some guys will respect you for it and some will think you are a tease. But, if the guy you are dating really cares about you, he will respect you and your decision. That is why I never go out alone without a group of friends. That is usually the best way to avoid the situation and it works.*

—Star, 14, California

So, you want to stay a virgin? Well then, go for it. I had a boyfriend who wanted me to sleep with him. He was a best friend as well as a boyfriend. I truly loved him and still do. I contemplated it for a long time, five months. I was almost ready to tell him I would sleep with him when we broke up. The guy I cared for and loved dumped me. So, even if you think it's right, are you 100 percent sure? I'd be sure before I ever make the same mistake again.

Sexuality · 143

—Joanie, 15, Colorado

The most difficult challenge I've faced as a teen is the temptation of having sex with my boyfriend. My boyfriend and other friends tried to pressure me into doing it, saying "Come on babe, I love you," and "You'll have the best time of your life." It's hard when dealing with peer pressure!

The fear of getting AIDS and/or becoming pregnant helped me NOT give in. I plan/hope to attend college on a basketball scholarship but my boyfriend said he'd break up with me, so I did it. Now I'm pregnant and who wants a player with a baby? What I say to young people is that it's your life, it's going to be yours forever. Some people say things to just get what they want, then they leave you. So be true to yourself!

—Carolyn, 15, Kansas

An 18-year-old guy from another high school was, or seemed so at the time, charming, and well, perfect. He was on the football team and captain of the basketball team. He was mature, or so it seemed, and popular. I was new in town, and thrilled when his friends liked me too. After six months, I was into alcohol, marijuana, and sex. Older guys use you. Going out with anyone more than two or three years older is a mistake. If you're a virgin, God, stay that way or at least ask yourself if he's pressuring you. Older guys do that. My life would be so much better if I hadn't taken that first beer.

—Starr, 16, California

One of the most important decisions I have made as a teenager was to give up my sexual purity. I talked to many friends, mostly older, who told me to wait for someone you truly love so it will be special. I was 16 and I don't regret it at all. I would warn younger people about a few things. First, always use protection no matter what.

Second, it is a big decision, so make sure you and your partner both feel the same about issues such as abortion and birth control. Also, when you give away your virginity you are giving a part of yourself away that you can never get back. You and that person will always have that special bond, so it is definitely something very important and it is not a decision you want to make quickly. Last, it is nothing like it is in the movies, you don't just wake up the next morning with your hair and makeup perfect. The main thing is make sure you are truly in love with the person. If you don't want to do it and your partner does, if he or she loves you, they won't pressure you. If you want to wait, your partner will respect you for your decision.

—Lauren, 18, California

Engaging in sex early in life ruins any kind of relationship later on. Because of sex, I was labeled and talked about constantly. I believe it changed my attitude about people in general and I went from a really sweet, nice girl to a slut and bitch. I couldn't trust anyone and even though it was a long time ago I still find it hard to trust.

—Natoshi, 18, California

I'm still a virgin, and very proud of it because it is hard to be a virgin. There are a lot of temptations out in the world. My advice is do what's right for you and only you.

—Michelle, 19, Georgia

I refuse to let someone else decide what I will do with my body. I am sexually active and have been for some time, but I decided when I was ready. If anyone put any pressure on me to have sex, I knew they didn't have my best interests in mind. I have always lost respect for people who try to encourage people to do things that would hurt them or that they don't want to do.

—Bob, 19, California

If you are in a relationship where an open discussion about sex is uncomfortable, get out of it.

—Patrick, 19, California

Every day I would hear another friend of mine brag about what he did or who he did the night before. These same people would also pressure us to drink, do drugs, and have sex. Don't be who your friends want you to be. I admit that I drink, but, regarding sex, I am waiting until marriage.

—Rebecca, 19, Washington

Wait, wait, wait. If it is that important that your partner have sex and can't understand your feelings, then it wasn't meant to be (trust me on this one). If it is right then you will know. I'm not giving you an age or a time, just wait until you feel it is right. And be safe if you do have sex. There is stuff out there that we don't even know about!

—Allison, 20, California

I wish I could say that I avoided having sex longer than I did. My advice is to know what you want. If that means having sex, don't make the decision on the spur of the moment. Think realistically about it, then act responsibly.

—Amy, 21, California

Do not have sex with a person until you feel 100 percent comfortable and close with the person. Trust and commitment must be established first.

—Dondi, 21, California

You are in control of your own body and mind—always maintain that control. As soon as you feel yourself starting to lose that control, get out of that situation.

—Vincent, 22, California

Try to get informed as much as possible; the more you know, the better off you'll be. Don't be pressured into having sex, only do it if you want to.

—Rachel, 24, New York

I had sex at a young age (16) and I do sometimes regret not waiting to really fall in love. What you think is love in high school is generally not what you think is love when you get older.

—Elizabeth, 25, Wisconsin

It took me years to really understand that I was free to make my own sexual decisions and had no obligation to the person that I was dating to be sexual with them. We need to debunk myths like "blue balls" [refers to uncomfortable pressure in the testicles of a sexually aroused boy] that make girls feel guilty about not being sexual with their boyfriends. I still have mixed feelings about it; my head knows the truth, but my emotions are still catching up. Listen very closely to yourself. If you can't tell whether or not you want to do something risky (being sexual, experimenting with alcohol or drugs, going somewhere unsafe), WAIT. Those opportunities will present themselves again.

—Jennifer, 25, Texas

I was pressured to have sex. Fear of getting pregnant was about the only thing that prevented me from doing it, but I engaged in a lot of sexual activities that I wasn't comfortable with, just because the pregnancy issue wasn't available as an excuse. What might have helped me cope was a better understanding of my own body and of human sexuality. I couldn't tell the difference between sexual arousal and panic, between physical desire and the desire for attention and approval. I felt like my body was something separate from me and that I was its custodian, but my job was more to negotiate between competing demands than to think about my own feelings. I didn't start feeling like my body was really mine until I was well into my 20s.

YOUR BODY BELONGS TO YOU. Nobody should be allowed to make you do something you don't want to or feel guilty about doing something you do want to. Don't say No when you mean Yes. Don't say Yes when you really want to say No. You can always say "maybe some other time."

Having sex is not an all-or-nothing proposition. You can have sex with one guy and not with your next boyfriend. You can have sex on Friday night and not be in the mood on Saturday night. You can engage in some sexual practices and say No to others. Doing so does not make you a prude, a slut, a tease, or anything else. You are an individual with individual needs and desires. What you do with a particular person at a particular time is a decision that you have to make each and every time; you are never obligated to do something just because someone hoped or thought that you would.

—Shelly, 27, Australia

I didn't know when to lose my virginity or under what circumstances. I want to share my experience because I was extremely lucky to have a positive first sexual encounter, after all those years of mental torture.

I have always been a physical girl; I love holding hands and kissing. I spent a lot of time "making out" with my boyfriends at 15, 16, and 17. I am extremely lucky that none of those boys date-raped me. I would advise young women to stay out of rape situations with any boyfriend they have even the slightest doubts about. I was fortunate that no boy tried to force anything on me and I stayed a virgin. Looking back, I realize that at that point sex scared and disgusted me.

By my senior year of high school I fell in love. We had long memorable kissing sessions that I still fondly recall. (REMEMBER, do not underestimate those wonderful make-out years. It's the most foreplay you'll get for the rest of your life, so make it last!) We had been going out for over eight months and he treated me with love and respect. I was getting very horny, so I decided to lose my virginity with him. (He was a virgin too but we figured it out!) Our sex was pure and lovely. We were monogamous for the following two years. The experience deepened our love. The down side of that was that I fell so deeply in love, I lost control of myself and became dependent on him emotionally.

I would recommend to young women that they give a relationship time to evolve before having sex—at least eight months. And also they should pay attention to their own emotions. If sex makes you feel scared, disgusted, or dirty, you're NOT ready. Wait for someone you know really loves you, someone who is going to hang around for a while. After all, sex is not good the first time, it only gets good after the 10th time or the 20th time. Treat your first sexual experience as sacred. You want it to be a pleasant memory for the rest of your life.

Definition of Terms

Abstinence: not engaging in sexual intercourse.

Coitus: penile-vaginal intercourse in various positions.

Cunnilingus: oral stimulation of the female genitals.

Ejaculation: occurs during male orgasm, forcefully releasing semen from the penis, nature's way of getting sperm into a vagina.

Fellatio: oral stimulation of the male genitals.

Monogamy: being faithful to one sexual partner.

Orgasm: the climax of sexual intercourse when muscular contractions in the genitals cause a highly enjoyable sensation.

Os: the opening of the uterus in the cervix, which can be seen at the end of the vagina in a vaginal examination.

Ovulation: usually mid-cycle, when the egg is released by the ovary into the fallopian tubes ready to be fertilized by sperm.

Secondary virgins: people who return to abstinence after having had intercourse.

Spermicide: chemical to kill sperm used with other birth control methods such as condoms or diaphragms.

STD: sexually transmitted disease, such as herpes or AIDS.

Withdrawal: removing the penis from the vagina before ejaculation in an effort to prevent pregnancy (an unsafe method).

Chapter 4

Stupidity

Andy Harvey

Drugs

> When you're young, everybody says they're not going to drink or use drugs. But the older you get, the more frequently you see these kinds of things. Finally it hits your friends and then you want to experiment also. Peer pressure plays a big part; you feel you have to join the crowd to fit in. When I was younger I thought it was cool to drink a beer, being a minor, when others had soda. By college, people drink or use drugs; you see it so much, you don't even think about it anymore.
> —Ace, 18, Texas

T he purpose of this chapter is to assist you in thinking about it. Drugs are big business. Billions are earned from selling legal and illegal drugs and alcohol and drug problems cost us about $200 billion a year. Drug use contributes to teen pregnancy, date rape, spread of HIV and other STDs, car accidents, suicide, and violence; how many personal stories have you heard to illustrate the point? Ads tell us if we don't feel happy, energetic, or healthy to take a pill or drink a beer, or to smoke cigarettes to be slim or macho. Surrounded by these messages, it takes will power to resist a quick fix, an immediate high. Longer-lasting and healthy highs stem from personal achievement and satisfying connections with people we care about.

Teen drug use is increasing while the percentage of teens who think drug use is harmful is decreasing. Drug use by teens more than doubled from 1992 to 1995 to 11 percent using drugs the previous month. This is down from the peak of 16 percent in 1979 according to Department of Health and Human Services. A 10-year study by the Carnegie Council on Adolescent Development reported in 1995 that nearly half of youth ages 10 to 14 are at risk of "seriously damaging their life chances" because of drug abuse, pregnancy, etc. Almost half a million teens binge drink weekly. More than half drink alcohol, 40 percent use drugs before leaving high school, and over one-third smoke cigarettes. Drugs and peer pressure are the worst influences on teens, report a representative sample of teens ages 13 to 17, surveyed for the Horatio Alger Association (only four percent say they have used drugs and nine percent smoke or drink).

In a survey of over 3,000 high-achiever high school students in 1995, almost half say it is easy to buy drugs at school—the most widely used drug is marijuana. They reported the "in" activities at their schools were in this order of popularity: listening to alternative music (85 percent), drinking beer, smoking cigarettes, drinking hard liquor, smoking marijuana, and using the Internet (50 percent). I'd prefer to hear that it's in to be creative, athletic, or a leader, rather than learn that four of the six activities are harmful.

Most drugs have side effects, including prescription drugs. When your doctor prescribes drugs for you, you may want to ask about the most common side effects listed in the *Physician's Desk Reference*. Is driving impaired? How does the drug interact with alcohol, over-the counter drugs, birth control pills, and foods? Is the drug addictive? How long before effects take place? What are alternatives to taking a drug, such as letting the body heal itself, or alternative practices such as dietary changes?

Mood altering psychoactive drugs are chemicals that change the way a person thinks, feels, or behaves, unlike drugs such as aspirin. Effects can be long lasting, as marijuana residues remain in the body up to four weeks and cocaine lingers at least three days after use.

Drugs can depress the body's immune system, especially with heavy use. Emergency room admissions are increasing, as these drugs can cause serious and permanent damage, as you'll see in some of the accounts that follow. The body develops tolerance, so the addict has to use more to get the same feeling. Many drugs are addictive and cause painful withdrawal symptoms when discontinued, including chills, cramps, nausea, insomnia, depression, and hallucinations. Heavy users often suffer from poor nutrition and poor health, as well as breaking the law. Sales of illegal drugs can be punished with up to 20 years in prison and a $250,000 fine. These penalties double with a second offense.

Why do teens use harmful drugs? Drug and alcohol counselor Dennis Hyde observes that the reasons can vary from curiosity to peer pressure to observing their parents use drugs, but mainly to escape from pain. Some teens are lonely or have unsupportive families. Many female addicts he works with were sexually abused. Chemicals numb the pain. He observes that a 12-step group can provide support and counselors can teach how to deal with the feelings themselves rather than repress them. He works with clients to identify the triggers to drug use, such as feeling left out or experiencing physical pain, and substituting positive ways to cope.

How do you know if someone suffers from "chemical dependency" on drugs? An addiction is a substance, person, or activity used to numb pain—anything that you are not willing to give up despite the cost. The addiction causes trouble, but the addict has lost control and continues in a downward path. Examples of legal addictions are work, food, sex, falling in love, or TV. Some signs of drug addiction are guilt about drug use, needing drugs to feel "normal," people complaining about your drug use, blackouts, using drugs frequently, using drugs to forget problems, lying, missing classes, withdrawal from others, and obsession with drugs. If the addict stops using drugs, physical and emotional withdrawal is painful. I haven't heard one story of drugs solving any problems in the long run.

Alcohol

If I drink enough, I will not remember how I feel. I mostly drink when I am feeling bad. Being drunk and having no worries does appeal to me; I forget about all the problems and pressures and have fun for a while. No, my mind is not centered, but it is a great release. Music is also a great release. It will help for the moment, but what about the next day? I remember how I felt listening to the music. A combination of both alcohol and music works great; I won't remember the pain, and I will keep out of trouble while under the influence. [Suggestions of other ways to cope with pain other than escape it?]

—Jeremy, 15, Canada

Alcohol is the drug most used by teens. It's seen as a way to be uninhibited; for alcoholics like Ryan (see below), it's an illness, probably a genetic predisposition. Children ages eight through 12 can name more brands of beer than former presidents of the United States, as they will see 100,000 beer commercials on TV by the time they are 18. It's not surprising that nearly two-thirds of high school students interviewed in a national survey said their friends were accepting of tobacco and alcohol use. Twenty-nine percent said it was easy to get alcohol at school and 61 percent said it was easy to get cigarettes at school (1993 National Household Education Survey, U.S. Department of Education).

University of Michigan surveys show that nearly 30 percent of seniors and 13 percent of 8th graders had more than five drinks in a row in the last two weeks (binge drinking). Eight million junior and senior high school students drink alcohol weekly and 454,000 are weekly binge drinkers. (Emma wonders, "Why not do surveys about the positive things and let people know that teens aren't so bad?")

Some believe that beer or wine contain less alcohol than hard liquor, but a 12-ounce bottle of beer contains about the same amount as a shot of 86-proof whiskey or a six-ounce glass of wine. Some cold relief medicines and cough syrups also contain up to 25 percent alcohol.

About 18 million adults have significant alcohol-related problems. These problems strike one out of every four families as there are over 10 million alcoholics in the U.S. Twenty percent of men and 10 percent of women are heavy drinkers, consuming two or more drinks a day. One in 10 drinkers will become an alcoholic.

The U.S. surgeon general estimates that alcohol is involved in 200,000 deaths a year, or 10 percent of the yearly deaths. Problem drinkers cause $15 billion in annual health care costs. Half of all traffic deaths are alcohol-related and drunk driving is the main killer of teens. (The number of people killed each year in drunk driving accidents in the U.S. is equal to the number of people who would be killed if a 747 jet crashed every day.) Alcohol and tobacco kill 20 times more people than all other drugs combined. A national study of college students found that those with poor grade point averages drank almost four times as much as "A" students.

Each year 36,000 babies are born with alcohol-caused birth defects because their mothers drank. Fetal alcohol syndrome is the third leading cause of birth defects and the leading cause of mental retardation in children. Children with alcoholic parents are seven to eight times more likely to become alcoholics.

Alcohol, a depressant, causes the heart to beat faster and weaker, mood changes, and inability to concentrate. Alcohol depresses brain functions and reduces inhibitions. It affects motor control so that balance is off and reactions are slower. Regular drinking raises the brain's tolerance to the drug so that addicts consume larger amounts. It can cause a person to pass out, as you may have witnessed. In large quantities it is a dangerous poison and can result in coma and death. Women are more sensitive to the effects of alcohol just before their period. The effects also worsen when drinking on an empty stomach, drinking rapidly, and in combination with other depressant drugs. Alcohol can change or intensify the effects of other drugs such as tobacco, tranquilizers, barbiturates, aspirin, and stimulants.

Heavy drinkers are more likely to suffer from cancers of the digestive tract and liver, mouth, hepatitis, breast, and pancreatitis. Over time, alcohol can lead to high blood pressure, heart disease, memory loss, stomach ulcers, nutritional deficiencies, destruction of liver tissue, sexual impotency in men, and disruption of the menstrual cycle in women.

About 20 percent of alcohol immediately enters the blood stream from the stomach. Alcohol increases the flow of digestive acids in the stomach which can irritate the stomach lining, causing nausea and vomiting. The rest goes into the small intestine, the blood stream, and to the liver. The liver can only process a small amount of alcohol per hour (about one-half ounce per 150 pounds of body weight), so the leftover goes back into the blood. The process of absorption is slowed by foods rich in protein or fat. Because it is a poison, the liver gives priority to cleaning alcohol out of the body, rather than to necessary functions such as maintaining stable blood levels of glucose to the brain. It also robs the body of important nutrients and vitamins—especially vitamins A, B, and C.

Parties are hot spots for pressure to drink. Alternatives are to plan other activities besides drinking, avoid drinking games and contests, provide nonalcoholic drinks, tell guests it's a drug-free party, choose designated drivers who will not drink alcohol, bring other friends who aren't drinkers, and let a friend who is drinking too much know you are concerned.

If you don't want to use drugs such as alcohol, plan what you will say if offered them. Heidi, 19, said, "As I entered the teenage years, I planned ahead about what I would do as I became involved in certain situations. When I was pressured to do drugs or drink, I already had my mind made up to say No." Other responses teens use are simply, "No, thanks," "I'm driving tonight," I'm high on my own," or saying nothing but indicating a full cup of soda. If you or a friend has an alcohol problem, talk to a caring friend or family member and call a hotline for information about local resources. Offer to go with your friend to an AA meeting and remember alcoholism is a disease, just like diabetes, which requires treatment.

—Christa, 15, Colorado

Getting involved in extra activities, such as sports and after-school clubs, made me stay focused and busy so I realized there was no time to be doing drugs, alcohol, and sex. I would tell younger teens to stay busy and to keep themselves clean. (Emma responds, "You don't decide whether or not to do drugs by if you have time. It's a moral thing.")

—Stephanie, 15, Ohio

My problem is trying to change the minds of the conformist student body at my conformist high school, or at least trying to make them see the moral and realistic side of an issue. This may seem like a petty problem, but in high school, drinking is life. For those of us who don't participate, we don't "really" experience high school, we merely go through the motions on our way to college. To the kids who don't want to live in a "bubbly" environment, I suggest scooping out the kid in the eco-club or that dorky drama boy so you have a pal.

Do not conform to the rules of adolescence. Do not feel obligated to go to the football games or to drink, or to feel like a geek if you skip the dances. Look at those floozy girls whose lives revolve around the dumb jocks who can't read the back of their jerseys and how they're going to kill their future because they want popularity and believe high school is life. Imagine returning to your high school reunion. Envision the head cheerleader all gross and a loser who did nothing with her life.

Live your life the way you want to and if kids bug you, then come back at them with a big vocabulary word or just smile and walk away. Get involved in stuff outside of school. Volunteer, go to uncharted land and meet kids. Talk to people.

—Jed, 16, California

I know a lot of people who use alcohol because they are too insecure to cut loose and have fun when they are sober. When they are drunk, it's a whole different story. I've even seen people drink bottles of cough medicine because of the alcohol in it. There isn't a person I know who hasn't used either marijuana or alcohol; that's kind of scary. I pick friends you can do things with besides getting drunk.

—Peter, 17, Texas

Alcohol use has spread throughout high schools everywhere. Almost every party has alcohol present. The individuals taking part in drinking seem to have fun and the consequences are not always seen. People would ask me to participate and it was always hard to decline. One of my friends, however, began looking up to me when she saw I did not drink. This encouraged me to continue turning away from alcohol. This was not, however, the major reason I decided not to drink. The major reason is that in the last two years our school has lost one kid due to drunk driving and almost several others. My advice to people who are fighting with the urge to drink is to talk to a friend about it. Above all be true to yourself and stand up for what you believe is right.

—Josh, 18, California

My town was small, so I never really had to deal with gangs or a lot of crime; however, what is notorious in small towns is heavy drug use. I saw many friends with great potential dwindle away in a puff of marijuana smoke or a drop of acid. I have stayed away from drugs but do confess to drinking. I think the key is that a person has to stay involved with something they enjoy while sober. I have always loved to golf, ski, and play basketball, so I never felt like I had to drink or do drugs to have a good time. I believe that it's impossible to keep kids from experimenting with alcohol and drugs; however, it is possible to keep kids from making drug or alcohol use a habit. My advice to kids is to learn to talk to your parents about life; some parents will understand, some won't; I know that mine did.

—Scott, 21, California

Throughout school I was always the straight "A" student because I felt I had to make my parents happy by being smart. I also was very active in sports and hung out with the kids who were studious. I was a junior in high school when I started meeting some new people and I was getting tired of feeling like I had to keep my parents pleased with me. I would go out with these people and drink, and I really enjoyed being drunk. I felt more free with what I wanted to do. I didn't communicate with my family very well and I stopped trying to be that perfect angel. I got into some heavier drugs and started sleeping with girls randomly. I knew I was having a problem with what I got myself into, but I didn't want to quit yet.

One night, though, I felt I was going nowhere with my life and felt I had no one to talk to and I went and got really drunk. I came home late when everyone was asleep in the house and I went into the bathroom. I don't remember too much of the night, but I guess I hit the mirror and took a piece to my wrists. My parents heard the noise and came in to find me with large gashes down my wrists and blood all over the floor. I was taken to the hospital and then my parents brought me home and let me sleep.

The next day they sat me down and asked me to explain what I was feeling and going through. I couldn't do it all at once or feel too comfortable with myself to say everything on my mind. But we worked it out over the following few weeks and we became a better family for the most part. I quit the drugs and drinking and they didn't expect the world of me. I got a job and met some new people who had the same interests as me.

I just have to say that if you are feeling pressured into being something you aren't, especially by your parents, go to them and say what is on your mind. Don't let it sit in you because you will do irrational things and cause harm to everyone—especially yourself.

—Beth, 22, Nevada

When I was 18 a truck I was in rolled over. I hit my head. I was drinking with friends. I now have a hard time learning. They took me to Reno. I flew in a helicopter. I do not remember that. People were scared. I was there for a long time. Then they said I could go home. My boyfriend left me. My friends don't say, "Hi, how are you?" anymore. I am in a special class. For people like me. My teacher says maybe someday I can learn a job. I talk OK in my head. I have a hard time to talk outside my head. Sometimes my talk in my head is fuzzy. That is when times are hard. Most of the time I am now OK, when I talk in my head. Paul says I am learning. Paul is my teacher.

Sometimes words go over and over inside my head. They get too loud. They get crazy. Paul says new one is quiet. Not words. Action. Calm. He says calm is action. It helps me talk outside my head. Paul says I need two mantras. One for to get strong. One for action.

I say don't drink in truck. You can get hurt. I did not think I can get hurt. Paul says when you don't think you are stupid. I was stupid. I would say blame me. I don't blame people. I made me hard to think in my head. If you drink be ready to get hurt. Do not cry when you get hurt. You did it yourself. People say do not drink. You drink. You get hurt. It is true. I know.

—Allison, 22, Missouri

Early in high school I dated the football hero who had an alarming drinking problem even at that early age. In our very traditional small town, as his girlfriend I was made responsible for his behavior. Even when we were in an off-again phase, people would talk to me about how he really listened to me and respected me. I should try to talk to him, then he would be OK. It became my job to "take care" of him and to correct his deficiency.

It took a horrible night of his drunkenness and pressure from everyone that ended with me in fear of being hit by this linebacker, before I quit believing I was somehow responsible for him. I woke up angry and swore that I was not responsible for him. The first several times I said that out loud to myself, then to friends and family, It was powerful. It was intoxicating. But I don't think his mother ever forgave me for not helping him. And, it took months before everyone else would accept my stance.

Refusing to back down and having the support of my family helped me to cope. It also helped to be angry. I needed the power that went with that feeling. I avoid circumstances where I know the point of the evening is to get plowed, with a simple, "I can't go tonight." No excuse or reason, just "I can't." Most people respect that.

[Allison developed effective "refusal skills" and resisted pressure to be a codependent, responsible for taking care of her alcoholic boyfriend (see the abuse section in Chapter 6 for more on codependency). We can't change someone else's behavior and instead should focus on getting our own act together. From another point of view, Emma adds "If everyone had the 'It's not my responsibility, let someone else deal with it' attitude,' the person with the problem could end up dead." We can offer support and information without feeling responsible for rescuing someone from their actions.]

—Ryan, 22, California

The most difficult experience I had as a teen was getting sober. The only way I was able to do it was knowing that my church youth group had given me a second chance (they kicked me out once for drugs). Whenever I felt like drinking or using, I thought of youth group, and drew strength from it. I finally realized that I could choose to pray that I would know the divine plan and have the strength and wisdom to carry out that plan. I also now know that God speaks through others as they pray in their own way, even if that way isn't the way I'd do it.

Without the foundation of my church, I wouldn't have been able to get sober; however, church made it more difficult in a way, as well. You see, I graduated from my church third-year religion class and high school within the same week. The people I looked up to had high hopes for me, and I expected a lot from myself. I was the star of my church, the perfect teenager, every parent's dream child. Then the last season of high school cross-country running ended. I decided to go to a party and get drunk for the first time, since I no longer needed to worry about being in shape for running.

I thought that one party couldn't hurt, but after that first party, the rest was history. How could I have a problem? I was admired by everyone at my church. When I realized that I did have a problem, and that I had disappointed all of those in my family and church who love me so much, I couldn't bear to face myself. I tried to kill myself by overdosing on crack cocaine. Luckily, I wasn't successful, and nobody said, "Shame on you, Ryan," like I expected. Instead, I had a huge network of friends and family who did everything they could to help me get better. Over two years later, I have gained back all my self-respect and all the trust from others that I had lost.

I'd tell other teens in the same situation to not be ashamed, that nobody sees them as bad people, or as lesser people. Nobody is angry at them for being sick. Nobody loves them any less than before and the road to recovery is a joyous one. I had a strong, spiritual foundation already established, so I was able to draw strength from this.

Therapy and prescribed medications also helped. I was 19 years old my first day of lasting sobriety. For many months I was too depressed to do anything and too ashamed to show my face in public. I spent some time in a recovery center. After that I went to daytime mental health care for several months. A psychiatrist prescribed an anti-depressant and an anti-anxiety drug. I was vigilant in telling him how the prescriptions were working, so he could try alternate medications when the first prescriptions were not effective. I knew that the purpose of the medications was to get me to the point where I didn't need them any more. With the approval of my doctor, I stopped taking them after six months.

The combination of therapy and medication helped me to get my mind together enough for me to get out and find employment. Having found a job, I began to see my life take a turn for the better. Every day I went to work was a day of new hope that I really could recover my self-respect completely, as long as I could remain sober.

I went (and still do) to a fair amount of Alcoholics Anonymous (AA) meetings—three to five per week. At first I struggled with the idea that I had a problem, but eventually I came to accept that I was sick and my life was out of control. I did anything and everything that my AA sponsor suggested, beginning with the 12 steps. An AA sponsor is a guide through the program of AA, and a mentor of sorts. My sponsor knew the feelings that I was going through. He constantly reassured me that everything was OK, that he'd been there, and that it would get better. He told me about the feelings he had and I knew he understood. He was constantly upbeat and compassionate. If he could do it, I could do it.

—Suzanne, 26, California

The biggest challenge I faced in high school was sticking to my beliefs when they went against what was popular. I didn't drink or smoke and there was a lot of pressure to do so. It was especially difficult for me because I moved to a new school across the country as a freshman in the middle of the year and had to figure out where I fit in with the already established groups or cliques. I chose not to go to parties where I knew there would be drinking, etc., and chose friends who had the same interests and values. And when I made friends who chose to party, I just didn't go with them to those particular events.

I really don't think I missed out on anything big; if anything, I think I prevented getting myself into situations that I may not have been able to handle. Stick to what you believe, even if it conflicts with what's popular or what your friends think because, in the end, you're accountable to yourself, not others. Not going to a party doesn't mean you have to stay home and do nothing. I focused on my classes and extracurricular activities, and preparing for college, which is how I met some of my closest friends.

—Michael Stephens, Ph.D., communications professor

On the one hand, young people have incredible insight. For example, young people are usually very skilled at recognizing the hypocrisy that exists in the adult world. On the other hand, young people can have difficulty seeing the connection between their present and future lives. I started drinking at 16 because it helped overcome the normal fears and feelings of insecurity that all young people experience.

As we become more tolerant to the effects of alcohol, we have to drink more and more to experience even the temporary relief that we once got after only a few beers. For some of us, this predisposition to drink more alcohol more frequently will become an obsession, as we try again and again to experience that pleasant sensation of well-being we first felt at 16 or younger. The trouble is, no matter how much or how often we drink, we will never be able to recapture that particular feeling. Drinking can destroy the health and sanity of the alcoholic and the people he or she loves and cares most about. I finally quit drinking at age 42 to save my self-respect.

Help for Alcoholics and Their Families

Adult Children of Alcoholics
1-800-344-2666 (for group meetings throughout the U.S.)

Al-Anon 1-800-356-9996
(for adult family and friends of alcoholics)

Alateen 1-800-344-266
(for young people, ages 12 to 21, with alcoholic family members or friends) (1-800-443-4525 in Canada)

Alcohol and Drug Hotline
1-800-821-4357 (referrals)

Alcoholism Helpline
1-800-ALCOHOL

Alcohol 24-Hour Hotline
1-800-821-HELP

Children of Alcoholics Foundation
1-800-359-COAF

Drug Abuse Information and Referral Line 1-800-662-4357

Helpline (alcohol, cocaine, gambling)
1-800-732-9808

Just Say No! International
1-800-258-2766 (1-415-939-6666 in California) (provides information about how to avoid alcohol and other drugs and how to set up Just Say No! clubs)

Mothers Against Drunk Driving
1-800-438-6233

National Clearinghouse for Alcohol and Drug Information
1-800-729-6686 (more than 700 free publications)

National Council on Alcoholism and Drug Dependence
1-800-475-HOPE

National Clearinghouse for Alcohol Information
1-800-729-6686

Co-Dependents Anonymous
P. O. Box 33577
Phoenix, AZ 85067-3577

National PTA Drug and Alcohol Abuse Prevention Project
700 N. Rush St.
Chicago, IL 60611

National Association for Children of Alcoholics
31582 Coast Hwy., Suite B
South Laguna, CA 92677

Stop Teenage Addiction Today
121 Lyman St., #210
Springfield, MA 01103

S.A.D.D. (Students Against Drunk Driving)
P. O. Box 800
Marlboro, MA 01752

Cigarettes

More than three million teenagers smoke cigarettes, over a third of teens—compared to 25 percent of adults, although tobacco use is the No. 1 cause of preventable death in the U.S.

Ads targeting youth have been effective. Every day about 3,000 young people start smoking and at least a third will die early as a result. Each year a million teenagers start smoking, more girls than boys. Smoking is more damaging to women, as they have smaller lung airways than most men (smoking causes the airways to swell and close slightly). Seventy-five percent of teen smokers have parents who smoke.

Nicotine in tobacco increases the heart and blood pressure rate, as nicotine is a mild stimulant—like caffeine. Smoking releases epinephrine, a hormone which causes stress, although smokers feel they have to smoke to calm down. Similar to other drugs, the body develops tolerance to the drug so more has to be used to get the desired effect.

This is not just a health issue for smokers, as a 1996 study reported that 88 percent of 10,000 blood tests showed significant exposure to tobacco even if the people didn't smoke or live with people who smoke (Centers for Disease Control). The smoke that escapes from a cigarette has 20 to 30 times more cancer-causing chemicals than the smoke inhaled through a cigarette filter. Children generally get 50 percent more exposure to smoke than adults, which results in 150,000 to 300,000 cases of child respiratory infections each year.

A large increase in the number of young teens who smoke began in 1991. A 1994 survey found that 19 percent of 8th graders had smoked in the last month, as had one-quarter of 10th graders (University of Michigan Survey Research Center). A 1995 survey found a two percent increase since the previous year in the number of 17- year-olds who smoke, to 33 percent (22 percent smoke daily). Teens who smoke tobacco are 100 times more likely to smoke marijuana and 30 times more likely to try cocaine than nonsmokers.

Overall, about 47 million Americans smoke and ninety percent of them started smoking as teenagers. More than 400,000 Americans die each year from cigarette smoking—18 percent of all U.S. deaths. More than 1,000 deaths a day result from smoking. A recent study estimated that passive smoking (inhaling someone else's smoke) is a factor in as many as 420,000 deaths each year. Smoking costs the country about $65 billion each year in medical costs and lost productivity on the job.

Smoking is the top preventable cause of death and disease in the world and one of the most dangerous forms of chemical dependency. Each cigarette contains at least 40 cancer-causing chemicals among the nearly 4,000 chemicals in cigarette smoke. You inhale arsenic, cyanide, formaldehyde, ammonia, tar, and carbon monoxide. Smoking is a major cause of cancer of the mouth, larynx, esophagus, kidney, pancreas, bladder, and lungs and may increase the risk of breast cancer. About 87 percent of lung cancers are linked to tobacco and passive smoking leads to higher rates of lung cancer for people who live with heavy smokers. Smoking can also cause emphysema and chronic bronchitis.

Thirty percent of heart disease deaths are tied to smoking, smokers have a 70 percent greater chance of having a heart attack than non smokers, and smokers die an average of eight years earlier than non smokers. Smoking during pregnancy causes about 20 to 30 percent of low-birth-weight births and about 10 percent of infant deaths. Cigarettes also are the leading cause of fire deaths in the U.S.

Smoking is the number one cause of premature death in women, causing about 20 percent of women's deaths. Lung cancer is the top cancer killer of women. Women who smoke while taking birth control pills after age 30 increase their risk of heart disease and stroke. Ads that suggest to women that smoking will help them lose weight or be liberated are part of the problem, as are brand names such as "Silva Thins," and "Slim Lights." The main reason girls are reluctant to stop smoking is the fear they will gain weight and advertisers prey on this fear. For example, an ad copy reads, "When you're wearing a swimsuit, there is no such thing as 'constructive criticism.' Virginia Slims: It's a *woman* thing." (Fewer than eight percent of teen girls smoked when Virginia Slims was introduced in 1968. Six years later, the rate rose to about 15 percent.) Most people do gain some weight after they quit, perhaps because their taste buds are working again or the body's metabolic rate slows down, making it more likely to store fat. Nicotine raises metabolism, the rate at which our bodies burn energy, and increases the heart rate, causing both weight loss and premature aging of skin. It also changes insulin levels, affected craving for sweets.

Using smokeless tobacco, such as chewing tobacco, is also dangerous. Nearly one in five high school males use spit tobacco. Chewing tobacco has many of the same risks as smoking, and is linked to cancers of the mouth, nose, and throat. It has 10 times the amount of cancer-causing substances found in cigarettes and is just as addictive. Chewing tobacco and snuff can also lead to loss of taste and smell, receding gums, and high blood pressure, as well as bad breath and yellow teeth.

Despite the proven hazards, fewer youths believe that smoking is dangerous to their health than in previous years, perhaps because tobacco companies spend over $6 billion a year on advertising. The companies maintain that nicotine is not addictive and smokers inhale just for pleasure, but tell that to someone who is trying to quit the habit. In fact, nicotine is probably the most addictive drug. The head of Philip Morris company, William Campbell, testified before Congress in 1994 that tobacco is not addictive, despite company research to the contrary since the 1960s. Drug and alcohol counselor Deanna Figueira's clients tell her that cigarettes are harder to give up than any other drug.

In 1980 tobacco companies spent $771 million on gifts for teens and this jumped to $3.2 billion in 1989, spent on caps, T-shirts, coupons, concert tickets, and other items to promote smoking. (These figures were given by the tobacco companies to the Federal Trade Commission.) By 1993, advertising and promotional item spending rose to $6.03 billion. A study of California youth found that in kids' decisions to start smoking, cigarette ads were more powerful than peer pressure or the example of family members who smoke (*Journal of the National Cancer Institute*). Teens are three times more likely than adults to respond to cigarette ads, as evidenced by the fact that 79 percent smoke three brands linked to Joe Camel, the Marlboro Man, or the fun couples of Newport (a study by Richard Pollay, *Journal of Marketing*, 1996).

The tobacco companies claim they do not target children. But why the cartoon figure of Joe Camel, introduced in 1988 by R.J. Reynolds? Ninety percent of kids ages 8 to 13 recognize Joe Camel. You've probably noted his male genitalia-like face and friends may have shown you the male figure in the front camel leg on the cigarette packages. Advertisers figure that sex gets the attention of kids as well as adults. President Clinton limited advertising to youth in 1996, although the new Food and Drug regulations could be tied up in courts for years.

How to Quit Smoking

◎ List your reasons for wanting to quit, post and read them every day. Write a good-by letter to cigarettes. Set a quit date and tell people about it. Some people quit gradually while some stop cold turkey. Throw away all cigarettes, lighters, and matches.

◎ Join a smoking cessation group sponsored by the American Heart Lung Association, the American Cancer Society, or other group recommended by your school nurse or your doctor. Avoid other smokers while you're quitting.

◎ Identify danger times for you, such as after a meal or at a party, and plan other things to do. Keep a journal for at least three days where you record when you smoke and why.

◎ Eat three meals a day to keep your blood-sugar level constant to reduce the urge to smoke.

◎ Drink lots of liquids to cleanse your body of nicotine and the over 300 toxic chemicals found in tobacco; it takes three to four days for this cleansing process.

◎ Avoid caffeine and alcohol.

◎ Ask a doctor to prescribe nicotine patches and/or see an acupuncturist to apply needles to help quit smoking, as the addiction to nicotine lasts several weeks after smoking the last cigarette. Hypnosis by a therapist works for some smokers.

- When you want to smoke, have a substitute ready: Call a friend, go for a walk, do an activity where you can't smoke like work out in a gym, snap a rubber band on your wrist, eat celery and carrots, chew sugarless gum, suck on a straw or hard candy or cinnamon stick, count backwards from 10 to zero, visualize a peaceful setting, and take a deep breath and exhale slowly.

- Eat a healthy diet and exercise to prevent weight gain.

- Reward yourself and keep adding to your list of benefits of quitting, including living longer and healthier, looking and smelling better, saving money, and being more kissable. Add the money you save by quitting smoking to your savings account.

In *The Last Puff* smokers describe how they quit. Health damage motivated some and others disliked the smell of their hair and clothes. Many found it helps to visualize yourself as a non smoker who is able to taste and smell perfectly, breathe deeply, and achieve a higher level of physical fitness. One man practiced saying over and over, "No thanks, I don't smoke."

Some start by limiting where they can smoke—such as not in the car or at home. They keep their hands occupied by playing with rubber bands and satisfy their oral needs with gum. When they feel the urge to smoke, they use self-talk, take a quick walk, or read their list of the negative aspects of smoking and the positive aspects of not smoking. Some distract themselves by going to movies or typing on the computer. They observe that their desire passes after about five minutes. Most report that the first week is the hardest, but they can never smoke even one cigarette again without starting up the addictive process.

—Emma, 15, California

No one wants to kiss you when you smoke. It's disgusting.

—Eric, 17, Texas

I had gone through the spring break of my sophomore year when my friends finally got me to do it. Now I smoke a pack a day, drink to get drunk, and have smoked pot. Until I did it, the fact that it was unhealthy was all I needed; other people use the fact that they lost someone using these drugs.

I advise that you not try it, though saying not to do it won't help, so think of this. How would you like a life of tar coughing, emergency rooms, stomach pumping, waking up in a pool of vomit?

—Darrel, 18, Colorado

My most difficult challenge was not smoking cigarettes. I knew I didn't like it and just because all my friends smoked didn't mean that I had to smoke to fit in or be cool. I would tell others to trust in themselves and do what they want to do, not what others think they should do to fit in or be cool. It's not worth it!

National Cancer Information Service
1-800-4-CANCER

Stop Teenage Addiction to Tobacco
1-800-998-7828

Americans for Nonsmokers Rights
2530 San Pablo Ave., Suite J
Berkeley, CA 94702

Badvertising Institute
25 Boyd St. #2
Portland, ME 04101

Office on Smoking and Health Centers
for Disease Control
Mail Stop K-50,
4770 Buford Hwy., NE
Atlanta, GA 303441-3724

Nicotine Anonymous World Services
Office
P.O. Box 5177
San Francisco, CA 94704-1103

Smoke-Free Education Services
375 S. End Ave., Suite 32-F
New York, NY 10280

Women and Girls Against Tobacco
2001 Addison St., Suite 200
Berkeley, CA 94704-1103

John Farquhar and Gene Spiller. *The
Last Puff: Ex-Smokers Share the
Secrets of their Success.* NY: W.W.
Norton, 1990.

Harlan Krumholz and Robert Phillips.
*No Ifs, Ands or Butts: A Smoker's
Guide to Quitting.* NY: Avery
Publishing, 1993.

Illegal Drugs

My dad and my brother do drugs, so naturally I have
seen and smelled them. A lot of my friends do them too and
when they ask me to and I say No, they make fun of me.
Sometimes I think about doing it just to get them off my back.
My boyfriend broke up with me because I told him I didn't want
to have sex with him and I really loved him; sometimes I think I
should just give him what he wants because I miss him so much

If I did drugs it would ruin my life. I would get addicted and I wouldn't be able to fulfill all of my dreams. If I had
sex then I could get pregnant and never graduate from high
school or go to college full-time. If you know it's not right, then
don't do it because
in the end you'll
regret what you're
doing.

—Melissa, 14,
California

Teen drug use expanded in the 1970s and 1980s,
declined through 1991, and then rose, according to
the University of Michigan Institute for Social
Research. Their 1995 survey of 13-, 15-, and 17-year-old students reported that drug use by the first group almost doubled since 1991, use by the second group increased by
almost two-thirds, and use among the last group was up
nearly half—to 39 percent. Forty-eight percent of high
school seniors had used an illegal drug at least once; more
than a third had used marijuana. About 800,000 high
school seniors use drugs every month. Drug use is 10 times
more common than parents suspect (U.S. Department of
Education).

"It's hard to say No to drugs because most teens have a hard time saying No to their friends," explained Devon, age 16. From our students' accounts of drug use, I see a desire to fit in, to escape loneliness, and avoid problems with parents. What themes do you see in the lives of drug users you know? What response works best for you if pressured to use drugs? A simple shake of your head and walking away is an effective refusal technique, refusing to be drawn into a discussion or debate. After learning more about the side effects of these drugs, including the possibility of brain damage, it seems if any enemy wanted to harm a country, they couldn't find a better way than to turn youth on to drugs. Read this section carefully if you're thinking about experimenting, or have friends who are addicts.

There is clear evidence of a close connection between drug use and violence, partly because some drugs increase violent behavior (PCP, ethanol, amphetamines, and cocaine). Teens who use illegal drugs and alcohol are more likely to fight and to be assaulted, according to the U.S. National Adolescent Student Health Survey. Drug use and arrests for violence rose together in the 1990s, especially in the suburbs.

The media are part of the problem. The Partnership for a Drug-Free America reports fewer anti-drug news stories and television themes; more drug abuse—specifically marijuana, is described favorably in songs and television.

Peer influence is a strong pressure to use drugs, especially for young people with emotional problems, according to Paul Kingery and other authors of an article, "Violence and Illegal Drug Use Among Adolescents" (*The International Journal of the Addictions*, 1992). Researchers followed 101 three-year-olds through their growing up years. In the interviews at age 18, roughly one-third had never tried drugs, another third had experimented, and about one-fifth were frequent users. This last group had psychological problems that showed up earlier when tested at age seven. (The research by J. Shedler and J. Block is described by Roland Lamarine in the *Journal of Drug Education*, 1993.) Problems are solved by facing them rather than running away.

—Dan, 15, Illinois

The most difficult challenge is trying (and succeeding) to stay off drugs and booze. It's tough; a lot of my friends love to go out and get wasted and it's hard not to join them. The best advice I can offer someone is to involve yourself in something in which you need to stay straight to succeed and keep on doing it. I play basketball and the team has a strict no drug/alcohol policy and random testing of players. (Emma reports, "We have this too, but it doesn't stop them.")

Other than that, my parents have been helpful and supporting (shocking I'm sure). Also my church youth group has people I can talk with—some go to my school. All I can say is I think I've been able to stay off drugs because I've always had something better to do.

—Joey, 15, California

I smoked pot for years, like many others, and mostly for the same reasons. Teenagers have a lot to think about: parents, friends, relationships, and—mostly themselves. Low self-confidence is one of the main reasons teenagers use drugs, but by taking care of yourself and keeping clean it will make you happy about who you are. Confidence helped me overcome daily use of marijuana and become happy.

—Wendy, 15, Illinois

I don't drink or do drugs, and this has helped me survive my life because I can think clearly and generally know what I'm doing. Drugs and booze, they're no good. If you don't believe me, think of it this way. Your mind is the one thing nobody can take away from you. Poor people, homeless people, prisoners, outlaws, everyone from every race—we all have minds. It is the one thing that truly belongs to you, so don't throw it away on drugs and booze! Do not mess up your life before it has started.

I have to watch the people I know, my best friends and my siblings, always either locked up in jail or so drunk or stoned they don't know what's going on most of the time. My brother was on pot when he was 13 and he's been drinking since he was 11. The same with my sister. They can't remember half the things they've done because they were wasted. I got one friend, he's 24, and he's really cool, but he's been huffing since he was 15 and eventually it's going to kill him. All my friends, they all end up in jail or dead from overdoses. Don't do that to yourselves or the people who care about you. There's more to life, there really is.

One more thing I have to tell you—take control of your own life. Don't let anyone make you do anything you don't want to do. Live for yourself. Make your own decisions. And if you sense danger—RUN.

—Joey, 16, Texas

The most difficult challenge is overcoming the lost generation feeling. It seems harder to find my place in the world and be happy. With all the negativeness, it almost seems as if the American Dream is dead. Honestly, at first I thought drugs would help, but they didn't, they actually enforced the negativism. For now, it is mostly fear of failure that keeps me going. I just don't know or understand any more. Probably just do what makes you happy and don't worry about what others say or think.

—Nick, 16, Texas

One night when I came home stoned, I was doing the dishes and trying to talk to my mom like a normal person. The whole time I was doing the dishes I thought, "Why am I doing this? Why do I want to waste my time doing something so stupid when I know I'll lose all of my freedom?" My parents give me more freedom than all of my friends and they don't need to find out that they have a son smoking weed.

When I was lying in bed just a half hour later, my brother came into my room to get something. I look up to my brother more than anyone. My brother then started asking me a lot of questions. For some reason he knew I was stoned and I could tell he was disappointed in me. Ever since then I know how dumb it was to lose family over some stupid high.

—Sara, 16, California

I feel the most difficult problem I face as a sophomore is drugs. Now I'm not saying I'm a saint in this matter because I'm not, but it's just so hard to go a full day without cutting class to go get high. My advice to other teens is don't get involved with drugs in the first place. If you do, then try to stop, get help, and most of all—know that you are not alone. There are tons of people who would love to help you. You just have to let them.

—Derren, 16, California

A lot of people use drugs to forget problems or use drugs such as pot to reduce stress. Drugs can be fun, but I don't know if that fun is worth the damage to my body. I've been around people who have tried to pressure me into doing cocaine and crack and I just laughed at them, said "f___ no!" and that was the end of it. I tried acid but I didn't like it very much. I got a bad smell in my nose and an awful taste in my mouth, and I hated how insecure it made me.

—Justin, 17, California

The most difficult challenge I have faced is turning down drugs. I have been approached numerous times in my 9th and 10th grade years about doing drugs and successfully turned down every approach. Don't give in. The people who push drugs are relentless. They push until you snap. I've found that if you listen to the babble once and then reply, "That's a bunch of crap," and walk away, they usually stop.

—Lauren, 17, Texas

The most difficult challenge I've faced as a teen is the drug situation. Almost everyone in my town who is 12 years of age or older does some type of illegal drugs, such as marijuana, X, rofenol, or acid—some older people I know even do cocaine. I'm proud to say that I've never tried an illegal drug in my life. What has helped me resist is that I see how they used to be before they used drugs, and then I see them now. Not one of them has changed for the better; as a matter of fact, most of them are now losers.

Don't hang out with people who do drugs, as they'll only pull you into it with them. Of course you'll know people who do drugs; you might even go to the same parties. You just need to know when to get away from them. You have to want to be a winner; you have to want to be something great in your future, or else it won't matter to you whether you're a loser or not.

—Susanna, 18, Massachusetts

About tripping, when people are flipping out, they need a responsible adult, a safe environment, and as long as it's not an OD, just supervision till they either ride it out, or excrete all the poison from their bodies. They DO NOT need lots of stuff happening around them like lots of people, music, and lights. They need to have someone TALK them through it (assuming they are coherent). Tell them it WILL end, they are not insane, they are just a kid flipping out on drugs. They most of all need to feel a sense of safety and trust with the people around them.

Most of the acid people take is mostly speed and strychnine, which tap into your subconscious so it's like you are dreaming when you are awake and it's harder to think yourself out of a bad trip. Kids need to know that acid sits in your spinal cord for the rest of your life, and that any drugs they take can have ANYTHING in them—Windex, rat poison, anything. BE CAREFUL!

—Michelle, 19, California

Find something that will give you a natural high—go bungy jumping, sky dive, cycle, do wall climbing. [Other ideas are water and snow skiing, roller blading, mountain biking, video games, creating art, watching a sunset or the night sky, reading an exciting book, hiking, climbing a tree, laughing, slumber parties, costume parties, singing with friends, dancing, holding hands, playing with a pet, solving a problem, nurturing a close friendship—you add to the list.]

—Jim, 20, California

My most difficult experience as a teen was saying No to drugs and dealing with peer pressure. One time I was stuck with a small group of peers and they began smoking pot—all of them but me. They pushed so hard, I gave in and tried it. Then they all moved on to mushrooms. It was then that I became very uncomfortable. I ended up walking five miles back to my house. I was told I was a loser and I had no spine. I soon learned that I was the only person there who really did have a spine.

—Elena, 21, California

I got sent to an insane asylum when I took two hits of acid. I stayed there for two days and was strapped onto a bed.

—Aaron, 22, California

The summer before my freshman year in high school I was drinking a lot, then was introduced to marijuana, and then the finale was cocaine. I was doing something every day and realized that I was having a bad attitude. School had also started and I would go to class high all the time. That was when I knew I had to take care of myself and get some help.

I did not communicate with my family at all, except for my brother, when we would get high together with our friends. I then went to my mother and father and told them that I had to get into a rehabilitation facility. I was only 14 years old. I stayed at a place for 40 days. Right away I knew I had done the right thing and I spoke very openly at the daily meetings we attended during our stay. I went to a therapist privately, too, and realized that I needed to develop a relationship with my parents. I had to explain that I could not be one of their perfect little boys. This had to be brought out to them while I was going through my treatment. Communication was so badly needed that once I got out and we had already started talking, I felt so positive and happy.

I knew drinking had become a problem because it was my way out of feeling lonely. I made the family come together all the time and speak honestly about what was going on in their minds. My brother was upset with me because it made him cry. But I have the best relationship with my family and don't get myself involved with drugs nowadays. I advise you to keep in honest communication with your family because they will always be there for you. Drugs are a way out but they will not solve your problems, so be open with your family from the start and hopefully everything will fall into place.

—Sarah, 22, California

I started using pot the end of my freshman year. I used it maybe seven to 10 times. I was at a party drinking and this older guy offered me some pot. He said it was "good stuff" and "very green." I took a lot of hits and it affected me more than I planned. I started freaking out; I didn't want to be left alone, and I didn't want anyone near me. I started to "logically" plan suicide, knowing that was the only way to come down. I swear I was high for three days. It was the worst experience; someone had to have laced it for my reaction to have been so extreme. One good thing came from this though; I stopped doing pot, and maybe that stopped me from progressing to stronger drugs. I started to respect my sanity and my brain more.

—Nicole, 23, California

My most difficult experience in high school was when I got involved with the drug crystal (methamphetamine), which led to increased drinking, smoking, and smoking pot. I had a really good friend who wanted to try the drug. I did it too because I was curious and didn't want to lose her friendship. She was very manipulative but it was ultimately my choice.

I started using the drug and did so for about three months when my parents confronted me with evidence (notes, drug paraphernalia, and behavioral changes) and I admitted to them I had tried it a couple of times, which was a lie, and I continued to use the drug and it got worse. I was using it before school, during break at school, and on the weekends for another two to three months, when I got caught again. Our parents decided we could not associate and we both received continuing counseling.

I decided that the shame, humiliation, and pain that I caused my parents and myself were not worth taking the drugs anymore. So I quit, but it took a couple of years to earn back the trust that I lost with my parents. A couple of friends also used the drug at the same time and kept using it. It was hard to see them lose part of their lives in some of the same ways that I had. I was very judgmental towards them, but I learned that they must come to the point of quitting on their own, with support from parents and friends.

—Laureate, 24, California

The ONLY, I repeat ONLY way for people to not get involved with drugs or alcohol or do other bad things is to NOT HANG AROUND OR BE FRIENDS WITH PEOPLE WHO TAKE THEM. This Mexican proverb is the first and last word on ANYTHING that has to do with peer pressure:

"Di me con quien andas, y te digo quien eres."

"Tell me who you walk with and I'll tell you who you are."

—Matt, 25, California

I did too many drugs as a teenager—lots of pot and a little bit of everything else, but no needles. I smoked pot three or four times a day and anything else when I could. In the beginning, it was like a game to do it around my parents without them finding out. Then it evolved into more of a lifestyle. I feel like I missed out on a lot of my teenage years because I was always stoned. Don't get caught in the drug trap. Try to enjoy high school and learn as much as you can. You will need it for college.

—Joe, 25, California

I entered a new high school when I was a junior. I was a total geek. No one liked me. To become popular I started using drugs. I didn't like using the drugs and I really wish I hadn't. I can't believe I was so stupid. I used weed, crank, cocaine—anything to give me a speedy, jittery high. Well, I became popular for the next two years with the druggies. All the real popular people had self-esteem as they were athletic. I tried to join the track team—try doing this when you're not on drugs. I really think I could have made it, oh well.

After graduation I went to a junior college, but I dropped out, and all of my druggie "friends" from high school stayed at home and sat on their rears. I did a lot of stupid things. I have a DUI and I became really depressed, so I decided I needed rehab. I went to rehab and I really enjoyed it. I have been off drugs and alcohol for six years.

I went to college and I joined the track team. It's great! What I have to say is, "Stay off drugs." I wish I had believed in myself, but oh well. I went through a bad trip to become popular. Yeah, I was really popular-NOT!

—Kitty, 25, Nevada

My father killed himself the day after my 15th birthday. My twin sister and I came home from school and found him in the living room. He had shot himself in the head. It was very messy. After the police left, the doctor gave my mother some medicine and she fell asleep. My sister and I cleaned up. Two months later my twin sister died in a truck accident when it lost its brakes and went off a canyon road. It took three days to find her. She was so messed up they would not let me see her. I never saw her again. I loved her more than I had loved anyone else ever before or since.

Whatever you do, don't start to do drugs. I started to do drugs and drink about a year after my father and sister died. I did drugs because they made me feel better inside and I wasn't depressed and sad all the time. I didn't cry all the time at night. But the drugs hurt me a lot. Some of the drugs I did hurt my brain. I used to get real good grades in high school and was on the honors list most of the time, but after I started to do speed I quit high school. Now I have a hard time remembering things, and it makes it hard to be in college trying to learn enough so I can get a good job.

I would tell younger people to get counseling instead of doing drugs. You will have to live with the pain forever. Drugs might seem like they help but they don't. I had to learn to live without my sister and father even if I was on drugs. Now I have a hard time learning anything else. Get counseling or talk to a minister. Many are trained in counseling and can help. I did drugs instead and caused brain damage. When you do a drug that makes your hair hurt, you should know the drug is no good for you.

—Ray, 41, Illinois

When I broke up with my girlfriend of two years, I started experimenting with marijuana and hash, then amphetamines and barbiturates, then LSD. I was 19. I began selling marijuana, first small quantities, then larger amounts. I also sold some mescaline (which, I suspect, was LSD ground up and mingled with powdered sugar and corn starch). I spent one year immersed in the drug culture. I took drugs to find the "answer to the mystery of life." Not surprisingly, there was no answer in drugs.

I overdosed on New Year's Eve a year later. A couple of friends and I bought some acid. We took the acid and waited. Nothing happened, so we took another hit. The next thing we knew, we were space rangers. The big difference between a big drunk and a "bad trip" is that with a drunk you throw up and pass out, but with acid, you stay awake for every second. It is terrifying—you can't shut it off. My friend said that he knew he had taken too much acid when he looked out of the car and saw ice forming on the wings. I started having convulsions. Of course, my friends were so far gone I spent about an hour with the dry heaves, lying alone in the back seat of the car.

Sometimes at college, I took mescaline. It really had little effect on me but I ended up drinking beer on the courthouse steps. I was arrested; the cops searched my car. For no reason other than luck, there were no narcotics in my car. Something clicked; I still don't know what to this day. I realized that life was what you make of it—no more and no less, and that a person could be in his life whatever he wanted. If a person wanted to be an environmentalist, or an engineer, or a doctor, the only person standing in his way was himself. The real roadblock to personal fulfillment is yourself, not someone else or through some wall.

So, I applied myself in school. I worked my way through college, graduated number one in electrical engineering, went to law school, graduated with honors, and am now a patent lawyer for a Fortune 500 corporation.

I have had personal problems since then. My life has not been a series of successes; there have been setbacks and problems. There are days when I struggle with the same things that led to drug abuse. The difference now is that when I have a problem, I look to my family, friends, and professionals, rather than a bunch of capsules in a plastic bag.

I think the best thing to say when offered drugs is No. You can't argue with people encouraging you to take drugs. There is no "put down" sufficient to dissuade them. Most people are going to experiment with drugs. And, in our society where we dispense drugs to cure depression like candy, drug use is almost a given. My biggest laugh is that kids with drug abuse problems get sent to mental health clinics where they end up taking lithium or Xanax for depression and then we tell them not to take drugs. Gheez...

How to Say No to Peer Pressure

Summaries of model prevention programs and research papers are available from the Office of Delinquency Prevention, Texas Youth Commission, P.O. Box 4260, Austin, TX 78765. prevention@tyc.state.tx.us

John Gibbs, et al. *The Equip Program: Teaching Youth to Think and Act Responsibly Through a Peer-Helping Approach*. Research Press (2612 N. Mattis Ave., Champaign, IL 61821).

Sharon Scott. *How to Say No and Keep Your Friends: Peer Pressure Reversal for Teens and Preteens. Positive Peer Groups and When to Say Yes! And Make More Friends*. Human Resource Development Press (22 Amherst Rd., Amherst, MA).

Drugs fall into the categories of stimulants, depressants, hallucinogens, narcotics, inhalants, cannabis, and steroids.

Stimulants

Stimulants/"Uppers" speed up the nervous system, making the user feel powerful and energetic and then depressed, edgy, and craving another rush. Stimulants include tobacco and caffeine in coffee and cola. They raise blood pressure and increase secretion of stomach acid. Cocaine and crack cause the heart to beat faster and increase blood pressure and body temperature. The rapid increase in the heart rate can lead to a heart attack or stroke. Stimulants can cause increased alertness, euphoria, insomnia, and loss of appetite. These drugs may also cause psychological disturbances mimicking panic attacks, manic stages, schizophrenia, or other loss of contact with reality (see mental illness section, Chapter 2).

Overdose of stimulants such as cocaine can cause agitation, hallucinations, convulsions, and death. A half-million Americans had to seek hospital emergency care because of problems with drugs in 1994; cocaine abuse was responsible for 28 percent of these cases. Signs of stimulant use are dilated pupils, rapid speech, restlessness, insomnia, anxiety, sweating, dry mouth, headache, sleeping less, loss of appetite, becoming argumentative, and purposeless, repetitive acts.

Cocaine ("coke," "toot," "blow," "snow," "flake") is a powder made from coca leaves. A study reports 134,000 teens use cocaine at least once a week.

It can be snorted, smoked, or injected, and is highly addictive. People often overdose on cocaine because coming down from the high often creates an intense craving for more of the drug to avoid the severe depression they feel as it wears off. There are about 2.5 million regular users in the U.S., which resulted in 109,376 hospital emergency room admissions in 1992 for seizures, shock, brain hemorrhage, coma, cardiac arrest, and paranoia.

Cocaine is an anesthetic that numbs tissue and stimulates the nervous system. Users feel hyper as their heart rates and blood pressure speed up; this can damage heart tissue and rupture blood vessels in the brain. The drug affects mood and relaxation by acting on the brain circuits that regulate pleasure, causing euphoria, a feeling you can do anything. Regular use may harm these pathways and also harms nasal tissue. Convulsions and respiratory paralysis are possible with high doses. Users may experience hallucinations and "coke bugs," a feeling that insects are crawling on the skin. Long term use can cause lung damage, ulcers inside the nose, paranoia (irrational fear of people and things), and hallucinations. Withdrawal symptoms include sleeping long hours, irritability, depression, loss of energy, and disorientation.

"Crack," or "rock," is very potent cocaine processed for smoking and is especially addictive. Dealers mix powdered cocaine with baking soda and heat it in an oven to produce smokable crack cocaine. Crack can cause permanent brain damage. A survey of teen crack users found that over half who traded drugs for sex were infected with an STD. Some experts blame much of the increase in violent crimes by youth on the epidemic of crack cocaine in the inner cities.

Methamphetamine is a central nervous system stimulant whose use has also reached an epidemic stage. These drugs ("speed," "ice," "crystal," "black beauties," "crank," "bennies," "whites," "white crosses," Dexedrine, Desoxyn, Biphetamine) increase blood pressure and heart rate, making the user feel wired, powerful, and energetic. Because it is usually injected or smoked, it causes a fast high and very high blood pressure that can lead to a stroke or heart attack. Meth-related emergency room visits rose from 4,900 in 1991 to 17,400 in 1994. (2,439 meth-related deaths were reported between 1991 and 1995.)

Meth is smoked, snorted, injected, or swallowed in tablet form, and produces a high that can last up to 14 hours—compared to just minutes with cocaine. Speed creates a feeling of euphoria because it floods the brain with dopamine, a neurotransmitter involved in feeling pleasure and motivation, and in motor control. Use over time reduces levels of dopamine and serotonin (another neurotransmitter), causing depression, loss of interest in normal activities, and inability to control body movement.

"Snot" is made by dissolving powdered meth in water and adding baking soda. "Ice" is a smokable crystal rock, made through a cooking process similar to making crack cocaine. It provides a buzz that lasts for about 12 hours, and the paranoia that follows the high can last up to two days. Ice destroys brain cells and, along with other amphetamines, alters the brain chemistry.

Meth users often report an increased sex drive and feel they don't need to eat or sleep. Some get very aggressive and argumentative. When they crash, they can get depressed and suicidal. In some cases, users develop extreme paranoia, psychosis, hallucinations, anxiety, fear of open spaces (agoraphobia), hear voices, and see something out of the corner of their eye. Meth can cause loss of appetite, loss of coordination, muscle tremors, insomnia, headaches, nausea, blurred vision, and heart problems. Some women start using crank to lose weight or fear they will gain weight if they stop using it. Long-term use causes damage to the organs, especially the lungs, liver, and kidneys, as well as the teeth and skin.

Manufactured legally for medical prescriptions, amphetamines are also manufactured and sold illegally as "designer drugs." Meth is be easily manufactured, but the chemicals can explode, catch on fire, and release toxic gases. The toxic waste products from the illegal labs are often just dumped into drains or streams, causing pollution.

MDMA or "Ecstasy" is an amphetamine-based hallucinogen, similar to mescaline and amphetamines. It can cause the user to feel in love and ecstatic, but can cause brain damage by destroying the brain's ability to produce serotonin. It can harm the brain cells that regulate movement, cause flashbacks, and increase blood pressure.

Depressants

Depressants/"Downers" slow down the central nervous system, as in the effect of sleeping pills. Alcohol is the most widely used depressant drug. Overdoses can result in coma, convulsions, or death. Taken in combination, alcohol and other depressants may cause coma and death. Depressants can cause a lack of concentration, muscle relaxation, slurred speech, and a staggering walk. Over time hallucinations may occur. Overdose of depressants such as Quaalude, especially in conjunction with alcohol, can cause weak and rapid pulse, coma, and death. Withdrawal symptoms include anxiety, tremors, delirium, and convulsions.

Barbiturates ("barbs," "goof balls," "blues," Phenobarbital, Seconal, Amytal) slow neural transmission, which slows reactions, slows the heart rate, and lowers blood pressure. Low doses are similar in their effect to alcohol. High doses cause wide mood swings, babbling, lack of coordination, and lowered blood pressure and heart rate. Over time these very addictive drugs damage the central nervous system, liver, and pancreas.

Tranquilizers (Valium, Equanil, Librium) relax muscles, cause drowsiness, confusion, and loss of coordination.

Methaqualone ("soapers," "quads," "ludes," "714s," Quaalude, Somnafac, Parest, Mequin) causes drowsiness, loss of coordination, dizziness, and slows the heart rate. It causes feelings of confidence and a euphoric high, followed by depression, and is very addictive. Much of "ludes" sold on the streets are something else, sometimes Valium or a more dangerous drug.

Hallucinogens

Hallucinogens cause changes in perception by scrambling the brain circuits that control judgment and concentration for up to 12 hours. Sense of direction, distance, and time becomes distorted. Visual and auditory hallucinations and anxiety attacks may occur, due to rapid mood changes. Hallucinogens also can cause flashbacks, paranoia, depression, and loss of contact with reality. Some people report spiritual experiences, although the possible side effects and flashbacks are a high price to pay. They caused over 8,000 emergency room visits in 1991 and about 110 deaths. Signs of hallucinogen use include enlarged pupils, increased blood pressure, tremors, flushed face, increased activity, increased sensory awareness, hallucinations, and anxiety.

Lysergic Acid Diethylamide ("LSD," "acid") increases the heart rate, blood pressure, and body temperature. The drug can interfere with vision and hearing, and can cause hallucinations, paranoia, panic, shaking, chills, and nausea. Flashbacks may occur weeks or years later. LSD can be either a depressant or a stimulant. Mescaline, MDA, DMT, STP, and psilocybin have similar effects.

Since psychedelic "magic" **mushrooms** ("shrooms") like psilocybin are in high demand and low supply, often grocery store mushrooms are treated with LSD or other drugs. Poisonous look-alike mushrooms are also a danger, particularly the fly agaric mushroom (*amanita muscaria*). Mescaline is made from the peyote cactus and has a similar effect to LSD. Users report feeling happy, seeing phenomena such as watching trees breathe, and experiencing intense nausea.

Phencyclidine ("PCP," "THC," "angel dust") has different forms: liquid, powder, tablets, or rock crystal. PCP is legally used as an animal tranquilizer. It is most often smoked, and acts as an anesthetic, stimulant, depressant, and hallucinogen at the same time. It produces a high similar to being drunk, or low dose effects compare with marijuana use. It can lead to brain damage, speech problems, paranoia, flashbacks, and interfere with memory. PCP can also cause depression, intense anger, hallucinations, amnesia, confusion, loss of coordination, delayed reactions, and distorted perceptions. It distorts the senses, including vision, and hearing. It increases the heart rate and blood pressure and can cause nausea and fever. PCP numbs pain; thus, combined with violent paranoid reactions, can lead to physical injuries. Higher dose effects can last for several days and cause flashbacks months after use. Overdose can cause convulsions, coma, psychosis, and death.

Narcotics

Narcotics numb the perception of pain, and the user may have a pleasant feeling of having no problems. **Heroin** ("smack," "dope," "horse") comes from the opium poppy plant. When melted, the powder is injected into the veins (most teens don't use this method), snorted, or smoked. Heroin, morphine, opium, codeine, meperidine, and methadone cause shallow breathing, drowsiness, and reduce hunger, thirst, and sex drive. Signs of use include needle marks, collapsed veins, glazed look, watery eyes, and lack of concentration. These drugs can cause loss of concentration and judgment. Overdose can result in coma, convulsions, and death.

Narcotics cause vomiting, euphoria, drowsiness, and slower heart rate. Highly addictive, over time they can cause lung damage and disrupt women's menstrual cycles. Withdrawal symptoms include irritability, tremors, panic, cramps, nausea, chills, and sweating.

Designer drugs made to look and act like heroin include fentanyls that can be hundreds of times stronger than heroin, and very easy to overdose. There is no quick way to tell fentanyls from heroin. Some users have become human statues, losing all ability to move.

Inhalants

Inhalants are usually household products, such as glue, paint, lighter fluids, cleaning fluids, hair sprays, butyl nitrite ("Rush"), amyl nitrite ("poppers" legally used for heart patients), or nail polish remover. They are sniffed or huffed, causing feelings of giddiness, loss of coordination, and sometimes violent behavior. Inhalants (vasodilators) expand blood vessels and cause blood pressure to fall rapidly, which increases the heart rate. Signs of use include slurred speech, appearing drunk, poor muscle control, drowsiness, shakiness, and nausea.

The chemical fumes cause headaches, dizziness, bloody noses, lack of coordination, heart palpitations, nausea, and loss of control over body wastes. Over time they can cause permanent brain, lung, liver, kidney, and nervous system damage, and can lead to death when used with depressants. Sniffing concentrated solvents or aerosol sprays can cause heart failure. Nearly 20 percent of adolescents report using these dangerous drugs at least once.

Marijuana

Cannabis, marijuana, and hashish ("pot," "weed," "dope," "bud," "smoke," "ganja," "reefer," "grass") are made from the *cannabis sativa* plant or the hemp plant, and alter mood, thinking, and behavior. Users usually smoke pot in cigarette form, the most commonly used illegal drug. Hashish, a more concentrated form, is usually smoked in a pipe. With years of cultivation, pot is now up to 20 times as strong as in previous decades. Some scientists consider it a hallucinogen. Marijuana acts both as a central nervous system depressant—causing relaxation, and as a stimulant—increasing heart rate. It causes short-term memory loss, reduces motor skills, and slows reaction time. A study reports that 17 percent of drivers killed in car crashes tested positive for marijuana use.

Marijuana smoking almost doubled from 1992 to 1994 among youth ages 12 to 17. Monthly use increased to 7.3 percent (1.3 million teens), compared to four percent in 1992. Twenty percent of eight graders have tried it. It can intensify feelings, acting as a stimulant to some users and a depressant to others. Heavy users may develop "Amotivational Syndrome," losing interest in school, relationships, exercise, etc. Pot causes sensory distortions, euphoria, lowers inhibitions, increases appetite, and interferes with memory and concentration. Overdose of cannabis can result in paranoia. High potency forms of pot can cause panic and anxiety attacks and resulted in more than 16,000 emergency room admissions in 1991.

Pot increases the heart rate, decreases the amount of blood flow to the brain, reduces coordination and slows reflexes, and long-term use can cause lung disease. It decreases the amount of testosterone, the male sex hormone, and can lower sperm count. It causes drops in sex hormone levels in both males and females. Long-term use can reduce growth hormone production, decrease the size of the testicles, block ovulation in women, interfere with memory, cause bronchitis, and weaken the immune system. Pot also reduces stomach acid secretions which can lead to more infections. Drugs like PCP are sometimes dusted on the marijuana leaves.

A complex mix of hundreds of chemicals, pot smoke has up to 50 percent more cancer-causing chemicals than tobacco. The chemicals trigger a rapid increase in the heart rate. One joint is as harmful to your lungs as four cigarettes. Both marijuana and tobacco produce carbon monoxide harmful to a fetus and put stress on the heart of the smoker.

THC, a mind-altering chemical, is fat-soluble, so it moves to high fat parts of the body such as the sex glands and the brain. Then the liver and kidneys break down the complex chemicals into those more easily flushed from the body. About half of these residues leave the body in 24 hours but the rest can stay for weeks, especially in the brain, testicles or ovaries, and other fatty organs. Marijuana widens the gaps between the nerve cells in the brain, making communication between the cells more difficult. It also causes packets of the neurotransmitters (the message senders) to become inactive, a sign of early nerve cell damage. Pot weakens the immune system by as much as 40 percent by damaging white blood cells (Harvard Medical School newsletter, Vol. 4, No. 5).

Some of the signs of marijuana use are bloodshot eyes, dilated pupils, "the munchies," dry mouth, talkativeness or withdrawal, fragmented thoughts, impaired short-term memory, drowsiness, dizziness, loss of coordination, inappropriate laughing, and relaxation.

Steroids

Steroids used legally to treat allergies and rashes are not the same steroids used to increase muscle mass, and mimic testosterone. Estimates are that six to 19 percent of high school students take steroids (one-quarter are female). The motive is desire to enhance athletic performance and perhaps to look more masculine. Anabolic steroids come in pills or are injected (this leads to another danger if users share needles infected with the HIV virus).

Steroids can cause liver damage and cancer, jaundice, cholesterol imbalances, heart disease, high blood pressure, and delay healing after a muscle injury. Steroids may lead to premature stopping of bone growth (the long bone can become prematurely fused), and interfere with normal hormone production. They can cause mood swings, paranoia, depression, hostility, and violent outbursts called "roid rages." Side effects in males include: stunted growth, premature baldness, increased hairiness, enlarged breasts, acne, jaundice, shrinking testicles, impotence (inability to get an erection), sterility, and puffy hands, feet, and face. Female use of steroids may result in similar effects and increased body and facial hair, smaller breasts, permanent enlargement of the clitoris, and disruption of the menstrual cycle.

Treatment of Drug Abuse

Mark, a drug counselor for a national 800 phoneline, reports that most teens who call say they are calling for a friend rather than for themselves. When they want to get help, he refers them to one of the 800 numbers listed below. They often want to know if withdrawal will hurt (many callers are using heroin or meth), and he tells them truthfully, Yes, it will. They may feel sick, depressed, and tired. If they are under 18, they may need their parents' permission to get into a treatment program. Sometimes callers report their parents are users or they don't want to talk with them about drugs, in which case, Mark suggests talking to a school counselor. He reports peer pressure can go both ways; often peers can help their friends get off drugs by telling them their concerns and offering support.

Mark thinks that teens turn to drugs to numb their pain, to compensate for low self-esteem or family problems, for a thrill, or to prove they're macho. He asks teens about their future goals and points out how school and job success don't fit with drug use. He knows of many people fired from their jobs after a positive drug test.

Drug prevention programs are obviously necessary but reach less than half of U.S. students. Many are cutesy, one-time school programs that lack follow-up or don't teach refusal skills. An analysis of 143 drug prevention programs for teens found that programs which involved youth in activities with their peers were the most effective in reducing drug use (Tobler's study was published in the *Journal of Drug Issues*). A study of school-based anti-drug programs in California reported that 90 percent of high school students felt the programs were not very effective (a study commissioned by the California Department of Education, 1995). Perhaps schools need to emphasize peer prevention programs.

The National Institute on Drug Abuse campaign "Coming Together on Prevention" identified three programs proven to decrease youth substance abuse: Project STAR, Strengthening Families, and Reconnecting Youth. The last program is a school-based curriculum (National Educational Service, 1610 W. Third St., Bloomington, IN 47404).

My feeling about drugs is that our minds and bodies are such precious gifts that it is our obligation to nurture and not pollute them, just as we should care for and avoid polluting the planet.

Help for Drug Users

American Council for Drug Education
1-800-488-DRUG

Center for Substance Abuse Treatment
1-800-662-HELP (referral)

Covenant House 1-800-999-9999
(provides information and referral
about drugs and other problems)

Cocaine Anonymous
1-800-347-8998

Drug 24-Hour Hotline
1-800-821-HELP
(drug and alcohol referral)

Helpline (alcohol, cocaine, and gambling) 1-800-732-9808

"Just Say No" International
1-800-258-2766
(in California,
1-415-939-6666)
(Groups around the country organize
recreational activities and work on
community projects to empower
young people and encourage the self-
esteem necessary to avoid drug use.
Their Youth Power program is
explained in training manuals.)

Marijuana Anonymous World Service
Office 1-800-766-6779
National Clearinghouse for Alcohol
and Drug Information
1-800-729-6686
(free information and catalog of
materials)

Narcotics Anonymous
1-800-662-4357

National Clearinghouse for Drug and
Alcohol Information
1-800-729-6686 (younger siblings
can call Wally Bear at
1-800-449-2559 to hear drug prevention messages)

National Council on Alcoholism and
Drug Dependence
1-800-622-2255

National Inhalant Prevention
Coalition 1-800-269-4237

National Institute on Drug Abuse
1-800-662-HELP
(provides referrals to programs in
your area)

Alcohol and Drug Problems
Association of North America
444 N. Capitol St., NW, Suite 706
Washington, DC 20001

Drug Abuse Prevention Office
U.S. Department of Education
400 Maryland Ave., SW,
Room 4145
Washington, DC 20202

Drug Information Association
P.O. Box 3113
Maple Glen, PA 19002

Families Anonymous, Inc.
P. O. Box 528
Van Nuys, CA 91408 (for
families of substance abusers)

Nar-Anon Family Groups
1-310-547-5800
P.O. Box 2562
Palos Verdes, CA 90274
(information and referrals for families and friends of
drug abusers)

Narcotics Anonymous
P. O. Box 9999
Van Nuys, CA 91409
National Association on Drug Abuse
Problems
355 Lexington Ave.
New York, NY 10017

National Child Safety Council
Jackson, MI 49204-1368
Don't Let Drugs Shatter Your Life!
booklet

National Family Partnership
11159B S. Towne Square
St. Louis, MO 63123

Parents' Resource Institute for Drug
Education (PRIDE)
40 Hurt Plaza, Suite 210
Atlanta, GA 30303

Pills Anonymous
P.O. Box 473, Ansonia Station
New York, NY 10023
(Modeled after Alcoholics
Anonymous, it assists with support
groups for pill abusers.)

Susan Cohen and Daniel Cohen. *What
You Can Believe About Drugs*. NY:
Dell Publishing, 1993.

*Making the Grade: A Guide to School
Drug Prevention Programs*.
Drug Strategies, 2445 M St., NW,
Suite 480, Washington, DC 20037

Parents Who Are Drug-Addicted

Alcoholic families just don't work. There's too much stress and no trust. If you have such a family, have will power and get help.
—Joe, 15, California

An estimated one in eight children has an alcoholic parent, or 6.6 million kids under age 18. A recent poll reported that one in every three American families has an alcoholic family member. Kids may feel guilt and self-blame, worry, embarrassment, lack of trust in relationships, confusion, anger, and depression. Seventeen percent of teens surveyed for the Horatio Alger Association report their parent uses drugs.

Claudia Black, an expert on ACoAs (adult children of alcoholics), reports that alcoholic families usually operate according to three rules: Don't trust others to follow through on their commitments, don't feel because the pain is ongoing, and don't talk about problems. Children of addicts may suffer from depression, anger, their own addictions (e.g. food) ignore their own needs, lack of trust in others, and stress-related health problems such as headaches.

Ms. Black finds that children tend to find various roles to adapt to problem drinking. The *hero* works very hard to achieve and tries to make the family look normal to outsiders, usually covering up her own feelings. This is often the oldest child. The *adjuster* tries to avoid rocking the boat and feels out of control of his life. The *placater* tries to take emotional care of the family, often ignoring her own needs. The *scapegoat* acts out the family's distress, relieves pressure by getting into trouble, and is labeled as the family's problem. This child is usually the one to get the family into treatment, although the only motive is to "fix" this problem child. Sharon Wegscheider Cruz adds the *mascot*, who acts like a clown to distract his parents from their fights, and the *lost child* who hides in her room to escape.

Children of alcoholics are more likely to become alcoholics and drug users and marry alcoholics than children with more healthy parents. Even if they do not become alcoholics, they learn unhealthy behaviors and dependencies. They have a tendency to be codependents who look for relationships with people they think they can help and rescue (see abuse section, Chapter 6). Feeling needed makes them feel they won't be emotionally abandoned as they were by the alcoholic parent. By focusing on caring for others, they avoid looking at their own fears and the feelings they weren't allowed to express to their parents. They can be addicted to the tension of highs and lows of trying to rescue an unstable person and confuse their excitement and pity with love.

To break these patterns, it's important to understand them and get support from other children of alcoholics in an Alateen group or some other 12-step support group. Children of alcoholics often need to learn assertive communication, to express their feelings, and to work on changing themselves rather than others. If you have a friend with an alcoholic parent, you might encourage her or him to check out Alateen.

—Barbara, 16, California

My grandpa, step grandma, mom, uncle, aunt, and uncle are or were all drug users and have been locked up numerous times. I'm upset a little about the way my family is, but I believe my sister and I had it better than any other drug-raised kids. We were always taken care of, provided for, and given attention. After being put away in foster care and taken away from my family I had to learn to do stuff for myself. It's really hard, but if my family had never gotten busted, I would still expect everyone to do everything for me. I would never get anywhere in this world.

—Jolene, 17, California

The most difficult challenge I faced as a teen is admitting that my mother is not good for me and that she will never change. She stopped doing drugs for a little while when she was with my stepdad. She slowly was getting back into pot and then started selling crank a little bit. That's when my stepdad left. We were close so we stayed in contact. She was hurting for money so she started selling it more and more. She became abusive mentally and physically both to herself and me. I was the only one living there with her.

I found out I was pregnant and our fights got worse. She gave me an ultimatum and that is why I moved out. I was one of the few lucky girls whose boyfriend was willing to take on full responsibility for a baby. Having my boyfriend and his parents around and letting me stay with them helped a lot. When my dad found out I was pregnant, he would not talk to me and still won't talk to me. My stepmom will though. She keeps communication open between me and my dad's family. The weirdest thing is that we never even really got along when we lived together.

Anyway, I am not talking to my real mother now (I have no contact with her) and she is out on the streets, homeless. I am not really sure if what I did was right or wrong, but I never wanted to believe my mother was not in her right mind.

—Steve, 21, California

Probably the most difficult experience I faced as a teen was the situation with my father. My father was an alcoholic and it tore our family apart. Being the oldest son, I had a huge responsibility to watch over my two younger brothers and it made me grow up faster than I really wanted.

I basically left my problems at home and focused my thinking on school and athletics. It really made me a better person. If it wasn't for athletics I would have probably dropped out of school to help support the family.

Children of Alcoholics

(See alcohol and drug section resource lists for organizations)

Claudia Black. *Double Duty*. NY: Ballantine, 1990. *The Missing Piece*. NY: Ballantine, 1995.

Sharon Wegscheider Cruz. *Another Chance*. Palo Alto, CA.: Science & Behavior, 1981.

Judith Seixas. *Living with a Parent Who Drinks Too Much*. NY: Beech Tree Books, 1991.

Paul Taylor. *Coping with a Dysfunctional Family*. NY: Rosen Group, 1990.

Techniques to Change Unhealthy Habits

B e specific about the goal you want to achieve and visualize your success. Start with changing just one habit or behavior so you don't feel overwhelmed. I'll use the example of quitting smoking, but substitute your own particular goal.

1. Learn about the problem (such as the health risks of smoking). The most effective way is to join a support group, such as a 12-step group.

2. Identify how you feel about the problem. (Why do you smoke?)

3. Make a commitment to change (quit smoking). Write out a plan of action, including possible obstacles and supports. Be specific.

4. Substitute healthy alternatives (such as exercise).

5. Analyze what situations trigger your habit. Keep a log of when you are tempted to engage in the unhealthy habit so you can watch out for dangerous situations (friends who smoke). Avoid people and places that encourage the problem (parties). You may need to change your group of friends, at least until you really quit.

6. Reward yourself for making changes (do something fun at the end of each day without cigarettes).

7. Seek out support from others (friends, family, counselors, support group) and express your feelings (i.e., how difficult it is to quit smoking). You might follow the model of Alcoholics Anonymous which pairs new members with a sponsor they can learn from and call whenever they start losing willpower.

8. Practice stress management and relaxation techniques (Chapter 2) and the wellness steps described in Chapter 1.

9. Set a time to evaluate how your plan is working and make changes if necessary. Be patient with yourself as the habit took root over time. It's normal to move forward two steps and one step back.

Four Steps to Change Habits

—Counselor Judith Eberheart, M.A.

Step One: First decide exactly what you want to change in your life. Not just generally, "I want to run faster," "I want to lose weight," or "I want to be healthier." Our mind responds to directions, but it needs specific goals to work towards. You must decide how much faster you want to run, how much weight you want to lose, or how you want to be healthier. Write in your journal: Something that I want to change about my wellness habits is_____.

Step Two: Devise a program. When you make bread you don't go into the kitchen, open the cupboard, toss a little of everything into a bowl and expect it to turn out as bread. No, you follow a careful, step-by-step proven plan that assures a successful loaf. The point here is that the plan must be a plan that suits you. Do not be discouraged when your plan doesn't seem to work. Find out what is not working and adjust it. Don't tell yourself that you can't or that you're not the type.

Charles Garfield, a psychologist, mathematician, weight lifter, and scientist with the moonshot, wrote a book describing the traits of successful people in different disciplines. He discovered that they worked for correction, not for perfection. The moonshot was off course 90 percent of the time. At no time did the scientists call off the venture because things weren't going perfectly. In fact, perfectionism is a trait that slows progress by "analysis paralysis." My plan for change is_____.

Step Three: Select your reinforcements, a way to reward yourself for success. You need to have a payoff for changing that is greater than the payoff for staying the same. Even though the habit you want to change is negative and harmful, there is some reason why you continue to do it. Be clear that you are getting some benefit or payoff from your negative behaviors. To change you will have to be willing to let go of the old desire in favor of a new one.

Selecting reinforcers may be an area where you will have to experiment. An imaginary reward that you create in your mind can be just as reinforcing as something real. My motivating reinforcers for this change are_____.

Even if you are on the right track, you'll get run over if you just sit there.
—Will Rogers

Step Four: Select techniques to help you along the way. Some supports can make the changes easier. Willpower works, but when we become tired, stressed, disappointed, and discouraged with lack of progress, willpower is overcome and the negative feelings and fatigue are victorious. This does not mean that you are doomed to failure. Remember, your efforts are not counted as failures, just lessons! Here are some power boosters that you can use for support in making a change and reducing stress.

Group support: Any wellness activity you want to pursue is easier in a group. The most successful self-help group in the United States is Alcoholics Anonymous (AA). Almost any activity is easier when there are others around for encouragement. When we are encouraged we get energy from others, just as when we are disapproved of we feel our energy taken away. When making a change, choose to be around people who support that change, not those who criticize, use sarcasm, or make negative comments. Local newspapers generally list meeting times and places of the various groups. Therapists and counseling departments should have lists of meetings for AA and Narcotics Anonymous and various other 12-step and codependency group meetings.

Visual Imagery: Our minds are very powerful tools. If we can visualize ourselves as persons with the changes we are planning to make, it is easier to believe that we can make the changes. Many athletes use this technique. Jack Nicklaus claims that his golf game is only 10 percent involved with the actual swing. "Hitting the specific shots," says Nicklaus, "is 50 percent mental picture and 40 percent setup."

Visual imagery is not only used in athletics, but business people use it widely in sales and promotion. Steven Covey in his best seller, *The 7 Habits of Highly Effective People*, writes that all things are created twice, the mental or first creation, and a physical or second creation. Take a few moments now to visualize the change you've written about for this chapter. Do this with the most vivid pictures possible, including smells, sounds, and emotions that accompany the pictures. Visualization gets better with practice.

If you have a substance abuse problem: Face it, identify the problem you're trying to solve, learn about the drug's effects, decide to quit, and find a support group. If you live with an addict, get support from a 12-step group where you'll learn healthy ways to cope from others with a similar challenge.

Chapter 5

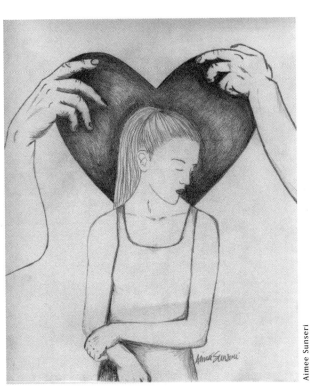

Aimee Sunseri

Family

The "Father Knows Best" type family popularized in TV sitcoms in the 1950s is a minority—less than 10 percent of families have an unemployed mother, employed father, and children under 18. People live in many different family types and these can change with divorce and remarriage. You may live in an intact nuclear family (the term for mom and dad in first marriage, and kids); in an extended family including grandparents, aunts, and uncles; in a single-parent family; in a stepfamily; in a family with unmarried adults living together, or in a foster family. About half of young people live with both parents, almost one-quarter live with a single parent, and about 21 percent live in stepfamilies. A major issue for families in an era when the majority of parents works outside the home, is turning off the television and spending quality time together. In any relationship, communication skills and having fun together help create harmony.

Adoption

I never remember a time when I did not know when I was adopted. My parents were told by the judge who signed the papers to tell me as soon as possible or he would not allow the adoption. My parents told me when I was around the age of two, so the knowledge has always been a part of my memories. I never really felt that it made me different, but it made me special, probably because that is how my parents explained it.

As I became older I asked questions about my birth parents. Because my adoption had been a private one through doctors, my parents knew more than most adoptive parents. I knew that I was my mother's sixth child and my birth parents were divorcing. My maternal grandparents had offered to pay the hospital bills if she would put me up for adoption. I believe that she made a sacrifice for me. I have always been curious about my brothers and sisters.

The casual question, "Are you related to...?" from a stranger always brought a faster heartbeat for me. As a student, many times you are asked to write an autobiography. It always seemed surreal to me. It was obvious genetically that I was not related to my parents. While their lives were my heritage, it always seemed like I was lying. It was not until later that I realized that the people who are your family are the ones that you choose to keep with you. You really do choose your own family, just like my parents chose me. You have the power to keep and make relationships, to shape and change them. Whether or not you look like someone does not matter. People who are not related to you can be parents, siblings, aunts, uncles, grandparents, and cousins.

I have never pursued looking for my birth relatives. That decision has been based on the fact that I already have a family with its own set of problems, connections, relations, and dynamics. I had to ask myself if I wanted to pursue a situation which could have a huge effect on my life—so far No. Having the knowledge I do have about my birth family has satisfied my curiosity. I may change my mind in the future.

I do think about my birth mother and I wonder what it would have been like to have lots of brothers and sisters. Around my birthday, I find my thoughts turning to them. I desperately wish sometimes that I could tell her I am alive and happy. I would like to reassure her that she made the right decision. These thoughts have never made me act though.

—Michele, 28, California

Surveys of parents and teens in more than 700 adoptive families show that the large majority of adopted teens is doing very well; most score high on measures of mental health, as reported in *Growing Up Adopted*. (The authors maintain that theirs is the largest study ever done.)

—Andrea Bowman did her psychology thesis on adoptees (CSUC, 1995). Here are some of the comments of those who searched out their birth parents:

A void has been filled within me. I know the answers now to questions that had always bothered me such as who did I look like and what were the circumstances of my birth.

I always thought something was wrong with me 'cause I was so different. When I met my birth mom, sisters, and aunts, they were all just like me. Not just looks, but personality, intelligence, outlook on life, likes/dislikes, etc. I had NO idea genetics determined so much! Now I know I'm OK. I had been in counseling for five years until then. Now I'm very comfortable with myself.

I found it disturbing and confusing. My adoptive parents were educated and refined. My birth parents were backward. I question what future I would have had in that environment.

I found my father. It changes so much. You know a lot more of detail about yourself— why they gave you up, where you get your looks. Many questions are answered.

Resources for Adopted Children

**Adoptive Families of America
333 Hwy. 100 N.
Minneapolis, MN 55422**

**National Adoption Information
Clearinghouse 1-301-231-6512
11426 Rockville Pike, Suite 410
Rockville, MD 20852**

Peter Benson, et al. *Growing Up Adopted*. Minneapolis: Search Institute, 1994. (700 S. Third St., Minneapolis, MN 55415)

Advice to Parents from Teens

(also see values section)

Adults should let teens have fun and not make so many rules and remember what it was like for them. They should be open and let them make their own decisions, but they also need to make sure that they know what is going on with their kids. They should give them responsibility, but not too much, and they should help them when asked, not when they feel like intruding when the kid did not ask. I could be unrealistic and say stop yelling. [Lindsey adds, "Also remember times are a lot different now and more rules are needed."]

—Sarah, 14, Nebraska

The Search Institute found that children develop best when their parents are caring, take time to talk, are approachable, discuss school and attend school events, help with homework, have clear standards for behavior, set rules and enforce the consequences if the rule is broken, limit the number of nights a child is away from home, and encourage participation in activities including religious services (from *What Kids Need to Succeed*). A poll of 1,400 high school juniors and seniors reported that students think parents should provide more structure, as in making sure homework gets done ("Teens Want More Rules, Attention," *San Francisco Chronicle*, May 12, 1992).

Teens point out in surveys for this book that parents may find it difficult to change the balance of power as their children travel toward adulthood. It's like renegotiating a contract between management and workers every few years which must be done, or else the workers/teens will do what they want to behind management's back. Parents have to let go of some control, while continuing to discuss important values and family rules.

Pushing too hard can create the opposite affect. Carla's mother said she wished she'd told Carla to relax and enjoy high school rather than pushing for good grades. Carla doesn't get them, to assert her independence. Mom didn't make a big point about not having sex, and Carla is a virgin.

Power struggles also can be limited by picking your battles. My skater son wears saggy pants revealing his underwear, but the pants don't harm him and it's more important to me to struggle over his daily chores. His friends can tell me what's on their minds without being condemned, although I do speak up about the hazards of smoking or whatever. In order for teens to continue confiding in their parents, they need to trust they will be loved. I don't like some of the experimentation my son has done, but I'm glad he tells me so I can provide information. The consensus of parenting experts is that effective discipline or limit-setting emphasizes consequences rather than lectures which get tuned out in parent deafness syndrome. For example, if a teen comes home past her curfew, it gets reduced by a half-hour the next time. If a kid leaves a bike unlocked where it can be stolen, it gets confiscated for a day.

—Barbara Osborne, high school teacher, in Seattle, told me:

Many parents aren't providing much direction. Too many students seem to be aimless, wandering, empty, hopeless, trying to find some soul to fill the emptiness. Teens feel they are neither fish nor fowl, caught between being a kid and an adult. The media teach them they deserve immediate gratification with food, sex and drugs. A ton of kids are on Prozac and other anti-depressant drugs, which cause the brain to lose some its natural ability to create endorphins.

Parents surveyed for my book for employed parents advise other parents to be consistent, honest about their feelings, admit mistakes, and not try to be a super-parent. They feel it is important to discuss issues with children, to listen to their side, and to explain reasons for parental decisions. A mother relates, "Always, always, always, I tell Melanie that I may be mad about something she has done, but that I love her even if I don't love some of her actions." A father of teenagers is proud that, "They have been taught how to think and how to make good, sound decisions by themselves."

The kids interviewed for *50/50 Parenting* agree that effective parents are neither permissive nor authoritarian but consult with their children in setting limits and then stick to them. They are scornful of permissive parents and see them as uncaring. They also advise parents to give kids responsibility and not allow them to "goof off," talk to them about when you were a kid, don't yell, and use praise more than punishment. "Give them freedom to do things and let them make mistakes. If they don't, they can't learn from them," explained a 15-year-old boy. "Nourish their goodness," said an 18-year-old girl. Research confirms that children's self-esteem stems from parents' warmth and acceptance, consistent but not authoritarian discipline, and respect for individual differences.

—John, 15, Missouri

Parents should have general respect for their children and treat them as intelligent people. Parents should give their children trust UNTIL they do something to lose it. Parents should not ASSUME their children are bad. If they do something wrong, they should be given an opportunity to earn trust again. Respect is different from trust, as you should always respect your child no matter what he or she does.

—Emma, 15, California

My parents have given me and my brother a lot of freedom to make our own choices. They support our choices and they support our decisions no matter how much they disagree with them. We have learned to be responsible for our actions and deal with the consequences. I think this is a better way to parent than to force lessons upon us. Let us learn our own lessons.

—Jennifer, 16, Texas

The major issues facing teens today are probably sex (to have or not to have, and if so, then what sort of protection?) and AIDS. Other problems are relations between adults and teens, the feeling that the earth is doomed, violence, drugs, weapons, the numerous laws and new rules in the schools that don't really work but make us feel like prison convicts, the sad state of the schools, the sad state of the economy, higher living costs, higher taxes, and lower wages.

What should adults do to make these issues more positive? Well, the nightly news could stop telling us all about how many people died in gunfights the other day (like they'd do that). And the government could stop funding stupid programs like prison remodeling, and fund schools and rebuild neighborhoods instead (like they'd do that).

We all know this stuff isn't going to get better, just worse. The adults could get more into educating the kids. (I know someone who thought that it's OK to litter, but then he didn't see the picture of "The Dolphin's Stomach Contents Upon Death"—plastic bags and soda can rings and bottle tops and all kinds of stuff.) I know a lot of parents who don't read to their kids. My mom read to me a lot, and I eventually taught myself at the age of three. I think that's the main reason I'm as educated as I am. I keep applying, day after day, knowledge that I learned reading as a little kid.

I know a lot of parents who smack their kids. My parents used to spank me, but they realized, I guess, that all it was doing was making me violent and bitter, so they stopped.

—John, 16, Missouri

If I get in trouble for something, I lose my driving privileges for a week. I can't stand not being able to drive. I love to drive; it relaxes me. (I've also noticed people hang out with you more when you can drive them around.)

—Jed, 16, California

My mom and I have a very open relationship; I can tell her anything. I know many kids who, if they told their parents some of the stuff they had done, would get in trouble. Parents should listen and know experimenting is part of growing up—they did it too. Parents should be a little lenient with their kids so they can experience the world. I was blessed with parents like this, but have a lot of friends whose parents totally shelter them and when they are on their own, they won't know how to handle it. Also, it's so sad when a parent only notices and remembers the negative things. It can be really hard on a kid, but just know the positive things you've done and be glad about that.

—Peter, 18, Pennsylvania

The world is getting crazier and crazier. It doesn't seem that there is any one group that can be blamed for the many troubles facing teens and young children, but obviously, some of it goes to the parents. I see too many parents setting terrible examples for their children. Just showing your child how important it is to have manners and be respectful seems to be missing from many families. Parents swearing in front of—

and all too often at children, or setting an example of "ME, ME, ME," instead of helping others—things like these are what parents contribute to the problems of children.

Another major problem is family values, actually being a family. Parents often want to use the media as babysitter/entertainer/role models. Then they turn around and criticize the media. I feel that if families did more things together that require each member to actively participate, family strength could be restored. Rather than saying "Kids, if you're good, I am going to rent a movie for you," parents should be telling their children that if they behave, mom or dad will take them to the park or a ball game—something that will seem fun and adventurous to the child. It will teach them to be a participant in life at an early age rather than sitting back and watching life.

The greatest change that needs to be made is a seemingly simple one. There is even a song about it, "R-E-S-P-E-C-T, find out what it means to me." If children would have more respect for themselves and the world they live in, many trivial childhood problems would be avoided. This would help children deal with other more serious problems like illness or divorce.

—Amy, 21, California

I wish my parents had pushed me more in school. People in this country are given a chance. This chance is yours to do whatever you wish with it. You can push yourself to study more, eat right, work out, and be friendly with others to help you succeed and benefit yourself, or you can hate every step of the way and do it for someone else. You can achieve your goals if you have the will and try.

—Jan Ross, parent (posted on the Internet)

We have been taking a class called the Parent Project. They teach that you cannot control your child but you can control his/her things. They advocate making a list of all the things and activities that really matter to your child. When you need to "punish" them, take these things away for a short period of time (about three days). Even more important than "punishing" inappropriate behavior, is to reward appropriate behavior. It seems that is always forgotten. Make a list of all the things your children like, then do those things to reinforce what you would like them to do.

—Kelly Lynn Baylor, psychology graduate student, has welcomed many teenagers into her home as a mother, foster mother, and friend.

"Punishment" is a nasty word that no teenager wants to hear. Adults have rules about what we can and can't do, too. The usual punishment for teens is restriction, but that doesn't work for either the parents or the child. The parents end up with a miserable, sulky teenager around the house (let's face it, you do make their lives miserable in that situation). You end up losing your freedom—not a good solution for either of you.

I figure if we can give criminals a second chance, why not our own kids? I call this system "probation." The teenager has a choice between restriction and probation, although I have never had a kid choose restriction once they have a chance for probation. Then the parent decides how long restriction should be. Let's say you blew your curfew and got in late, so your parent gives you a week of restriction. Probation is double the amount of restriction time, so probation would be two weeks.

During the probation period the teen cannot for ANY reason make the mistake that got him or her in trouble. For example, he must be home on time, with no reminders and no excuses, for the whole two-week period. If she blows it, the original punishment takes place, but if she makes it through the probation period, then the original punishment never happens.

This punishment is about responsibility. It lets you dig yourself out of a hole (a skill you will definitely need later in life) by taking responsibility for your actions. It works for the parents because they are paying attention to and correcting the very behavior you blew. It takes some of the "butting heads" out of the parent-child relationship by putting the responsibility right where it belongs, on the person who broke the rules. (A good book is Denise Chapman Weston's *Playful Parenting*, Tarcher/Putnam.)

Resources for Parents of Teens

(see also parent involvement section in Chapter 7)

The Parents' Music Resource Center
1500 Arlington Blvd.
Arlington, VA 22209
(from grades 6 to 12, youths average 11,000 hours listening to rock music)

National Parenting Association
65 Central Park, W., Suite 1D
New York, NY 10023
(NPA started in 1993 to provide parents with information and to organize. Task forces include prevention of youth violence and how to involve fathers with their children, etc.)

Carol Eagle. *All That She Can Be: Helping Your Daughter Maintain Her Self-Esteem*. NY: Simon and Schuster, 1993.

David Elkind. *Parenting Your Teen*. NY: Ballantine, 1994.

Sheila Fuller and L. Rudd. *The Parents' Pipeline Guide, 1994*. (P.O. Box 11037, Greenwich, CT 06831-1037.)

Jeanette Gadeberg. *Raising Strong Daughters*. Minneapolis, MN: Fairview Press, 1995.

George Gallup. Scared: *Growing Up in America and What the Experts Say Parents Can Do About It*. Ridgefield, CT: Morehouse, 1996.

George Homes. *Helping Teenagers into Adulthood: A Guide for the Next Generation*. Westport, CT: Praeger, 1995.

Myriam Miedzian. *Boys will be Boys*. NY: Doubleday, 1991.

Tom McMahon. *Teen Tips: A Practical Survival Guide for Parents with Kids 11-19*. NY: Pocket Books, 1996.

Linda Meyer. *Teenspeak: A Bewildered Parent's Guide to Teenagers*. Princeton, NJ: Peterson's Guide, 1994.

Michael Riera. *Uncommon Sense for Parents with Teenagers*. Berkeley, CA: Celestial Arts, 1995.

Jacqueline Shannon. *Why It's Great to Be a Girl: 50 Eye-Opening Things You Can Tell Your Daughter to Increase Her Pride in Being Female*. NY: Warner Books, 1994.

Olga Silverstein and Beth Rashbaum. *The Courage to Raise Good Men*. NY: Viking/Penguin, 1994.

Laurence Steinberg and Ann Levine. *You and Your Adolescent: A Parent's Guide for Ages 10-20*. NY: Harper, 1990.

Nick Stinnett. *Good Kids: How You and Your Kids can Successfully Navigate the Teen Years*. NY: Doubleday, 1996.

Anthony Wolf. *Get Out of My Life, But First Could You Drive Me and Cheryl to the Mall?: A Parent's Guide to the New Teenager*. NY: Noonday Press, 1991.

Bettie Youngs. *Safeguarding your Teenager from the Dragons of Life: A Parent's Guide to the Adolescent Years*. Deerfield Beach, FL: Health Communications, 1993.

Kidsrights 1-800-892-KIDS (resources for parents and professionals who work with children and youth)

For Fathers

We're seeing increasing interest in studying fathers' interaction with their children and encouraging fathers to stay involved with their children after divorce. A major issue facing families today is children's lack of contact with their fathers: The average amount of one-to-one contact is less than 30 minutes a day, according to Professor Henry Biller. About 30 percent of our families are headed by a single parent, usually the mother. Almost one in three babies is born to an unmarried mother, although these figures may be inflated by counting married women who keep their maiden name as single. About 40 percent of the children who live in single mother families haven't seen their fathers in at least a year and only about a third see their fathers an average of once or more each week. Organized movements are underway to support fathers, as listed in the resource section.

How to Be an Involved Father

Over 300 parents who share parenting equally (interviewed for *50/50 Parenting*) explain their techniques.

✪ Appreciate that men and women have different parenting styles and that one is not better than another. Women are not innate authorities on parenting; it's not instinctual or otherwise child abuse wouldn't exist.

✪ Participate in a class or support group of fathers, without women in the group.

✪ Structure regular activities such as driving kids to activities, bedtime rituals, and cooking Sunday dinner together.

✪ Turn off the television.

✪ Talk with your own father about parenting.

✪ Cut back on time spent at work and make time with family a top priority.

✪ Speak up for changes at the workplace, such as flexible work hours, noontime parent education workshops and support groups, and time off to volunteer in schools.

Fatherhood Organizations

American Fathers' Coalition
2000 Pennsylvania Ave., NW,
Suite 148
Washington, DC 20006
afc@capaccess.orghttp://www.erols.
com/afc
(AFC is an umbrella organization of
fathers' groups throughout the country whose primary purpose is to promote positive father-inclusive
policies.)

Children's Rights Council
220 Eye St., NE, Suite 230
Washington, DC 20002-4362
(provides information and resources
about joint custody and divorced
fathers' and children's rights)

Father-to-Father (men helping each
other, started by Al Gore)
Children, Youth, and Family
Consortium
University of Minnesota,
12 McNeal Hall
St. Paul, MN 55108
To get a Community Starter Kit, call
1-612-626-1212
http://www.cyfc.umn.edu/
FatherNet.htp

The Father Policy Institute, Family
Resource Coalition
200 S. Michigan Ave., 16th Floor
Chicago, IL 60604
(Studies public policy impact on low-
income fathers, such as state welfare
laws, and provides technical assistance to service agencies. Fathers can
call for referral to agencies.)

Fatherhood Project, Families and
Work Institute
330 Seventh Ave., 14th Floor
New York, NY 10001
(provides information about how to
create a father-friendly workplace
and involve men in early childhood
education)

Joint Custody Association
10606 Wilkins Avenue
Los Angeles, CA 90024

National Congress for Fathers and
Children 1-800-733-DADS.
(Provides educational material on joint
custody and fathers' rights after
divorce, local chapters, a computer
information bank of case laws, and
telephone advice from board members.)
The E-mail address for FREE, equality
exchange for fathers' rights, is
shedevil@vix.com. Type JOIN FREE
<your name> in the subject line and
in the body of the text.
The National Coalition of Free Men
can be joined by e-mailing a request
to ncfm@liii.com. Their web site is
www.ncfm.org

National Fatherhood Initiative
1-800-790-DADS
www.register.com/father
(Membership provides a
newsletter, discount on fathering
resources, conferences, "Father
Facts" brochure, and a media
information kit.)

*Modern Dad, for a New Generation of
Fathers* magazine
7628 N. Rogers Ave.
Chicago, IL 60626-1214

Balance Magazine:
http://www.agt.net/public/
dolphin
The Fathers' Advocate:
guympall@freenet.edmonton.ab.ca

Child Abuse and Neglect

> *The most difficult challenge I faced as a teen was being molested by my cousin's husband. Tell someone right away even though the person told you not to say anything, or said, "It's our little secret, nobody has to know about what's going on between us." Whatever you do, don't keep it to yourself; it will just eat you up inside and eventually you'll spill your guts. Tell somebody.*
> —Corinna, 16, North Dakota

Child abuse is an act that harms a child's physical or emotional health and development. *Time* magazine reported 850,000 proven cases of child abuse or neglect in 1992. Each day 8,189 children are reported abused or neglected in America and a child dies of neglect or abuse every seven hours. The levels of child abuse and neglect more than doubled from 1986 to 1993. "Violence toward very young children has reached the level of a public health crisis, and is similar in scope to the destruction of teenagers by street gunfire" (The U.S. Advisory Board on Child Abuse and Neglect 1995 report, "A Nation's Shame").

Sad Facts

* Nineteen percent of youth ages 11 to 17 report they or someone close to them had suffered from scars, broken bones, or bleeding caused by an adult and 15 percent say they know someone who has been sexually abused (1995 national study by Kaiser Permanente and Children Now).

* Almost three million kids were abused and neglected in 1994 (triple the number of reports in 1980) and 2,000 of them were killed.

* Every 26 seconds a child runs away from home.

* Every 53 minutes a child dies from poverty.

* Every two hours a child is murdered, according to the Children's Defense Fund.

Most victims know the perpetrator of the abuse. Four kinds of abuse are physical, sexual, emotional, and neglect. Verbal abuse usually includes frequent criticism, name calling, belittling, humiliation, and emotional blackmail as tools to keep the abuser in control and feeling powerful.

Child sexual abuse refers to sexual activities involving a child and an adult or significantly older child. It includes rape, incest (sexual contact between relatives), molestation, indecent exposure, and child pornography. The Department of Justice estimates that pornographers make between $2 and $3 billion a year. Most of their victims are between eight and 16.

One of every four girls and one of every seven boys will be a victim of sexual assault before their 18th birthday. The peak age for abuse is between ages seven and 13. In 1991, there were 405,000 reports of child sexual abuse. About half the sexual abuse cases are incestual. Threats and bribes keep children from telling anyone and they are often told it is their fault. Many abusers were themselves abused as children in an ongoing cycle of abuse. Most offenders are heterosexual men whom the child knows as a family member or friend of the family. Some abusers are adolescents.

Abuse is more likely to occur in families where alcohol and drugs interfere with parents' better judgment and in families who live in stressful conditions, such as poverty and unemployment. A majority of wife beaters also abuses their children. A large majority of prostitutes, runaways, male criminals, and about a third of women prisoners, were abused as children. A 1989 study reported that half the adults admitted to a mental health facility had a history of sexual abuse. Recent studies find that a majority of women in treatment for drug abuse suffered sexual abuse as children.

Almost half of abuse victims never told anyone, according to a national survey by Patterson and Kim. Often children repress and forget their memories of abuse until something triggers the memories as they get older. Some suffer from post-traumatic stress disorder, similar to war veterans or survivors of disasters. Victims of child sexual abuse may feel helpless, guilty, angry, depressed, blame themselves, and have low self-esteem. Some become drug abusers, develop eating disorders, or become sexually promiscuous (many sexual partners). This problem is too overwhelming to handle alone; most victims of child sexual abuse need professional counseling to work through the pain and shame.

Because of child abuse, over 400,000 children are in the child welfare system. As the need for foster homes increases, however, the number of people willing to serve as foster parents has declined. In many states the amount paid to foster parents is less than the cost of boarding a dog in a kennel, another example of the low value actually placed on care for children.

Some states provide parent education and support programs for parents. Hawaii's PREP Program, Missouri's Parents As Teachers, Minnesota's Early Childhood Family Education Program, Maryland's Family Support Centers, and Connecticut's Parent Support Centers are useful models for other states.

Teens who are "resilient," who do well despite difficult family situations, usually have at least one healthy adult who cares about them and is available to provide support. If you or a friend suffers from abuse, you must speak up and get help. You may want to start with one of the hotlines to learn about resources in your area.

—Dana, 21, California

When I was a junior in high school, I started having flashbacks of incidents in my life that I had blocked out. My frail, frightened mind had shut out the memories of molestation when I was three to five years old. Through a series of haunting dreams and disturbing flashbacks, I rediscovered the pains of my childhood. I really don't know what triggered my memories. I think that I finally came to a point where I could handle the information. I believe God knew exactly when He wanted to pull me through these deep wounds. Also, I had just become very good friends with my current husband.

Along with the memories, the feelings of loneliness, fear, filthiness, and guilt revisited me. Another struggle was that no one in my life knew, not my parents or anyone, and the fear of them finding out became overwhelming. It's so strange that when I saw other kids on TV who'd been molested, I could see them as victims, without blame, without looking at them as "dirty." But, when it came to me, I could not remove the sick, dirty feelings.

The man who did these things to me was a very intelligent, well-liked professional who loved kids and happened to be dating my mother. My biological father left my mom before I was born and this was the first man she dated since then. He must have seemed safe because he truly doted on my brother and me. I feel sad because my mom worked so hard during those years to provide for us; the sacrifices she made were incredible. She broke up with him one year later because he was selfish. He fits the classic pedophile type perfectly. [A pedophile is a sick person sexually attracted to children. These men can be very charming and skilled in getting children to trust them or scare them into not telling about the sexual abuse.]

When I was six, my mom married my stepdad, a wonderful, loving, supportive man who truly is my daddy! I feel I had a wonderful upbringing and never wanted to hurt my folks with this information. If I thought it would really help my healing, of course, I'd tell them. My mom would probably suffer unnecessary guilt over it. She worked too hard back then for me to put her through that.

Two things really assisted the healing process in my life. One was my best friend (now my husband). For three years he was the only one who knew. He was so great it helped me fall in love with him. I met my husband in junior high, but we did not become good friends until we were 16. We started dating at 17 and 18. It is a super friendship and a wonderfully satisfying marriage. We've grown up together and love each other very deeply. I know he'd do anything for me.

The other thing, and most important, was my relationship and faith in God. As a Christian, I believe in Jesus as my Savior. He really did save me from the evils acted out on my small body. He helped me to forgive the sick man who did it, and saved me (through the Bible and prayer) from my own sexuality becoming perverse. I now have a very healthy sexuality and understand that I was a victim. I believe that part of why this happened to me was so I could help some of the millions of still-hurting, still-bitter people who have suffered the same trauma.

I worked out the vocalization of pain and crying through the memories during prayer time. I felt that talking to God about my hurts was a very freeing experience. Bitterness is more a hindrance than an empowerment. That will always be a part of who I am but it does not have to control how I am!

I recommend that youths with similar experiences seek out someone to confide in. Some friends may disappoint you, but don't give up; someone will listen, will cry with you, will pray with you if you so desire. School counselors, teachers, and parents are usually the wisest choices. Very few classmates have the maturity to really help you but there are exceptions—I am living proof. Also, don't lose hope when it's hard; life is hard but you can overcome the anger, rage, and pain.

—Isabella, 21, California

I wish someone had told me that past family life doesn't necessarily doom your future. I used to beat myself up about what a loser I was and that I would never amount to anything because I'd had such a crummy family life. You make the choices that determine where you're going in life—not your family, your childhood, or your past mistakes.

—Bryar, 25, Canada

The most difficult issue I faced as a teen was that I was abused physically, sexually, and emotionally by my mother. This is still a topic that receives almost no exposure, and it shows no sign of changing. When you are not believed it is upsetting to say the least.

I had many unhealthy coping mechanisms. What really got me through was stubbornness, and a belief that what was happening to me was for real. Despite the preaching of "professionals," I knew I wasn't making it up. My advice to someone younger would be to tell and keep on telling. I found someone who believed me.

—Jim, 29, California

My mother became pregnant with me at the age of 15. My father was 18 at my birth. He became an alcoholic, a heroin user, womanizer, and a wife abuser. My mother, after three years of his actions, left him. Unfortunately, she left my brother, who was four months old, and me with him. He was very abusive, mentally and physically. He stabbed me, threw lit cigarettes at me, beat me, put lit cigarettes near my eye, and held the back of my head. He used to laugh so hard when he moved his hand and I fell to the ground.

Eight years later my mother found us and had my brother and me come out to California for the summer. We came out here and were told we were not going back to New York. This was good news for me. When I was about 15, I got involved in the Police Explorers, a youth group organization run by the Boy Scouts for teenagers interested in law enforcement.

My mother began to feel threatened by the amount of time I was spending with other Police Explorers, both male and female. My success in school was a threat to her as well, because she only finished the 9th grade. She became very jealous. She began to restrict my travel and impose mandatory attendance at dinner. The tension became very great and I expressed this tension to my friends and their parents. I received three offers by these parents to have me move in with their families. I was not only flattered, I accepted one of the offers.

My mother told me I could go and I began to pack my bags. At the time the police department had a psychologist, who knew my mother and me because of my brother's arrests. She stepped in and told my mother to back off and suggested I tough it out for two years. At 16, two years is one-eighth of your life, a very long time. Her points to stay were valid, i.e., my own room and not imposing on another family. I unpacked my bags and my mother and I gave each other space.

My suggestion to teens is to stay focused on the goal of staying at home until you have a job that can sustain you. The teenage years are short, despite appearances. Being on your own can force you to make decisions that have negative repercussions. I know this through the young people I see on the street as a police officer. Many found themselves easy prey for the vultures of our society, the pimps and drug dealers.

—Rosie (posted on the Internet)

I was raped at eight years old by my godfather and it continued until I was 12 because my mother and father thought my godfather was such a wonderful person. My mother beat me when I told her he was a bad man. Also, my parents believed "Children are to be seen and not heard" and children were also "natural born liars." He was such a GOOD man in her eyes. He bought me candy, toys, took me places, and he LOVED me— what a BAD little girl I was! This is the very first poem I ever wrote. I got the idea to write it after a walk against domestic violence.

> "Breaking In"
> To some having their house broken into was traumatic.
> The trauma to me was that my body was broken into.
> For others they had their family or friends or the police to turn to.
> Whom did I have to turn to? I had no one to turn to.
> People listen and look with awe and say "Oh, my, your house was broken into."
> For me, what did they say? "Is that true? I find that hard to believe."
> Well, it is true; I didn't lie.
> My body was broken into by my godfather.
> From the house they stole TVs, VCRs, stereos, and other material values.
> From my body he tried to steal my heart and soul; these are my values.
> He may have got them for a while.
> He only got them from me when I was a child.
> Now I have grown to adulthood and can fight back.
> I'm getting my heart and soul back, and I'm gaining lots of new values.
> How do I buy back my heart and soul and all my other stolen values?
> With my insurance, of course. The insurance that people will listen and care.
> The insurance that it wasn't stolen, just lost. I'm finding it all over.

—Kelly Lynn Baylor tells her story of abuse.

I know the pain of abuse firsthand. I was physically, sexually, and emotionally abused as a child. My abuse was horrendous, and although I have worked very hard in therapy to transcend the abuse, I must live with the consequences every day of my life. My body is covered with scars from cigarette burns and cuts, and today I use a wheelchair to get around because of brain damage suffered from the abuse. But, with the help of therapy, I have built a wonderful life for myself.

Abuse falls into four categories that may overlap. First, there is deprivational abuse. Parents are required to provide a clean place for their children, to feed them, provide clean clothes that are warm enough for the season, and provide medical care if needed. If any of these basic elements are missing, it can be considered neglect, which is a form of abuse.

The second category of abuse is emotional abuse. This is when a parent or significant adult makes frequent demeaning or hurtful statements to a child. If an adult you care about is constantly telling you: "You're worth nothing," "You'll never amount to anything," or "If only you'd never been born," this is emotional abuse. Words can hurt and they do make a lasting impression.

The third category is physical abuse. According to the law, physical abuse is leaving a mark on the child or causing injury to that child. You are past the age of being spanked, so an adult should NEVER touch you in anger. If you are being hurt, it is NOT your fault and there is NEVER a valid excuse for hurting you. (Many times abused children are left with touch deprivation for a lifetime because they didn't get enough nurturing touches from their parents; to satisfy this need, nurture pets or plants, sleep with stuffed animals, and wear clothes that feel good to touch like the inside of a sweatshirt).

The last kind of abuse is sexual abuse to which teenagers seem particularly vulnerable. I want to say this loud and clear—it is NEVER OK for an adult to touch you in your private areas or request that you touch theirs! I don't care if you are prancing around with very little on and acting like Madonna, you are not responsible for enticing an adult. It is ALWAYS up to the adult to set the limits and maintain the boundaries. The appropriate response in the example I gave is for the adult to say, "Go put some clothes on and stop acting like that." The sexual feelings you have at this age are natural and normal. It is not OK for an adult to take advantage of them.

It is very common for a child to think that abuse happens only to the next guy and that my parents must have a good reason for doing what they are doing. If an adult is hurting you in any of the ways I have described, then you are being abused, and it is NOT your fault. Abuse is NEVER, and I do mean NEVER, the child's fault!

If you are being abused, it is very important that you get some help. Talk to someone you trust about what is happening, preferably an adult. Now that I have said that, there are some things you need to know about what can happen when you do that. Too many teens I have worked with have been caught by surprise by what happens after they talk to someone.

Certain adults are "mandated reporters." Under the requirements of the law, the adult must report it if they suspect abuse or if they are told about abuse. They have no choice in the matter. These are adults who are in official positions that deal with children, like teachers, doctors, and counselors. Mandated reporters make a complaint to child protective service workers who investigate the complaint, with their primary intent being to find the truth and help the child. However, their investigation can have negative consequences for teenagers.

If the caseworkers feel the case is serious enough they may take you out of the home and put you in a foster home. Although every attempt is made to put you in a foster home near your school and friends, this may not happen. I am telling you all of this not to discourage you from getting help, as I am an adamant supporter of reaching out for help, but because you need to know what will happen and have that play into your decision.

If you are being abused, running away from home, using drugs, or committing suicide to stop the pain, are NOT the answers to the problem of abuse. If you feel you cannot take it any more and are considering running away or committing suicide, then please reach out for help. There are phone numbers in this section that can put you in touch with caring people who will help. You do not have access to money and there are people out there who will take advantage of that fact and hurt you more. Committing suicide is final. It will end the pain of the abuse but it will also end all the possibilities of a wonderful future.

When I was younger I tried running away from home and I tried suicide, but thank God, I did not succeed! I was able to find a therapist who genuinely cared. He was able to help me not only learn to live with the pain of my life but to turn it around and use it as a positive force in my life. I do have to live with the physical realities I was left with, but I also get to laugh and experience joy in a way I never knew was possible. Now I am an honors graduate student, studying to become a counselor to teenagers in trouble. I have a wonderful grown son and many other kids I have helped raise.

There is a life after the abuse and you can have it too. You may have to fight for it, and get some help finding it, but it can be yours. Having been abused is not a life sentence of pain and agony. The world can be yours for the taking once you get help. A wonderful man once helped keep me alive with this hopeful bit of wisdom: "I want you to know that all you have to do is grow up and your life will be your own."

Hotlines for Abused Youth

Believe the Children (Child sexual/ritual abuse)
1-708-515-5432
(referral to support groups)

Childhelp National Child Abuse Hotline 1-800-4-A-CHILD

ChildLine: Abuse Hotline
1-800-932-0313

Kid Save 1-800-543-7283
(information and referrals for adolescents in crisis)

National Clearinghouse on Child Abuse and Neglect
1-800-394-3366

The National Child Abuse Helpline
1-800-422-4453

National Committee to Prevent Child Abuse 1-800-CHILDREN
(for new parents)

National Organization for Victim Assistance 1-800-TRY-NOVA

National Resource Center on Child Sexual Abuse 1-800-KIDS-006

National Resource Center on Child Abuse 1-800-227-5242

Nine Line 1-800-999-9999 (general questions and help)

Parents Anonymous 1-800-421-0353 and in California
1-800-352-0368 (for parents who feel out of control with their children)

Windgate Internet home page:
http://home.aol.com/jmwindgate
(links for reporting child abuse, sexual abuse, sexual harassment)

Organizations to Prevent and Treat Child Abuse

Believe the Children
P. O. Box 797
Cary, IL 60013

C. Henry Kempe National Center for the Prevention and Treatment of Child Abuse and Neglect
1205 Oneida St.
Denver, CO 80220

International Cult Education Program
129 E. 182nd St.
New York, NY

National Committee for Prevention of Child Abuse
332 S. Michigan Ave., Suite 1600
Chicago, IL 60604-4357

National Organization on Male Sexual Victimization
918 S. Front St.
Columbus, OH 43206

National Resource Center on Child Sexual Abuse
107 Lincoln St.
Huntsville, AL 35801

Groups for Incest Survivors

VOICES in Action, Inc. (Victims of Incest Can Emerge Survivors)
1-800-786-4238
(provides referrals and a newsletter)

Incest Survivors Enlightened and
Empowered
P.O. Box 82,
Milton, VT 05468-3524
(a newsletter, resource and
referral service)

Incest Survivors Anonymous
P.O. Box 5613
Long Beach, CA 90805-0613

Incest Survivors Resource Network,
International
P.O. Box 7375
Las Cruces, NM 88006-7375

Survivors of Female Incest Emerge!
P.O. Box 2794
Renton, WA 98056-0794

Books About Child Abuse

Womontyme Distribution Co.
P.O. Box 50145-CIP
Long Beach, CA 90815-6145
(The *Helping Hands Catalog*
offers books and tapes including
sexual assault, incest, domestic violence, codependency, multiple personality disorder, and ritual abuse.)

Louise Armstrong. *Rocking the Cradle of
Sexual Politics: What Happened When
Women Said Incest*. Reading, MA:
Addison-Wesley, 1994. (The author tells
what happened since she broke the
silence around incest with her autobio-
graphical book *Kiss Daddy Goodnight*.)

Ellen Bass and Laura Davis. *The
Courage to Heal*. NY: Harper and Row,
1988. A workbook was
published in 1990.

Suzette Haden Elgin. *You Can't Say
That to Me! Stopping the Pain of
Verbal Abuse*. NY: John Wiley and
Sons, 1995.

Mike Lew. *Victims No Longer*. NY:
Harper and Row, 1990.

Domestic Violence

I was almost 10 when my father began to physically abuse my mother in my presence. When it began, I was so in shock that I couldn't do anything but watch my mother go down. The second time I saw him hurt her was about a week later and I decided that I had to do something about my situation. My father never really abused me although I was always afraid that he would.

I used to look up to my father. I thought he was the most intelligent man in the world. I also thought that my parents were the perfect couple, so I tried to pretend that it didn't happen the first time. My life was too perfect. I had no responsibility other than school, and I knew that little girls should not have to go through what I went through.

When I was 13, I developed an ulcer. By that time, I was dealing with the beatings about every two or three weeks. I started going through phases where I would only drink liquids for a month because my stomach could not handle any more pressure.

I was a cheerleader in junior high and in high school and I am now a cheerleader in college. My brother is a star football and baseball player. Even my closest friends thought that I had the perfect family. I guess I hid it extremely well. The first time I told anyone that my mother was a battered woman was about a year and a half ago.

What I hated most about the whole ordeal was when my father would hit my mother, I would be deathly afraid to try to stop him. And I hated myself for fearing him so much when my mother needed my help. My mother would always tell me to run, but I would always find a way to stop him. Once I told him to beat me instead because it hurt me less than seeing him hurt my mother. When that didn't work, I told him that I hated him. For this, he threw me up against a wall. I was right; it did not hurt me as much.

When I was a junior in high school, after the divorce, I began to see a therapist. She was fun to talk to, but she didn't help. There was nothing she told me that I had not learned on my own through experience. As an observer, a lot of things seem more clear to me than they may seem to others. I can spot an abusive relationship a mile away. I plan on doing something in the future to help victims in this situation. I'm also deathly afraid of becoming a victim. Because of this fear, I am often too skeptical about relationships. I am afraid that I have somehow been psychologically damaged by what has happened without my knowledge. I am afraid of somehow damaging my future children.

—Toneka, 19, California

Acts of domestic violence occur every 18 seconds in the U.S. Domestic violence is the major cause of injury to women, more so than auto accidents. Watching music videos may illustrate the cultural message that aggressive men dominate clinging women, even chain them or throw them around. From three-to-four million women are the victims of domestic violence each year and one-third of murdered women are killed by a husband or boyfriend, according to the Justice Department.

Strangers commit less than one-quarter of the assaults against women. Poor women ages 19 to 29 are most likely to be assaulted, but men are also victims of domestic violence. If you or a friend faces this problem, you might start by calling an 800 phone line to find out how to get help.

Resources to End Domestic Violence

Domestic Violence Hotline
1-800-333-7233

Family Service Association
1-800-221-2681

National Council on Child Abuse and Family Violence
1-800-222-2000

National Family Violence Helpline
1-800-222-2000

National Coalition Against Domestic Violence
1-800-799-SAFE

National Coalition Against Sexual Assault
P.O. Box 21378
Washington, DC 20009

Barrie Levy. Skills for a Violence-Free Relationship: Curriculum for Young People. Southern California Coalition on Battered Women, P.O. Box 5036, Santa Monica, CA 90405

Counseling

I had to learn that my parents are who they are and I am who I am. Counseling helps you to understand you are a good person and you are OK. It helps you build your self-esteem and learn how to do things the healthy way.

—Jennifer, 18, California

Just as athletes have coaches and musicians have music teachers, many of us need to learn how to talk about our feelings with a trained communication expert—a counselor. Otherwise our unconscious patterns influence our choices in irrational ways. In families we often get in ruts, replaying an old tape over and over, and may need a neutral outsider to show us how to change our behaviors and approach conflicts. Counseling is not for crazy people but for people wise enough to get a coach. To find a therapist, ask your school counselor, clergyperson, or friends who have gone to a good counselor. Some groups offer low-cost counseling for teens. Group counseling often works well for teens.

Some Questions to Interview Counselors to Find the Right One

1. What is the fee? Is insurance or Medicare accepted? Sliding fee scale? Can you meet in person at no cost to interview him or her?

2. What kind of therapy is most often used (behavioral, cognitive, play therapy, etc.)? What experience does the therapist have treating your kind of situation? Some specialize in abuse issues, eating disorders, or drug treatment. What training does the therapist have?

3. How soon can you schedule an appointment? Do your schedules fit? Is the therapist available to talk over the phone?

—Jill, 21, California

I was terrified to start therapy. At the same time, I was desperate and not getting any better. It had become too much to handle alone. I recommend speaking to a professional as soon as possible. I was molested as a child by an uncle. It happened on two occasions.

Don't be afraid to ask the therapist questions. Be picky. What are their focuses and experiences? What techniques do they use? Where do they stand on privacy issues? I wished I had asked more questions. I really didn't know what to expect. At my first appointment the therapist asked me what was happening and why I was there. She also went through paper work and some of her policies. I was as honest as I could be at that stage of my self-disclosure. I told her about my depression and the molestation. The first few sessions were uncomfortable, but not as bad as I had expected. We tried to get a feel for each other's style of communication.

At times it is difficult for me because I tell my therapist personal things and I need the affection a mother gives. To help me she can only get emotionally attached to a certain point. I am her client first and foremost. I need to give her time and room to help me. She is a wonderful resource and reference point.

I found a couple of things to be useful in my therapy. Write important points down that you have learned through reading, a group, or a therapist. Write down questions and feelings that are unclear, to share with the professional. Involve your parents if possible; it will help the family to be educated on this issue. My parents pay for my therapy but are not really involved.

Sometimes I leave therapy feeling relieved. Sometimes I leave a session feeling hopeless (this seldom happens). Until actually receiving counseling I would have never expected the degree of dedication required. It is full of ups and downs for me. I also feel frustrated a lot. It is natural to realize that my progress will move forward and back. That is part of learning. Remember to be patient with yourself and take a lot of breaks (walking, reading, movies, etc.). Take one day at a time. Treasure small triumphs because they will eventually add up to a huge triumph.

—Amy, 22, Washington, DC

I think the most important thing to tell teenagers is that therapy isn't just for crazy people. I think we all need therapy to one degree or another. So many young adults nowadays have so many issues that they are dealing with and they keep them all locked up inside; it isn't until later they realize they need to be dealt with.

It wasn't until I was in college that I started to deal with my mother's death. It was then that I decided to go into therapy. I had a lot of guilt surrounding my mom's death, and I wasn't able to let go of any of that until I admitted that I wasn't crazy just because I was seeing a therapist. It wasn't until then that I could really work on my issues.

My mother died of cancer when I was 16. This has probably had the greatest impact on me so far in my life. I grew up in a family where no one showed emotions, everything was just OK all the time. When my mom died, a friend suggested therapy to me, but that was completely out of the question. I didn't want anyone to think I was crazy! I had no natural supports around me to get me through this experience. I had to do it on my own, which led me into sexual promiscuity, drugs and alcohol, and depression.

—Alanna, 22, California

Getting along with my parents when I was a teen was the hardest. We fought over friends, school, boyfriends, and colleges my senior year. To cope, I started going to a psychologist to help me work through a lot of things. My advice would be to find someone you can talk to, either a friend, adult, or therapist.

—Topher, 24, California

My father died when I was 16. He had a massive heart attack. That tore me up for a long time. I was the oldest child, so I had to stay strong to help my mom. It was devastating for her too. I went to counseling for several months. Don't think that it's not macho to go to counseling. Those people helped me through a really tough time.

—Elizabeth BeMiller, California

(The mother of 17-year-old Heidi explains what they learned about communication from a counselor.)

Through referrals from our local school, we found a youth services clinician, Sandy, to work with us. At first my daughter, Heidi, worked with her to discuss her own issues and to establish if she could trust her. After several sessions, I was invited to join them. I was both excited and anxious—excited at the opportunity to communicate, and anxious about revealing my iceberg [her unspoken unconscious feelings].

Instead of my usual, "You should have ..." or "How could you ...?" I acknowledged Heidi by looking directly at her, paying close attention, and nodding to signal that I was with her. I validated her by paraphrasing what I heard her say. She expressed that she wasn't trying to take away my control (by sneaking out of her window at 2:00 a.m.) but needed to help a friend get home. I acknowledged that she had not intended to disobey the rules and that it was important to help her friend. When she heard me feed back what she had said, she faced me with more interest and elaborated with more of the circumstances. Clearly she felt my response demonstrated that her feelings were real and had validity.

As I was describing my values, perceptions, and intentions, we uncovered the primary unexpressed feeling—FEAR. With difficulty, I explained that the pain I carried related to substance abuse. I described how it felt to endure the substance abuse by Heidi's father that led to his eventual suicide. I described the pain from my son's long separation from the family, the uncertainty of never knowing whether he was alive or dead, and the damage done by his heroin dependency. For the first time, I was able to realize and express that underneath my anger with Heidi was the fear that I would lose her too. At that moment a momentous shift occurred.

Heidi helped me to understand how my fears, expectations, and suspicions affected her. She noted that she was an "A" student, an all-league athlete, and a performer in the university symphonic band. She asserted that she shouldn't be compared to her family members. I acknowledged what she said and empathized again by saying, "It must be difficult when I'm on your back constantly."

Then, while uncovering a big chunk of my iceberg, I realized Heidi's achievements were raising my fears. Heidi's father, in his early 20s, functioned at a high level also. I realized Heidi's brother was a gifted and talented student in grammar school before gradually losing interest in school and dropping out. Because alcohol and drugs were prominent in her father's and brother's demise, I linked Heidi's achievements and party behavior to an anticipation of repeated pain.

By continuing to uncover each other's iceberg, Heidi and I were able to agree to some responsibilities. Heidi, after listening with new ears to the family background, was willing to take a step toward assessing her use of substances. After attending several weekly teen meetings devoted to information about substance abuse and self-analysis, she made the decision to adopt her own program. She enlisted the support of her friends in respecting her decision not to drink. She also called upon me for support, primarily for acknowledging her progress and listening to the challenges she was experiencing.

I agreed, when relating to her, to work at separating our past history with other family members. Also, I agreed to give her more freedom out of respect for the level of accomplishment and sense of responsibility she demonstrated. Now I'm finding it much easier to acknowledge, validate, and empathize because I'm not carrying the burden of responsibility for her behavior—she is.

Resources for Families

Independent Order of Foresters
1-800-922-4-IOF (Canada
1-800-268-6267)
(a fraternal benefit society that provides information on coping with family stress and effective parenting)

KidsPeace 1-800-25-PEACE
(resource material and referrals for family crisis)

Carolyn Foster. *The Family Patterns Workbook*. NY: Tarcher/Perigee,1993.

Kimberly Wood Gooden. *Coping with Family Stress*. NY: Rosen, 1989.

Joyce Vedral. *My Parents Are Driving Me Crazy*. NY: Ballantine, 1989.

Death of a
Family Member

(For resources, see the grief section in Chapter 2.)

> *My mother drowned five months ago on a trip to Mexico. I really can't talk about my problems with anyone, because I just break down crying. But I can talk to my brother because he has the same issues. I miss her a lot, but I guess it was her time to go, and someday it will be my time. This pain will be inside me forever, so I will just have to work through it step by step, day by day. I feel her spirit, like when I see a butterfly, because she liked them a lot and so do I.*
>
> **—Morgan, 13, California**

—Amy, 21, Michigan

The biggest challenge I faced as a teen was the death of my father. He died of a sudden heart attack when I was 13. Although my parents divorced, my father and I were fairly close. I took the loss badly and sort of diverted my attention from growing up and onto death. I became fascinated with death of all kinds. The effort to join my carefree friends was hard and I still haven't reached that goal. They all seemed petty and cheap. That was the challenge I faced—coping with death, my separateness from my friends, and how in the world I fit into the big picture.

What helped me cope? I started writing things down and have kept a diary/journal/scrapbook ever since. I found a one-in-a-million friend in a boy about a month after my dad died. I tried to commit suicide and he saved my life, literally. He is still my friend to this day. He was the only person I would talk to after the death, and he pulled me out of a dark world of despair and cynicism.

I found more friends and became a rebel. I smoked, drank, took a lot of drugs, and lied my way through my teens. Most of my friends were just like me, searching for something that could be found in each other, or not at all. They were mostly boys, too, which I find interesting considering that I had no male role models at that time.

I think specifically my friends allowed me to forget the past in a really weird way. I talked, and they understood (but not really), at least they pretended to; they were my glue because they kept my mind on what crazy thing I could do next.

I have a feeling many teens go through this—especially if they are from so-called dysfunctional [not a **healthy environment, as when parents have a drug problem**] homes. Yep, friends, drugs, and oh, music—a big, huge factor. I used to lock myself in my room after school and not come out for the rest of the night because I was too busy listening to other people's pain and music. It was scary, wonderful, heart wrenching, and glorious, the most important way to get through the teen years.

I love my mom dearly, but when I was growing up, I hated her. I guess that's fairly typical, but ours was a stormy relationship from the time I turned 13 till about my 19th year. After my dad died, my mom tried hard to make things normal. My mom is a very strong person (sometimes to a fault) who tried to make everything go away. I felt like it was bad to talk about it in front of my mom. Maybe that explains my attachment to my friends later. Many years later I ended up seeing a shrink and working some stuff out with my dad at the cemetery, which caused lots of tears. But, as a teen, I rarely cried for my dad in front of my mom because I was scared of looking weak.

—Sonia, 21, California

At the age of 19, my sister committed suicide (shot herself). This was an overwhelming shock to the family because we didn't see it coming. However, I had seen a change in her attitude, but felt I was too young (14) to discuss her personal life with my mother. Since we shared rooms, I heard and saw a lot of things my mother didn't (anger, sadness, and depression). After our father's death from alcoholism, my sister began to withdraw from the family. I was 12 when my father passed away, too young to really understand, but my sister was a senior in high school and took it really badly.

My other four siblings had married and moved away, so they had the support of their spouses. However, my sister and I didn't have anyone and my mother put tremendous pressure on my sister and me. We needed to get jobs at a very young age to survive because my father was the one who had brought in the income. I believe my sister couldn't adjust to the changes and she cracked under pressure.

The loss of my two loved ones gave me incredible strength to survive and love myself even more. I began to accept my life style and commend my mother for doing the best she could. I found my strength through her love for me. However, there are times when I feel tremendous pressure from my siblings and mother. The guilt of my sister's death led to their desperate need to smother me. That's what bothers me to this day; they're frightened that I may have this side to me (suicide potential). It's hard to tell them that it's OK for me to be unhappy at a given time—it's healthy. I would recommend that any teenager who has experienced anything similar should focus all the negative energy into something positive. That means loving yourself and accepting each hardship as a learning experience, as things happen for a reason.

—Genia, 22, Tennessee

The death of my father when I was 16 was painful. It may sound cliché, but time has helped a lot. I would advise not shutting out the rest of the family members and to keep the deceased close in memory and in love.

One of the things that I've found most helpful is asking the people who knew him best what he was like. Even though I was 16, I discovered there was a lot that I never knew about him as a person. When I can get other people from his past to ramble on about things they did together or things he said, it is one of the most wonderful things in all the world! It makes me miss him and points out just what opportunity has slipped through my fingers, but it also makes my memories of him richer.

—LouAnn, 23, Iowa

My most difficult challenge in high school was the loss of my mom, between my sophomore and junior years. What helped me was setting a goal, trying to make a "dream" come true. I traveled to Australia and I got involved in a drama club. I also turned to close friends and their families.

—Johanna, 24, California

My mother died from cancer when I was 16. It was, and still is, the most traumatic and pivotal event in my life. I was the third of four children, the youngest girl, and the closest to my mother. It is difficult for some to understand the intense bond I had with my mother but we were truly best friends, an inspirational image for one another.

My mother was the bond that kept our family together. After my mother died, my sister and I took on the role of mom—caring for our 10-year-old brother, cooking, cleaning, and keeping up our dad's morale. It is a frightening feeling to see your only parent break down; however, that was the case for some time. My mother was a nurturer and I took on that role. She always had a smile on her face and rarely complained. I did that too. My grieving process was hindered by this need to put on a good face, smile, and be tough as well as my need to be there for my father and brother. It was probably the worst move I could have made, but "when times are tough, the tough get going." I learned to live with that phrase, having a Marine Corps Colonel for a father.

At this point, however, he could not be so tough for he had lost not only his soul mate, lover, and friend, he had also lost the support that he so desperately needed that my mother gave as a nurturer. My father's grieving was overwhelming. There were a few times when he said to us that he "just couldn't go on." That scared us beyond belief because like most who lose a parent, even though we are not terribly young, the thought of losing our father too was terrifying.

As I came into my own grief at 19, when my father was coming out, we went through a period of adjustment that is still not complete. I had never disappointed him. I was strong and successful initially, but during my freshman year in college, I felt the shock of my mother's death and all that I had put "on hold" while finishing high school and caring for my father and brother. Cut loose from my daily obligation to "hang tough," I fell apart without my mother's confidence behind me. I had little motivation to succeed. This regression, so to speak, led to my dismissal from college and my father's tremendous disappointment.

This period lasted for another three years. I am now getting things in order in college and resolving my grief for my mother. My mother asked me to be like a rubber ball and bounce back. "That is our purpose. It may take a few more bounces than anticipated, but you must bounce back."

Divorce

My parents have been divorced for six years. Having an extremely close knit family, it was extremely hard to face each day. My younger brother, older sister, and I became a support for each other and often for our parents. Divorce is awful. Every day, even now, I still struggle. I don't think it will ever get easy. We stick together and try to stay strong. The fact that we are so tightly knit has helped me cope with this challenge, because although we aren't a complete family any more, we are all just as close, if not closer. Be your own person, no matter how much you love them and want them together. You'll be all right, take everything in stride. Remember, none of it is your fault. You are a great, strong individual.

—Krista, 16, Washington

Over a million divorces take place each year, half of them involving children, so over a million children experience their parents' divorce. Almost half of recent marriages in the U.S. end in divorce, one of the highest rates in the world. A survey of nearly 20,000 teenagers by *Sassy* magazine revealed that most teens do not want relationships like their parents': This included 78 percent of the boys and 63 percent of the girls. The average cost of a wedding in 1990 was $16,144, according to *Brides Magazine*. It would make a lot more sense to spend some of that money on pre-marital counseling and counseling during the marriage.

One in four adolescents grows up in a single-parent family (compared to only 12 percent in 1970). Of those with one parent, 88 percent live with their mothers. By 1994, single-parent families comprised nearly one in three of all U.S. families with children. Nearly 4 in 10 of the single parents were never married (compared to only 13 percent of families in 1970). The poverty rate among children in female-headed families is 54 percent, compared to 11 percent in married couple families. After a divorce, the standard of living goes up 10 percent for the men, and declines 27 percent for the women. U.S. children are owed more than $34 billion in unpaid child support.

David Popenoe, sociology professor, reported in his book *Life Without Father* (Martin Keller Books), children from single-parent families have two to three times the risk of: living in poverty, dropping out of school, becoming pregnant as teens, and getting in trouble with the law.

You hear a lot about how kids of divorce have more problems. Researchers such as Constance Ahrons (*The Good Divorce*, Harper Collins) point out that problems make news. They agree that the majority of children experiencing a divorce go through a crisis period for a few years following the separation, especially boys, but most get on track again. It's not the divorce that is the long-term problem, it's feeling caught in continued conflict between parents and the loss of effective parenting that hurts kids.

As Dr. Ahrons reports, "It's not the divorce so much as the way parents handle it." She estimates that about half the parents are able to reduce conflict, keep a routine so that kids feel secure, and work together to parent well. Kids with these kinds of effective parents develop similarly to kids with married parents.

Some counties require parents to attend seminars for divorcing parents and some state laws permit judges to order parents to attend these seminars. For example, the Juvenile and Domestic Relations Court in Alexandria, Virginia, requires a three-part seminar for any parent who files a child custody petition. Montgomery County, Maryland, has a similar requirement. Connecticut and Utah require almost all divorcing parents to attend seminars.

I surveyed 268 children of divorce for *How to Survive Your Parent's Divorce*. They said the main reason their parents couldn't get along was they were too different. Some parents got married too young and grew apart, had different values and interests, didn't communicate well, or a parent had alcohol or drug problems. Some parents found a new love while still married which, needless to say, was not popular with others in the family. Those who had little contact with their fathers after the divorce reported it was because he had a new family, his new wife was jealous of the children from his first marriage, their own mother kept them from their father, he moved away, or he had an addiction or violence problem that made him unsafe to see. Sue relates, *My mom uses visiting my dad as a punishment to me so I go there upset. I think mothers play a big role in the relationship between distant fathers and their children.*

Advice from 268 Youths
About How to Cope After Divorce

○ Don't blame yourself.

○ Take it one day and one step at a time.

○ The divorce does not mean your parents don't love you.

○ Talk about your feelings.

○ It's natural to feel upset, sad, and angry. Get support.

○ Don't listen to criticism of a parent by the other parent.

○ Your main responsibility is to take care of yourself.

○ Learn about the stages of dealing with grief (see Chapter 2).

○ Things will get better.

The young people agree that divorce is painful but report that, if kids have continuing support and love from caring adults, they will do fine. Julie's is the ideal situation: "I don't believe the divorce phased me that much. I don't remember a time when my father wasn't there when I wanted him to be." What these young people learned from their parents' divorces is to wait to marry until they know their partners well and to learn to be good communicators.

Lindsey, a reader, asked me to write more on "what we can do to make sure we don't get in a relationship like our parents." To pick the right partner, wait until you're in your 20s, and spend time with a counselor identifying your family's relationship patterns to analyze what you want to keep or change. Remember that often what originally attracts a couple later repels them. (For example, she wants a daddy to take care of her and he likes feeling important. Then she matures and feels stifled by her husband.) Make sure your partner is your best friend, and study and practice effective communication skills.

Avoid getting married just because the timing is right, everyone else is getting married, the other person seems so sure, you're sexually attracted to each other, she's attractive, and he's a good provider. (These ideas are developed more fully in *Everything You Need to Know to Succeed After College* along with an extensive list of questions to discuss with a potential mate.) PREPARE and FOCUS are useful "premarital inventories" that reveal problems that might lead to divorce if ignored; many clergypersons use these tests as part of counseling engaged couples.

A group of my college students who believe that their parents are very happily married report they communicate well, are best friends, are loving, spend time together, respect and support each other, give and take, and work at the marriage.

"They work together, they see eye to eye."

"They still hug, kiss, and flirt together."

"They know that marriage takes a lot of work."

"They compromise."

"They go out and have fun."

Just because your parents are divorced doesn't destine you to the same fate. Ask them about what they've learned and practice effective relationship skills with your friends.

—Suzanne, 18, California

My parents were recently divorced and three of my best friends' parents are getting divorced. I think it is pathetic that almost 50 percent of marriages end in divorce. Because of this statistic and because of the hopelessness about love I have received from my parents' lost marriage, right now I feel that I will never get married.

Because my friends and I have one another to counsel, we have continuously talked about our similarities and differences compared to our parents, the need for equality—no male dominance, and most importantly seeing how a boyfriend treats his mother.

If anything positive has derived from the high rate of divorces, it is that our generation is more cautious and more self-demanding before settling down permanently. But it has almost made me cautious to a negative extent. I'm scared as heck to settle down. Our parents seemed to demonstrate that their marriages didn't work; with more technology, more stress, and less free time for basic communication, why would mine? [Because you're more aware that a good relationship requires ongoing nurturance and you're less likely to marry for the wrong reasons.]

—Diana, 22, California

Do not sacrifice yourself to anyone. I was close with my dad. When he left, I was heartbroken and still am. I haven't seen him since I was eight. My mom was very emotional, but tried to stay strong. I had to be strong for everyone. My sister hates my dad. She remembers things that I must have blocked out. I defend him to everyone, so I am that way myself. I really don't express my feelings very well, except for anger. That is what my mom showed to us. I am still trying to deal with the challenge. Everyone thinks I am mean and hard-core, but I'm not. My advice is to take care of yourself first, because if you don't, you'll be a mess later.

Resources for Children of Divorced Parents

The Association for Children for Enforcement of Support
1-800-537-7072
(has local chapters and helps get fair child support)

Children's Rights Council
1-800-787-KIDS.
(information for children and parents, specializing in shared custody information)

International Youth Council/Parents Without Partners
1-800-637-7974 (support groups for teens)

Big Brothers/Big Sisters of America
230 13th St.
Philadelphia, PA 19103

Shapes: Families of Today: A Curriculum Guide on Today's Changing Families for Children Ages Eight to Eighteen. Families in Transition Project, Stepfamily Association of America, P.O. Box 91233, Santa Barbara, CA 93190-1233.
(a four-meeting curriculum guide for teachers and counselors)

Stages, Guidance projects, Irvine Unified School District, 5050 Barranca Pkwy., Irvine, CA 92714.
This school-based program for children deals with transitions, including divorce, death, and moves. A curriculum is available for 7th-12th graders (also available in Spanish).

Gayle Kimball. *How to Survive Your Parents' Divorce.* Chico, CA: Equality Press, 1995.
(lists more resources)

Family Fun

> *My parents and I do stuff together a lot—hiking and swimming are some things we do. I'm lucky because it really enables me to get to know my parents as people. If your parents don't spend enough time with you, then think of an activity that would be fun for both of you and ask them to do it. If they say No, then tell them you feel you aren't spending enough time with them and when can you do something together?*
>
> **—Jed, 16, California**

> *Don't be talked out of continuing to be "young," playing, creating art, etc., that is considered "babyish" but is really wonderfully human.*
>
> **—Dina, 20, California**

G ood times are the glue that holds relationships together, so it's helpful to establish a regular schedule of family fun time. My students and I asked over 200 employed parents what their families do for fun. In order of frequency, they said: sports, travel, watch videos or movies, cook and eat together, play games, go shopping, talk with family and friends, visit friends, and go to church or church-based activities. How would your family answer this question?

I've collected other ideas for family fun. Some teens commented that some of these activities are for youngsters, but we all have a young kid inside us who enjoys being invited to play. I do anyway. Make your own list, with your family's help, that suits you better if these ideas don't seem enjoyable to you.

Fun Family Activities

* Put on rock 'n roll music and dance in your living room.

* Paint a family mural on a big piece of butcher paper (sometimes you can get the ends of paper rolls free from newspaper publishers). Finger paint or toe paint.

* Make chalk drawings on the sidewalk near your home.

* Make crafts together—get ideas from a craft store and library books and magazines.

* Bake bread together.

* Tape record family singing and interviews with each other to listen to when you pull out the photo albums.

* Send copies of the tapes to relatives you don't get to see very often.

* As part of a family member's birthday, look at his or her photo album. As an ongoing activity, write in the album the delightful quotes that person says.

* Rent a video camera, write and direct a movie with your family and friends as actors.

* Organize a block party in your neighborhood with potluck dinner and games. Or organize a scavenger hunt, with clues to finding the next object.

* Play 20 questions, to figure out the animal, mineral, or vegetable object the other person has in mind with Yes or No answers.

* Design a coat of arms for your family, studying encyclopedia pictures to see how shields are designed.

* Plant a vegetable and flower garden in pots or in your yard.

* Have a family "fight" with a squirt gun, whipped or shaving cream, or jello.

* Watch the clouds or stars together describing what images you see.

* Play games in the car, such as competing to spot all the letters in the alphabet on road signs, or see who can see the most Volkswagen bugs.

* Tell a round-robin story, where each person makes up a section as you go along.

* Improvise a dialogue as actors, perhaps using accents.

* Create your own plays or do charades.

* Sing rounds and make up rap songs.

* Copy the leader's hand clap or dance step.

* Take dance lessons as a family (ballroom, square, folk).

* Play non-competitive "New Games" as well as sports (see Terry Orlick's *Cooperative Games and Sports Book*, Pantheon).

* Go skating or bowling.

* Visit a museum or historic building, and play tourist in your town.

* Visit different churches, synagogues, mosques, and temples.

* Write regular family letters to politicians urging them to support something you believe in, such as environmental cleanup, or write to protest ads you think are a bad influence.

* Read funny books out loud.

These books are recommended by counselor Judith Eberhart: Robert Fulghum, *It Was on Fire When I Lay Down on It* (Faucett, Columbine), and *All I Really Need to Know I Learned in Kindergarten*; Robert Byrne, The 637 *Best Things Anybody Ever Said*; and Ashleigh Brillant, *I May Not Be Totally Perfect, But Parts of Me Are Excellent* (Woodbridge Press). Emma books by Ralph Moody and Farley Mowat are funny.

Our family has rituals to celebrate the seasons and holidays. For example, we backpack and make fruit pies in the summer, dress up for Halloween in the fall, watch migrating water birds and ski in the winter, and hike to see wildflowers in the spring.

Ask each other some of the 260 questions in Gregory Stock's *The Kids' Book of Questions* (Workman Publishing) like "If you could pick any one food and have nothing else during the next week, what would you pick?" or "Would you rather be a rich and famous movie star or a great doctor who saves a lot of people but is not wealthy or well-known?"

A family I know has an instant party bag, with balloons and streamers, to celebrate someone's achievement, such as a good grade on a test. When someone has an occasion to celebrate they pull out the bag at dinnertime.

One of your projects could be tracing your family history. See *Suggestions for Beginners in Genealogy* (send a self-addressed envelope with two first-class stamps) to: The National Genealogical Society, 4527 17th St. N., Arlington, VA 2207-2399.

Do volunteer work together or save and invest money (see Chapter 10) to give to a charity.
Giver's Charity Rating Guide (reports on 300 charities)
American Institute of Philanthropy, 45789 Laclede Ave., Suite 136, St. Louis, MO 63108-2103

Please let me know your additions to this list.

Marge Kennedy.
100 Things You Can Do to Keep Your Family Together, Princeton, NJ: Peterson's, 1994.

Family Meetings

Weekly family meetings keep communication healthy.
Everyone can add discussion topics on a list posted on the
refrigerator during the week. Take turns being the leader of
the meeting. Start with what you liked and appreciated about each
other during the past week. Include decisions such as where to go on
a vacation or what to buy for your home. Schedule fun times and
other events on your family calendar: Each person can have her/his
own color of ink, with a color for the family as a whole.

Family meetings shouldn't be gripe sessions where people just complain or parents discipline, as no one will want to come.
They should end with a fun activity so people look forward to them.

Parent educator Kathy Lynn makes these suggestions
for an effective family meeting:

○ Meet at a regular time to discuss the next week's activities and chores, as
well as to iron out conflicts and discuss gripes.

○ Use an agenda to organize the meeting. Take minutes so that people can
refer to decisions.

○ All participants have equal opportunity to add topics to the agenda and to
speak about them.

○ Make decisions by consensus [each person explains his or her position without interruption; after hearing everyone, it is usually clear where the group
agrees] except for set family rules.

Family Communication

Kathy Lynn. *Parenting Today Newsletter.* 1205 Kingsway, Vancouver, BC, Canada V5R 1L1.

Michael DeSisto. *Decoding Your Teenager: How to Understand Each Other.* NY: William Morrow, 1991.

Alex J. Packer. *Bringing Up Parents: The Teenager's Handbook.* Minneapolis: Free Spirit Publishing, 1993.

Mary Pipher. *The Shelter of Each Other: Rebuilding Our Families.* NY: Grosset/Putnam, 1996. (She suggests turning off the TV and creating small rituals, as at dinner time.)

Paul Swets. *The Art of Talking with Your Teenager.* Holbrook, MA: Adams, 1995.

Moving

The most difficult challenge I faced as a teen was moving from Chicago to Texas. This was a big change in my life; this meant that I had to start my life all over again and make new friends. For the first two years I really did not accept anything, but these last two years I have finally learned to adjust to my situation. Several of my new friends helped me get over the anxiety I felt from being relocated to another city. The advice that I would give to teens facing this dilemma is just to accept what is going to occur and go with the flow.

—George, 17, Texas

My most difficult challenge was changing high schools my junior year after moving to a different state. I didn't know what the students would be like at the new school, but I wanted to fit in. I wasn't sure how I would be treated in a school where most of the students knew each other. I felt confused and out of place for the first week or so, but eventually made the transition to a smaller school.

The best way to handle such a situation is to just be yourself. I tried being friends with everyone, but soon discovered that was not possible. It is best to just act normally and soon others will discover your personality. Joining extra-curricular activities, such as sports and other clubs, helps in such a situation because it introduces you to a large number of people.

—Darren, 21, California

Parents

The most difficult challenge that I've faced and still am facing is dealing with parents and the differences between them and me. It takes A LOT of patience and communicating to get past the differences. Although there's a lot of arguing, I have to stick with them because they're trying to understand me and vice versa. They're not experts and neither am I; there's a lot of give and take. If you do fight a lot with your parents, you need to try to work with them. It's frustrating and challenging because sometimes you think you'd be better off without them, but really in the long run you need them more than ever. It's not easy being a parent when your child disagrees with you. And it is hell being a child when your parents don't agree with you.

—Chris, 16, Wisconsin

As a teen my ultimate challenge is my mother. Though she doesn't admit it, she's having trouble accepting my privacy and independent needs. I try to put myself in her place in understanding her point of view. We discuss this problem often and I've found that being honest with her works best.

—Sam, 17, Illinois

The main theme you'll read in young people's stories is teens want independence and parents want to continue control over their kids. The job of an adolescent is to detach the close bonds with their parents in order to become adults (they reunite after the young person leaves home). The changing power dynamic as you get older requires much discussion to renegotiate attitudes and family rules. Youth emphasize the importance of honest communication to work out a new balance of power.

College students advise you to respect your parents. (Danisha comments, "Probably because most of them are out from their parents' house.") They have probably experienced most of your challenges, so it pays to listen to their suggestions and share your concerns. "Teach them, because it was 30 years ago when they were in high school. Be their friend," says Kim. "Realize that in a couple of years you'll be sitting down with them and discussing 'kids these days.'" You'll be in their place someday, so act the way you'd like to be treated by your kids, students advise, as what goes around comes around.

Surveys indicate that young people generally feel close to their parents. A 1995 survey of over 3,000 high-achiever high school students reports that most (83 percent) have a great deal of trust in their parents. Over half (53 percent) regularly share an evening meal with their families. These students reveal the person they confide in most is a friend, and, secondly, their mothers. Students who are not close to their parents are much more likely to be sexually active, drink, and be unsatisfied with their lives. Two-thirds of the students plan on being equally strict with their own children. The most common forms of punishment in their families are loss of some privileges and being grounded.

Another national survey reports 89 percent of teens say their parents are interested in them and 75 percent say their parents understand their problems. Most (94 percent) are happy with their mother and 81 percent with their fathers. About half, though, say they'll raise their own children differently, providing more freedom and understanding (1996 poll for the Horatio Alger Association).

A KidsPeace poll of 1,023 kids ages 10 to 13 found that 73 percent can count on their parents to be there when they need help and 71 percent trust their parents to do what is best for them. Most (93 percent) feel always loved by their parents. When asked about a role model they look up to, teens most often name one or both parents.

Only 23 percent of students in 5th, 6th, and 7th grades do not feel comfortable talking with their parents about difficult issues, such as sex or drugs. A major change occurs by age 13, when 43 percent of 8th graders say they do not feel comfortable talking with parents. The greatest fear (65 percent) of this age group is that a parent might die. A majority (53 percent) is afraid their parents will not have enough money to pay the bills and fear poverty. Forty-seven percent say they think their parents might not "be available."

A survey by Teenage Research Unlimited reports that teens rate their mothers as first on their "most admired" list, while dads came in third. Teens with two parents at home report they seek advice first from their mothers (44 percent), then from their friends (26 percent), and lastly from their fathers (10 percent) (1995 survey by Children Now and Kaiser Permanente). A survey by the Barna Research Group found that teens more often seek help or encouragement from their friends (72 percent) than their mothers (54 percent) and their fathers (38 percent). Fathers ranked higher as to how much influence they have on their teens; 60 percent of teens said their dads had a lot of influence on how they think and act, compared to 70 percent for moms.

Kids are four times more likely to talk to their moms about problems than anyone else, agrees the KidsPeace Preteen Survey, as 71 percent of the youth are most comfortable talking with their mother, while only 13 percent pick their dad. Another 14 percent say they feel comfortable talking with both parents. Why do you think these kids enjoy talking with their mothers? What can dads do to achieve this close communication with their kids? You might discuss this with your father and go over the active listening skills in Chapter 2; sometimes dads don't listen well because they think they're supposed to solve problems and they were trained to view their main contribution as breadwinning.

Fathers

—Scott, 16, Illinois

I had to face certain problems with my dad by going to a therapist and then communicating with him at home about the problems. With every problem or difficulty you come across you have to look at it from all points of view instead of thinking that you are automatically right. In everything there is good and bad, so when faced with one, always consider the other.

—Justin, 18, Wisconsin

My father denies my identity. He denies me the right to be anything he feels is "not socially acceptable." To him I am first and foremost a reflection on his quality as a person, not an individual. I just relax. When it started I was 15, so I just vented my frustrations briefly and then said to myself, "36 months and I'm gone." I'm down to three months and still reasonably sane. [I'd suggest making more of an effort to communicate, as Scott did, otherwise these issues surface in a different form later.]

—Nitz, 19, California

I was born into a family that owns a small construction company. As a child I taught myself how to operate all of our heavy machinery. As I grew older I was making a grown man's salary operating a dozer. My family was very proud of me, but I was always being lectured on how I was not doing my job right. Not meeting my parents' expectations was my deepest worry. I was never told or taught how to do something the right way, it was just expected of me. No matter how hard I tried, I was not doing a good job.

After working for four years, being chewed out every day, I wondered if it would ever stop. I would stand tall and take my scolding like a man [note his definition of masculinity], but afterwards I would break down inside. I couldn't figure out why my work looked so good to me, but was wrong. After years of hiding my feelings inside, I realized I needed to approach my father. He needed to know how I felt.

I wish I had confronted him earlier. I told him to remember I was only 17, and taught myself how to run the equipment. After he realized he had been treating me like I should know everything, he broke down and cried. He then agreed he had been too hard on me, and expected too much from me. After this talk, things changed.

I find my father giving me better explanations than he did in the past; often I'll even get a demonstration. Many teens also feel they do not meet their parents' expectations about work, school, sports, or other activities. I feel parents do not realize it. If you face these kinds of problems, you need to step up and talk about them. If you don't, it could carry on throughout your whole life.

—Brandon, 20, California

My dad was the most important influence on me while I was in high school. I moved in with him because of differences with the law. He straightened me out and helped me in school and in life. He taught me a lot of lessons about life and how things work.

Mothers

—Misty, 15, Michigan

I'd say the most difficult problem that I've faced during my teen years has been "the mom." It seems since I turned about 12 or 13 she and I have not gotten along too well. We disagree on just about everything. I have other problems with peer pressure and stuff, but I've got to face her every day.

I write a lot of poems and stories to cope. I spend a lot of time away from home or in my bedroom. My advice is this: Parents most likely will disagree with you sometime in your life and what you should do is grin and bear it. You've got to realize that they were young (with the dinosaurs) and don't want you to go through the same mistakes and problems that they did. I didn't realize that and now our communication is gone.

—Kathleen, 15, California

My father died when I was nine, of cancer. I never took it in a negative way exactly. I miss him a lot but I feel like it has made me a better, stronger person. When politicians say that kids aren't as good or as smart if they live in a single-parent family home, I can say I hold a 4.0 grade average, I'm in student government, I play three sports, and I'm a volunteer in my community. I can credit that all to my mom who has been great. My motto is "Make the best of things."

—Susanna, 18, Massachusetts

For almost my whole life, until very recently, I had very, very low self-esteem because my mom and I had a control conflict; she wanted control over my life, and so did I. For most of my life I had no choice because she was bigger than I was mentally and physically, but as I got older, I took control.

To deal with a controlling parent, you must first have someone give you a reality check, or else you really think what you are going through is normal, which it isn't. A good friend, peer, or adult, can really be helpful in telling you that you have every right to be angry. Also, having mediated conversations (i.e., with a counselor and with the parent) is also helpful. A lot of times, I think the parent doesn't realize that she is being so out of line, and I also believe that most parents have good intentions. They just have a warped sense of what is normal child/teen behavior, or a warped sense of discipline.

Mediated, rational discussions about everyone's needs and desires is always necessary. When there is a lack of communication between two parties, no good can come from it, and harmony is based on communication. When one party is dominant by nature (the parent), the child really needs someone of equal status to the parent (another adult) to be an advocate. This is a tough job, because a lot of controlling parents are extremely threatened by another adult telling them they are treating their children wrong.

Being at college, away from my parents, has helped a lot. It is hard, and a lot of what I feel is subconscious and deeply ingrained, so I know it will take a very long time, but I'm working on it, successfully.

—Koren, 20, Pennsylvania

I would have to say the biggest challenge I faced as a teenager was winning back my mother's trust. I did some pretty stupid stuff in my early teens that really worried and scared her, and it took me a long time to convince her that I had really changed for the better. But by the middle of my junior year, my mom was relaxing a little and trusting me more than she had before. I never showed her that she couldn't count on me again, and now we have a really good relationship and talk all the time. Looking back now I understand why she got so overprotective and overbearing, but I still think she could've looked a little harder at my progress and listened when I told her I wasn't doing illegal, immoral things any more.

Parents

—Landon, 16, California

The most difficult challenge I have faced is trying to please other people, namely my parents. Most of my friends accept me how I am and are proud of me for what I have done. My parents and coaches, on the other hand, are a totally different story. I can never totally please them. It's the same old story; you get a 4.0 grade point average, they ask you, "Why aren't you taking honors classes?" You win the game with a three-pointer at the buzzer against the cross-town rival, and they ask why you dribbled the ball off your foot in the first quarter. I know parents and coaches want the best for you, but come on, let up a little bit. Don't ask questions like "Why can't you do better?" Show your love by being happy for us like we just won the lottery.

As a teenager you can take criticism one of two ways. You cannot listen to what they say and be happy with your own performance and know in your heart and mind that you did the best you possibly could; or you can try to keep pleasing everyone else and tear yourself apart doing it. What has worked for me is somewhere in the middle. Do your best and work hard, but don't be motivated to please your parents; do it for yourself. It's your life and you can be as successful as you want; you get out of it what you put into it. Live your life to your standards, not someone else's.

—Jill, 17, Wisconsin

I'm 17 and I still have a 12:00 curfew. I used to think my parents were so uncool. I set my mind to hating them. I was a problem child right from the beginning, but I never believed that I was the problem. I hated my parents every time they said No to me. We fought all the time; I loved to yell "I hate you!" to them and slam the door in their faces. I thought they didn't understand me, just like most kids do. I used to think they enjoyed making me angry, and that they got a kick out of grounding me.

NONE of that was ever true. They punish us BECAUSE they love us. I understand that now, but it's too late. Things have changed for the worse at my household, as my parents have stopped trying to set me straight. And now more than ever, it seems like they don't love me any more. They just couldn't handle it any more. Now THIS is the biggest challenge of all, trying to undo too many years of my screwing up!

What helped me to cope with this challenge was my older sister and myself. I have an aunt, I hardly ever get to see, who is a drunken bum. She ran out on her family when they tried to help her get her act together. I just didn't want to end up like that, and my sister helped me to realize that. I love my family more than anything, and I don't want to do any more damage. I realize now that my parents aren't and never were the problem, I WAS!!!

My advice to anybody else in my situation would be to grow up and realize what you'll lose before it is gone. It can be good if you want it to be, and you'll get more freedom in the long run if you stick around and do what is asked of you now.

You've got your whole life ahead of you to party and be on your own; just give your parents 18 years, and make them good ones. Your parents will not always be there for you when times get tough, but they are now and all they want is to help make it easier.

—Jen, 18, California

Honesty has always been the key to a successful relationship with my parents. Things tend to be bad when they have reason to distrust you. When I'm honest, they don't have any doubts about the things I do or friends I'm with. Honesty has also gotten me into trouble, but it's still worth it to tell the truth. It always works out better in the long run. Trying to respect their opinions usually proves to work because, even though it doesn't always seem like it, they know a lot more than we do and are wiser than we are because they've been through a lot more learning experiences. The relationship always seems better when you try to think of them and act towards them like they are your friends and not just parents.

—Zak, 19, Pennsylvania

Understand where your parents are coming from. They've been through a lot and they've made a lot of sacrifices. Don't take them for granted. Their advice will someday be your own.

—Julie, 20, New Jersey

Develop a relationship based on trust. Set ground rules that you can both follow and then don't keep trying to change it. If they see you are responsible and that you trust them to trust you, it will be easier.

—Mgamboa, 21, California

My parents and I got along well until I began to realize that I needed to make changes in my life and beliefs to become my own person. They respect my decisions more these days because I take the time to explain why I need to do something or why I believe something. They still voice their disapproval, but they respect my decisions more often than not. I'm still working on this one.

—Megan, 23, New York

The biggest challenge for me as a teenager was trying to have fun and trying new things (some of which weren't necessarily safe), while still maintaining a trusting relationship with my parents. I didn't cope very well with this dilemma, and looking back, I wish I had been more honest with my parents and myself about who I was and what I was doing. I know our relationship would be better today had I confided more about my life, including stuff about alcohol and sex, with both my mom and dad.

—Andrew, 24, Oklahoma

Family is first, FAMILY IS FIRST, FAMILY IS FIRST. The family, no matter what they impose or tell you, only love you and want the best for you. When times get tough, and they do, your family will be there more often than anyone else, if you decide that they are important also.

Family Patterns

—Janice Gagerman, D.S.W., Social Work professor and therapist

Some of the most important experiences you will have as an adult will be your interactions with family members, close friends, and sexual partner. Your styles of interaction with others are shaped by your early experiences with the important adults in your life. You will most likely repeat these patterns with your friends. If you and your parents treat each other with respect, and your parents encourage and support you during difficult times, then most likely this is the way you relate to your friends. You will be drawn to people who remind you of these "character styles" you learned, saw, and felt.

A child who grows up in an abusive home seeing her parents fighting, many times chooses boyfriends who are similar to her father's style of interaction, because she knows how to respond to him. I have worked with many women who "know" that dating a man who is kind to them would be better than dating a man like her abusive father. However, many times these women cannot stay with these kinder men, since they are more accustomed to relating to men who are abusive.

Some people are able to change and choose partners who are kind and considerate, even if they grew up in difficult environments. Most likely these people had counseling in order to address these issues and make changes in how they act, think, and feel about themselves. If you feel the style of interaction you grew up with may cause you to have difficult times in future relationships, seek help to make changes. The longer you wait to make these changes, the deeper these patterns set in.

Time with Parents

—Phil, 19, Connecticut

I grew up in a middle-class environment in New England where both my parents worked to keep up with the Joneses. I hardly ever saw my parents together at one time. I missed a sense of family unity. My father was busy working with his father in "the business." My mother was always working and socializing with the big mucky-mucks. How impressive they were—except they seemed to forget one thing; money can't buy love.

—Lance, 23, California

My mom wasn't home very much and she was a single parent. There was hardly ever food in the house and there was no guidance. I made some pretty weird things for dinner, did the dishes, kept the house clean, did homework, and went to bed. My advice to other teens is to keep your head up. Strive to do your best. Be positive and bold, but realize your place in this world—you're a teen, not an adult.

Parents spend about 40 percent less time with their children than a generation ago, according to researcher John Robinson. Almost 20 percent of 6th to 12th graders have not had a conversation with a parent in the previous month that lasted for at least 10 minutes (Peter Benson, Search Institute). In interviews by the Barna Research Group with a national sample of teens, the top vote getter for how they would do things different from their parents was spending more time with family (followed by more freedom and independence for kids). They average 40 minutes a week discussing "things that matter" with their fathers (for those whose dads lived in the home) and 55 minutes with their mothers. They spend more time with their friends (15 hours a week) than their families (13 hours). Parents average 50 hours a week working and commuting, versus only 12 hours on family activities (*Time: A Precious Commodity,* by Jeanne Hogarth and Christiann Dean, Cornell University Press)

A majority of parents also says they would like more time with their children and point to work as the main barrier to reaching this goal. One in two fathers, one in eight mothers, and one in three single parents regularly work more than 40 hours a week, according to the National Commission on Children. Television becomes a third parent; the average American youth will spend 15,000 hours in front of the television set by the time he or she is 18, compared to 11,000 hours in school.

A study of Boston families where both parents worked found that fathers did about as much child care as mothers once the kids were in school, so kids in these families get more attention from their dads. Generally these parents were happy with the job they were doing as parents, although many would trade job advancement for more time with their families (R. Barnett and C. Rivers, *She Works/He Works,* Harper, San Francisco).

Time magazine quoted a survey of people in their 20s (by Leo Burnett ad agency) that reports that this generation is angry and resentful about their lack of time with parents. "The flashback was instantaneous and so hot you could feel it," says research director Josh McQueen. "They were telling us passionately that quality time was exactly what was not in their lives." A 20-year-old interviewed for the article says, "I don't want my kids to go through what [loneliness] my parents put me through."

Many teens feel lonely, agrees Jerry Johnston, author of *Who's Listening? What Our Kids Are Trying to Tell Us.* He gave talks to teens in over 3,000 schools where many students told him they feel no one is listening to them or cares about them; he says too many teens are sad, lonely, and angry.

Newspaper columnist Richard Louv spent three years traveling around the U.S. talking with youth. He reports that kids don't see their parents a lot because of work and divorce. Kids are understanding of their parents' responsibilities but also angry and disappointed about not getting enough time with them. They want more opportunities for fun with their families. He said many parents feel isolated, lonely, guilty, and sad because they know their children are not OK. He concludes, "The isolation from adults that many children feel is acute, painful, and ultimately numbing." They turn to their friends for support, some become depressed, and some turn to drugs, alcohol, and gangs.

The *Who's Who Among American High School Students* survey of 2,000 high achievers in 1987 reported about 80 percent feel loneliness, isolation, and worthlessness, plus pressure to get good grades. Their main worry is that they will fail. In a nationwide poll of teens, four in ten say their parents (either sometimes or often) do not make time to help them and half say the television is on during the family dinner hour. Time with parents does not correlate with whether their mother worked outside the home or not (1994 telephone poll of 1,055 teenagers, ages 13 to 17, by the *New York Times* and CBS News).

	Single-Parent Households	Two-Parent Households:
Want more time with mother	21%	14%
Want more time with father	45%	23%
Cares for self after school	25%	15%
Mom misses important things a lot	13%	5%
Father misses important things a lot	32%	10%

(Princeton Survey Research, 1994, national poll of youths ages 10 to 17)

How does your family create quality time together? How much is the TV on in your house and in your friends' homes? What effect do you think it has on family conversations and activities? Take a look at the sections on family fun and family meetings to get ideas for activities you'd like to do together.

Barna Research Group. *Today's Teens.* Glendale, CA, 1991. (interviews with a national sample of 710 teens in 1990)

Jerry Johnston. *Who's Listening? What Our Kids Are Trying to Tell Us.* Grand Rapids, MI: Zondervan, 1992.

Richard Louv. *Childhood's Future.* Boston: Houghton Mifflin, 1990.

Poverty

I feel the most difficult challenge I faced as a teen was living in the ghetto. This was a challenge for me emotionally and physically. It was a drain on both my mother and me each day. The atmosphere was chaotic and I chose to stay inside our "safe haven" (home) and write and reflect on my life. I did not have many close friends then; however, my mother was there to teach me the difference from right and wrong. I felt that my mother played an important role in helping raise me. She taught me about the world and my heritage. She made me have pride in myself.

Living in a crime-infested area is hard, because you see many youths your age turning to violence, crime, or sex. My mother was there for me, when the other mothers weren't, and her support was vital to my upbringing.

I would encourage other young adults and teenagers in the ghetto to realize there's a whole world out there. I want to point out that having someone positive in one's life makes a difference. If you don't have a parent, seek a counselor, mentor, friend, police officer, or anyone who can bring positiveness to your life.

—Cathryn, 19, California

Nearly one in four American children lives in poverty. Children make up over 40 percent of the poor although they are only 25 percent of the total U.S. population. Ten percent of children live in "extreme poverty," double the percentage in 1975. Children under six have the highest poverty rate of any group in America (nearly 26 percent) and 33,000 American babies die before their first birthday. Children's poverty rate is about double that of the elderly.

Poor children are three times more likely to die from disease and accidents, are 1.3 times more likely to have a learning disability, twice as likely to drop out of school than middle-income children, and less likely to go to college. Poverty breeds long-term problems for children's health and educational success. It's the main cause of violent crime, teen parenting, and school dropout. Common sense and research confirm that money spent on pregnant women's care and children's health and preschool education saves money in the long run. To me, it's morally wrong to have inner city children living in third world conditions, viewing wealthy families on TV, and then just condemning frustrated youth for acting out. They need access to good education and jobs.

The Index of Social Health (Fordham University) tracks 16 categories of American life. By 1995, these conditions for children had gotten worse: children in poverty (22 percent, up from 15 percent in 1970), child abuse, and drug abuse. In 1994, over 15 million American children were poor, compared to around nine percent in Australia and Canada, the countries with the next highest rates.

The poverty rate has gotten worse since 1965 rather than better, as you would expect of a mighty industrial nation. Most of the increase in the poverty rate took place in the 1980s. The U.S. has the biggest gap between rich and poor of any industrial country. The top 20 percent of earners make more than the middle 60 percent. The three percent of Americans who make more than $100,000 a year control about 22 percent of the nation's income.

Families are likely to be poor if the parents were teens when they had a child, if parents have low levels of education, and the father is absent. Almost 75 percent of children in single-parent families will experience poverty before they turn 11. More than one child in eight lives in a family receiving an AFDC check (Aid to Families with Dependent Children, or welfare, usually received by single-mother families). (It costs an average of $145,320 to raise a child to age 18 in the U.S.)

Although about 70 percent of welfare recipients are children, welfare serves fewer than 60 percent of all poor children in the U.S. and welfare reform in 1996 reduced this percentage. Over nine million children lack health insurance. One-fourth of U.S. babies are born to mothers who did not receive adequate prenatal care and one-quarter of a million low-birthweight babies are born every year.

Despite widely believed myths, welfare benefits consumed about one percent of the federal spending in 1995, the majority of recipients are white, and welfare families don't have more children than families in general. A person who works full-time at minimum wage earns below the poverty level for a family of four. To support a parent and two children and their child care requires earning at least $9 an hour, more than many current welfare recipients can expect to earn.

Poverty and racism intertwine. One-fourth of all Latino families live in poverty and Native Americans have even worse poverty rates. Black children are three times as poor as white children and black infants are more than twice as likely to be born with low birth weight. Black workers' wages, as compared to white workers, dropped to 73 percent by 1990.

At least 100,000 children are homeless each day in America, according to estimates by the National Academy of Sciences. In 1994, one in four homeless people was under the age of 18. More than one-third of the homeless are families rather than single individuals.

One in eight children don't have enough food to eat. Five million children younger than age 12 go to bed hungry, skip meals, or eat small portions because their parents run out of money to buy food, according to a study released by the Food Research and Action Center in 1995.

—Carina, 21, California

I wanted to have all the nice clothes and cars that the others had. My parents said we can't and that's that. Clothes and a car don't make you more fun or improve your personality; you do, and that doesn't cost a thing.

—Carol-Lynn, 29, Nevada

Our family was very poor. We lived in a falling-down rotten-wood house and wore secondhand clothes. We cooked on wood fires. We did not have TV. Sometimes we did not have running water when the water line would freeze or the pump would break and we did not have the money to fix it. That would mean that we had to go to the bathroom in the outhouse and go to school without a shower. We would wash with a washrag and warm stove water, but that is not really clean. It also meant that we had to go to school in clothes that were not always clean. We would try very hard to be clean, but it was always difficult.

It was hard being poor. I never had records or tapes like my friends. We only got one radio station in our canyon so I never really knew what the music was that my friends were talking about. When all my friends got new dresses for dances and special events, I had to go to the Salvation Army, the best of the two thrift stores in town. I knew people talked behind my back, but what could I do? My father was land poor. He raised some cattle, but never had enough to get really good stock, and he would break horses he would capture. A horse kicked him in the chest and killed him when I was 18. But I had moved from the ranch then, married, worked as a butcher.

Even when a stack of meat fell on me and broke my back, I knew things would be better. And they were. By the time I was 20, I could stand up, and by the time I was 21, I could walk again. By this time my husband had left me and my mother was dying of lung cancer. But things would get better.

I was not poor any more. I was not rich, but I had my life and reasonably good health. I had a child and I could take care of my mother. I learned that if you want to do something you can do it. All you have to do is to believe. The doctors told me I would not walk again. But I did. I did not want to be dirt poor and I wasn't, and I am not now. I had hope and a belief that God would not leave me in dirt. I believe that my positive outlook on life made all the difference in my life.

Don't worry too much about being poor. All you have to do to get a good job is to go to school or work hard from the ground floor and up. I started sweeping sawdust and soon I was a butcher with good benefits and good pay. I made more in a week than my father made in a month. But you have to believe in yourself, you have to believe that you can do something. I see a lot of people who had more than I did, who now have less because they didn't believe, or they believed in the wrong things.

Running Away from Home

When my brother ran away from home, it was the worst experience of my young teen life. I talked to older people and adults about my brother and why he went. They told me he'd be all right and he probably needed time away. My advice, if this ever happens to you, is to talk to an adult. They'll really help you cope with the problem.

—Candi, 14, Virginia

A majority of runaways is escaping from an abusive environment. Two-thirds of all runaways who look for shelter were physically or sexually abused by a parent. Many have parents who are drug and alcohol addicts. An estimated three million children run away from home each year.

Estimates are that 300,000 teens live on the streets in the U.S. Pimps and drug dealers prey on them, so by age 21, young people who live on the street are 13 times more likely than other teens to be infected with the HIV virus. If you know a runaway, give him or her the 800 phone numbers to call to find out alternatives to living on the street, such as group homes or foster care.

I was a street kid for most of my teenage years, sort of a runaway, except at night I usually went home. I lived on cola because you could buy one glass and have unlimited refills, and free samples in grocery stores, or I'd eat from dumpsters. Mostly my thing was panhandling. Me and my sister, we'd go to the mall or the train station and beg, "Mister, you got a quarter?" Then usually the cops would come around and we'd run for it. I don't know how we escaped some of those times.

Also, we escaped from other people. My sister, she's 16, and guys are really attracted to her. We'd be wandering around, a truck would pull up next to us and the guys would ask, "Wanna go for a ride?" One time my sister agreed to go the movies with some guys. Only they didn't really take her to the movies. So after that we didn't go with anyone—ever. Unfortunately, sometimes they'd chase us.

We spent most of our time looking for food or money and trying to escape from people. It got crazy sometimes. But it was also a lot of fun because we could do whatever we wanted. Also, you meet a lot of people. After my sister moved away, I sort of got adopted by these real cool homeless people and I stayed with them for a while. They're the only real family I ever had. You don't realize how great a lot of people are until you're in the position where you need food or money or someone's shoulder to cry on, and a complete stranger is willing to help you without asking anything in return.

The worst part, believe it or not, was when I unfortunately was forced by child protective services to go home. The streets aren't so great, but I would have sooner starved than go home, back then. And now, here I am—total culture shock, I'll tell you that much. I can't go into why I stopped hanging out at home, except that I had this gut feeling I couldn't survive that insanity any more. Anyway, right now I am working hard in school and I have an after-school job and buy my own food and clothes. I'll probably move out next year, if I find a place. Until then, I guess if you can survive the streets, you can survive anything.

—George, 18, California

I can still remember the worst day of my life. I don't mean being turned down by the finest girl in school or slipping and sliding at the biggest game of the year. Me and my mom got into a gigantic confrontation. I was being my rebel self and was yelling at my mom, saying all these wicked things. We were both seriously pissed off at one another. And boom, what she always said she was going to do happened. My mom kicked me out of the house. It wasn't like leave for a little while to cool down, it was get out. I was like, "Yeah, yeah." Five minutes later there was a police officer at my house. I remember thinking to myself that she is trying to scare me. Little did I know! I played Billy, the bad ass; my mom said to get my stuff. At this point it was too late to plead at all. Boy, I sure cried that day. The cop took me away.

I went down deep into the East Bay, a place I never heard of, where I was left by the cop. I was like, "Dude, when are you going to take me home?" He looked at me and shook his head, "Boy, you just don't get it do you?" I answered with a wet sobbing No. The cop told me that this place was a group home; I did not understand. My mom had never told me of such a scary place. It was about 1:00 p.m. when I got there and the cop left me. A guy who worked there sat down with me and explained the program to me for about two hours. By this time the shock had left, for the most part.

It looked like a regular house, however, on the inside there were little signs that read "TV hours, do not do this, do not do that." The place smelled real bad and six other kids lived there. I was used to my brothers and my mom and dad, not six people I never met before. My stomach was tingly for a few days. I met the other five guys who were all older than me.

After a couple of months or so, I moved to another group home where I lived for about two years. This place was much nicer. It was long-term placement; the people there were cool and more mellow. It was Rojon, Jim, Mike, me, and two young ladies I did not like very much. Rojon and I became the best of friends for the most part. Ro, Jim, and Mike looked out for me and one another. I had a really good time there, most of the time. During this time I was about 13 or 14, my parents and me would spend time together; however, I felt strangely more at home with the fellas. We played basketball, movies, videogames, and picked up girls together that endless summer.

No one knew that we lived in a group home except a couple of teachers. The first day of high school was pretty bad for me as I kept thinking about home and going to school there. But I got over it quick. Me and Rojon made names for ourselves; we would dance all the time at school which was good due to it put us on the map socially. No one ever knew that we danced at home for hours the night before.

The only time things got sticky was when I would cuss a teacher out and he/she would want my parents' work numbers. Boy, did that ever put me in an unsafe spot! Then suddenly I would get that splash of dry wet heat that just paralyzed me! That feeling was around for about five years or so. So that's how some teacher would find out about my living situation. I use to get in all kinds of trouble left and right, mostly for talking back and cussing in class at the teacher. None of them wanted me in their classes due to my behavior. However, that all changed when I finally got over my mom kicking me out and started to do things with a lot of my friends.

Now life was good even though I had more than the average person to deal with. Going back to school for my 10th grade year was the best thing I ever did. I got into a lot of clubs at first and that helped to relieve some of the stress from my home life which was the most difficult part. I started to cope a lot better when I stopped blaming my parents. It was not easy to leave my past behind me, yet it had to be done.

With the way the government is going, troubled youth with no home and no family will be left out in the cold. As far as suggestions for those who may be going through hard times, if you like to argue, you should get involved in your high school and clubs on campus you feel strongly about. Find a teacher who is willing to help you and wants to help you, not only as a student, but also as a person. If I got this far, anyone can make it to college.

Information for Runaways

Angels' Flight Crisis Center for Runaways 1-800-635-8651

Child Find of America 1-800-I-AM-LOST

Covenant House 1-800-999-9999 (information and referral)

Family Reconciliation Services 1-800-422-7556

Home Run 1-800-HIT-HOME (national hotline for runaways)

National Center for Missing and Exploited Children 1-800-843-5678

National Runaway Switchboard 1-800-621-4000

Options House 1-800-225-4325 (24 hours)

Runaway Hotline 1-800-231-6946

Vanished Children Alliance 1-800-VANISHED

National Clearinghouse on Runaway
and Homeless Youth
P.O. Box 13505
Silver Spring, MD 20911-3505

National Network of Runaway and
Youth Services
1319 F St., NW, Suite 401
Washington, D.C. 20004

National Foster Parents Association
226 Kitts Dr.
Houston, TX 77024

*The Heart Knows Something Different:
Teenage Voices from the
Foster Care System.* NY: Persea
Books, 1996.

Louise Armstrong. *Solomon Says: A
Speakout on Foster Care.* NY: Pocket
Books, 1989.

Help for Teen Prostitutes

Children of the Night, Los Angeles, 1-
800-551-1300 (provides services)

The National Center for Missing and
Exploited Children
1-800-843-5678 (refers to local
agencies to find and
assist children)

Paul and Lisa Program
1-800-518-2238
(helps young prostitutes and teaches
prevention
programs in schools)

WHISPER 1-612-724-6855
(Offers help to anyone who wants to
leave prostitution—accepts collect
calls to Minnesota.)

Prostitutes' Education Network:
http://www.creative.net/~penet/

Siblings

*My little brother is mentally disabled. He can be very diffi-
cult to deal with at times. It's almost like he's a full-grown four-year-
old. Learning how to deal with a 13-year-old throwing a tantrum in a
video store is quite a task. I've learned over time how to prevent
these situations. It's hard for me to see him so frustrated over a simple math problem. I try as hard as I can to be patient with him and
help. To a teen with a dis-
abled sibling: Be patient. My
parents have been very helpful in this situation.*

—Kathryn, 15, Virginia

Puppies give each other practice working and
playing together, and so do brothers and sisters. Although the bickering is annoying, it's
wonderful to have a sibling when you're an adult.
My brother and I fought and now we're the best of
friends, mutual supporters.

Kelly Lynn Baylor suggests that sib-
lings get to know each other as individuals, looking
past labels that get put on "the smart one," "the
clown," the athletic one," or whatever. If your sibling irritates you, remove yourself from the conflict
and walk away. If you respect yourself and others,

disputes can be worked out rationally.

If a conflict continues, she suggests writing a contract you both sign and post, including sanctions for not following through. For example: We agree that we have to get each other's OK before borrowing anything. You can't help yourself without asking in advance: If you forget to ask me, I get your skateboard for a week. If you argue over chores, see if you can trade so you are both doing a job you don't mind doing, or alternate jobs everyone dislikes.

Some researchers think that birth order influences our personality development. In *The Birth Order Book* (F.H. Revell), Keven Lehman categorizes birth order differences this way:

    a. perfectionist, reliable, well-organized, critical

    b. mediator, avoids conflict, has many friends, a maverick

    c. manipulator, charming, blames others, a good salesperson.

These traits supposedly describe first, middle, and last-borns. People often say that first-borns' parents expect them to be high achievers, middle children often feel they get the least attention, and last-borns get babied. How true are these generalizations for you and your siblings?

—Emma, 15, California

Having an older brother can be both great and a pain. We now have a great relationship. Often he waits up for me if he gets in before me. We talk about anything and everything. My brother and all of his friends are very protective of me. I hang out with my brother and all his friends a lot, so they are all like brothers to me.

—Lindsay, 17, Wisconsin

The hardest thing for me in my preteen years was getting along with my older sister. But as we both grew older and I entered high school, our relationship began to get better. If someone is having a problem with their sibling, I suggest to just give it a little bit of time. In the long run, your sibling will be one of the most important and closest friends.

—Nick, 18, California

There are so many issues dealing with my younger brother: privacy (invasion of and respect for) and sharing (clothes, borrowing money, trust, getting your fair share). A younger sibling has to measure himself against the accomplishments of older siblings and feels less powerful. Older siblings see their younger siblings receive privileges and rights earlier and have them at the same school.

—Melissa, 21, California

My challenge was trying to follow my sister in school. She did everything: cheerleading, student body president, 3.5 GPA. I coped because I had a strong group of friends and my parents didn't expect me to be like my sister. Just realize that everyone has her/his strengths; you don't have to do or accomplish what other people have done. Be yourself.

Stepfamilies

My dad married a woman who is 16 years younger than he.
She is a control freak. Everything has to be her way and she
always has to have the last word. Her mood swings are unbear-
able. They just had another child. I often feel like a leftover. They
sometimes make remarks that make me feel so unwanted. She is
very two-faced. When it's just her and me, she is a jerk, but when
my dad is around she is an angel.

Every day I just talk with my friends about it a lot. I don't
think things with her will ever change, so I just try to suck it up
and move on. I sometimes confront her about it. Confronting the
situation always
makes me feel better.
All I can say is, "Look
for the best in life."
Even though she is
rude and unsociable
to me, I have a beau-
tiful little brother to
play with and watch
grow up.

—Robin, 15,
California

One of every four children will live in a stepfamily. Researcher Mavis Hetherington found that 80 percent of children in stepfamilies do not have damaging emotional problems or school difficulties. She also found that boys tend to have an easier time adjusting to stepfamilies; girls have the hardest time when they live with their father and stepmother (perhaps because the females compete for the man's attention). Kids do much better when they have a continuing relationship with both biological parents. Researchers at the University of Missouri found that kids do best when their family is nurturing and stable, no matter what type of family they live in.

Jan Lawton, an Australian psychologist, reports that after five years or more, remarried couples report greater satisfaction with their marriages than couples in first marriages. Second marriages are more likely to end in divorce in the first several years, however, mainly because of problems with "his" and "her" children. Once they learn how to combine families, they can flourish.

Stepfamilies are complicated. Kids are coming and going. There are ex-spouses and grandparents in the picture. Stepparents can be jealous of their mates' longer history with their kids, and kids can be jealous of attention to a new person. Young people who didn't grow up together become stepbrothers and stepsisters. A family of two kids can expand to a blended family of six kids. An only child or the oldest can become the baby in the family.

Each family has its own rituals that may conflict with the other family's way of doing things. One family watches television at dinner, the other doesn't. This family opens Christmas presents on Christmas eve. The other one opens them on Christmas morning. How can these differences be resolved?

People may expect the new stepfamily to be like a first marriage family or like the "Brady Bunch," an unrealistic expectation. Expectations are a major problem in relationships, especially if they are unspoken and no one talks about their disappointments and frustrations. It's much easier if you do not expect your stepfamily to be like your original family. If you expect a dog and get a cat, you'll be sad. If you expect a cat and get one, you can handle it.

Youth surveyed for *How to Survive Your Parents' Divorce* advise that you enjoy having more family and friends and give the stepparent a chance. A frequent remark is that it takes time to get adjusted to a stepfamily, "because no one really knows how to act or react to everyday situations."

Adjusting to a Stepfamily

"It's hard to adjust: Just try to get along."

"Understand that it's all new to the stepparent, too."

"Be tolerant." (A reader comments, "It's harder than that for most kids!")

"Be patient with your stepparent."

"Keep an open mind about a new family structure."

"Be prepared for different philosophies."

"It's more love to go around. Try to be understanding about how difficult it is for everyone to adjust to a new family situation."

"It's hard at first. You feel like you have to do things to get attention from your real parent. It's hard to share your parent. But, after getting used to it, our stepfamily was great."

"It's hard to bond the way you do with a parent. Instead, be best friends with your stepparent on a special level."

"Be honest with your parent. My stepmother would try to hurt me by saying my father didn't want me. This hurt very badly and I wish I'd talked to my dad about it more."

"When a stepparent becomes controlling, which happens, you need to communicate and let them him/her that you are having a hard time taking rules. Build a respect that allows give and take."

Here are their negative and positive reactions to having a stepparent:

"It is very awkward having another woman getting my father's attention. We're not as close."

"My stepmother is very jealous of me and my mother; my dad and I drifted apart."

"I resent seeing more of my stepfather than my own father."

"It's like having a new friend in the family that you are supposed to treat as a parent."

"My stepfather became my 'real' dad."

"The first time my future stepfather came to the house, I liked him right away and told my mom that she should marry him."

"When my dad got a girlfriend, we got even closer."

Judith Bauersfeld, a leader in the Stepfamily Association of America, would like you to think about the stepparent's point of view. She explains, "Difficulty usually comes from some frustration or confusion on their part." She encourages you to talk about the kind of relationship you would like in order to understand each other's point of view. Being a stepparent can be hard and she asks that you think about what it's like for him or her. Check out your assumptions, essential to good communication between any two people.

Wendy Geis-Rockwood, author of the curriculum for *Shapes* groups for changing families, suggests that if you are having a hard time with a stepparent, speak up about how you feel. A parent's remarriage may trigger the stages of grieving you first went through during the separation, as it reminds you that your parents are not going to get back together. Some kids think if they are obnoxious, they can get rid of the stepparent, but it is not going to bring their parents back together. All the adjustments and complexities mean that good communication and conflict resolution skills are vital (see Chapter 2).

The National Survey of Children found that over a third of the children in stepfamilies will experience another divorce, and 10 percent will experience three or more divorces. Because of the previous histories, stepfamilies can benefit from working with a counselor before they move in together. There are good books about stepfamilies, such as those by therapists John and Emily Visher (who live in a large stepfamily themselves and are thriving). Stepfamily support groups and newsletters are also available to help.

—Lee, 18, California

My mom and stepdad have come a long way since their marriage when I was eight. By working everything out as a family, we all became really close. My parents have always done everything for me, even sacrificing themselves by giving up things they want so that I have everything I need. Their advice has been so good and they've always accepted me and forgiven me for the times I've screwed up.

I had a little rebel streak in me through high school and dealing with my parents. They seemed so off base in their decisions, but instead of getting on the defensive, rebelling, and completely disrespecting them, I changed my attitude. I realized they are really only trying to look out for my best interests, protect me, and prove their love for me.

—Devin, 21, California

I have two stepfamilies, one sister and a stepbrother. My birth parents divorced when I was four. My mom started seeing Mark shortly after. So as far as I can remember, Mark has been a part of my life. He and my mom are married now and have been together a long time. Mark never tried to take the place of my birth father. My dad was always visiting and calling and we managed to stay close despite my parents' divorce.

I think what has helped me to make room in my life for two full-time dads is not thinking of them both as my dads. Rather, I tried to remember that I only truly had one dad (biological), but there was room in my life for a friend. Mark started out being a good friend to my sister and me and now we think of him in much the same terms as our dad. We have never called him "dad" and sometimes it is hard to say "I love you" to him, but that's only because he's different from our dad.

My biological father remarried when my sister and I were teens. I had a much harder time accepting my stepmother than Mark. She was much younger than my dad and came with a one-year-old son, Joe. He was cute, but my sister and I were not very excited about having a baby brother. My dad and Lois married after he knew her for not even a year. Lois never tried to be a mother to us, but something was still awkward among the three of us. Since we didn't live with my dad, we were never forced to get to know his new family. Eventually we did get to know one another and, with time, we all have become one happy family.

I think what helped me deal with my dad's marriage was realizing that Lois made my dad happy. And while I may not have chosen her for my stepmom, my dad chose her to be his wife. I had to accept this and respect his decision enough to let him be happy. Joe, my new brother, was a tougher issue to cope with. He called my dad "Dad," even though Joe was not his biological child. My sister and I wanted to know when Joe would be told that our dad was not his "real" dad. When Joe was old enough he was told. By this time my sister and I had grown to love him as a brother and accept that our dad is his dad too. Learning to share our dad was the hardest part. Realizing that there was enough of him to go around gave us two great new people in our lives. I think that the key to dealing with stepfamilies is learning to accept your stepparents and share your biological parents.

—Steffani, 23, California

My parents divorced when I was really young and within a year, a lady, my stepmom, moved in with us. When I was 10 and 15 they had a girl and a boy together. Now they had their own family and then there was me. I felt like an outsider because my brother was with my mom and stepdad as their family. I stayed in my room during all my free time. I drank a lot on the weekends and gained 20 pounds. I would have to say I went through a depression where I had suicidal thoughts.

I coped by having a few very close friends to talk to and there was one family that was always there for me. They would give me support and I would hang out at their house a lot. I became serious with a guy and that changed my life around for the better. I had a more positive attitude, accomplished all my tasks, and was given more freedom.

For other teens who might be in a similar situation, I would suggest that there be someone on the outside whom you can go to for support and comfort. Also, I wish I had taken a stand and talked with my dad and stepmom to say what I was truly feeling. I had this problem of keeping everything in and stressed on everything. So I think you should sit down and discuss your feelings with your parents, tell them you want to talk as friends, and for them not to get upset at what you say, but to work the problem out *together. One last note for teens with stepparents, once you move out, you do become a friend of your stepparent. I get along very well with my stepmom now and I say exactly what I'm thinking, especially when she says something I disagree with.*

Stepfamily Association of
America 1-800-735-0329
(provides education and support
through local chapters and sells
books, videos, and tapes)

Stepfamily Foundation, Inc.
333 W. End Ave., Apt. 11C
New York, NY 10023

Values

There is so much peer pressure these days to "fit in" and "be cool." One thing a lot of kids knock is Christianity. I know myself that when you are around a bunch of friends and peers you tend to lose part of your identity as a Christian teen. A lot of times you don't realize what you are doing or how you are acting. I admit that I could be a whole lot better witness but I am too worried what my peers might think of me. The best thing you can do to help yourself live a better Christian life is to read your Bible, fellowship with other Christians, and pray to God. You might lose a few popularity votes but, trust me, in the long run it's worth it.

—Elaine, 14, Virginia

Values are what you think is right and wrong. Since they are the principles that shape your decisions and goals, it is essential that you give some thought to what you think is important and ethical. Students think the greatest crisis facing both their generation and the country is the decline of moral values and increase in crime, according to a survey of high-achiever students in 1995. Another national survey of teens found that their top issue or concern is "having life goals or purpose" (followed by a tie between "knowing God" and doing well in school, then their health, destruction of the environment, and peers). (The Barna Research Group, 1990 survey of 710 teens)

Part of growing up is defining your beliefs and principles. For example, some of my values are that you can count on me to do what I say I'll do, I make decisions on the basis of principle rather than how other people will respond, and I stick up for the underdog. Think about the Golden Rule of do unto others as you would have them do unto you; or, as you plant seeds, so shall you harvest.

How would you respond to the following polls about values? First, what's your definition of success? Teens are becoming less materialistic. In 1993, only 32 percent of teens agreed with the statement that "Success means making a lot of money," compared to 61 percent just four years previously (Teen-age Research Unlimited, Northbrook, Illinois). A 1992 Gallup poll of teens ages 13 to 17 reports that 67 percent believe that personal happiness is more important than being rich, 58 percent want to help those less fortunate, and 25 percent agree that "Making money is what it's all about." The Barna Research Group asked teens about their ideal future: 80 percent ranked close personal relationships as top priority, followed by marriage (60 percent), with a high paying job and being known as a person of integrity tied for fourth place.

A poll of youth ages 12 to 17 finds that only 16 percent say religion is not very important to them. Over half attend religious services about every week. Religion is a little more important to girls (53 percent) than boys (44 percent) and important to more Southerners than teens from other regions. (The telephone poll of 503 youth was conducted by Associated Press in 1995.) The Barna survey found that 60 percent of teens are religious and half attend religious services; 71 percent prefer to be experimental rather than traditional (29 percent). A 1996 poll reports religion is important to seven in 10 teens and 51 percent attend religious services regularly (poll for the Horatio Alger Association).

A 1993 Gallup poll looked at teens' religious preferences:
47 percent are Protestant, 30 percent Catholic, 13 percent no religion, five percent other religion, three percent Mormon, and two percent Jewish. A Gallup poll for America's Youth in the 1990s also asked about religious beliefs:

> 95% believe in God or a universal spirit
> 52% have confidence in organized religion
> 39% consider their own religious beliefs very important
> 25% believe religion can answer today's problems.

A 1995 poll of thousands of college freshmen nationwide (by UCLA) reports that belief in religion sank to a record low since the poll was first taken in 1966. Also, the percent who favor legalizing marijuana was the highest in 15 years, 58 percent favor legalized abortion, 43 percent think casual sex is OK, and 31 percent favor outlawing homosexual relationships.

A 1994 survey of 3,177 high-achiever high school students by Educational Communications Inc. raises concerns about values. More than three-fourths said they have cheated and two-thirds said it "didn't seem like a big deal." When asked if they would have sex with a "reasonably attractive stranger" for one million dollars, 43 percent of the boys and 25 percent of the girls said Yes. About a fourth are sexually active, and of those students, more than a third said they would have sex without a condom. Seventeen percent said they had stolen something from a store in the past five years. They believe the greatest problem facing the country is the "decline of the family." How would you respond to these questions?

Schools in some cities teach "values education," as in Baltimore, St. Louis, and Roswell (New Mexico). In Roswell, they emphasize values of trustworthiness, respect, caring, citizenship, justice, kindliness, consideration, and responsibility.

The Search Institute in Minneapolis does thousands of youth surveys to find out about their values. The Institute encourages the following values as a starting point. Rank them in order of importance to you.

Examples of Values

❖ Equality: All people have the same rights regardless of skin color, gender, national origin, or sexual preference.

❖ Honesty: meaning what you say.

❖ Promise-keeping: doing what you say you will do.

❖ Respect: treating yourself and others with consideration.

❖ Responsibility: carrying out your obligations.

❖ Self-control: being in charge of your actions and words.

❖ Social justice: treating all people fairly.

Another way to think about your values is to describe your dreams for the future. See what comes up in your mind as you complete these sentences in your journal. When I'm an adult:
I'll always _____. I'll never _____. My dream is to _____. I'll be admired for _____. I'll be known for _____. I'll change _____. I hope _____. I'm afraid _____. I'll never forget _____.

In the 1995 survey of high achievers (72 percent female), students identified what they most want in life:
family (32 percent)
career success (18 percent)
security (17 percent)
making a contribution to society (15 percent).

—Anna, 15, New Jersey.
I suppose the most difficult challenge that I face is knowing what to do in life. I feel like there are so many opportunities, and I'm afraid to miss them. That sounds bourgeois, I know, but I'm afraid that I'll look back, 10 years from now, and say, "Wow, I had a lot of potential, and I really blew that one." I want to live a spiritually guided life. I want to be right with God. I'm not sure how to do that, or even how to get in touch with God, or even what God is or how I should know God.

My main solace is writing, writing, writing. I write down my fears and thoughts, and later I look back at them and am wiser for having read them. I know more about myself. Asking myself questions on paper helps me to work through the puzzles in my head, as do late-night talks with similarly minded people. So does listening to the wisdom of others by reading holy books, talking to a parent or a teacher—just being open and listening to advice.

Life is hard. Don't try to do it by yourself, or try to solve it all at once. Don't be afraid to ask for help, and don't be discouraged by false starts or periods of feeling nothing. Don't accept mediocrity or depression; do something with your life.

—Jeremy, 15, Canada

I am expected by my parents to go to church every week by my parents, but I really do not believe in god. There are just too many questions. If there is a god, why such an imperfect world? If there is a god, why so many different versions of our beginnings? If there is a god, why so much scientific proof against it?

[My belief is that the world is imperfect because we have free will in order to learn and grow. Just as steel needs to go through intense heat to burn out impurities and become strong, so do we learn from our mistakes. I believe this is the symbolic meaning of the biblical story of expelling Adam and Eve from the Garden of Eden. Our job is to learn lessons from our challenges, and listen to our conscience or higher guidance.

As to a scientist's view, when Albert Einstein was asked if he believed in God, he said he believed there was Something that explained the spiritual harmony of the universe: "I maintain that cosmic religious feeling is the strongest and noblest incitement to scientific research." I like to think about tiny molecules having the same design as enormous solar systems. People who study quantum physics and chaos theory often arrive at a spiritual view of the universe because of the amazing patterns and order, even in seemingly random drops of water, as the following books explain.

Fritjof Capra. *The Tao of Physics*. Boston: Shambhala, 1991.

Michlo Kaku. *Hyperspace: A Scientific Odyssey Through Parallel Universes, Time Warps, and the Tenth Dimension*. Oxford University Press, 1994.

Brian Swimme and Thomas Berry. *The Universe Story: A Celebration of the Unfolding of the Cosmos*. NY: Harper Collins, 1992.

James Redfield and Carol Adrienne. *The Celestine Prophecy: An Experiential Guide*. NY: Warner Books, 1995.

—Camilla, 17, Mississippi

The main way that I "tap" into God is through daily devotions and youth retreats. Everybody needs renewal every once in a while, just like a car needs new gas sometimes. In life, everyone has ups and downs, mountain top experiences and valleys. We all want to stay on the mountain, but coming down is part of life. Surrounding yourself with a group of religious friends will definitely keep your spirits higher than a valley.

Talking with others about faith also strengthens your faith. If people ask you questions, you are forced to think and respond to them. There are so many ways to tap into God, individually and as a group, but I encourage you to try to encompass God in your daily walk so that you can stay on the mountain top all year.

—Nate, 18, California

As I entered adolescence, I rejected all my parents' values and beliefs and formed my own, which were basically opposites of theirs. As I grew older, I realized that my views weren't really my actual heartfelt opinions and that I only adopted them because they were different from my parents. Our values are pretty much the same now.

—Jane, 18, Ohio

What really turned me on to the "wrong" path was a constant struggle I had with the mold people tried to put me in. I attended church school all my life where I was having God, an "acceptable" moral code, and how I should act shoved down my throat so much that I finally choked. It suddenly dawned on me how disgusting these people were who were meant to be my role models. I simply rebelled against everything I was taught. It was just like when you eat too much. If you are fed enough of something that doesn't taste good to you to begin with, you just throw up, and it all comes out in a mixed mess at your feet and appalls everyone around you.

I was taught that I should look a certain way—plain, not much makeup, cute little loafers, and my hair in a ponytail—that's how everyone looked at my school. I wore very eye-catching (to say the least) clothes, eyeliner so thick that I looked like a raccoon, with blackish lipstick to match. I wore combat boots from the army surplus store and dyed my hair blue and wore it straight down in my face. I looked ridiculous most of the time but convinced myself it was better than what "they" wanted from me.

I was taught premarital sex was wrong: I began to sleep around. I was taught "Just say No!" so I began drinking heavily and smoking cigarettes and pot in large amounts. I was the complete opposite of everything I was taught and, by God, it was fun! A year later I had a serious drinking problem, I was labeled a slut by the people I wanted to be my friends, I had a cough that wouldn't go away, my grades dropped, my parents worried, and I was an emotional wreck. What started out as a "good time" had caused my entire world to collapse.

What put me back on track was something inside myself. I finally saw through all the makeup and dye and thrift store clothes. I was trying too hard and I knew it. Instead of being what "they" wanted me to be, I was being a complete opposite of it and I was neither. I had tried both extremes and didn't buy into either one. I finally began to "just be me." With a lot of support from family and friends, I became what I am today. I regained my self-confidence (actually got more than I had ever had) and began to act like the person I always knew I was.

I finally learned, as anyone has to, that being yourself is what matters. I didn't learn it from a music video or a quiz in a teen magazine, or even in school. I learned it from the most important source of all—experience. I slowly pulled myself out of the hole I had dug and began to see everything come together for me. I had a job, car, boyfriend, bigger group of friends, and good grades. It wasn't easy for me to do all this and took about two years before it all came together, but when it did, it was so, so worth it.

—Amber, 18, California

The most difficult challenge I faced was deciding my morals/values. I'm talking about personal issues: Is sex bad? Are all men really mean? My friends cheated in school, one is bulimic, one is mentally depressed. My grandfather died. It's all happened to me. Life can be really tough sometimes, but all you can do is know that you can always depend on yourself (and a good hug) to get you through.

My family is extremely close; I never realized it until I saw what my friend's family is like. We always have dinner together (or some activity) and I don't mind being there. They don't control my life (Mom began to let me have some freedom at 16), and they've always encouraged me and let me know that my opinion and judgments count. My mom is very much my friend. My grandmother is very close to me too. They never made fun of me when I cried over a boy, or a test, or anything else. Sure, my friends are helpful, but they aren't quite the same. I always tell my sister that I'm always here for her and that she can come to me about anything.

—Amanda, 21, Indiana

High school is a stage where a teenager establishes what is important: Use your high school experiences to help establish various values. Remember to respect those with wisdom—parents and advisors, but cultivate your own personal beliefs. Learn to question, and understand why you hold your own personal beliefs, values, and goals.

—Mike, 22, California

I got caught cheating on a test when I was 14. My parents were called and had to come to school and talk with my teacher and the administration. The worst part of it was the only thing they did to me was tell me how disappointed they were in me and how I let them down. I tried as hard as I could to regain the respect I lost. I put more time into studying and I was able to retake the test. Now, whenever I think about cheating, I think back to the disappointment in my parents' eyes and the urge to cheat is gone.

—Suzanne, 22, Canada

I was a geek, picked on in school, and had a lot of intellectual interests I could not share with anyone I knew. I liked poetry, religion, esoteric stuff like astrology and reincarnation, history, and philosophy. I turned to the Bible. I figured if people hated Jesus with all his wisdom, I shouldn't expect any less. I think the important thing is to stick to your convictions and be proud of your individuality. Conformism reigns because people don't have the guts to show their real selves. We're all individuals. The ability to express it is an act of courage, being true to one's nature. Developing a moral and intellectual backbone is essential. MORALITY IS A HABIT. The more you practice, the more committed you are to it, and the better you become. Consequently, you are truer to yourself. You don't sell out to worldly interests like popularity and peer pressure. God loves you.

—Tim, 24, California

*My high school music teacher loaned Richard Bach's **Illusions** (G.K. Hall) to me. It was a different way of looking at life, fun reading, but challenged me, made me think of things I'd never thought about before. Then I discovered **Autobiography of a Yogi** by Paramahansa Yogananda (Self-Realization Fellowship). The divine shone so clearly through Yogananda that it made it seem possible for me. I also enjoyed **Zen Without Zen Masters** (Camden Benares, And/Or Press) and **The Celestine Prophecy** (James Redfield, Warner).*

—Said, 24, California

When I was 12 years old our family escaped from Iran. My younger brother and I were the only ones who lived. After the shah was overthrown, a religious government came to power in Iran. This government took everything away from people who were not followers of Prophet Mohammed and who did not do what the government said to do.

My father said we must leave our country and go to another one. He said that if we stayed in Iran we would die. One night we started across the desert. There were patrols in cars and trucks we could not approach. Patrols hid in piles of rock and in holes in the desert. They looked out with special glasses that could see in the night. We had to be very careful. We had to go where there were no people, no food, and no water. There were fewer patrols there. One night my mother could not walk because she had hurt her foot the night before. My father sent us on and tried to carry my mother. Two days later he said a patrol had found them and killed my mother. He had a bullet hole in his leg and in the front and back of his torso. He almost died because we had not found water in many days and did not have medicine.

One day we slept in an old ruin wall. A man who seemed friendly gave us water and food, but soon came back with his friends and took away my sisters. They put ropes around us so that we would die in the sun or be shot by patrols. My brother found a piece of an old bomb and we worked all day and all night and cut our ropes. Three days later a land bomb went off near us while we were walking and I was cut on my leg in many places. It hurt a lot but we continued across the desert and the canyons.

My brother and I escaped from many patrols and hid from all people until we reached the mountains of Pakistan. We did not know it, but there is no water in those mountains. We almost died. We would have died except that one night a woman heard me crying and praying because I thought my brother was dead. I was afraid because I was all alone and we did not have food or water. The lady worked for the government of Canada as a nurse at a refugee camp. She took us 20 miles to the camp. A doctor in the camp said that I would not walk right again, and in an operation, took two rocks and some metal out of my legs. He said he was surprised that I could walk and did not die from infection or loss of blood.

It is important that I have faith in God. A big problem to one person may be a small problem to another. It is very difficult for me to walk upstairs, but I can do math very well. Some would look at me and wonder why he can't walk upstairs, that is so easy. But we all face many problems.

I would tell younger people to look at others who have faced great problems and see for yourself how others have solved the problems. I would tell them that often the way to solve a problem is the same no matter what the problem is. I would tell them that no problem is unsolvable, that there is a solution for all things. Many times a person must just wait and be quiet and not move and have faith that the problem will be solved. Many problems have their own solutions inside them. When facing a problem, admit that you cannot change it. Then when you know you are powerless, God will allow an answer to appear. He will give you strength to ace your problem and do what is right.

—Juan, 29, Nevada

When I was 14, I was caught with seven grams of marijuana. I was living in Guatemala where using drugs is not the same as using them in America. In America, you have constitutional protections and you only go to jail for a short time, if at all, on a first offense. I was poor and my parents were poor and could not pay money to the police or to the judge. I never went to the judge and was put in a prison right away. I think it was because the government wanted to show America it was getting tough on drug users. I went to prison for five years. I got out when I was 19 years old.

Prisons are different in Guatemala, too. If you have money you can buy good food or clothes or a good room. I was poor so I had to eat food that other people threw away, and some of the clothes I got I took off dead people before other prisoners or guards found them.

Sometimes the guards would come and take me into a room and beat me or tie me up and burn me. They were often young men who just liked to hurt people. Sometimes they would hurt people so badly the people would die. Sometimes they raped me. Sometimes other prisoners would too. Most of us who were young would stick together to protect ourselves from other prisoners or from the guards. Some boys were only 10 years old.

At first it was hope that helped me the most. But soon you learn there is no such thing as hope. Then it was friendship that helped me the most. But you also learn that there is a limit to friendship and devotion. We were friends, but we learned that friends are not always friends. I was not always able to be a friend to my friends.

I finally learned that only a belief in God could help, the God beyond God that people talk about. And not even Him so much as the belief in Him. It was the Belief that helped me the most. If you believe in something it will get you through almost anything. It got me through five years in prison in Guatemala. It got me into America when I ran away from my country. And now I am an American where I have constitutional protection. Belief made me an American citizen. Believing is helping me go to school to become a counselor so I can help other people learn how to believe. It is a hard thing to do, but if you do not believe, you will die. Believe me, I saw many people die who did not believe.

In America things are so easy, it is hard to know that Belief is important. I would tell people to Believe (it only works if it has a capital on it). Without Belief in something: God, Self, Dreams, anything, there is no strength to grow or to live. Very few Americans I meet know how to Believe. I would tell younger persons to look inside themselves, look at their dream of God, and Believe it.

Mary Halter and Barbara Fierro Lang. *Making Choices: Life Skills for Adolescents*. Santa Barbara, CA: Advocacy Press, recent edition. (P.O. Box 236, Santa Barbara, CA 93102) (Designed for classroom use, the book encourages thinking about personal values and gender stereotyping, and includes a student workbook.)

Kelley Kline

Chapter 6

Friends

Friends can provide tremendous support and understanding, or peers can make us feel out of it and pressure us to engage in activities against our better judgment. The challenge is to find friends we trust and respect to help build a buffer against peers who may be hurtful. The main advice from youth is to be yourself, create your own identity, and realize that the popular group in high school may not be the successful ones at your five-year class reunion. (Notice how many times the word *cool* is used in this chapter and what it suggests about how to behave. Would we be happier if it was considered in to be "warm?")

Abuse in Dating

My freshmen year in high school, I had a very abusive boyfriend, but because he never left bruises, no one ever found out. I had no friends to go to; he almost ruined my life.

He moved out of state, otherwise I may have stayed with him longer. I really did not have any clue as to how I should have dealt with it. Now, I have rules about the people I date. Boyfriends aren't allowed to call me fat or ugly, and I won't date someone who tries to take away my friends. Now no one I date is ever allowed to hit me— one strike and he is gone.

—Robin, 18, Colorado

Estimates are that one quarter of high school students are in abusive or violent relationships. Girls may stay in the relationship because they blame themselves for doing something to "deserve" the abuse. In a study released in 1995, 15 percent of girls ages 14 to 17 reported being the victims of attempted date rape, 40 percent had a friend who had been beaten by a boyfriend, and 26 percent knew someone who was a victim of sexual abuse (a telephone survey of 1,000 11-to-17-year olds, by Children Now and Kaiser Permanente).

The logical action is to get out of an abusive relationship, but the abuser often gradually wears down the self-esteem and strength of the victim by alternating put downs and affection. Similar tactics are used to torture prisoners of war. Abusers are often very controlling, jealous, try to keep their victim isolated from others, blame others, and have sudden mood swings. Feeling weak and dependent obviously makes it hard for someone to break away from that control.

Also, abusers tend to be apologetic and affectionate after violently venting their negative feelings. Some people get hooked on the excitement of building tension, blowups, and making up in the cycle of abuse. As with any problem, recognizing it is half the battle. Talk to an expert who recognizes the cycle of abuse, such as a school counselor or a 12-step codependency organization (modeled on Alcoholics Anonymous) to find out about support groups.

You've probably heard people talk about being a codependent; 12-step support groups look at their attraction to unhealthy romances as an addiction. An anonymous Internet writer describes the dynamics of codependency.

We were dependent personalities, terrified of abandonment, willing to do almost anything to hold onto a relationship in order not to be abandoned emotionally. Yet we kept choosing insecure relationships because they matched our childhood relationship with dysfunctional [often alcoholic] parents. We confused love with pity, tending to love those we could rescue. Even more self-defeating, we became addicted to excitement in all our affairs, preferring constant upset to workable solutions. The solution is to become your own loving parent. Support groups assist in the healing process.

We can get hooked on an unhealthy relationship just as people can get addicted to a drug. This usually occurs when two patterns developed in childhood fit each other like a key in a lock, as when an alcoholic and a rescuer are instantly attracted and feel at one with each other. Popular songs refer to this unhealthy dependency as if it were a natural part of love: "Without you I'm nothing," "You're my other half," "When I lost my baby, I almost lost my mind."

In an unhealthy relationship we're unhappy, frustrated, unconfident, and anxious. The other person is usually unavailable in that he/she doesn't want a committed relationship or isn't capable of one. If you find yourself controlled, put down, threatened, isolated, and manipulated, then leave. You can't change the other person's behavior, but you can stop playing the game.

We often gravitate to the familiar, as when we repeat our parents' relationship or react against it, so it's wise to spend some time thinking about their interaction. A counselor can help by pointing out patterns so close to us we can't see them. Danisha comments that some people don't like talking to someone they don't know, and feel more comfortable with a friend. In such cases peer support groups may be more useful. The neutrality of counselors and their skills in getting at buried feelings is hard to duplicate though.

Robin Norwood, author of *Women Who Love Too Much* (J.P. Tarcher) suggests that codependent persons should focus on their own growth rather than trying to change their partners, stop being the rescuer or the victim, and find a support group or counselor. We all need to take time alone rather than hopping from partner to partner. Your challenge is to figure out the differences between infatuation, lust, codependency, desire for attention, and love (see the love section). Your task is easier if you've been able to closely observe a loving couple; if you not, you can learn on your own by reading, talking with a counselor, and analyzing your interactions.

—Brad, 20, California

My ex-girlfriend was very codependent and controlling. I thought I was in love, but I was too involved for my age (16). From what I know now I would not have had such a serious relationship at that point in my life. Then I ignored the problems, rather than face the facts. Problems included her threatening suicide and unwanted sexual advances.

I put myself in a bad situation by trying to rescue her from her bad situation. To change that I would no longer attempt to rescue anyone from their problems by having a romantic relationship with them. [Perhaps he was codependent in trying to rescue her.]

—Tamara, 22, California

When you see red flags, get away, it's not worth it. I started dating Mark when I was 18. I'd graduated from high school and I thought I was in love. He was a sophomore at CalTech and very cute. We dated for three years. Throughout those years, he raped me, hit me, and emotionally abused me. When Mark was abusing me, I didn't mind the physical parts, it was the emotional. He would tell me I was fat and stupid. After a while you believe it. [The abuser does this to lower self-confidence and create dependency.] I was at a junior college, and I had a really low GPA. (Now I am graduating from college and raised my GPA.) I blocked everything out, but started remembering after we broke up the last time.

After we broke up, he stalked me, followed me, and made my life a living hell. This was a really hard time in my life. I still am trying to remember what he did to me. I went through counseling, which I am still in, and I cried a lot. I am now helping other rape survivors.

—Tamara, 23, Illinois

I came from a good home, no divorce or abuse. Unfortunately, at 17, I found my way into the arms of a 25-year-old abuser. I was attracted to the fact that someone older liked me. If I had only listened, I would have realized that from the beginning he was trouble. He was in the military and that kept him somewhat straight because, if he was late or belligerent, he would get his pay docked. He was an alcoholic and mentally abused me in every fashion. I wish someone would have been there for me.

I was at boarding school because my parents lived overseas. I was a senior in high school and very independent. I thought I could handle it but I lost my friends, my social life, and some very precious time—three years to be exact. I moved out to San Diego to be with him. He never wanted me; he used me and verbally abused me.

When he got out we moved back to Illinois, where our parents were. Ironically, he broke up with me and forced me out of our home. I left and thought it was the end of the world. My therapist made me write down all the terrible things he did to me. When I would get the feeling that I wanted to go back to him, I would reread those passages and it made me stronger.

The story doesn't end there. He decided that he wanted me back and if he couldn't have me, no one could. I am still in hiding today because he stalked me. I have gotten orders of protection but the law doesn't help. He has to actually put his fist to my face before they will help me.

I don't know what to tell young girls who are in bad situations. I think building self-esteem and self-worth needs to begin at home and, if not there, in after-school classes. If I had been smart enough to realize that I was worth more, I would have been a lot better off. This man stripped any self-worth I had away from me.

If someone keeps pushing you away, you should go, get on with your life. He isn't worth it anyway. Someone who makes you feel that bad IS NOT WORTH IT. There are so many good people out there. Mine came along when I least expected it. Now, I am happily married, but still battle with things in our relationship. My husband is a beautiful man who is trustworthy and a hard worker. He never abuses me but I still revert to my old defensive ways when I don't have to.

—Jennifer, 25, Texas

A guy I was involved with was a very bad influence. We started as friends and I really opened up to him about my insecurities and inner thoughts, but he wound up twisting it around to manipulate me emotionally and sexually. It was an emotionally abusive situation, and it took me years to be able to trust myself, let alone trust men.

Ending Abusive Dating Relationships

Leah Aldridge, et al. *A Relationship Violence Prevention Curriculum for Youth Ages 12-19.* (Equity Resource Center, has many other resources, 1-800-225-3088)

Melody Beattie. *Codependent No More. Beyond Codependency.* SF: Harper, 1989.

Harriet Braiker. *Lethal Lovers and Poisonous People.* NY: Pocket Books, 1992.

Barrie Levy. *In Love and Danger: A Teen's Guide to Breaking Free of Abusive Relations.* Seattle: Seal Press, 1993.
(includes emotional, physical, and sexual abuse, dating violence, and what to do about it)

Brenda Schaeffer. *Is It Love or Is It Addiction?* San Francisco: Harper, 1989.

Cliques

Teenagers form cliques with others who have the same problems and interests as themselves. When I walk down the hallways at school, I see the "rednecks" talking at their lockers, the "sluts" walking with their boyfriends, the "jocks" discussing last week's game, the "preps" talking about their political views, the "nerds" debating which computer program is best, and the "rejects" watching their feet as they shuffle slowly down the hall. People can be way too critical. The teachers suggest getting help from a school guidance counselor. Sometimes they can help, but other teenagers can give advice too. As Shakespeare wrote, "To thine own self be true."

—Kristen, 15, Illinois

Belonging to a group which accepts and likes you is an issue for most of us. School is easier if we have a group of friends with common interests who appreciates us for who we really are. But what do you do if your clique's expectations of you sometimes conflict with your values, or if you have to hide parts of your personality to fit in? Danisha observes that, "Often people are put down and ridiculed for having the confidence to be themselves." Some people are content with a few good long-lasting friends.

Most of the college students I surveyed remember high school cliques of preppies, jocks, skaters, stoners, and nerds. Some also named surfers, cowboys, aggies, gangsters, mods, rockers, rock-a-billies, metalers, head bangers, druggies, loadies, wedge heads, punks, skinheads, freaks, hippies, geeks, bookworms, brains, snobs, actors, cholos, homeboys, slackers, and quaddies. "What's the point?" asked a reader. I'm curious about how people identify themselves (and the names sound poetic); please let me know about the cliques in your school.

"People aren't always what they seem. They're usually more. Find out what they dream and see," Toki advises. "Visit" different cliques to learn about them. Treat people as you want to be treated, look for what you have in common, and don't judge by appearances. To get along with various ethnic groups, students advise that you make an effort to learn about them, ask questions, be open-minded, and concentrate on the fact that we are all human.

—Melissa, 15, Texas

The most difficult challenge I face as a teen is finding who I am, not who people want me to be. Realizing I am an individual, not part of a clique, and that I will always be different from everyone else helps me cope with trying to find myself.

Don't conform, no matter what. If you conform to others' standards, you lose a part of yourself, your identity. If anyone ever tells you that you are "weird" or "different," thank him or her. It is probably the best compliment you will ever receive.

—Justin, 16, California

People look at you like you're crazy or bad because you have a different style and because you dress unique. Most people judge you by the way you dress, which is wrong. They think you have to look like other people or you aren't a person. Sometimes the way you dress is describing the way you feel inside, not perfect, and you're your own person.

—Jed, 16, California

In junior high, it was all about popularity, the in-crowds, and outcasts. I felt this a little bit, but I've always had close friends who supported me so I didn't need to join any clique. In high school, it was like a breath of fresh air. The cliques are still there, and the popularity thing is still there, though not as much, and it isn't as important. I think as people grow up even more, they will ditch the cliques. I am pretty mature for my age, so I have trouble associating with the insecure and immature people who feel they need to be in cliques. The women like mature men, so it's all good.

—Dawn, 18, Kansas.

As in most high schools, ours had about 50,000 little "groups" or "cliques" one could be in. What helped me cope with this was that I just got involved. I joined clubs, I did marching band, I became active in our theater. I would say GET INVOLVED. Find a club or activity that interests you, and join up. Clubs and activities come with peer groups to associate with. If all you do is sit on the side, then you are not trying to meet people and find your niche.

—Jen, 18, California

The main groups in my high school were the jocks, aggies, the really popular crowd, geeks, skateboarders, thespians, and the "rebel" crowd in their black leather jackets. When I first changed schools, I got a lot of first impressions from the different people I saw and prejudgments from comments I heard about the different groups. Starting out like this I almost developed prejudices against certain groups. After a little while, I started to give the people I had avoided a chance. I realized how much I had been missing out on.

I discovered that the most judged people were also the least judging. I've found that the people I never expected to have anything in common with are the friends I really value.

—Riadh, 18, California

The most difficult challenge I faced as a teen so far is popularity status. When it comes to friends and popularity, many people—including myself—put up a false front to make friends, but what I find hard is putting up that false front. I don't want to at all, but that false front appears. Well, I just found out that being myself made people like me more and they found out that I'm a pretty cool guy.

—Kerryn, 20, Australia

The main groups in high school were the westies (heavy metal), the surfies, the rurals (from out bush) and the regular people. We all had different interests, different styles, but we all got along OK, because we had such a small school.

—Sara, 22, Missouri

High school is a time for people to want justification for their own feelings and to feel the kinship of others who feel that same way. This leads to cliques and gangs. A gang is a clique that uses physical violence instead of social violence to intimidate and harass others that they feel are beneath them. Avoid them. Don't join a clique, don't allow your group of friends to become closed, and don't confront a clique.

Each group has its own perspective, values, and goals, so enjoy the ideas they have to offer. Don't write them off. I've been impressed with some of the stuff I've heard from people I'd previously labeled and written off as techno-geeks without a clue.

The students who run for student office should be thanked for warning other students that they are the "popular crowd," and if you dare not think like them, dress like them, talk like them, and generally abandon all vestige of your own sense of self-worth when you are near them, you will incur their wrath, and the lemming-like pack-wrath of their flocks.

As for the group of students who say, "Look at me, world! I'm DIFFERENT! Please, someone, look," for all their talk about not caring about what other people think, they do. The evidence is on their tattoos, their ripped leather jackets, their motorcycle boots, etc. They do care, and they want to shock.

Look at them, and remember to not put the opinions of others so highly that you don't care how you feel about something. That's the most important "secret" of high school. A lot of people will tell you that you won't feel good about yourself unless you act like them, dress like them, think like them. Ask yourself, "Do they feel good about themselves? If they're so insecure and need other people to affirm their behavior, do I want to be like them?"

Friends · 255

Denis Lang. *But Everyone Else Looks So Sure of Themselves: A Guide to Surviving the Teen Years.* White Hall, VA: Shoe Tree Press, 1991.

Lee Peck. *Coping with Cliques.* NY: Rosen Publishing Group, 1992.

Dating

T he dating ritual can be exciting or humiliating. Concentrate on developing genuine friendships with both sexes and learning as much as you can about the other sex. You don't need to rush into having a boy/girlfriend before you set the foundation of your own style, values, and goals.

The consensus of college students I surveyed is that it's smart to date various people in high school rather than pair up with one person, and that it's a burden for guys to have to initiate relationships. Sue adds, "Don't just focus on the popular guys, you'll be missing out on some really nice boys." To minimize the nervousness of a first date, think about doing something active during the day, like taking a hike or bowling—something that doesn't put you in the date mode so you have to think about how close to sit, to hold hands or not, or to kiss good-by. Going with a group to an evening activity such as a concert or a film is also safe.

A survey by Teenage Research Unlimited, 1993, reports that teenagers' favorite activity was dating. However, the most time was spent— you guessed it—television. Another survey looked at the most common leisure activities of high school seniors (University of Michigan Institute for Social Research, 1990). In order of most frequent activity, teens watch television, hang out with friends, read, play sports, and spend time alone.

Fond Memories

A third survey asked teens about the best time they've had so far (make your own list before you read on):

- ⮑ getting their driver's license (12 percent)

- ⮑ winning a sports championship (11 percent)

- ⮑ starting high school (nine percent)

- ⮑ sneaking out late at night (eight percent)

- ⮑ losing their virginity (eight percent)

- ⮑ academic achievement (eight percent)

- ⮑ first party without their parents (seven percent)

- ⮑ going to the prom (six percent)

- ⮑ getting a job (four percent)

- ⮑ community recognition (three percent).

(1993 poll by Teenage Politics: Public and Personal, BKG Youth)

Anthropologist and author Desmond Morris observed courtship practices around the world, and found a common pattern that's interesting to observe. First, societies somewhat separate elementary school age boys and girls in different groups so that they'll be excited about discovering each other later in adolescence. Teens "parade," walking around looking at each other, checking each other out for sexual attractiveness as a potential mate. They meet during a common activity and talk to each other while leaning forward and smiling to show interest. When they start a romantic relationship, it's like a return to infancy in that they use baby names (including "my baby"), cuddle, rock, feed each other, and so on. When they're a couple, they show "tie signs" in public to keep other suitors away, like handholding and arms around each other.

Starting A Relationship
—Christine, 16, Texas

The most difficult thing I've faced as a teen has definitely been being in a relationship. I feel that, from experience, anyone 16 and younger should avoid a steady relationship. You become, in a way, secluded because you are so dependent on one particular person. And in the long-run, you end up getting hurt. As a teenager, I feel the best thing to do is to stay out of a relationship and date people.

—Andy, 17, Texas

My problem has been lack of independence, which I can successfully blame for my ineptitude in attaining girls. [His expression suggests dating is like going hunting and needing to catch something to prove your masculinity, a belief that puts a lot of pressure on a guy to be somehow more than just himself.] *Girls go for the carefree guys but, when your parents limit your independence, they also limit your carefree side. I wasn't allowed to stay late and socialize with girls, leaving an open door for the guys who could stay longer. The carefree guys with more independence were allowed to have cars before I did. This limited my social appearances since I didn't want to be dropped off and picked up at a party. But now that I've got my own vehicle and can stay out long enough, my status has dramatically changed.*

—Josh, 17, Texas

Choosing the right girl to date has been difficult. I find myself liking the wrong girls for the wrong reasons, either purely for looks or social standing or what not. One must go through the stupid act of courting someone based on superficial reasons. Have as much fun with as many people you can, but be sure to learn from your mistakes.

—Peter, 18, Pennsylvania

In junior high I was known for being a nerd, geek, etc. It was not a pleasant thing. Junior high may have been hell, but at least it was something that I could latch onto. When I entered high school, immediately I felt intimidated. There were so many older kids! How many were nice? How many weren't so nice? The status quo I had in junior high and the security that came with it suddenly came crashing down. No one knew who I was here. I thought about it, and soon concocted a plan that would make everyone know who I was.

Nicole was a rather popular girl throughout junior high, an excellent golfer. She was the only freshman on the varsity golf team. Because of her excellent golfing ability, she became well known in the school. As the person actively chasing her, I also became well known. Even seniors knew who I was. A year after the fact, one of them asked me in a class, "You're the one who was in love with Nikki, aren't you?" It just goes to show that I became known in the school, even if it were for something like that.

Also, in my own class, I became hugely popular, as kids told me that "I finally found my hormones." The whole experience of falling in love made me feel very insecure and very immature. My grades suffered horribly. I didn't care, though. When my parents questioned my grades, I told them they were bad because of a hard class I was in. I never told them about the lassie who didn't like me. I felt so insecure that I nearly took my life a few months later. After finding the wisdom not to take my life, I swore off girls forever. The first and only love I had at that point put me in a very bad position and I didn't want to repeat it.

But two and one-half years later, I communicated my interest to another girl. The results were mixed, partly because I was afraid the same thing was going to happen. This year, there were three girls I liked. With two of them nothing resulted, but the third I asked out. She told me she couldn't that day and seemed somewhat surprised that I asked her. I didn't call again, and decided I'd wait until college. [Girls, please note how difficult it can be for boys to initiate dating, so try to be empathetic. The following is an Internet dialogue between Peter and me.]

GK: I think meeting people is like going fishing. You keep casting, not waiting for the perfect fish. You don't have to ask girls out on a formal date; lunch or a walk or something casual is a lot easier. So is talking on the phone for some people. You need to practice getting to know them and see how to play the game.

Peter: I've always viewed it as a burden. Ever since Nikki, I could never view it differently.

GK: It's time to change your attitude because thoughts are very powerful—they generate results. I would keep thinking a positive direction like "I will meet the right girl at the right time." It really is fun once you get the hang of it. It should be enjoyable, not a burden. Think about it as a game, where you see how many girls you can get to know a little and make each one feel good about you being interested in her as a person.

Do your best to meet girls and initiate conversation, but what is important is that you try, not that they respond. Don't judge yourself by results, just by effort. Eventually you'll meet someone you click with, but it's good to practice first to gain self-confidence. That's very attractive in itself.

Peter: I guess you're right, but how do I just change my attitude that quickly? It isn't easy. I'm under the impression that I'm NEVER going to get a girl. How can I start to talk to her? What should I say? I want to try to at least DATE a girl soon.

GK: Find something in common. If you share a class, ask her what she thinks about it. If you don't share a class, say, "Hi, are you a freshman? Me too, how's it going?" If she responds, say something like, "Let's go have a soda and talk more about this" (see Cane's advice below).

Peter: I'll try. But I don't want to say the wrong thing that will paint me in a bad light.

—Dave, 21, California

I was really shy in high school so I'd have to say that asking girls out on dates was a pretty tough thing. Mostly my parents supported me and my friends gave me the self-esteem and confidence to overcome my fear of rejection. I think the best advice I can give is that No is the worst a girl can say, but you'll never know unless you ask.

—Darin, 23, California

I dated as much as possible! I got experience by dating a lot and having a lot of female friends who gave me good advice. Have lots of female friends and treat women with respect.

—Jennifer, 25, Texas

I think it's really important to have good, platonic [nonsexual] friendships, not just dating relationships. I grew up in a family of girls and I really never had close male friends (who were not potential dating partners) until I was in college. I think I sort of assumed that, if I got along with a guy, that meant I must want to date him.

—Tim, 27, California

The girlfriends you can catch by being "on the prowl" are the ones that you will look back on and say, "I didn't want that person in my life." The ones you grow to be special friends with, after first being good friends, are the ones that will stand a chance of being friends with you during (and after) a relationship.

How to Ask a Girl Out

—Cane, 29, California

1. *Never come across as desperate. No matter how much you like a girl, she should never know that you've got a huge crush on her until after you've gone out several times.*

2. *First things first, spend some time around her so she has some idea who you are. This can be as simple as smiling at her and saying hello on a regular basis. Then try to find something in common—art, computers (careful with this one unless you're sure she really likes them), sports, etc. What you're trying to do is have a casual friendship with her before you ask for her phone number.*

3. *After you've gotten her number and before you call her, think about what you'll say. Have a legitimate reason for the first call, homework, school activity, etc. When you call her, if her mom or dad answer the phone, introduce yourself to them; this is important! You want her folks to be comfortable with their daughter spending time with you. But, be careful; if her parents like you too much, she'll probably lose interest in going out with you.*

4. *Do NOT ask for a date on the first call! Also, be nice; if you can fit it in the conversation without it being strange, compliment her on something, hair, clothes, etc. Then, after talking about what you called her for, unless she continues the conversation, say thanks and goodbye! The Cardinal Rule of Women: Women are like cats, they only become interested in something that they have to chase. This doesn't mean that she'll pursue you obviously, but if you entice her interest, you'll notice that she'll be around where you are more frequently and will smile at you more.*

   Once you're dating, to have a smooth first kiss, don't try to go into it "cold," after doing something together with no touching, such as eating dinner. Wait until you've held hands, so it's natural to take both of her hands when you're saying goodnight. If she pulls her hands away, it's not time to kiss. If she keeps them in yours, or touches you, that's a signal to go ahead and kiss her. The first time, kiss and leave, so she doesn't feel overwhelmed and is intrigued.

—Jack Kammer, author of *Good Will Toward Men* (St. Martin's Press)

Young women often explain that they usually don't initiate relationships because "men don't like it." That makes me laugh because what men like didn't stop women from demanding equality in the political and work world. I think a much more honest reason why women don't initiate is that initiating doesn't serve their purposes. If a woman initiates a date, she's much less likely to have the young man scrimp and save to take her to a fancy restaurant for dinner. But, she's much more likely to start a relationship free from traps and friction rooted in sexism.

Ten Red Flags to Watch
For in Starting a Relationship

—Stan Morgan

1. The person's relationship with parents and parents' relationship with each other.

2. How many dating relationships he or she has had, how long they lasted and why. If someone has a lot of short romances, for example, you might want to know why.

3. Honesty is important. Does she tell little white lies or change her stories over time? With some people you can tell if they're telling the truth by looking into their eyes.

4. Communication is essential. Is the other person willing to share his feelings, compromise, and resolve conflicts fairly?

5   Is the person overly focused on their appearance and clothes?

6. Is he or she too eager to please, too generous, or wants to move too fast? You want to be with someone who is independent.

7. What are his friends like?

8. If the person has a quality you don't like and says so, believe her. Don't expect to change it.

9. Is there more than a chemical/sexual attraction? Do you have some common interests? Take time to become friends before you move into the sexual area to make sure.

10. Does the person smoke or use drugs? What about other values?

Aaron asks, "What's good conversation for first dates?" Your goal is to get to know each other, make the other person feel appreciated, and have fun. Find out what interests the other person, about her or his goals and beliefs, as if you were a reporter interviewing a famous personality. You can talk about school, music, sports, films, politics, family and childhoods, or whatever interests you share.

You might take turns asking and answering questions: What are five things you like about yourself? What are three things you like about me? What five things make you happy? Most thrilling adventures? How do you think you'd be different if you'd been raised the other gender? What are your favorite foods, movies, music, colors, etc.? If you could travel anywhere in the world, where would you go? If you could have lunch with any living famous person, whom would you pick?

After reading this, Jessica adds, "Don't make it sound like an interview or 20 questions." Some people don't like to be asked such direct questions, so make a genuine effort to get to know the other person and let him or her know you are interested. Guys need to make a special effort to ask questions of their dates rather than try to impress her by talking about themselves.

Maintaining a Relationship

—Tom, 22, California

Getting along with either sex requires respect, honesty, and a lot of humor to deal with the hard times. Basically, just be yourself and listen to the other person.

—Susie, 27, California

I always had a list of what I want in someone. The list is really lengthy, but I knew someone had to have all those qualities because I felt if I had them, there had to be someone else who had them too. After endless dating experiences, some of my friends said, "Susie, you will never get married, you are too picky." I would say, "If I don't get married, I don't care. I know what I need and want and I will not settle for any less. I'd rather be alone than lonely in love." I adopted the motto, "I will not marry someone I can live with, I will only marry someone I cannot live without."

I feel there are so many divorces because people marry for the "I can live with this person" reason. I believe many times people marry someone they are with because they are getting older and feel their time is running out to find the right person. Other times, the woman gives the man the "marry me or I am leaving" ultimatum, and the man is not ready to let go of the relationship yet, so they marry. Sometimes, people just feel that their relationship and all its imperfections is the best that it gets. In all these cases, people are settling.

I feel I am very lucky to have found John; he is definitely someone I cannot live without and I can place a check mark by each item on my list. Romance and passion are what I thrive on, so it is easy for me to keep the relationship alive. I hate the thought of being married and having it get monotonous, so I constantly do and plan things to keep our relationship interesting.

Some of the items on this list are what I call "Rules for Romance." We always give each other cards for no reason at all and leave them all around the house as reminders of our love. We celebrate our monthly anniversary. We call several times a day to say "Hi," or "I love you." We always kiss hello and good-by. We treat each other like a guest whenever possible (for example, when I am getting something in the kitchen for myself, I'll ask John if he needs anything).

My theory is this: In the beginning of relationships, people go out of their way to impress the other person. They try to always look nice, they are affectionate, they kiss a lot, play a lot, and spend a lot of time getting to know each other—sharing, talking, and listening. Then after they "have" each other by becoming an item, a sad and strange phenomenon happens—they change.

The marriage moves to the back burner and work, chores, and daily life take precedence over the relationship. They take it for granted, pure and simple. The little things they used to do, they don't. They get out of shape, stop complimenting, and start nagging. They are too tired to kiss and make love because all their energies are put into other obligations. No wonder the divorce rate is so high; something has to give.

A relationship is an obligation and a commitment. A relationship is like a garden; if you tend to its needs you have a beautiful garden; if you neglect it, it grows weeds and part of the garden dies. It is much easier to spend a little time tending it every day than to replant.

Maintaining a relationship is similar to maintaining a car. Both require gas, servicing, and maintenance to keep running. Take time to nurture each other by sharing activities you enjoy, talking, and cuddling. Many couples make the mistake of forgetting to keep courting each other. My college students shared how they create romance: surprise gifts, love notes (sometimes hidden), flowers, picnics, really listen to each other, candlelit dinners, watch a sunset, hold hands, eat finger foods such as strawberries, listen to music, make a photo album, create a handmade card, plan a surprise party, paint a T-shirt, tape your favorite songs, dance, hike, walk in the rain, compliment each other, and "kidnap" your sweetheart for a special date.

Overall, in the surveys, college guys emphasized treating young women with respect and as equals. "If you don't see women only for their physical attributes, you'll find that you treat them with much more respect," Toki reports. "Try to downplay sex issues, find a middle ground," Will says. Females emphasized being friends first and understanding gender differences. Erika suggests, "Realize that under most circumstances men and women communicate and react differently. Be patient."

> Gregory Godek. *1001 Ways to Be Romantic*. Weymouth, MA: Casablanca Press, 1993. Also, *Romance 101* and *The Portable Romantic*.

Breaking Up

—Kelley, 16, California

I was always very unsure about myself from junior high up till the 10th grade, when I had my first true love. It gave me direction and confidence but it ended and I felt like I was dying. It seemed so bad at first, but I realize there is so much more left of my life and more to experience. I think I'll do OK without her.

—Tracy, 17, California

I just recently came out of a relationship I've been in for 14 months. He was my best friend and only love. My world revolved around this person and without him now I feel like only half a person. [This is not healthy love and if you feel like this, consider it a danger signal. You should feel expansion rather than shrinking of your self, stronger rather than weaker.] *He was my very best friend and now I feel very sad and alone. It is hard to remember who I was before him. I still feel very strongly about him and wish that he acted more like he used to. I find it hard to love myself when he can go on without me.*

I talked to my friend in my church youth group, a good listener, and all-around beautiful person. She helped me to do things that I enjoy doing and to discover life again for myself. She is one of the few who can make me smile. I also learned to live day by day and let time heal.

Life can get very hard and sometimes almost doesn't seem worth living, but the moments help when you discover a new friend or see a rainbow. Time does heal and surrounding yourself with positive things that make you smile on the outside often can make you smile on the inside too.

Don't lock people out. Remember that you can love again, although you don't believe it until it happens again. Avoid what hurts you in your life, at least until you can face it when you are stronger. I still feel alone, sad, and weak. I try to keep busy every day. I am growing stronger, but very slowly. When I feel depressed I talk to people and cry, sleep, and remember to eat. Life starts up and you have the power in you to change. Don't give up on yourself. You are a lot stronger than you might think.

[Kahlil Gibran writes in *The Prophet* (Knopf),

Love one another, but make not a bond of love:
Let it rather be a moving sea between the shores of your souls.
Fill each other's cup but drink not from one cup...
And stand together yet not too near together:
For the pillars of the temple stand apart,
and the oak tree and the cypress grow not in each other's shadow.

Losing yourself in another person is not love, it's dependency.]

—Jenna, 17, California

The most difficult challenge I've faced as a teen was breaking up with my first love. I was totally heartbroken, and still am after a year and a half. I was devastated and I lost a lot of weight (which wasn't too bad). I never ate or smiled or wanted to do anything. I was in a serious depression for about eight months, I felt so hurt and rejected. I've never had a whole lot of self-esteem anyway, so this practically buried me in the dirt.

Just remember that you can't let anybody change who you are. There are better guys out there, especially the one you're going to marry. With every heartbreak you learn. Guys are stepping stones to find out what you want in a husband. It's hard to let your guard down and trust someone, but love is a risk. If you want to take the risk of something beautiful, there's always the risk of getting hurt. Be happy in yourself and love yourself before you can learn to love someone else.

—Molly, 18, California

I started going out with Nick when I was 15. I liked him for a long time before we ever started going out. I was young and he was my first love. It was about 10 months into our relationship and things were getting real serious between us. The pressure was on to take a further step into our relationship, a step I didn't quite know if I was ready or willing to take—sex. I knew I loved him, and cared for him a lot, so one day we had sex. This brought us closer together than ever and I knew, at least I thought I knew, I was meant to be with him. Our relationship went on throughout my junior year, and then one day in September of my senior year, it all came crashing down on me, the day I thought would never come; he broke up with me.

"I think we need to see other people." Those words I repeated over and over again in my head trying to figure out, "How could he have done this to me?" I felt as if my whole world was gone, as if I was nothing and my life was ending. I felt as if I had been violated; I felt as if I had been used. Two years of my life with him just washed away with eight words: "I think we need to see other people." I was a 17-year-old basket case. I felt that I would never get over this ordeal, but time went on and things got better. I finally lost my interest in him and started my life over.

Three months after the big break-up, guess who wants to come back? You guessed it—Nick! By this time I couldn't care less about him, and basically told him I was not interested anymore. Now Nick and I are good friends, but never anything more. The moral of this story is sex does not mean forever or love, just passion.

The most difficult experience I faced as a teen was breaking up with my first girlfriend. She broke up with me. That was pretty hard. I was going to kill myself with a .357, when my dad found me sitting out in our orchard with a gun in my hand. My dad and I really became close after that. He made me realize that these things happen all the time and that it will probably happen again. He told me to pick myself up and move on. I did and things are much better. When you go through a break up, it's going to be tough for awhile, but it will get easier. Find someone to talk to about it. Don't be afraid to find another girlfriend.

Relationship Danger Signals

—Judy Bordin, Ph.D., child development professor

1. **Frequent quarreling**: A pattern develops where couples/friends argue, split up, and get back together, over and over. They argue about each small issue that causes a breakup, never looking at the large picture or the common themes in these episodes. For example, one person in the relationship is late for events, doesn't keep commitments like phone calls and appointments. The real issue here is the level of responsibility to the relationship, not each tardy or missed commitment.

2. **Uneven course**: This pattern involves a roller coaster ride in a relationship. The relationship is either really good or really bad. There are no in-between times. Numbers 1 and 2 undermine the confidence that one has in that relationship. Can I count on you? Can you count on me? Can you count on you? Can I count on me?
THE DEGREE OF CONFIDENCE IN A RELATIONSHIP IS AN INDICATOR OF WHETHER OR NOT THE RELATIONSHIP WILL WORK.

3. **No mutual respect** or a lessening of respect:
   trying to change someone
   critical/giving advice to someone
   sarcasm (do you hide your spear within a smile?)
   teasing/belittling the other's wants and desires
   refusal to listen to the other's point of view.

4. **Brings out the worst in you**: A danger signal is when you experience an increase in your own "nonhelpful" habits. These are individual but may include substance use, poor self-control, lying, changes in eating habits, or procrastination. What is the worst in you? Has there been an increase in this behavior recently?

5. Intolerance of partner/friend by **friends or family** or your partner/friend doesn't care for your friends or family. Your true friends and family know you well. Listen carefully to what they say. You don't have to agree with them, but it is to your benefit at least to listen to their options.

6. **Continuous depression**: A lack of energy or enthusiasm for things and events. The relationship seems to define you and determine your self-esteem or feelings.

7. **Overcontrol/possessiveness**: A partner or friend who tries to or does make decisions for you and demands all your time may seem flattering. Episodes of jealousy and control are indicators of concern and the most consistent pre-characteristic of batterers. Be very concerned about this danger signal.

These danger signals are beginning indicators that something is wrong or may go wrong very soon. Even with one signal present, your self-esteem may plummet. This is especially true in intimate relationships. So, if you have found any of the above patterns with a partner, read on:

1. Remember that you are a worthwhile person, with or without a partner.

2. Take time to ponder and analyze the relationship. Observe and think about what is happening.

3. Find support by writing in your journal or talking to someone you trust who is neutral. Get your thoughts straight.

4. If you decide to talk to your partner: Timing is everything, know what you want, figure out and communicate exactly what you think is happening, stick to the point and to the present. You have two ears and one mouth; use them in that proportion.

To cope with a break up, allow your pain and anger to surface and be worked through and released. Talk with trusted family members and friends until the emotional charge is gone and you are free to think about solutions. Keep busy so you don't get bogged down in depression. Think about the lessons involved, why you were attracted to the person, what you learned, how you grew as a person, and what you will do differently in your next relationship. This is the way we learn about our unconscious feelings and become aware of behavior patterns/habits/beliefs that get in the way of love. Pain is often the best teacher, although certainly not enjoyable. If we grow from it, it allows for deeper love next time. Students' stories remind us that time does heal the pain of breaking up and we do meet new loves.

Benjamin Darling.
*Tips for Teens: Telephone Tactics,
Petting Practices, and other
Milestones on the Road to Popularity.*
San Francisco: Chronicle Books,
1994.

Friends

The most difficult challenge I face as a teen is my friends. They play a major part in my life. Sometimes I like to impress them which sometimes can get me in trouble by going against what my parents say. For a lot of teens, their friends are a major part because they make us feel like somebody cares when we are feeling down. We depend on our friends.

Sometimes your friends rule your life. If your parents say you have to be home at a certain time and your friends get to stay out later, go home when you are told. Maybe next time you can stay out later since you went home when you were told to last time and they can now trust you.

—Melissa, 16,
California

Being a good friend doesn't just happen. It requires effort to work through disagreements, examine your irrational behaviors, keep secrets, listen, affirm, and stick to your values. The young women I surveyed were more likely than the men to mention difficulty with gossip, back stabbing, jealousy, and competition among friends. Kristen wrote that "High school was a really hard time for me. People can be mean. These are the years when friends dump each other and experiment with feelings for attention." Stacie recommends, "Women need to unite as allies."

Males have their power struggles too. "Always stand up for yourself because if you come off as being weak, you will probably get stepped on for four years," suggests Christopher. "When you're at the top, there will always be people who try to drag you down. When people give you negative messages, they usually don't really believe what they're saying," says Apollo.

A popular teenager, Derren makes friends by using these techniques: Risk rejection by saying hi to kids you don't know, listen well to people and ask them questions to show your interest in them, have the courage to be yourself, pick friends who like you for who you are, and don't discriminate against unpopular students. Liking yourself is important if you expect other people to like you.

To make new friends: Form a study group with fellow students in a class, join a school club, join a sports team, participate in a religious youth group, do volunteer work, get a part-time job, let friends know what you're looking for in new friends, look past clothes and outward appearance, or reach out to shy people.

Dale Carnegie suggests in his widely read book *How to Win Friends and Influence People* that you show genuine interest in the other person, smile, use the person's name in conversation with him or her, and make the other person feel important by listening and asking questions. The importance of listening comes up a lot.

—Amber, 19, California

I always thought I was old enough and ready to get seriously involved with boyfriends. Now that I look back on everything, I wish I had spent more time with my friends because those are the memories that I really cherish. Always remember that friends are going to be there much longer than boyfriends.

—Corina, 19, Oregon

Treat friends like they should be treated and realize that even the most unlovable people are important. Work on listening skills.

—Heidi, 19, California

Relationships take time, patience, effort, and communication. You'll only get out of them what you put into them.

—Jon, 20, New Jersey

In high school I was friends with everyone, but out of school I only had a couple of good friends. Outside of the school setting I didn't really fit in with my school friends. I didn't feel accepted into their groups, probably because I went to a private high school where juniors got brand new BMWs for their first cars. I couldn't really relate to that.

I learned to be myself. The "cool" kids in high school are losers in college because no one cares about their crap anymore. Also be positive because no one likes a depressing lump.

—Allison, 20, Oregon

Finding a close circle of friends is the hardest question for me. I tend to be a quiet person and many take that as an attitude of snobbery. I also get along with a variety of people but don't open my personal self very easily. I used to worry if I had enough friends. But now I have realized that the friends I have would drop everything to help me if I needed it. And this is more important to me than the large number of friends I had in high school whom I hardly trusted.

Finding the friends I have now was work in a sense. Or perhaps it would be better to say that finding them was luck (or fate) but keeping these relationships has been work. I have learned to open myself more and to value the little quirks of people rather than finding fault with them.

—Karen, 21, California

Be the kind of friend you want to have. If you don't know what that is, make a list of the things people do that make you feel special.

—Rae, 21, California

I learned from experience and got hurt many times. Eventually I learned that if somebody has something to tell me then they will. Otherwise it's none of my business. Avoid gossip!

—Cheryl, 24, California

I made a lot of friends and developed a support network of other geeks, freaks and weirdos. Even though I always wanted to be a part of the "in" crowd, I realize now how lucky I was not to become part of it. Last year, when I went to my five-year reunion, I saw that most of the "in" crowd were tied to the small town we went to school in. I, on the other hand, have had the chance to really experience life. I moved to Southern California to go to grad school, where I've met some famous people through my involvement in different organizations, and I feel like I'm making a difference in people's lives. Although I'm sure my classmates have found their own happiness, I know I couldn't have been happy with their life styles.

Eda LeShan. *When Kids Drive Kids Crazy: How to Get Along with Your Friends and Enemies.* NY: Dial Books, 1990.

Gangs

Every gang has its color and the most popular colors are blue and red—blue as in Crip and red as in Blood! They are the most definite colors on the street. Also they are archrivals so they are always at each other's throats. There are four ways that I know of to get into a gang: One is to get jumped in when the most powerful people and you fight for 30 seconds. Two is to get walked in and that is only if you know the leader of the gang and you are good friends or intimate. Three is to get trained in when all the guy or girl gangsters get in a line to have sex with you. Last is to do something "worthy" like steal something or kill someone of the rival gang. After you are officially in the gang you can't get out until you are jumped out, or if you are pregnant by the leader of the gang, or you are dead.

In schools many adults who work there think most problems at the school are usually gang-related somehow, so they ban anything that is gang attire. To them that means no solid colors of any clothing or pagers allowed! I see they are trying to protect us but usually the person in a gang stands out in the school crowd. If you are in a gang there is usually a rival gang there, so they are always fighting or hurting each other. This usually does not happen until you start high school. The kids in junior high usually have brothers or sisters in gangs so they want to act all hard because of that. But basically gang violence doesn't happen in school; it happens on the streets and in the neighborhoods. They fight because of color or ethnicity.

—Nancy, 14, California

The U.S. Department of Justice reported that in 1980 there were 2,300 gangs with nearly 100,000 members. By 1996, the numbers increased to 16,000 street gangs with more than 500,000 members. As a result, youth gang murders more than quadrupled between 1980 and 1993. Although the number of youth in gangs is small, gang violence can change the atmosphere of a school or town, creating a climate of fear. Gang-related crimes numbered more than 580,000 in 1993.

A gang is a group of three or more people, with a common name (i.e., Crips and Bloods exist in 33 states), who commit crimes—usually violent conflicts with other gangs, drug dealing, random shootings, and robbery. Although many gang members end up in prison or dead, the gang provides a kind of family, a way to get respect by being tough, and excitement. Some youths join to get protection from other gangs. Members often do not do well in school or get much support from their parents, so they turn to gangs for recognition.

These problems cross class and racial lines. Chico police officer Daniel Fonesca sees gang members from middle class families whose parents throw money at them rather than give attention. He sees girls forming gangs too; sometimes they're more violent to gain respect. He also sees kids getting involved with gangs at increasingly younger ages because they want to "be somebody." The main reason kids leave a gang is the near death or loss of a loved one to gang violence.

Signs of gang activity are common: graffiti (called "tagging," although a skateboarder notes that skaters tag too), flashing hand signs, "flying their color," certain makes of shoes and clothes (football team jackets of the right color, gang color bandannas, baggy pants), markings on clothing (i.e., the number 14 stands for the 14th letter of the alphabet, for "Norte" gang), tattoos, pagers, and weapons. Gangs often pick names describing their neighborhood or ethnicity. Individual members have nicknames, called monikers.

To avoid confrontation with a gang, police officer Fonesca suggests avoiding them by not even watching their activity. If necessary, go to the library after school, because they won't be there. Since "dis'n" someone, or disrespecting them is so important, don't confront a gang member.

As a police officer/counselor who works with gang members, Denise Cangiano concentrates on teaching family communication skills. She emphasizes that parents should praise their children whenever possible and get involved in their activities. "Feeling understood and OK is the big thing," she observes.

Gangs are not just an inner-city problem; they're spreading like an infectious disease into all areas. Cities and schools need to proactively set up alternative programs to provide youth with something to do and a sense of belonging. Research by Brian Tarcy found successful school strategies to provide alternatives to gangs: teaching alternatives to violence such as peer mediation, providing after-school activities like sports, developing strong school spirit, and providing adult mentors who work individually with at-risk students.

Robert Montoya (a gang counselor at Harry S. Truman Middle School in Albuquerque, New Mexico) brought together students from rival gangs. They rebuilt a car into a low-rider to raffle off to one of the students, volunteered at homeless shelters, and painted a mural. The school also provides support groups for students (i.e., coping with parents' divorce, alcoholism, or understanding Attention Deficit Disorder).

Administrators at Jordan High School in Long Beach, California, organized a "peace offensive" by paying 125 student leaders to attend a four-day retreat to promote "better human relations." The leaders learned skills for conflict intervention and peer group counseling. Discussions between leaders continued throughout the school year. These kinds of programs could be helpful in every school with gangs.

—Lucy, 16, California

The most difficult challenge I am still facing is my gang ties. I'm not sure if I would say don't be in a gang, because it's not all bad, but I would tell them to be careful. I've been shot two times. My friends help me with this and I also release my pain by writing.

—Nydia, 16, California

The most difficult challenge I have faced as a teen has been staying out of gangs and the crazy life. I can think of many times when I almost slipped, but I eventually made it through.

My real friends and teachers I am close with helped me and guided me. I would tell anyone facing the same situation to look towards the future; every time you look at the future you will realize that gang life has no place there and may take your future away from you.

—Erlinda, 18, California

I loved hanging around gang members but stayed away from the violent part. At least I tried. Only a couple of times did I see them fight. Once I watched as people got jumped in. Once you start gang banging, you've got to watch out; you're never safe. You might be at the wrong place at the wrong time.

—"Loner," 18, Massachusetts.

I'm a girl who's not afraid of anything, except losing my family. I'm an ex-gang member, who never cared much about my life until I started losing my friends to drugs, AIDS, drive-by shootings, and playing Russian Roulette. There were times I wanted to kill myself because I was afraid of facing the real world, and afraid someone else would shoot me.

When I was gang banging, I never really cared much about the people I was with. All I cared about was killing people, and selling drugs to my own people. I felt that I had to prove to my friends that girls could kill people and not feel remorse. That's what I did for two years. I'd always thought that to be in a gang, you had to be tough. Not really. All it takes is a stupid person to do it, and I was one. I think if you're smart enough, you'll stay away from gangs. If you're in one, and you want to get out, all you have to do is move away from the gang. Another thing you should stay away from is drugs. They don't lead to anything except a miserable life. I'm getting my life back together now. Pretty soon, I'll get my GED and I'll move on to college, God willing.
Quoted from *Teen Voices*, Winter/Spring, 1994. (Women's Express, 316 Huntington Ave., Boston, MA 02115)

—Rocky, 21, California

Growing up in the inner city in Los Angeles brought forth many challenges for me in the form of drugs and gangs. I started taking part in gang activity in the 4th grade. At that age we were into gang banging and girls. As I got into more and more trouble, I wanted to find a way out because things were going badly for me. I remember when I brought home a sign-up sheet for Little League baseball. That sheet of paper made a big difference in my life and made me who I am today. When I started playing baseball in the 5th grade, I still had my affiliation with the gangs. As I got into junior high school, I joined the football and basketball teams.

I was in junior high when I started to drift away from the gangs because of all the time sports required. I seemed to change my friends from gangsters to athletes.

Though I was still affiliated with the gangs, I was constantly struggling between friends. After I came home from practice I would hang out with my gangster friends. It was hard to stay away from them because they lived in my neighborhood.

When I got into high school, things changed for me completely. I kept playing baseball and football. By playing sports in high school I could keep my focus on school and not on gangs. After completely leaving the gangs behind, I started to work on my baseball career. I saw that I had a chance to become a good baseball player, so I concentrated on that sport the most.

During my junior year I received letters from colleges to play baseball for them which made me very excited. I started to work hard and try to receive good grades so that I could get a scholarship. Everything was going well for me until I tore my rotator cuff [muscle in the shoulder] my senior year. Colleges turned their backs on me and I had nowhere to go. I was then forced by my parents to go to school up north so that I could get out of the inner-city life.

—David, 23, California

There is an episode of one year where I was lost and trying to find myself within a gang. My father was killed by a drunk driver when I was 12 and I had no father figure to go to when I was in trouble or had important questions to ask. My mom was there but we all need both a mother and father or there is a feeling of loss.

I was a junior in high school and became involved with a gang because I looked up to the close comradeship they had with each other. I wanted to have an older male figure to go to and this was my choice. The gang was called the "Older Generation" because it wasn't only people from high school; there were a variety of ages. I felt like I found my family of males that I had needed.

I ended up getting the shit kicked out of me one night when the gang was out patrolling for trouble. Well, this scared me badly because I was left to defend myself, and I could have been killed if I hadn't kept up my strength and got away. So I decided this was not the way my life was to go and I wanted out. I first had to find myself and come to terms with my inner problems and how I could communicate with my family better.

I went to a therapist and let it all out, even cried until I had no more tears left. The therapist wanted to know what was a positive note in my life and the only thing I had, an ex-girlfriend but still, a good friend was gone and doing her own thing, so I felt that I had nothing. By talking with the therapist I came to see that a gang was not for me but I had to find some positive activities to keep me focused. Then I got involved with theater and acting which changed my whole way of thinking and feeling.

I suggest that if you feel lost or without a confidant, don't run to the trouble spots; go to someone you feel safe with and talk about whatever is on your mind. Get all the negative out of you and move on.

Gang Prevention

Gangs and Schools. Holmes Beach, FL: Learning Publications 1-800-222-1525

Gangs in Schools: Breaking Up Is Hard to Do. The National School Safety Center. (4125 Thousand Oaks Blvd., Suite 290, Westlake Village, CA 91362)

Brian Tarcy, "On Safe Turf," *Teaching Tolerance,* Fall 1995. (free magazine from SPLC, 400 Washington Ave., Montgomery, AL 36104.)

Margot Webb. *Coping with Street Gangs.* NY: Rosen, 1995.

Homosexuality

Definitions

Of every 1,000 youth, 40 to 100 are lesbian or gay and 10 to 20 have a lesbian or gay parent. Homosexuals are people who are romantically and sexually attracted to the same sex, while heterosexuals are attracted to the opposite sex. Homophobia is the irrational hatred or fear of homosexuals. We usually refer to homosexual men as gay and homosexual women as lesbians, but the term gay also refers to both genders, when speaking about the gay community. Bisexuals are attracted to both sexes and may have boyfriends and girlfriends.

Beth, a reader, 15, adds some other terms which she feels should be included.

It was great to see so much of the text coming straight (pardon the pun) from the mouths of US! It's confusing to some people that "queer," "faggot," and "dyke" are such derogatory terms, yet we (gay people) use them to refer to ourselves. This confused me when I was first coming out, but I now realize it's about reclaiming the language so that it can't hurt us. "Queer" and "dyke" are so widely used by the gay community now that it's much less effective for people to call us that in order to make us mad.

You didn't say anything about "the Closet" which is a terrible but extremely important institution to discuss. The Closet is this imaginary yet very real place—a dark, hidden place—where gay people have had to stay for who knows how long. We stay there out of fear, out of pressure from family and peers, and out of insecurity about ourselves. Being "in the Closet" means not letting people know you are gay/lesbian/bisexual.

"Coming Out" is the act of acknowledging your homosexuality and telling other people about it and/or not denying it when someone asks you if you're gay. Being "Out" is being out of the closet. Some of us are partly in and partly out; I'm out to a few people but haven't come out to a lot of people in my life yet. Being "Outed" is having someone else, often against your will, tell people that you are gay. All of us hope that one day the closet won't exist, but right now it is very strong and there are so many people there.

Homophobia

—Ashley, 15, California

This is one of the worst problems in school. All day long I hear words like "fag." I really respect someone who doesn't give into the put downs towards gay people. It's not necessary to sell yourself out so you don't get labeled.

—Lemur, 19, Washington

A friend came out to me in 9th grade. Like most outspoken girls, I got "lesbian-bated," [called gay] in junior high, so I was familiar in a small way with just how much this hurts. The real crisis was figuring out how to react to people in my school who made homophobic remarks. My friend was in so much pain that he seriously considered suicide and for a while I reacted to homophobes as if they were murderers. It took me a while to realize that they weren't hateful for the most part (just clueless) and that I was overreacting. When I got to prep school I joined a group aimed at educating students about gay/lesbian issues and learned other ways of dealing with my frustration over the issue.

—Andy, 20, Maryland

I suffered culture shock after my freshman year when I moved from suburban Chicago to a suburb of Richmond, Virginia. I went from a very liberal, open-minded town to a town that seemed to consist only of farmers, pickup trucks, and racists.

During that summer, I became friends with my next door neighbor. It happened that he was gay, but he respected my sexuality and we became friends. When classes started in September, I quickly learned how bigoted and closed-minded this town was as I was labeled "queer" because of my friendship with this guy. It wasn't until my senior year that I was able to truly make any real friends at this school (other than my girlfriend whom I still date).

I think what helped me cope the most was my thick skin—that and my very supportive girlfriend. I would advise others in a similar situation to remain true to themselves. There were always people in school whom I could talk to. I would also advise them to be the aggressors in relationships. If they were in a similar situation to mine and did not make an effort to be friendly to people and get to know them, many of the people wouldn't have been friendly towards me. Mostly, it comes down to the fact that most people treat you how you treat them.

Other advice would be not to try confronting the ignorant people who weren't willing to give them a chance in the first place. In my situation, confronting them would've gotten me two things—a butt whipping and being laughed at. I chose to let the comments and snide remarks blow off to the wayside. If anything really got to me, I found someone whom I could trust to talk to.

—Kevin, 21, Iowa

In high school a friend of mine "came out" as gay. Most of us in his group of friends felt really odd at first being seen with him in public, because we didn't want others to think that we were gay too. The more we decided to ignore what other people thought, the easier it became. After a while we realized that all our friends—the people whose opinions really should matter to us, were behind him. Once we established that loudly and openly, there was nothing for us to fear. By then, anyone who didn't support him seemed like the outcast, not the ones who did.

Bisexuality

—Jake, 17, Pennsylvania

Bisexuality is about love. It's about being with who you want because you LOVE them, not because you can't get someone of the opposite sex. There are so many stereotypes about bisexuals—most aren't true. But all the stereotypes are fueled by ignorance. The best quote I've ever heard about bisexuality is from a friend of mine. He said, "I desire a person, not a gender." I guess bisexuality is just being nondiscriminatory. It's about looking past someone's outsides (well, not all the time—lust does play SOME role) and looking to their heart. I fell in love with a girl. That was just luck. I could have just as easily fallen in love with a guy. C'est la vie.

—Megan, 17, Illinois

I'd say the most difficult challenge I faced was when my best friend, who is bisexual/experimenting, told me she was in love with me, not just a friendship, but sexually in love with me. We had a really great relationship for a while, friends sharing everything, including the physical contact that we both needed. But then she decided that it wasn't working emotionally for her, and it came down to just fooling around, kissing and stuff like that. Now we can hardly be friends, and I still love her. She was the first one who truly understood me and now a lot of that understanding is gone.

I was helped while it was happening by inner strength. No one knew what we were doing, so I couldn't really talk to anyone. After we had the big split, I got brave and told another one of my friends. We were close, but I wasn't sure our friendship could handle this (he's pretty conservative), but now, he's my best friend in the whole world and we share so much of each other's lives. My advice is be friends first (that's how my current boyfriend and I started out), but be sure you're prepared to risk the friendship. I'm not sorry I did what I did, but I'll be sure to be more careful next time. Saying "let's just be friends" doesn't always work.

I'm straight, occasionally bi-curious, and even that made me occasionally suicidal about six months to a year ago. I hate to think how badly off I'd be if my homosexual tendencies were stronger, because this conservative area makes me feel that the way I feel is wrong.

—Susanna, 20, Ohio

Many young girls I have met (my past self included) don't know that their same-sex crushes in early adolescence and feelings of tenderness toward their girl friends are quite normal. I've found that the first urge is either to suppress those feelings or to think, "Eww! I must be one of those queers!" This awkwardness greatly limits the range of relationships open to girls. Most loving actions are often seen as "weird." Realizing my bisexuality, I feel comfortable admiring the beauty of the women around me.

Lesbians

—Jessica, 15, California

The most difficult challenge I've had to deal with is acceptance by parents and friends about my sexual preference. I am not offended by ignorant people's remarks because I realize their fear. The main thing that has helped me is realization about the mentality of all the insulting people who are frightened. My advice is don't deny these feelings because it will cause great emotional turmoil.

—Beth, 15, New York

Please, please mention that you CAN know what your sexuality is at a young age and you CAN know it without having had romantic or sexual experiences with anyone. So many of us feel insecure because of getting mixed messages about how much experience we have to have to "know." You have to allow yourself to be confused for a while. Clearness comes in its own time.

My parents are always trying to keep me in the closet for "my own safety," which is a bunch of b.s. and makes me doubt myself a lot. For other people who are struggling with issues of being lesbian, gay, or bisexual, all I can say is there's nothing more helpful than getting in touch with other people who are going through what you're going through. My e-mail and pen-pals have been more valuable to me through this whole process of coming out to myself and others and recognizing who I am than anything else. Also, it's very helpful to read a lot of books and magazines and talk to a lot of people and realize that there's a thriving community of people who are gay or who care that gay people are happy and have equal rights. I got a P.O. Box of my own when I realized I wanted to get some stuff in the mail that I didn't want my parents to see and question me about. Know that you were made to be yourself for a purpose. Trust in yourself, trust that things will work out.

It's important to erase all stereotypes of gay people you have in your mind. Some of us think we have "gay-dar" (the ability to see a stranger and know if he/she's gay), but the truth is that you wouldn't be able to tell most gay people from anyone else if they didn't tell you they were gay.

—Sue, 18, Maryland

I think what I hate about my queerness more than anything else is that the terribly complex creature who is ME is constantly getting reduced to a single characteristic. To try to avoid this happening, I don't come out to people I've just met, because I want them to know a few other things about me first. I want them to pay attention to who I am before I tell them I like girls and everything else stops mattering.

But after this initial withholding of information, inertia takes over. I keep making excuses about why it isn't the right time to come out to a friend, until finally the excuse becomes, "I can't tell her after such a long time, she'll think I don't trust her." Of course that is exactly the truth. I'm so afraid to come out to anybody because I'm terrified that everybody would leave me and I'd be left alone. I feel like maybe if I wear a skirt, keep my hair long, get good grades, and don't let myself think about sex, the people who would otherwise hate me automatically for being a lesbian will say, "Look, she isn't so bad." Who am I kidding? The people who will hate me for being gay will hate me no matter what other parts there are to my personality.

—Deanna, 22, Georgia

I came out to myself, actually said I was gay, when I was about 20. But I was always aware of my feelings. In fact I was scared from a very young age that I might be gay. In my mind, from what my church said, my family said, people at school said, and the media and so on, being gay was the worst thing imaginable. Certainly, being a Southern Baptist, I did learn that it was wrong to be gay. And definitely there were the typical anti-gay insults in my high school: "dyke," "queer," "fag," etc.

But what probably made it toughest for me to deal with the reality of my affectional orientation was the lack of acknowledgment of gay men, lesbians, and bisexuals. Gays weren't talked about in History, English, not even in Sociology or Political Science. The only time they (we) seemed to be paid attention to was in a negative light of news clips about outlandish behavior. All I knew of lesbians was the "Dykes on Bikes" images and man-hating feminist stereotypes, etc. Of course, I didn't identify with those. How could I be a lesbian if I liked men and didn't even own a leather jacket?

Coming out would have been a lot easier if I had been offered information other than negative rumors and stereotypes. If I had the opportunity to see real, live, out, adult, gay-identified people who lead happy, healthy lives, I may have realized sooner that I could be who I am and have a happy, fulfilled life. As it was, all I knew was that gays got kicked out of church, kicked out of the Scouts, kicked out of their homes, kicked out of the military, left by their friends, abandoned by society, etc. It doesn't have to be that way and often isn't! I wish I would have known that then.

Gay Men

—Tony, 17, North Carolina

I was your typical boy next door: blond hair, blue eyes, Boy Scouts, and Little League. I made good grades and made my parents proud. I had the letter jacket and the cheerleader girlfriend. I knew that I didn't particularly have a lot of interest in girls, but I hoped it would come.

Then I won an award to go to Europe for a year and everything changed. As my environment changed, so did my outlook on things back home. My "inlook" changed as well. I really started to listen to my feelings and living how I wanted to. I realized (LET myself realize) that I was attracted to guys, and that I was gay. This was really traumatic; I was raised in a really strict, REALLY religious home. Homosexuals were people who were outcasts, so I had become an outcast.

One night, at a seminar relating to my exchange program, I had to talk to someone and I started talking to one of the counselors. It turned out that he was gay as well and he has helped me a lot. He really helped me to accept myself and the feelings that I have. When I first met him, I wanted to be "normal" and have the feelings that everyone told me I should have. He taught me to accept my feelings and really helped my self-confidence.

Since the seminar, he and I have become really good friends. He introduced me to a lot of his gay friends and I go to a gay youth group with him. I met his parents and we talked together about how they reacted when they found out he was gay. I haven't told my parents yet, but his parents really helped me with ideas. He also took me to my first gay bar. It was really a shock to see so many men together, out in the open! That was actually the most assuring part; if so many people could have the same feelings then I wasn't as alone as I had thought.

I don't expect my church to accept me once I make it known. I am certain that they will not ask me to leave, but slowly they will get me out. I have actually heard my pastor preach about homosexuality as the "unforgivable sin." This is still a big point of worry for me. This is a part of my life, and I have always thought of myself as religious. [Some churches welcome gays.]

It's hard, but you're never really as alone as you think. I had this sense of overwhelming loneliness because I was sure I was the only one who had ever had this problem. I tried to change, but it COULDN'T be changed. If I could do it all again, with the little that I know now, I wouldn't fight it like I did. It's not something to be ashamed of.

—Bill, 23, Montana

My most serious problem was alienation from the heterosexual community and complete isolation from the gay community. This was the problem with which I was most occupied as a youth. Growing up in the state of Montana, knowing that any homosexual act is a felony, is minor compared to the ignorance and disdain that parents and the community at large hold on the subject matter. My advice for a closeted gay teen is first to to become comfortable with an individual identity. Do not identify yourself strictly as gay or lesbian but as the individual you really are and with those interests and abilities that define you. It is important to build confidence and independence as an individual free from any negative, puritanical attitudes aimed at homosexuals. If you are able to be confident and, most importantly, proud of yourself, then you will have fewer problems introducing yourself as an individual and not as a label.

Also of importance is to think constantly of the fact that your perceptions of the gay community are probably based on stereotypes reinforced in society. You must think of yourself and how you as an individual do not fit those negative stereotypes. Do think that you are capable of serving your country, of having a safe and healthy sex and romantic life. The felony status of homosexuals in most states is archaic and should be repealed [note, in 1996 legislators in Utah banned gay student clubs from high schools]. Do not think of your gay element as in any way preventing you from pursuing your goals and interests. You are stronger in many ways than your straight counterparts who do not have to face these challenges. Take absolute control over yourself and your future. Think and never stop thinking.

—Neal, 24, Maryland

During the last two years of college I had activism to thank for my sanity. I got very involved in university politics relating to Queer Equal Access Rights, as I call them. OUT (the Gay, Lesbian, and Bisexual People's Union and its members) provided me with ample amounts of support, encouragement, and love.

—Bryan, 26, Wisconsin

If I had had the information I needed when I needed it, my life would have been much easier. The first thoughts that I might be gay came in 9th grade when I realized that I was more attracted to guys than girls. As I look back now, I realize that I "knew" I was gay back in early grade school. I was able to ignore these feelings during high school in a number of ways. First I convinced myself that the only place there were gay people was on TV and in California. It was not possible for a farm kid to be gay.

In college I got the old "date girls, pretend you're not, and it will all go away," which I did. I had the absolute worst luck dating and this made my self-esteem drop. By the end of my third year in college, I was at the point of not going to classes and really not wanting to go on. I tried counselor after counselor and ended up at a psychiatrist who put me on antidepressants.

I began dating a girl who I had been friends with and we began making plans for the future. When it got to the point of knowing we were close to being engaged, I lost it. I had tried suicide three times before then and I knew if I did not do something, the next time I would not be so lucky.

I checked myself into a psychiatric hospital where I stayed 10 days. These were 10 days of hell because I found it was not a good hospital. When I finally admitted I was gay, the hospital went to extremes. Without saying who, they announced that someone in the group was dealing with sexuality issues and there were a dozen rules about what could or could not be worn, what could or could not be said, etc. I decided that I was not being helped and left.

What helped me deal with being gay was my summer job. I was a camp counselor in northern Minnesota. I spent the summer working with kids and with a great bunch of fellow counselors. I found out that I could be who I was and that there was nothing wrong with that. I never told them that I was gay, but just the way we all interacted helped me see this. From then on, it was mostly smooth sailing.

The famous sex researcher, Professor Alfred Kinsey, discovered that human sexuality is on a continuum. Imagine a line where people at one end are heterosexual, people at the other end are homosexual, and people towards the middle are bisexual. Generally, researchers think about 10 percent of the population are gay or lesbian, but many more have engaged in sex play with their same sex in their youth. Most people now think that our sexual preference is not something we consciously select or get from our family, but part of our physiological makeup, just like right- or left-handedness.

One of the most common put downs youth still use is calling someone a fag, queer, or a pervert, illustrating the homophobia in our culture. Some people envision gay men stalking young boys, when in fact most child molesters are heterosexuals. People who are homophobic also tend to feel prejudice against other minority groups and need to look down on others. This fear of homosexuality may stem from people's insecurities about their own sexuality. The U.S. is more homophobic than many other countries with a longer history.

Homosexuality is still illegal in about half the states, but mental health professionals are changing their views. In 1974 the American Psychiatric Association stopped classifying homosexuality as an illness, but still acknowledges treatment of "Gender Identity Disorder." Girls might be suspect if they have "intense negative reactions to parental expectations or attempts to have them wear dresses or other feminine attire" and identify with "powerful male figures such as Batman or

Superman," to quote the American Psychiatric Association's *Diagnostic Manual*. The consequence of this stereotyping is that gay and lesbian youth are more likely to attempt to commit suicide than heterosexual teens (a national study estimated that one-third of teen suicides are gays) and about one-fourth of homosexual teenagers leave home. It's estimated that up to 500,000 homosexual youth live on the streets. Being a teenager is difficult, but establishing your identity as a gay person in a homophobic society is truly a deeper challenge.

Organizations for Gay and Lesbian Youth

National Gay/Lesbian Hotline
1-800-347-TEEN
(Thursday to Sunday)

Parents, Families, and Friends of
Lesbians and Gays 1-800-4-Family
E-mail:
PFLAGNTL@aol.com http://www.crit-path.org/~maggie/pflag/

Dignity, Inc. (Catholic)
1500 Massachusetts Ave. NW
Suite 11
Washington, DC 20005

The Gay, Lesbian, and Straight
Teachers' Network
2124 Broadway, #160
New York, NY 10023
(Packet for teachers, *What You Can Do: Ideas and Resources for Educators Working to End Homophobia in Schools*)

LAMBDA Legal Defense and
Education Fund
666 Broadway
New York, NY 10012

Lesbian and Gay Youth Pen Pal
Network
P.O. Box 460268
Indianapolis, IN 46220-071

National Center for Lesbian Rights
462 Broadway, Suite 500A
New York, NY 10013
(defends the rights of lesbians and gay men at no cost)

National Gay Alliance of Young Adults
P.O. Box 190426
Dallas, TX 75219-0426

National Gay and Lesbian Task Force
2320 17th St., NW
Washington, DC 20007
ngltf@ngltf.org

National Lesbian, Gay, and Bisexual
Student Caucus
815 Fifteenth St., NW, Suite 838
Washington, DC 20005

National Gay Youth Network
P.O. Box 846
San Francisco, CA 94101

!OUTPROUD, The National Coalition
for Gay, Lesbian and Bisexual Youth
P.O. Box 24569
San Jose, CA 95154-4589
http://www.cyberspaces.com/out-proud/

Books for Gay and Lesbian Youths

Naiad Press 1-800-533-1973
(sells lesbian books and videos)

InsideOUT magazine: the essential queer youth magazine
P.O. Box 460268
San Francisco, CA 94146 (will mail without their name if you ask)
http://www.youth.org/io/

Mary Borhek. *Coming Out to Parents: A Two-Way Survival Guide for Lesbians and Gay Men and Their Parents*. Cleveland: Pilgrim Press, the United Church Press, 1993.

Daniel Cohen and Susan Cohen. *When Someone You Know Is Gay*. NY: Dell, 1992.

Gilbert Herdt and Andrew Boxer. *Children of Horizons: How Gay and Lesbian Teens Are Leading a New Way Out of the Closet.* Boston: Beacon Press, 1993. (a description of a gay and lesbian youth group developing a supportive community)

Ann Heron, ed. *Two Teenagers in Twenty: Writings by Gay and Lesbian Youth.* Boston: Alyson Publications, 1995.

Kevin Jennings, ed. *Becoming Visible: A Reader in Gay and Lesbian History for High School and College Students.* Boston: Alyson Publications, 1994.

Rachel Pollack and Cheryl Schwartz. *The Journey Out: A Guide for and About Lesbian, Gay, and Bisexual Teens.* NY: Viking, 1995.

Janice Rench. *Understanding Sexual Identity: A Book for Gay Teens and Their Friends.* NY: Lerner, 1990.

Bennett Singer, ed. *Growing Up Gay/Growing Up Lesbian: A Literary Anthology.* NY: New Press, 1994. (more than 50 coming-out stories by adults and teens and including resources)

Mitchell Sterrill, et al. *The Gay, Lesbian, and Bisexual Students' Guide to Colleges, Universities, and Graduate Schools.* NY: New York University Press, 1994.

Internet Sites

Coalition for Positive Sexuality
http://www.webcom.com/~cps/cps/resources.html

GLB Youth Advisor
http://www.usa1.com/~furball/glb/glb.html

IFGE International Transgender Resource Guide
http://www.transgender.org/tg/ifge/intlist.html

Justin's Life, a gay youth's home-page, with his journals
http://www.koool.com/mylife.html

Lesbian and Gay Youth and Coming Out
http://www.ncf.carleton.ca/freeport/sigs/life/gay/out/menu

Resources for students and schools:
http://www.cyberspaces.com/out-proud/html/school.html

The Student Center: An organization for college students, high school students, and teenagers
http://www.infomall.org/studentcenter/

The Ultimate Gay Youth Page, Alix's resource page
http://www.fornext.com/gayyouth/newlife.htm

Youth Action Online
http://www.youth.org/

L.Y.R.I.C. youth talkline e-mail:
lyric.talkline.info@tlg.net. (information and referrals)

Love—What Is It?

I have been dating the same female for two years. We are planning to get married. I love her more than anything in the universe. I KNOW this is love. How? When I touch her my heart beats faster. She can look as dirty or grungy as I've ever seen and I stay with her because of what she says and thinks. I know it's not just sex either. I've been approached by other people to sleep with them, but I don't want to.

I can tell the difference between lust, infatuation, and love. It's not always easy, especially at first. But once you've been around someone long enough you can begin to tell. Lust is easy to detect. You see someone, find them attractive—you know the rest. Sex is probably the easiest emotion to notice. I mean, it's all over the media so we should be able to notice it. Love is what binds people together, sex is what keeps people busy for 10 minutes.

Obsession is longing for someone because you need them to fulfill something you can't yourself. Infatuation is NOT love; neither is lust. Infatuation, much like obsession, leads nowhere.

Love is something humans have been contemplating for centuries. When I had my first serious girlfriend, I fell in love with her at first sight. Not long after meeting her we began dating. Well, one night I was on the phone with her and I told her I loved her for the first time. What she said in return I will never forget. She said, "Are you sure? How do you know?" Now, when telling your first love that you love them for the first time, that's not the answer you want. Nonetheless, I had to come up with an answer; this is what I got. Love is the strongest of all emotions. It's about doing ANYTHING for another person. I would die for my future wife— anything. That's what love is all about. It's about helping, caring, and being true to yourself and your partner.

—Jake, 17, Pennsylvania

We use the word "love" loosely, saying, "I love peaches," or "I love to play basketball," or "I'm falling in love," or I'm "lovesick" as if struck by a virus we have no control over. Love is deep caring, strong emotional attachment, attraction, tenderness, and enjoyment of the person you love. Love is making a commitment to work on a relationship with your partner. It builds on respect, similar interests and values, and complementary personality traits. In contrast, you can be sexually attracted to and infatuated with a person you don't even like or who isn't kind to you.

There are different types of love, as between family members, best friends, or sexual partners. Romantic love includes sexual passion, fascination with the other person, and intense feelings. Infatuation is short-lived as it's based on an image or idealized fantasy about the person. It may develop into love but is not love itself. Love is a whole different ball game from the infatuation generated by excitement and uncertainty about getting to know a new person. Infatuation doesn't last over time, because love means trust and intimacy which are wonderful but not unpredictably exciting.

Being best friends is the important path to love. The hallmark of friendship is that the pair likes to talk with each other and spends time communicating. Couples talk about their experiences, goals, thoughts and feelings, which requires turning off the television. David (a husband and father) reports, "Not being afraid to talk about things carries a vitality in itself. That's what a relationship is about and what keeps it meaningful. Communication is at the heart of it." Honest disclosure of feelings prevents manipulative behavior (when people are indirect about what they feel and want) and generates trust, an important ingredient of any friendship.

A study of 161 long-term happily married couples reported that the spouses became more interesting to each other over time. The authors defined the four keys to a successful relationship as friendship, commitment, agreement on fundamentals, and humor (Jeanette and Robert Lauer, 'Till Death Do Us Part, Harrington Park Press). Friendship develops from enjoyment, taking time to have fun together and to enjoy each other's sense of humor. Pair bonding increases with the shared memory of good times.

—Sara, 18, Maryland (from her zine "Out of the Vortex")

Romantic relationships are to me like pot is to this one friend of mine. She will smoke at a party and then the next morning says, "That was really dumb and pointless and hurt me way more than it benefited me, so I'm not going to do it anymore." That is, until the next party where she comes face-to-face with weed and then says, "Oh well, it's here, so I might as well smoke it."

Whenever I come out of a romantic relationship, I am so consumed with guilt or pain (depending on whether I am the dumper or the dumpee). I always say, "That hurt both of us more than it benefited either of us; it's obvious that I can't get romantically involved without screwing people over, so I'm just going to be asexual for a while." But this resolve of mine only lasts until I meet the next spirited, intense, principled, and intelligent person. I convince myself that this time can be different, this one I can make work.

I still dream of a true heart-soul-mind-body connection complete with total communication via telepathic link-up, even though the one time I experienced that, it ripped me apart, it was so intense. Is infatuation an addiction? [It can be and typically lasts about 90 days; it's certainly not love, which deepens over time.]

—Janet, 19, Michigan

The most difficult challenge was realizing I was no longer in love with my boyfriend of three years and yet I still loved him. The two conflicting feelings did not make any sense to me. We were the typical high school couple and many people, including ourselves, believed we were going to get married after college. However, I discovered my change of heart the second semester he was away at college and I was still a senior in high school. I went to visit him as often as I could and he came home to visit me also. But something had changed and we always fought. I loved him and wanted to make the relationship work so we both talked and tried to resolve things. However, they always seemed to resurface and we would end up going in circles.

I talked to a friend about it one day and he asked me if I was still in love with my boyfriend, and if so why. I answered that, of course, I was still in love, but to my amazement, I couldn't answer why. He told me to think about my inability to answer the question.

After thinking for a while and talking to my friend more, I realized that I loved my boyfriend as a person and a friend, but I was no longer in love with him. I did not understand how that could happen. How could I stop loving the person I had loved for three years? When did it happen? My friend could not answer these questions for me, so I talked to my mom about it. She helped me a lot by talking to me and assuring me that it was not my fault, that things like this happen, especially considering that I had never dated anyone but him. She suggested talking to him about seeing other people while we still dated and see if I still felt the same, and no matter what he said, to just trust myself and stick to whatever plan I felt was right.

I followed her advice and did tell him how I felt and that I wanted to see other people. He was very hurt by it all and accused me of cheating on him and falling for someone else. He could not believe I no longer loved him. His accusations hurt me a lot but I again followed my mom's advice and did not cave in to his ideas that I was wrong.

By dating other people, I found that I really was interested in and attracted to other people. The confirmation of my lack of feelings for my boyfriend showed me that I was not just fed up with the fighting in my relations and that things definitely had changed emotionally between the two of us. I stopped seeing him entirely after that because he could not handle simply being my friend. The loss of his friendship and caring devastated me since he had become my best friend. But, again, my mom helped me through it by talking to me and caring. She told me he was just upset and would come around after awhile. Just as before, she was right. He and I are friends now and do not regret any part of our long relationship. My mom was there for me and got me through the hardest time in my life. Someone older has enough experience with life to give you some great advice. They might even have a similar story.

Love is what you feel when you're happily content to simply sit in silence with someone and not feel uncomfortable about that silence; just thinking of the person brings an "ahh" smile to your face. Love is what will always be there for you; it's what you feel for your family and good friends, a combination of trust, respect, admiration, and happiness.

Love, in love, and infatuation are kind of like a flower growing. Infatuation is the first bud of spring that courageously pushes up through the snow and all the excitement of the people who see that bud and the promise that it holds. In love is the flower blooming and getting stronger with its petals open, ready and willing to give all that it can. Love is the flower pressed into a book for safekeeping. And, even though it's faded and withered, just looking at it brings on a rush of feelings for all it stood for and the contentment and happiness it stands for now.

—Avonel, 20, California

When I was 14, I was in a position that acceptance was of the utmost importance: I guess a lot of us felt that strange, terrifying pressure. I would have done anything to fit in because much of the time I felt utterly alone, freakish, and unattractive. At 14, it was a dismal scene for me until one day I heard a rumor that a real popular guy wanted to go out with me. A strange excitement filled my life.

Anyway, what started with rumors became a "relationship." I was the popular guy's girlfriend; suddenly my status went up and I felt like I had finally gotten some acceptance I wanted from this niche of kids at high school. My boyfriend was the way to happiness. I confused these feelings with love. It was like the story of the handsome prince who comes to the maiden's rescue and everyone lives happily ever after.

The only other information I had about love was that you were supposed to be extra nice and happy all the time. In other words, don't get angry, don't try to get what you want, make him happy. Since this fantasy was running around in my head, I refused to see that my "boyfriend" was abusing me emotionally. He was obviously only after one thing and he was extremely determined to get it from me. I didn't understand that all he wanted was a way to what he thought manhood was. He had to be a stud; it would add to his status.

He toyed with me. He told me he loved me, he promised to buy me things, to display me like a trophy. He controlled me, he decided what I would wear, where I would go, who I would be seen with. I was not to go anywhere until he called me every night, but most of the time the call never came. He taunted me by talking to me about this other girl he wanted. Every time we were together and alone he tried to get me to have sex with him.

Part of me wanted to excuse this behavior because it made me feel wanted. I was having enough fun just going on dates and making out, I didn't need to have sex. But the emotional abuse, the pressure he put on me slowly wore me down until I gave in and I lay there crying. My first experience with sex was awful. I hope no one has to go through that sort of manipulation, but I think it happens frequently to high school girls. If I had had more self-esteem, more support, more knowledge about what love was really about, I think I could have avoided this situation. There should be a mandatory class in freshman year of high school that teaches self-worth.

Intimacy Enhancers

Intimacy means "into me see." To learn about yourself and your partner on a deep level, here are some discovery tools with the "onion model" in mind. A Texas husband interviewed for *50/50 Marriage* said his relationship with his wife is like peeling layers of an onion, continually finding something new about her to explore. That's the best image I've heard of a great relationship, just as tending a garden is the best image of how to maintain it.

◎ The most powerful step is to take regular time to listen to each other, giving total attention without offering advice, judgment, or interjecting our own experiences. This exchange should occur at least once a week for a half-hour or more of quiet time for each person (see communications section in Chapter 2).

◎ Discuss your dreams with each other, remembering that their language is symbolic and visual rather than literal. Record your dreams in a journal, a valuable tool for intimacy (see the identity section in Chapter 2).

◎ Do exercises together to explore your inner child, as described in Lucia Capacchione's *Recovery of Your Inner Child* (Simon and Schuster).

◎ Say at least one thing you like about your partner each day, establishing a habit of offering praise. Make a list of qualities and attributes you like about your partner and share them.

◎ Understanding goes a long way towards replacing irritation with empathy. Take the Myers-Briggs personality inventory published in Keirsey and Bates' *Please Understand Me* (Prometheus Nemesis Books).

◎ Make a list of how you feel most nurtured and appreciated by your partner and what you think is nurturing for him or her. Follow through with at least one enjoyable activity from your list each week.

How to Love

Erich Fromm. *The Art of Loving*. NY: Harper Collins, 1989.

Terence Gorski. *Getting Love Right: Learning the Choices of Healthy Intimacy*. NY: Fireside/Parkside, 1993.

Harville Hendrix. *Getting the Love You Want: A Guide for Couples*. NY: Harper Perennial, 1990.

Peer Pressure

Guys always pressure you to have sex. It seems like everyone else is doing it, so why not you? People do drugs to fit in, or because they get pressured. You have to be stronger than the peer pressure. You have to respect yourself. Don't do it if you think you'll regret it later. Be yourself and don't be scared to say No. You'll like yourself much better.

—Alicia, 15, California

Two-thirds of young adolescents, ages 10 to 13, say peer pressure would lead them to do something they wouldn't normally do (1995 survey of 1,017 youths in the KidsPeace Preteen Survey). In the same year, a survey of 3,000 high-achiever students found they feel the most peer pressure to: get good grades (67 percent), drink alcohol (33 percent), cheat (26 percent), skip classes (20 percent), and have sex (20 percent). Of these students, 59 percent consider themselves popular and most (85 percent) are happy with their level of popularity.

Loud and clear, the number one message from students I surveyed is to be true to yourself rather than trying to be popular or cool, the word used most often in their stories (interesting, because it implies not showing feelings, being aloof, as in our expectations for men). *High school reality is fake, false, virtual. The people who are the most popular, become less and less through life. The geeks in high school become the power brokers in business, government, and religion,* Jeff believes.

Refusal Skills

If you feel pressured to do something you feel is wrong, i.e., use drugs, or have sex, students suggest:

★ Think through your position ahead of time. Define your boundaries.

★ Learn about the consequences.

★ Say No and walk away and notice the respect you'll receive for standing up for your beliefs. "I've found that doing the opposite of what's expected can bring satisfaction. People look up to you and soon they will follow," Sara states.

★ Select your friends carefully. A former drug abuser reports, "It's mostly who you hang out with. I fell into that trap. It's hard to get out of it too."

Take time to think about the consequences of peer pressure: "You want to give me a ride even though you've been drinking? Drunk driving is the main cause of teen deaths; I'm not ready to die." Suggest an alternative like "Let's call a cab/parent/friend to pick us up." State your decision simply without trying to justify it; "I'm not going to ride with a drunk driver." If you try to back up your decision, the other person may argue with your points. All you really need to say is No, mean it, and walk away.

—Lucie, 15, South Africa

A big problem here in Cape Town is peer pressure and "who's cool" and who's not and that's quite a big thing to try to be cool. Lots of people get caught up in things beyond their control, like drinking, smoking, drugs, and sex because of it. I think it's a big challenge to stand up for yourself, be your own person, and not give in to other people you consider "on a higher level." I think that is such bull; I don't see how some people can be cool and others not. Everyone's just different and different groups of friends have different interests and that's why there ARE different groups in the first place. It's got nothing to do with not being cool enough to be in one particular group.

My advice to people who are facing the problem of peer pressure is not to be insecure. Your personality and your characteristics are what you were born with and that's who you are, so don't go trying to change into someone else to be accepted. Find friends interested in you for YOU and not for what you do, because those friends won't be true friends and they aren't worth it. Believe me.

—Tricia, 15, California

I just decided one day that I didn't have to be just like everybody else to be cool. You can't please everybody, so please yourself, be an individual. If you're always conforming to society, you can't find yourself and you won't be happy. Also, people might tease you, but just ignore them. That's their personal way of saying, "I have no confidence in myself. I wish I could be more like you."

—Natalie, 16, California

Social pressures are really hard. People, when they're young, say, "Oh, I'll never do those drugs," but a lot of them do. I've had coke and crank chopped right in front of me and offered to me a thousand times, but once people get the point that you don't do that stuff, they don't ask. Always let people know you're a strong person and no one will ever pressure you.

—Emiliano, 17, California

I think the biggest challenge as a teenager is trying to be cool and liked. When I was around 13 to 15 my whole life was trying to impress girls and other people. But now I realize it's how I feel about myself that's most important. My friends and family helped by caring about me no matter how I acted or looked. I've had friends before who just liked me for money, my car, or anything else. Do what YOU want to do and don't worry about other people. When it all comes down to your true friends, they will like you for who you are.

—Jane, 18, Ohio

When I got into trouble it was basically because my friends, who were mostly older than me, were doing those things (i.e., drinking). I got sucked in and reveled in all the attention, not to mention how grown-up and invincible I felt. Now I wish in a way that I hadn't grown up so fast, but then, it made me who I am today. I got out of it simply because it was made obvious to me, on a Christian teen retreat, that I didn't need to do those things and that there were other ways of life and people who liked me the way I was. It was such a release for me to know this! It was a long journey, but I made it and I am stronger and more compassionate.

My advice to teenagers is if anything makes you think twice, it's probably not worth it! Also trust your gut. If you feel weird about it, don't do it. Don't do things just because your friends are. And try to remember that your parents usually are not your enemies.

—Leo, 18, California

Many kids have been very hurt thinking that they are not "cool" like the other kids. Personally I have experienced just a little of that, but I do know friends who've had that mentality for so long that they themselves think they're inferior! The truth is, everyone wants to be "cool." Sometimes popularity can alter one's judgment.

Let's say that Student A is socially acceptable. Kids think he's cool while Student B is the opposite. Now, an event has been planned at school that requires all students to dress up and wear a tie. If Student A shows up with a black shirt with white trousers and sport jacket, while wearing a bright white bow with little sprinkles of silver, other students would think that Student A's outfit qualifies as "Cool." Yet if Student B does the same, it would just be "lame" or "nerdy." Simply because Student A had been "cool" before, whatever he does later would most likely be cool. Of course, there is a limit to this "coolness." It will eventually wear off. This holds true for both sides of social acceptability.

—Todd, 22, California

My biggest dilemma during high school involved my confrontation with conformity versus individualism. It seemed like I was constantly running the gauntlet for a group of guys I considered "close friends." Most of these "friends" didn't share the same perspective on loyalty that I deemed essential in my friendships. Many of my friendships were based on a daily perception of popularity. If I had made a game-winning touchdown in football or a game-saving goal in soccer, I had the most loyal friends in town for that day or week. However, when I stopped glittering, I was just an acquaintance to my buddies.

I began to ponder the thought, "Are these friends really worth having?" Some months I wanted to cut my ties with my "close friends," to enjoy the freedom of individualism. It was a good feeling to be myself. I came to realize that I would lose some friends if I chose the path of individualism. After months of jumping back and forth between being myself and conforming to the ideals of my peers, I decided to take the lesser of two evils. Turns out that I made the right choice. Being a victim of conformity is like being a painting never unveiled, as you will never know its quality until you open it.

—Charlie, 24, California

The pressure of trying to be or do what people expected was not only peer pressure, but pressure from my parents, teachers, and relatives. I still have trouble with this, but I am definitely my own person and move at my own pace. My advice to someone younger would be that you can't please everyone and you shouldn't always try. Do what makes you happy, go at your own pace. Life's too short to be angry. Use and appreciate what you have.

—Nancy, 24, Arizona

The most challenging part of my teen years was that I was an intelligent young woman in a smallish suburban school. I did not fit into the cheerleader/makeup/boys crowd. I excelled in my classes and then had to deal with the "goody-goody/teacher's pet" attitudes. Not to mention that boys rarely seem interested in a smart girl (with glasses to boot!). It's hard to really pin down what helped me deal with it; my parents supported me and helped instill pride and self-confidence as a result of the work I did. And like many "nerds" I had a small, tight-knit group of nerdy friends.

Maybe the key is that no one truly feels like they belong at that point in their life. I had my share of experiences with peer pressure. And my first boyfriend in high school tried to pressure me into having sex with him (I am sure you'll hear about that from lots of people). In that case I realized the relationship wasn't worth much if the only way to keep him was to do things I was not comfortable doing at that point in my life. If he truly cared about me why was he not listening to what I said and felt?

Put Downs
and Bullies

Be nice to everyone. Even if people are mean to you, maybe
the niceness will wear off on them. And always remember that if a
teenager wants to get the best of you, if you show them that you
don't care what they are doing to you; they usually give up or
don't even
hardly bug you.
—Missy, 14,
Michigan

Put Down Responses

Ignore put downs so the person doesn't get
your attention and reaction. The bully's motive is to play the
"I'm up, you're down, I'm in control and you're not" game to
feel more powerful, so don't play. For example, another professor who was trying to intimidate me, called me at home, raising
his voice, using crude language. I hung up, and he didn't call
back. If it continues, though, action must be taken or the bully
will keep testing your limits to see how far he or she can push.
Try assertively to tell him to stop, state a consequence such as
telling school authorities, or try to negotiate a solution (probably unlikely because power struggles are not reasonable). You
can try a sympathetic or adult approach to throw her off guard
or let her know she's being childish:

"You sound angry" (or frustrated, upset, hurt...).

"That's one way to look at it."

"I'm going to ignore that childish comment."

"What goes around comes around."

"We often criticize in others what we don't like about ourselves."

"Right."

Emma thinks some of these remarks might make more trouble, so use your own judgment. If these techniques don't stop the person, you might ask your friends to stay around you or ask an adult for help. If you are bullied at school, talk to the vice-principal. You don't have to put up with cruelty. Practice the assertiveness skills discussed in Chapter 2.

—Anna, 15, New Jersey

When someone threatens you, talk a mile a minute and try to show them why it wouldn't be in their best interest to beat you up. It might confuse them long enough for you to get away. "Discretion is the better part of valor."

—Anne, 15, Virginia

The most difficult challenge I face as a teen is verbal abuse from my peers. I never had a problem with this before I entered the 8th grade, but the older I get, the more abuse I get. I consider myself a very easygoing and friendly person. I try to get along with everybody. Lately kids my age have been putting me down, flipping me the bird, and even meddling with my personal belongings. The worst experience I've had with this was when a 10th grade girl constantly told me I was no good at playing the trumpet. She told me I could never get anything right and called me stupid. Soon she started using bad language and even threatened me.

It got to the point where I couldn't stand being put down anymore. I tried to fight back by telling her all her faults, but that just made matters worse and made me feel lousy. I finally found that the best thing to do was just ignore her. There will always be people in the world who are so insecure inside that they put others down just to make themselves feel better. The best advice I can give to people in this situation is don't resort to their level. Have confidence in yourself and know you're being the best person you can be. Don't let their comments bother you because most likely that person is jealous of you and really needs a friend.

—Brian, 16, Texas

The most difficult challenge I had was overcoming my fear of people. I always thought they'd make fun of me forever. The things that helped me cope were my parents and sincere friends. People aren't jerks forever; it'll mellow out. Myself, I wanted to die, but DON'T DO IT! I am glad I didn't.

—Natalie, 16, California

My reputation was at stake. Rumors were going around and even people who knew me had a hard time not believing them. People you don't know hear these things and feed those rumors to other people. I just held my head high and people confronted me about them and I told them they were lies. I told them I'm not worried because the kind of people who believe that b.s. are not worth being my friends. Also, let people know it's your life and not their business! The person who was talking shit has a horrible reputation and ended up looking even worse. I didn't lose anything or anybody.

Always tell the truth. Lying eats you up so badly. People always find out. And if your reputation is ever at stake, people will believe the one who always tells the truth, even if it's hard to admit.

—Jed, 16, California

If you are confronted by a bully or someone who is dis'n you, you should attempt to get out of it so neither of you loses face. For example, if he pushes you and says, "Come on, wimp," then just look at him, smile a fat grin, and say, "You know, dude, you're not worth my time," and walk away. If it's someone who is talking smack, who you don't think will want to fight you, then something like this will work: "Pull your head out of that hole, then talk to me, I can't hear you." Or, "If I was as stupid as you are, I'd probably be talkin' smack to me too." There are many ways to avoid fighting. If you're really afraid to fight or of getting beat up, then you might want to try something like karate; it really boosted my courage. I don't back down to anybody and I don't get into fights either. I stick up for myself and I'm much more confident because of it.

—Navy, 19, Maryland

If you engage in put downs, ask yourself this: Why do you do it? Because you're bored? Because you make yourself feel better by making someone else feel bad? If your peers are doing it, is that really the type of friends you want? What if the tables were turned?

There will always be someone who feels superior to you. What goes around comes around. Think about how the other person feels. You could damage that person's self-esteem for life. Put yourself in their shoes. If your friends choose to act like immature morons, find new ones, or tell them that they're immature morons. I bet deep down inside they all feel what they're doing is not right, but each one is too much of a coward to admit it.

—LouAnn, 23, Iowa

I always stood up for the underdog; it was hard in high school but I'm so glad I did!

—Rebecca, 23, Australia

I was the main source of ridicule amongst my peers, no one else seemed to flack it as bad as I did, except my best friend. The extent of the teasing was so persistent and offensive, I had to build a subconscious wall so that I wouldn't get hurt as much. That's how I never let them see that the teasing got to me after the initial two years. I never was very popular in high school, but that didn't bother me as they were no longer teasing me after the first two years.

Understanding
the Other Sex

Understand that men's and women's approaches to life are different. Women tend to be relational, men tend to be goal-oriented [our survey responses back up her point]. *Generally, when women have a problem, they want support. When men have a problem, they want advice. Read John Gray's Men Are from Mars, Women Are from Venus (HarperCollins), a great book about cross-gender communication.* [See also books by Deborah Tannen on this topic.]

—Sara, 22, Missouri

Females are more people oriented and males more achievement oriented, according to the survey for this book of 1,5000 youths. The following results of their responses to their most difficult challenges are listed in order of frequency. (See the appendix for more details).

Female Issues:

1. **Peer pressure**
2. **Sex**, pregnancy
3. Getting along with **parents**
4. (tie) Getting along with **friends**
5. School, grades, getting into college

Male Issues:

1. **School**, grades, getting into college
2. **Drugs**
3. **Peer pressure**
4. Getting along with parents
5. Sex

The top four issues for females were about people, compared to two for males. The top issue for females was peer pressure, while males' was achieving school success. Other interesting differences: Males were more likely to mention jobs and money (15/6) and sports (40/4)—also achievement issues. Females were more likely to mention the death of a friend (17/5) and eating disorders and body image (10/1)—not achievement–oriented.

In the long surveys, males emphasized high school sports and coaches, trying hard to do your best, the importance of respecting other peers and adults, and were more likely than females to encourage having sex as a teen. Females more often mentioned the problems of friends gossiping behind their backs and the importance of being true to yourself.

—Vincent, 22, California

Be sensitive to girls' upbringing. Try to understand that men usually like showing their feelings in action and women like telling their feelings. Try to allow girls some freedom to do what is natural for them.

—Rebecca, 25, California

I read a lot of books written from a teenage guy point of view. It took me till I was in college (and had a couple of good friends who were real honest men) to find out that most of the guys I idolized as a 15 year old were as sweaty and insecure and emotionally deranged as I was. I tended in high school (and unfortunately still do) to put so much importance on whether this or that guy liked me, whether he talked to me in class. I would constantly put my entire self-esteem on the block for the price of one word from some totally confident guy in the coolest clothes. But you start talking to these guys four years later, or reading books, and you find out they're almost as raked over the coals about their bodies as we are. They're sure they're repulsive to all women and they don't know what anybody wants of them.

The Male Role

(see also masculism section in Chapter 11)

Men are expected to hide their feelings, not seek help, know the answers, compete, and take risks to prove their courage. A 1988 survey of 2,000 adolescent males revealed that boys want to be viewed as strong, unemotional, and self-confident (NIH's National Institute of Child Health and Human Development). In other words—cool. Their worst fear is "acting like a girl." However, being more progressive than earlier generations, most do not think it is unmanly to talk about their feelings or do housework, according to psychologist Joseph Pleck who studied the data. He believes that our definitions of masculinity still promote some negative male behaviors such as unhealthy risk-taking, date rape, and not using condoms. Pressures to compete and perform push guys into actions that may be harmful to them, such as fighting, playing sports with an injury, or not asking for help when they need it. The equation of manliness with coolness is very limiting. For example, in my interviews with youth activist groups, I find girls frequently outnumber boys because, as Tesmer, 15, confirms in Seattle; "Social change is not seen as cool. Community service, helping people, is seen as a girl thing."

Author Warren Farrell observed that boys learn to be either a "physical-striving man" or a "job-striving man," but either way they feel pressure to prove themselves as "success objects," while women are treated as sex objects. Few men arrive at a point in their lives when they feel, "I'm a success, now I can relax."

In discussion groups conducted for Children Now and Kaiser Permanente in 1995, researchers found major differences between teen boys and girls. "The teenage boys come in the room and take up a lot of space but they can barely talk. They're in significant trouble but they don't ask for help.... Even the appearance of fear seems to make them feel they would be putting themselves in more danger," reports Maryann O'Sullivan of Children Now. In contrast, she continues, "The girls come into the room full of words. They cry. They talk across the table to other girls they had just met. They talked about their friends.... We may be seeing the beginning of a lifelong pattern—do these boys grow into fathers who have trouble communicating?" In a *USA Weekend* magazine survey of 222,653 students, they agree girls behave more responsibly (99 percent of girls and 73 percent of boys), although parents don't give girls more freedom or later curfews (57 percent of girls and 43 percent of boys think parents give boys more freedom). Parents still are likely to assign chores on the basis of traditional roles, with boys more likely to mow the lawn and girls to clean house. And its still OK for girls to cry—gender roles change slowly.

Although men have most of the power and prestige, the pressures of their role are stressful. Men comprise most of the prisoners, victims, and perpetrators of serious crimes, sex offenders (93%), drunk driving arrests (87%), drug abuse arrests (83%), and serious drug addicts (80 percent). The life expectancy of white men is 73, compared to 79 for women. The rate for black men is 64.5, compared to 74 for women.

Pressures of Masculinity

✳ Boys are the majority of truants, delinquents, and dropouts.

✳ Four times as many boys than girls were arrested in 1992.

✳ Boys are three times more likely to abuse alcohol and 50 percent more likely to use illegal drugs.

✳ The main cause of death among white males ages 15 to 24 is accidents. Teenage boys are more likely to die from gunshots than natural causes.

✳ Males commit suicide two to four times more often than females (although females attempt it more often).

✳ Boys receive lower grades than girls and are more likely to have to repeat a grade or drop out.

✳ Boys are 80 percent of the students in school programs for emotionally disturbed youth (and more than 70 percent of students with learning disabilities).

✳ Boys are 71 percent of students suspended from school.

(Myra and David Sadker, "The Miseducation of Boys" in *Failing at Fairness: How America's Schools Cheat Girls*, Charles Scribner's Sons)

What can young men do to break out of harmful stereotypes and pressures? List the social expectations you feel as a male. Decide what you think is unfair or unhealthy for you. Take a stand, explaining that sexism hurts males as well as females. For example, perhaps you decide it's unfair to pay for everything on a date with a girl who has more money than you. Date girls who are willing to pay their share. Read books about men's liberation to become aware of stereotyping and how other men move towards equality for both sexes (see the masculism resource section in Chapter 11).

Men need to understand that women may funnel various emotions, including anger, through tears. Women need to understand that men may funnel all kinds of emotions, including grief and fear, through anger. In workshops I led with Randy Crutcher around the U.S. on "Bridging Men's and Women's Worlds," young men explained that they do in fact have deep feelings and sensitivities but are expected to hide them. They reported that women are often content to be just friends with nice guys but are attracted to jerks who seem cool. Men get mixed messages—be tough/be sensitive, be liberated/pay my way, open the door for me/don't open the door for me, be successful/have time for me.

Women may condemn men as being insensitive without thinking about the cultural definition of masculinity—the tough Rambo or Terminator, the aloof Marlboro Man, and other hunks who put the dreaded wimp to shame. Many best sellers tell women that men are jerks and that foolish women love too much and pick immature Peter Pan types who never want to grow up emotionally or make a commitment. This "male-bashing" does not account for the restrictive ways in which we bring up boys and the expectations women have of men to be Prince Charming.

Making an effort to understand the pressures on the other gender builds empathy and a sense of being understood and supported by one's partner. This is one of the most important gifts we can offer. For example, instead of being irritated at a guy because he talks about himself a lot, realize males are taught they have to compete and perform for female attention. Let him know you appreciate him and let him know what you think, even if he doesn't ask. Instead of being irritated at a young woman who won't give you a direct answer about what she wants to do, realize females get trained to be unassertive and indirect. Let her know you like having a friend who shares decision making and initiating activities.

—Nick, 15, California

I think if I believed and fell for the whole macho bit, then I would probably feel pressure from that group of guys. But I realized in advance that it is dumb to take advice from these people or be pressured by them.

—Regan, 15, Canada

This past weekend I was an usher at my cousin's wedding in Calgary. Being the first man to see the bride in her gown was kinda special to me, and seeing all those people at the wedding with lifelong companions. Seeing how happy they were made me feel different than I have ever felt before. I grew up with my cousin and his bride, he was like a brother to me.

When they came down the aisle at the end of the service, I actually shed a tear for the first time in my life since I was four years old and E.T. died. Just thinking of the fact that he married his first girlfriend in life makes me happy. If it was that easy for him, I MUST be able to find someone who makes me that happy, right? [Males aren't supposed to cry, so Regan waited 11 years, but how are they supposed to express their grief and joy?]

—Kelly and Jed, 16, California

People are prejudiced against boys too. They make fun of us or put down boys who don't fit the standard. It's harder on boys to be members of society than girls, because girls don't have to fit any mold. We have to be masculine; if you aren't confident and cool, people make fun of you. Girls still expect guys to ask them out, and go by the old rules of paying on a date. You have to hide your feelings, you can't just bawl like girls can. You have to be able to talk the talk, and walk the walk. It's not as bad for a girl to be a nerd; other girls are nice to them, but jocks make fun of the nerds.

—Jake, 17, Pennsylvania

Many people (like my father) can't get over the fact that many of the gender roles are either breaking down or changing these days. I love it; I think this is what my generation is going to accomplish. The 1960s had the freedom of sex, drugs, and rock 'n' roll. My generation will have gender-role breakdowns.

I've definitely felt pressure about what I'm "supposed" to do. For instance, most of my friends are girls because—gasp—I think girls are smarter. If there's one thing I can't stand, it's stupidity/ignorance. I find that females are more open to ideas (and thus more intelligent), so I tend to gravitate toward them.

I do get shit from some of the macho-type guys. I've been called every name you can think of about it (faggot, fairy, etc.). I just take it all in stride. What else can I do? I find, even these days, that many of the old stereotypes hold up, but not by as many people. It's the jocks/preps that get on my case. Every once in awhile I wear these neon pink and yellow sunglasses: Man, do I get shit about them.

—Peter, 18, Maryland

I don't really feel too many pressures to fit the "masculine role" anymore, although I can't say that I am completely unconscious of my actions. I used to be very conscious of them. I am lanky and often stereotyped as a "pretty boy." I used to get bothered all the time about my actions, whether it was standing with my hand on my hip, crossing my legs while I sit, etc. For a while I became very self-conscious about my every move. As the comments became less frequent, my worry about how I moved left also.

As far as trying to fit the masculine stereotype now, when I first went off to college, my goal was to become friends with "normal" guys. So, at first, I hid parts of my personality. For example, the things that used to get me so much ridicule of gayness in high school (musical taste, hatred of violence, and just plain old sensitivity), I just kept to myself until I knew that these friends were for real. Now that I know I can trust these male friends of mine, I am completely open with my personality. I take some playful teasing about things, but none of it is meant in a hurtful way.

—Kevin, 21, Iowa

Being profeminist, and indeed, something other than traditionally masculine, can be very hard. In high school, I felt pressure to have sex and to make jokes about "chicks" and "bitches." I remember bad feelings about not being a natural athlete. (Everyone always expected me to be a basketball player because I'm 6'4". I've always been a horrible basketball player!) I remember the fear that people might label me as gay, even to the extent that it was hard to be friends with other people suspected of being gay.

Being a feminist liberates men from behaviors and attitudes that blind us and keep us from experiencing life and others to their fullest. Perhaps this can best be seen in the way we are taught to see womyn [he prefers this spelling as it isn't added onto "man"] as sex objects. This makes it so our first reaction when meeting someone of the opposite sex is to "check her out." We are so busy looking for potential mates in females, that we neglect to see them for the different types of people they actually are-possible friends, co-workers, peers, teammates, teachers, artists. In short, we are blinded from seeing that womyn have a lot more to offer us than sex.

These aren't the only ways rigid gender roles hurt us as men. There is the rather cliché examples of how men are oppressed because they "aren't allowed to cry." For me, in particular, the most important examples of how I am hurt by rigid gender lines have more to do with things like homophobia and the ideal of man as provider. Even as a long-time profeminist, it is difficult for me to embrace my male friends, or to admit too openly that I care about them, because I worry about being seen as gay. Internalized homophobia also keeps me from exhibiting my feelings, like being nurturing, or even simply being emotional (good or bad).

As a man, I am taught that my role in a family will be that of "provider." I should put making money as a priority in my life. All my life I have been talented with computers and good at math and science. I know my parents were disappointed when I decided to be neither a doctor nor a computer programmer, both of which would have offered me a more stable, larger income than that of a philosophy professor.

Overall, I think we need to ask ourselves as men: Who do we want to be? Do we want to continue taking advantage of the unfair privileges society gives us over womyn? Do we want to engage in relationships that are fundamentally unequal and domineering? Do we want to treat womyn as mere sex objects or as true equals? Would we rather be uniformly what traditional masculinity prescribes that we be—aggressive, violent, egotistical, competitive, heterosexual, and emotionally detached? Or do we want to have the freedom to combine whatever set of gender traits to be who we really are—whether it be nurturing or athletic, sensitive or strong, homosexual or heterosexual or bisexual?

The only way I can like myself is to act true to what I believe. I don't want to be sexist, racist, or homophobic, and I'd find it hard to live with myself if I acted differently.

—Zacks, 28, California

The standard feelings of inadequacies were present during my teen years, but the most difficult thing I had to deal with was discovering emotion beneath the exterior I showed to the outside world. I did this through trust and conversations with friends and my mom. Don't worry, it's normal.
[Note the theme of expecting males to suppress their feelings to the point they lose touch with them. I hope female readers encourage men not to hide their feelings. Many men have told me women say they want sensitivity, but freak out when they actually see it, especially in the form of tears.]

Becoming a Man

—Bruce Drobeck, Ph.D., family therapist, board member for the Men's Health Network

One of my best friends in high school, "Rowdy Red," was one of these guys who was always pushing the limits. Not only did Rowdy push the limits, but he often took his friends along with him. Rowdy frequently dared us to do things that varied from risky to close to suicidal. Sometimes we would balk, but in the end Rowdy would always win, because he knew exactly what to say: "You haven't got a hair on your ass if you don't_____." You can fill in the blanks with such things as "run that red light" or "dive off that cliff." We would laugh at Rowdy, but we usually did what he said.

Looking back, it's almost comical to see how easily Rowdy pushed our buttons. But there is a more serious side to this matter beyond hairy asses. My friends and I blindly followed Rowdy on the same potentially destructive path that many teenage boys have followed for years in our society. We risked our lives trying to prove our manhood. We did not question it, we just did it. Most of us were lucky enough to survive it. Now, I wonder how many teenage boys do not survive the car wrecks, the fights, the drug overdoses, etc., trying to prove they are men.

Certainly, teenage girls have their own set of worries and concerns. Probably the most life-threatening aspect of girls' development during adolescence is anorexia. I would see this as something of a parallel to boys killing themselves proving they are men. However, some theorists would argue that an anorexic girl is not trying to prove herself to be a woman but trying to avoid developing into a woman. (By the way, there seems to be an increase in the use of steroids among teenage boys, indicating that the emphasis on physical looks is becoming just as much of an issue for boys at this age.) But girls do not seem as concerned with proving they are women. They develop breasts, have periods, then someday they have children and they are women. Rarely do you see a teenage girl fight (or drive drunk) to prove her womanhood.

For teenage boys becoming a man is a complicated issue. In some so-called primitive societies, there are specific rituals and rites of passage that lead a boy into manhood. Once the boy has undergone these rites of passage, there is no question about it, he is a man. In our society, we have a number of formal and informal rites of passage, such as getting a driver's license, graduating from high school, getting your first job, smoking, drinking, and first intercourse. But at which point can a boy say he is now a man? If graduating from high school, getting drunk, or getting laid is the answer, why do so many men spend the rest of their lives trying to prove they are men?

Based on years of experience as a man, a husband and a father, I propose another image of what it means to be a man. Being a man is not about having the biggest muscles, or the biggest penis, or the biggest bank account, or the most women. Being a man requires following your own instincts, having values and standing up for what you believe. Being a man means care and concern for others. This care and concern goes beyond your immediate family to care about the community and society at large. Being a man means that you realize you have feelings, which can include tenderness, kindness, sadness and anger, and realizing that it is OK to express these feelings.

If you are trying to figure out what it means to be a man, I would suggest that you find a mentor or role model who seems to have a sense of values and integrity. Find a mentor who seems more concerned about others than he is concerned about proving his own masculinity. Find a role model who can express a whole range of feelings, not just anger. Your role model can be your father, your grandfather, a teacher, a coach, an uncle—it really does not matter who it is. What does matter is that you find someone, other than another teen, who can show you the way to manhood. Find an alternative to getting drunk, driving fast, and running red lights. I wish Rowdy Red could be here to tell you how he became a man. Unfortunately he did not live long enough to figure it out.

Bottom line, I don't think it's easy for males or females in our society to develop into healthy adults. I think our traditional sex roles are toxic for both sexes.

Why We Need a Men's Movement

—Warren Farrell, Ph.D., author of *Why Men Are the Way They Are* (McGraw-Hill) and *The Myth of Male Power* (Simon and Schuster)

The feminist movement has done a wonderful job freeing women from stereotyped sex roles, but no one has freed men from those roles. The result is that the suicide rate of girls has gone down, while the suicide rate of boys has gone up. Girls used to be less than half of college students; now boys are less than 50 percent of college students. Boys are dropping out of school, joining gangs, and committing murders at alarming rates.

What is the relationship between gender roles and suicide? When society gives its approval only when we fulfill strict roles, we feel like a failure when we don't meet those expectations. It used to be that girls who didn't want to be homemakers felt like failures. When we define only one type of girl or boy as a success, everyone else feels like a failure, which increases suicide rates, dropout rates, etc.

If the 21st century is to serve boys well, it will teach boys that power is not about earning money that somebody else spends after he dies; it is about control over his life. He will begin to put this into practice by making sure he doesn't feel he has to pick up the check, risk the rejection of the first kiss, ask her out, drive, be successful in sports, be career oriented, bring her flowers, and be the only sex to register for the draft. The failure to fulfill an expectation produces depression; the choice to pursue or not pursue an option creates empowerment. The 21st century will be wonderful for boys if we make as much progress freeing boys and men from stereotyped sex roles as we did in freeing girls and women in the 20th century.

The Cage of Masculinity

—Sociology professor Don Sabo, Ph.D., co-author of *Sex, Violence, and Power in Sports: Rethinking Masculinity* (Crossing Press)

While growing up, boys learn various cultural messages about masculinity. We learn to behave "like men," which means not to behave like women. We're told don't be a sissy or a wimp. Keep a stiff upper lip. Big boys don't cry. Take it like a man. Be independent, try not to depend on others. Be tough and aggressive and keep your feelings to yourself. In fact, if you can hide your feelings even from yourself, so much the better. Strive for success and superiority over others.

Each of these cultural messages becomes a bar in the cage that takes shape in a man's gender identity. By the end of adolescence, the cage of masculinity has become so rigid that men have difficulty breaking out of it. Young boys are often taught to endure grief, anxiety, feelings of inadequacy, or pain in stoic silence. Boys who are "too emotional" run the risk of being labeled "sissies," "wusses," or "queers." The suppression of emotions is a built-in requirement for many adult roles that men pursue.

Everybody has an emotional life, yet, historically, men's roles have allowed fewer opportunities for the expression of emotions than women's roles. For example, I remember holding back tears in a movie theater with a date. I believed that the "boyfriend" was supposed to be stoic, unsentimental, and in control of his emotions. As a linebacker on high school and college football teams, I learned to be tough and to mercilessly beat up on other players. These were the rules to live by. Even though I experienced sadness, hurt, or compassion on the inside, I rarely showed these sentiments on the outside.

One result of traditional masculinity is that men are not only less likely to express emotions, but they are also less able to recognize, label, and experience an emotion when they actually experience it. This lack of recognition can lead to confusion, anger, or brooding silences in a man. Women may view this as intentional withholding when the man is truly not conscious of a set of feelings. As men increasingly participate in less rigid, more nurturing roles such as parenting and, as the masculine stereotype continues to wane, men may feel free to explore and express their feelings more openly.

What Young Men Wish Women Understood

(quotes from my college students' discussions)

♦ *We need space, time alone or with the guys. This doesn't mean we don't care about you. Leave us alone when we're watching football. Don't expect us to be sweet, nice, affectionate, and sensitive to you when our buddies are around.*

◆ We may not want to talk about our problems like you do, but just do sports or something to forget a bad day. As Kyle said, "Why do women want to know what I'm thinking? I don't like to be put on the spot." We don't like it when you ask, "What are you feeling?" all the time.

◆ We don't like it when you tell your friends what bugs you instead of telling us directly.

◆ We were raised to be in control, and are afraid of being controlled. Our whole lives are "have to's" (have to be good in sports, have to be strong, have to make money, and have to be the problem solver).

◆ We were raised to find solutions rather than dwell on the emotional aspects surrounding a problem.

◆ We're expected to be good at so many roles—the loving boyfriend, but be tough when necessary. We feel it's our fault when you're unhappy, that we're not doing something right.

◆ We're not all rapists, egotistical jerks, or insensitive macho pigs. Don't transfer your bad experiences from another guy to me.

◆ We have feelings just like you, but have different pressures not to show our feelings. Just because we don't show feelings, doesn't mean we don't have them.

◆ We like it when you are interested in sports and have common interests.

◆ You say you want to go out with caring, sensitive guys but always seem to be attracted to macho jerks.

What do men wonder about women?

—Aaron, 20, would like to ask women:

1. Do women truly want independence or do they want to return to the 1950s?

2. Are men judged by the cars they drive and the gifts they give, or is honesty and purity of heart the most important?

3. Do true gentlemen still exist in women's eyes?

4. What careers do you think should have more men?

5. Are women capable of unconditional love, other than their children?

6. Is romance still alive? What is romantic?

7. Is there good common ground for first dates, allowing for both men and women to feel safe?

Other questions my male students want to ask young women:

1. Do you think about marriage, look at *Bride's* magazine and such?

2. *Do you think men are stupid?*

3. *Do you think men think they're dominant but women really are?*

4. *Do you want a boyfriend to be in charge, a kind of dad?*

5. *Why are you so moody?*

6. *Why do you change your mind so much?*

7. *Why don't you give men some space?*

Bruce Glassman. *Everything You Need to Know About Growing Up Male.* NY: Rosen, 1991.

Ray Raphael. *The Men from the Boys: Rites of Passage in Male America.* Lincoln, NE: University of Nebraska Press, 1988.

Female Role

(also see sexism section in Chapter 7)

—Lisa, 19, Washington

I think the biggest problem girls have is that we worry too much about the other sex. Time and time again, I see girls deliberately acting dumber to get the appropriate nonthreatening image. My advice is it's fine to want to be attractive, but you need to have the self-esteem to put your own goals first. I've been happy to find out that there ARE guys who are attracted to their intellectual equals. We shouldn't settle for less.

—Esther, 22, Massachusetts

There are many challenges to becoming an engineer, in classwork alone. The difficulty for me though was how the majority of my peers treated me in high school. Most of the guys in my school had a picture of a smart girl as being boring on a date, which is just not true. I didn't miss a prom, but I always went with friends. Not being asked out does pull down your spirits quite a bit. I have seen, and this troubles me greatly, other smart women act less intelligent because of this. In every case, it has only hurt them in the end. [So we equate femininity with not being smart in technical fields?]

Once I got to college, I found men who appreciated me for just that, me. That's the way it should be. My recommendation to young women is to tough it out. Know that you will be appreciated once you've left the high school atmosphere. And most importantly, be yourself, as trying to change to impress someone else just doesn't work for them or you.

What Young Women Wish Men Knew About Women

(from discussions in my college classes)

◉ Women are as intelligent as men. We can do anything men can. I hate being underestimated because I'm a blond.

◉ Women deserve to be listened to, even while telling about their day. Look at my face when I'm talking, not my breasts.

◉ Don't try to solve my problems, just let me know you understand them. We often feel guys don't really listen to us.

◉ Some women do get moody with PMS, but when I'm upset it's not usually that. Some men seem to think that women have PMS all month long. We do have ups and downs in our feelings and it's not because we're mad at you.

◉ Crying is not a sign of weakness. We don't have to smile if we don't want to.

◉ It is intimidating and degrading to be yelled at on the street by a group of men.

◉ We wish you'd tell us what you really feel. Why not say what you mean instead of making a woman go crazy while you hide behind your front?

◉ Interactions with men our age don't necessarily mean we want to go out with them or are sexually motivated. Just because we kiss a guy doesn't mean we want to go to bed with him.

A cross-cultural theme tells women to focus on their appearance to attract men. Wellesley College researcher Deborah Tolman suggests that this is a way to keep women in inferior positions. You might try looking at media images of girls and women, keeping that idea in mind. Is the emphasis on the woman's mind and personality or on her body parts? Are just parts of women's bodies shown without the whole person? Are grown women shown in girlish poses? Do females cling and gaze adoringly at men who coolly look away? Do you see evidence of plastic surgery or anorexia?

Television is a useful tool for seeing how our culture defines the female role. TV teaches that men are more important, more powerful, more knowledgeable, and more numerous. Men are most of the anchors on national news programs, narrators of commercials, and the most important characters. On prime time television, men still outnumber women three to one and are usually the initiators of action. Female characters are often younger than the men, attractive, blond, nurturing, or victims.

On Saturday morning kids' shows, fewer than one quarter of the characters are female and even fewer main characters are female. In cartoons, the girls are sidekicks to the main male characters. Think of the Smurfs—with only two girls, or the Ninja Turtles and April, and the lone Power Ranger female dressed in pink. Most of the main Sesame Street characters are male (Big Bird, Cookie Monster, the Count, Elmo, Grover, Oscar—and then there's Miss Piggy and Prairie Dawn).

A visit to the boys' and girls' sections of a large toy store is revealing: "Boys are portrayed as powerful G.I. Joes and girls as passive Barbies," Emma notes. The boys' section is mainly military themes, professions and athletes (doctor, police, basketball player), and action toys, weapons, and vehicles. The girls' section is mostly pink and the toys are mainly about looking attractive (make-up kits and sexy dolls) and housekeeping (ironing and dishwashing sets). Girls' board games include uncreative activities like shopping in a mall and "guess who likes you," referring to a boy calling a girl.

Look at video games to see what they teach about sex roles. The males fight each other and rescue the fair maiden in distress. If a female is not portrayed as passive, she is very buxom and warlike; for example, one of these characters says, "Your missing teeth will remind you of my victory." The games teach that a female can't be both feminine and powerful.

Because of the sexist attitudes illustrated in the media, numerous studies report that girls' self-esteem drops around age 12 or 13 when they hit puberty. *Meeting at the Crossroads* (Lyn Mikel Brown and Carol Gilligan, Ballantine) describes a five-year study of a girls' school in Cleveland, Ohio. The Harvard University researchers found the pressure to be "nice" and "fit in" resulted in the girls' "loss of voice" or confidence to speak their own minds and be independent. Girls create a "cover girl" to fit the cultural definitions of femininity. Exceptions are girls Dr. Gilligan refers to as "the resisters." (Project on Women's Psychology and Girls' Development, Harvard Graduate School of Education, Larsen Hall, 14 Appian Way, Cambridge, MA 02138.)

Andrea Johnston cofounded "Girls Speak Out" with feminist Gloria Steinem, organizing consciousness-raising sessions for girls ages nine to 15 in many states. She observes that girls struggle to hold onto their true selves in spite of pressure from the outside. Young girls feel powerful and clear, but may gradually lose touch with their feelings as they try to please and take care of others. Some lose their clarity, become confused, and less willing to take risks. A 12-year-old wrote, "I'm a strong woman, not an object for the public." In contrast, a 16-year-old wrote, "I'm burned out from listening to others. I don't have time to think about me." Another girl, 16, wrote, "I don't know myself anymore. It seems like I'm nothing, I'm supposed to please others and neglect myself." Ms. Johnston says that reminding girls they can stay in touch with how strong and unique they are as they grow up is a next step in the women's movement.

Tim Flinders, an elementary school teacher of gifted students, is researching these observations in his school district in northern California. He also finds that "confident, bold, combustible, clear-thinking girls with wild dreams" go through a wall around 6th grade and come out silenced in the 9th grade. They may be nasty to each other, but that's typical behavior for the "underclass." Girls act as if it's not feminine to be too honest, self-confidant or smart, since they are supposed to be nice and kind. They learn to be compliant and obedient, a kind of self-suffocation which gets them good grades but not the skills needed to get to the top. He asks that you look at newspaper photographs and count the suits to be reminded about male privilege. Men are born into an aristocracy, responding to his work with girls as if he is a traitor to his class. But he points out the heavy price men pay; the culture says you can have power and prestige and we'll take your soul. The culture needs to be more caring about both sexes, Mr. Flinders concludes. (He recommends E. Debold, et al., *Mother-Daughter Revolution: From Good Girls to Great Women*, and Susan Crawford, *Beyond Dolls and Guns: 101 Ways to Help Children Avoid Gender Bias*, Heinman.)

Evidence of the lack of respect for women can be seen in kids' replies to this question: "How would your life be different if you woke up tomorrow and discovered you were the other sex?" Think about your own answer before you read on. Dr. Alice Baumgartner asked that question of 2,000 Colorado students in grades three through 12. She and her colleagues at the University of Colorado found that both girls and boys shared a contempt for females. The girls felt they would be better off as males, have access to better jobs, get paid more, be taken more seriously, get more attention from their fathers, not be judged by their appearance, be able to play more team sports, be stronger, and not have to worry about being raped. In contrast, the boys hated the thought of becoming female, being restricted, serving others, worrying about their appearance, and not having as much fun.

Professor Cynthia Mee interviewed 2,000 students in grades five through eight in various states. She asked them the best and worst thing about their gender. She was struck by the agreement by both sexes that boys can do more, have more fun, have fewer domestic responsibilities, and are better than girls. The girls had a much harder time than the boys trying to think of good things about their gender and a much easier time thinking of the bad things. Girls frequently responded: "People don't take us seriously. I don't get to do boy things. Guys take advantage of us. We can never get as good a job as men. Being ladylike. People don't think we're as good as boys. PMS." ("Middle School Voices on Gender Identity," *Women's Educational Equity Act Publishing Center Digest*, March, 1995) Sex role stereotypes create limitations for both sexes. If we're aware of the restrictions, we can move beyond them towards equitable relationships (see the sexism section in Chapter 7 and feminism section in Chapter 11).

Youth Publications and Internet Networks

Zines have been around since the late 70s and are now reaching a critical mass. [Thousands of personal zines are available on the Internet. The magazine *Factsheet Five* reports there are more than 40,000 zines worldwide.] *This is how I started writing zines. I got involved with small punk bands and local shows when I was a high school student in Florida. I got roped into it by friends because it seemed interesting. When I worked with male musicians, I wasn't an equal partner; guys would get thanks from bands at the end of a performance—not me. People assumed I was somebody's girlfriend, no matter how hard I worked. When I coauthored a zine with a guy, people referred to it as his zine. This motivated me. I decided I had to do stuff on my own. But*

I still get that, like reviews of my zines credit the guy who drew one cartoon.

I moved to Staten Island. Since I had trouble finding reviews of girls' zines, in 1993 I started publishing a newsletter where I review about 50 zines or comic books by girls. They usually have something to do with female experience in high school and college, like my math teacher who told me I shouldn't get too excited about math because in another year I wouldn't know how to add. I get letters from girls who say they really believe in empowering girls but they mistakenly believe they can't be a feminist because they wear dresses, shave, take baths, and have boyfriends.

It seems the majority of zines are by college-age people, some are in high school, and some older ones are in the punk scene. The majority used to be punk, but now they're less than half the zines. Readers just need to send me two stamps to get my newsletter.

—Sarah, 2?, New York

Action Girl Newsletter
P.O. Box 060380
Staten Island, NY 10306

Periodicals with Youth Writers

Factsheet Five
P.O. Box 170099
San Francisco, CA 94117-0099
(This magazine reviews and catalogs hundreds of zines.)

Global Teen Club International: An International Organization of Ethnically Diverse and Socially Aware Teenagers.
33120 Oak Rd., Suite 309
Walnut Creek, CA 94596-2076
(International contributors write articles about activities in their areas.)

HUES (Hear Us Emerging Sisters)
P.O. Box 7778
Ann Arbor, MI 48107
hues@mail.lifeplay.net
http://www.lifeplay.net/magazines/hues
(A pro-woman magazine started by three 19-year-old University of Michigan students)

New Moon: The Magazine for Girls and Their Dreams
P.O. Box 3587
Duluth, MN 55803-3587
(stories by and about girls internationally, for girls 8 to 14)
http://newmoon.duluth.mn.us/
~newmoon.

New Youth Connections: Youth Communication
144 W. 27th St.
New York, NY 10011
(Written by teens, published monthly during the school year, has large circulation, and co-produces a radio show)

react is distributed in newspapers and on the Internet as *virtually react.* The goal of the interactive news and entertainment weekly is "to help young people get involved in the world and be heard." The print magazine includes an 800-number phone line, fax line, e-mail, and snail mail addresses for readers to respond. http://www.react.com includes news, polls, games, reader letters, and sound and video clips.

REAL Girls
P.O. Box 13947
Berkeley, CA 94712-4947
(A quarterly of "first-person stories
about a girl and her life;" "We're not
interested in stories about how to
get a guy, new hair styles for fall, or
what color eye shadow goes with
what lipstick.")

Teen Voices
316 Huntington Ave.
Boston, MA 02115
(a quarterly "nonexploitative"
magazine written by girls)

Voices of Youth
P.O. Box 1869
Sonoma, CA 95476
(a national magazine of writing and
art by high school students)

Writes of Passage
817 Broadway, 6th Floor
New York, NY 10003

Periodicals for Youth

(some published by newspapers)
Careers & Colleges magazine
989 Sixth Ave., 6th Floor
New York, NY 10018

Dream Scene Magazine
38 Rossi Ave., Suite 1
San Francisco, CA 94118-4218

Exploring Magazine (Boy Scouts)
P.O. Box 152079
Irving, TX 75015-2079

Keynoter
3636 Woodview Trace
Indianapolis, IN 46268-3196

Noise
P.O. Box 3204
Burbank, CA 91504

NY Connection
144 W. 27th St., Suite 8R
New York, NY 10001

The Mirror
1100 Denny Way
Seattle, WA 98109

San Jose Mirror
1650 Los Plumas Ave., Suite J
San Jose, CA 95133

SF Teen
McLaren Lodge, Parks and Recreation
San Francisco, CA 94117

Young Adult Press
P.O. Box 21
Mound, MN 55364

Young Scholar
4905 Pine Cone Dr., Suite 1
Durham, NC 27707

(Magazines for teen girls include
Seventeen, Y.M., Sassy, 'Teen, and
Quake. A magazine for boys, called
Dirt, was distributed by the
publishers of *Sassy*, but it folded.
I know of no mass circulation
magazine for teen boys—any ideas
why? Entertainment magazines for
teens of both sexes include
Mouth2Mouth, react and *Vibe.*

Computer Networks

Internet newsgroups include forums for
students and for kids, as well as special
interest groups revolving around music
groups, computers, games, comics, etc.
Commercial online services,
including America Online
(1-800 827-6364), provide discussion
groups for youth. CompuServe (1-800
848-8199) has Students' Forum, including a message board, chat rooms,
libraries, and games. Prodigy (1-800-
776-3449) offers "Just Kids," with chat
rooms, games, contests, etc. and Delphi
has Just for Teens (1-800-695-4002).

Internet Web sites with Resources for Youth

About and For Kids and Teens
http://www.slip.net/~scmetro/
forabout.html
(a useful list of teen resources)

E-mail Address Sites
http://sunsite.oit.unc.edu/~masha/

FishNet
http://www.jayi.com/opin.html

Global Village News shares news written by students around the world. It is located on the newsgroup K12Net bbs, Channel 11. On Usenet, choose
>>K12.sys.Channel 11<<

www.geekgirl.com.au/geekgirl/
006high/index.html

HIGH SCHOOL CENTRAL
http://www.azc.com/client/enn2/
hscentral.htm

Yahooligans has 1,000s of fun sites:
http://www.yahooligans.com

(see *Tech Girls' Guide to the Internet*,
IDG books, 1996)

Online Shorthand

These symbols can also be used when typing a letter but are most frequently used in computer chat groups.

:) smile

{ } hug

:D laughing

LOL laughing out loud

;) wink

OTF on the floor laughing

:X my lips are sealed

BRB be right back

:* kiss

:(frown

{{{***}}} hugs and kisses

—"—"-@ a rose

IMHO In my humble opinion

ROFL Rolling on floor laughing

Chapter 7

Nathan Allen

School

Your main job now is getting the most out of school. You spend a lot of time there and it's the pathway to career success. Besides learning to communicate effectively, think logically, manipulate numbers, understand the world you live in, and be an informed citizen, you learn to interact with people from different backgrounds. Despite their importance, most Americans agree schools are in trouble; too many are unsafe, overcrowded, and unable to give students individual attention. As a result, more than 40 percent of students score below basic reading and math skills and about one-quarter of high school graduates lack marketable skills.

You can help make your school a better place for younger students who follow you by getting involved in activities, becoming a leader, attending school board and PTA meetings to offer a student view, starting a new organization, doing volunteer work, or whatever it takes to make a positive change.

Advice About How to Succeed in High School

When you enter high school there are so many new things to spend your time on, like athletics, football games, and dances. You can sometimes forget the report that's due or the science project. I tried day planners and organizers. The things that have worked best are determination to get things done and realizing my priorities.

—Jenny, 14, California

Advice from My College Students

—Courtney, 19

Don't be fake to try and fit in. It will only ruin you in the end.

—Amy, 20

Don't see people of your same sex as competition, but as allies.

—Rachel, 20

Look past the exterior and get to know people in different groups.

—Greg, 21

Even if you think your parents are not the best, ask them for advice. They've done everything you want to do. You'll be surprised about how much they know and can help.

—Lolly, 22

Get involved with sports, clubs and/or work. The more active you are, the more focused you become in school because you have to manage your time.

— Joe, 23

Take a class on study habits and memory retention.

—Meredith, 23

Teachers are usually very nice and will do anything they can for you if you get to know them.

—Adam, 24

The best way to be cool is to enjoy yourself, trust yourself, and know that you are OK the way you are.

—Pete, 25

Set goals, make plans to reach them, and follow through.

Define Your Goals

Respond to these questions in your journal or discuss them to clarify your goals.

1. What are your favorite subjects? What kind of job might build on these interests?

2. Which subjects are hardest for you? Does your school have tutoring services? What activities are most challenging for you? You might want to experiment with running for an office or another challenge that stretches you.

3. What are your goals for school achievement this semester? By graduation?

4. What is your plan for achieving these goals? Rewards for achieving them?

5. What study schedule works best for you?

6. Who is your favorite teacher of all time? Why?

7. Sometimes students feel subtle pressure not to do well in subjects considered more appropriate for the other gender, another ethnic group, or for "geeks." Have you felt this irrational stereotyping and, if so, how did you respond?

8. What do you want to do after high school? Interview people with interesting jobs, counselors, teachers, your parents, and parents of friends about how to achieve your goal or figure one out.

9. What activities would you like to learn more about, i.e., drama, sports, chess, video making, a foreign language, music, ballroom dance, or other opportunities at your school?

10. Which clique are you most curious about? Make an effort to get to know someone who seems the most different from you on the surface.

—Eric, 15, Colorado

When I first got into high school it was very different from junior high. I didn't have much time at home because football practice was long, I got home late, and had to do a lot of homework. I used my time in school as much as I could to do work so I sometimes wouldn't have homework.

—Rebecca, 17, Texas

I have to cope with different obstacles thrown at me at the same time. These obstacles included the challenge of adjusting to high school, harder work, drugs, alcohol, first loves, sex, and looking into the future. When these challenges approached me, I could usually depend on a friend or a sibling. Parents are sort of off limits for some problems because if I go up to my mother and say, "Jimmy wants to have sex and I'm not sure if I'm ready," or "Karen wants me to smoke out with her tomorrow," then my mom would ground me or tell me not to hang around with them.

People my age who are stressing about all the different obstacles, really need to have someone to talk to. If they feel like they cannot talk to anyone, they should talk to themselves. Writing down how they feel or writing a letter to someone (and not giving it) is much better than keeping it all in.

How to Succeed in High School Books

Terry Dunnahoo. *How to Survive High School*. NY: Franklin Watts, 1993. (principles of good study habits, preparing for college, and staying healthy)

Barbara Mayer. *How to Succeed in High School*. Lincolnwood, IL: NTC Publishing Group/VGM Career Horizons, 1992. (asks questions to get you thinking about your values, attitudes, grades, communication, friends, parents, money, and goals)

Marian Salzman. *Greetings from High School*. Princeton, NJ: Peterson's, 1991. (interviews with students and information about coping with teachers, friends, and parents)

Z.D. Schneider. *Countdown to College: Every Student's Guide to Getting the Most Out of High School*. NY: College Board, 1989.

Dropping Out and the GED

In my freshman and sophomore year I was failing a lot of classes and thought of dropping out. The thing that helped me was a teacher. That, and my mom saying that I would go to school until I was 50, kept me from dropping out. My advice to someone younger is to hit the books. It might suck now but it will pay off in the long run.

—Adam, 17, Wisconsin

More than 2,800 kids drop out of school each day. A dropout has less than a one-in-three chance of finding a job. The main cause of dropping out is not feeling connected to school, often connected to poverty and failing in school. The dropout rate is linked to income and ethnicity, so that low-income, Native American, and Latino students are more likely to drop out, but poverty is the main cause. The more education your parents have, the less likely you are to drop out; but the two causes intertwine, since education is linked with earning power.

A 1995 survey of California dropouts found that they were more likely to use drugs and alcohol and be in gangs than teens who stay in school. Nearly one of three dropouts started using drugs before age 12. Among female dropouts, over one third are pregnant or parenting. Girls who succeed in school and whose parents have higher incomes and education are least likely to become pregnant as teens.

The high school graduation rate has stayed about 87 percent since 1990. Each year, over half a million teenagers drop out of school, although education is the single largest expenditure in state budgets. The good news is 79 percent of Americans ages 25 and older have at least a high school degree, up from only one third of the population in 1950.

Each yearly class of dropouts costs about $240 billion in lost earnings and taxes and each dropout can cost up to $90,000 in welfare, prison, and other social programs, according to Bill Honig (former California superintendent of public instruction). Dropouts average $13,697 a year in earnings, compared to $37,224 for college graduates (Census Bureau, 1995). An alternative to going to high school or dropping out is getting a GED and going to a community college.

Alternatives to High School

—Kelly Lynn Baylor, psychology graduate student, offers some advice.

Some of you may wake up every morning dreading the thought of going to school. If your parents approve, and if your state offers it, you may have an alternative choice. Most states have a way of testing out of high school once you reach age 16. I am not talking about the GED which you cannot take until you are 18. There is another exam that is more difficult that tests whether you have the basic knowledge expected of a high school student. In California, it is called the High School Proficiency Exam and takes approximately four hours. This test is not easy to take and you will have to study or have already attained a lot of knowledge.

To find out if such an exam is offered in your state, talk to your high school counselor. This is not an easy out, but taking the exam is better than quitting or flunking out. If you pass the exam you will receive the equivalent of a high school diploma.

This step should not be taken lightly. Even though this legally gives you the equivalent of a high school diploma, it is not considered as strong as a diploma. Employers will question why you didn't stay in high school, and wonder if you have the knowledge to do the job. Community colleges will admit you with just your equivalency diploma but other colleges will also want you to take the SAT, or other college entrance exams. Whether you decide to take the exam or not, it is important for you to know you have a choice.

—Jason, 27, California

My biggest challenge was moving to California from Iowa and having to change high schools and being the outsider at a new high school. What helped me cope was the GED (Graduate Equivalency Exam). It allowed me to finish school early and move on.

—Noel, 32, California

My most difficult challenge as a teen was trying to stay in school and to keep from ultimately dropping out. Peer pressure, lack of family encouragement, and simply my own lack of interest in school played a large part in the direction I eventually chose to take in life. The decision I made then still affects my life today in many aspects.

I grew up in the Philippines with four brothers and two sisters. My parents did the best they could to support the family. Mom washed clothes for the neighbors to earn small cash while Dad drove a jeepney (a small bus). Both Mom and Dad only got as far as elementary. School for us was just a place to go because we were not old enough to work. In short, we were never encouraged to pursue higher education.

Coming to the U.S. at the age of 12 was a total culture shock. There were new faces, different races, and English language to tackle. After two years in the U.S., I met some friends to hang out with. Unfortunately, they were the kind who got a big kick out of skipping class and smoking pot. I got so involved I ended up joining a gang. They say that once you get a taste of skipping classes you get used to it. All I wanted was to feel wanted and hang out with the fellas. Well, I got so used to it that I was set back twice in junior high and also twice in high school.

I remember my parents telling me that all I needed to do was to find any paying job and I'd be fine. Because there wasn't anybody to encourage me and I couldn't count on me to get motivated about school, I dropped out. At that time I didn't have anyone I could call my role model or someone I could talk to for advice.

After being in the work force for more than 15 years with three different companies, I find no satisfaction in what I do. I finally realized that although I have potential to do certain jobs, because a degree is not in hand, I'm limited to a certain position in the workplace. The choices you make in your teens, whether they're right or wrong, will affect you in the future.

National Dropout Prevention
Center and Network
205 Martin St., Box 345111, Clemson
University
Clemson, SC 29634-5111
(provides technical assistance to
schools, research, and a database)

Geoff Martz. *Cracking the GED*. NY: Random/Villard Books, 1994.

Murray Rockowitz, et al. *Pass Key to the GED*. Hauppauge, NY: Barron's, 1995.

Employer/School Partnerships

(You may want to show this section to school administrators and the chamber of commerce.)

Employers are assisting schools and parents in improving education. Their concern was first triggered by the National Committee for Economic Development's 1983 report on "A Nation at Risk." A decade later, over 150,000 business/school partnerships were in place. Despite these efforts, the Business/Education Council leaders were disturbed by the lack of "broad-based measurable results" ten years later. Jerry Hume, chair of the board at Basic American Co., points out, "When we look at the skills level of our incoming work force and find a 50 percent failure rate of the entry-level employee when tested at the 8th grade level, certainly reform is not working." The "Employer Promise for Learning" is a recent project of business leaders and the U.S. Department of Education to form partnerships to improve education.

RJR Nabisco is a model company which supports education. Their employees have access to: time off to attend school conferences, a workshop series on how to be leaders on their school board or in the PTA, grants of $2,000 to help school leaders with special projects, a Scholastic Savings Plan where the company will match employee contributions of up to $1,000 a year for four years to save for their kids' college expenses, and help with paying interest on college loans.

Employer/School Assistance Options (with examples)

✪ school reform/restructuring (RJR Nabisco)

✪ provide on-site elementary school classrooms (Hewlett-Packard)

✪ adopt-a-school (provide tutors, lecturers, field trips, science materials, computers, etc.)

✪ science and math enrichment (Amoco, Hewlett-Packard)

✪ mentor individual students (Coopers and Lybrand)

✪ school-to-work preparation (Bank of America)

✪ provide child care on school sites (Pratt Whitney)

✪ assist in preschool readiness programs (Honeywell, Minneapolis Way to Grow)

✪ outings for school-age children on school holidays (John Hancock's "Kids to Go" for children 6 through 14)

✪ provide management training to school administrators (Xerox, IBM, Bank of America), and loan executives to schools

✪ train parents to become leaders in school organizations (Southern California Gas Company)

✪ education telephone lines for homework assistance, college planning, selecting a school through SchoolMatch (a database)

✪ encourage employees to start second careers as teachers (IBM, General Electric)

✪ give employees paid time off work to help in schools (Stride Rite)

✪ organize employees and retirees to provide tutoring (McDonnell Douglas)

✪ computer Internet linkup (Genentech)

✪ lobby government for tax increases for education and keep the spotlight on the need for better schools (American Business Collaborative)

Business and Education Coalitions

American Business Collaborative (1-617-965-6469, provides funding for after-school and other family-friendly programs), The Committee for Economic Development, The National Alliance for Business, American Business Conference, the National Association of Manufacturers.

The Business Roundtable, 1615 L St., NW, Suite 1350, Washington, DC 20036.

Chamber of Commerce, Center for Workforce Preparation, 1615 H St., NW, Washington DC 20063.

Fortune magazine organizes an annual conference of business and education leaders and issues special education editions.

Ethnicity

Racism is a big problem. Teens seem to hang in ethnic groups. As you walk around campus you see whites, blacks, Asians, all in different groups. They seem to have a problem with each other.

—Bryan, 14, California

Stereotyping occurs when we assume everyone in a group is the same. Prejudice occurs when we prejudge people we don't know by the group they belong to because of their ethnicity, gender, sexual preference, music preferences, cliques, hair color—you add to the list. Most young people seem to feel racism is widespread but they are not personally part of the problem. A 1993 poll of U.S. college freshman found that 86 percent agreed that racial discrimination is a major problem, but less than half (42 percent) felt that helping to promote racial understanding was a very important goal (poll by the UCLA Higher Education Research Institute).

A 1995 survey (of the 276 members of the Teen Board for the magazine *Careers and Colleges*) reported that 77 percent observe racism in their high schools, but only 20 percent believe that it is a serious problem. Many reported social segregation in their school, as with people eating lunch with only people of their own ethnic group. Forty-three percent believe that teachers and administrators discriminate against students of color.

By the year 2000, over 40 percent of public school students will be ethnic minorities. In states like California, white students are already a minority. If American ethnic groups were ranked like countries for their incomes, health, and political power, European Americans would rank first in the world, African Americans would rank 27th, and Latinos would rank 32nd, according to the 1995 UN Human Development Report. Asian Americans with college degrees earn 26 percent less than whites with similar degrees and are underrepresented in executive positions. Although minority students are about one-quarter of recent high school graduates, they are only 16 percent of the four-year college students, partly because of increasing tuition costs.

By around 2050, people of non-European ancestry will be almost half the U.S. population. The Census Bureau reports that currently, 74 percent of the population is European American, 12 percent African American, 10 percent Latino, 3 percent Asian, and .7 percent Native American. In 1990, only eight percent of the population was foreign born, compared to 16 percent in 1910.

In a global economy, we need to learn about multiculturalism. If you could shrink the world's population to only 100 people, representative of the existing human ratios, there would be: 57 Asians, 21 Europeans, 14 North and South Americans, and eight Africans. Of these 100, 70 are people of color and non-Christian. Half would suffer from malnutrition and only one would have a university education (United Nations data).

To combat racism, you can let people know you disapprove of racist and sexist slurs and jokes and speak out against stereotyping and prejudice when it occurs. Do not expect one person to speak for their whole culture. Learn more about the ethnic groups in your area, perhaps by listening to their radio stations and reading their magazines and books. If people eat lunch in segregated groups at school, take the radical step of asking a person with a different background to eat with you. If you have spiritual beliefs, think about how racism contradicts the belief in divine intelligence and love.

Don't make assumptions that others do things the way you do. For example, in some cultures people stand close together and look at each other in the eyes when talking. In other cultures direct eye contact, touching, and standing close are considered rude. People may have different beliefs about time, such as the importance of promptness. In some cultures people consider it rude to say No directly, while others don't like beating around the bush.

If you're the brunt of racism, pick your battles. Sometimes it's not worth your energy to do anything but ignore a stupid comment. But similar to any form of bullying (see Chapter 6), if it continues, let school authorities and other adults know what's going on. Ask your student government to find out what other schools do to educate students about racism and sexism on campus and provide support groups.

—Candice, 14, California

The most difficult thing I've faced as a teen is all the prejudice that goes around. When someone would say or do something bad, I would try to ignore it. Sometimes it would get so bad that I would go to the principal or counselors. Since then I haven't had a real problem with it. You should solve it now or it will turn into something more than you can handle. Talk to someone immediately.

—Brandon, 15, Colorado

The most difficult challenge I have to face right now is racism. It is really hard to concentrate on doing good in school when people are expecting you to fail. The main thing that helped me cope with this challenge was talking. At my school there is a club based on the racial tensions and pressures of school life. My advice to someone younger is to talk about your problems, because a person is not going to know they're doing something wrong unless you tell them your feelings about it.

—Adimika Meadows, 17, Washington

All my life, I thought my education was complete. I was told about the cowboys and Indians, that sex is bad, and that it doesn't matter what color you are because "we are all special." Those points were valid in my young life but did not prepare me for the challenge I was going to meet—life.

Life was filled with surprises such as racism, poverty, teen pregnancy, gay/lesbian youth rights, and sexually transmitted diseases. All the once-important slogans I chanted as a child: "Say No to Drugs," "Petting is a No-No," and "Don't Talk to Strangers," were not relevant. My candy-coated education did not prepare me for the experience of growing up.

I once thought that all cowboys were European Americans, when the reality is many were African Americans. I was told that the Indians were friends of the Pilgrims, but not told that we snatched their land. My white male, Eurocentric [concentrates on the culture of European males] school education taught me segments of the truth, but what is a fraction of the truth going to do for me if I want to excel in college?

Multicultural education is not an option in my high school. When school books date back to 1972 and only mention black people in history during the segment on civil rights, you know that your education is outdated. [A reader noted, "I'm experiencing this in my history class right now."]
[(This quote and the next one are from Tony Watson, "Youths Map Solutions," *The Seattle Times*, Section E, November 29, 1994.)]

—Tesmer Atsbeha, 17, Washington

The greater problem at my high school is the polarization and resulting self-segregation throughout the student population based on race and culture. Because of this separation, miscommunication is frequent and a continuous tension pervades everyday schedules.

One of the sources of this separation is the inequality of resources that begins at the elementary school level and tracks students of color into regular level classes with the poorest quality teachers, most uncreative curriculum, and a lack of role models and necessary services.

This ultimately turns the high school into a system of haves and have-nots, and although we share many triumphs, the victories are soured by the knowledge of the number of students who are falling through the cracks without a side glance from teachers and administration. Thus only the community notices and often by then it's too late for many students.

In my school, we already have a group working for interactive learning and improved communications. In addition to proposing forums, we decided to add mediating and cross-cultural communication skills as part of a proposal for a new curriculum. Included in that is the use of non-Eurocentric history of America, which would spread greater respect for the contributions of people of color and possibly eliminate stereotypes generated by a single class perspective that can lead to misunderstandings and conflicts.

—Camilla, 17, Mississippi

The most difficult thing that a teen has to face is discrimination by other teens. People discriminate against you not only by race, but by religion, how you dress, how *you wear your hair, or how rich you are. The way I cope is to be happy with who I am. Those people are not worth being friends with if they are going to ridicule me.*

—Mgamboa, 19, California

For me, nationality is something that should be treasured and respected. I like learning about other cultures because it enhances my own life. When you shut out others based on color, you can lose out on knowing really wonderful people. Respect other people's interests and they'll respect yours.

—Scooter, 19, New York

Be open and willing to learn about everyone else, and always remember there is nothing wrong with asking questions. It's better to ask questions rather than to assume things based on stereotypes that are usually wrong anyway.

—Lupe, 20, California

Talking with others and finding out about them is the only way to know and understand. Don't be afraid to be open-minded, as when someone changes their attitude, they change their whole world.

African American Students

—William, 17, Washington

A lot of teachers put you down. Teachers say you're not going to pass (the one I'm thinking of was an African American). In my high school, the AP classes are on the third floor, mainly white kids. This discourages other students.

More than half the 31 million African Americans live in the South and/or in central cities. Forty-six percent of African American youths ages 18 and younger live in poverty, compared to 16 percent of European American kids. The results of poverty for black youth present a sobering picture:

- Every 46 seconds of a school day a student drops out.

- Every 104 seconds a teen gets pregnant.

- Every 43 minutes a baby dies.

- Every four hours a child is killed by a gun.

By 1992, 12 percent of African Americans over age 25 earned a bachelor's degree from college, compared to 22 percent of European Americans. Education pays off: The median earnings for African Americans workers over 25 with college degrees was $30,910, compared to $18,620 for blacks with just high school degrees. However, black men with professional degrees earn 21 percent less than white men with similar jobs and degrees, according to the Department of Labor's Glass Ceiling report. Black women with college degrees earn almost $2,000 less than white women, although they are catching up. Whether we go to college or not has a lot to do with whether our parents went, as well as their income. Unless intervention is offered to break the cycle, it continues, like the old saying that the rich get richer and the poor get poorer. Schools that provide outreach and mentoring programs can make a difference.

—Natoshi, 18, California

The most difficult challenge I faced as a teen was racism. I moved to rural Northern California from L.A. my sophomore year. It was a drastic change, as I ended up in the agricultural classes. Since there weren't very many African Americans in that class, they figured us to be all the same, but they really didn't know me. It took them a while to really get to know me and realize I was not like everybody else.

In a world history class they made a lot of racist comments that hurt. But I had to learn that you can't get mad at petty comments. You have to worry about more important things like your health. Don't take heed to what everybody says, cause either it will hurt you or get you in trouble.

—Seymour, 22, California

The most difficult challenge I faced as a teen was playing three sports a year, and being the only African American on the team. What helped me is talking to my parents and meeting friends in school who supported me also, as an athlete and a friend.

—Adarian, 27, California

Being a black male in America is a very trying experience. We are not given from birth the same things as our white counterparts, things such as pride and respect. We have to earn them.

How do we handle racism? Don't play the game. The next time someone calls you a name, say to them, "Prove it." Prove that you are a stupid cracker, spic, or whatever they choose to call you besides your given name. The next time someone says that "All whites are superior to blacks," say to them, "Prove it." The next time someone says, "Girls can't learn math," say to them, "Prove it." Don't accept what someone tells you on the strength of them saying it, without them being able to put actual facts up for support.

Difference is what made the human race. The difference between male and female populated this planet. The difference in skin color allows some of us to live in certain places. So remember, differences are good, they allow us to exist on this planet.

National Black Child Development
Institute
1023 15th St., NW, Suite 600
Washington, DC 20005

The Black Collegian
1240 S. Broad Ave.
New Orleans, LA 70125
(magazine for college students
published four times a year)

National Scholarship Service and
Fund
for Negro Students
Martin Luther King Jr. Dr.
Atlanta, GA 30314
(provides scholarships and free
information about colleges)

Black Community Crusade for Children
and Black Student Leadership Network
(publishes a newsletter called
*WeSpeak! A Voice of African American
Youth* and initiates campaigns)
Children's Defense Fund
25 E St., NW
Washington, DC 20001

Joan Carroll. *The Black College Career
Guide.* Covington, KY: Masey Young,
1989. (describes black colleges,
including curriculum, costs, and
financial aid)

Audrey Edwards and Craig Polite.
*Children of the Dream: The Psychology
of Black Success.* NY: Doubleday,
1992. (interviews with successful
African Americans—a common theme
is pride in their ethnicity)

Ed Smith. *African Americans Students
in Interracial Schools: A Guide for
Students, Teachers, and Parents.*
Garrett Park, MD: Garrett Park Press,
1994.

Errol Smith. *37 Things Every Black
Man Needs to Know.* Valencia, CA: St.
Clair Rene, 1991.
(overcoming racism)

Erlene Wilson. *The 100 Best Colleges
for African-American Students.* NY:
Plume, 1993.

Asian American Students

—Ken, 16, California

The biggest problem I've faced is overcoming stereotypes about Asians, that they're only smart and can't play sports. I play multiple sports for my high school and keep up good grades, with a chance to win an all-league award. I learned to work hard at whatever I do, giving it my all. I would say to just have fun in high school and keep your own values.

—Moon Jee Yoo-Madrigal, Ph.D., professor of Asian American Studies

As Asians, we come from many different places with different languages, cultures, and histories, but here in this country, we share one sobering and ultimately transforming experience. Being outsiders, we're made to feel inferior for having the wrong skin color, the wrong accent, the wrong clothes, eating food with unpronounceable names, and celebrating holidays no one else has ever heard of. Being an outsider is the common American experience. It is, in fact our single common bond.

Historically, racism against Asian Americans was masked by the tide of discrimination against blacks and Jews. During the 19th and 20th centuries, Asians were discriminated against through laws that restricted their economic and sociopolitical advancement and laws which prohibited marriage between Asians and whites. Asians had to attend segregated "oriental schools" and live in segregated residential areas, until the historic Brown v. Board of Education court ruling in 1954.

Despite all these hardships, Asian Americans made tremendous contributions. From building the transcontinental railroad which opened the West to East in 1868, reclaiming the California swamp land making it some of the richest agricultural land in the U.S.—from farmers to rocket scientists, Asians made their mark in the U.S. through hard work and perseverance.

I have acquired an American "cultural identity' intermingled with my original Korean and Asian identifications, but my identity, like yours, reflects myriad cultural influences, and role expectations, which I have fused, adapted, and integrated in my own individual way. Each of you will develop your own version of cultural identity.

"The republic of learning knows no national, no cultural boundaries."

—Nora, 17, California

Growing up in a predominantly white and conservative town has definitely shaped who I am today. Being a half-Korean and half-Filipino girl, racism is not a very big issue in my life, partly because many people seem to deny it exists. It doesn't happen often, but I have felt it from both sides, from my own race and from non-Asians.

When I was in 8th grade, like most girls my age, I wanted to be popular. I had just become friends with a girl from the "in " crowd. One night, Barb, my other friend Darci, and I were at a Chinese restaurant. We came upon the subject of race and Barb said, "I just don't think you belong here." OK, where am I supposed to go? Send half my body to Korea and the other half to the Philippines? At the time, I was dumbfounded because that was the first time I'd experienced blatant racism. I was truly speechless and couldn't stick up for myself or my race, so I just shook my head and chuckled in disgust. I hope someday she will learn that the United States was formed with the hope and foresight of all people and races.

The next year I started high school. My character is somewhat complex. I am a studious Asian girl, honors student, and play a few instruments classical-style, but I also listen to punk music and have a unique style of dressing. The way I dress is a mixture of classical and modern with a touch of punk, but it is definitely not trendy, core punk, or gangster, like the Southeast Asians wear.

There is a small, distinct minority of Southeast Asians in my hometown, and because of social and cultural similarities, they group together. One day at the mall, some of the Asian guys made some "cat calls" at me and I guess the girls they were with got mad because they thought I was a sellout. They followed me around the mall, mad-dogging me. It hurts when people think I'm a sellout because I am very proud of who I am, my parents' accomplishments, and my ancestors' accomplishments. The fact that I am the only Asian girl in all the classes I have taken greatly hampers my chances of making Asian friends. My advice to other teenagers is to go where you're comfortable. Conforming to societal molds is not a must and one shouldn't shed his or her character to the norms. Never lose your identity—your style, your experiences, your family, your culture.

—Fue, 21, California

I was about seven years old when I came to the United States from Laos. Since then I have faced culture loss because we don't have time to practice both the old traditions and learn the new ideas and methods in America. Some of the strengths and beauties of preserving the old traditions are that it gives us a sense of identity. I feel we should preserve our language, art (needlework on tapestries), music (traditional instruments), religion (shamanism), and rituals (funeral, wedding, and other traditional ceremonies). Even though I want to preserve our culture, I know we will eventually lose it like most other groups that came before the Hmong.

When I was growing up, a part of me got really involved in school athletics, and other organizations. Feeling a sense of belonging, I was able to adapt better than others. I also became more outspoken than other Hmong students.

—Xsue Thao, 27, California

I used to think that America is a wonderful land, a paradise, a place where I could peacefully sleep. But I never thought that people would hate each other so much. My first year in America was terrible. I started to speak the language that isn't mine; I started to go to a school that was different from those that I used to attend. I don't mind what people think and say about me, but please don't hurt my feelings. I'm so concerned about how I'm going to be able to survive in this new land since the native people aren't very happy to see me being in their country. I love this nation as much as any other folks do. How come people look at me like I did something real wrong? Isn't it because I don't look like them? My friends, don't hate each other because our colors are different. Please keep in mind that we are all the same in the eyes of God, and let's share this only earth that we have with one another.

Coalition for Asian Pacific American
Youth (CAPAY)
c/o Institute for Asian American
Studies
University of Massachusetts
100 Morrisey Blvd.
Boston, MA 02125-3393

Leadership Education for Asian
Pacifics
327 E. Second St., Suite 226
Los Angeles, CA 90012-4210

Latinos

—Iliana, 15, Texas

The most difficult challenges I faced as a teen have to deal with racism and favoritism. Support from my parents helped me cope with this challenge because they taught me to ignore the ignorant. If a younger person was facing the same problem I would tell you to keep pride in who you are.

—Amy, 15, Colorado

The most difficult challenge I have faced is trying my hardest to succeed in school and elsewhere without any minority support and hardly any other Hispanics in the honors classroom. I have tried to push other minorities and let them know they can do just as well as someone who is not a minority. When others try to push me down, it makes me work harder to be the best. My advice is to work as hard as you can and you will always succeed. What is difficult is easy, and what is impossible is only difficult; it just takes longer.

Over half the Latinos in the U.S. lack adequate literacy skills to read and write English. As a consequence, the high school graduation rate is 54 percent (compared to 87 percent for whites and blacks in 1995). Latino students have the second highest dropout rate because of language barriers and working to help support their families. Also, school may seem like an alien Anglo culture where they feel out of control and frustrated. Only 57 percent graduated in 1994 and one-third of these went on to college.

In 1992 only nine percent of Latinos age 25 and over had four or more years of college, compared to 22 percent of European Americans. The gap has more than doubled since 1970. The connection between education levels and income is shown by the fact that nearly three times as many Latinos have incomes below the poverty line as European Americans (in 1991, 29 percent of Latinos had incomes below the poverty line).

Successful outreach programs demonstrate that high percentages of Latino students will graduate if given adequate encouragement. An example is the Calexico school district, on the California border with Mexico, where 95 percent of the students are Mexican American. Most graduate and many go on to college because they work individually with an adult mentor, plus an extensive bilingual program offers core courses in Spanish.

In Watsonville, in northern California, a program of peer counseling and monitoring attendance succeeded after three years in keeping 72 percent of the targeted students in school. In contrast, only 22 percent of a comparable group of students stayed in school without a support program. These successful programs should be available to every student who speaks English as a second language. Having a mentor to show interest in your school success makes a major difference.

—Art Sanchez, Ph.D., psychology professor

As Latinos living within the United States we should expect to be burdened by others who have prejudiced and racist attitudes towards us sometime during our lives. Unfortunately, some of us will experience this more than others. This of course depends on "how we appear to others"; for example, the shade of our skin color, the clothes we wear, and the manner in which we speak English. The more we are seen as different, the more likely we will experience prejudice.

If you should experience this, remember *cada cabez un mundo*, every person contributes through his/her experience an importance and uniqueness to the world. Also remember that we are a culture that values *personalismo* and that applying personal informal attention to relationships helps to break down prejudices. During difficult times draw on your inner strength—*fuerza de espiritu*. Our families and our culture have taught us to be tough, determined, and strong willed during these times. You have seen others in *la familia* endure, then move forward in life, as can you.

There are several other aspects of our culture that I believe can help guide our decisions and help us to make the best choices for our future: *respeto* (respect for others), *confianza en confianza* (mutual trust), *simpatia* (maintaining closeness to others), *orgullo* (pride), and *verguenza* (shame). As you make personal choices, see if you can find a balance between these cultural aspects and your personal self. Look to those whom you respect, feel a closeness to, and trust. And when others are in need, be that person for them. Lastly, make decisions for which you and your family can be proud.

—Maria Lopez, instructor, Ph.D. student

The young girl sat at the kitchen table, gazing at the dreary rain outside the window, tears streaming down her cheeks. This young girl is 17, a junior in high school, from a strict Catholic family, not married and pregnant! "What can I do now?" she thought.

Actually, it's not surprising that this young lady found herself in this predicament. She grew up in a small rural town, one of the few Mexican families, raised in an all white environment. She experienced a very tumultuous adolescence; feelings of isolation, emotions of anger, hostility, and confusion. Her world was in conflict with the world surrounding her. Although she had achieved considerable popularity in school, she still lacked a sense of belongingness. She was a member of the school's majorette team, elected cheerleader and songleader each year. She was well-liked by her peers, adding to her confusion. Why didn't she "fit" in? Why was her background so different from others? How to balance between two worlds, different languages, different cultures, different sets of expectations? It seemed that the confusion destroyed her inside.

Being pregnant, the right thing to do was to marry. She married in her senior year. However, she continued to attend high school much to the administration's chagrin. The school policy was that pregnant girls did not attend school. Against all odds, she graduated from high school with a three-month-old baby girl to watch her receive her diploma. These experiences created a determined spirit so vital to her survival. That was in 1976, a young girl, Maria, at 19, with a child to raise, alone.

The story you have just read is my life. Currently, I teach college classes, am a doctoral student, and am considered a leader in my community. I have been able to strive, attain, and progress in the face of adversity. I would like to share some of my strategies for success with you.

One of the most important things that I can share with you is to educate yourself. Know who you are and what a wonderful proud legacy you have. As women in a mostly male, mostly white environment, we often think badly about ourselves. We must learn from our mistakes and make them work for us. Educate yourself. Build knowledge. Begin to take a good look at yourself and your life. Learn as much as you can about your life, yourself, your loved ones, your heritage, and your future. When you begin to recognize the achievements around you, you begin to see a brighter future. When you compare the barriers that we Latinas have faced: racism, sexism, and poverty, we can be proud that we have survived it all. Consider yourself a survivor. Know that you have a right to dream your dreams, strive to achieve your goals, and live your life peacefully.

Prepare yourself. Find your voice, and when you find that voice, I challenge you to have the confidence and courage to use your voice. Stand up for what you believe in and know that you have a right to think the way you do. Look for people who can help you. This is the key to success. No one, nothing operates in a vacuum. We cannot manage all the many pressures without some help from somewhere. Seek out and find those who will understand you, those who will nurture you and believe in you.

ERIC Clearinghouse for Bilingual
Education 1-800-647-0123

ASPIRA
1112 16th St., Suite 340
Washington, DC 20013-1492

Committee for Hispanic
Children and Families
140 W. 22nd St., Suite 301
New York, NY 10011

LULAC (League of United Latin
American Citizens)
2100 M St., NW, Suite 602
Washington, DC 20037-1207

The National Association of
Latino Arts and Culture
1300 Guadalupe St.
San Antonio, TX 78207-5519

National Council of La Raza
1111 19th St. NW, Suite 1000
Washington, DC200036
hn2263@handsnet.org

National Hispanic Scholarship Fund
P.O. Box 748
San Francisco, CA 94101

MALDEF (Mexican American Legal
Defense and Education Fund)
733-15th St., NW, Suite 920
Washington, DC 20002

United Mexican American Students
P.O. Box 207, UMC, Room 182
Boulder, CO 80309

University Latino research centers:
The University of Texas at Austin,
Hunter College—CUNY, UCLA, Florida
International University, Michigan
State University, University of
Arizona, University of New Mexico,
and Stanford University.

Andrea Bermúdez. *Doing Our
Homework: How School Can Engage
Hispanic Communities*. ERIC
Clearinghouse on Rural Education and
Small Schools, P.O. Box 1348,
Charleston, WV 25325-1348.
(describes how to involve parents
and do parent education)

Libreria y Galeria San José distributes
books by Latino authors in English
and Spanish. P.O. Box 8068, San Jose,
CA 95155-8068. Another catalog is
available from the *Art Publico* Press,
at the University of Houston,
Houston, TX. Counselor Juan Zertuche
recommends Victor Villaseñor's books
Rain of Gold and *Macho*, the poet
Cherie Moraga, and Internet: Latino
Links and Latino Web.

Native Americans

—Shor-tay, 18, California

The toughest thing in my teen years is the struggle between two worlds. It's not easy being white and Indian, but being raised white and trying to connect with my Indian side is the hardest part of all. I used to not care about my Indian side, until the day I went to my first powwow. The beating of the drums matched the beat of my heart, the regalia of the dancers matched the dreams of my ancestors, and the songs of the drummers sang songs of a hundred years. It sparked the flame that I now so dearly love, so I'm learning more about my culture from the college Indian club and Four Winds Indian education.

My family and white friends don't want to understand why I need to know the other part of me, why I care. The only thing that helps me cope is being around my Indian friends who understand me, who are there for me, and teach me about my ancestry. Around my Caucasian friends I rarely talk about my Indian side because it seems they don't care.

The most oppressed group in the U.S., Native Americans have the lowest life expectancy, lowest per capita income, the highest rate of many diseases and alcoholism, the highest school dropout rate (36 percent), and unemployment ranging from 50 to 85 percent. These facts are striking evidence of the harmful effects of racism and poverty.

The Bureau of Indian Affairs operates 187 schools with about 47,000 students on reservations around the country. The schools are in decay. The director of the BIA's (Bureau of Indian Affairs) Office of Indian Education Programs, John Tippeconic, admits, "In some cases we are probably putting some kids in danger, in unsafe conditions." In South Dakota, for example, public schools spend an average of $4,045 per student. At the Indian school in Oglala, the average spending is $2,515 per student, despite a federal government treaty promising Indian children education equal to the average for their state. American history teaches us that treaty breaking is a long tradition. Native American youths deserve equal opportunity for education and health care.

Native American Organizations

American Indian College Fund
(represents 29 tribal colleges)
21 W. 68th St., Suite IF
New York, NY 10023

Elementary/Secondary Office of
Indian Education Programs
1849 C St., NW, Mail Stop 3512, MIB
Washington, DC 20240
(coordinates contacts with
reservation schools, etc.)

National Indian Youth Leadership
Project
P.O. Box 11849
Albuquerque, NM 87192

United National Indian Tribal Youth
4010 N. Lincoln, Suite 202
Oklahoma City, OK 73105

Multicultural/Anti-Racism Education

CHIME/NCAS (clearinghouse for
immigrant education)
1-800-441-7192
(resources including racism,
multicultural education, and school
restructuring)

National Education Service
1-800-733-6786
(books for teachers about "managing
the diverse classroom")

Tools for Empowering Young Children,
by Louise Derman-Sparts and the
Anti-Bias Curriculum Task Force.
1-800-424-2460

Black Pax
P.O. Box 603
Wilton, CT 06897
(Send a self-addressed stamped
envelope with 52 cents postage to
receive a list of multicultural, anti-
sexist children's books.)

National Coalition of Advocates for
Students
100 Boylston St.
Boston, MA 02116-4610
ncasmfe@aol.com

National Institute Against Prejudice
and Violence
31 S. Greene St.
Baltimore, MD 21201

Students Organized Against Racism
Box 3558, Connecticut College
New London, CT 06320

*Sources: Diversity Initiatives in
Higher Education*
(a directory of college programs and
services for students of color)
Office of Minorities in Higher
Education 1-800-666-1728

Teaching Tolerance (includes ideas
for classroom use, no charge)
Southern Poverty Law Center
400 Washington Ave.
Montgomery, AL 36104

J. Banks and C. Banks, eds.
*Muticultural Education: Issues and
Perspectives*. Boston: Allyn and
Bacon, 1993.

Deborah A. Bymes and Gary Kiger.
*Common Bonds: Anti-Bias Teaching in
a Diverse Society*. Wheaton, MD:
Association for Childhood
Educational International, 1992.

*In Their Own Voices. Teenage Refugees
Speak Out* (a series), and other
books for teens on history, conditions, and politics of other countries. NY: Rosen Publishing Group,
1996. 1-800-237-9932

Susan Kuklin. *Speaking Out:
Teenagers Take On Race, Sex, and
Identity*. NY: G.P. Putnam's Sons,
1993.
(interviews with 25 students and
five teachers in New York City)

Jane Pratt and K. Pryor. For Real:
*The Uncensored Truth About America's
Teenagers*. NY: Hyperion, 1995.
(interviewed 23 teens)

Renea Nash. *Everything You Need to
Know About Being a Biracial/Biethnic
Teen*. NY: Rosen Group, 1995.

Racism and Race Bibliography

(This list was compiled by Wellesley College students Nikki Morse and Johari Townes.)

Nonfiction:

Borderlands/La Frontera.
Gloria Anzaldua

Out of My Father's House.
Anthony Appiah

The Fire Next Time.
James Baldwin

Faces at the Bottom of the Well: The Permanence of Racism.
Derrick Bell

The Cry and the Dedication.
Carlos Bulsolan

Reflecting African Americans: African-American Cultural Criticism.
Michael Dyson

Everyday Racism.
Philomena Esed

African Americans' Skin, European Americans' Masks.
Frantz Fanon

Monitored Peril: Asian America: A Politics of TV Representation.
Darrell Hamamoto

Under Western Eyes.
Garrett Hongo

Racism 101.
Nikki Giovanni

Autobiography of Malcolm X.
Alex Haley

Breaking Bread.
bell hooks and Cornel West

The Politics of Diversity.
John Horton

An Ocean Between Us.
Evelyn Iritani

Makes Me Wanna Holler.
Nathan McCall

Getting Home Alive. Rosario Morales

Assata: An Autobiography.
Assata Shakur

Racism and the Underclass.
Penna Shepard

A Different Mirror: A History of Multicultural America. Ronald Takaki

Race: How Blacks and Whites Think About the American Obsession.
Studs Tercel

Race Matters. Cornel West

The Asian American Movement.
William Wei

Impacts of Racism on White Americans. Benjamin Bowser and Raymond Hunt, eds.

On Being White. Marylin Frye

Novelists

Chinua Achebe, Dorothy Allison, Maya Angelou, James Baldwin, Toni Cade Bambara, Gwendolyn Brooks, Bebe Moore Campbell, Olivia Castelano, Sandra Cisneros, Ralph Ellison, Louise Erdrich, Nikki Giovanni, Rayna Green. Susan Griffin, Lorraine Hansbury, Zora Neal Hurston, Jamaica Kincaid, Barbara Kingslover, Maxine Hong Kingston, Paula Marshal, Gabriel Garcia Marquez, Terry McMillan, Toni Morrison, Gloria Naylor, Ntozake Shange, Amy Tan, Alice Walker, Margaret Walker, Richard Wright

CLNet's Diversity Page includes resources about ethnic groups, women, and gays and lesbians: http://latino.sscnet.ucla.edu/diversity1.html
This Internet page provides information on listservs (discussion and information networks), gophers (searches for information), web sites (information provided by organizations or individuals) as well as newsgroups.

International Education

I go to an all girls' high school, so I only really meet male friends at socials and when Boys High and Girls High join together for productions and sports events.

No difference is made between Maori people [the native people are Polynesians] *and English people in the school system, although traditionally Maori students haven't performed as well. The Maori culture has placed more emphasis on whanau (family) working together and spirituality than individual achievement. This is changing though.*

We have six periods a day (six classes), and each teacher can set us 15 minutes of homework each. We should have about an hour and a half a day, but usually only get between 30 to 60 minutes.

Our school year is from February 1 until about December 16. The school I go to has a three-term year, which means we get two holidays that last about two weeks each during the year and a six week holiday over Christmas (our summer). We have primary, intermediate, and high school. Primary goes from age 6 to 10, intermediate 11 to 12, and high school 13 to 18. Each school operates differently.

—Sian, 13, New Zealand

I think you'll be struck, as I was, by how similar the issues, slang, and cliques are for teens in English-speaking countries across the globe. It's easy to meet some of your peers and get to know more about their youth cultures by surfing the Internet youth discussion groups (see Chapter 6). You can be a foreign exchange student or sponsor one in your home.

—Kirsty, 15, Scotland (an island off the coast)

My school is basically made up of three large buildings and a number of temporary huts. The oldest of the three buildings was declared a fire trap ten years ago; it is a danger to anybody who crosses its festering threshold. Many of the classroom ceilings have fallen in through damp, and books can't be left leaning against the wall for more than a couple of days or the ink runs.

I don't really get too much homework. It all depends on the teacher as the better teachers tend not to give out much homework, because they manage to get the work done in class. I'm in fifth year so I usually get a bit of homework, but not much, because I was lucky in what teachers I got this year.

There isn't much local slang for different types of people. To me there are ravers, sluts, metalers, druggies, swots, teeny-boppers, and fashion victims. There are no universally accepted "types" here; if people are excluded they're excluded on their own. There aren't many problems with bullying, although there used to be when I first started school here.

I don't do anything after school because there is nothing. I usually just play piano and use the Net. I live too far away from anyone to be part of their social circle. The main problem is that I don't drink so I don't have much in common with most of the kids here. The only thing to do (quite literally) is go to the Friday night dances.

—Lucie, 15, South Africa.

School in Cape Town is completely different from school in America, or so I've heard. It's a lot more formal. We wear a uniform and there are only girls at my school. In a typical school day, we have four classes of 35 minutes each before little break. Most classes are doubles, so that's two lessons of one hour and 10 minutes. After a little break we have another three lessons and then big break, which is 50 minutes long.

In summer we sit on the grass lawns with our lunches and we just talk and some gossip or "skinner," as South Africans say. And then we have another three lessons and school ends. After school, we have all the extra activities: I'm in the choir and the orchestra and I play tennis, indoor hockey, and I do athletics in summer till about 5:30.

—Regan, 15, Canada

I'm taking IB (International Baccalaureate) Physics and "Information Technology In a Global Society" (quite a name). It's a pilot class for the rest of the world, and I am in the first ever class. For normal classes, I'm taking English, algebra, and gym. Gym is a great class, as we spend almost no time at the school. We've gone curling, scuba-diving, bowling, played racquetball, squash, tennis, and golf. I get along OK with all of my teachers, except my physics teacher; we just don't like each other.

My lunch hour is usually spent playing basketball in the gym (1.5 hours), and after school it's home to watch the Simpsons. Homework takes about two hours on a normal day.

The jocks pretty well rule the school. The skaters skateboard and wear the giant corduroy pants. There are trolls, all the people who have the colored mohawks, body piercing, vinyl clothing, and chains. There are bangers and all the losers who drop out of school, steal alcohol, and do nothing but get pissed or high. Then there's people in-between. That's most likely where I am.

—Michele, 18, France

The French school system is not the same as in the U.S. The only condition to be graduated from high school is to pass a very formal exam called le baccalauréat at the end of the senior year. I would advise a student to begin to work a long time before the exam and not one week before, as I did.

—Yasuko, 20, Japan

Japanese children are in school 243 days a year, for eight hours a day—compared to 180 days in the U.S. for 6.5 hours. But Japanese children have different kinds of problems because they are under rigid adult control all the time. Almost all Japanese children go to preparation school, piano lesson, penmanship class, and sport clubs after their school. They are busy every day. They don't have their free time. They do what parents say to do. They don't have creativity; they are like robots.

Japanese parents invest in their children's education too much. Usually at 9-10 p.m., we'll see a lot of elementary school children going home from preparation schools by the subways. Parents have a desire to let their children enter high-level famous schools, so they give a lot of attention to their children. They try to make a good environment to study. A lot of mothers cook a meal in the night and carry it to their children's desks. Thus, Japanese children receive too much supervision and pressure from their parents.

—Becky, 23, Australia.

School started at 9:10 a.m. and finished at 3:30 p.m. I usually got in about 8:30, sometimes 8:00, according to whether I had choir practice or not. There were eight classes, which we called periods, which lasted 40 minutes each. Some of those were double periods for the same subject. We had three periods, then morning recess, then another two periods, then lunch from about 12:45 to 1:30, then three more periods. The homework depended on the year that you were in. In Year 11 and Year 12 there were at least three hours of homework each day.

People did all sorts of different stuff after school; some went home and either did their homework or watched television, and others either played on the streets or at each other's house. Still more used to hang around the shops. The dating scene is fairly casual. You usually meet people at social activities, through school, and through friends. The different groups were skaters, surfers, and the geeks (computer freaks and squares).

You have to complete Year 12 to be able to get into university. The different courses at university had different requirements, TEE subjects and non-TEE subjects. These subjects were divided into two different groups, humanities and sciences (something like that, I forget). You had to do at least three subjects, one from each group.

—Catherine, 25, France

At age 16 students are free to turn school down. Classical high school is very selective, does not demand any creativity but scholarly discipline. For the last two years of learning, pupils specialize according to their results and to their choices: arts and humanities, scientific, economics courses, etc. It doesn't mean that you will officially stop studying the rest, but how much time in the week can you devote to Latin or poetry when you have 15 hours of math, 12 of physics, and three hours of biology? I'd say students sit in class 30-40 hours a week, and spend 25 hours or more doing their homework.

There are other parallel school systems, like music school and sports lycee, and Lycee Professionnel which teaches technical skills to prepare to be cooks or craftsmen, etc. The technical *le baccalauréat*, will be taken at 17, as for the "classical" pupils, it paves the way to technical higher education.

All candidates who passed the BAC (60 percent to 70 percent people pass vs. 55 percent 20 years ago) can go to university and that's what they will most likely do, since it is synonymous with social achievement and a good career—but only if you finish it first, which is rare. Registration fees are rather cheap (averages $500). Universities are nationally funded by the French government, so they do not have much money for the curriculum (ratio averages one professor for 200 students at college).

Foreign Exchange Programs

American Field Service (AFS)
1-800-237-4636

American Institute for Foreign Study
1-800-888-2247

Open Door Student Exchange
1-516-486-7330

Sports for Understanding
International Exchange
1-800-424-3691

Youth for Understanding
International Exchange
1-800-424-3691

Work, Study, Travel Abroad:
The Whole World Handbook. NY: St. Martin's, recent edition. (see high school programs)

E-mail pen pal in another country:
dvandeve@nylink.org.

Involvement
in Activities

I believe strongly in trying on different hats to see which one looks right: Be as many selves as you want. Participate in anything that is interesting—even fads. When I was in high school and the early days of college, I wore a myriad of styles, changed my handwriting once a month, joined clubs and abandoned them, touted ideas and forgot them, all in search of those ideas and feelings that repeated, that I felt most comfortable with.

The basic thing I've come away with from high school and college is the idea that both are really protective shells, although one can put cracks into them and invite the outer world in. The air is purer and one can dedicate themselves to this idea or that in the university, but once one gets out into the working world, one sees that there are many more types of people and greater areas of gray, where pure ideas smudge and don't quite work. Gathering as many different ideas and experiences as possible in college and high school prepares you to deal with a greater range of individuals and settings once you graduate. It develops your sense of tolerance and respect.

—Andrea, 21, Florida

Students at McAteer High School in San Francisco formed SPAM, Students for Positive Action at McAteer. Laura Horsefall, explained, "I can't change my schedule, I can't change my teachers, but at least I can change my campus." SPAM planted a Peace Garden in big tubs in an outdoor walkway, lends portable gardens in buckets to a teacher or student having a hard day, tapes up paper bags for trash, collects food and clothing for the homeless, works with community groups, and posts signs in the halls asking, "If we don't change the world, who will?" None of these projects take much money. Of course those who participate are empowered as well as enjoying their campus environment more.

The National Household Education Survey of students in grades 6 through 12 reported that 70 percent had participated in school activities such as sports, clubs, or student government during the past year. The most involved students were likely to have very involved parents. The same survey found that 58 percent of students had participated in non-school activities during the current school year, such as team sports, scouting, or church groups.

There are over 400 national youth-serving organizations. Together the 15 largest agencies (Scouts, YW/MCAs, 4-H, Boys and Girls Clubs, etc.) serve about 30 million youth each year. However, about 30 percent of young adolescents have no such programs available to them, especially in low-income neighborhoods. The 1988 National Education Longitudinal Study of 8th graders found that only 17 percent of students in high-income families did not participate in an organized activity, compared to 40 percent of low-income youth. Again we see the effects of a society divided into haves and have-nots.

Peak experiences in high school, for college students I surveyed, include participating in sports, social activities, creative ventures such as drama or video production, and leadership positions. "The way you change things is by getting involved," Meredith found. From the other side, Abbi reports, "You miss a lot of things when you ditch a lot and all you get into is trouble." If no club interests you, create one that does.

Students report that participating in many activities, besides being fun, is a good way to make friends, and a boost to college admission. It motivates you to keep your grades up to be eligible, and teaches vital time management techniques by juggling many responsibilities.

—Allison, 22, Missouri

Don't let other people who may not appreciate their education distract you from getting what you want. I knew I wanted to go to college, to get out of the small town. I took my studies seriously despite being labeled a brain. I was also a cheerleader, sang in choir, and was very active in Future Homemakers of America. I think those activities were very important in helping me develop leadership qualities and dedication to goals. I think as colleges get more expensive and more selective, those qualities will become ever more important.

Organizations for Student Activities

Junior Achievement (for economic education) 1-800-THE-NEW-JA

Division of Student Activities, National Association of Student Councils National Association of Secondary School Principals 1904 Association Dr. Reston, VA 22091

National Education Association Student Program (future teachers) 1201-16th Street, NW Washington, DC 20036-3290Z Marla@aol.com

United States Student Association 1612 K St., N.W., Suite 510 Washington, DC20006 ussa@essential.org

Latchkey Kids

Beginning in the 7th grade, I was a latchkey kid. From 2:30-5:30 every day I was alone. This eventually opened the door to independence and a life of alcohol and drugs. I was from an upper-middle-class family but hung out with people who were poverty stricken. For the most part, my parents were ignorant about what I did when they weren't home. But eventually, as usual, they found out what was going on. It took many years to fix what had gone on in my own life, but in my heart I know those things wouldn't have happened if I hadn't been home alone.

—Kathleen, 20, California

About three-fourths of parents of school-age children are employed. Overall, 44 percent of all school-age children with employed parents are latchkey kids (refers to wearing a key around their neck to let themselves into their home). Looking at children ages five to 14, 1.6 million were latchkey children in 1994, according to the Bureau of the Census, although researchers believe the numbers are higher than parents report. By age 10, 60 to 70 percent of children are latchkey kids. About two-thirds of junior and senior high school students are home alone. Low-income children are not more likely to be latchkey children than high-income families. Polls of teachers and principals agree this is the major reason children have difficulty in school. The risk of abusing alcohol, drugs, tobacco, and sex increases with the amount of time students spend unsupervised.

When the Camp Fire youth organization asked 509 teenagers how they had felt at age 12 about going home to an empty house after school, they were almost evenly divided between liking it and finding it stressful. Almost three-fourths said they believe latchkey kids (ages 12 and under) learn personal responsibility. Kids who like it least feel afraid because they live in the city, have to stay inside, or have unkind older siblings.

Some city governments sponsor telephone lines youth can call when home alone, such as Irvine, California. A long-lived phone service, PhoneFriend, began in Pennsylvania: A manual is available to help others start a phone line.

AAUW State College Branch
P.O. Box 735
State College, PA 16804

Reform Models

Students should have representation in school management, although there seems to be a real fear of sharing power with students. Models I've heard of are Andover and Brookline High Schools, MA; Hanover, NH; and Warwick, RI. Our generation is mad about the shit we're being given, like pollution and rapists, without being given the tools to change it. Schools should be reformed to provide those tools and understanding of issues like multiculturalism. We need to create a vision of what we want, as well as what we don't want.

—Grant, 18, Washington

The school restructuring movement began in the late 1980s to try to give teachers, parents, and students more control in improving education. For example, Peter Negroni, Superintendent of Schools in Springfield, Massachusetts, set up management teams at all the district's 40 schools. He asked them to reconsider old assumptions about teaching and learning: six 45-minute classes for 180 days, grouping students by age and tracking them by test scores, the lecture format with students seated in rows, and top-down school government—and proceeded to make changes. Business provides over half of the funding for U.S. reform efforts.

The typical U.S. student spends only three hours per weekday studying academic subjects, half of what students spend in Germany and Japan. Education Secretary Richard Riley suggested expanding school hours, "fundamentally changing the structure and rhythm of American life. We are putting parents in a terrible bind between the demands of work and helping their children grow and learn." (Olivia comments, "If school got any longer I think I would truly go insane. I ride my horse, read, do art, and play the piano after school. I love doing those things and have to do them.")

Many school reformers follow the example of the Coalition of Essential Schools, directed by education professor Theodore Sizer, in their efforts to redesign the American high school. The coalition consists of over 700 schools in 20 states. As explained in his books, *Horace's Compromise: The Dilemma of the American High School, Horace's School,* and *Horace's Hope* (Houghton Mifflin), Sizer believes students learn more when they discover answers to questions rather than listening to lectures. He advocates integrating subject matter in themes with teachers working in teams and designing materials for their students rather than relying on standard textbooks.

Coalition schools have succeeded in reducing dropout rates and increasing college entrance in poor neighborhoods. Students demonstrate their mastery of the curriculum by assembling portfolios of their work, rather than taking multiple-choice tests. For example, to graduate from Central Park East High School in East Harlem, students must defend their portfolio of 14 subjects before a committee. Content includes a post graduation plan, autobiography, scores on state competency tests, a history research paper, evidence of knowledge of a second language, and community service.

School restructuring is underway in California, Florida, Illinois, Kentucky, New York, and other states, as tracked by the National Center for the Organization and Restructuring of Schools. Some states have officially established state coordinators to encourage reform efforts (e.g., Arkansas, Colorado, Delaware, Illinois, Indiana, Maine, New Mexico, Pennsylvania, and Rhode Island).

At Horace Mann middle school in San Francisco, shared decision making with teachers, administrators, and students is the key to restructuring, according to science teacher Roberto Bonilla. The principal becomes a partner, rather than the director. Students serve on the faculty council but are the weakest link in shared governing, Mr. Bonilla observes.

Horace Mann places students in "families," two for each grade. Families take four core subjects together. Student families go on camping trips together and do projects and fund-raisers. Classes meet every other day for an hour and a half, with shorter, 45-minute wrap-up sessions on Fridays. Teachers interact to plan themes.

The program has resulted in more contact with parents as teachers focus on the students in their family group. "Kids feel looked at and talked about; you can't fall between the cracks," Mr. Bonilla says. Students who do not live up to their teachers' expectations serve detention after school and write a letter to their parents explaining why. The restructuring program has attracted many gifted children, although previously the school had the lowest achievement scores in the city.

Technology transforms the curriculum in Harvest Park Middle School in Pleasanton, California. "The kids are the teachers," reports teacher Clark Fuller. If you visited the school, you might find a student doing historical research with a laser disk, using the Internet and e-mail to ask NASA a science question, making videos, scanning a picture onto a computer paint program and editing it, using a computer for rocket building, or loading a new Hypercard program.

The federal government is involved in reform efforts. President George Bush proposed "America 2000," a plan to increase the high school graduation rate, improve math and science education, provide voluntary national tests for student achievement at various grades, give parents choices over schools their children attend, award grants to schools that improve their performance, and encourage employers to bring the classroom into the workplace. President Bush stated, "Our challenge amounts to nothing less than a revolution in American education."

Congress passed Goals 2000 in 1994, based on goals developed by the nation's governors, plus two new goals calling for greater parental involvement and expanded professional development for teachers. The plan continued the previous administration's emphasis on establishing academic standards and testing students to make sure they reach them. The legislation funded money for states to work on school improvement or reform programs.

By spring 1995, 37 states had received more than $70 million in federal seed money for school reform. For example, Oregon developed student certificates in Initial Mastery and Advanced Mastery in areas such as arts, business, and industrial and engineering systems. However, a 1995 report looking at progress during the five years since the governors proposed the goals found little to be happy about. High school graduation rates were about the same (86 percent) and reading achievement of seniors declined slightly. (Math achievement of 4th and 8th graders did go up and more women earned college degrees in math and science.) However, 1996 legislation made Goals 2000 a toothless tiger by allowing the states to spend the money on computers rather than enforcing standards.

Everyone agrees our schools need improvement, but it seems few reforms have been made since your parents were in school. This might be an interesting dinner-hour discussion for your family.

School Reform Resources

National Committee for Citizens in Education 1-800-NETWORK

U.S. Department of Education
1-800-USA-LEARN
http://www.ed.gov
(materials such as a report on *Strong Families, Strong Schools* and *Team up for Kids!*

The Business Roundtable
1615 L St., NW, Suite 1350
Washington, DC 20036

Center for Restructuring/American
Federation of Teachers
555 New Jersey Ave., NW
Washington, DC 20001

Coalition of Essential Schools
Brown University, 1 Davol Sq.
Providence, RI 02903

Educational Resources Information
Center (ERIC)
U.S. Department of Education
Office of Educational Research and
Improvement
Washington, DC 20208-1235

Educators for Social Responsibility (ESR)
23 Garden St.
Cambridge, MA 02138

Foxfire Fund
P.O. Box B
Rabun Gap, GA 30568

Kentucky Education Reform Task Force
Office of Communications,
Department of Education
Capital Plaza Tower
Frankfort, KY 40601

National Clearinghouse on
School-Based Management
P.O. Box 948
Westbury, NY 11590

National Coalition of
Advocates for Students
100 Boylston St., Suite 737
Boston, MA 02116-4610
(catalogue)

National Coalition of Education Activists
P.O. Box 405
Rosendale, NY 12472
(a newsletter titled *Action for Better Schools*; audio tapes of conference speeches; help finding speakers, trainers, and other resources for better schools with a vision of social change)

National Society for
Experiential Education
3509 Haworth Dr., Suite 207
Raleigh, NC 27609-7229

Parents' Institute for Quality Education
Policy Studies in Language and Cross-
Cultural Education
San Diego State University
San Diego, CA 92182-0137

Rethinking Schools
1001 E. Keefe Ave.
Milwaukee, WI 53212

School Development Project/Comer
Project for Change in Education
55 College St.
New Haven, CT 06511

School of the Future, Dept. P
Utah State University
Logan, UT 84322-1400

*New Schools, New Communities
newsletter*
Institute for Responsive Education
605 Commonwealth Ave.
Boston, MA 02215

*Education: How Can Schools and
Communities Work Together to Meet
the Challenge?*
Study Circles Resource Court
P.O. Box Pomfret, CT 06258
(a guide for organizing study circles
to improve schools)

Partnerships in Education Journal
P.O. Box 210
Ellenton, FL 34222-0210
(includes information on local
newsletters to exchange)

Larry Martz. *Making Schools Better:
How Parents and Teachers Across the
Country Are Taking Action—and How
You Can Too.* NY: Times Books, 1992

Mary Susan Miller. *Save Our Schools:
66 Things You Can Do to Improve
Education.* San Francisco: Harper,
1993

Daily Report Card is a weekly
Internet publication:
listserv@gwuvm.gwu.edu

Educational Research and
Improvement Center:
http://eric.syr.edu/

Experiential Education:
http://www.princeton.edu/~rcurtis.ae
e.html

K-12 Resources:
http://web66.coled.umn.edu

Services at School

I feel that having professional counselors in the schools is extremely important. My junior year in high school I had three friends die in a car accident. This was very hard to deal with because it was difficult to grasp the idea of three 16-year-old guys dying. At my high school we had a grief counselor come to talk with us. It helped a lot!

—Alison, 21, California

The school of the future will be a community center, according to Thomas Shannon, director of the National School Boards Association. Ahead of the pack is New Jersey with one of the most extensive school-based networks of services for youth. "One-stop-shopping" for services at school include personal counseling, drug abuse counseling, family planning, telephone hot lines, and job services.

Another leader is Kentucky, the first state to enact a comprehensive reform plan, including state learning goals and training educators to implement the goals. Family resource centers and youth service centers exist in schools in all low-income neighborhoods. When a teacher refers a student, the center coordinator visits the home to assist the family in connecting with useful services or bringing services to the neighborhood. High school-based centers assist youth with job placement and health referral. By 1993, 373 school centers were in operation in Kentucky.

In Denver, seven Family Resource Schools provide adult education, parent education, support groups, tutoring programs, summer programs, and child care. A Collaborative Decision-Making Team governs each school program, including parents, school staff, and business leaders. New York City has Beacons, begun in 1991 with 10 school-based community centers. Each center receives $450,000 from the city Department of Youth Services.

School-based health centers are numerous in states like New York and Connecticut. Louisiana approved an adolescent school health initiative in 1991 and funded 19 centers by 1993. The poor marks for children's health (see wellness section in Chapter 1) indicate all states should join the 22 states that currently mandate health education in elementary school. A comprehensive program includes healthy school food, physical education activities, wellness programs for the school staff, and outreach to parents in wellness education. A curriculum called *Know Your Body* (the American Health Program) provides teaching materials. If any of these programs interest you, propose them to your school administrators.

School Wellness Efforts

The American Health Foundation
800 Second Ave.
New York, NY 10017

EarthSave's Healthy School Lunch
Program
706 Frederick St.
Santa Cruz, CA 95062
earthsave@igc.apc.org
(how to establish a healthy school
lunch program, Action Guide)

The American Health Foundation
800 Second Ave.
New York, NY 10017

School Services Organizations

National School Organizations
Council of Chief State School Officers
One Massachusetts Ave, NW, Suite
700
Washington DC 20001-1431

National Association of State Boards
of Education
1012 Cameron St.
Alexandria, VA 22314

National Federation of State High
School Associations
P.O. Box 20626
Kansas City, MO 64195-0626
(a federation of state associations
and 20,000 high schools)

National PTA (Parent Teacher
Association)
700 N. Rush St.
Chicago, IL 60611-2571

School-Linked Family Support
Services (technical assistance)
Family Resource Coalition's
Families/Schools/Communities
Division
200 S. Michigan Ave., Suite 1520
Chicago, IL 60604

Twenty-First Century Schools
Bush Center, Department of Child
Development
Yale University, New Haven, CT 06520
(elementary schools)

Peer Counseling

—Kim, 13, California

I became a peer counselor in 7th grade. I was voted in by my peers. The thing I've gotten most out of being a peer counselor is that I've learned people trust me. My listening skills have increased so much. You get a lot of new friends that you can really trust. I learned that the people you least expect to have problems probably have the biggest problems. Also, confidentiality is the most important thing in the whole world. Trust is a must.

[When I asked Kim and two other peer counselors at Chico Middle School what issues they hear about most, they said friendship problems, sex, drugs, abuse, and eating disorders. They explained their main job is to listen, suggest options, suggest that a decision be made, and then do follow-up.]

—Kyle, 16, Colorado

I am a peer counselor at my high school and I know how to handle personal problems through the training I received. I coped with a date rape of my best friend mainly by being there for my friend whenever she needed to talk. Helping her through her pain brought me through mine.

The majority of schools in the U.S. have some form of peer counseling, emphasizing active listening skills (see communication skills in Chapter 2). Some schools provide peer support groups led by an adult counselor to help students going through painful transitions such as their parents' divorce, the death of a family member, or a move. An example is "Stages" provided for students in Irvine, California. Various curriculums are available to assist in the start-up of these support groups, listed in *How to Survive Your Parents' Divorce: Kids' Advice to Kids.*

Peer Counseling Resources

Peer Resources
1052 Davie St.
Victoria, B.C. V8S 4E3
Canada
http://www.islandnet.com/~rcarr/peer.html
(Peer Resources is a leading authority on peer helping and the creator of Canada's National Mentor Program Strategy.)

Leaders' Guide for Natural Helpers.
Comprehensive Health Foundation
22323 Pacific Hwy. S,
Seattle, WA 98198

J. Tindall. Peer Counseling: *In-Depth Look at Training Peer Helpers.*
Muncie, IN: Accelerated Development, 1989.

Service-Learning

—Ben Jones, 18, Texas

I hate seeing other people unhappy. As president of the student council, I emphasized community service. We did three canned food drives, a road and park clean-up, and Christmas tree recycling. We also worked on safety campaigns, such as handing out statistics on drunk driving. When a boy from India came to our school, speaking no English, and in a wheelchair, people pushed him around. I told the administration I was going to get out of each class five minutes early to take him to class. People started treating him better and that made me happy.

—Lester, 19, Pennsylvania

I'm most proud of my extensive involvement with community service. I went to a Catholic high school, and we had a Christian Service program. One student from each Catholic high school in the archdiocese was recognized for community service, and I was selected from my high school.

Some school and community groups cooperate to provide students with academic credit for volunteer work in the community. They focus on experiential learning and providing service. Examples of projects are tutoring elementary school students and "adopting" an elderly "grandparent." StarServe, a service learning organization, suggests that students identify important community issues by reading newspapers and interviewing officials, neighbors, and family members. They recommend that students work with people different from them, write about their experiences, and seek public recognition for their efforts by informing the local media about successes through press releases and videos shown to the school board and other groups.

In 1992, Maryland became the first state to require community service (75 hours) to graduate from high school, followed by New York. In Atlanta students are also required to perform 75 hours of service at approved nonprofit organizations. Under national service corps legislation, students can earn part of their college tuition by doing volunteer work in community programs, such as child care centers (1-202-606-5000). The National and Community Service Trust Act of 1993 promotes integrating service learning into the curriculum.

In Maine, KIDS (Kids Involved Doing Service) as Planners grew out of a 1988 state law that requires each city to develop a comprehensive plan every five years. Students work with their city government to identify problems, research a plan of action, and implement it. Adult volunteers with professional expertise work with the students. For example, a high school English class in Auburn researched a plan to transform the littered property next to their school by building a mountain bike trail, walkway, and lighting. Local businesses and the city council worked with students to get a $15,000 federal Community Development Block Grant to put their plan into action. The students learned skills by writing, using the computer to prepare professional reports, researching, public speaking, designing maps and illustrations, and exploring the plants and animals. A geometry class designed and built a greenhouse on the land to operate as a student-run business. The KIDS as Planners process being used in over 50 towns across New England is protecting wildlife, documenting local history, designing parks, and other projects (see the activism section in Chapter 11).

Community service is part of "values education," which some educators believe all schools should teach. Examples of schools with a values program are Guager

Junior High in Newmark, Delaware; Hebbville Elementary in Baltimore County, Maryland; and in the Sweet Home district in New York. (The Thomas Jefferson Center foundation specializes in values education, and Thomas Lickona's book *Education for Character*, Bantam, discusses these issues.)

Service Learning Resources

National Information Center for Service-Learning
1-800-808-SERVE
(provides technical assistance, information, referral, publications, newsletter, and Internet newsgroup)

National Service Learning Center. Guides to Developing Service-Learning Programs.
1-800-808-SERV

StarServe 1-800-888-8232
(provides materials to classrooms about community service)

Corporation for National Service
1201 New York Ave., NW
Washington, DC 20524

KIDS Consortium
Southern Maine Technical College
2 Fort Rd.
South Portland, MI 04106

National Association of Service and Conservation Corps
666 Eleventh St., NW, Suite 500
Washington, DC 20001

The National Center for Service-Learning in Early Adolescence
Center for Advanced Study in Education
University Center of the City
University of New York
25 W. 43rd St., Suite 612
New York, NY

National Service-Learning Cooperative/Clearinghouse
University of Minnesota
1954 Buford Ave., R-290
St. Paul, MN 55108

National Youth Leadership Council
1910 W. County Rd. B, Room 216
Roseville, MN 55113

The Youth Voice Project, Department of Communication Studies
Bingham Hall, University of North Carolina
Chapel Hill, NC 27599

Rich Cairn and J. Kielsmeier, eds. *Growing Hope: A Sourcebook on Integrating Youth Service into the School Curriculum*, 1991.

Close Up Foundation. *Active Citizenship Today Handbook for High School Teachers*, 1994 (44 Canal Center Plaza, Alexandria, VA 22314)

Carol Kinsley and Kate McPherson, eds. *Enriching the Curriculum Through Service Learning*. Alexandria, VA: ASCD, 1995.

Sexism

Boys

Boys are more likely than girls to have learning disabilities, to be hyperactive, to have severe emotional problems, and be in special education classes. Elementary school may be difficult for high-energy boys who learn best by doing. Since most of the teachers are female, their teaching style may be geared to how girls learn best (see the male role section in Chapter 6). Girls get better grades overall, although boys do better on major tests like the Scholastic Aptitude Test required for college admission. Recent studies find that among high school and college seniors, females are slightly more likely to plan to go to graduate school, law school, or medical school. Emma observes, "Many times boys think that it is not macho to get good grades, so they don't try." Jed agrees, and adds "They don't want to be nerds or it's a rebellious way to get back at your parents."

Professor William Purkey, of the University of North Carolina, studied 400 students in his state in grades six through eight. He believes that "boys have a much lower image of themselves as students than girls do." They brag as a "shield to hide deep-seated lack of confidence. Girls, on the other hand, brag less and do better in school."

In a survey of 222,653 students grades 6 through 12, most think teachers are tougher on boys (75 percent of boys and 60 percent of girls), few think boys get more positive attention in the classroom, and one-third of boys think teachers call on boys more often (42 percent of girls think boys get called on more). (The 1996 survey respondents were readers of *USA Weekend* magazine.)

Boys catch up, though, as men are still more likely to have the support systems to gain graduate school and professional degrees than women, just as whites get more degrees than people of color because of the resources available to them

—Ken and Joe, 16, and Andy, 18, California (from a discussion with male readers who felt this section was biased towards girls)

Girls are more devoted to school and to doing what they're told. Guys want to have fun and rebel against their parents. Some girls are more like guys, the ones who were tomboys. Girls are treated just as good if not better than guys, in the classroom. My English teacher makes fun of guys, jokes about how women are better. Some male teachers are more flirty with the girls, let the girls do more, like go to the bathroom. It depends on the teacher—some favor one sex over the other, and whether there are more boys and girls in the room. The dominant group speaks up more, you get power from guys supporting you. Girls pack together and agree on everything.

Outside of classes, I do know a lot of friends who see girls as nothing but a vagina on legs and who call them bitches and chicks. I can't put them down for that, because I call them chicks too. It's just how society is, but you need to respect women and treat them well. Girls sexually harass guys, too, but we know they're just joking. For example, girls held up signs rating boys on the water polo team, with numbers from one to 10.

There are women who contribute to sexist views of men. Men don't rule society, it's a conglomerate, like cells in a brain. Guys don't get any more special training than girls do; if girls want to take math and science, no one is stopping them. You should ask students if they can name 20 famous men, as well as women; but if they can, keep in mind those were times when women weren't equal to men, not like today. You mention that girls do better in all-girls' schools; boys probably do better in all-boys' schools, too, because there are less distractions. Boys don't get any training to deal with their problems either.

I would really like to hear from you about your observations of equality in your classrooms.

Men's Studies

**American Men's Studies Association
22 East St.
Northampton, MA 01060
(offers a newsletter and directory of
college Men's Studies courses)
AMSA-List@cc.yse.edu**

**Eugene August. *The New Men's
Studies: A Selected and Annotated
Interdisciplinary Bibliography*.
Englewood, CO: Libraries Unlimited,
1995. (describes over 1,000 books
about men)**

Girls

—Liesl, 14, Massachusetts

Last year, I had a teacher who made sexist comments about his wife. I felt very uncomfortable sitting in his class listening to this. A few months later, one of my friends complained to the principal about him and the teacher apologized to the students. But some of the boys found out that my friend was the one who complained, and they got mad at her. They said, "His jokes were the only interesting things in the class."

A lot of the boys were saying, "Women are good for three things: cleaning, cooking, and getting beer for their husbands," and other sexist comments. When I told a teacher, all he said was, "Boys will be boys. Don't let it bother you." It does bother me. When sexist comments are made to me, I feel ashamed to be a female. I've been brought up to believe that everyone should be treated equally, but maybe I'm wrong.

(Quoted in "Lynn Minton Reports," *Parade* magazine, November 5, 1995)

We need to examine gender stereotypes to see how they affect students' goals, expectations, assumptions about their abilities, options, and future roles. I asked students (in workshops I led at three high schools in northern California) to write down what they want to achieve by age 25 and what things might stand in their way. "Motivation and money," said some of the girls. A girl who wants to go into politics wrote, "I don't have a lot of money to go through graduate school. Even my parents don't think that I will make it because I am female."

Just as women in the work world sometimes report being treated as if they are invisible, girls get less attention in the classroom. Although boys talk three times more than girls, it seems normal for girls to be good listeners, so we don't notice it, even when specifically watching a video looking for sexism in the classroom. Boys get called on more often, get more attention and eye contact, more specific dialogue and feedback on their work, encouragement to figure out a solution on their own, and are expected to take math and science.

Boys influence the topics of class discussion more than girls; for example, if they groan when the teacher starts talking about sexism, she is likely to drop it. Teachers permit boys to call out in class, but if girls do it, they are scolded for not being ladylike. That concept has done a lot to limit girls! Boys are more often allowed to interrupt teachers, and girls and teachers also interrupt girls more than they do boys.

Boys often monopolize science equipment, computer monitors, and verbal math contests. Schools do not teach girls how to cope with being ignored, discrimination, sexual harassment, low self-esteem, and fearfulness about risk taking. Studies indicate that girls who attend all-girls schools tend to have higher self-esteem and take more math and science. Observe genders in your classrooms, marking number of speakers, interruptions, length of discussion, teacher questions, etc.

—Sara, 18, Maryland

Before I finished my first semester of 9th grade, I concluded my high school was a hostile environment for women [this is illegal according to Title IX of the Civil Rights Act]. I endured physical and verbal abuse, belittlement, and classroom discrimination. The girls I talked to had experienced the same. Although these encounters with sexism disturbed me, it didn't immediately occur to me that I might have an opportunity—even a responsibility, to battle gender bias at my high school.

*This powerlessness changed in 10th grade, after I interviewed a prominent fig-
ure in the National Organization for Women (NOW) for an English assignment. I asked
her what I could do to improve the atmosphere for women at my school. She suggested
that I establish a women's issues group. I set to networking, meeting with the school
administration, collecting student support, writing a charter, and our NOW club was
born (see the feminism section in Chapter 11).*

—Tracy, 20, California

*Girls are treated differently in schools. I can remember three male teachers I
had between grades 7 and 12 who treated girls as prizes. So, that "good girl" image
remains. One high school teacher was known to comment on girls' legs, figure, and
attire, and ignore their responses in his class. Girls often got out of assignments by
flirting or saying they had cramps. It really disgusted me.*

—Amy, 22, New York

*I remember thinking that it was odd that my 5th grade teacher had me and my
girlfriends give him back rubs, that the girls' soccer team had to wear the boys' old uni-
forms, that I had to endure endless comments about my appearance in my advanced
math classes, and that I was the only female in my advanced science classes. When I
started sharing these memories with other female friends, we all had the same reaction:
"That happened to you, too?"*

—Stephanie, 26, Oregon

*Never letting anyone tell you that you are ugly, fat, "just a girl," or whatever, is
so important. I think an interesting exercise is to sit down and think about men and
women in different areas of life. TV characters, your family, school books, friends—who
has the power, who is represented, who does what? Nothing will ever change for girls
unless they are aware of the world they live in.*

Teachers

Teachers usually think they treat boys and girls equally and are surprised to watch videos of themselves spending much more time interacting with boys.
Teachers can close the gender gap in the classroom by calling on girls as much as boys
and asking them thoughtful questions; boys got 81 percent of the "high-level" questions
asked in secondary school science classes observed by Roberta Barba and Loretta
Cardinale in Pennsylvania. (They also saw teachers shaming boys on the sports field by
calling them girls.)

Teachers need training to become aware of bias which is so common it
seems natural. GESA (Gender/Ethnic Expectations and Student Achievement) is a program for teacher training, which assists teachers in looking at their biases (Gray Mill
Foundation, Rt. 1, Box 45, Earlham, IW, 50072). The underlying philosophy is that teacher
expectations for their students get results. Kim Harper, a teacher who participated in
the GESA training reports, "I think everyone realized after going through it that to a
certain degree we all discriminate a little bit. That was the most eye-opening aspect of
the program."

Tips for Teachers

- Expect the same achievement and behaviors from both sexes.

- Assign duties to students on the basis of ability rather than gender.

- Use nonsexist language, as in avoiding the use of he and man to refer to women and referring to women's marital status but not men's (as in Miss and Mrs. instead of Ms. and Mr.). Use humans or people instead of mankind, police officer instead of policeman, etc.

- Create a classroom environment which includes female and ethnic role models, as on bulletin boards.

- Use curriculum that includes the contributions of women and men and various ethnic groups.

- Encourage both sexes to participate in sports and class dialogues.

The Hidden Curriculum

The hidden curriculum is the lack of female role models in books and course content. Professors Myra and David Sadker asked students in classrooms nationwide to name 20 famous U.S. women, not including athletes, entertainers, or president's wives—unless they were famous on their own. Few students could answer their question. Can you? This is not surprising when even new history textbooks still give almost no space to women, according to the Sadkers.

They counted the number of women listed in texts and found few. For example, in the 1992 text *A History of the U.S.* (by Daniel Boorstin and Brooks Mather Kelly), only three percent of the people discussed were female. In Addison-Wesley's *World History* text, the index lists 596 men and 41 women. The Sadkers typically found twice as many males in illustrations as females. Emma adds, "Some books have a special section devoted to women in history, which I find sort of insulting. They should just be included in the rest of the text."

Science, Math, and Girls
—Lisa, 19, Washington

STICK WITH MATH! This is a mistake so many girls make, and I made it. Having ditched math too early has put me in the annoying position of having to do high school work over to take classes I really need. Don't let anyone pressure you out of taking math classes!

Women will continue to earn less than men and have fewer real job choices until girls get training in technical courses that lead to careers in high-paying jobs such as engineering and computer science. Women earn less than 10 percent of the bachelor's degrees in engineering, for example. Science and math are still seen as male fields. For the last four decades, when asked to draw a scientist, students usually drew men. In recent drawings, all the boys and 84 percent of the girls drew a male scientist. This mirrors what students see in science texts, as over two-thirds of the illustrations are of men. Boys are much more likely to take physics, to control science laboratory equipment, and to speak more often and louder in science classes.

Despite the myth that males are better at math, gender differences are small and declining. Hundreds of studies show that generally girls do slightly better on school math. Sex differences in verbal and math abilities have almost disappeared on most tests during the past two decades, with the exception of the SAT and the National Merit Scholarship. Females get better grades than males in high school and college and their grades are more accurate predictors of their college grades than their SAT scores.

Some schools are making an effort to encourage girls' interest in science and math and to change teaching to fit their less competitive, more collaborative style. Doug Kirkpatrick has been a science teacher in a Walnut Creek, California, middle school for 32 years. For the last seven years he has been part of an effort to change science teaching to make it relevant to students and to create gender equity.

His feedback from girls is that they did not expect to like science, but they do like his class. Each computer in his 8th grade classroom is named after a scientist. Half of them are women such as Sally Ride and Grace Hopper. Mr. Kirkpatrick tells his students how women scientists like Rosalind Franklin are short-changed by historians. He uses examples such as whether tin foil keeps a baked potato hot rather than sports imagery to explain heat conductivity.

Mr. Kirkpatrick thinks the main block for girls is lack of confidence and it doesn't help that all but one of the science teachers in his school and the local high school are men. (Fewer than a fifth of the nation's scientists and mathematicians are women.) One of his students, Autumn, 13, said, "I wouldn't go into a math or science career. The thought of all those guys scares me. It would make me too nervous. I'd think, 'What if they make fun of me because I'm a girl?'" Or as Lin Lee, one of the few recent female computer engineering graduates from U.C. Berkeley said, "Sometimes I wondered, do I have a chance in this field?" Systematic efforts such as Mr. Kirkpatrick's do make a difference in changing girls' attitudes.

—Shelley, 22, Massachusetts

I definitely felt that, as a woman, I was "strongly encouraged" to excel in the liberal arts and not so much in math and science. What was a minor deficiency in high school developed into a major problem once I got to college, where, because I had not taken math courses EVERY year in high school, I was too intimidated to take a college level math course.

—Kirsten, 21, Massachusetts

At some point I learned that normal is better than different, and smart was different. But I always liked math, and physics was a real-world application of math. Senior year I took AP Physics and AP Calculus, and discovered/decided this being smart thing was cool. My calculus teacher was especially cool, a very strong woman. The labs where we got to measure gravity and torque and voltage were what really interested me.

So I applied to colleges as a physics major, mostly. Then after winter break, an engineer from Bose came to our classroom to talk about this competition thing for high school students paired with companies/universities and I got involved in that. OK, so I was mostly there to flirt with one of the guys, but in the process I discovered that I liked building things, and I began to apply as an engineering (ece) major.

At CMU, I've been in classes where the ratio of male to female was as bad as 5:1, and it's never been anywhere close to 50:50. I believe the ratio for the entire school is 5:3, and for ece it's between 7:1 and 10:1.

Professors notice more easily when I don't show up for class. I've gotten more confident about asking questions, though that probably has more to do with the personality of the teacher and my maturity than anything else. The professor I've felt most comfortable with has been the sole woman professor on the staff, but that isn't to say I've had uncomfortable experiences with any other faculty. I've only once experienced what I consider discrimination, but that wasn't in my department. A math professor didn't call on me even though for several minutes I was the only one with my hand raised to answer a question he had asked. I don't think I get any special treatment one way or the other.

I think the most challenging thing facing me is not taking the easy way out by playing dumb and having things explained to me rather than figuring them out for myself. It's something I have to fight on my own, for the most part, although my boyfriend tells me when he thinks I'm giving up too quickly.

—Ruth, 24, Nebraska.

I'm in chemical engineering. I liked math a lot in high school. My peak junior high experience was participating in MATHCOUNTS, a mathematics competition for 7th and 8th graders and winning the Oral Presentation round. Don't let anyone say you can't do something because you're a girl or that what you're doing is unfeminine. I'd like to think this goes without saying, but maybe it doesn't. For me, most of the harassment had stopped by high school, thank goodness.

I went into engineering because I wanted to solve problems, have a practical impact on the world, and help repair some of the environmental damage. It didn't hurt when I found out engineers make a lot of money.

What should you do if you want to go into something like engineering? Take all the math you can while you're in high school. If AP courses are available, they will help you cruise through some of your freshman science courses and are well worth the effort. Take computer programming classes, especially PASCAL and FORTRAN (primitive languages, but all the universities seem to use them). A drafting course may be helpful; most of that is done on AUTOCAD now, but some universities, like the one I attended, do require hand-drafting.

What should you expect once you get to college? There are campus groups like SWE (Society for Women Engineers), that can be great resources. Ours has plant tours, workshops on fixing your bike or your car, and mock interviews. It's also a great place to meet other women engineers as sometimes it can be a bit lonely. The upside of this is that at an engineering school, even former wallflowers can be very popular.

Science and Math Curriculum

Girls and Science: Linkages for the
Future
American Association for the
Advancement of Science
1333 H St., NW
Washington, DC 20005

Association for Women in Science
1522 K St., NW, Suite 820
Washington, DC 20005

Girls Inc. National Resource Center
441 W. Michigan St.
Indianapolis, IN 46202

Computer Equity Trainers/Women's
Action Alliance
370 Lexington Ave., Suite 603
New York, NY 10017

Women and
Mathematics/Mathematical
Association of America
1529 Eighteenth St., NW
Washington, DC 20036

National Science Foundation/Targeted
Programs for Girls
4201 Wilson Blvd.
Arlington, VA 22230

Women's Educational Equity Act
Publishing Center
55 Chapel St.
Newton, MA 02160
(many materials i.e., pamphlet *"Girls
and Math: Enough Is Known for
Action"* for students and teachers)

Solutions

What should be done about sexism? Some high school girls are organizing for gender equity; an example is the Grrrls' Clubs started by Amy DeBower in Madison, Wisconsin (her fax number is 608-251-4896), or chapters of national feminist organizations described in Chapter 11.

The AAUW (American Association of University Women) report *How Schools Shortchange Girls* reviewed over 1,300 studies and articles. It recommends that teacher training programs include gender and multicultural education, that women be included in school materials and curriculum, and that community and schools work together to present role models of women in math and science professions.

Title IX states, "No person in the U.S. shall, on the basis of sex, be excluded from participation in, be denied the benefits of, or be subjected to discrimination under any education program or activity receiving federal financial assistance." This includes access to sports, access to any course, counselors not steering students away from non-traditional courses for their gender, and equal access to teachers' instructional time. Sexual harassment is a form of discrimination and is therefore illegal. States have added their own companion laws, codes, or regulations to enforce gender equity.

You might want to investigate your school's plan to implement Title IX and the state laws. Your school district is required to have a person in charge of enforcing Title IX/gender equity, although you may have to be very persistent in tracking that person down, and be prepared for lack of knowledge. When I called my school district office, no one knew what I was talking about, and I had to be persistent; try asking who is in charge of "sex discrimination." When I finally tracked down the person in charge, he told me he didn't know about the particular state codes he is supposed to enforce or much about students' rights under Title IX because he works mainly with adult staff. When I pressed him, he said he would find and mail me some information. I had to call back and remind him.

An example of a school district that took Title IX seriously is Los Angeles, the second largest district in the country. (I use past tense because as I write, the school board is trying to remove the director of the Commission for Gender Equity, the only staff person.) The Commission has the only fully-funded position devoted to gender equity in the U.S. Having one person in charge has resulted in action, such as trainings at every secondary school about how to stop sexual harassment, establishing Playground Parity—a program to match high school and college women athletes as mentors to elementary school girls, promoting girls' access to advanced math and science classes, providing speakers, assisting Women's History Month coordinators in every school, and establishing a parenting teen advocate at every secondary school. One person can make a significant difference.

All states are required to employ a Sex Equity Specialist to implement Title IX and their salaries are funded by Title IV of the Civil Rights Act—or at least they were until 1996, when all funding for this purpose to state Departments of Education was cut. The Women's Educational Equity Act (1974) allocated grants to fund compliance with Title IX and is also on the chopping block in terms of future funding. If schools don't obey the law, they can have federal funding cut, but this has never happened, although many schools ignore Title IX. You should also be aware that vocational education is covered by the Carl Perkins Act, which requires full access to auto shop for girls, to interior design class for boys, as well as access to disabled people.

If you discover sex discrimination and can't get information from your school district, you can contact the U.S. Office for Civil Rights (330 C St., SW, Washington, DC 20202). They're understaffed (looks like gender equity is not a high priority), so my guess is you'd have to be persistent.

Gender Equity Organizations

Equal Employment Opportunity Commission 1-800-669-EEOC

American Assoc. of University Women Educational Foundation 2201 N. Dodge St. Iowa City, IA 52243-4030 (provides grants to promote educational equity for girls)

AAUW National Coalition for Women and Girls in Education 1111-16th St., NW Washington, DC 20036 *How Schools Shortchange Girls. Growing Smart: What's Working for Girls in School* (1995). 1-800-225-9998, ext. 330 (also sells videos)

Center for Research on Women at Wellesley College, Publications 106 Central St. Wellesley, MA 02181-8259

Kathryn Wheeler. *How Schools Can Stop Shortchanging Girls (and Boys): Gender-Equity Strategies,* 1993.

Educational Equity Concepts (bias-free materials for teachers) 114 E. 32nd St. New York, NY 10016

Equity Newsletter, **The Marymount Institute 100 Marymount Ave. Tarrytown, NY 10591** (describes how to make classrooms gender fair, includes recent research, resources, and legislation)

Equity Training Concepts 3 Gaiser Ct. San Francisco, CA 94110

Feminist Press City University of New York 311 E. 94th St New York, NY 10128 (books and course materials)

Foundation for Role Equit Education newslette P.O. Box 254 San Diego, CA 92112-254

National Center for Curriculur Transformation Resource on Wome Institute for Teaching and Researc on Women (ITROW

Towson State University
Towson, MD 21204-7097
(Provides a newsletter
and resources for universities)

National Coalition for
Sex Equity in Education
One Redwood Dr.
Clinton, NJ 08809

National Women's History Project
7738 Bell Rd.
Winsdor, CA 95492-8518
(provides material for elementary
and secondary school courses, teacher
training, and for girls)

National Women's Studies Association
7100 Baltimore Ave., Suite 301
College Park, MD 20740

Parents for Title IX
P.O. Box 835
Petaluma, CA 94953
(provides resources for
filing claims in schools)

Project on Equal Education Rights
1413 K St., NW, 9th Floor
Washington, DC 20005

Project on Equal Education Rights.
*Anyone's Guide to
Filing a Title IX Complaint.*
(1-212-925-6635)

Women's Educational Equity Act
Publishing Center
Education Development Center
55 Chapel St., Suite 200
Newton, MA 02158-1060
(Their catalogue has materials for
various grade levels and
subjects, such as "Checklists for
Counteracting Race and Sex Bias in
Educational Materials.")

Women's Feature Service
20 W. 20th St., Suite 1103
New York, NY 10011
wfs@igc.apc.org Women's Equity
Resource Center web site:
http://www.edc.org/home.html

Educational Equity Discussion List for
teachers, parents, and students.
MAJORDOMO@CONFER.EDC.ORG

University of Wisconsin Women's
Studies Library
wiswsl@macc.wisc.edu
http://www.library.wisc.edu/libraries/
Women's Studies/
(includes links to other websites,
women's studies research centers,
course materials, newsletters, and
databases)

WomensNet
http://www.igc.apc.org/womensnet/
(an international news service provides
bimonthly bulletin by mail or e-mail)

Books About Gender Equity

*A Resource Directory for Sex Equity in
Education.* Department of Public
Instruction, Drawer 179
Milwaukee, WI 53293-0179.

Girls, Inc. *Past the Pink and Blue
Predicament: Freeing the Next
Generation from Sex Stereotypes* (441
W. Michigan St.,
Indianapolis, IN 46202)

Mindy Bingham and M. Stryker.
*Things Will Be Different for My
Daughter.* NY: Penguin, 1995.

Tim Flinders. *A Gender Primer:
Helping School Girls Hold On to their
Dreams: An Introductory Sourcebook
for Teachers and Parents.* Two Rock
Publications, P.O. Box 2773,
Peteluma, CA. An expanded version is
Rosie Unbound, Dell, 1997.

Susan Klein, ed. *Handbook for
Achieving Sex Equity Through
Education.* Baltimore. MD: Johns
Hopkins University Press, 1989.

Myra and David Sadker. *Failing at
Fairness: How America's Schools
Cheat Girls.* NY: Charles Scribner's
Sons, 1994.

Janice Streitmatter. *Toward Gender
Equity in the Classroom.* NY: SUNY,
1994.

Sexual Harassment

One bright sunny day, I was waiting for my bus after school. There was a big blond boy named Jason. He always bothered me every day at school, but this time was worse. Anyway, I was standing and I didn't know he was behind me, when suddenly out of nowhere, he just grabbed my breast like it was nothing!

My God! You don't know how humiliated and frustrated I was!!! When I turned around he was laughing his ugly head off, while I felt like I wanted to kick him in the groin. But I thought of a better idea. That idea was reporting the harassment to a teacher or anyone.

The next day, I reported it to my teacher. She wrote him up on a yellow piece of paper and sent it to my assistant principal. Later on, I was sent to this office to answer some questions. When I was there I saw Jason. You know what he did to me? He practically begged me to lie to the assistant principal by saying it was an accident! Can you believe that?!? I held up my nose and proudly said No. I told my assistant principal the truth. Then Jason got suspended for two days. I've never talked to him since.

The reason I wrote this is that if any of you get harassed or raped, you should report it immediately, or as soon as you can. If you don't do it, those chauvinists will keep on doing it to you. [Quoted from *Teen Voices: The Magazine For, By and About Teenage and Young Adult Women*, Fall, 1993]

—Durkhy, 16, Georgia

Sexual harassment includes pinching, patting, grabbing, sexual comments and gestures, sexual pictures and messages, ongoing staring at body parts, rumors, graffiti, bra snapping, skirt flipping, flashing, forced kissing and other sexual contact. In contrast, flirting is enjoyable to both people involved. This problem affects four of every five teenagers in schools around the U.S., although few report it. A survey of almost 223,000 teens found that three of four were sexually harassed (1996 *USA Weekend* magazine survey). Researcher Louise Fitzgerald found about 30 percent of female college students are harassed during their college career, but only three percent report the incidents.

Sexual Harassment

- A survey of 2,000 girls, "Secrets in Public," was reported in *Seventeen* magazine (September, 1992). Eighty-nine percent of the girls had experienced sexual comments, gestures, or looks, and 83 percent had been touched, pinched, or grabbed. Over a third experienced daily harassment at school. In a 1996 University of Michigan study, 83 percent of girls and 60 percent of boys said they'd been sexually harassed.

- A Harris poll (sponsored by the AAUW, "Hostile Hallways,") of 1,600 8th through 12th graders reported that 66 percent of the girls and 42 percent of the boys had been touched, grabbed or pinched in a sexual way at school. Many of the boys said they thought the girls liked it. More than half of the assaults were physical— being grabbed and touched, or seeing a boy expose himself. Boys were much less likely than girls to fear coming to school because of harassment, partly because they don't fear being raped or physically assaulted by girls.

Of these 1,600 students, 39 percent of girls and eight percent of boys said they were afraid to be in school. Girls of color were especially likely to be targets. Only seven percent of the victims told the school staff about their sexual harassment and only one in five told a family member. The outcome is that more than 40 percent of girls say they feel less sure of themselves and about one in three doesn't want to go to school or talk in class.

This atmosphere of intimidation makes learning more difficult. The Supreme Court ruled in 1991 that Title IX of the Civil Rights Act prohibits sexual harassment in the schools and that schools can be sued for monetary damages for intentional violations of the statute. The courts have defined two kinds of harassment: (1) pressure to have sex, as in return for a good grade, and (2) a hostile environment. Perhaps the first court case holding a school liable for not taking steps to prevent sexual harassment was won by Katy Lyle, a student at Duluth Central High School in Minnesota, whom the court awarded $15,000 in damages.

Some schools are responding to this problem. For example, California, Minnesota, and Maryland's Montgomery County, require schools to have sexual harassment policies in place. The National Association of State Boards of Education developed a model policy to end sexual harassment.

If this happens to you, tell your parents and school administrators, keep a written record of the incidents, find out who is responsible for sexual harassment prevention at your school, and tell that person what happened. If no one responds, contact the U.S. Department of Education's Office for Civil Rights in your state or you can file suit in state or federal court.

How to Fight Sexual Harassment

For information about sexual harassment 1-800-4-ACHILD

American Society for Training and Development
1640 King St.
Alexandria, VA 22313-2043

NOW Legal Defense and Education Fund
99 Hudson St.
New York, NY 10013
(a kit for how to reduce sexual harassment in schools)

Secrets in Public: Sexual Harassment in Our Schools
Center for Research on Women
106 Central St.
Wellesley, MA 02181-8259

Sexual Harassment: It's Not Academic
(pamphlet about how to stop harassment in schools)
U.S. Dept. of Education, Office for Civil Rights
Washington, DC 20202-1328

Tune In to Your Rights: A Guide for Teenagers About Turning Off Sexual Harassment
P.E.O., 1005 School of Education
University of Michigan
Ann Arbor, MI 48109-1259

Montana Katz and Veronica Vieland. *Get Smart! What You Should Know (But Won't Learn in Class) About Sexual Harassment and Sex Discrimination*. NY: Feminist Press, 1995.
(includes date rape and sex discrimination, geared for college students)

June Larkin. *Sexual Harassment: High School Girls Speak Out*. Toronto, Ontario: Second Story Press, 1994.

Nan Stein and Lisa Sjostrom. *Flirting or Hurting? A Teacher's Guide on Student-to-Student Sexual Harassment in Schools, Grades 6 Through 12*. NEA Professional Library, 1994. Order from Center for Research on Women, Wellesley College.

Susan Strauss. *Sexual Harassment and Teens*. Minneapolis: Free Spirit, 1992.

Beth Vanfossen, et al. *Sexual Harassment: A Topical Bibliography*, 1995. (TSU-ITROW, Towson State University, Towson, MD 21204-7097)

Social and Academic Problems in Schools

In my sign language class today, Zane had some balloons, and he made them into balloon animals. Sara and I practiced signing cuss words and Susan and I folded paper cranes. Zondra fell asleep and never even participated once. We all sang "Happy Birthday" to Susan and Stephanie, and pushed them both around in a rolling chair. The teacher played with us too. I love high school. It's not just ASL class—it's every class. Mom just frowns when we tell her what we did. Sure, we're learning stuff, but Mom thinks we're not learning anything. I aced every class this six weeks. I was absent for an entire week.

Somehow, they only marked me down for one absence. How did they do that??

—Jennifer, 16, Texas

Schools face expanding social problems. In California, for example, in an average group of 100 students, 21 do not speak English fluently, 17 live below the poverty level, and seven live in families suspected of child abuse. At the same time, class size is increasing. David Hamburg, author of *Today's Children: Creating a Future for a Generation in Crisis* (Times Books), says that the U.S. commits "atrocities" on our children. Too many are "lost to drug abuse, crime, and teen pregnancy, but also to more subtle corrosives like malnutrition, illiteracy, and poor self-esteem."

Only 66 percent of students give schools a "B" or "A" grade, down from 75% in 1983 (poll for the Horatio Alger Association). Almost half (45 percent) say lack of discipline is a major problem and 27 percent report gangs at their schools. In a 1995 survey of 3,000 high-achiever students, they pinpoint the most serious problems facing their schools as student apathy (43 percent), lack of funds (18 percent), cliques (12 percent), and alcohol abuse (10 percent). Students generally graded the quality of their education as a "B" (50 percent) or "A" (29 percent), although only 30 percent reported their school is very challenging (54 percent spend seven hours or less per week studying).

Elementary and middle school principals observe that only about a quarter of their students are adequately prepared by their parents for school success (a survey of 10,000 principals by the National Association of Elementary School Principals in 1991). The principals said that building children's self-esteem is the most important contribution a parent can make. Kindergarten teachers reported in 1991 that 42 percent of their students are less prepared to learn than five years before (a Carnegie Foundation survey). Emotional difficulties, caused by "divorce, neglect, low self-esteem and separation of family members," are the most common health problems facing elementary school children, 92 percent of teachers agreed.

Despite these social problems, the U.S. lags behind 18 other industrial nations in teacher-pupil ratio (it has more students per teacher), trailing countries such as Libya. The U.S. pays teachers less than teachers in most other developed nations. A Japanese teacher with 10 years experience earns $44,200, compared to $26,000 in the U.S., or $29,900 in Canada.

Yet the U.S. has the world's largest education budget. The U.S. is second only to Canada in the percentage of gross domestic product it spends on education (seven percent, compared to 7.4 percent in Canada). By 1993, the U.S. average spending per student was $5,686 (a total of $353 billion). New Jersey and New York are the highest spending states, and Idaho and Utah the lowest. Unlike other countries, more money in the U.S. goes to support services (i.e., counselors, bus drivers, administrators) than to teachers.

Spending on education doubled in the last decade, yet literacy skills have decreased. A 1991 study by the American Association of School Administrators discovered that one in eight U.S. school buildings is unsafe or substandard. Cutbacks in physical education programs contribute to the fact that only 32 percent of our children reach or exceed minimal fitness tests; this deficiency will affect health insurance costs in the future. School reform is desperately needed—see that section in this chapter.

Poor Literacy Skills

* One in four high school seniors lacks basic reading proficiency.

* Each year 700,000 new graduates are functionally illiterate (very poor readers).

* A 1993 Department of Education study, "The Reading Report Card for the Nation and the States," found that two-thirds of high school seniors did not have more than a superficial understanding of what they read. The more television children watched, the poorer their reading skills.

* Twenty percent of U.S. high school graduates cannot even read their own diploma (1992 report by the U.S. Labor Secretary).

* Almost half of all American adults, more than 90 million, are functionally illiterate (a 1993 test of 26,000 adults by the Department of Education).

* In a random sample of 2,000 Oregon adults, only 35 percent could determine the correct dosage of medicine using a chart of children's age and weight.

* Employers report large numbers of job applicants unable to pass simple skills tests. For example, New York Telephone tested 60,000 applicants to find 3,000 who qualified.

Employers pay a high price for poor educational outcomes. The yearly cost of offering education at the workplace is $200 billion. One in three companies offers new employees remedial training in basic skills, according to the California Business Roundtable. Employers spend around $25 billion a year on initial and remedial training for new employees, as when Domino's Pizza spent $50,000 to teach its bakers to read well enough to follow simple dough-making instructions.

Poor Math and Science Test Scores

Ninety percent of U.S. students score below international averages in math and science. Thirteen-year-olds in Jordan were the only students to score lower than U.S. students on math in 1992. Only five percent of high school seniors can perform any advanced math, according to a 1990 National Assessment of Educational Progress. Fewer university students receive science, math, and engineering degrees than competitor nations (15 percent in the U.S., compared to 32 percent in Germany, and 26 percent in Japan and the United Kingdom). Nearly 40 percent of students tested in 1992 failed to meet basic proficiency skills (a Department of Education test of nearly 50,000 students).

A survey of adults confirmed that their inadequate knowledge of science; a majority do not know that the Sun and Earth are both in the Milky Way galaxy, and a third think that dinosaurs and humans lived at the same time. Twenty percent tested think the sun rotates around the Earth and fewer than 10 percent can explain what a molecule is, according to a survey of 2,000 Americans released by the National Science Foundation in 1996.

On the positive side, 14-year-olds scored above average in reading, when compared to students in other industrial nations (a 1993 report by the Organization for Economic Cooperation and Development). Seven of eight Americans ages 25 to 29 have high school diplomas or the equivalent, and a quarter of adults have a college degree—one of the highest rates in the world. Only Canada and Norway have higher rates of college graduation.

Sports

—Derek, 16, South Dakota

You can go out and give it your all and forget about your problems.

A total of 5,794,429 students participated in high school sports in the school year 1994-1995. Girls were 2,240,461 of the athletes, an increase of 115,706 students from the year before. The most popular sport for girls was basketball, followed by track, volleyball, softball, and soccer (National Federation of State High School Associations).

Although Title IX (see sexism section) requires gender equity in schools, more money is still spent on boys' sports like football. Title IX ironically reduced the number of women coaches from 100 percent to 39 percent as co-ed terms were added. Two decades after Title IX, girls are only 37 of the players participating in high school sports and 34 percent of college athletes. Colleges still spend three-fourths of their sports funds on men. Girls drop out of sports at six times the rate of boys; 72 percent of girls drop out by age 14, according to an article by Jane McConnell in *Women's Sports & Fitness* magazine (September, 1994). None of the schools in violation of Title IX have lost federal money.

—Jenny, 17, California

The biggest challenge for me is getting respect as a female athlete. My friends are there for me if I need them. I have yet to be respected by people as an athlete, but would tell others to talk to someone, i.e., the coach or the athletic director, and make sure they know you're serious.

—Anthony, 22, California

The pressure of performing well in athletics was intense. I tried not to put so much pressure on myself to do well, but instead I concentrated on trying to be a team leader by trying to get everyone involved. That helped me with my challenge.

—Cheryl, 24, California

As a teenager, I was under a lot of pressure. Getting involved in extracurricular activities helped. You shouldn't be afraid to try new things. I once thought I was a horrible athlete but, after joining the track team and winning an award based on my spirit and dedication, I realized I could make a contribution to the team, even if it wasn't as the fastest girl in the league.

—Joe, 24, California

I had to deal with not being on our basketball team because the coach also coached football, so he chose all the football players who tried out. I coped by playing hoops constantly and getting recognition from my people.

Sports Organizations

The Women's Sports Foundation (scholarships) 1-800-227-3988 (publishes a *Women's Athletic Scholarship Guide* for colleges)

Black Women in Sports Foundation P.O. Box 2610 Philadelphia, PA 19130

National Intramural-Recreational Sports Association (NIRSA) 850 SW Fifteenth St. Corvallis, OR 97333

Midnight Basketball Leagu 3628 Cousins D Landover, MD 2078

National Association for Girls an Women in Spo 1900 Association D Reston, VA 2209 (resources include a newsletter calle *GWS New*

Violence in Schools

*I was scared to death when I started high school. The sec-
ond week of the semester, there was a stabbing of a friend of
mine. A friend got killed at a dance at another school this year. I
wish I'd been better equipped. All students should have skills in
conflict management. There would be a lot less violence. My school
just got a grant to start peer mediation to hear both sides—usually
to correct misunderstandings, such as, "I didn't know you and
Chris were together."*

**—Chanda, 15,
Washington**

Violence permeates schools and guns have replaced
cars as the status symbol for some students.

California State Senator Teresa Hughes reports, "We
live in a society where children going to school has
become comparable to soldiers going off to war."

In a survey of 3,000 high-achiever students, over half reported problems with violence at
school, including fist fights between students (47 percent) and students attacking teachers (17 percent). Over
one-quarter knew someone who brought a weapon to
school and 12 percent feel unsafe at school. These students say the main problem is apathetic parents.

School Violence

- Young people between the ages of 18 and 21 commit 36 percent of violent crimes in the U.S. and homicide is the second main cause of death for this age group. Over one-quarter of high school students are afraid of their peers.

- Over 400,000 crimes are reported in U.S. schools each year, along with 50 killings or suicides at or near schools.

- A national survey of 10-to 13-year-olds found that 22 percent change what they might do or where they go during school hours to avoid physical threats. About a third do not feel completely safe at school and 42 percent don't feel completely safe in their own neighborhood (1995 KidsPeace Preteen Survey).

- One in 13 juveniles was the victim of a violent crime in 1992, according to the Justice Department. In suburban schools in Colorado and Ohio, 44 percent of boys and 14 percent of girls report being hit at school.

- 270,000 guns are brought to school on a typical day. One-quarter of high school students have carried a weapon in the past month (U.S. Centers for Disease Control report). One in 14 students was threatened or injured with a weapon on school property during the previous year and about a third had property stolen or damaged at school.

- A survey of 11,000 students (grades 8 and 10) reported that 61 percent had been robbed, attacked, or threatened at school in the previous year (The National Adolescent Student Health Survey released In 1988).

Students at high-risk of violent behavior lack these skills: empathy (understanding the viewpoints of others), control over their impulses, problem-solving skills, assertiveness skills, and anger management. "Second Step" is an example of a school-based curriculum to teach students "prosocial" skills. School violence should be tackled, not just defensively with metal detectors and guards, but proactively by teaching students alternatives to violence and by involving parents. Some schools train peer mediators to help settle conflicts. Mediators learn how to be good listeners, to encourage the two persons to listen to each other, and identify solutions.

Rick Harwood teaches at Reiner Beach High School in Seattle, where he reports many students feel scared, frustrated, and angry about their futures. Concerned about violence, he started a prevention program expanding on the Community Board, Inc. (San Francisco) training manual for conflict managers and on resources from the National Association of Mediation. Student mediators are on call for two to three periods. The main problems they hear, as in other schools, are rumors and misunderstandings between friends. The pair in conflict repeat the other person's feelings and propose solutions. The outcome is a major reduction in the number of fights and weapons. The school also provides a drug and alcohol counselor and support groups for students in recovery, another way to prevent violence.

In New Jersey's SAVVY Program (Students Against Violence and Victimization of Youth), empowered students learn ways to prevent violence. The program began in 1993 with a statewide conference of 22 schools. Representatives of each school received training and created an action plan for their school district. SAVVY projects include peer leadership groups that perform conflict resolution skits, peer conflict mediation programs, and conflict resolution groups.

Programs such as New York City Schools' Resolving Conflict Creatively Program make a major improvement in reducing violence, according to students and teachers. Students and teachers trained in conflict resolution at Washington Elementary School in Daly City, California, report that problems in the schoolyard are down by around 80 percent. These guiding principles are posted around the school: Talk and listen to each other, find out what you both need, brainstorm ideas, and use "I messages" as you negotiate. The Violent Crime Control Act of 1994 set aside funding for Community Schools Youth Services to create after-school programs in low-income neighborhoods.

Although ending sexual harassment in schools should be included in efforts to prevent school violence, a survey of 51 teen violence prevention programs found that only four specifically mentioned prevention of dating violence (as reported in the 1991 AAUW report). Schools with prevention programs do cut down on violence.

—Tristan, 17, California

Five years ago, as part of her Senior Project, a girl decided to institute a student court program at our high school. (A Senior Project is part of the graduation requirements; students are required to investigate, write a report, and give a speech on either a career they are interested in or a project that would help the community.) The school was plagued by crime, such as vandalism and innumerable counts of disruption in the classroom. All too soon, this girl graduated and the idea of a student court was dropped, although the student government position of Judiciary Commissioner was created. Last year I was elected to this position. I set up a Student Court Program. I now have it running smoothly in the following way. On Monday, one of the deans will call me in to say that we have a case. On Tuesday, I select the jury, by drawing names out of a can, and send out call-slips to the selected jury members. Then, on Thursday, I send out reminder slips to the panel members. They all show up at noon (hopefully) in the conference room and we proceed with the trial.

The dean outlines the events from the administration's point of view. The student then gets a chance to defend him/or herself. We ask questions, then I ask the student to step outside the room, and the jury members and I discuss punishment options. Although going to Student Court is optional, the punishment is binding. The carrot on the string is that the crime gets erased from his/her record. The students are much harsher on their peers than would be thought, which greatly increases the effectiveness of the program. Crime at school is way down, at times so much so that we may not get a case for a month.

—Jayson, 24, California

I was a skinny young boy who never got into trouble. I had many close friends I socialized with. I played sports outside of school every day with my friends. I had many friends, but there was a group of students who just didn't like me and had no reasons. I didn't even know these students. These kids were a bunch of bullies led by one boy who got his friends to pick on me. They called me Mama's boy because of the way I dressed in nice clothes that had style. I had a nice car that I drove around in.

Many of these kids were jealous of the things I had. They would threaten to beat me up every day. Some of the kids carried knives. I would ignore them and walk away. They would throw anything they got their hands on.

Throughout the days they slowly broke me down by the harsh punches and words that were thrown out at me. I told my parents and the principal. It took me away from my studies and I had a lot of anger inside me toward these kids. I tried many times to ask why they disliked me. There were no reasons. It's the way I looked and acted; it was just me they disliked. At times I wanted to gather a bunch of my friends to beat them up. I was angry but I realized that I could change everything by going to a different school. I didn't like running away from my problems, but quitting that school and getting away from that environment was the best choice I could have ever made. I went to a different school and was lucky that the kids accepted me for who I was.

Programs to Prevent School Violence

(Also see the violence section in Chapter 1 and neighborhood organizing in Chapter 11)

Educational Development Center
1-800-255-4276
(*Violence Prevention Curriculum for Adolescents*)

California State Department of Education. *Safe Schools: A Planning Guide for Action. School Community Violence Prevention.*
1-916-657-2451

The Bureau for At-Risk Youth,
Violence is Preventable
645 New York Ave.
Huntington, NY 11743

Coalition to Stop Gun Violence
The Educational Fund
100 Maryland Ave., NE
Washington, DC 20002

Conflict Resolution and Peer Mediation
Resolving Conflict Creatively
163 Third Ave., #239
New York, NY 10003

The Educational Fund to End Handgun Violence
100 Maryland Ave., NE, Suite 402
Washington, DC 20002

ESR National Conflict Resolution Program
23 Garden St.
Cambridge, MA 02138

Fast Track, Dept. P
1211-18th Ave. S.
Nashville, TN 37212 (school program for "anti-social" kids)

Institute for Peace and Justice
4144 Lindell Blvd., #124
St. Louis, MO 63108
Kathleen McGinnis. *Educating for a Just Society (grades 7-12)* (includes conflict resolution, ageism, racism)

Kids Against Crime
P.O. Box 22004
San Bernandino, CA 92406

Men's Contact and Resource Centre,
Boys Talk Program
P.O. Box 8036 Hindley St.
Adelaide, S.A. 5000, Australia

National Crime Prevention Council
1700 K St., NW, 2nd Floor
Washington, DC 20006-3817

National School Safety Center
4165 Thousand Oaks Blvd., Suite 290
Westlake Village, CA 91362

Resolving Conflict Creatively Program
National Center
163 Third Ave., #103
New York, NY 10003
(The center provides booklets and videos describing the RCCT program in New York City schools which sell a curriculum called *Resolving Conflict Creatively Program* to teach students "emotional literacy," how to negotiate a solution, and peer mediation.)

Second Step,
K-8 violence prevention curriculum
Committee for Children
2203 Airport Way, S.
Seattle, WA 98134-2027 (includes
videos, leader and parent guides)

*The Prevention of Youth Violence: A
Framework for Community Action,*
Centers for Disease Control and
Prevention, U.S. Department of
Health and Human Services, Public
Health Service, 1993.

Books

*Safe at School: Awareness and Action
for Parents of Kids Grades K-12.*
(Includes information on gangs,
environmental hazards, sexual
harassment, etc.) Minneapolis: Free
Spirit Publishing.

Annie Cheathan. *Annotated Bibliography
for Teaching Conflict Resolution in
Schools.* Cambridge, MA: Educators for
Social Responsibility, 1989.

Allan Creighton, et al. *Helping Teens
Stop Violence.* Oakland Men's Project,
1992. 1-800-788-3123.

Roger Fisher and William Ury. *Getting
to Yes: Negotiating Agreement Without
Giving In.* Cambridge, MA: Educators
for Social Responsibility, 1991.

Gail Sadalla, et al. *Conflict
Resolution: A Secondary School
Curriculum.* The Community Board
Program (1540 Market St., Suite 490,
San Francisco, CA 94102).

Ron Stephens. *Safe Schools: A
Handbook for Violence Prevention.*
This and other resources available
from National Educational Service,
P.O. Box 8, Bloomington, IN 47402.

Renée Wilson-Brewer, et al. *Violence
Prevention for Young Adolescents: A
Survey of the State of the Art.* Newton,
MA: Education Development Center,
1991.

Chapter 8

Bryce Harmon

Good Grades

Achieve Your Goals

My most difficult challenge as a teenager is finding out who I am, where I belong, and how far I am willing to go to meet my goals. I've learned to set my own goals and to strive to reach them, to look ahead into the future and not to look back on my mistakes but learn from them. I've learned that I don't need to meet anyone else's expectations but my own and to have morals and self-respect.

—Nancy, 14, California

The main point of school is to learn, right? Although grades may not reflect your knowledge, high marks are what it takes to get into college, and your ticket to the career of your choice. The secret is to conquer procrastination, set aside daily time to study, and use your study time efficiently. Your goal is to develop your mental muscle, so to speak, so you learn a lot in a short period of time and avoid spacing out. Learning is a discipline, similar to becoming a trained athlete. It's enjoyable to expand your mental abilities and learn more about your world.

—Derek, 15, California

There is so much expected of you—to do well in school, but then there is so much expected by your friends to be cool. I get by with grades that are very good, but I know I can do better. I never let school get in front of my friends though. That way I can still go to a good college and stay popular.

—Amber, 15, California

Being a teenager is sometimes very difficult. There are many challenging things I face everyday, such as drugs, smoking, alcohol, peer pressure, and trying to fit in. The thing that I have most trouble with is a place I go almost every day. It's a place where it is supposed to be fun and exciting, a place where you have a lot of friends, also a place where you learn new knowledge. Yes, I'm talking about school.

The problem with that is when I think of my school, I think of a horrible, boring, dirty place where teachers don't care how you're doing. To most teachers, it's just a job. When a teacher doesn't care, the students can tell. It makes me feel discouraged and not want to go to school. But the truth is, I do care. School has always been difficult for me. I have to struggle very hard just to get a passing grade. It also doesn't help that I don't like being there. One of the ways I keep myself from not giving up is I tell myself, if I ever want a good job, I have to stay in school and try my hardest. The advice that I'd give to anyone who asks is always try, never give up, and think about your actions.

—Mina, 18, Texas

As an honors and AP [advanced placement] student, I am faced with competing against others in grades, work excellence, and GPA. For today's fast-paced, high-tech society, high intelligence (based on grades and classes) is highly competitive and much sought after.

The only way I've found to deal with this challenge is by thinking of my future and how school will aid me in college and in my career. Good education is achieved in good schools which, in turn, accept only good students. This thought has helped me study more and pay more attention. I keep telling myself that I am doing it for myself because I want it, and I do. I want the challenge. I want to be good. That is why I study and try to process everything I hear so I can understand and will myself to do better.

I know that many young people are confronted with the same problem. Those who want to be someone, and feel good by achieving something through their hard work, should never give up. If a course is hard, stick to it. Don't drop out. Challenge yourself, tell yourself to do better. Pay attention in class and, if necessary, go to a tutor or have a study group. Set goals and strive to achieve them. Once achieved, set them again, only push yourself harder to do better. And always remember, all your hard work is never in vain. You do it for you and you only.

—Timothy, 19, Michigan

All I can say is to never fall behind on assignments, read all the assigned material, and study as much as you can. Try not to feel that you always need to have fun. There will be time for that when you're not cramming for an exam because you're all caught up with everything.

—Bob, 21, California

The future belongs to those who believe in their dreams.

—Octavio, 24, Oklahoma

Knowledge is power that may bring us closer to understanding truth. Truth will help us to understand ourselves so that we can grow and be happy in the future. To learn is like traveling; you can go to many places. The more you learn, the easier understanding others will be, so that we can all get along.

—Sean, 26, California

My most difficult task as a teen was keeping my head into my studies. I played sports as well as partied a lot. A balance of education and recreation is important, but I wish I realized then how my lack of effort in education would affect my college career and beyond.

Take a step back and look at the people around you, and try to imagine where they will be in 20 years. Then look at yourself and see where your life is headed. Support from my family and friends as well as coaches pushed me to succeed.

Frederick Hageman.
Making the Grades: How You Can Achieve Greater Success with Less Stress in School and Beyond.
Rising Crescent Publishing.
P.O. Box 7703-A,
Berkeley, CA 94707-0703.

Concentrate in Class

Review your notes every night simply by reading over them. When my teachers told me this I didn't listen. I never thought I had enough time. I realize now that it would have only taken about 15 minutes each night and it would have helped my grades tremendously. [Underline or highlight your notes as you read over them to keep focused, then read only this information to review for a test.]

—Amanda, 17, Wisconsin

Sit at the front of the class. Raise your hand and answer, even if you think you may be wrong. Don't procrastinate. If you see a problem, don't ignore it, it won't go away. If you are experiencing personal/emotional problems, talk to someone, if possible a professional. Work on resolving your problems as they can be a distraction from your education.

—Lisa, 25, California

Sit in the middle or in the front of the classroom (picture a "T") and make eye contact with the teacher, as students who sit in this "T" zone tend to do better. Don't sit near a talkative friend or where you can look out a distracting window. Take notes to concentrate on what the teacher is saying and prevent spacing out. Ask questions and participate in class discussions to keep your mind processing the information. Keep a calendar or appointment book to record in one place when assignments are due.

To get motivated to concentrate, visit colleges when students are on campus and get inspired by the atmosphere. Do some job shadowing to see what it's like on the job. Interview recent graduates from your school to learn about the choices they made and take advantage of the career information in your school library to imagine yourself putting your current studies to use. These steps will demonstrate why studying is in your best interests.

Essay Writing

When responding to an essay question, first make an outline. To think up points to support your thesis or central idea, try "clustering," drawing a circle with your theme written inside. Then draw lines radiating from the circle, like a starfish, labeling them with points to support your thesis. Do this quickly, without judgment—just brainstorm. Then list the most important points you intend to use and number them in the order you'll explain them. On tests, you may want to do the outlining and clustering on your answer sheet so your teacher can see your organizational skills.

The first paragraph of an essay should tell the reader your theme, its importance, and the three to four main points you will provide to prove or support your central idea. One way to organize your theme is to set up a "strawman" and knock him down, along the lines of some people believe that _____, however, the facts indicate otherwise. Then, in the body, develop the points in the order listed in the introduction. Be sure that your points follow one another logically and each specifically proves your thesis or central idea. Follow your outline. In your conclusion, summarize the most important points, and if appropriate, suggest future trends.

The comments that I write most often on my students' essays are: be specific instead of vague, illustrate a general statement with examples, explain how this information proves your theme, and connect and build transitions between each new idea. Think about, "digest," and analyze the information you present rather than just summarize other people's thinking. To analyze ideas, think in terms of comparison and contrast, causes and effects, why, and so what?

Style

—English teacher Susan Suntree offers two main tips about **style** from Stanley Oropesa, of the UCLA Writing Program.

1. Less is more. Be as direct and honest as possible. This will give your work elegance and impact. Two popular words—*it* and *there*—signal that your style might be too wordy or flabby. Likewise, eliminate weak passive verbs: *is, are, were, have been.* [Substitute action words. For example, instead of, "Women have been paid less," write "Women earn less." Ask your English teacher to go over this in class because it's a major pitfall for writers. Whoops, I just used a passive construction. How about, "The passive voice trips up writers." A computer grammar checker will point out passive construction.]

2. Try role playing. Assume the voice or style of a close friend, teacher or boss. Write your ideas as s/he might express them. Use writing in another person's voice as a way to find your own. If you are having trouble, write as if you are the instructor.

Learning Disabilities

> *The most difficult challenge is my learning disability (LD). I had to learn about my LD and how to use my Individual Education Program (IEP) to assist me in the classroom. My advice is to ask about your learning disability and learn about it.*
>
> **—Troy, 17, Wisconsin**

About 10 to 15 percent of students are learning disabled (LD). This has nothing to do with their intelligence or emotional health, but with how their minds process words or information. Learning disabilities are probably caused by a genetic difficulty in the nervous system that makes it difficult to receive information from the senses, process it, and communicate it.

LD students may have trouble understanding instructions, remembering what they hear, and with reading or math. The student may have difficulty remembering instructions and following through on them. Learning disabilities are treated with special educational therapy and some schools provide an LD resource room and teacher.

Attention Deficit Disorder (ADD) is a neurological problem that begins in childhood. About 20 percent of the population will be diagnosed as having ADD. Some of the symptoms are restlessness, inability to concentrate, easily distracted, forgetfulness, mood swings, irritability, impulsiveness, and poor sense of direction. ADD is treated with medication, therapy, and education. The medications most often used (Ritalin, Dexedrine, and Cylert) cause an intense rush for most people, but improve concentration for people with ADD. Some are also hyperactive, referred to as ADHD.

For people who like herbal remedies, nutrition specialist Donald Payne suggests taking the herbs ginkgo bilobia (it takes three weeks to have an effect) and DMAE (dimethylminoethanol) daily. DMAE aids the brain transmitter that affects memory and concentration. He also recommends eliminating sugar, junk foods, soft drinks, chocolate, preservatives, and artificial food coloring from the diet.

Dyslexics have a reading problem caused by their brains reversing some letters and words. They may have difficulty seeing the difference in *no* and *on*, hearing the difference in letter sounds such as *pin* and *pen*, and confusing 25 with 52, or *b* with *d*. They may have difficulty writing what they hear or speaking what they read. Dyslexia is eight times more likely to affect boys, left-handed people, those with high math ability, and kids with a family history of reading problems because it is inherited. Up to eight percent of students are dyslexic.

—Andy, 18, California

I didn't have a problem with ADD until the age of 10. In the 4th grade I started losing interest in school, fiddling with my fingers, tapping my feet, daydreaming, sleeping, and drawing. I was also obnoxious, interruptive, and loud, but that was a personal problem. One of the most widely used drugs by doctors to cope with ADD is Ritalin. I took this drug from grade 6 to grade 9. Ritalin helps you concentrate and pay attention in school, but the downside was it made me sleepy in the early morning and kept me up at night. While on Ritalin, your sleeping habits change, you eat less, and it can make you nauseous if you don't eat after taking it.

After Ritalin, I went to Tophranil, which is an anti-depressant. This drug is rather mellow, it helps you sleep at night and in the morning, you're easy to wake up. The only side effects I can think of is that if you forget to take it one day, or if you're weaning yourself off of it, you feel paranoid or out of it for about 72 hours.

After all the drugs, counseling, and thousands of dollars spent, I myself found the way to cope. I take a tape recorder to school and record my teachers, take notes on everything, write myself notes, and try to concentrate on what's going on. I recommend the video "Where There's a Will, There's an A." It does work if you apply yourself. I was skeptical and said, "Yeah, right," but I sat down and watched it. I get good grades now and I am about to go to college. Most of it is in your head; if you have the will, there's a way. It's possible.

ADD

—Edward Hallowell, MD.

If you know someone like me who's acting up and daydreaming and forgetting this or that and just not getting with the program, consider ADD before he starts believing all the bad things people are saying about him and it's too late.

It's like driving in the rain with bad windshield wipers. Everything is smudged and blurred and you're speeding along, and it's reeeeally frustrating not being able to see very well. Or it's like listening to a radio station with a lot of static and you have to strain to hear what's going on. Or, it's like trying to build a house of cards in a dust storm. You have to build a structure to protect yourself from the wind before you can even start on the cards. In other ways, it's like being super-charged all the time and people are calling you disorganized and impulsive; it's just that you have all these invisible vectors pulling you this way and that which make it really hard to stay on task.

Plus, you're spilling over all the time. You're drumming your fingers, tapping your feet, humming a song, looking here, looking there, and doodling. People think you're not paying attention or that you're not interested, but all you're doing is spilling over so you can pay attention. On the positive side, we're highly imaginative and intuitive, have a "sixth sense," and can feel a lot.

The treatment is anything that turns down the noise. Just making the diagnosis helps turn down the noise of guilt and self-recrimination. Building certain kinds of structure into one's life can help a lot, as does working in small spurts rather than long hauls, breaking tasks down into smaller tasks, and making lists. Get help where you need it and get enough exercise to work off some of the noise inside. Find support, get someone in your corner to coach you, to keep you on track. Medication can help a great deal too, but it is far from the whole solution. The good news is that treatment can really help.

Learning Disability Organizations

National Center for Youth with Disabilities 1-800-333-6293

Orton Dyslexia Society 1-800-ABCD-123

Council for Exceptional Children 1920 Association Dr. Reston, VA 22091

Council for Learning Disabilities P.O. Box 40303 Overland Park, KS 66204

Foundation for Children with Learning Disabilities 99 Park Ave. New York, NY 10016

Learning Disabilities Association 4156 Library Rd. Pittsburgh, PA 15234 (a grassroots organization for parents and teachers that provides information about the latest research and legislation)

National Center for Learning Disabilities 381 Park Ave., Suite 1420 New York, NY 10016

National Institute of Dyslexia 3200 Woodbine Ave. Chevy Chase, MD 20815

ADD Resources

Attention Deficit Disorder Association 1-800-487-2282 Challenge (referral to support groups) 1-800-232-2322

American Academy of Pediatrics, Publications P.O. Box 927 Elk Grove Village, IL 60009-0927

Children and Adults with Attention Deficit Disorders 499 NW 70th Ave., Suite 101, Dept. P Plantation, FL 33317 (information packet)

Kate Kelly and Peggy Ramundo. *You Mean I'm Not Lazy, Crazy, or Stupid?* NY: Scribners, 1995.

Patricia Quinn, ed. *ADD and the College Student: A Guide for High School and College Students with Attention Deficit Disorder.* NY: Magination Press, 1994.

Books for Learning Disabled Students

Pamela Espeland, ed. *The Survival Guide for Teenagers with LD*. Minneapolis: Free Spirit, 1990.

Mary Ann Lisiscio. *A Guide to Colleges for Learning Disabled Students*. Orlando, FL: Academic Press, 1986.

Kathleen Nadeau. *Survival Guide for College Students with ADD or LD*. NY: Magination Press, 1994

Parents' Educational Resources Center. *Bridges to Learning* booklets provide information on reading disabilities. 1-800-471-9545

Learning Styles

We don't all learn the same way. It's helpful to identify how you learn best, and be aware of your teachers' styles. School counselors should be able to give you tests to let you know your style.

☆ Some learn best by hearing (an auditory learner), such as listening to verbal instructions from a teacher.

☆ Some by seeing/reading (a visual learner), like reading or drawing a diagram or chart.

☆ Some learn by touching (tactile learners).

☆ Others by doing (kinesthetic learners), such as learning geometry by making three-dimensional shapes.

Most of us remember better if we combine methods, such as learning a new vocabulary word by seeing it on a flashcard, saying it out loud, and writing it.

Students generally remember:

- ○ 10 percent of what we read
- ○ 20 percent of what we hear
- ○ 30 percent of what we see
- ○ 50 percent of what we see and hear

- 70 percent of what we say out loud
- 90 percent of what we do.

This indicates that it's a good idea to talk about what you are learning in a study group or to practice explaining a difficult idea to a friend or family member.

Another way to think about learning style is whether you are global—the right hemisphere of the brain is dominant, or analytical—the left hemisphere of the brain is dominant. Rita and Kenneth Dunn have written over 10 books on learning styles. They believe that about 55 percent of the population are global thinkers, about 28 percent are analytical, and the rest are "integrated" learners who don't favor either hemisphere.

If you are a global thinker, you like to understand the overall concept before tackling details. You tend to be intuitive and see patterns in things. Globals like some background noise and low lights when they work, and they may like to have something in their mouth (eating, chewing gum, biting on a pencil). They often like to learn in a group, while analytical thinkers learn better on their own.

Analytic thinkers like to work step—by—step in logical progression from point A to point B. They like to do one thing at a time until finished, while globals like to take breaks and have several projects going at the same time. Analyticals like to work quietly, with bright lights to help them concentrate, and rarely eat when they are working. Analyze your learning style in your journal and keep watching how you learn best.

Rita Dunn. *Teaching Secondary Students Through Their Individual Learning Styles.* Boston: Allyn and Bacon, 1993.

Thomas Armstrong. *Seven Kinds of Smart.* NY: Penguin/Plume, 1993.

Memorizing Skills

To memorize information, connect it with something you know. To memorize lists such as the names of human bones or state capitals, take the first letter of each word and make up a word with those letters (acronyms) to remind you of all the information. Or make a sentence with words that start with the same letters as the list you are memorizing. Or picture them on different parts of your body, from head down to feet. Your brain learns by stimulating various senses, using pictures, sounds, and feelings. For example, let's say you want to memorize a list of prominent women. Think of Eleanor Roosevelt sitting with a red rose on top of your head. Sandra Day O'Connor could be your sunglasses with an S on one lense and an O on the other. The idea is simply to attach new information to something you already know and can visualize. (By the way, do you learn about women and minority scientists, writers, and leaders in school? If not, ask why.)

To memorize vocabulary or facts, use a separate flashcard for each word, with the definition on the back of the card. Quiz yourself until you know each word or fact. To memorize a quotation or speech, break it up into parts and memorize the first part, then the second, then the two together, and so on.

Note-Taking Skills

J ill, a Harvard law school student, suggests, "Look at someone's notes who makes good grades and see what s/he finds important enough to write down." Lecture notes not only help you study for tests, they keep you focused in class. When I study for a test, I underline the key information in my notes, then write the most important ideas on index cards and quiz myself on them.

Take class notes in outline form so you have to think about how one point fits in with the other:

I. Main division
  A. First topic
    I. sub topic
      a. fact

Later write key information in the margin of your notebook and quiz yourself on those "cues." As you review your notes each evening, mark questions to ask the teacher the next day. Some people take notes only on the right page, leaving the left/facing page for notes from the textbook on the same topic. Invent your own note–taking abbreviations for commonly used words and note your code in your notebook, or learn some shorthand.

Oral Reports

—English teacher Susan Suntree, M.A

+ Keep breathing, relaxing your belly, and feeling your feet on the ground.

+ Highlight your notes and speak from note cards: Do NOT read word for word or you will put your audience to sleep.

+ Pick a couple of people in the audience to talk to, especially at the beginning of your speech. Think about what you're saying rather than how you're doing.

+ Pay attention to your posture. Don't lean on the podium or stand on one foot or hip. Watch for wiggling and jiggling your foot or other distracting nervous movements.

+ You don't have to deliver the perfect speech. If you're human, your audience can identify with you.

+ Don't apologize for anything. Just notice what has happened—an awkward pronunciation, a dropped note card—take care of it, and go on.

Parent Involvement in Schools

olls of teachers rank parent involvement as the number one cause of
students' school success. Parents' involvement reduces student
absences from school, limits television viewing, and increases reading
outside of school. Unfortunately, however, parent involvement in school
drops as their children reach high school. Although 73 percent of parents of
children ages eight to 11 are involved, nearly half the parents of high school
students do not attend school events such as back-to-school nights or
Parent–Teacher Association meetings. Working mothers are just as involved
as full-time homemakers (with kids in 6th to 12th grades), with one-fourth of
both groups highly involved in their children's schools. Forty percent of
mothers who work full-time have low involvement, as do half of homemakers.

Students who repeat a grade (19 percent) are more likely to
have uninvolved parents, as are students suspended from school for behavior
problems (15 percent). The most active parents tend to be college graduates,
with higher income and two parents at home. Students' achievement relates to
their parents' education, therefore youth with college-educated parents are
almost twice as likely to be high achievers as students whose parents didn't
finish high school. (The National Household Education Survey of grades 6 to 12)

Sadly, more parents watch television with their children (52
percent) than read with them (48 percent). American 13 year olds watch more
television (three hours a day average), do less homework, and are outper-
formed in science and math by students from other nations. A 1993 U.S.
Education Department study of gifted students found they average less than
one hour per school day studying, the same finding a a 1996 poll of represen-

tative teens for the Horatio Alger Association. Parents can reverse these trends by spending more time reading and conversing than watching television.

Progressive California legislation, The Family School Partnership Act, requires employers to allow parents to take off up to 40 hours a year to participate in school activities. The law, however, only applies to employers with 25 or more employees and parents must use vacation time or take unpaid leave. State governments and employers can do a lot more to enable parents to be involved in schools.

Parent Involvement Resources

American Federation of Teachers' Learning Line 1-800-242-5465

Education Today. *Parent Involvement Handbook.* 1-800-927-6006

Family Education Network 1-800-927-6006

National Parent Information Network (articles, experts answer your questions, discussion forums, resources, models) 1-800-583-4135 http://ericps.ed.uiuc.edu/npin/npin-home.html

Center for the Study of Parent Involvement John F. Kennedy University, 12 Altarinda Rd. Orinda, CA 94563

Family Involvement Partnership for Learning (More than 150 national organizations are working with the U.S. Department of Education, Washington, DC 20202-0498

U.S. Department of Education *Community Update newsletter* (free) 1-800-USA-LEARN for resource information listproc@inet.ed.gov (Type in subscribe EDInfo, your first and last name) to receive messages several times a week on topics such as updates on legislation, how to prepare for college, and technology resources.)

National PTA catalogue 135 S. LaSalle St., Dept. 1927 Chicago, IL 60674-1927

James Lengel and D. Kendall. *Kids, Computers and Homework.* NY: Random House, 1995. (includes websites and software)

Terry Mallen. *Taking Charge of Your Child's Education: Nine Steps to Becoming a Learning Ally.* Seattle:, WA Acumen Press, 1995.

Internet Sources

CIA World Factbook: http://www.odci.gov/cia

Classroom connect: http://www.classroom.net

AskERIC answers education questions: askeric@ericir.syr.edu

An evaluation of Internet education sites: http://cciweb.com/iway500/educat.html

Index to treasures on the Internet: http://pen.k12.va.us/~cfifer/trea-sures.shtml

parentsoup@aol.com (ask experts)

PTA's Children First is found in the Parenting subcategory of the Home and Family Category.

Time Management

I don't have enough time to accomplish everything I wish to accomplish. It does not matter how hard I try or how early I start, I still don't have enough time. All the things that I wish to accomplish are important to me and I don't want to give any of them up.

I haven't really found a good way to cope with my challenge. I have learned, though, some things help me to cope a little. Prioritizing has helped me to accomplish things, such as home-work, band auditions, and college and scholar-ship applications. Unfortunately, there are things I never do finish. Make sure you know due dates or make due dates for things that you need to get finished.

—Judy, 17, Illinois

Billie Jackson, head of the Student Learning Center at California State University, Chico, explains the difference between an "A" and a "C" student. Organization is the key. "A" students start ahead of time; they don't cram for tests the night before. They do more than just the minimum require-ments. They think and talk about what they're learning to integrate it with what they know, and put new vocabulary to use. They write down assignments in one place and have a notebook with sections and pockets for each subject.

Ms. Jackson observes that effective stu-dents have a study schedule. This involves a quick review of the text and class notes after class. They review as soon after class as possible in a Sunday-through-Thursday schedule for homework, with intensive review the night before a test. The secret to learning is to review infor-mation three to four times a week. Write down the most important points to remember on flash cards and quiz yourself as part of the review process.

I suggest you keep a log of how you spend your time in a typical day, marking down what you do and for how long. See if how you actually spend your time matches your goals and values. Remind yourself that you can take charge of your life. Two people presented with the same problem can react very differently, one by giving up or avoiding the problem, and the other by getting the help needed to solve the problem.

The main enemy is procrastination, "the unjustified avoidance of a specific task that should be accomplished." Putting off doing work robs you of energy and confidence, and makes the task you've put off seem twice as hard. In contrast, getting a job done adds to your energy and confidence. Some of the causes of procrastination are perfectionism, feeling overwhelmed or unable to do the task, and not liking or caring about the task. To conquer this enemy, decide what you really do want or have to achieve and do it in small steps.

It's normal to think of excuses to avoid studying (such as you really need to clean your room or make a phone call) but stick to your schedule. If you're like me, the more difficult the assignment, the more excuses automatically pop into your mind, but once you get started, you'll get on a roll. Just expect the excuses to come up, tell them you'll plan time for fun, but now you need to be on task.

The single most important path to school success is to break a big assignment into small pieces and complete something every day. For example, the steps to writing a research paper include: go to the library, do a bibliographical search, read the most important articles first, write a rough draft, revise the draft, and type the final draft. Schedule when you will take each steps.

Start now. Get help if you can't achieve a task on your own. Don't expect perfection and do visualize yourself achieving the end goal, such as turning in a research paper that reflects your best work. As you plan, remember that most things take longer than you think they will. Schedule open blocks of time to catch up as well as to relax and play. Carry reading material for times when you know you will have to wait, such as for a doctor's appointment. You might want to ask successful people you know how they manage to get a job done well and still have time for fun. For me, a routine is the key: exercising every day, dancing every Friday, and so on.

Be aware of when you work best and try to schedule your most challenging work then; if your brain is zonked by 10:00 p.m. that's obviously not the time to study for a difficult exam. Sometimes it's best to start homework with your easiest assignment, because finishing it gives you the sense of accomplishment to go on to the next assignment. Usually it's best to do your hardest homework first when you have the most energy. If preoccupied with a personal problem, to clear your mind, write about it in your journal or write a very frank letter and tear it up. Negative self-talk is another enemy, so tape up positive messages around your work space, such as "I am capable of deep concentration and remember what I read." Most people can concentrate for about 45 minutes before they need to take a break, so build a change of pace into your schedule.

Work in an area set aside for concentrated effort, free from distractions. Choose the same place (i.e., your desk or the library) for study and use only that place for it. At home, make your senses happy when you sit down to study by having a neat space, a beautiful picture, a favorite photograph, unbuttered popcorn to eat, juice to drink, relaxing background music, and a list to check off your accomplishments. Set boundaries: Work with your back to traffic flow, keep your door closed with a "Genius at Work" sign, and let the machine answer your phone. Say No to the phone, people coming into your space, and other interruptions.

Good Grades · 389

—John, 17, Wisconsin

     The most difficult challenge I face as a teenager is trying to find enough time to be with my family, friends, and girlfriend, while trying to participate in school events, do my homework, and hold a job at the same time. It can be very frustrating at times and makes me a little depressed because I can't find time for everything and everyone.

     I decided to work just on the weekends. [A good idea because when teens work long hours, grades drop.] *This allowed more time to do homework, and get enough sleep. I started spending Friday nights after the football game going out with the guys, spending Saturday night with my girlfriend, and Sundays with my parents. Schedule your time so that you are not rushing yourself, and do not overload your schedule so that you can't get everything done.*

—Daniel, 19, California

     I needed time management with all the sports and the student body positions I held, so I learned when my best study hours were and used my time to the best of my ability. Set aside a specific time for studying and stick with it. Self-discipline is hard but necessary.

Getting Organized

Claudine Wirths. *Where's My Other Sock? : How to Get Organized and Drive your Parents and Teachers Crazy.* NY: T.Y. Crowell, 1989.

Computer software is available to help with organizing: Nolo Press' "Personal Record-Keeper" and "Campbell Services' OnTime" are examples of programs to assist in record keeping and planning.

Reading Strategy

I'm a slower learner than other teenagers in my class. I've always caught on to a concept one niche slower. It's been difficult to sit in a math or science class and not understand what in the world the teacher is talking about. With the world growing in technology, it's important to know and understand math and science. What I have caught on to is that if you want to really catch on, you study AHEAD. Don't just read the chapter your teacher said to read for that week. Read one more, then review the notes. By doing this, you can at least kinda know the information. Because you have read so much, when you have a question, you know exactly what you don't know.

—Jayna, 16, California

By 12th grade, only four percent of students are advanced readers, 30 percent are proficient/adequate, 70 percent are basic, and 30 percent are below basic (the 1994 National Assessment of Educational Progress was given to 27,400 students). Scores dropped slightly since the test scores in 1992. A 1988 study of 8th graders found that they averaged only two hours a week reading for enjoyment and spent 21 hours a week watching television and only six doing homework. The moral is to establish a reading habit by reading every day. Reading novels increases your speed and having a dictionary nearby helps you to learn new words as you read them—helpful for doing well on the verbal section of the SAT.

When you read for schoolwork, never read without taking notes because, like listening in class, it's easy to space out if you don't involve your body by writing. We've all had the experience of reading a page without remembering a word on it. To prevent this, take notes and work in blocks of time with beginnings and ends. When I correct five term papers, I get a break to briefly do something else. After each set, I feel a sense of completion that keeps me from feeling overwhelmed by the stacks of papers and keeps me paying close attention when I'm reading. Take a short time to stretch and walk around when you start losing concentration or you'll waste your time.

When you read a text, Billie Jackson suggests that you try a reading strategy called SQ4Rs (survey, question, read, recite, record, and reflect). First quickly *survey* the headings, bold type, charts, and questions at the back of the chapter to create memory hooks. The main idea of each paragraph is usually in the first sentence. Ask yourself *questions* as you read each section. Answer these questions after you read each section; *recite* the answers out loud to engage your various senses; *record* your key answers in your notebook; and then *reflect* by relating the new information to what you already know. These steps engage your brain, like putting a car in gear.

You might want to take a speed reading workshop to learn how to increase your comprehension as well as speed. To increase your reading speed, read in groups of words, never word—by—word. To practice reading in word groups, swing your eyes from line to line, faster than is easy for you. Practice skimming and scanning your text looking for the main ideas. Don't move your lips or say the words in your mind, because you want to read in sentences.

—Mgamboa, 21, California

I wish someone had told me to read more and told me what kinds of books to read. Also, I wish I had had more direction in high school on how to discover what I wanted to be (major) and what classes I should take. [Use your counselor, career center, college admissions offices, and local librarian to analyze your interests, strengths, and books to assist in your search.]

READ*WRITE*NOW! is a national campaign to encourage students to read 20 minutes a day during the summer break from school. Materials are available from 1-800-USA-LEARN.

Family Involvement Partnership for Learning 600 Independence Ave. SW, Washington, DC 20202-8173

Research Papers
(also read the essay writing section)

When assigned a research paper, find a guidebook in your library, such as Phyllis Cash's *How to Write and Develop a Research Paper* (Prentice Hall), or *The Perfect Term Paper* by Donald Mulrerne (Anchor). Make sure you are absolutely clear on the assignment; I mark down the grade on my students' research papers if they didn't follow the directions, as when they merely describe a problem rather than discuss how to solve it, as assigned. If you're not crystal clear what the teacher wants, ask, and he or she will appreciate your desire to do the task well.

Take research notes on index cards rather than trying to organize notes on various topics on the same page of notebook paper, which is too time consuming. Use only one topic per index card. List on the card the last name of the author (or number your bibliographical sources on a separate page and refer to this number), page number you are quoting, and the theme number. If you want to get fancy, you can use color-coded cards, such as writing theme B information on green cards. For example, if you write a paper on the achievements of the Civil Rights movement, school integration could be theme A, equal opportunity to use public facilities like drinking fountains could be theme B, and so on. A card might look like this:

When finished with all your reading and note taking, divide the cards into theme piles, in the order you'll write about them. Then organize the first topic cards into an order that makes sense to you, type from them one by one, and continue on to the second theme. You may decide to move cards into different themes where they fit better. This is much easier than trying to write from notes with many themes on one page. But if you choose this approach, color code the themes, e.g., underline school integration information in red, and refer only to the red sections as you write that part of your essay. A third technique for note taking is to type notes or scan text directly into your computer and then cut and paste and elaborate. The danger of this method is relying too much on copying rather than analyzing.

After your first draft, read your essay out loud to yourself or a family member, so you can hear where the paper needs more explanation or connection between ideas. My high school composition teacher told us to write essays for someone stupid, so you'll explain the connection between ideas that may seem obvious to you.

It's important to allow time to reread various drafts of a major assignment. You'll be surprised at how differently you see your writing after some distance from it. No professional writer ever turns in a first draft and you shouldn't either. I've gone over this book countless times, making corrections each time, but I'll bet you can still find errors. Please let me know.

Internet encyclopedias:
http://www.yahoo.com/refer-
ence/enclyclopedia

Maps, search engines, Library of
Congress, public libraries online:
http://www.slip.net/~scmetro/for
about.htm

(see Parent Involvement
resource list)

Teachers

The most difficult challenge that I face is grades and teachers. I think that I don't give teachers the respect they deserve. I really need to be more positive about my relationship with teachers. My grades keep going downhill and I think it's because of my lack of respect for my teachers. [Linnea adds, "I see them get torn apart every day."]

I'm trying to be polite to my teachers. I now always say thank you and please. I go in before and after school to my classrooms and just visit with my teachers. I think that if I get to know them they will understand me and I will understand them, which lets us know what each other's expectations are. Also, if you get to know your teachers, when they are lecturing, it is not so boring! Surprisingly I'm more interested in what they have to say because I know them as people, not just a teachers. Especially if you really dislike a teacher, it will help immensely to get to know them as a friend/person and not as an authority figure.

—Tiffany, 16, California

College students I surveyed report that their teachers had the biggest impact on high school success, followed by their parents and friends. Coaches were especially influential for athletes who felt inspired, challenged, and supported. Ken reports his coach taught him, "If I try my hardest in school and running, no matter how I do, I will succeed in the long run." Stay after class to talk to your teachers and let them know your interests and problems. Most teachers are genuinely interested in helping their students.

As a teacher, I do pay more attention and give the benefit of a doubt in grading students who talk to me about their goals for the course, let me know they're interested, and speak up in class. If a subject is difficult for you, stay after class to get more explanation or find a tutor. Don't wait to do this until you feel discouraged and left behind.

To get along well with teachers, college students' main advice is to respect them. Nod when you agree, ask questions, and participate. If you disagree, discuss it after class "so they don't feel their power is threatened." An argument that "uses logic works far better than excuses," Michael said, and "They don't like you to talk when they're talking."

You will probably need letters of recommendation for colleges or jobs. It's especially important to get to know your advisor/counselor as he or she can be supportive throughout your high school years. Advisors usually have many advisees and only have time to give special attention to the ones who make the effort to talk with them. Check in with your counselor at least once a semester.

—Jeff, 15, California

Some overbearing teachers can't teach very well and don't care about their students' problems because they have tenure and expect you to dedicate your life to their class. Take up an alternative hobby that relaxes you and relieves your overstressed mind. Don't let yourself get intimidated by teachers. There's nothing you can do to fight them and if you do, you only get into trouble.

—Olivia, 15, California

So many kids would expand their whole being in school, but some teachers just stifle everything wonderful about us. My history teacher right now is giving a disgustingly awful lecture. Freedom of speech shouldn't end when you go to school. Every day you sit biting your tongue when you want to say what you think.

—Sara, 22, Missouri

Brown-nose, get on their good side, tell them what they want to hear. Some will up your grade if they see you as an enthusiastic and participating student, so give them what they want, and you are more likely to get what you want (assuming you want the grade). It sounds cynical (and it is) but it can work.

—Rebecca, 25, California

Don't expend too much energy getting angry at bad teachers. There are far too many of them, but when you leave high school they become bad professors and bad bosses. So learn now as much as you can in spite of them. And if you find good teachers, do everything you can to milk them for all they're worth. If you can, find a teacher who can be your mentor, someone you can trust and talk to. I think this is the most valuable friend you can have in school.

Test-Taking Strategies

If I can't do it myself, then what's the point? was my attitude and that hurt my grades. My advice is if you need help with school, get it.
—**Shabba, 17, California**

Never cram. Learn the material as you go. Pretend you're reviewing for a test every week and when you find things you don't understand or aren't clear about, get your questions answered right away.
—**Corina, 19, Oregon**

How to Ace Your Tests

◆ When studying for a test, quiz yourself on questions you think might be on the test. Find out as much as you can about the form of the examination. Will it be essay or multiple choice?

◆ Study with small groups, take turns quizzing each other, as the best way to learn is to teach.

◆ At test time, start with deep breaths from your lower stomach area. Quickly imagine the most calming place for you, such as a beach, a lake, a mountain top, or a sand dune. Look at the teacher for a moment to focus and then get started. Read the instructions carefully. Tilt the paper and sit up so you're not bending over in a tired position.

◆ During the test, if you feel anxious, take deep breaths, visualize getting your test back with an "A," imagine an invisible wise person helping you, or use positive self-talk. Tense and relax your feet, ankles, calves, and other muscles.

◆ Look over the test, making sure you understand all the directions and scoring. Read the directions twice before you begin. Answer the easy questions and the ones with most points first. Budget your time, checking your watch frequently.

◆ Your first idea about a right answer is probably the best one.

◆ Write as legibly as you can—a felt tip pen helps, so the teacher won't have to struggle reading your essay answers.

In true and false tests, words like "all" and "always" often flag a "false" statement. There are usually more true than false questions on a test. Longer statements are likely to be correct.

For multiple choice questions, answer every question, marking ones you're not sure about to recheck if you have time. In choosing the right answer, eliminate the answers you know are wrong. Read multiple choice statements, noting whether each is a "T" or an "F," so that you can respond to an "all the above" choice. When two out of four choices are opposites, pick one of the two as the best guess. Often, B, C, and D answers are the best guesses in five-answer multiple choice questions. Avoid pairs, so if question 5 is B, avoid B in question 6 unless you know it's the right answer. "All the above" and the longest answers are usually good guesses. If two out of four choices are almost the same, pick the longest of the two. The best strategy, of course, is to consistently review the course material so you don't have to guess. Your work will open up options to good colleges.

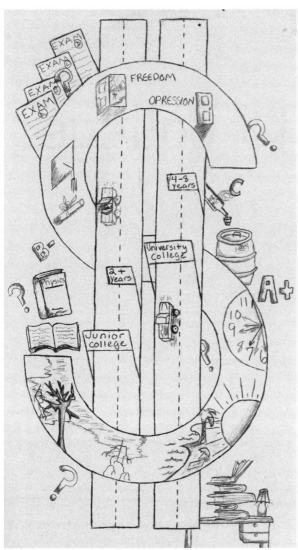

Joanna Ledyard

Chapter 9

Topics
(This chapter is arranged chronologically rather than alphabetically.)

College

Why Go to College?

What if you are in high school and you hear all this stuff about colleges or other things, but you don't know what you plan to do with your life?

[Read the career choice section in Chapter 10, job shadow, visit colleges, talk to your school counselor, and check out the career choice books listed at the end of this section. Keep your options open by taking college preparation classes in a variety of areas. See Ted's quote below.]

—**Jason, 15, Ohio**

A 1992 Gallup poll asked teens about their plans after high school: 68 percent plan to attend college full-time, 18 percent plan to attend college part-time, only five percent want to work full-time, and five percent intend to join the armed services. In a 1996 national poll, 67 percent of girls and 54 percent of boys said they plan to go to a four-year college. Despite the large majority of teens with college aspirations, only 23 percent of adults ages 25 to 34 had earned a college degree in 1992 (87 percent had graduated from high school).

About two of three high school graduates go on to higher education; of about 12 million college students, women are the majority of undergraduates. More than half of students work for pay and about five million students receive financial aid. Surveys indicate that many students feel overwhelmed by all their tasks, partly explaining the alarming fact that less than a quarter of students who enter college finish their degree. Pay attention to this statistic and plan how to complete your education, a major advantage in a tight job market—plus, it expands many horizons, socially and intellectually.

—Michelle, 19, Georgia

What worked for me was realizing that even though I didn't know consciously what I wanted to do—I didn't even know that I wanted to go to college until my junior year—I should keep my options open by doing the best I could. That gave me the incentive to do as well as I could, even though I had no specific goal to achieve.

—Lynn, 20, California

I went straight to college after high school. I highly recommend this because my friends who got jobs after high school, intending only to take one year off, got used to the money coming in and didn't want to go to college anymore.

—Ted, 25, California

If you're finishing high school and trying to decide what to do with your life, don't freak out. You're probably going to live a long time, so don't feel pressured into having to go to college right now or decide what your major will be. Some of us can use some time to think, to work, to earn some money, and to explore what we want to do with our lives without feeling so pressured.

If you do know that college is where it's at for you, then spend time talking to people you respect: cool teachers, friends of your parents, or people in the community who have interesting careers. Ask them how they decided what they wanted to do with their lives. There are lots of good books in the library about career choices that might have some helpful suggestions, and talk to your high school or local college career counselors.

If you're having trouble making up your mind, listen to your heart because often when your mind can't decide, your heart simply knows. That's not to say you shouldn't be practical in your career choice, but it also needs to be something you're going to enjoy. Even after you've made a choice, if you can see you made a mistake, don't be afraid to stop and change directions. If there is anything worse than making mistakes, it's knowing you're about to screw up, and then going ahead anyhow.

—James, 29, California

Attending college has helped me to gain a broader perspective of my place in the world. It helped me understand that I am not just a citizen of the small town where I attended high school, but that as a citizen of the world, the things I do have an impact on others around me. Also I have learned about my African heritage, which gives me a totally different outlook on life. I believe that it is important for high school students to have role models who are in college, or work in a higher education setting. I found role models are very important in the success of students.

Your Career and Major Choices

College Board. *The College Board Guide to 150 Popular College Majors.* NY: College Board, 1992.

Mindy Gingham and Sandy Stryker. *Career Choices: A Guide for Teens and Young Adults—Who Am I? What Do I Want? How Do I Get It?* Santa Barbara, CA: Academic Innovations, 1990. 1994 workbook, *Career Choices and Changes.*

Joyce Mitchell. *The College Board Guide to Jobs and Career Planning.* NY: The College Board, 1994.

Fred Rowe. *The Career Connection for College Education: A Guide to College Majors and Related Career Opportunities.* Indianapolis, IN, 1994.

Harlow Unger. *But What If I Don't Want to Go To College?: A Guide to Successful Careers Through Alternative Education.* NY: Facts on File, 1992.

How to Get Into College

Colleges really do look at the classes you take, so take the hardest ones you think you can handle. Get to know teachers because they can write good recommendations and are more willing to provide academic help when they know you personally. Do extracurricular activities because those make high school fun, help you organize your time, and make colleges rate you higher because of your leadership and involvement.
—Julie, 20, New Jersey

Don't wait until you're a senior to prepare for college admission. College students suggest that you:

* Take the PSAT and SAT early, after studying.

* Visit colleges you're interested in and learn about them.

* Talk to counselors to make sure you're taking the classes required for college admission. Get their help with your college applications.

* Apply to many colleges, even if you don't think you can get in. (My students picked their college because of location, atmosphere, academic programs, and friends.)

* Learn how to prepare financially for college, including financial aid possibilities, and how to apply for scholarships.

Trust your abilities. "Nobody thought I was college material, but here I am, a college junior," Russell notes. Most students advise going right to college after high school graduation because many of their friends who took time off to work never went back. Some feel a community college is a good transition, inexpensive, and allows you time to mature and to figure out a major. Others think it's important to leave home because "you learn so much living away from your parents and friends."

College Entrance Tests

Take the PSAT [Preliminary Scholastic Aptitude Test] as a sophomore to see what you need to study. The Scholastic Assessment Test (SAT) has two parts. SAT I tests general verbal and mathematical intellectual abilities. SAT II subject tests cover specific subject areas: Literature, American History, Biology, Spanish, and Mathematics. You may take up to three subject tests on one test date.

Take workshops and study with guidebooks or computer study programs before taking the test so that you know what type of questions to expect and build your knowledge of vocabulary and math formulas. You may take the SAT more than once, but previous scores are reported. You may cancel your score on the day of a test by telling the test supervisor. A fraction of a point is subtracted for every wrong answer (but not for a question left blank) to discourage guessing. If you can eliminate answers you know are wrong on a multiple-choice question, it's a good idea to guess at the correct answer. (See the test taking section in Chapter 8.)

The Enhanced ACT Assessment has four tests: English, Mathematics, Reading, and Science Reasoning. All questions are multiple-choice and there is no penalty for guessing. Please do thorough preparation for these tests as good scores will help you get accepted to the college of your choice.

—Shelley, 22, Massachusetts

You can take the PSAT as a diagnostic tool for determining how you will score on the actual test. There are also preparation books and courses such as the Princeton review. I did participate in one of those courses and found it very helpful. I feel that my score was probably higher as a result of taking the course; however, had I not somehow picked up a math phobia during high school, I believe I would have done better on the math section.

Some colleges consider samples of your written work, research, or art work as part of your admissions portfolio, so find out if the schools you are applying to will accept submissions like that. I submitted a chemistry research paper I wrote to Wesleyan. I applied there as a biology major, whereas I applied elsewhere as a liberal arts major. Obviously, what you submit should be relevant to the image you are portraying to the school in terms of your essay answers, etc. I did not get into Wesleyan. I have no idea if it had anything to do with this "biology" approach; however, in hindsight, I would not have submitted the paper. It was really just a regurgitation of some stuff I read, and if you submit something, it should be really groundbreaking and include a lot of your own ideas.

Many colleges have specialty programs you can apply for as well. The way most work is the school will still consider you even if you do not get accepted into the special program, so there is no need to think that this might hurt your chances. Smith has a STRIDE program, for example, for freshmen who are good students to get paid for doing research with a professor. Students should definitely look into these kinds of opportunities when applying, because they can really make or break your collegiate experience.

Also, early decision is great for students who know what they want. [A binding early admissions program requires any student who applies early—usually by November 1—to promise to attend that school if admitted. Some colleges have nonbinding early admissions. Colleges with binding policies send each other the names of the students who accept early admission to make sure they keep their agreement. Some students are afraid they will lose out on financial aid if they don't apply early. However, some admissions officers say early decision forces students to decide too early in their senior year.] It is likely that you will get in on early decision, you know much earlier, and don't have to deal with all the stress of applying to many schools.

But for those who don't know (and most won't), make sure their parents don't get them all in tizzy about the whole thing. It is a big deal and a serious deal and all that, but transferring is common, and easy, so there is no need to make the decision out to be life or death. It is only final if you decide it is final.

—Seth, 21, Virginia

Getting into the Ivy League requires demonstrating you have multiple talents and have been a leader in everything you have done. To get into a state university in your own state is easier. Just have good grades, a decent SAT or ACT, and say something intelligent for the essay.

—Kieran, 23, Maryland

To get accepted, for me it was grades, SAT scores (take a prep class, they give such good tips!!!!), essay (have a LOT of people like your English teacher and your mom proofread it!), and a good interview (there's lots of good books on how to do good interviewing). Also, connections help a lot of people get in—if your teacher who writes your recommendation went to the school, if your guidance counselor did, etc.

To select a college, look at the overall student body; are there lots of students who share your interests? Is this a place where you can feel comfortable? Are you going to be one of the only black-gay-liberal-conservative-religious-Jewish-nerdy-whatever students on the campus? The quality of the faculty. The location. Size—how much assertiveness do you have to handle a large place where it takes lots of effort to get the attention you need? Visit and stay two days or more if possible, and stay with a student. Read a lot of DIFFERENT college guides to get a complete picture.

—Marge, 24, California

Pay attention in class. Don't talk to your friends in class. Apply to colleges and take the SAT even if your counselors tell you not to.

—Louis, 25, Colorado

Learn how to take a test. The college entrance exams measure your ability to manage your time and take an exam, not necessarily what you know.

Getting into College

SAT, College Board Admission Testing
Program
Box 592
Princeton, NJ 08541

ACT, American College Testing
Program
P.O. Box 168
Iowa City, IA 52243

The Education Today College Guide.
Educational Publishing Group. 1-800-
248-EDUC

Careers and Colleges Magazine
989 Ave. of the Americas
New York, NY 10018
(designed to give high school seniors
and juniors information about college
and career choices)

U.S. Dept. of Education. *Preparing
Your Child for College, A Resource
Book for Parents.* (free)
1-800-USA-LEARN

Sarah McGinty. *Writing Your College
Application Essay.* NY: The College
Board, 1991.

Marianne Ragins. *Winning
Scholarships for College: An Insider's
Guide.* NY: Henry Holt, 1994.
(suggestions for test-taking, essay
writing, interviewing, and applications)

How to Select a College

The most difficult challenge I faced as a teen was deciding what college to apply to. The whole senior year is one of the most stressful times for teens. It makes them realize that they are finally on their way to becoming adults. During my senior year, I have worked harder than ever. My grades have gone up, my electives are broader, and my attitude for life has become real. It's hard to choose what college to go to, and to get accepted. I was one of those students who blew off their grades until the end of the junior year when I realized anyone could get an A, so right away my grades became A's and B's.

I am applying to five colleges, and of those five, I might be accepted to one. It's unfortunate now that I look back and see all the time I was lazy. Now the hard thing is to go to college and be accepted, and choose my career, something I will do day after day for the rest of my life. [People change jobs five or six times and learn new skills.]

—Adriana, 17, Texas

Some students prefer to attend their local community college because tuition and other expenses are lower. The estimated average tuition is $1,099 a year, compared to an average of $2,365 for four-year colleges (1993-1994). Some students want to sharpen academic skills in smaller classes or get help figuring out what they want to study. Community colleges usually have "articulation programs" with nearby four-year colleges that specifically prepare students for

College • 405

acceptance. Some want a two-year technical training course or certificate program to learn drafting or to become a paralegal or nurse, etc.

—Tina, 17, Washington

I found as much information as possible about the colleges and made a list of pros and cons for each college and the factors that were important to me in a college. My advice is to get information from many colleges, go to visit many colleges, and ask questions.

—Liffy, 18, New York

I've heard numerous tales of students visiting colleges during the summer or vacation periods. But visiting when there are no students on campus and no ordinary activities is practically useless. All campuses look like lovely parks when vacant, but it's the student life that makes a college's real identity.

—Scooter, 19, New York

I made a list of what I was looking for, i.e., a very competitive school, a school with a Jewish population, a city school where I could have the opportunity to work in city politics, price range, a 500-mile radius from my parents' house, and a handicap accessible school. With the list I looked through the Barron's Book of Colleges and was able to narrow it down to three schools. I made sure one was a safe school where I knew I would get in with the grades I had.

—Michelle, 19, Georgia

First, I decided I wanted to go in-state because of lower tuition and state grants. Then I looked at factors such as cost, reputation, majors, surroundings, and the like. Whenever I found a school that I thought fit my needs, I applied to it.

—Lester, 19, Pennsylvania

I applied to 11 colleges, mainly because I did not know where I wanted to go or what I wanted to do. I got rejected at three, got deferred one semester at two, and got accepted at the remaining six. I did not want to go to college a semester late. And I decided that a private education would be a much better investment in my future, as well as a guaranteed graduation in four years instead of the average five years. I narrowed it down to two universities. I visited both schools and waited for financial aid awards, but what it came down to was my impressions during my visit (the type of students, energy, and dedication) and the reputation of the school.

College Rating Books

College Board's College Handbook. NY: College Board, recent edition.

Editors of the *U.S. News and World Report. America's Best Colleges.* Yearly edition (includes entrance requirements, expenses, financial aid, and popular majors)
Money magazine, *Time,* and *Newsweek* also publish guidebooks.

Lisa Birnbach. *New and Improved College Book.* NY: Simon and Schuster, 1992.

Jack Gourman. *The Gourman Report—Undergraduate: A Rating of Undergraduate Programs in American and International Universities.* Los Angeles: National Education Standards, recent edition.

Edward B. Fiske. *The Fiske Guide to Colleges.* NY: Times Books, Random House, recent edition

Peterson's Guide to Four-Year Colleges. Princeton, NJ: Peterson's, recent edition.

Frederick Rugg, ed. *Rugg's Recommendations on the Colleges.* East Longmeadow, MA: Celecom, recent edition.

Lucia Solorzano. *Barron's 300.* Hauppauge, NY: Barron's Educational Series, recent edition.

Community Colleges

American Association of Community Colleges
National Center for Higher Education
One Dupont Circle, NW, Suite 410
Washington, DC 20036-1176

ERIC Clearinghouse for Community Colleges
UCLA, 3051 Moore Hall
405 Hilgard Ave.
Los Angeles, CA 90024-1521

Financing College

To acquire student loans, parents need to file their federal income tax VERY early and the student must have his/her Free Application for Financial Aid completed and sent early also. Loans are not the only option. With today's costs of education, if they relied only on loans, it would take forever to pay them all back after graduation. There are alternatives, but most students and parents are not even aware of all the available free money out there for them. The American Association of Fund-Raising Councils reported that private foundations, corporations, and charitable organizations gave away over $75 billion dollars through grants, awards, fellowships, and private gifts in 1994.
—Peter Doelger, Ohio

(conducts computer searches: 76345.2771@compuserve.com)

Start your scholarship search in the 10th grade so you can satisfy requirements such as volunteer work for nursing or science courses for engineering students. Some parents are able to establish savings accounts for their children's college education, such as investing in tax-free EE series savings bonds, stocks, bonds, or money market certificates. Just a little money saved every month earns significant interest over the years.

College costs are growing much faster than the average family's income. The average annual cost in 1995, including room, board, and fees, was $9,285 for public and $19,762 for private colleges (the College Board). Expenses include tuition and student fees, textbooks and lab fees, room and board, transportation, and medical care. Personal expenses include clothing, insurance, transportation, phone, laundry, and entertainment. You might check with college students you know to see what else to add to the list of expenses. Budget these costs against your money supply, which may include your paycheck, parents, savings, scholarships, work study grants, and loans.

The cost of four years of college can be $50,000 for public colleges and $120,000 for the most expensive private schools. A study of young men who attended colleges of varying quality found those who graduated from the top 20 percent best colleges earned about 20 percent more than those from the bottom 20 percent; there were no significant differences between public and private colleges, according to a study by Dan Black, et al., at the University of Western Ontario.

Scholarships and grants do not have to be repaid and fall into two categories. Need-based programs evaluate your family's financial resources, while merit-based programs are based on grades, athletic or artistic abilities, ethnic group, community involvement, etc. Don't assume your parents earn too much money for you to apply. Develop your talents so that you will stand out through your athletic, musical, dramatic, or other achievements.

Sources of financial aid include federal and state governments, colleges and universities, and private organizations such as unions, businesses, foundations, service organizations, and churches. Call the federal government 800 number listed in the resource section, your state higher education agency in your state capitol, and college financial aid offices. Check out local sources, including service clubs and businesses, where your chances are better than in national competitions for scholarships. See if your parents' employers or unions provide scholarships. Low-income students should check out Upward Bound and Educational Talent Search programs for high school students, funded by the federal government.

High schools often provide financial aid workshops and counselors can help you get started in the application process. Financial aid directories should be available in your high school or local library—ask librarians for assistance. Computer software lists scholarship sources, as well as information about colleges and careers; for example, the College Board program called *Expan* includes *Fund Finder*. With over 3,000 colleges, it's worth a search to look for compatible schools you may not know about, suggests student advisor Diane Dickerson in Boston. Private financial aid companies will search for aid sources for you but may not deliver much in return for your fee. You still have to apply directly to the source of funding.

Approximately $30.8 billion was granted to college students in 1994, about half the total amount spent by students on their college education. About 30 percent of undergraduates receive some federal government aid. Borrowing for a college education increased from $16 billion in 1992 to about $27 billion in 1995, according to the Education Resources Institute in Boston. Almost 50 percent of students (about 15 million) use student loans. The increase is partly due to changes in federal law in 1993 making more students eligible to borrow more money under the federal guaranteed-loan program. The average student graduates with $11,000 in debts.

Financial aid applications are available from high school and college financial aid offices; the sooner you turn them in the better. Request financial aid information from the colleges you are considering.

To be considered for federal financial aid, you must file the Free Application for Federal Student Aid and provide a copy of your parents' tax return and your social security number. Your family's financial need is determined by the difference between what it costs to go to college and what your family can afford to pay. A standard formula calculates your family's financial need based on income, savings and assets, expenses, debts, and number of children. About six weeks after you file your FAFSA, you will receive a Student Aid Report that tells you whether you're eligible for a grant, loan, work-study, or a combination. Send a copy to your college financial aid office. Then apply for scholarships and loans. Keep copies of all documents you send in case they get lost.

Five Federal Aid Programs

✪ Pell Grants: All students in need were eligible for up to $2,300 a year in 1994. (1-301-722-9200)

✪ Supplemental Educational Opportunity Grants: for students with exceptional financial needs, up to $4,000 a year. This grant is usually awarded in combination with a loan or work-study.

✪ Guaranteed Student Loans: The government backs up loans from private lenders such as a bank and pays the interest while you're in school full-time. The government also provides unsubsidized Stafford Loans, not based on need, and does not pay the interest while you're in school.

✪ Perkins Student Loan Program: Low-interest loans of up to $3,000 a year can be partially or fully canceled if you teach in certain schools after graduation. These loans are hard to get, as they are for students with "exceptional financial need," like single mothers. There are also special federal loans for students going into health care and the military provides some educational benefits.

✪ College Work-Study: The government pays part of your wages for working part-time for your college.

Keep in close contact with your school counselor and the financial aid offices of the colleges where you apply. Don't take these programs for granted as Republican efforts to balance the budget in 1996 proposed eliminating the student loan program and freezing Pell Grants without consideration of enrollment increases.

—Brad Glanville, Ph.D., professor, author of tax books and *How to Raise Money-Smart Kids* (in press)

Let's say you're 15 and want to go to college in four years. Well, the bad news is that unless mom and dad started an investment plan for you when you were much younger, you are in a tough situation. Had they opened up an aggressive growth mutual fund when you were five and put $100 a month into the fund, you would have $25,000 (to possibly $60,000) in that fund to withdraw for college expenses. Of that money, $12,000 would be available for your education without taxes, as the amount originally invested.
But if that's not the case, and mom and dad don't have the money in hand to put you through college, you can still take action. Aggressive investing is too late now, because you need to have six to 10 years for investing if you intend to ride out the frequent dips and slips of the stock market. Instead, you and your parents can set up a frequent savings plan, a monthly contribution that will accumulate in the most tax-advantaged way. For example, one or both parents may be able to start a 401k or a 403(b) tax-deferred retirement plan. If so, they can have money withdrawn from their paychecks—before they pay taxes on it—and have an investment firm place the money into a relatively low risk investment,

such as bonds or income mutual funds. When it's time for you to go to college, money can be borrowed from the retirement plan in the form of a low cost loan. Alternatively, the money can be drawn out, the taxes on it paid, and the money left could be used to send you to college.

If you have a source of earned income (like house cleaning or a paper route) you might consider placing the money into a tax-deferred Individual Retirement Account (IRA). This would have been a smart idea when you were six or seven, because it would have grown tax free. The down side to the IRA is a 10 percent penalty applied to the money when you withdraw and you must also pay taxes on the withdrawal. Still, many IRAs grow very fast because of the delayed taxes.

Another strategy your parents can use is the "second mortgage." If your parents' house is worth more than the mortgage (the "first") they now have, it is possible to borrow that extra money out by taking out a second mortgage, often called a home equity loan. The interest on these loans can be tax deductible for your parents. Check the yellow pages for a college investment planner in your area.

Financial Aid Organizations

To determine your financial need, write to need-assessment services such as:
American College Testing Program
Box 168, Iowa City, Iowa 52243

College Scholarship Service
Box 6300, Princeton, NJ 08541

1-800-4-FED-AID answers questions about federal government financial aid. Ask for a free copy of *The Student Guide*. Call 800-433-3243 for a FAFSA, the application for federal student aid.

ConSern Loan Program
1-800-767-5626
(administers federal and private loans)

Nelli Mae (New England Loan and Marketing) 1-800-634-9308
info@nelliemae.orghttp://www.nelliemae.org
(This non-profit organization assists students in getting private and government grants and loans. Send for their free pamphlet, *Steps to Success: A Comprehensive Guide to Preparing and Paying for College*. It includes a useful reference section and timelines to follow.)

Sallie Mae (Student Loan Marketing Association) 1-800-831-LOAN
(The largest servicer of federally guaranteed college loans has a Signature Student Loan Program to allow students to combine their loans with a single lending agency.)

Scholarship Bank 1-800-322-4432

Financial Aid Books and Pamphlets

How Low-Income Families Pay for College, order number ED 260 673 from ERIC Document Service, 1-800-227-3742.

Higher Education Opportunities for Minorities and Women: Annotated Selections (Washington, DC: U.S. Government Printing Office).

John Bear and Mariah Bear. *Finding Money for College*. Berkeley, CA: Ten Speed Press, 1993.

Laurie Blum. *Free Money for College*. NY: Facts on File, 1992.

Kalman Chany. *Paying for College*. Princeton, NJ: Peterson's, 1996.

College Scholarship Service. *College Costs and Financial Aid Handbook*. NY: The College Board, recent edition.

Willis Johnson. *The Big Book of Minority Opportunities*. Garrett Park, MD: Garrett Park Press, 1995.

Anna Leider. *College Loans from Uncle Sam. Don't Miss Out*. Alexandria, VA: Octameron, 1992.

Paying Less for College: The Complete Guide to Over $35 Billion in Financial Aid. Princeton, NJ: Peterson's, most recent edition.
(a guide to over 1,600 colleges, plus other funding sources) See also, *Peterson's Top 1,000 Private Sources of Financial Aid*.

Cynthia Ruis McKee and Phillip McKee. *You Can Go to College Almost for Free*. NY: Hearst Books, 1993.

John Schwartz. *College Scholarships and Financial Aid*. NY: Macmillan, 1995.

Gail Ann Schlatter and R. David Weber. *Directory of Financial Aids for Women*. San Carlos, CA: Reference Service Press, 1993.

Preparing for Freshman Year

Take campus tours and go to any special Senior Days and other orientation to the campus programs offered at your schools of choice. To incoming freshmen I would have to say go to class. It is so easy to skip classes because, especially if it is a large lecture, they NEVER take attendance.

For what to bring to college, it really depends on where you live. Take a tour of the dorms before you move in to get an idea of the room size. Deciding what to bring also depends on where you go to school. If you go to a school far away from home, I would say bring just about as much as you can: all your clothes, dorm refrigerator, stereo, and things to make it seem more like home. If you are going close to home, then you probably don't need as much. Your goal should be to make it as homey as possible.

The best way to meet people on campus is to live on campus. The dorms are a great way to meet people, and they offer special activities. My dorm floor has activities like an intramural flag football team and a floor slumber party. Whenever you go out to the lobby, there is always at least one person out there to talk to.

Another way to meet people is to join organizations. Just as in high school, it is a great way to find a place on campus where you belong. My school has an annual Activities Carnival where all the clubs and organizations set up tables and students can look at them, and sign up. [Look for these tables during registration.]

To select classes, you have a faculty advisor in your major who will help. The best thing as a freshman is to take as many of the basics as possible, the classes that most majors require. That way if you change your major two years down the road, all you need is that major's specific classes. Depending on how the school works, it is probably best to take no more than 15 credit hours your first semester. You will be adjusting to campus life, away from your parents, and there are a lot of activities in the fall.

—Dawn, 18, Kansas

A 1995 survey of more than 2,500 colleges by American College Testing found that one-third of freshmen did not return for their sophomore year, the highest rate since the survey began in 1983. Another 1995 survey by the American Association of State Colleges and Universities reported that its members graduate only 40 percent of their freshmen after six years. Some colleges provide freshmen courses on how to survive college: For example, the University of Maryland offers "The Student and the University." I advise taking such a course and reading success guides.

The Difference Between High School and College

—Karyn Buhler, college student, Colorado

☆ In college, you can blow off studying by writing lists like this.

☆ In high school, you can't go out to lunch because it's not allowed. In college, you can't go out to lunch because you can't afford it.

☆ In college, when you miss a class (or two or three), you don't need a note from your parents saying you were skip... uh, sick that day.

☆ In high school, it never took three or four weeks to get money from mom and dad.

☆ In college, your dad doesn't pay for dates.

☆ In college, there's no one to tell you not to eat pizza three meals a day.

☆ It's much more time-consuming to run between classes to that place where you know he/she will be in order to "just happen to bump into him/her."

☆ In college, weekends start on Thursday.

☆ In high school, when the teacher says, "Good morning," you mumble back. In college, when the professor says, "Good morning," you write it down.

☆ In college, any test consists of a larger percentage of your grade than your high school final exams ever did.

☆ In high school, if you screw up you can usually sweet-talk your way out of it. In college, you're lucky to ever talk with the professor.

☆ In high school, you're told what classes to take. In college, you get to choose; that is, as long as the classes don't conflict, you have the prerequisites, the classes aren't closed, and you've paid your tuition.

☆ In high school, you have to live with your parents. In college, you get to live with your friends.

☆ In college, there are no bells or tardy slips.

☆ In high school, you do homework. In college, you study.

☆ No food is allowed in the hall in high school. In college, food must be provided at an event before students will come.

—Timothy, 19, Michigan

My entire first year of college was just a little bit better than a disaster. I graduated from high school with high honors and I had a 3.55 GPA in almost all college prep courses. I had always considered myself a rather intelligent person. When I got to college I experienced the freedom of being away from home and not having somebody looking over my shoulder constantly. There was nobody to tell me to do my homework or to go to class. I really didn't have any direction in life.

I finished the first semester with a 2.07. That was quite a shock after what I had done in high school. The problem was that I wasn't mature enough to notice the warning. I didn't do too much better the second semester. The basic problem was that I was not mature enough to handle the "freedom." I did not have enough self-discipline to make myself do what I needed to do. I just wanted to sit around and slide through. I was having too much fun. I could basically do whatever I wanted with little or no repercussions. It was great, or so I thought.

My life's dream has been to become an officer in the U.S. Army. I am in the ROTC program at Michigan State University. I noticed that I was at risk of not attaining that dream because of my performance that year. Some maturing happened over the summer. I realized more and more that I could accomplish my goal, if I put some effort into it. I started thinking about how I was going to do this. I realized that I just have to work hard. That's one thing that I learned on my high school swim team: You can't accomplish something without hard work. The thing is, I don't think it was the desire to accomplish my goal as much as it was the fact that I realized I had greatly disappointed my parents. I come from a very close family, and it hurt to know that I had let them down. I started applying myself to my classes and taking them seriously. I also became more active in ROTC which gave me a sense of purpose and direction. I finished the first semester of my sophomore year with a 3.1 and a 2.5 cumulative GPA. There's still a lot of room for improvement, but I'm happy.

I think the main thing that should be put in a book for teens is that you can't accomplish anything without hard work. Nothing in this world is handed to you. You also need to have self-confidence. Out in the real world nobody really cares if you make it or not, so you have to care. All you need to have is a dream. If you have one and you work towards accomplishing it, nothing can stop you.

—David, 18, California

When you're in college, you have no parents to go home to, you have no curfew, nothing. You can do what you want, up to a point. That's what hurts me. I take advantage of that and it's hurting me a lot. School isn't going so well. I put off my school work for something else almost all the time. Slowly but surely I'm trying to get on the ball.

—Sonia, 20, California

The most difficult challenge I faced was moving away from home to go to college at age 18. It was scary and confusing. It is a great experience, but I was homesick and scared. What helped me was joining a sorority. It helped me keep busy and I met a lot of nice girls.

—Shelley, 22, Massachusetts

The most important thing I wish I had known before going to college was about STDs. [see Chapter 3] They are common, and so is casual sex at parties and dorm-like environments. Students in general really have no idea what is going on with STDs, but these diseases are often not as serious for men as they are for women. Women should definitely have had a few gynecological examinations before they go to college, so they are not embarrassed to go to the college health service for exams BY THEMSELVES!

Sexually active high-schoolers need to get an AIDS test and be screened for other diseases, like herpes and warts. I know at least four friends who have had warts. Some of the people I know haven't been treated, which is very serious because it can lead to cervical cancer. They can be detected by a pap smear.

The problem is that the vagina is affected by hormone changes that are often caused by stress; thus the kind of stress that one encounters in college is likely to exacerbate these problems. I am willing to bet that a large percentage of college women are suffering with yeast infections or worse and are oblivious to what they need to do for treatment.

Steady, sexually active relationships are common in college and I know three women who got pregnant and had abortions. It is not uncommon at all, and it is a miserable experience to go through. It is also expensive. I am shocked at how little accurate information there is for men and women (especially teens) about these topics. If you were to put some real information in your book you would be doing the young people of the world a great service. Safe sex involves a LOT more than just wearing a condom.

—Rebecca, 25, California

Just before I went to college I read a book called Where There's a Will, There's an A. Great book, I recommend it. It had lots of helpful little tidbits about how to impress teaching assistants and stuff, but mostly its theme was simple. You are able to get A's in college, if you know how to play the game, if you know how to study, if you know how to work smarter—not necessarily harder. If you want to, you can get A's. My first two years in college, I had an average of 3.9 although I was a C student for most of high school.

Success in College Guides

Surviving the Freshman Year. Energeia Publishing (Box 985 Salem, ORE 97308)

Arthur Chickering and Nancy Schlossberg. *How to Get the Most Out of College: A Guide to Succeeding at the College of Your Choice.* Boston: Allyn and Bacon, 1995.

Melinda Dalgarn, ed. *Smart Start.* NY: McGraw-Hill, 1994.

Scott Edelstein. *The Truth About College: How to Survive and Succeed as a Student in the Nineties.* Secaucus, NY: Lyle Stuart, 1991.

Joshua Halberstam. *Acing College: A Professor Tells Students How to Beat the System.* NY: Penguin, 1991.

Greg Gottesman, et al. *College Survival: A Crash Course for Students by Students.* NY: Macmillan, 1996.

Paul Grayson and Philip Meilman. *Beating the College Blues: A Student's Guide to Coping with the Emotional Ups and Downs of College Life.* NY: Facts on File, 1992.

Martin Nemko. *How to Get an Ivy League Education at State University.* NY: Avon Books, 1992.

Where to Live

—Mai, 19, Georgia

Live in a coed floor dorm. That is the best way to get to know the opposite sex. I think I learned a lot from the freshmen experience because I have to deal with the guys who are always around.

—Shelley, 22, Massachusetts

FOOD was one big problem in the dorms, especially since at home I was being fed healthy and low-fat foods. I don't know if I necessarily gained the freshperson 15 pounds; however, my eating habits definitely affected my ability to study and just generally feel good. Because I was eating so poorly, my energy level was very sporadic and so were my moods. This is easy to see in retrospect, although at the time I was totally unaware of how I was being affected by poor nutrition.

In terms of looking for a school, the meal program is definitely something to consider. Try to pick a meal plan that gives you as much flexibility as possible. For example, it may sound good at first to buy the full plan and have meals fixed for you in the dorms all the time, but chances are that after two weeks you will be so sick of the dorm food that stale cereal sounds better. Many schools now offer alternative programs and are even contracting with local restaurants to provide alternative meals. Another drawback of the meal plans is that they often restrict WHERE you can eat, which is a real pain if you take an evening class on the other side of campus, or if the dining hall where you are supposed to eat is a long walk from your dorm. Whether parents and teenagers realize it or not, this will have more of an impact on their student's first two years in college than most other things.

—Steve, 24, Australia

Find some new friends in the city you are moving to through social clubs and other organizations. If you don't like the people you are meeting you don't necessarily have to see them again. This is a somewhat callous way to view things but it works. In my first year of university I must have met several hundred people but ended up with a few good friends who could be relied upon. Take control of your life and decide what you want to do with it.

To be successful in college and get the most out of the activities available to you, review the time management strategies in Chapter 8 and stress management techniques in Chapter 2. If you schedule daily time for studying, go to class regularly, concentrate, and stay away from the heavy drinkers and dopers, you'll have time to play. Interaction with new people and activities is a fun and vital part of your college education.

Chapter 10

Heather Neumann

Work and Money

Living on Your Own

Managing your Money

Work

Reading about how to earn and manage money may not be as interesting as sex and love, but a job takes up more time than those other activities once you complete your schooling. You may refer to some of these sections in the future, after you leave home. If you are looking for a job or want to buy a car, the information in those sections will be useful, and it's smart to start investing now.

Now is also a good time to check out different careers through job shadowing or summer jobs to give you a better idea of what college to go to and what to major in when you're admitted. Let's say you think you'd like to be a vet. A summer job or volunteer work might reveal that you get bored sterilizing cats and dogs and giving them shots and want to check out being a pharmacist or a biologist. This kind of work experience looks terrific on your college applications, as well as adding jingle to your pocket.

Living on Your Own

Decision Making

The most difficult challenge in all my teenage years was when I had to decide whether I should leave school during the final exams of my junior year to go see my grandmother who was very sick. My parents gave me the choice of staying to take my tests or leaving with them to go see her. With a lot of hesitation, I decided to take the test, then leave immediately after that. Everything went well on the tests so I got the first flight to Miami to see my grandmother, who had just gotten out of a successful surgery.

I would advise people to weigh the situation and make the best decision in the long run, because usually nobody can help you make tough decisions like mine. I hope you get something from my situation, because I learned how to weigh the good and the bad in the difficult decisions I must make.

—Orlando, 17, Texas

Peter Castle, career counselor, suggests we should note the difference between a bad decision and a bad outcome. We may have no control over the outcome and decisions are calculated risks. Make the best decision possible and know that you did, no matter what the outcome.

Techniques for Decision Making

—Jacqueline R. Sheehan, Ph.D., therapist

A lifeline is one way of looking at influences in your life that affect your decision making. Begin by drawing a horizontal line across a page. At the left end is your birth and at the right end is your present age, as in the lifeline example below. In between, begin to mark places where important influences affected you.

For instance, one young woman noted that at age five she was the only one of five siblings not in school. She remembered thinking that school must be a glorious place to be and couldn't wait to get there. Another influence was her dynamic 6th grade teacher who encouraged her in science and political thought. Yet another influence was the death of a parent and her fear of poverty. Finally, she noted she had made her choice of a college major (political science) based on what important people in her life had told her she was good at, rather than by making a more comprehensive assessment of herself. By seeing the graphic portrayal of the importance of the opinions of others, she was able to put more emphasis on her personal needs.

Example of Elena's Lifeline

year 5	11	18	25
Positive image of school	Influence of teacher	Choice of major	

Decision making is a learned skill, not unlike learning computer programming. What keeps so many of us from actively learning decision making is that there is always an element of risk. Unfortunately, this fear can be so paralyzing for some people that they will decide not to decide, which places them in the even riskier position of passively accepting whatever choices other people may toss their way.

Decision making is, for the most part, a process of choosing between several options. Most decision-making systems are variations on the old system of listing the negatives and positives of a potential option. List as many options as occur to you for a specific decision you are considering. Under each option, list the weighted advantages and disadvantages. Weigh the options in the following manner:

3 = very important
2 = somewhat important
1 = of limited importance

OPTION ONE _____

ADVANTAGES

WEIGHT
1. _____
2. _____
3. _____
total _____

DISADVANTAGES

WEIGHT
1. _____
2. _____
3. _____
total _____

Continue with the next option, giving numerical values to the advantages, then seriously consider the option with the highest points. You can use this ranking system for other purposes as well. In relationships, you can rank your preference on a one to 10 scale, with the person with the strongest preference making the decision, such as what movie to see or where to eat lunch.

—Andy, 18, California

If you don't make a decision, you get the short end of the stick. You get stuck with what's left over.

—Amy, 27, New York

I grew up in a very rural area in the South, in a middle-class family, but with few resources available from my school in terms of learning about careers, sexuality, relationships, etc. It would have been perfectly acceptable for me to choose not to go to college and to get married right after high school. I desperately needed more role models (particularly female) who were accessible or at least visible in my high school years.

My family is an excellent example of the typical "bible belt" in which there wasn't a great deal of openness about drinking, sexuality, and drug use—although all these things were easily accessible to me at a very young age. As a result, I could not go to my parents with any of these issues and, for the most part, found out about them the hard way.

One interesting yet ironic thing about my life is that I was a straight "A" student and graduated second in my class. Because I was considered smart by both my parents and my teachers, it never occurred to them that I could also be experimenting with all the same temptations that every other teenager had. In retrospect, I think I walked a thinner line than most teenagers between success and failure because my authority figures never dreamed of what we were up to most of the time.

My greatest challenge as a young woman was to keep my own focus on my dreams of achieving more than others in my family had achieved. I knew very well what I wanted to be as an adult, but I still had to fight the same desires/passions/reactions of any typical teenager, which could have truly knocked me off track. Though I consider my naive experimentation with alcohol, drugs, and sexuality to be rather typical of any teenager in today's world, I cringe when I consider all the horrible things that could have happened to me.

I constantly reminded myself of what I wanted to achieve in life. I kept diaries in which I wrote about my dreams and I forced myself to refer to them from time to time to see if I was still on track.

One blessing in disguise was my parents were very strict with curfews and with the places I went and the people I could hang out with. I hated their "overbearing" parenting at the time but I realize now that they kept me out of a lot of trouble—although I managed to get into plenty without their knowing.

My advice to those younger is to think very carefully about what it is that you want to get out of your life. Not so much that you need to decide on your career, but decide what steps you must take to reach what you define as happiness. To me this meant that I did not want to have children or to marry until much later in life, perhaps even in my 30s. Therefore, if I chose to be intimate with high school or college boyfriends, then I absolutely had to take steps to prevent any "accidents" from happening. I would urge young people to be very realistic with themselves and take full responsibility for their decisions at an early age.

Food Purchase

Plan your meals for the week and add to your shopping list at the same time. Type out a standard shopping list to duplicate so you won't have to start from scratch each time you make your list. Keep a list on your refrigerator and check it off as you run out of food.

Don't shop when you're hungry because it clouds judgment about food purchases. Look for unit pricing, the cost per ounce or pound. This allows you to compare products in different size packages. Compare unit prices by dividing the cost of the item by the number of units, such as ounces or grams. One item may cost more than another but be a better buy because it contains more.

Read labels, remembering that the greatest quantities of ingredients are listed first. Do you want to pay for mostly water or sugar? Avoid foods with lots of chemicals, food dyes, preservatives, flavor enhancers, salt, and fat. Processed foods cost more and packaging may contain suspect chemicals called phthalates.

Shop at different stores for a while and compare prices for the same items. Check for food coupons in the newspaper.

The Basics for Cooking Quick Gourmet Meals

—Joan Jackson, chef

A quick meal does not necessarily mean a meal of prepared store-bought foods. These foods contain higher amounts of sugars, salts, and fats than their homemade equivalents, and consumers pay the high price of preparation and packaging. It is very satisfying to know that the pantry and freezer are stocked with home-prepared foods, just waiting for final assembly or heating.

1. Maintain a pantry of little jars of condiments to aid in the assembly of a variety of quick, savory dishes. For example, have basil pesto, cilantro pesto, chutney, olives, a few bottled salsas, various types of mustard—including spicy brown, sweet hot, and Dijon style mustards; hoisin sauce (a tangy Asian sauce found in most supermarkets) and soy sauce, as well as an assortment of vinegar, including balsamic, rice vinegar, and both red and white wine vinegar. Also, bottled capers and marinated artichoke hearts will keep for months, and will add the kick needed in many a meal.

2. When cooking rice, prepare at least twice as much as needed, then freeze the remainder in meal-size portions in freezer bags, labeled and dated. Keep an inventory of several types of rice including basmati, wehani (available in most health food stores) or another robust brown rice, and pearl grain white. Rice will reheat in a microwave, in the oven, or on the stovetop. Try reheating some rice in a casserole in the oven with ingredients such as cooked bits of poultry, artichoke hearts, and canned whole tomatoes. Try frozen rice thawed and tossed with Italian salad dressing and crunchy vegetables as a salad.

3. A well-stocked pantry should contain bottles of plain vegetable oil, pure olive oil, peanut oil, and sesame oil. Mix the oils with herbs, garlic cloves, or sun-dried tomatoes. Invest in an assortment of herbs including oregano, basil, bay leaves, dill, tarragon, mint, and cilantro (coriander). Also, have small supplies of the following spices: cinnamon, cloves, nutmeg, cumin, garlic powder, several different curry blends, and ginger.

4. Keep packages of pasta of different shapes on hand for quick hot or cold dishes: fusilli for salads, linguine or penne for hot meals, and small shapes like elbow macaroni or orzo to add to a soup to make into a full meal. When preparing pasta, prepare extra portions and freeze or refrigerate leftovers. Leftover spaghetti, unseasoned, can be added to beaten eggs and vegetables to make a quick frittata [a fluffy omelet]. Cooked pastas are quick to reheat in the microwave, covered, or on the stovetop in a covered pot at low temperature adding of a few tablespoonfuls of water to prevent burning.

5. Soak beans in water to cover and store in the refrigerator several hours or overnight. Then drain off the water, rinse, add enough water to cover the beans again, and bring the beans to a boil. Boil hard for five minutes, then reduce the heat to low and cover. Cook for a few hours, without salt or seasonings, until tender. This can take as little time as 40 minutes for some small beans such as limas, or up to three hours for large red kidney beans. Always cook extra beans and leave some unseasoned. When tender, drain and rinse some of the beans for a bean salad, and season the remainder to taste. Bean salads can be quickly assembled from cooked beans, or in a pinch from canned beans, with a few simple additions.

6. Save the cooking water from simmered meats, poultry, and fresh vegetables with the exception of broccoli, cauliflower, and cabbage which may be too strong tasting. Freeze in ice cube trays, then label and store. These cubes of flavored ice will assist in building the flavors in a dish, whether in gravy, as part of the liquid in cooking rice or pasta, or to create an assortment of quick soups. Add to these any of the frozen cooked beans, pasta or rice, add a few chopped vegetables, and season with herbs, salsa, pesto, or chutneys to taste, and the basic soup is made.

7. With leftover vegetables, pour enough Italian salad dressing over them just to wet all the pieces, and store in a tightly sealed jar in the refrigerator. The vegetables can be eaten as a side dish or appetizer for another meal and will be delicious from marinating in the dressing. Add the leftover vegetables to soup, casseroles, and stews in the last few minutes of cooking, just long enough to heat them through.

8. What to do with leftover meats [vegetarians can use tofu or rice and beans]:
Chop finely and mix with mayonnaise or dressing as a sandwich filling.
Combine them with salsa and cheese and use to fill tortillas. Mix the meats with egg and bread crumbs, capers and chopped celery, and form into patties. Coat with crumbs then fry. Serve hot with fresh fruits and marinated leftover vegetables. Stir them into a pasta sauce and serve hot, over pasta.

Juggling Work and Family in Your Future

—Leanna, 17, California

The most difficult challenge I've faced so far was balancing a part-time job, a full school schedule, and having to do my share at home. My advice is to set your priorities: Work first—play later. I went to work an hour early to do my homework in the break room so I wouldn't have any distractions. When you're off, you're free to do what you want.

The juggling act Leanna experiences now will become more complicated with a career and family of her own. Each semester I ask my college students to write an essay predicting a typical weekday 15 years in the future; their responses consistently reveal a lack of realism. Taryn's is a typical female focus on bending job around family needs:

> *At age 35 I am an attorney in a small law firm. I have two young kids. At 6:30 my husband and I wake. We take turns with breakfast and getting the kids up and dressed. The kids get dropped off at daycare (or school or grandparents). I'm at my office by 8:00. My job affords me a certain amount of flexibility with my schedule which means that I will be able to spend weekday hours with my kids. Sometimes my spouse and I will meet for lunch. We both work until 5:00, then pick up the kids and go home. We have a light meal, made by either of us, and then maybe go to the racquet club for some exercise. A nice hot tub and a few games with the kids and we go home. We relax and go to bed fairly early.*

To contrast Taryn's plans with a Maine high school student who also intends to be a lawyer, Josh plans on living in Boston, being married, and the father of a child. His essay focuses on the kind of law work he will do, his interest in getting involved in politics, and his financial situation.

> *My work consumes most of my time. I sometimes have to work on weekends and late evenings. During the free time I do get, I spend time with my family. The responsibility I have of providing for and protecting them is very scary. This idea may be the reason behind my working so hard. I try to spend every moment I can with them.*

Although they are both lawyers, she works shorter hours than he does and discusses the details of caring for a family. She expects short work hours and flexibility, and he assumes he will have the main money-making responsibility—common gender difference noted in the essays. Similarities are that both genders usually expect both partners to work and be actively involved with their children, although they still see the man as more responsible for work and the woman for the household.

What is unrealistic about this future described by so many of my college students? First, the divorce rate in recent marriages is almost 50 percent, so many will be single parents, remarry, and then form stepfamilies. Second, few jobs allow much flexibility, suburban dwellers may add several hours to their workday by commuting, and many people work much more than 40 hours a week. Millions of children are latchkey kids and many others are cared for in a patchwork child care arrangement, combining babysitter, friend, center, after-school program, etc.

In a 1996 *USA Weekend* magazine survey of 22,653 students, 20 percent of boys and five percent of girls do not expect their future spouse to work ouside the home and 82 percent of girls and 79 percent of boys expect to share child care equally. However, the tasks they do at home now are still segregated, with 52 percent of girls and 27 percent of boys reporting they babysit and 50 percent of girls and 39 percent of boys helping with dinner. Over half who live in a two-parent home see their mothers do more chores than their fathers.

Life Management Courses

Students need information about the strains of "role-overload," as they try to live up to media portrayals of glamorous careers, romantic marriages, and smiling, well-behaved "Gerber babies." Couples who try to be equal partners state they require "continued negotiations and struggle to maintain balance."

Home economics courses have expanded from teaching about foods and clothing to balancing work and family, career planning, and life management skills. The courses are called Life Skills, Life Management, Life Planning, Independent Living, Work and Family Life, or Consumer and Family Studies, depending on the state. They are usually electives taught by home economics teachers. A few states require a family life course and many (over 12) require it as a component in health courses. You might investigate your school's course to prepare you for life after graduation, or propose one if it's not available.

Family Life Courses

☆ In Florida, Life Management Skills is a required high school course.

☆ New York requires a Home and Career Skills course for middle school students and established a Family Life Education Regional Training Network to assist school districts.

☆ Ohio's Work and Family Life Program aims to empower students to cope with their future roles by teaching them how to problem-solve, make decisions, prioritize, set values, plan and reason, as well as how to be an effective parent, cook, and family member. Half the junior high students who take these classes are boys, as well as a third of the high school students.

☆ Utah requires a "Technology, Life, and Careers" course of 7th graders and offers an elective course in most of its high schools titled "Adult Roles and Responsibilities."

☆ Virginia requires a Family Life Education component (K-12) in courses like health, science, and social studies. The program must discuss family living, community relationships, parenting skills, and child abuse.

☆ Texas requires that an elective Life Management Skills course be offered in the 7th or 8th grade.

☆ Tennessee requires Family Life classes in counties with high teen pregnancy rates.

Since 1986, New York State has required all middle school students to take a Home and Career Skills and Introduction to Technology course. I visited Janice Brown's classroom in Harlem where, like the home economics course I took in junior high, students were baking muffins. The difference was boys were doing it too, and students also practice sewing and shop skills, discuss career options, and learn life management skills such as problem solving.

At least they are supposed to have these experiences. But in our unequal system of education, these African American students have no textbooks or instructional videotapes (just occasional handouts), their school has not replaced the shop teacher who retired so they can't use the power tools, and their teacher has 350 students. The yearly career fair has not been held for two years due to lack of funding. About 60 percent of the students will drop out of school. When Ms. Brown taught the same course in a wealthy Long Island school, she had access to all the texts, videos, and other resources she requested.

Renting an Apartment

Find out about rental agreements and leases, security deposits, giving notice to move out, potential rental increases, and if the landlord or renter pays for gas, water, power, and garbage disposal. Make sure you agree with the security deposit policy. Check for adequate storage space, natural light, laundry facilities, parking, soundproof walls and noise level of neighbors, kitchen appliances, deadbolts on doors, neighborhood safety, fire extinguishers, smoke alarms, and closeness of public transportation. Walk by at different times to check noise levels. Talk to other tenants about how responsive the manager is about making repairs.

When you first get the key to your new home, walk through with the landlord and make a list of any problems you see, with both signing it. You have a right to live in a home that is safe and healthy. If you need repairs, call the landlord, then document your requests with a letter, and keep a copy. If the landlord doesn't respond within a reasonable time, write to him or her that you will arrange to have repairs done and subtract the cost from your rent. Keep the receipt from the plumber, or other repair person.

When you are ready to move out, again walk through the place with the landlord and agree in writing on how much of the security deposit will be returned. Communication, cooperation, and maintaining the property are the keys to a good land-lord-tenant relationship. Remember, you'll need a reference letter for your next rental.

Travel Tips

—Kerryn, 20, Australia

I went to South America for a year after school, and that taught me a lot. I changed so much over there that it is hard to say what hasn't changed since high school. The main thing, I suppose, is that I lost my fear of the unknown, my fear of being the only one who doesn't know. Now I'm not afraid to ask and make a fool of myself.

If you get the chance to do it, GO! It is the most life changing experience I have ever had, and it was the perfect time for it. I was so much more ready for university after going away. It changed my whole outlook.

Travel with a guidebook geared for your style. Books published by Lonely Planet Publications, Moon Books, Let's Go! Harvard Student Agencies (St. Martin's Press), and Student Travel Catalog (Council on International Educational Exchange) are useful for student travelers with limited budgets and a desire for locations off the beaten track. Train passes purchased in the U.S. are cheaper. Also get a list of youth hostels and college dorms for inexpensive places to sleep.

Pack very light and leave space to buy clothes and other souvenirs. Take a money belt to wear under your clothes to carry your passport and travelers' checks, or at least take a fanny pack that can't easily be grabbed by a thief. Take a money converter guide or calculator to refer to when you make purchases. Include some quick energy food such as granola bars for the inevitable times when you are hungry but can't find good cheap food. Depending on your destination, you might want to consider carrying a light backpacking water filter. Take earplugs and a scarf to cover your eyes to sleep when it's noisy and bright, and first aid and sewing kits. You might want to ship inexpensive clothes and jewelry home to sell to your acquaintances to help pay for your trip.

When you arrive at a new city, take an orientation bus tour to get a feel for the layout and highlights of the city. Then use your travel book and ask questions of locals and other tourists as you visit places on your own.

When you're older, keep in mind courier air flights that allow you to travel very cheaply in exchange for carrying documents and/or use of your baggage space (Association of Air Travel Couriers, 1-407-582-8320). If you'd like to live in a different country while you're in high school, investigate student exchange programs (see international education section in Chapter 7).

—Brandon, 20, California

On my solo travels through Europe and California, I learned to blend in and do the chameleon thing. Getting to know the locals and their ways is my favorite thing to do. It is not a good idea to upset any of the local customs. Carry yourself in a positive way and do good wherever you go. [Young Americans sometimes get drunk on holidays in other countries. Please don't give your country a bad reputation.]

—Dondi, 21, California

I spent a year in Europe and Argentina. I highly recommend it. I learned more in that year about me and life than I have in four years of college.

—Rebecca, 25, California

I left for London with a student work visa and $500, found a job, a flat, worked for nine months in London, and then traveled all around the continent and managed to have money to send home. It's definitely possible.

American Youth Hostels
733 15th St., NW, Suite 840
Washington, DC 20005

Del Franz, et al., eds. *Work, Study Travel Abroad*. NY: St. Martin's Press latest edition

Managing Your Money

Balancing a Checkbook

Some teens have their own checking account, receive a certain amount from their parents each month and/or their own paycheck, and are responsible for paying all their personal expenses. To keep track of your money, record each check number, date, and amount in your register to keep track of your expenditures. Check the instructions on the back of your bank statement. You might want to use a computer program, such as Quicken, to assist you with your financial record keeping.

—Bob Brandt, accountant

The reason to balance a checkbook is to have an accurate account balance.

1. Enter a checkbook balance in your check register. Go back to the last balance and add all deposits and subtract all check amounts.

2. Subtract from your checkbook balance any monthly service charges, ATM (automatic teller machines) fees, ATM withdrawals not entered, other bank charges, and all automatic withdrawals/payments (some people have their paycheck directly deposited to their bank account) not previously recorded. List all these in your checkbook.

3. Verify your outstanding checks. Mark off in your checkbook register all checks paid by the bank. List on a piece of paper all checks written and not paid by the bank and total this amount.

4. Reconcile balances.

Enter the ending balance as shown on bank statement.	$ _____
Add all deposits which are not shown on statement.	+ _____
SUBTOTAL	= _____
Enter total of outstanding checks from Step 4 above.	
This total should agree with your checkbook balance.	$ _____

If your checkbook does not balance:

Verify that the previous month's statement balanced properly. There might be a check written a couple of months ago that has not cleared. Make sure you include this check in Step 4.

Compare the amount of each item listed on the statement against the amounts entered in your checkbook. Sometimes you may forget to enter a check in your checkbook, or enter the wrong amount.

Review all additions and subtractions for errors as well as balances brought forward in your checkbook register. Determine that all credits shown on the statement are entered in your checkbook. Unless the bank has made an error, the amount from this total should agree with your checkbook balance.

Budgeting

You can start the saving process now. To budget, keep records of what you spend and what you earn. Carry around a small notebook and write down everything you spend earn for a month. Keep track by putting receipts for purchases in labeled envelopes, such as "food," "transportation," and "fun."

When you add the totals, decide if your spending habits match your income, financial goals, and priorities. If you want to save and invest, put aside that money as soon as you receive it. Money tends to burn holes in our pockets, so don't carry more in your wallet than you really want to spend.

A poll of employed high school seniors said they spent their money this way: personal expenses (40 percent), car expenses (16 percent), saving for education (nine percent), long-range savings (seven percent), and six percent on family expenses (The University of Michigan, Institute for Social Research, 1990).

How to Budget

1. List your gross (total) income and net income (what remains after deductions such as income taxes).

2. List your regular expenditures such as lunch money and bus fare and make a second list of infrequent expenses such as auto insurance or holiday gifts. Divide these costs by 12 months and include them in your monthly budget. Also include "mad money" for unexpected expenditures.

Some expenditures you might list in your budget:
food, clothes, transportation, magazines and books, films and CDs, other entertainment, sports, hobbies, grooming (i.e., shampoo), and savings/investments. Remember to separate them by fixed and irregular expenses. Income may include your paycheck, allowance, gifts from relatives, and returns on investments.

3. You might want to set aside money to invest in a savings account, credit union, treasury bills, bonds, or stock market. You are never too young to start investing and enjoying the return on your savings. You can join an investment club and/or consult with a stock broker or financial planner. Some families invest together. Shop around for a financial institution just as you would for any consumer service. Find out about service charges, transaction fees, broker fees, interest rates, and services.

4. If you have a positive balance, the money left over is discretionary income which you can decide how to spend or save.

5. If you have a negative balance, consider where you can cut back on spending and increase earnings.

6. Reevaluate your budget spending plan after a month of keeping track of expenditures and income.

Set up a file drawer with labeled file folders for important documents such as a copy of your birth certificate and social security card, school papers you want to save for future reference, useful tips, and product warranties and receipts. A cardboard box and dividers work fine as a file container. When you need information, you will know exactly where to find it.

Car Purchase

—Vincent Petkus, dealer/shop owner

The majority of car purchases are made on a whim, on the basis of emotions; this error is costly. Take the time to do your homework. Study *Consumer Reports, American Automobile Association reports*, automotive magazines, newspaper advertisements, and interview car owners to determine the best car for your particular needs.

Think about your needs over the next five years (the average duration of a loan). What is a realistic monthly amount you can afford to spend on repaying a car loan, insurance, gas, and repairs? If your family belongs to a credit union, start there to research where you can find the most inexpensive car loan. Auto manufacturers sometimes have special offers with low interest rates.

In a showroom, check the car sticker on the car to see the manufacturer's suggested retail price. Dealers who buy large numbers of cars can probably afford to sell them less expensively than a low-volume dealer. Tell them what you want to pay or what you can pay elsewhere and refuse to play the game of haggling.

Test drive cars you are interested in but beware that some predatory dealers are trained in high pressure tactics to get you to buy a car. The most common tactic is known as the T-O approach, using a series of salespersons and a well-tested sales formula. The first in the chain is the greeter, a friendly person who walks up to you in the showroom and suggests that you test drive a car. Then a sweet-talking floor manager takes over, offers to get you financing for the car, tries to get some commitment on your part, and tries to make you feel guilty if you do not express interest in buying a car from them. The third person is the finance and insurance person, an experienced salesperson who types up a worksheet and attempts to manipulate you into signing. The sales manager is brought in at the end to close the deal.

An alternative to a dealer is a broker who buys cars at discount and sells them cheaper than a dealer because he doesn't have the high overhead of showrooms and multiple salespersons. The broker will charge a percentage or a fee.

If you plan to buy a used car, the older the car and the more mileage, the more likely you are to have problems. Many used car dealers just wash and wax the car before putting it up for sale. Some sellers turn back the odometer. Check for wear on the driver's seat, pedals, and tires if you suspect the odometer reading is inaccurate. Some used car sellers also use tricks like putting oil additives in the engine to keep it from smoking until you change the oil. Get a trusted mechanic to check out a car you are thinking of buying; he or she should be able to tell if the vehicle has been in an accident or has engine problems. Ask why the vehicle is for sale and ask to see repair and service records. Take your time; test drive the car first thing in the morning when it has not been warmed up. Get agreements in writing, including a warranty.

The same principles apply to selecting a shop to repair and service your car. Ask acquaintances about their experiences, call the Bureau of Automotive Repair, the Better Business Bureau, and the American Automobile Association to find out their list of approved mechanics in your area. Get estimates in writing and, when in doubt, get a second opinion as you would in selecting a surgeon. Do service your car every 3,000 miles.

When buying a car, first go to the library and check the vehicle pricing guidebooks and consumer guides. *Consumer Reports'* yearly April issue reports on new and used vehicles; their CD-ROM *Consumer Reports Cars: The Essential Guide* rates new and used cars. Look at car magazines such as *Car and Driver* that provide information about new vehicles and the repair record of recent used vehicles. Research the car's fuel economy, safety features, ratings, and performance. The Auto Club has an inexpensive vehicle pricing service (1-800-621-8851). *Consumer Reports* (1-900-446-0500) and the Used Car Price Line (1-900-737-CARS) also provide car prices for a fee, while lenders and insurance companies may give you the same information for free. Your state Department of Motor Vehicles can tell you about the previous owners of a car and its mileage the last time it was sold.

When you negotiate with a dealer, tell him or her you want to deal with just one person. Start from the dealer's cost rather than the sticker price, be aware of add-on costs such as extended warranties, shop at the end of the month when salespersons are eager to meet their monthly sales quotas, and handle each transaction (trade-in, financing, purchase) separately. Ask about warranties and guarantees. Make sure both the manager and the salesperson sign the sales contract—after you have read every word. For used cars, check with car rental companies and newspaper ads. The seller is responsible for providing a clear title.

James Ross.
How to Buy a Car. NY: St. Martin,
1993.

The American Automobile Association,
a *Car Buyer's Handbook* and brochures
on buying a used car, buying a new
car, and financing a car.

Clothes and Other Purchases

To save money and have fun, organize a party to swap used clothes with your friends. Give each person play money for the clothes they bring. Each person then selects the items he or she wants. If several people want the same item, they can bid for it with their play money, as directed by an auctioneer.

Shop at thrift stores, second-hand stores, and yard sales. (I wore a red ruffled dress to a dance and was told it was the best dress there. I got it for $4 at a used clothing store. I went to the very elegant Black and White Ball, a fund-raiser for the San Francisco Symphony, wearing a black velvet and white taffeta dress I bought at a Junior League thrift store for $16.) Some girls buy clothes in the boys' section of a department store where the prices are lower.

Avoid clothes that need expensive dry cleaning. Read the hang tag on the garment for cleaning instructions. Natural fiber fabrics are cotton, linen, ramie, wool, and silk. Manufactured fibers include rayon, triacetate, nylon, acrylic, and polyester and usually need gentle washing and low temperature drying. Some fabrics have a finish added such as permanent press; remove from the dryer immediately to prevent wrinkles or remove when damp and hang.

Avoid impulsive buying. For a costly purchase, compare prices at various stores and compare brands by doing library research in consumer magazines.

To return an item, place the item in its original package, save sales receipts and warranties, and keep a record of whom you talked with, when, and about what. If you do not get the action you feel is fair, write a letter to the head office of the store, the manufacturer, or the chamber of commerce. Keeping phoning, asking for specific action, and writing letters to document your conversations. If all else fails, you can go to small claims court for amounts under $5,000.

Credit

—Andy, 18, California

Get one credit card when you're young, but only use it in an emergency, like when you're traveling, and pay the bill immediately.

Establish a good credit history, as you will need it to buy a car and later a house. Credit bureaus keep track of your credit history (e.g., TransUnion, Equifax Credit Information, and TRW, Inc.) and sell their reports to businesses. Ways to develop good credit include paying off a car loan and establishing a work record. Another way to build a solid credit history is to use a credit card or store charge card, wisely and make full payments on time to prevent paying interest. Credit cards charge a yearly fee, so shop around for the best deal for you. Find out about initial fees, interest rates, amount of credit available to you, and penalties for late payment. Read the fine print of any credit agreement. Compare the credit cost of an item you want to buy with the cost of a cash purchase.

Consumer Credit Counseling Service
1-800-388-2227
(provides referrals to local
nonprofit credit counselors)

Investing

—Ray, 29, Illinois
Most definitely, I wish someone had taught me about investing. There are so many ways to invest earnings safely. I had to learn this after college and it wasn't even very difficult to master.

—Paula Kamen, author
Ken Kurson started a zine for 20somethings about money. It's called *Green* ($10 a year). The angle is that it gives financial planning advice to people like me, who are usually nauseated by it. It tells you what things like the Dow and no-loads are and has a sense of humor. Ken is a former punk rocker, so the magazine reflects his irreverent style.

Green
245 Eighth Ave.
New York, NY 10011-1607

Newspaper columnist Ann Landers defines maturity as "being able to pass up the fun-for-the time and select the course of action which will pay off later." She believes it is the ability to stick with a project or person through hard times or until it is complete. It means living up to your responsibilities and keeping your word, and is "the ability to make a decision and stand by it."

Investing requires mature, long-term thinking and self-discipline to save money. One of the most important rules for investing is to start early so your money has a chance to grow, like planting a tree in your yard. If you invest $50 a month at eight percent, in five years you will have $3,674. In 25 years, you will have $47,551.

Investors usually aim for a "diversified portfolio," ranging from Treasury Bills, Certificates of Deposit, bonds, money market funds, mutual fund stocks, growth stocks, established large company stocks, and international stocks, to gold and silver coins. Various financial companies offer college savings plans for your parents and grandparents to invest for you. Your family might consider starting a savings program now. The stock market offers the highest returns on investments, if you invest well. Now is a good time to learn about the market, especially if you like legal gambling.

If interested in socially responsible mutual funds (they do not invest in funds which pollute, sell tobacco, have racist and sexist practices, etc.), Morningstar Mutual Funds newsletter rated these four as the best: Pax World, Parnassus, Dreyfus Third Century, and Calvert Social Investment Managed Growth. These ratings change, so do current research and send for the *Financial Planning Handbook for Responsible Investors* from Co-op America (1-800-713-8086). For a list of socially responsible mutual funds, call 1-202-872-5319, or see the *Good Money Quarterly Report* (1-800-223-3911).

Some families form investment clubs to pool money to invest in the stock market, with each member contributing say $20 a month and voting on how to invest the group money. The National Association of Investors, one such organization, suggests: Invest regularly, reinvest your earnings from stock interest and dividends, invest in growth companies, and diversify your purchases to reduce the risk of losing money.

Investment Options

—Taryn Sievers, stock broker

Simply put, there are two things you can do with your investment money: Loan it out or buy something. When you loan your money, you get interest. This type of investment is a debt instrument. When you buy something, you hope the value of what you purchased increases. This is owning an equity.

Think of a debt instrument as an IOU. If you loaned a friend money for a certain period of time at a set rate of interest, she/he would pay you the interest and the money at the end of the period. This is how bonds work. Often debt instruments are called fixed income investments because they provide dependable income.

Equity is ownership. When you purchase stock, you are buying a slice of the company. If you own AT&T stock, you are a part owner of American Telephone and Telegraph Company. If the company does well and makes money, the value of the AT&T stock will go up and so will the value of your shares. Of course, values can drop too, although with investments such as land or gold there will always be some value attached to the asset. There are no guarantees or fixed income rates on equities. Some equities pay dividends that are distributions of the corporate profits. If you own shares in a company that continues to excel, your shares can continue to increase in value indefinitely.

If you are under 18, your investments have to be placed under the name of your parent or guardian, as "custodian" or "trustee" for you. They can legally sell or trade these investments.

Money Markets

These investment pools invest in short-term loans to banks, governments, and major corporations. They are perfectly liquid in that you can get your money at any time with no penalty. They pay a slightly lower rate than certificates of deposit and usually more than bank passbook savings. Often they provide check writing privileges and are used as a place to keep reserve cash. Money market rates are very sensitive to interest rate fluctuations. In 1980 they paid 14 percent, while in 1996 the rates were around three percent.

U.S. Treasury Securities

Worldwide these are considered the safest investments. When you buy them, you are essentially loaning money to the U.S. Treasury to finance the government deficit. Due to the risk-free nature of these securities, the interest rate is usually low. All interest earned on U.S. Treasury securities is free of state and local taxes and there are other special tax-free features for those intending to use the money for a college education. There are three types:

✪ Treasury bills mature in one year or less and come in $10,000 minimum denominations. These are purchased at a discount and mature at $10,000.

✪ Treasury notes mature in two to 10 years, come in $1,000 minimum denominations and pay interest semi-annually.

✪ Treasury bonds mature in 10 to 30 years, come in $1,000 minimum denominations, and pay interest semiannually.

✪ Series EE savings bonds are issued by the U.S. Government and are purchased at half the face value. If you hold the bonds five years or more, you will earn six percent retroactive to the purchase date. For current rate information, call 1-800-US Bonds.

Certificates of Deposit (CD)

You loan money to the bank for a set period of time, at a set rate of interest. The longer the term of the CD, the higher the rate you will get. Amounts up to $100,000 are insured by a government agency. Interest rates are usually slightly higher than those for treasury securities. If you have to cash in a CD early, you pay a penalty.

Municipal Bonds

Municipal bonds are similar to corporate bonds except states, cities, counties, and other municipalities issue them. The interest earned on municipal bonds is entirely tax-free but the interest rate is therefore lower.

Common Stock

Stock is ownership in a company. The value of the stock relates directly to the success of the company. The stock market fluctuates daily, as does the value of your stock. There is no maturity date on stock; you can buy and sell whenever you like. Over the last 60 years, the average share of stock listed on the New York Stock Exchange increased at an annual rate of about 10 percent.

Choosing individual stocks involves considering the amount you are going to invest, the risk you will take, how much time you are willing to be in the market, and how closely you want to follow the market.

Mutual Funds

The second way to invest in the stock market, without having to select different stocks yourself, is to invest in mutual funds. A stock mutual fund is like a basket of different stocks. By buying into a mutual fund, you own a little bit of different stocks for a small amount of money (usually the minimum is $500 to $1,000). Professional managers manage mutual funds so you don't have to decide what and when to buy or sell. You are automatically diversified so your risk is spread out. If you are in a fund with 100 stocks in it, and one falls in price drastically, it is unlikely that the other 99 will fall at the same time. Dividends are paid quarterly and you can either choose to receive or reinvest them. Ask your investment advisor or broker about "loads" (sales charges) and management fees.

Investing Tips

Money Minds 1-800-ASK-A-CAP
(Certified public accountants and financial planners answer questions ranging from tax returns to how to invest, for $3.95 a minute.)

Mutual fund investing information is provided by Morningstar Mutual Funds in a rating service carried by many libraries and in an investment newsletter. 1-800-876-5005. http://networth.gal.com.

The Handbook for Learn-by-Doing Investing and monthly newsletter *Better Investing*
National Association of Investors Corp.
711 W. Thirteen Mile Rd.
Madison Heights, MI 48071

The Mutual Fund Investment Kit
Mutual Fund Education Alliance
1900 Erie St., Suite 120
Kansas City, MO 64116-3465

Richard Maturi. *Main Street Beats Wall Street: How the Top Investment Clubs Are Outperforming the Investment Pros*. Chicago: Probus, 1994.

Mary Rowland. *A Commonsense Guide to Mutual Funds*. NY: Bloomberg Press, 1996.

Internet Investment Resources:

Bulletin boards where members exchange tips—misc.invest.stocks.

Invest-o-rama!: http://investorama.com (links to financial sites)

"InvestQuest" lists addresses for companies. Their worldwide web address is http://invest.quest.columbus.oh.us/

"Networth" is a source of information on stocks, accessed through a search tool such as Netscape. NETworth: http://networth.gal.com

Yahoo investment sites are reached at http://www.yahoo.com/Economy/Markets_and_Investments/

Global Network Navigator Personal Finance Center http://gnn.com/gnn/meta/finance/index.html

Saving Money

People tend to be savers or spenders. Which are you? What attitude toward saving, spending, and going into debt did you learned from your family? Do you agree or disagree with these old sayings?

- *Money burns a hole in my pocket.*
- *Money talks.*
- *Money doesn't grow on trees.*
- *You can't take it with you.*
- *A penny saved is a penny earned.*
- *Love of money is the root of all evil.*
- *Money can't buy you happiness.*
- *Easy come, easy go.*
- *It's easier for a camel to go through the eye of a needle than for a rich person to enter heaven.*

Ways to Save

—Taryn Sievers, stock broker

- Buy at the end of the season when stores try to decrease their inventory.

- Utilize newspaper ads. Used items like computer equipment can be bought at substantial discounts. Remember thrift shops, second hand stores, and garage sales.

- Stick to your list when you shop. Studies have shown list keepers spend less than those who wing it.

- Try to carry as little cash as you need. The less cash you carry, the less you will spend.

- Make long distance calls on the weekends and evenings.

- Borrow free video tapes and books from the library.

- Lower the temperature gage on your hot water heater to 120 degrees, install a low-flow shower head, and use the washing machine and dishwasher only when full.

- Put your change in a container each day and add it to your savings account each month.

Theft Prevention

In a file folder keep serial numbers and sales slips of valuable posses-sions, such as a bike or car. Engrave possessions such as a computer with your Social Security number. The police department will probably lend you an engraver. Secure your computer to a wall bracket; the hardware is available from computer stores.

Engrave your bike with an Operation Identification number recommend-ed by your local police or with your driver's license number. Lock your bike with a U-shaped lock made of steel that can't be sawed, or a case-hardened chain or cable and lock. Put the cable through the frame, both wheels, and a bike rack or other fixed object.

Over one million vehicles are stolen each year (not including bikes). You can buy anti-theft devices including steering column locks, alarms, switches that stop the fuel system, and locks for tape decks and gas tanks. If you can't afford a real alarm now, some people use LED lights on their dashboard as a decoy. Park your car in well-lighted areas. Keep your car's vehicle identification number (VIN) in your file of important papers at home. (Car manufacturers must engrave a VIN on a metal plate on the dashboard and in several other hidden places.) Don't leave the vehicle registration and other identification papers in your glove compartment, although the registration must be available to show to police. You can solder the bolts of your vehicle license plates to prevent theft.

Terilyn Davenport. *Starting Out: Step-by-Step Guide for Teens Succeeding in the '90s*. 1994. Step-by-Step (P.O. Box 1492, Cupertino, CA 95015). (Discusses money management, how to get a job, moving into your own apartment, etc.)

Work

Affirmative Action

I believe affirmative action will make a small impact on getting a job, and a huge impact on salary. Women still only make 72 cents to a man's dollar for equal work. This has gone up since affirmative action started, but it obviously has a lot further to go. I hope that the presence or lack of affirmative tive action will not have a huge impact on my career, but I have dreams of being a lawyer and I think it will have a dramatic impact in that field.

—Kate, 21, New York

Judy Meadows and Miranda Johnson, Darmouth students, comment from the Internet.
[Some argue against affirmative action on the grounds that people who work hard become successful, no matter what their background, and don't need affirmative action.] *If this contention is taken to its logical extreme, then the success of Frederick Douglass demonstrates that slavery was not truly a problem. Although born as a slave, Douglass managed to learn to read and write, to escape from slavery, to write and autobiography... and to become a leader in the abolitionist movement. Why couldn't all other slaves do the same?*

Few will deny that racial discrimination is still a problem in this country, and that due to various histories of discrimination, ethnic minority groups have disproportionate rates of impoverishment. For every dollar earned by a white man, white women make 80 cents, black men make

73 cents, black women and Latino men make 63 cents, and Latinas make 56 cents. [People of color suffer from unemployment at about twice the rate of whites and have nearly three times the poverty rate of whites.] Because 85 percent of available jobs are filled by word of mouth and whites hold 90 percent of the managerial positions in private industry, many of the benefits of family networks for jobs [and college admission to children of alumni] will continue to accrue to other whites.

A large poll of college freshmen in 1995 found that half believe affirmative action should be abolished, with women more in favor of affirmative action than men. However, when asked if there should be special consideration for race in college admissions, 70 percent of the freshmen agreed. Most of my students have strong opinions about affirmative action but not facts.

You've probably heard people talk about affirmative action in terms of quotas (as in a court requirement to hire five percent women fire fighters) or reverse discrimination against white male workers. Neither is accurate in terms of the law or its impact. Look at any large organization in your town or nation—government, corporations, or educational institutions—and see who makes the most money, manages the organization, and has the high paying, high status jobs. Neither the law (Executive Order 112546 established by President Lyndon Johnson) or its main regulations require or allow employment preferences for ethnicity or gender. (An example of an employment preference is veterans' preference laws that add points to their government job application scores.)

Affirmative action only requires employers who sign contracts with the federal government to be equal opportunity employers by not discriminating and by showing good faith efforts to establish written goals and time tables to hire underrepresented groups (people of color, women, Vietnam era veterans, etc.). The only time quotas are required is when a court imposes them on an employer proven guilty of violating Title VII of the Civil Rights Act, which prohibits discrimination on the basis of race, color, religion, national origin, and sex. Title VII of the Civil Rights Act provides far more protection against discrimination on the job than affirmative action.

Employer affirmative action programs often include outreach to hire qualified women and people of color, training programs to give all employees a fair chance for promotion, and establishing goals and timetables to measure progress toward hiring underrepresented groups. Companies rating in the top 100 on affirmative action open up their talent pool and earn almost twice as much a return on their investments, according to a U.S. Department of Labor study.

You've probably heard of reverse discrimination against white males, but they have benefited from the GI Bill, government price supports to big businesses and large farms, and the old boys' network in getting jobs, scholarships, and promotions. Only one-third of the population, they are 97 percent of school superintendents, 95 percent of top business leaders, 90 percent of U.S. Senators and 80 percent of members of the House of Representatives, 88 percent of tenured professors, and 85 percent of law partners in large law firms. The 1995 report by the federal government's Glass Ceiling Commission (the result of legislation introduced by former Republican Senator Bob Dole to look at the invisible barriers to advancement of people of color and women) reported little progress for people of color and women employed in business. Stereotyping continues, along with fear of change. The playing field is not yet level.

Equal Employment Opportunity
Commission 1-800-669-4000
1801 L. Street, NW
Washington, DC 20507

http://www.law.ucla.edu/student/clas
smat/civaa

Attitudes Towards Work and Your Future

—Maran, 16, California

From the end of my freshman year, people have been asking me about my future, telling me it's important that I prepare well for my career. And they wonder why we can't just sit back and "enjoy our childhood!" As a junior, the pressure is even greater. Luckily, now I know what I'm going to do for the next two years. I'll go to the community college and get college credits and high school credits. So that's a load off my shoulders!

Talking to my friends helps somewhat, knowing that they're in the same boat as me. They're stuck without a clue about what they want to do with the rest of their lives. It is an important matter, but people (adults especially) place too much importance on striving forward, thinking about your future—so much that you have no time to live in the present!

—Sarah, 17, Wisconsin

The most difficult challenge I face as a teen is the question of what the future holds for me. Will I be struggling to survive or will I be successful when I'm out of school and on my own? Will I be able to afford the nice things for my children given to me as a child? Will I succeed in college and make a difference in others' lives? I try to take one thing at a time, to not look too far into the future, or I may really disappoint myself. You can't be too critical of yourself, either.

Many young people worry about the possibilities for their future success. A 1994 MTV Jobs Poll found, "The one thing that is clear to today's young work force is that the old rules don't apply. The classic elements of the American dream—marriage, owning a home, a secure job with a clear path for advancement, seem to many of today's young workers to be out of reach." Eight in 10 young adults polled think now is a bad time to start a career. Half of the young people with jobs doubt they will achieve their career goals. In a 1996 survey, almost 65 percent said they believe the American dream is nearly impossible to achieve. Teens' main goal is to be happy (a successful career was #1 in the 1980s survey). In 1996, career success was fifth on the list of goals (a survey of 938 teens for the Horatio Alger Association).

Similarly, a survey of 3,000 high-achiever high school students in 1995 reported over half think they will have a more difficult time than their parents paying for their education, getting a good job, and buying a house. Although a poll of college freshman around the country also found that over 50 percent students are pessimistic about the nation's economic future, 89 percent of these same freshmen are optimistic about their own individual careers and financial prospects (the Higher Education Research Institute at UCLA).

Top Career Choices

Girls

1. Nurse
2. Teacher
3. Physician
4. The arts
5. Business
6. Law/communications (tie)

Boys

1. Business
2. Computers/electronics
3. Lawyer/pro athlete/the arts (tie)
6. Physician

A 1991 Gallup poll

What differences do you see in these choices? Girls are still more likely to select helping professions such as teaching and medicine, while only one of the boys' top choices was a helping profession. Emma believes, "It's all in girls' heads. They think that's all they're supposed to do."

In your planning, keep in mind that researchers predict the following **future trends**:

◎ Increasing use of computers, robots, telecommunications, and other technology will continue to replace factory workers, secretaries and other clerical workers, salesclerks, bank tellers, telephone operators, librarians, and middle managers. Millions of existing jobs will be replaced by machines, according to Jeremy Rifkin (*The End of Work*, Tarcher/Putnam).

◎ People will work at home more and work fewer hours, so the neighborhood will become more important.

◎ Housework will be increasingly mechanized with computerized devices to regulate security, temperature, lighting, start food preparation, and provide entertainment and education.

◎ People will change jobs often and need to revise and update their skills and knowledge.

◎ Employers will assist with child care and eldercare and provide increased flexibility in working hours to accommodate workers' family responsibilities.

Futurists also predict these workplace changes:
Smaller companies will contract for services only as needed rather than hire as many permanent employees, technicians will be the new elite, more companies will organize in changing work teams (they break up after they complete a project and regroup and are self-managed), will produce services (i.e., heath care) and information (i.e., accounting) rather than manufactured products, customized manufacturing (such as having jeans made to fit your measurements), global competition, and demand for special-

ists and those who can integrate information. Education will be a lifelong process. Keep these trends in mind as you define your career goals.

Choosing a Career Path

—Corina, 19, Oregon

Start right away looking at different occupations. It would have been much better had I visited different companies, universities, etc., to discover for myself what kinds of jobs are out there. Also, ask lots of questions.

—Rebecca, 25, California

I had a friend in high school who knew she wanted to be a doctor of some sort, and didn't really need money, but wanted to improve her chances of getting into a good school. So she worked a lot at the local state hospital, and volunteered in the area a good deal. She had fun doing that, strengthened her desire for her career, and it did help her get into school. I, on the other hand, waited tables and that was brainless and fun and paid well. But it's easy to get stuck in a McDonald's type job if you're not careful, so I'd say if you can afford to, and you have an idea of what you want to do, try to get a job in that area.

How to Choose Your Career

—Kelly Lynn Baylor has been an accountant, illustrator, magazine publisher, freelance editor, and is studying to be a counselor.

Choosing a future career is one of the most important jobs a teenager faces. Try volunteering in a place where you think you would like to work. If that is not possible, talk to people in that profession to see what their jobs really entail. What you have heard about a job, and how the media portray some jobs, may not be accurate depictions of the day-to-day realities.

Within each major field are several subfields that can offer exciting possibilities. For instance, do you like science and art? You don't have to make a choice between the two. You could work as a scientific illustrator or an art restorer. The one thing that is vitally important in your career is to feel passion for the job you are doing.

Find out about the life style that goes with a career. If you know you want to have kids someday, then it is not wise to choose a career that will keep you away from home much of the time. Do you want to live in a big city? If the answer is No, then don't choose international banking, a profession that exists only in large cities.

My son wanted to be an architect, but he is not an aggressive student. He is more laid back and loves to go rock climbing and mountain biking. To be an architect he would have to compete to get into one of the top universities. Instead, he has chosen to be a graphic illustrator which does not require such high level competition, but uses the same essential skills. It is also a job that he can do anywhere and it will blend in well with his love for the outdoors rather than a city environment.

After you have given a career serious consideration and chosen what seems best for you, remember it is not a decision written in stone. Many students enter college with one career in mind and switch somewhere along the way. Even if you go all the way through college and into your chosen profession, you are still free to change. The days of having one career in your life are long gone.

Determining Your Interests

There are over 7,000 occupations available. To learn about your options and identify your interests and strengths, take advantage of career information at your school career center, community college, or the local library (see Chapter 9 for useful books about career choices). Computerized career guidance programs are available, including: Eureka, Discover, Sigi Plus, and Major-Minor Finder. Popular career assessment "tests" are Holland's Self-Directed Search, Strong Interest Inventory, and the Myers-Briggs Type Indicator. Ask your school counselor for more information.

John Holland, a psychologist, developed a widely used profile of personality temperaments and their compatible work environments. You may want to take his personality inventory as part of the information you gather in making a career choice. He created a diagram of six different types in a hexagon to show that the closer two types are, the more similar, and those across the hexagon from each other are the most different.

Holland's themes are realistic (likes to work with objects or be outdoors), conventional (likes to work with data and follows through on instructions), enterprising (likes to influence people), investigative (likes to analyze and solve problems), artistic (likes to use imagination and creativity), and social (likes to help people). Which seems most descriptive of your interests?

Rank which of these job categories interest you most. The clusters are defined by the Department of Labor, with examples.

Agriculture: farmer, geneticist

Business and office: accountant, computer programmer, bookkeeper, bank teller

Communications and media: graphic artist, technical writer, camera person

Construction: carpenter, surveyor, draftsman, architect

Consumer education and home economics: dietitian, home economist, nutritionist

Fine arts and humanities: historian, clothing designer, museum worker, singer

Health: nurse, doctor, veterinarian, physical therapist, dentist, medical technician

Hospitality and recreation: hotel manager, chef, ski instructor

Manufacturing: tool designer, electrical engineer, factory worker

Marine science: oceanographer, marine biologist, fish culturist

Marketing and distribution: salesperson, retail store manager, market researcher

Natural resources and environment: forest ranger, soil conservationist, urban planner

Personal services: waiter, counselor, cosmetologist

Public Service: teacher, armed forces, firefighter, government agency worker

Transportation: taxi driver, pilot, merchant marine, flight attendant

I surveyed my high school class after getting their addresses in a reunion effort. At midlife, after establishing careers and families, their advice to you is to "follow your passion." Select a career you enjoy and then work hard at it. "Take risks to get where you really want to be." "Go for it." "We make our own luck." "Don't let other people limit your goals." Most of them had worked for two to five employers. (The survey was returned by 13 women and eight men.)

In your career planning process ask yourself: What do I like to do? What do I value? What work experiences have I had—including volunteer work? What skills have I developed? Do I want to work with people or things, indoors or outdoors, at a desk or moving around? What kind of lifestyle do I want? How do I spend my leisure time? How many years of training am I willing to do? Do I mainly like to work alone or with a group? Do I want to work in a city, a smaller town, or the country? Is my main goal to make money, to help others, to create, to lead, to be challenged, to learn, or something else? Do I want a career that usually requires many years of training and a commitment to move forward in my field, or do I want a job where can I forget about work when I'm home?

Job satisfaction stems from feeling that you: make a difference, have prestige, like your co-workers, have an interesting job, feel challenged, learn new skills, have some say in decision making, feel the employer cares about you, think your salary is fair, have the potential to move upward, have reasonable work hours and job security. Think about these factors in deciding what kind of career you want.

Job Availability

Between 1992 and 2005, almost 18 million college graduates will compete for 14 million new jobs that require a college degree, according to the Bureau of Labor Statistics. Although the number of jobs requiring higher education is increasing, from now until 2005 an estimated 30 percent of new college graduates will be unemployed or underemployed/overqualified. In comparison, during the period from 1984 to 1990, an average of 20 percent of each graduating class was "underutilized." One out of three college graduates works in a job that doesn't require a college degree, compared to one in five graduates in the 1980s.

About half of recent college graduates earned less than $21,000 a year in 1992. One of the reasons for this decline in earnings is that technology has eliminated many jobs and layoffs increase the pool of workers competing for jobs. The encouraging news is that college graduates' pay almost doubles with experience by the time they reach 30. College grads earn an average of 77 percent more than high school graduates, and the gap is widening. (In 1993, 47 percent of people ages 18 to 24 had some higher education, compared to around a third in 1980.)

A sign that good jobs are hard to find is that one in eight adults ages 25 to 34 was living with parents in 1993 (up from one in 11 in 1980), according to the U.S. Census Bureau. Since both house payments and rental costs are high, many young adults are moving back with their parents; 58 percent of unmarried people aged 20 to 24 live with their parents. Home ownership among people ages 25 to 29 has fallen to 35 percent.

About half of the job offers to graduating college seniors are to students with technical majors, such as engineering and computer science (mostly male majors). In 1996, electrical engineers started at $37,662, and accountants at $28,971, compared to $21,973 for English majors and $20,041 for sociology majors (an annual survey by the National Association of Colleges and Employers). Experience and technical know-how gained through internships, volunteer work, and part-time jobs are more important than the particular major, according to Donald Casella, the director of the Career Center at San Francisco State University.

High school graduates find it harder than earlier generations to get blue-collar jobs requiring physical labor, especially in unionized industries like car manufacturing. Entry-level wages for male high school graduates fell nearly 30 percent from 1979 to 1993, to an average of $7 an hour. College-educated men are doing better, but their wages fell eight percent to $12 an hour. Women with college degrees averaged $11 by 1993.

Positive news is that the U.S. is still creating about two million new jobs each year. The job growth rate will be 1.5 percent from 1992 to 2005, according to projections by the Bureau of Labor Statistics. Service industries will provide more than half of the new job growth in this period (business and health services will provide the most). Unfortunately, these jobs are usually poorly paid. Actual production of goods will not grow much, but most of these new jobs will be in construction. Agriculture is not expected to produce additional jobs.

The training you get for a specific occupation will likely be obsolete in about five years. You will probably have seven to nine jobs in your lifetime, because people are more likely now to make lateral moves as well as vertical moves up the career ladder. (Lateral moves are to a related or different field in a position that is not higher than the previous job.) Expect your education to be a lifelong process.

The National Association of Colleges
and Employers
62 Highland Ave., Dept. P
Bethlehem, PA 18017
(offers publications such as Planning
Job Choices)

How to Get a Job Now
—Andy, 18, California

When you fill out an application, use black or blue ink, not pencil, and your best handwriting, or type. Pick up two applications in case you mess up. Read everything carefully. Make your answers thorough and complete. Where they ask the times you can work, be as broad as possible, like for the summer put 6:00 a.m. to 9:00 p.m. Don't turn in a folded or wrinkled application. It has to be perfect.

When you turn it in, look nice and neat. Ask to speak to the manager, introduce yourself, look eye to eye, shake hands, and say, "nice to meet you." Come back within a week, and then every week, to check and to show you're interested and eager. I've gotten jobs over people who were more qualified because of this.

In an interview, answer fully, not just Yes or No. Don't look away or fidget. Ask yourself before what you think they'll ask, so you can answer so they'll understand. When you leave, be courteous, shake hands. You have to be nicer, more respectful, more enthusiastic, to get selected. I got a job as a cook because I was willing to work 12 hours on Mother's Day and didn't complain. I did everything quickly and asked, "What else can I help you with?" I got hired on a regular basis.

About five million young people ages 12 to 17 are employed. Studies show that working over 20 hours a week results in lower grades. On the average, each month 1.1 million teens and 1.2 million young adults are unemployed and looking for work. The unemployment rate for teens was 24 percent in 1992, compared to eight percent for adults. The rate of black teens who can't find a job is double the rate for white teens.

Six Steps to Land a Job

1. Determine your **goals and priorities**. Do you want a job that will look good to a college or future employer? Is your priority finding a job that fits into your schedule, pays top dollars, or brings you in contact with interesting people?

2. **Network** with every resource possible: friends, parents of friends, friends of your parents, teachers, neighbors, your school job placement center, counselors, newspaper want ads, chamber of commerce, government and private employment agencies, office bulletin boards, and telephone book yellow pages. Look in reference books such as Standard and Poor's *Register*, available in the library. Research small but rapidly growing companies, such as looking at *INC.* magazine's yearly issue on that topic. Or create your own job taking care of children, gardening, making casseroles and running errands for busy parents, or selling handmade craft items.

3. Create a **résumé**. Take time to do this carefully as it gets you in the door for a job interview where you can sell yourself in person. Include your name, address, and phone number at the top. Use subheadings such as (a) work experience and volunteer work (list in chronological order with the most recent job first, and include your job title and duties), (b) education and other skills that prepared you for the job, (c) a list of references (or write that they're available upon request so you can alert the people they may be called), and (d) personal (your interests, achievements, language skills, and hobbies).

   It's fine to use bullet format rather than paragraphs. Make sure you have a good editor check for spelling and grammar errors and make sure you use action verbs rather than passive voice (see the essay writing section in Chapter 8). Leave adequate margins to make the layout pleasing to the reader's eye. If possible, use a computer and have it laser printed. Use heavy bond white or cream–colored paper. Change your résumé to target the different jobs for you apply. Talk with secretaries and other employees to find out about the workplace, and try to do library research.

   You can attach your résumé to a job application, which ideally should be typed as well. You're probably competing with many others, so sell yourself well. Give the employer a reason for him/her to call you rather than 100 other applicants, and don't provide any reason to immediately toss your application (by not answering questions, messy writing, or not knowing about their workplace).

   Keep a "master application" with dates and addresses of your prior jobs and education so that you have this information in one place when needed for a specific job application. This information is not part of résumés.

4. Dress your best and **ask to speak to the manager** when you hand in your résumé and application. Again, do research about the workplace beforehand so you know what they want in an employee. Briefly tell the interviewer what you like about their business and what you have to offer. Call back regularly to let them know your interest. (I have gotten jobs simply because I kept in such regular contact they got tired of talking to me and put me to work.) A reader adds, "Walk the line so you don't annoy them."

5. Make phone calls, use e-mail, faxes, voice mail, and stop by to **follow-up** with employers because they probably receive many applications. About half of adult job searchers are eliminated after their first phone call, so practice what to say and get a critique from an adult before calling.

6. To **prepare for a job interview**, practice first with an adult and videotape the interview, pretending your dining room table is the interview space. Often the most qualified person on paper loses out to a person with more energy, enthusiasm, effective communication skills, courtesy, and persistence, who demonstrates he or she has prepared for the interview.

Practice answers for these **interview questions**:

O Tell me about yourself.

O What is your best quality? Your worst quality?

O Why did you apply for a job with us?

O What do you expect from this job?

O What are your career goals?

O Who has influenced your development?

O Why should I hire you for this job? What are your strengths? Your weaknesses? To this type of negative question, answer in a way that puts you in the best possible light. A response might be, "I tend to be a workaholic/perfectionist/too invested in my work" or mention other traits that might seem desirable to an employer. If you lack a skill they're looking for, tell them how you might learn it, such as taking a class.

As you watch the taped practice interview, look at your posture (lean forward a little to show interest), eye contact (look the interviewer in the eye), hand gestures (shouldn't distract), phrases you repeat (OK, yeah, you know, uh, um, like, just, totally), and your clarity of expression. To come across as confident, make your statements declarative rather than frequently using a questioning inflection, don't rush, look at the interviewer, and occasionally repeat his/her last name in your responses. Often interviewees are nervous and talk too much, so take time to think through to-the-point responses. Also prepare questions to ask the interviewer to demonstrate the research you've done about what's important to that employer.

Be aware of proper manners as unintentional rudeness can quickly disqualify an applicant. When meeting a new person on the job or socially, introduce yourself with your first and last name, say something affirmative like "I'm glad to meet you, Mr./Ms. X," and shake hands. Technically, a woman determines whether she wants to shake hands or not by being the first to offer her hand, so if she doesn't offer, don't extend your hand. If you're introducing people who don't know each other, start with the person who deserves the most respect, such as the oldest or the boss: "Ms. Boss, I'd like you to meet my friend Kelley Chu." Stand when an elder enters the room you don't know, and hold doors open for him/her, to show respect. Don't start eating a meal until the host begins or tells you to begin eating. When you leave a telephone message on a recorder, always leave your phone number and say it slowly.

Job Interviewing Tips

—Madelyn Jennings, vice-president for personnel, Gannett (the large media company which owns *USA Today*, etc.)

★ Always arrive 10 minutes early. Wear business attire appropriate to the position for which you're interviewing.

★ Bring extra copies of your résumé to help you fill out the application quickly, neatly, and accurately, or to provide it if needed.

★ Don't smoke or chew gum.

★ Listen carefully to questions. Don't interrupt the interviewer. Don't rush too quickly to answer: It's fine to pause to organize your thoughts.

★ Never use clichés, such as "I like working with people," because it makes you sound unoriginal.

★ Make sure you pronounce and spell the company name and the interviewer's name correctly.

★ Shake hands firmly before and after the interview. Refer to the interviewer by name as you answer his or her questions. At the end of the interview, say what you liked about the interview and what impressed you about the company. Summarize your strong points in a follow-up letter to the interviewer, being sure to use his/her name.

—Aaron, 20, California

Go to video stores and restaurants. They always need some sort of help. Movie theaters have a high turnover as well.

—Brandon, 20, California

I see hundreds of money-making opportunities daily. It only takes an open mind and a little motivation to do what you want to be doing to make money. I found my best opportunity to be distributing environmentally-conscious products. Money opportunities are everywhere, just go looking for them.

—Josh, 20, Indiana

I grew up pretty fast, after getting kicked out of the house at 15. At first I felt pretty sorry for myself, but as I look back now it really made me learn how to stand on my own two feet. I worked at restaurants and still finished high school. It wasn't easy getting home at 2:00 a.m. after work and getting up at 7:00 a.m. to get to my first class. My moral of this story is that you can go through life feeling sorry for yourself about how life just isn't fair, or you can take that energy and work hard, laughing at the cry babies. My personal motto is "things happen for the best."

—Joe, 20, Virginia

Developing independence requires you to realize that you're dependent in some way, so make a commitment to minimize this dependence. From the financial standpoint, I started out cutting grass, and through a series of contacts at school, I was able to jump up to part-time computer salesman. It took me from 6th grade to 11th grade to move beyond lawn care, but once you get the ball rolling, things can happen fast!

My father's initial reaction to my independence was to try to squelch it by cutting me off financially; having already secured that portion of my life, I was able to continue independently building the rest. His next reaction was to react very forcefully whenever It came up in discussion; after a time he realized how unreasonable this was and sought counseling. Since then he has changed much for the better. The root cause was he was a very young father who saw his life as a failure and was very insecure; when he saw someone as an affront to his authority, he was enraged by it and tried to secure control over it. It helped that I had a strong peer group and understanding relatives. Sometimes you just need a shoulder to cry on, and I did my share.

It can be tough, but the key is to have a definite direction and be motivated. Once that's established, even though it's not easy, it's not nearly so hard to strike out on your own path.

—Allison, 22, Missouri

Start small. Don't think you are going to be able to go out and begin working for a Fortune 500 company wearing suits when you are 15. You should be willing to do a variety of things if called on. You also need to be eager to learn new skills and possess the basic responsibilities like being on time and honesty. So many of my friends in high school got jobs and then lost them over little things like consistently coming in late to work, helping themselves to a candy bar without paying for it, or just general laziness. Don't be afraid to let family and friends of the family know you are looking. My first job was with my mom's work. My second was with Wal-Mart, and it helped that I knew someone who worked there.

National Youth Employment Coalition
1501 Broadway, Suite 1111
New York, NY 10036

Martin John Yate. *Knock 'Em Dead:
The Ultimate Job Seekers Handbook.*
Holbrook, MA: Bob Adams, 1994.

A social security number

This is required by an employer, and some require a copy of your card. If you don't have one, call the Social Security Administration at 1-800-772-1213. You can get a work permit through your school.

The Internet Computer Online Job Search

The Online Career Center lists jobs and stores your résumé (three pages or less) for six months. This is a free service. The e-mail address is info@occ.com. If you don't have access to a computer, you can mail your résumé and a $10 check to Online Résumé Service, 1713 Hemlock Ln., Plainfield, IN 46168. Commercial online services also provide career information.

Pam Dixon. *Be Your Own Headhunter: Go Online to Get the Job You Want.* NY: Random House, 1995.

Peter Weddle. *Electronic Résumés for the New Job Market.* Manassas Park, VA: Impact Publishing, 1995.

So much information is available on the Internet that it is a resource for almost any job you might want. More than 23 million people use the Net on a regular basis. It is an international network linking regional computer networks funded by universities, schools, government agencies, and businesses. Imagine a giant spider web joining many different webs built by various spiders.

The Net began in the mid-1970s as a tool of the Department of Defense for military research. Beginning in the mid-1980s, universities formed regional networks connected to the Internet, assisted by National Science Foundation funding. In the 1990s most new users were members of the general public like you who have access through school, work, regional networks, or commercial services. They use the Internet most frequently for e-mail communication, but also to read bulletin boards (discussion groups), mailing lists (receive news bulletins from organizations such as a political party), and information resources (articles and library sources).

Tools are available to search for information without having to know where to look for it. Gopher, Mosaic, Telnet, and Netscape are examples of the search tools or "engines." For example, I typed in "teenager" to get information for this book as well as contact youth newsgroups.

To get online, you need a computer, a modem that connects you to the Net by your phone line, and the telecommunications software to connect you to the Internet. Many books are available to guide you through your journey on the Information Highway, such as *The Internet for Dummies*, by Levine and Baroudi (IDG Books).

Job Training

Search for local job training and mentoring programs offered by your school, city, an employer, or a service organization. For example, the city of Tallahassee administers a Summer Youth Employment Program, where teens earn minimum wages to work for the city for eight weeks. The Career Shadowing Program matches high school seniors with a professional employee for a day. Their Student Apprenticeship Program trains teens for city jobs for a year and gives them preference in employment after they graduate from high school. In San Francisco, in the "Say Yes" program, youth work for government and nonprofit agencies; companies make tax deductible contributions to pay their salaries.

Overall, European employers do a better job of providing on-the-job training, reports Labor Secretary Robert Reich. He explains the U.S. has "one of the worst systems among industrialized countries for getting young people (who are not going on to college) from school to work. About two-thirds of youth don't go on to college and three-quarters don't graduate from a four-year college."

The 1990 Commission on the Skills of the American Work Force concluded, "America may have the worst school-to-work transition systems of any advanced industrial country. Students who know few adults to help them get their first job are left to sink or swim." This is a major issue for the young adults who do not receive college degrees.

Some high schools provide co-op (cooperative education) programs where local employers train students. Others give students training in print shops and auto repair centers on campus. The School-to-Work Opportunities Act of 1994 helps fund job training which combines vocational skills with school learning. It encourages employers, schools, students, and workers to form local partnerships. All states initially received development grants ranging from $200,000 to $750,000. Each program must include work experience and mentoring. ("Job shadowing" and "mentoring" are supervised worksite programs.) However, Congress reduced funding, so you might want to check on the funding level for your school system.

Government job training programs include the Job Training Partnership Act (JTPA) which provides vocational training and job placement for low-income and high-risk youth ages 16 and older. The goal is to train youth to match the needs of local employers. JTPA job labs also offer high school completion programs.

The Carl D. Perkins Vocational Education Act of 1984 provides the largest amount of federal dollars for vocational education and programs for single parents, girls, women, and other underserved groups. Some states funnel this money to Regional Occupation Programs (ROP) to teach vocational skills.

> **Job Corp. (ages 16 to 24)**
> **1-800-624-9191**
>
> **Regional Occupation Programs**
> **check with your school counselor or**
> **look in the phone book under**
> **government—county education.**

Progressive employers encourage their employees to mentor local high school students, in a one-on-one relationship that pays off. Examples are Procter and Gamble in Cincinnati, Ohio; and in Philadelphia, Project BEGIN (Business Education Goes into Neighborhoods) links businesses and students, organized by One to One. Kansas City has the most ambitious program, YouthFriends—a cooperative effort of schools, nonprofit agencies, and community leaders. It aims to match 30,000 volunteers with kids aged five to 17 (1-816-842-0944).

The new emphasis on preparing youth for work after high school raises some concerns: Does this force teens to make career choices too early? Is there too much emphasis on skills rather than becoming a well-informed citizen? Do businesses and industry have the resources to provide work-based learning experiences? Clearly more needs to be done to train youth for jobs after high school.

Information line of the Department of Labor's Training and Technology Resource Center 1-800-488-0901

Jobs for the Future 1-800-899-3411 (JFF works to develop new systems for linking employers with schools.)

Junior Achievement 1-800-THE-NEW-JA

The National School-to-Work Learning and Information Center 1-800-251-7236 (provides information, assistance and training)

WEEA Equity Resource Center 1-800-225-3088 "School-to-Work Jump-Start Equity Kit"

Council of Chief State School Officers One Massachusetts Ave., NW, Suite 700 Washington, DC 2001-1431

ERIC/ACVE 1900 Kenny Rd. Columbus, OH 43210-1090 wagner.6@osu.edu (materials on service learning, job trends, etc.)

National Alliance of Business 1201 New York Ave., NW Washington, DC 20005-3917

National Commission for Cooperative Education 501 Stearns Center 360 Huntington Ave. Boston, MA 02115

(provides information about the schools that offer practical earn-and-learn options)

School-to-Work Opportunities Information Center 330 C St., SW Washington, DC 20202-7100

S2WTP, discussion forum. To subscribe, send a message to majordomo@cccins.cccneb.edu with this command in the body: subscribe s2wtp your internet address.

How to Find an Internship

Association for Experiential Education 2885 Aurora Ave. Boulder, CO 80303 (publishes *Jobs Clearinghouse*, a monthly newsletter that lists internships)

National Society for Experiential Education (NSEE) 3509 Haworth Dr., Suite 207 Raleigh, NC 27609

Internships: Over 35,000 Opportunities to Get an Edge in Today's Competitive Job Market. Princeton, NJ: Peterson's, recent edition.

Garrett Martin, et al. *The National Directory of Internships*. Raleigh, NC: National Society of Experiential Education, 1993.

Starting Your Own Business

—Maisie Jane, 20, California

I felt that being able to do things my own way and making my own time schedule were critical for creating happiness for myself. This led me to start my own almond flavoring business, Maisie Jane's California Sunshine Products. Starting my business at the early age of 17 was on the unique side, so I got some strong responses from the community, which worked to my benefit. People love to see young adults initiate an idea and become successful.

Do you feel like you're stuck in a whirlwind being whipped around in a million different directions by people telling you what they think you should do with your life?

Especially being a young adult, people don't seem to trust our judgment. I know that sometimes you feel like screaming, "I have a mind of my own!" The first step to success is feeling confident in your own ideas. The problem is we become too critical and doubt overcomes confidence. When you see this approaching, tell yourself, "I will never know until I try."

Once you accomplish this confidence, you are ready to take action to create your own niche. How do you acquire motivation? Well, motivation is positive energy, right? It comes from being confident, excited, and happy about something. Therefore, the livelihood you choose must be something that you enjoy and feel good about doing.

It's true that having your own business brings on a lot of responsibilities. But I believe if you master the technique of being responsible at an early age, it won't be such a dramatic change once you're through with the party stage and have to provide for yourself. I don't believe that work and responsibility are the only thing life should offer, though. Fun and relaxing time is essential for a balanced life! While you're young, try to engage in activities or jobs that you have a real interest in and stay focused on a balance of pleasure and work. This will bring you true peace with yourself.

The teen owners of "Food from the 'Hood" in South Central Los Angeles offer these suggestions, as reported in the Spring, 1995, issue of *Careers and Colleges*.

★ Read business magazines such as *Business Week, Inc.*, and *Entrepreneur*, including back issues, and ask the librarian to suggest helpful books.

★ Write out a business plan. Have backup strategies in case Plan A doesn't work.

★ Whenever you meet people who own their own business, ask them for advice.

★ Use the services of a business advisor, lawyer, and accountant. Hopefully they'll donate their consultation time. [Ask the business department of the nearest college.]

★ Enjoy your work and make it fun, or it probably won't be successful.

Resources for Young Entrepreneurs
Co-op America 1-800-424-2667

An Income of Her Own
1-800-350-2978
(organizes seminars and Camp $tart-Up)

The National Education Center for Women in Business
1-800-NECWB-4-U

Small Business Administration 1-800-8-ASK-SBA

Center for Student Entrepreneurship
Wichita State University
Wichita, KS 67260

National Foundation for Teaching Entrepreneurship
1-212-232-3333

Private Industry Council—check the phone book.

William Stolze. *Startup: An Entrepreneur's Guide to Launching and Managing a New Venture*. Rochester, NY: Rock Beach Press, 1994.

Internet Business Library:
http://www.bschool.ukans.edu/intbuslib/virtual.htm

Success on the Job

If you're employed, watch adults to analyze their dynamics so that when you start full-time work you'll be aware of some of the games being played. New employees should study the culture of their workplace to learn its informal rules and expectations for behavior and performance, as if they were anthropologists studying a new culture. Interview successful workers about how to excel, how to work for a promotion, and what taboos or no-no's exist in the organization's culture.

—Shirley Sloan Fader, an expert on work issues, suggests these seven techniques for success:

1. Complete your assignments without being reminded.

2. If something prevents you from working on your main task, such as a computer crash, work on something else.

3. Don't aim for perfection. Get the job done well by the deadline.

4. Do more than you were assigned.

5. Some bosses will indirectly ask you to do something, such as saying, "We need more ink in the printer," rather than, "Please get more ink."

6. Try to take care of disagreements among co-workers on your own rather than asking the boss to solve them. Give co-workers praise and appreciation when appropriate.

7. If you need to talk with your supervisor, ask for a convenient time to meet rather than when she is on her way out the door.

A seven-year study of engineers at AT&T's Bell Labs identified the characteristics of the star performers. Their main skill is the ability to take the initiative. They also build informal employee networks of information for problem solving, manage their time effectively, are active followers, exhibit leadership, recognize other viewpoints than their own, are effective team members, make effective presentations and written reports, and understand office politics (a study by Janet Caplan and Robert Keeley).

Success from a Latina Point of View

—Sylvia Lopez Romano, Ed.D., is a student affairs administrator at Arizona State University

My career in higher education administration spans 18 years; during this time I have learned the hard way. At age 16, I dropped out of high school, married, and raised five children. This was culturally acceptable, for it wasn't expected that a Mexicana would do anything else but marry and have children. Latinas were subordinate to their mates and their families. I never dreamed of returning to school until my last child entered school and my husband and I decided that my becoming a teacher would be a positive move for our family. The cultural norms dictated that what was good for the family should be good for me.

Going back to school opened up a whole new world. I earned two B.A.'s, an M.A., and an Ed.D. These accomplishments by a dropout and teen parent followed a nontraditional avenue to success. Juggling a household of five children, a foster child, a husband, full-time employment, and college classes taught me that organization and follow-through are essential for success in any venture.

The most important strategy for success is to know your personal definition of success. This definition determines your happiness and your self-esteem. Do not allow society, family, or friends to define your view of success, which I personally gage by my internal feeling of peace. Other strategies for success include obtaining skills in organization, planning, goal setting, timing, and producing quality work.

Balancing work and family requires mental and physical well-being. Developing self-esteem requires determining your own goals and priorities. This may feel like going against the family or cultural group, but if you remain true to yourself, your contributions will reflect the positive energy you gain.

A mentor once criticized me for working hard. She insisted that working hard did not pay off; rather, working smart is vital. What I learned is that without the support of decision makers, hard work does not result in advancement. Time spent with your supervisor discussing projects will benefit you later.

We need a new paradigm: Latinos need to begin to think like winners. Shift your thinking from being oppressed to being a survivor, a talented individual. The world is yours for the taking with proven methods for success.

—Matthews Jackson is vice-president at Butte Community College, Oroville, California, and presents an African American view.

Probably the single, most significant characteristic held in common by African Americans who have gotten past the glass ceiling is their unbridled belief in themselves, confidence borne of the knowledge that they are valuable as human beings and capable as managers and workers. Usually, this self-esteem is encouraged in individuals long before they ever get into the work realm, by parents, a mentor, or a teacher who convinced the person of his/her own personal worth and dignity.

However, for African Americans, there is a delicate balancing act. Our sense of confidence is frequently labeled as arrogant (code for not knowing our place). So, while we must convey a strong message of self-assurance, we must at the same time possess a dignity and presence which can only be construed as confidence. If we expect others to be comfortable with us, we must be comfortable with our own personhood first.

Even the most gifted of us know that there is absolutely no substitute for preparation. Few acquire success by being average; indeed, the Willie Mays complex is still at work. To climb the ladder of success, African Americans must usually prove that they are not only equal to their white peers, but must frequently outperform them simply for the privilege of working.

Preparation includes understanding the culture and values of the employing organization. It means being conscious of office politics. Acquiring an influential, in-house mentor who is willing to serve as your guide is a critical factor in succeeding and being accepted in the organization. Preparation also means cultivating an area of expertise within the organization that is perceived as valuable.

Successfully shattering the glass ceiling is possible; with a steady growth of African Americans in decision-making roles. It is a part of the evolution from slavery to emancipation to civil rights to economic success. See yourself as a player in this transition. Cultivate strong self-esteem, be diligent about your preparation, have a vision, prepare a plan, be self-critical, demonstrate humility, be a team player, and you will acquire success. Do not use your blackness as an excuse for failing or a reason for succeeding. You are, first and foremost, a valuable person.

Successfully Working with Difficult People

Many power games go on in the workplace when people are competing for advancement; you will probably be tested, subtly or not so subtly. You will inevitably run into difficult people who play power games at work. Try disarming them by finding a point of agreement or getting them to buy into your success by asking their advice. Susanne, a professor, gave her voting proxy to a man she was having some difficulties with, telling him she agreed with his viewpoints. "Massaging his ego" worked, she says, for "he has been like sugar ever since."

Some may want the ego satisfaction of getting you upset, angry, or hurt-any negative reaction to their verbal attacks, because they like to feel up to your down.

Don't give them the reward of seeing you upset, as this reinforces bad behavior. (This is using the psychological behavior modification principle of rewarding good behavior to reinforce it and ignoring bad behavior to eliminate it, just as elementary teachers give gold stars or time-outs to their students.) Some power-hungry people will try to intimidate or threaten you. Ignoring unacceptable behavior will sometimes be enough to discourage it, while at other times it has to be confronted with an ally to help you.

If you feel overwhelmed, say, "I'd like some time to think about this; I'll get back to you," and leave or hang up the phone. Use assertiveness techniques by firmly repeating what you want, such as, "I expect courtesy from a co-worker." Use direct eye contact and confident body language and practice in front of a mirror.

Susanne advises you to find out who is influential and why, then zero in on a powerful person to fight for you. This person will be flattered by your respect and become personally involved, "buying into your progress." Mentors can provide some protection from the hazing or testing process that often greet new employees. The goal is to not fight battles without allies or go out on the front line alone.

Just because someone is friendly doesn't mean he or she is trustworthy or has a perfect memory. Put any important agreement into writing, signed by both parties. Even if someone is totally honest, he/she can forget or misunderstand, so it's VERY important to put agreements in writing. (The emphasis here is on the basis of my mistakes.)

About half of American women will experience sexual harassment on the job. It's illegal: Title IX covers educational institutions and Title VII of the Civil Rights Act covers employment. Sexual harassment is unwelcome sexual advances on the job that create an offensive work environment or interfere with the individual's work performance. The courts ruled that an employee can receive money for damages incurred in a hostile work environment. This includes sexist posters on the wall, sexist jokes and name calling, as well as touching and pressure to have sex. Men can be the victims of sexual harassment as well as women and are included in the law.

If someone harasses you, it's important to document his or her actions in writing. Write a letter to the harasser describing the facts of the incident as if it had been video taped. Then describe how it made you feel and the impact on your work performance. Ask for a specific change and state that if the problem happens again you will make a formal complaint. Keep a copy of the letter and perhaps send it registered mail. If the harassment continues, contact the person in charge of preventing discrimination at your job site.

Equal Employment Opportunity
Commission 1-800-669-EEOC

Joel Friedman, et al. *Sexual Harassment*. Deerfield Beach, FL: Health Communications, 1992.

Women and Work

A *USA Weekend* magazine survey of 222,653 students reports the majority do not believe men and women are paid equally for equal work (67 percent of girls and 52 percent of boys). In general, they think males have more career opportunities (82 percent of males and 81 percent of females), although a majority think a female will be elected president in their lifetimes. Both sexes worry more about finding a good job than finding a good spouse—73 percent of girls and 72 percent of boys.

Questions and Answers to indicate a woman can't depend on the handsome prince to support her. She needs job skills, as 90 percent of women eventually will become the head of their household due to divorce or widowhood.

Percentage of men's earnings earned by women? **74 percent**

What percent of jobs can support a family of four above the poverty line? **20 percent**

What is the average cost of a house in the U.S.? **over $100,000**

What percent of wives are employed? **A Louis Harris poll looked at middle-class families earning $25,000 to $50,000 and found that in 82 percent of these families both partners must work.**

What percent of mothers of infants under one year are employed? **over 50 percent.**

What is the current divorce rate? **Almost 50 percent—the average marriage lasts less than seven years, with 1.8 children.**

What is the average child support payment? **Around $250 month. A study of 1,000 representative children found that only one in six saw their father once a week or more.**

What percent of women don't have a husband to share breadwinning? **About 14 million women lived alone in 1994 and about 31 percent of families with children were headed by a single woman. Women are three-fifths of Americans living in poverty and two-thirds of those who earn minimum wages.**

Average age of widowhood? **56**

What percent of women have a company-sponsored pension? **Women are half as likely as men to be covered by their employers and are also less likely to have health insurance. Only nine percent of women over age 40 receive a retirement benefit. Over 90 percent of men are qualified for Social Security benefits, compared to 77 percent of women.**

More and more Americans are insecure about their financial futures. Paychecks are dropping for college-educated men as well as men in blue-collar jobs. The overall median income has declined. As a result, wives and mothers also have to work. By 1990, three-fourths of women aged 25 to 54 were in the work force.

Women in the Workforce

✧ White males will comprise only 31 percent of the new workers between 1992 and 2005.

✧ Women are 47 percent of the work force and 57 percent of women are employed (68 percent have a child under age 18).

◆ Women accounted for 60 percent of the growth in the work force between 1982 and 1992.

◆ Women-owned businesses employ more Americans than the large Fortune 500 companies and women are projected to own half of the small businesses by 2000.

◆ Women earn over half of the bachelor's and master's degrees, 40 percent of law degrees, and a third of the master's degrees in business.

◆ Women of color (nearly one in four American women) earn significantly less than white women. African American women's share of professional degrees (i.e., law, medicine) declined in the 1980s and the gap between the earnings of white women and blacks and Latinas increased.

◆ A look at median income in 1993 reveals:

   White men—$31,089

   White women—$22,023

   Black women—$19,816

   Hispanic women—$16,758

◆ 80 percent of working women earn less than $25,000 a year, partly because two-thirds of them work in female jobs in the "pink-collar ghetto" such as clerical work.

◆ Women professionals earn less than men in their fields; for example, women physicians earned 54 percent of what male physicians earned in 1991.

◆ Women are 74 percent of the teachers but only six percent of school superintendents,
50 percent of new accountants but only 15 percent of accounting firm partners,
23 percent of lawyers but only 11 percent of partners in law firms,
48 percent of all journalists but only six percent of the top jobs,
40 percent of middle managers but four percent of top jobs, and
72 percent of elementary school teachers but only 29 percent of the principals.

The Rules of the Work Game

To succeed and be able to implement change for others, women need to learn how to play the work game. Research indicates that women do not make it to the top because of discriminatory corporate promotion systems, not because of women's abilities. A survey of senior executives found that formal criteria accounted for only 44 percent of the criteria for the review process. Informal standards included networking skills, personality, loyalty, ability to play politics, and integrity.

Succeeding in large organizations requires planning strategies, as if preparing to win a military battle or a chess game. Strategy includes long-term planning, something many women neglect because they focus on other people. The head of a large banking chain (NationsBank), CEO Hugh McColl, Jr., advises:

Women have to push harder. They often feel that things will be done fairly, whereas men don't believe that, and in reality it's often not the case. So women must ask their bosses what's needed to get to the next level. They then need to make sure they get those opportunities, and ask for feedback every step of the way. (Fortune, *September 21, 1992)*

Women need to establish long-term goals for their careers, and plan how t
achieve them. Women are taught to have less sense of control over their lives than men, so
this too requires rethinking. They are also less likely to take calculated risks, or delegate
work to others, according to a survey comparing the attitudes of male and female managers

Risk-taking requires women to develop self-esteem and assertiveness
(see Chapter 2). In laboratory tests, women are likely to pay themselves less than men
for equal work and to join men in rating what men do higher than women doing the
same task. A study of managers found men feel more confident than women about taking a job for which they are not trained, expecting to learn on the job.

Since power plays go on at work, observe that powerful people are likely
to touch, take up space with their bodies and possessions, intrude into other people's
space, and make declarative rather than questioning statements. Subordinates—usually
women and children—disclose more about themselves, take up less space, allow themselve
to be interrupted, smile more, and ask for attention with phrases like "Listen to this." To
prevent being interrupted, the speaker can keep talking or firmly state that she or he
would like to finish the thought. Women can avoid unnecessary apologies and revealing
their personal issues, take the initiative to shake hands or speak, lower voice tone, make
statements rather than questions, take space such by spreading out papers, and look people in the eye. When my women students introduce themselves the first day of class they
are more likely than the men to use tentative language ("just," "maybe," "kinda"), shrug,
smile, cock their heads, use a questioning inflection, speak fast and softly, and other
apologies for being the center of attention. This reduces their power as speakers.

Playing the game well requires some emotional detachment, which boys
learn by playing sports where rules and winning are more important than the feelings of the
players. Boys often learn a put-down humor which, combined with the fear of being a "sissy,'
teaches them to armor themselves. Girls, however, are likely to stop playing a game if feeling
get hurt. The work world runs according to boys' rules, as explained in an old but unfortunately still useful book—*Games Mother Never Taught You*, by Betty Harragan (Warner Books).

Taking time to recharge emotional batteries is important. Having to work
harder than men to achieve recognition, facing discrimination, and doing more family
work and child care is exhausting. To avoid burnout, women have to develop support systems and regularly take time to do what they like to do. Women often have to unlearn the
workaholism and perfectionism that they developed to prove their abilities. Learning whe
to say No is crucial, since one of women's primary problems is having too much to do.

Career Planning for Girls

Take Our Daughters to Work Day
1-800-676-7780
Ms. Foundation for Women
(The foundation started the National
Girls' Initiative in 1991 to fund
girls' programs. It began the Take
Our Daughters to Work Day on April
15, 1993. A curriculum for boys is
available too.)

Women's Educational Equity Act
(WEEA) Publishing Center
1-800-225-3088
(guides for career planning and mentoring for girls)

Apprenticeship and Nontradition
Employment for Wome
P. O. Box 249
Renton, WA 9805

U.S. Department of Labor Women'
Bureau http
www.dol.gov/dol/wb/welcome.htm

Jolene Godfrey. *No More Frogs to Kiss
99 Ways to Give Economic Power t
Girls*. NY: HarperCollins, 199!

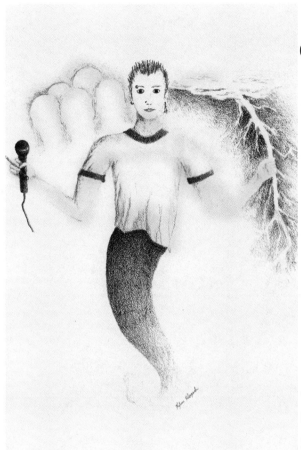

Kylene Klopsch

Community

Advocacy and Activism

Never doubt that a small, dedicated group of people can change the world:
Indeed, it is the only thing that ever has.

—Margaret Mead

To refuse to participate in the shaping of our future is to give it up. Do not
be misled into passivity either by false security (they don't mean me) or by
despair (there's nothing we can do). Each of us must find our work and do it.

—Audre Lorde

Shallow understanding from people of good will is more frustrating than
absolute misunderstanding from people of ill will.... We will have to repent in
this generation not merely for the vitriolic words and actions of the bad people, but for the appalling
silence of the good people.

**—Martin Luther King,
letter from Birmingham
jail, 1963**

Teens report there is nowhere to go and
nothing to do, police and merchants are
suspicious, the media trashes them, it's hard
to find a job, and schools need major improve-
ments. As Max asks, "Where are we supposed to
go? What are we supposed to do? Everything we
do seems wrong."

Some teens organize, speak up, and do something about these problems in their towns. You can too if you get a group together to focus on the most pressing problems. For example, do teens need more activities? Organize a group to work with the recreation department, the school board, the city council, or other groups with power and money and you'll be amazed at how much respect you generate. Danisha (an activist with the Seattle Young People's Project) points out, "You can't complain about a problem unless you're doing something to change it." Organizing is a skill which takes practice, but you can learn the basics from this chapter. I'd like to hear about your efforts.

A poll asked teens about the greatest problems facing the U.S. Their responses were AIDS (21 percent), the economy (15 percent), crime and gangs (13 percent), education (10 percent), intolerance and racism (six percent) and environmental destruction (five percent). (Poll by Teenage Politics: Public and Personal, BKG Youth, 1993) A poll asking about the worst world problems got these responses from teens—crime and decline in values (Horatio Alger Association, 1996).

There's work for us to do. American young people are more likely to be poor, drug addicted, murdered, jailed, or pregnant than youth in any other industrial nation. Over 15 million children lived in poverty in 1994. In a ranking of 15 major industrial nations, the U.S. is at the bottom in infant mortality, health care coverage, preschool attendance, and science test scores. Despite these problems (or because of them?) young people have gotten less interested in keeping up with politics; those interested fell from 57 percent in 1966 to only 28.5 percent in 1995 (a UCLA poll of 240,000 college freshmen). Yet community activism can make a difference.

We can learn from the elderly who influence politicians by writing letters and telephoning in large numbers. In the 1995 national elections, 60 percent of the elderly voted, compared to only 39 percent of the 58 million parents with children at home, and less than 20 percent of young adults. The Association of American Retired Persons has a huge membership, with an annual budget of $300 million, compared to $66 million for the American Rifle Association, and a puny $13 million for the Children's Defense Fund—the leading lobby group for children.

It's not by chance that the federal government spends about one-tenth as much on each child as on the average senior citizen. California politician Willie Brown observes, "Neglect of children by our government and political leaders is a national disgrace. America has abandoned children. For every $1 spent on youth, $8 is spent on old people. That makes no sense whatsoever." Youth and their families need to organize as powerfully as the elderly and in coalition with them.

Teens have time to take action. A study of young adolescents (ages 9 to 14) found they spend 32 percent of their time in school and 3.5 percent studying, while 42 percent is free time. Of that time, 21 percent is spent watching television and 15 percent on outdoor activities, hobbies, and with friends (a report of the Task Force on Youth Development and Community Programs). Just a few hours of volunteer work a week can cause significant change.

Adultism is something for young activists and their adult advisors to think about, a new word to add to the list of racism, sexism, classism, and so on. Adultism occurs when adults systematically don't notice, listen to, trust, or allow youths to participate in decision making. Mike Males, author of *The Scapegoat Generation*, writes, "We have lied about today's adolescents in every conceivable negative way to every conceivable profitable end." He believes that adults cause most of youth's problems, by abusing them, raising them in poverty, having sex with girls, etc. Adults cite statistics about teen problems to blame them, he says, without pointing out that adult rates are usually higher, as for single parenting, suicide, or drug-related deaths.

Strategies for Youth Activists

✳ Start small and concentrate on goal that no one else is focusing on, that is widely desired and easy to understand.

✳ Select a reachable goal that can be achieved fairly quickly, such as setting up a Youth Commission. The project should have an end that can be celebrated, publicized, and evaluated.

✳ Empower the members of the group by making decisions as a group and giving each person a task to accomplish and report on to the group.

✳ Study potential resources (city budget, service organizations, religious groups) and needs (do surveys, polls, search census records). (See *Know Your Community*, Family Resource Coalition, 200 S. Michigan Ave., 16th Floor, Chicago, IL 60604.)

✳ Write out a plan of action, including committees, tasks, and due dates. If you need money, develop a fund-raising strategy.

✳ Involve and talk with influential people about your goal, including city officials, school administrators, chief of police, religious leaders, business leaders, service groups such as Rotary Club, media, and leaders of neighborhood associations.

✳ Establish links with other groups having similar goals (e.g., teachers' associations, religious youth groups, Junior League, and youth-serving organizations). As a youth activist, Danisha emphasizes, "This is essential!"

✳ Publicize your goal with photo opportunities for media. Send out press releases and organize press conferences to announce the results of a study or poll at a place with photo opps, such as youth volunteers in action at a nursing home. Piggyback on national events, like Mother's or Father's Day, elections, or local events such as the first day of the school semester. Call radio and TV station public service directors or station mangers to find out the format and length of their public service announcements (PSAs). Include how your information can help the listener or viewer and whom to contact for more information.

✳ Put a human face on your campaign by presenting individual examples and getting press coverage of activist young people.

✳ Select the most powerful facts that fit on one page to inform local leaders about your issue. Be brief, as decision makers have much to read and are short on time.

✳ Frame your message as broadly as possible, as six in 10 adults live in households with no children under 18. Point out, for example, that youth are future workers, voters, and taxpayers.

✳ Exert power as a group, by collecting petitions to present to officials, organizing a candidate's forum to feature your issues, endorsing candidates for office, boycotting a business, getting your message in the media, organizing a speakers' bureau, registering voters, and attending meetings of the city council and school board as a group—while wearing a symbol of your cause. For example, when a group of us tried to start a family task force, we wore pink and blue armbands to the city council meeting.

* Evaluate the success of each effort, analyze what you've learned and can apply to the next goal, then reward yourselves.

What to Include in a Press Release

1. Your organization, address, and phone number, and a person to contact

2. Date and time for release of story or write "For Immediate Release"

3. Headline

4. Dateline begins the first paragraph (your city and state). Double space. Be brief: Keep it under two pages long. Answer who, what, where, when, and why. Include brief, juicy quotes from your leaders or community leaders. Type "more" at the bottom of the page, then end the release with ###.

Organizations to Include in Your Youth Campaign

Ask groups like these about additional contacts for coalition building. The chamber of commerce has a directory of many groups.

◆ Private nonprofit organizations: churches and synagogues, NAACP, Urban League, college and university student groups such as fraternities and sororities, veterans' groups.

◆ Business groups: chamber of commerce, corporate foundations.

◆ Professional groups: medical associations, social workers associations, teachers' and other unions.

◆ Volunteer service organizations: Salvation Army, Goodwill, Rotary, Lions, Business and Professional Women, American Association of University Women.

◆ Community agencies: city and county social service agencies, mental health agencies, police department, judicial system, housing authority, school district, tribal councils, neighborhood associations, tenant councils, librarians, hospitals.

◆ Youth groups: Big Brothers/Big Sisters, Girl Scouts/Boy Scouts, Boys Club/Girls Club, Campfire, YWCA, YMCA.

Examples of Youth Empowerment Programs

Activism 2000 Project

      Adalis Santiago, Massachusetts, reports, *Our project gave me the opportunity and motivation for speaking up for what I want and not holding back on what I think is best. As a student I feel proud of what we accomplished, and as a teenager, it is good to know that older people will understand and hear your words.*

Activism 2000 is a resource center that teaches young people, especially those under voting age, how to lobby to influence politicians. Projects include organizing state Youth for Justice Summits, lobbying to preserve the National Service Trust Act, lobbying in Virginia to prevent state budget cuts for youth programs, a statewide effort to get high school students elected on every school board in Illinois, and opening a shelter for runaways in St. Paul, Minnesota.

Activism 2000 provides resource materials, including the book *No Kidding Around! America's Young Activists Are Changing Our World and You Can Too*, by director Wendy Schaetzel Lesko. She suggests projects for youths.

Use your age to get your foot in the door and do not underestimate the power of your voice. Investigate an issue you are passionate about, absorb different points of view, mobilize support, publicize your campaign widely, and meet face to face with community leaders and elected officials who are responsible for developing new programs or policies, or enforcing existing laws. Wake up to your power!

Produce a 30-second public service announcement, write a letter to the editor of the local newspaper, speak up before your school board, invite speakers to address school groups, encourage your student council to work for a school health clinic, train to be a peer mediator, investigate how easy it is for minors to buy cigarettes, organize a youth summit, clean up the environment, and testify before the city council on proposed laws which affect youth.

Activism 2000 Project
1-800-KID-POWER
ACTIVISM@aol.com

Children's Defense Fund's
Black Student Leadership Network (BSLN)

BSLN is a national organization of college-aged African Americans who are activists for youth in their communities. Members receive leadership and advocacy training. The Black Community Crusade for Children organizes the Black Student Leadership Network, trains college students to work with disadvantaged children in summer Freedom Schools, backs a Cease Fire violence prevention media campaign, and organizes a Religious Action campaign to strengthen youth and family ministries. BSLN provides assistance with Beat the Odds celebrations to honor "remarkable young people." To check on your local Congressperson, request CDF's annual Congressional Voting Ratings.

Children's Defense Fund
1-800-ASK-BCCC
E-mail: hn3208@handsnet.org
Web site:
http://www.tmn.com/cdf/index.hdtml

Coleman Advocates for Children and Youth

Coleman is a nonprofit educational agency and a model for other cities as one of the most successful local advocacy groups for youth in the U.S. In the 1980s Coleman began focusing public attention and pressure on city officials. They sponsored candidates' forums on children's issues and lobbied the city of San Francisco to adopt a Children's Agenda in 1987 (policies covered housing, education, health, recreation, and juvenile justice). Coleman recommends how to vote on local ballot propositions affecting youth and evaluates the voting record of supervisors and the mayor in an annual report card.

In 1989, the city created an Office for Children. Another groundbreaking victory was the adoption of the Children's Amendment in 1991 by San Francisco voters, setting aside a percentage of the annual property tax for children's programs and requiring the city to develop a yearly Children's Services Plan. The effort was spearheaded by Coleman's director, Margaret Brodkin. From 1991 to 1995, the city spent $31 million on new children's services.

A 1993 poll of 8,000 students in social studies classes asked about their priorities for spending the Children's Fund money. Their top issues were: child care for poor families, sex education, services for homeless kids, after-school jobs, and "teen club" recreation programs. The Youth Vote, followed by a press conference, became an annual event. In the 1995 Youth Vote, youth employment and training got the most votes, followed by health services, after-school activities, and help for homeless kids.

Coleman organized a Kids' Network of thousands of citizens who receive a monthly alert about children's needs, including a youth issues action postcard. A hotline updates telephone callers about children's issues in the city (1-415-206-1023). As a result, in 1995, San Francisco was probably the first city to defeat a curfew measure on the ballot and to require the city government to consult a Youth Commission of young people before passing legislation that affects youth. The commissioners must be between the ages of 13 and 23, appointed by the supervisors and the mayor. (Their 1996 goals were to address homelessness, jobs, day care for teen mothers, poor maintenance of parks, and police harassment.)

Coleman administrator Carnella Gordon-Brown says the main problem in lobbying for teens is that adults are afraid of young people. Many adults stereotype teens as violent, disrespectful, and bizarre dressers. Coleman's first task is to change how the public thinks about youth, to look at them as individuals, most of whom don't get in trouble.

Coleman sponsors a youth board called Y-MAC, Youth Making A Change, comprised of 15 high school students. Y-MAC's goal is to create a positive youth agenda. Middle school students were involved at first, but the two groups were too different to mesh. Members earn about five dollars an hour, six hours a week. The founder, Carol Callen, recruited the first members in 1992 by visiting schools and talking to receptive teachers and youth agencies. She reports girls tend to be more involved, as boys think "it's not cool to be too enthusiastic." (We see that word cool again, a major roadblock.) Ms. Callen believes that the underlying effort is to rebuild community and struggle against people's lack of connection with each other.

The five principles the youth decided upon as their operating principles are CROSS: *Chaos* and noise are part of youth organizing, mutual *respect*, *ownership* (teens are in charge), *skills* building (including public speaking, multicultural understanding, and goal setting), and *slow* down. Members do not want to be rushed to the next project before celebrating and reflecting on the completion of their current action.

Y-MAC members organize activities including a citywide dance, youth conferences, newsletter, and youth "Speak Out," and attend board of supervisor meetings to lobby for youth. They want a more positive media portrayal of young people to change the media focus on youth drug abuse and violence. Y-MAC joined with other youth groups to defeat curfew legislation in a Youth Uprising Coalition which continues to meet, expanding their platform to jobs and education.

Coleman's suggestions for a successful youth summit are: include everyone involved with youth issues—especially youth, demand specific and measurable goals, have skilled facilitators, and focus on prevention measures which build on the strengths of youth, families, and the community.

Y-MAC got a major boost from foundation funding for a full-time adult director. A spin-off was the formation of a parents' board called Parent Advocates for Youth, with a parent representing each neighborhood in the city. The parents also receive a stipend, attend dinner meetings, and work on achievable goals such as making parks safer. They succeeded in getting $1.5 million added to the city's park budget.

In 1995, Coleman's YouthTime campaign aimed to "provide somewhere to go and something to do." The campaign defined goals that probably apply to your city as well. One of the goals is to make sure elected officials commit to youth as a city priority. At the YouthTime kick-off campaign, the four candidates for mayor of San Francisco were invited to speak to an audience of about 500 youth and adults.

Other goals of the three-year YouthTime campaign to consider duplicating in your planning are: offer something to do in every neighborhood; increase funding for the Recreation and Park Department to expand youth services and make parks safe; encourage the media to cover positive youth activities; encourage the school district to establish Beacon Schools throughout the city (using the model of New York City Beacon Schools which provide youth with full services, including after-school recreation); establish a city-funded youth center run for and by youth; equip public libraries with access to the Internet; expand job training and job experience; establish a phone referral YouthLine run by and for youth (modeled on the NYC YouthLine); encourage businesses to provide teen activities such as teen nights; and stop unreasonable curfews and other "overly punitive policies."

Coleman Advocates for Children and
Youth
2601 Mission St., #804
San Francisco, CA 94110

Margaret Brodkin (director of
Coleman). *Every Kid Counts: 31 Ways
to Save Our Children*. San Francisco:
Harper Collins, 1993.
(Other materials include
videos and reports.)

Seattle Young People's Project

Kids do more than talk about a perfect world. They work to make one. *For far too long society has ignored, dismissed, or rejected young people's ideas, opinion, and beliefs. Youth are thoughtful, angry, creative, articulate, passionate, and urgent and they deserve to be heard! SYPP is a rare organization dedicated to empowering youth to speak out, stand up and take action on the issues that affect their lives. Youth empowerment is our mission and guiding force.*

By 1993, youth were involved in internships and organized more than 650 young people. About 600 members receive a quarterly newsletter and phone calls to get their input and inform them about events. Girls outnumber boys by about two to one.

Teens vote on their preference for initiatives to work on and can join one of the initiative task forces. Issues revolving around school have been most popular, including violence, multicultural and health education, and sexual harassment. Danisha emphasizes the importance of a youth-run, youth-led organization,.

We have a number of initiatives that focus on the concerns and interests of Seattle's young people. The Anti-Violence Initiative recently held a youth/police forum and a rally and candlelight vigil for youth killed in our country. Puget Sound Student Alliance held a weekend retreat to come up with ideas to help implement a multicultural curriculum in our schools and held a rally outside of the school district offices. Queer Youth Rights is publishing their third zine and doing panels in local high schools about homosexuality, as well as outreach in the community to queer youth. The Sexuality Harassment and Assault Initiative is working on surveys and putting on trainings. Urban Agenda is a newsletter for and by youth of color. Empowered Youth Educating Society works on securing the rights of youth through lobbying at the city and state level. All are youth initiated.

SYPP is managed by a full-time paid director, six youth staff members paid for eight hours of work per week, and a board of directors chaired by a teen. Funding sources are one-third private foundations and two-thirds individual donors. The budget for fiscal year 1994 to 1995 was $90,000. SYPP avoids government funding because of the restrictions and strings attached.

The Seattle Young People's Project
1265 S. Maine St., Suite 310
Seattle, WA 98118

Youth Power

Youth Power is a program sponsored by "Just Say No." The underlying belief is that youth need opportunities to experience success in a caring and supportive environment. Their projects dovetail with other programs in schools or community groups. (1) The "Just Say No" club works to create a drug-free community. (2) The Transitions Project teaches youth to help others through difficult changes, such as starting junior high school. (3) The Peer Tutoring Project trains youth to tutor other students. (4) The Community Service Project trains youth to help solve community problems like loneliness of single elderly people.

JSN chapters empower youth by working on community projects including adopting a grandparent, stopping smoking, and reducing teen pregnancy. Headquarters provide youth organizations (such as city recreation programs) with training and technical assistance with this empowerment model. Director Sam Piha reports that doing community service gives youth the "opportunity to stretch their vision of who they are in their community." Sue Wigg, director of the Jamestown, North Dakota, chapter found their information alone doesn't change behavior. Involvement and looking to kids for answers works better than adults preaching.

"Just Say No" International
1-800-258-2766

Youth Leadership Institute

YLI is a youth development agency based in the San Francisco Bay Area. Founded in 1991, YLI integrates six independent programs: Friday Night Live and Club Live (drug and alcohol prevention recreation programs for youth); Teens Kick Off (an educational theater program where young people perform their own life stories and issues); the Youth Mentor Program (matches young people with mentors under age 25); the Advanced Leadership Training Program (training for interns ages 17 to 25 in community organizing, media advocacy, and public policy); The Marin Youth Commission (young people lobby city and county government); and the Youth Grants Board (a re-granting program where young people distribute $25,000 a year to youth-initiated efforts).

YLI programs rely on organizing young people to take action. Jane Reed, the Advanced Leadership Training Director, reports:

How to Organize

1. **Listen:** Leaders should listen to the needs and issues expressed by young people. The key is listening to what they want to do and to their ideas for solutions. A leader provides ideas, suggestions, training, and support as the group carries out the plan. If youth seem apathetic, start by listening to their concerns, including their anger. The group may need time to vent frustration. The effective leader then channels the anger into action. Some of the issues young people defined as pressing include: HIV/AIDS, nothing to do, ageism/nothing teen-friendly, racism, sexism, sexual preference, images of youth in the media, and affirmative action.

2. **Train:** Even though it is important for the young people to carry out their own ideas, they need adequate training to do this. Basic skill training includes communication, group facilitation, event planning, conflict mediation, and team building. More advanced training includes community organizing, public policy, and how to get your message out to the media.

3. **Define a collective vision:** To build cohesiveness in a group, identify common issues. While a group of young people may seem incredibly different, there are probably commonalities, such as women's issues and HIV/AIDS.

4. **Start small and celebrate victories** to help the group gain confidence and feel successful.

5. **Think about the larger social environment.** Too often the focus is on the problem of the individual (for example, he drinks too much, so he needs counseling). One might also approach the problem by considering the prevalence of alcohol advertising to youth (such as Budweiser cartoon frogs), and become politically active to remove such advertising. Young people might consider the broader social issues, such as why we see more alcohol and tobacco ads in low-income neighborhoods. By examining the larger picture, the focus is not only on individual young people, but on the root causes of problems.

Youth Leadership Institute
1115 Third St.
San Rafael, CA 949901

—Shannon, 14, Connecticut

There is a lot of discrimination against teens. Adults act like it is the teens who rob, kill, kidnap, and are the cause of every bad thing that goes on. Then they say that we are maniacs and weirdos because we like baggy clothes, nose rings, ripped clothes, and colored or shaved heads. We just like to be different. It is our lives and we are almost grown. Now we even have dress codes. If an adult was wearing a nose ring, for example, nobody would tell him or her to take it out, but with a teenager they make us. Right now I want a nose ring, but I can't have one. So personally that part of being a teenager sucks majorly.

—Tovah, 15, New York

A challenge for me as a teenager is growing up in a really screwed-up time and recognizing what bad shape the world is in. Changing the world is in our hands but it's easy to get discouraged when we see what's out there. You have to always remember your Self—and that capital "S" is there for a reason. You have to remember that force inside you which is your true being.

—Emma, 15, California

Many adults look down on teens. They don't trust us. If you walk into a store, a salesperson will follow you around so you don't steal anything. Ladies have called my brother a pervert for being in the girls' section when he was waiting for me while I was trying on swimming suits.

—Katy, 16, Colorado

Being a teenager, it's difficult staying happy and calm when this time and this world throw me different mountains to climb every single day. There is so much stress living up to expectations you have inadvertently set for yourself. And as you get older, it all gets harder. The best advice is to get involved in the world that needs you so much. There are too many teens walking the wrong road in life. Being a leader and getting involved in as much as I possibly can saved me and led me down the path of success!

—Andy Pokorny, 18, North Dakota

We're the generation to build and invent. We grew up so fast, we're street smart, we can read adults, and we know how to manipulate others because we have to. Adults underestimate youth. If they label us as goof-offs, they create a self-fulfilling prophecy.

Here's how I became an activist to inspire positive living. I've been so blessed: It has snowballed and I'm loving it. I moved to my mom's house in the 9th grade. The first friends I made in the new town didn't drink or do drugs. A couple of them led a "Just Say No" club and asked me to help with a JSN walk. That started everything. I became a teen leader in charge of a Just Say No! club of elementary school kids. They loved it when I listened to them and set boundaries for them. We played games, analyzed smoking ads, and so on.

The idea was to establish a strong support system of friends who don't drink, smoke, and use other drugs. I've learned that the way to keep kids out of bad situations is to get them involved in activities with their friends. It makes a big difference if the cool people in school, the strong leaders, participate. And parents need to take more responsibility to set limits. Saying things like, "I'd rather have my kids drink in my basement where I know what they're doing," is crap.

All of this led to my involvement in the National Student Safety Program. The organization started with an emphasis on traffic safety and wearing seat belts, but expanded to educate youth about AIDS, teen pregnancy, racism, homophobia, rape, and gangs. In my high school we organized drug-free events such as a bonfire after the homecoming game, a Spring Fling softball tournament, dances, and a sleigh ride. Everyone turned out.

I eventually became the national president of the NSSP, traveling and speaking all over the country. I plan to make motivational speaking my career. The motto on my business card reads, "Seeking Out and Inspiring a Positive Direction."

What It Takes to Be an Effective Youth Activist

1. Walk your talk and talk about your walk.

2. Find your passion. If music and protecting the environment are what energize you, use them both to make a difference in your community.

3. Put your passion into action, learning the skills you need, such as public speaking or how to publicize events.

4. Before you get burned out, pass the torch on to someone else.

—Giulia Campanaro, 19, Maryland

I'm student Area Coordinator of the Philadelphia Area for Amnesty International and the mid-Atlantic representative on their National Campus Advisory Committee. Some key points that I found to be useful in student activism:

⇨ The unique aspect of students is that they can be either highly spirited and dedicated or they can be apathetic. The student activist's job is to target these different groups in different ways. For example, if the student is dedicated and hard-working, give him or her tangible and productive tasks. For the apathetic student, take an approach which pulls them in—how does this apply to them? Make it fun, that's what draws them in.

⇨ Give student activists things to do. Don't let them simply be participants.

⇨ Another unique feature about working with students is that you are usually dealing with an educational system. You must work closely with the administration and make sure they are aware of your intentions. Educate them initially about what you are working on and make them a part of the planning process.

As a student area coordinator, I work closely with student leaders. Students are unique because they have so many other priorities and it is difficult to coordinate schedules. Also, student activists are likely to be involved in various similar activities which occupy them as well.

During my first year as a student area coordinator I worked to organize a human rights freedom festival involving several student groups. Many times it is easy to want to do everything yourself as the organizer. But I found that assigning important tasks to each reliable student group ended in success. For example, one school handled live music, another got goods for a raffle, another gathered information and xeroxed flyers, etc. Each group did what they were asked except for the group who was supposed to handle the food. Up to the actual day of the event I thought that they were handling the setup. In fact, I called constantly and checked in with the coordinator of that group and she assured me everything was going well. To my disappointment on the day of the event there was no food and we received complaints. Although this was a small down-

fall to the event. I was proud of the hard work everyone else put into it and amazed at the empowerment that this kind of responsibility gave young student leaders.

Amnesty International has a student action network with staff just to work with students and they make it easy to get started [1-800-266-3789]. They also have a children's action network and a women's rights network. You can subscribe to their youth magazine SAY by calling the 800 number.

—Elena, 20, Ohio

An idea for a project is to start a newsletter of local teens' successes to counteract the media's negative images. Or hold a mock election during presidential or other races; it will get kids interested in the issues and spark discussions, as well as get people used to voting.

When leading a group, be mature and serious about the group's goal when talking to adults so they take you seriously. Take a break now and then (like a group party or outing), to help the group become friends. Have a rotating facilitator. College students are great resources for anything a group wants to do; they have time, energy, and age.

Organizations Focusing on Youth Issues

Children Now 1-800-CHILD-44
http://www.dnai.com/~children

American Youth Policy Forum
1001 Connecticut Ave., NW,
Suite 719
Washington, DC 20036-5541

Center for Campus Organizing
P.O. Box 748
Cambridge, MA 02142
cco@igc.apc.org

The Center for Youth Development
and Policy Research
1255-23rd St., NW, Suite 400
Washington, DC 20037
(The center does research, analyzes policy, provides information about youth programs, and provides technical assistance.)

Children's Policy Institute
P.O. Box 4387
Charleston, WV 25364

Family and Youth Services Bureau
P.O. Box 1182
Washington, D.C. 20013

Family Resource Coalition
200 S. Michigan Ave., 16th Floor
Chicago, IL 60604

Families USA
1334 G St., NW
Washington, DC

National Association for the
Advancement of Colored People
(NAACP) Youth Section,
4805 Mount Hope Dr.
Baltimore, MD 21215

National Children's Advocacy Center
106 Lincoln St.
Huntsville, AL 35801

National Clearinghouse of Families
and Youth
P.O. Box 13505
Silver Springs, MD 20911-3505

National League of Cities
Successful Programs for Youth.
1301 Pennsylvania Ave., NW
Washington, DC 20004

National Resource Center for Youth
Services
202 W. Eighth St.
Tulsa, OK 74119-1419

People for the American Way
2000 M St., NW, Suite 400
Washington, DC 20036
(keeps track of censorship efforts in schools and public libraries)

Public Allies
1511 K St., Suite 330
Washington, DC 20005.
(A 10-month paid apprenticeship
program in nonprofit and government
agencies teaches leadership and
organizing skills.)

Serious Teens Acting Responsibly
(STAR)
South Carolina State University
1890 Research and Extension,
P.O. Box 7659
Orangeburg, SC 29117
(assists in the development of local
youth leadership, activism, and entrepreneurship programs nationwide)

With a Growing Voice newsletter
UNPLUG!
360 Grand Ave.
Oakland, CA 94610
(works on commercial-free, equitable
education; the newsletter is about
young people creating change.)

Works in Progress, Applied Research
Center
25 Embarcadero Cove
Oakland, CA 94606
(reports on community issues and
organizing)

YouthAction (*Breakdown* newsletter is
written by young people)
1830 Connecticut Ave., NW
Washington, DC 20009
(YouthAction works with community-
based organizations in low-income
areas "to develop opportunities for
young people in social, environmental,
and economic justice efforts." It provides youth organizations with training,
technical assistance, and networking.)

Youth Action Program
1280 Fifth Ave.
New York, NY 10029

YouthBuild USA
P.O. Box 440322
Somerville, MA 02144
(They train youth in construction
skills for 12 to 18 months by
rebuilding abandoned buildings to
produce housing for low income people. Students attend academic and
leadership classes as well.)

Youth Communication
144 W. 27th St.
New York, NY 10011
(Director Keith Hefner started a group
called Youth Liberation when he was
15. Now, as the adult manager of a
teen newspaper staffed mainly by
young people, he suggests that any
youth program benefits by having a
specific product, such as a newsletter
or an event to aim for and to evaluate.
The project should formally teach skills
and should recognize the necessity for
"a healthy dose of adult direction.")

Youth Policy Institute
1221 Massachusetts Ave., NW,
Suite B
Washington, DC 20005-5333
(publishes *Youth Record: The semi-
monthly report of federal youth-relat-
ed policy*)

International Youth Activist
Organizations

Coalition of Children of the Earthways
(CCE was formed in 1990 after the
Children's World Seminar presented
the Children's Declaration for Peace
to the Dalai Lama. In 1993 the
Children's World Conference on
Human Rights met in Vienna.)
Peaceways Activities
324 Catalpa Ave., #318
San Mateo, CA 94401

4th World Movement
7600 Willow Hill Dr.
Landover, MD 20785

Global Family Youth Clubs
112 Jordan Ave.
San Anselmo, CA 94960
(Teams of youth work on peace building, preserving the environment, etc.
John Server, peace educator, observes
how important it is for youth and
adults to work together. "I'm amazed
at the level of wisdom, sense of
knowing, that emerges when adults
listen to kids," he says. The lone
ranger's [the person who works
alone] work is not sustained over
time, so team-building is important,
requiring skills in communication,
problem-solving, and conflict resolution. This creates a deep level of
trust and open communication.")

World Wide Free Press
http://www.wwfreepress.com/wwfp/
This Internet publication provides
information about how to change
society, e.g. information on nuclear
testing.

Youth Organizing Books

Active Citizenship Today Field Guide.
Los Angeles: Constitutional Rights
Foundation and the Close Up
Foundation, 1995. One edition is for
middle-school students and another
is for high school.
(CRF, 601 S. Kingsley Dr., Los
Angeles, CA 90005)

The Kids Count Data Book (ranks
North Dakota as the best state for
children's well-being and Mississippi
as the worst)
(Center for the Study of Social
Policy, 1250 Eye St., NW,
Suite 503, Washington, DC)

*National Guide to Funding for
Children, Youth and Families.* The
Foundation Center (79 Fifth Ave.,
New York, NY 10003-3076). They
also have a *National Guide to
Funding for Women and Girls.*

*The Role of Youth in the Governance
of Youth Service Programs.*
Constitutional Rights Foundation for
Youth Service America.
(YSA, 1101-15th St. NW, #200,
Washington, DC 20005)
YSAsysop@aol.com (database of ser-
vice organizations)

Nancy Amidei. *So You Want to Make a
Difference: A Key to Advocacy.*
Washington, DC: OMB Watch, 1991.
(1731 Connecticut Ave., NW, 4th
Floor, Washington, DC 20009-1146)

I. Shelby Andress. *Working Together
for Youth: A Practical Guide for
Individuals and Groups.* Lutheran
Brotherhood for RespecTeen, distributed by the Search Institute (has
many other resources about how to
build a healthy community for youth)
1-800-888-7828

Steve Fiffer and Sharon Sloan Fiffer.
50 Ways to Help Your Community.
NY: Doubleday, 1994.

Paul Fleisher. *Changing Our World: A
Handbook for Young Activists.* Tucson,
AZ: Zephyr Press, 1993.

Penelope Leach. *Children First: What
Our Society Must Do—And Is Not
Doing for Our Children Today.* NY:
Alfred A. Knopf, 1994.

Frances Moore Lappé and Paul Martin
DuBois. *The Quickening of America:
Rebuilding Our Nation, Remaking Our
Lives.* San Francisco: Jossey-Bass,
1994.

Barbara Lewis. *The Kid's Guide to
Social Action: How to Solve the Social
Problems You Choose and Turn
Creative Thinking into Positive Action.*
Minneapolis: Free Spirit Publishing,
1992.

Mike Males. *The Scapegoat
Generation: America's War on
Adolescents.* Monroe, ME: Common
Courage Press, 1996.

Peg Michels, et al. *Making the Rules:
A Guide for Young People Who Intend
to Make a Difference.* Minneapolis,:
Project Public Life.
(130 Humphrey Center, 301 19th Ave.
S., Minneapolis, MN 55455)

*David Walls' Activist's Almanac: The
Concerned Citizen's Guide to the
Leading Advocacy Organizations in
America.* NY: Fireside, 1993.

City Youth Programs

W endy Schaetzel Lesko travels around the country as a consultant for youth-led campaigns such as prevention of AIDS and pregnancy. She observes this generation is interested in problem solving, rather than confrontation with adults. When teens are encouraged to work with adults to make an impact on their communities, their self-esteem soars and everyone benefits.

She reports an exciting but tardy trend, beginning in the early 1990s, for city officials and youth-serving organizations to include youth on their boards. For example, in Indianapolis, the "Youth as Resources" board is one-third teens. The board funds local projects like a babysitting co-op to prevent child abuse by giving parents time out.

Although teens are often cynical about the way adults have wrecked things and are absent from their children's lives, she finds youth are very protective of children and make a big impact when they mentor elementary school children. As an example, one of the few successful programs to prevent teen pregnancy paired teens in Atlanta as big sisters to young girls.

The evidence is clear that the social support that allows families to flourish has worn thin. In my suburban and mostly white college town of Chico, surveys by the Pacific Wellness Institute found that one-fourth of 8th graders reported carrying a weapon, nearly half had been in a fight during the previous year, one-fourth were sexually active, and one-fifth reported feeling frequently depressed. Nearly one in three Chico children lives below the poverty line, and child abuse and teen pregnancy rates in the county have soared.

The Search Institute in Minneapolis has identified programs communities can use to nurture their youth: parent education, parental involvement, child care, youth activities, youth empowerment, family-friendly work environments, mentoring, and caring schools. Their studies show youth develop best when they have a positive school environment, a supportive family, are active in a church or synagogue and in structured youth activities. Danisha adds, "And jobs, real jobs!"

Efforts are underway to empower communities to develop neighborhood organizations. Cities with effective citizen participation efforts (such as Portland, Oregon) recognize distinct neighborhoods, do outreach to all households, fund neighborhood organizations, and involve neighborhoods in city planning.

Donald Fraser, former mayor of Minneapolis, used to think that social services were the county's responsibility rather than the city's. Experience taught him that only city government is charged with thinking about community and developing mutual responsibility on the local level. Mayor Fraser realized, "These children are our community's treasure. Minneapolis will not squander this treasure. We will instead create the kind of community that values its children and families above all else." Now every city policy in Minneapolis is tested against the question of whether children will gain.

Most cities, however, still wait for families to fall off a cliff before helping them. Fraser realized that the protective umbrella of services for families has eroded and needs to be replaced by informal support systems in neighborhoods. Families are like plants that grow in soil, he says, and community is the nourishing environment families need to thrive.

Chico, California

My students and I organized a Youth SpeakOut, with video documentation. We organized meetings with high school and junior high students throughout the semester to identify their top issues, then solutions and goals were debated in breakaway groups at the SpeakOut. The event started with a welcome by the mayor who read a proclamation we wrote declaring Youth Day in Chico. The most popular task group was "things to do," followed by developing "positive media" coverage of youth, then teen sexuality and pregnancy. The groups reported back on their short- and long-term goals, approved by the 80 participants, well-covered by the local TV news. We provided pizza and a band as an incentive to attend—food and awards are very helpful organizing tools!

Our work paid off when a Youth Council was selected to provide ongoing leadership. The council planned a monthly event, but members gradually lost interest and energy for organizing faded without a paid staff person. I couldn't put the necessary energy into making the council ongoing, along with teaching and family responsibilities. We learned an organization requires a consistent paid staff person to keep recruiting and training new student leaders.

—K.C. Somers, 17, Colorado Springs, Colorado

My involvement in the Teen Action Council is an eye-opening insight into the real world, such as when I've attended meetings with adults as a spokesperson for teens. It's made me a lot more responsible. We have to use teamwork; working with so many different kinds of personalities, as cochair, I have to bring them all together. I get good grades, I'm athletic, but this completes and broadens my whole personality. This prepares me for a possible career in public administration, or maybe I'll be a lawyer [he went to the Air Force Academy after graduation].

It all started when I was in 8th grade. The city council and the mayor of Colorado Springs sponsored a "Teens Talk: Adults Listen" forum to find out what teens wanted. About 150 of us met in a dozen small groups to discuss topics such as after-school activities and the availability of transportation to these activities. We reported back to the whole group, with an adult facilitator. A notebook reported on our ideas to the city council and community. [The *Youth Policy Project* reports that at the forum, teens said their best times were with friends and family, and doing exciting things without adult supervision. Their worst times revolved around trouble with the law and parents, death, relocation, social rejection, and conflicts with friends and family. Youth wanted more activities coupled with transportation and affordability.]

We filled out a form if we were interested in joining a youth council. I said I was interested, and in the 9th grade I became a member of the first Teen Action

Council. It was staffed by the city's Department of Community Service which hired a part-time professional to work with us. There were about 10 of us that year. At first adults ran the meetings and we weren't very serious or organized. We didn't feel needed or respected yet, as we had to develop a relationship of trust. Teens have to be involved in the planning because we know what works with other teens.

We knew that kids wanted something to do so we wrote a booklet listing activities for teens. We knew teens wanted a more positive image in the community, so we organized a teen talent day at the mall. We didn't get a lot of people as the publicity wasn't great. But we learned.

By the time I was in 10th grade, we got stronger and more organized. In the fall we contacted every high school principal (about 20) and asked for two (four for bigger schools) council representatives, half male and half female, including minorities. We suggested that they not be in student government because those people were already overcommitted. The principals usually gave our requests to a counselor who tended to select teens who spoke out. Some of them ignored our request at first. We did the talent day again and organized another citywide teen forum where this time the teens ran the meeting. We said if they want to change the bad reputation and lack of respect for teens, this was our opportunity to be heard. We had the meeting organized to the minute.

At our once-a-semester Teen Action Council meetings we started to click. We set four goals for the year. First we set up a phone line for teens to find out about weekly activities since they often didn't know what was going on. About 4,000 kids call each month. The TV news station updates the activities tape and PepsiCo helps pay for the costs. Second, teens said they wanted to work, so we organized a job fair in the spring. Employers come to one place for a day, the YMCA, instead of teens having to go to them. We got about 500 kids. Many of them were 14 and 15, so this year we are going to especially look for jobs for this age group.

Third, teens wanted to improve their public image, so we are organizing STAR (Super Teens Are Recognized) awards. [The first group of 11 teens was selected in 1996, honored at the city council meeting and at a Toast to Teens banquet.] Our fourth goal is to identify unmet community needs, which happens at our twice-a-year Teen Action Council meetings.

We asked council members to serve on Teen Action teams to meet monthly to implement our goals. About 15 of the 45 members were interested, a few more girls (they tend to be a little more organized) than boys, and almost half minority members. A problem is that we're mostly seniors, so we're asking principals to select sophomores for the next council [32 members were active the next year]. I've been cochair in my junior and senior years, along with a girl. The cochairs are hand-picked by the previous chairs and our adult facilitator, as we don't want it to be a popularity contest.

We break up in small groups a lot; we try to separate good buddies. Our problem area is staying on focus after a long day at school, basketball practice, etc. Sometimes we get a little goofy. Having a city staff member makes our work possible because we sometimes experience ageism when we ask businesses to post a flyer for the job fair. We've learned to go ahead and try an idea to see if it works.

Success Tips

I asked the Teen Action Council in Colorado Springs to comment on what makes a youth activist project successful. The high school students suggest the following:

☆ Have a common goal.

☆ Work hard on publicity.

☆ The leader is what makes a program work. Make sure leaders are sincere and sensitive about the problems of the group.

☆ Keep the group small or work in small groups.

☆ Set an achievable, worthwhile goal and stick to it.

☆ Work hard as a team.

☆ Work with adult advisors who take you seriously and let teens have a voice.

☆ Helping elders or children will always leave a lasting impact. Also, we can help our future by planting trees and promoting earth-help projects.

☆ Offering rewards seems to get the most participation. Student Council helped collect 10,000 cans for Care and Share. Our group offered prizes for winning classes—a pizza party.

☆ Communicate effectively.

—Cindie Myers and Patty Cameron, their advisors, suggest:

☆ Projects need to be teen-driven, not adult-directed. Let teens own the project.

☆ Give teens the responsibility for the outcome but guide them through the process.

☆ Set clear guidelines so that everyone understands what is expected from the project and from each teen. Given time and guidance through the process, teens can reach consensus on the most amazingly controversial challenges.

☆ As an adult, believe that teens can do it. In our work with teens, we appreciate the way they dedicate their time to complete a project and resolve their differences.

☆ Find teens who are truly interested and believe in the project; avoid getting bodies for the sake of numbers.

Minneapolis, Minnesota

Minneapolis is out in front in its efforts for youth. The Youth Coordinating Board is an intergovernmental organization which is a developer and advocate for working together to promote healthy youth development. The board includes representatives of the city, school board, county, parks and recreation board, and library board.

Examples of activities are "A Day of Listening," where students spent the morning job shadowing and the afternoon presenting essays on "What It's Like to Be Young in America Today." "Dancin' in the Streets" was a weekend recreation program. A campaign encouraged adults to sign this pledge: "In all of my interactions with young people, I will treat them with respect, and affirm their dignity and value to our community."

The Youth Coordinating Board in turn established the Minneapolis Youth Organization. It involves youth in bettering the city through Youthline Teen Advisory councils, youth policy forums, youth service days, the Neighborhood Youth Leadership Academy, the Downtown Youth Center, and festivals. Danisha comments, "I think this type of activism should be the focus, rather than dancing in the streets and I hope this is youth run." The Department of Park and Recreation Board's Youthline provides youth ages 12 to 16 access to community involvement (volunteering, sports teams), arts (music, visiting museums and theaters), and life skills (classes in personal development). Activities are planned by teen advisory councils, girls' groups, and parent support groups.

Minneapolis Youth Coordinating Board
202 City Hall
Minneapolis, MN 55415

Santa Monica, California

Santa Monica's youth empowerment program (first called Kids City, then Youth in Action, because youth did not want to be called "kids") unfortunately ended in 1993, perhaps a victim of their successful activism—a lesson to other such efforts. Kids City, for youth ages 11 to 18, was funded by the city council in 1989 as part of a 10-year Youth Action Plan. The city manager appointed a Committee for Youth to survey students and adults and hold community forums, culminating in a report on youth needs and an action plan for the 1990s. The report concluded that many young people feel "fragile and vulnerable," powerless, and lacking in self-esteem. As one high school student wrote, "We are not social blemishes. Don't deal with us; talk to us—get our opinions. We know a lot more than we're given credit for."

Youth in Action ran a downtown storefront where teens met to organize other students. The city paid the salaries of 10 peer organizers who worked eight hours per week along with the adult staff. They also conducted leadership training in the schools. The first Youth SpeakOut, in 1990, was attended by 300 youth who adopted a Youth Agenda.

Youth in Action published a series of newsletters titled "Da Scoop," got free condoms available in the high school, initiated leadership training programs in the middle schools, set up support groups for African American and Latino males, twice defeated curfew legislation proposed by the police chief, made a videotape of the SpeakOut, and organized job workshops. They made presentations to the board of education, the planning commission, and the city council.

The city, however, ended the program. Success in empowering teens may have led to Youth in Action's downfall; for example, a critic wrote in the local newspaper against giving youth "free rein." The police did not like youth opposition to the proposed curfew, and some adults were offended by "Da Scoop" newsletter articles criticizing school policies such as the dress code. Others were unhappy about the youth's success in getting condom distribution in the high school. The youth were such effective speakers that school board member Peggy Lyons said, "I'm getting more lenient by the day as I listen to the students." Former director Elena Chavez notes that the majority of youth active in the program went on to college, including the students of color who got more involved after she replaced the mainly Anglo staff.

Seattle, Washington

Kidsplace advocacy group was started by the city and community groups in 1983. Its purpose was to make Seattle the best city in the country for families with children, a response to the fact that the number of children living in the city dropped over a third in the 1970s. Around 7,000 kids were asked how to make Seattle a good place for them, which resulted in six task forces working on 30 goals. Results were more bike lanes, an annual KidsDay, a city child advocate, expanding playground and park programs, reduced bus fares, and expanded multicultural opportunities for kids. A KidsBoard gave their feedback to city and county officials.

Kidsplace had two main goals, advocacy and youth recognition. Leaders disagreed about which goal was most important. As a result, Seattle Youth Involvement Network replaced Kidsplace in 1991 to empower and involve youth in their community. This mission has expanded to focus on advocacy, youth involvement, and youth recognition. SYIN receives funds from the city ($95,125 in 1996), and receives additional support from local businesses, foundations, and individuals. Current focus is on expanding the number of businesses and individuals involved with SYIN.

The focus on youth advocacy led to improving relations with the police. Students and police worked together to produce a video and handbook titled "RESPECT." Another handbook, the "Youth Yellow Pages," lists resources ranging from AIDS, to Things to Do, to Volunteer Opportunities.

At "Youth Summits" students discuss issues and solutions. High school students at the 1994 Youth Summit identified their goals as mandatory multiethnic classes, youth attendance at school board meetings, and less police harassment. "Seattle Youth Involvement Day" provides information about how youth can get involved in their neighborhoods.

The Seattle Youth Report, 1996, compiled the responses of thousands of youth over the previous two years about ideas for improving Seattle with a focus on neighborhoods, schools, and the city as a whole. Goals included establishing a Teen Center, creating more jobs, and forming a Youth Force effort to train youth living in violence-prone neighborhoods to reduce violence.

Seattle Youth Involvement Network
172-20th Ave.
Seattle, WA 98122

Other City Youth Programs

➤ Detroit, Michigan: The Detroit Youth Advisory Commission sponsors an Open Forum Speaker Series where youth discuss issues with public officials once a month.

➤ Frederick, Maryland: The Department of Youth Services established a 12-member Youth Services Commission, which includes five youths, to make recommendations to the mayor and city council. (The Youth Services Department provides tutoring, counseling, recreation, dances, computer training, etc.)

➤ Kent County, Michigan: High school juniors are appointed as student representatives to over 100 government boards and commissions.

➤ Lincoln, Nebraska: A Youth Advisory Council plans drug and alcohol-free activities, such as a New Year's Eve party and night splashes in the city's public swimming pools, and a street dance.

➤ Louisville, Kentucky: Neighborhood Youth Boards encourage youth to discover neighborhood needs and create programs to meet them. The 16 boards have organized activities such as bringing meals to senior citizens and youth dances.

➤ New Haven, Connecticut: The Board of Young Adult Police Commissioners, composed of high school students appointed by the mayor, meets once a month to advise police and improve relations with youth.

➤ Pasadena, California: The Pasadena Youth Council is composed of high school and college students who advise the Commission on Children and Youth and other community groups.

➤ San Francisco's Mayor's Youth Forum developed Education and Training for Social Change, a model youth development/leadership program for interns in government and community service. (25 Van Ness Ave., Suite 750, San Francisco, CA 94102)

➤ Tallahassee, Florida: Mayor Dorothy Inman Crews realized escalating problems of teen dropouts, pregnancy, and crime are symptoms, not the core problems. Instead of just responding to crises, the city mobilized youth programs, especially in targeted low-income neighborhoods. The city developed neighborhood service centers to coordinate services, including libraries, health clinics, child care, after-school tutoring, job services, and elder programs. The city helps fund summer recreation programs in every neighborhood, as well as youth employment and apprenticeship programs.

City Neighborhood Organizing
—Wakako, 20, Japan

I learned to be responsible, to take care of younger children, to respect others, to be creative, and to express my own ideas as well as do teamwork. Most of us learned our values through the community activities. I never felt we didn't have enough time for family togetherness, although both my parents work. I grew up in a safe community with strong bonds with neighbors, so children could be left unsupervised after school.

Teens can get involved in or start neighborhood activist groups dealing with issues such as safety and recreation activities. It's easier to have an impact on a small area than a large one.

The Japanese provide a model of neighborhood associations and organizations to provide family support. A small neighborhood organizes a *han*, which joins with perhaps eight other *han* to form a *chounai-kai* of around 100 families, which becomes part of a larger *jichi-kai*.

These associations speak up for neighborhood needs to the city council, organize neighborhood cleanups, and plan recreational activities: baseball games, seasonal parties, potluck dinners, special days for parents and children, and festivals.

General meetings occur each year, and leaders meet monthly. Families pay a small amount, supplemented by a government subsidy, to fund these activities.

Minneapolis uses a Neighborhood Revitalization Process to organize neighbors. The city provides staff to assist volunteers in developing and implementing neighborhood plans. Every homeowner was mailed a survey with their tax statement, asking how to make their neighborhood a better place to live. Minneapolis encourages block clubs and neighborhood watch programs. Over one-third of the city's blocks are organized and new block leaders are trained each month by the police. Neighborhood youth leaders are trained in the Youth Leadership Academy. Community meeting spaces are available in libraries, parks, and schools—a good example of collaboration among agencies.

Neighborhood Organizing
(see violence sections in
Chapters 1 and 7)

Center for Community Change
1000 Wisconsin Ave., NW
Washington, DC 20007

Communities That Care
Training—Developmental Research
130 Nickerson, Suite 107
Seattle, WA 98109
(provides training and materials
about how to "reduce adolescent
problem behaviors")

Comprehensive Community-
Building/Urban Strategies Council
672 Thirteenth St., Suite 200
Oakland, CA 94612

National Neighborhood Coalition
810 First St., NE, 3rd Floor
Washington, DC 20002

Neighborhood Revitalization Program
and Resource Exchange
Crown Roller Mill, #425, 105-5th Ave. S.
Minneapolis, MN 55401

Neighborhoods, U.S.A.
Mid City Station, Box 307
Dayton, Ohio 45402

Dale Blyth. *Healthy Communities,
Healthy Youth*. Minneapolis: Search
Institute, 1993. 1-800-888-7828

Maritza Pick. *How to Save Your
Neighborhood, City, or Town*. San
Francisco: Sierra Club Books, 1993.
(explains how to contact neighbors,
face officials at public hearings, and
set up campaign committees and fund
raisers)

Raquel Ramati. *How to Save Your Own
Street*. NY: Doubleday, 1981.

Environmentalism

I'm president of my high school's Environmental and Social Action Club. In the last three years, we've gone from 10 people who sometimes showed up for meetings to 30 or 40 people at lunch meetings every week. Our club has worked well because it has a regular meeting time and place and projects the kids care about. We can decide Monday that we want to have a "Homecoming for the Homeless" and have kids sitting in cardboard boxes at the football game on Friday night. Our club is made up of students who really care, and because we don't have a lot of paperwork to do, we can move fast on an idea. One success-ful project puts everyone in the right frame of mind for doing another.

—Robin, 18, Colorado

National polls show that about 75 percent of young people consider the environment to be one of the main problems facing their gener-ation. A UCLA poll of thousands of college freshmen found that almost 87 percent believed that govern-ment is not doing enough to control pollution.

Steps You Can Take to Save the Environment

☺ Recycle your family's cans, newspapers, cardboard, glass, plastic, tin, aluminum, and car batteries. Some recycling centers pay for these products.

☺ Recycle your food scraps and plant cuttings by creating a compost pile, either in your yard or a community garden.

☺ Turn off the lights when you leave a room and use energy-efficient light bulbs.

☺ Use paper and other products made from recycled materials. Buy unbleached and uncolored paper products. Buy in bulk and choose unprocessed foods rather than many little cartons, trays, and other packaging. Buy products that are biodegradable if you can.

☺ Avoid using unnecessary throwaways such as paper plates and plastic cups. Shop with a fabric tote bag rather than using plastic or paper bags. Don't buy disposable razors, cameras, etc. Use rechargeable batteries. Avoid prepackaged meals.

☺ Use organic nontoxic household cleaners (Household Products Recycling and Disposal Council, 1913 I St., NW, Washington, DC 20006).

☺ Stay informed and support environmental groups by becoming a member and reading their newsletters.

☺ Encourage people to quit smoking as cigarette smoke contains many toxic chemical pollutants.

☺ Reduce the amount of animal grazing and deforestation by cutting down on your red meat consumption. Your body is better off without high fat foods.

☺ To prevent further thinning of the ozone layer, avoid the use of chlorofluorocarbons in aerosol spray cans, refrigerators, foam plastics, and some solvents.

☺ Avoid use of pesticides and herbicides in your garden, except for organic pesticides, and try to buy organic foods grown without pesticides. (National Coalition Against the Misuse of Pesticides, 701 E St., SE, Washington D.C. 20003)

☺ Use public transportation and bikes rather than cars.

☺ Earth Day 2000 publishes a list of companies that make false claims about their products (1-800-999-0979). Some companies claim their packaging or polystyrene products are recyclable when they're not, claim No. 3 plastics are recyclable when they're usually not, or claim their refrigerators are "ozone-friendly" when they contain ozone-destroying gases. (Consumer's Resource Handbook from U.S. Office of Consumer Affairs, 750-17th St., NW, Washington, DC 20006. See also Samuel Epstein and David Steinman, *The Safe Shopper's Bible*, MacMillan.)

☺ Write letters to elected officials, companies, and the media.

—Tovah, 15, New York

Each year thousands of teenagers across North America are choosing vegetarianism in response to the cruelty of an animal-agriculture-based society. "Vegetarian" refers to anyone who doesn't eat any type of meat (including fish and poultry) or slaughter byproduct (gelatin, rennet, etc.).

People choose vegetarianism for a variety of reasons, including a meat-free lifestyle's benefits to human health, world hunger, and the environment. People are often motivated to 'kick the meat habit' when they learn about the cruel ways in which animals are treated in factory-farms. In the class on "Hog Farm Management," farmers are advised to "Forget the pig is an animal. Treat him just like a machine in a factory." This is just one of many motivating factors for people to oppose the slaughter and consumption of animals. Dairy cows, veal calves, and egg-laying chickens are also treated in outrageous ways, so many people choose to reduce or eliminate their consumption of related foods.

The food options for vegetarians are limitless! Using just what you can buy at your local supermarket, you can prepare all kinds of vegetarian foods made from fruits, vegetables, beans, grains, nuts, and seeds. It's good to do some research about vegetarian nutrition before you go veggie.

The Vegetarian Youth Network
P.O. Box 1141
New Paltz, NY 1256
VYNet@mhv.net
(Send self-addressed stamped envelope if you want a reply.)
http://www.geocities.com/RodeoDrive/1154

http://mars.superlink.com/user/dupre/navs/index.html
(North American Vegetarian Society Page)

Environmental Groups

Environmental Protection Agency Hot Line 1-800-424-9346

Carbon Dioxide Campaign
Children's Earth Fund
40 W. 20th St.
New York, NY 10011

Children's Alliance for Protection of the Environment
P.O. Box 307
Austin, TX 78767

The Children's Rainforest
P.O. Box 936
Lewiston, ME 04240

Environmental Action
1525 New Hampshire Ave., NW
Washington, DC 20036

Environmental Defense Fund
1616 P St., NW, Room 150
Washington, DC 20036

Friends of the Earth
218 D St., SE
Washington, DC 20003

Global Response: Environmental Action Network
P.O. Box 7490
Boulder, CO 80306
majordomo@ipc.apc.org and write "subscribe globersmember."
(This international network for students provides a newsletter called *Young Environmentalist's Action*, in Spanish and English, that suggests actions to take and addresses.)

Global Tomorrow Coalition
1325 G St., NW, Room 915
Washington, DC 20005-3104

Green Peace
P.O. Box 1808
Merrifield, VA 22116-9947
(confrontational group that fights to protect whales or stop nuclear testing, etc.)

Kids Against Pollution (KAP)
275 High St.
Closter, NJ 07624

Kids for Saving the Earth
P.O. Box 47247
Plymouth, MN 55447-0247

Mothers and Others
for a Livable Planet
40 W. 20th St.
New York, NY 10011

National Recycling Coalition
1101 30th St., NW #305
Washington, DC 20009

Partners for the Planet
136 Main St., Dept. P
El Segundo, CA 90245
http://www.interverse.com/inter-
verse/partners

Save the Whales
P.O. Box 2000
Washington, DC 20007

Student Conservation Association
P.O. Box 550
Charlestown, NH 03603

Student Environment Action Coalition
1400-16th St., NW, Box 24
Washington,DC
20036seacdc@igc.apc.org

Mail Preference Service
Direct Marketing Association
P.O. Box 9008
Farmingdale, NY 11735
(If your family gets junk mail, you can
ask that your name be removed from
mailing lists. This will be good for
only five years or until you send for a
mail order purchase. If you mail order,
specify that you do not allow your
address to be sold, rented, or traded.)

To stop telemarketing phone calls,
write to Direct Marketing Phone
Preference Service
(P.O. Box 9014
Farmingdale, NY 11735-90014)

YES! (Youth for Environmental Sanity)
706 Frederick St.
Santa Cruz, CA 95062
(YES! is a group of 17- to 25-year-olds
who perform national tours with multimedia presentations to provide examples of how to solve environmental
problems. They also provide organizing
manuals, a newsletter, and camps to
teach how to "turn the world's biggest
environmental problems around.")

*50 Simple Things Kids Can Do to Save
the Earth*. Berkeley, CA: Earth Works
Group, 1990. Also, *50 Simple Things
You Can Do to Save the Earth* and *Kid
Heroes of the Environment*.
1-800-826-4216

Pat Suiter, ed. *Green Guide, An
Educator's Guide to Free and
Inexpensive Environmental Materials*.
San Francisco: Sierra Club, 1991.

Earth Day: www.earthsite.org

Feminism

My favorite definition of feminism is it's the radical notion that women are people. [The early church had serious ongoing debates over whether women have immortal souls, rather than just being baby-makers and helpers.] *In the 19th century, women couldn't vote and, if they married, their husbands had total authority over their property and children, and could legally beat and rape their wives.*

—Elena, 19, Ohio

A United Nations platform for action was proposed for three decades in four UN Conferences on Women (Mexico City, Copenhagen, Nairobi, and Beijing). The proposal about girls aimed to eliminate all forms of discrimination against girls, insure their equal access to education and health care, protect them from violence and economic exploitation (such as prostitution), and ensure that they develop a positive self-image. Girls got involved in the Beijing conference and continued to network.

—Allyson, 20, Canada

Third wave feminism is a 90s phenomenon. Feminism in the 1980s was riddled with racism, androcentrism [human centered, rather than including other creatures], *ethnocentrism, classism, and ableism* [ignoring the needs of disabled people]. *Third wave feminism proposes to be more inclusive, to not see sex/gender as the fundamental and universal system of oppression experienced by all women in the same way to the same degree. Third wave is largely influenced by a younger generation of feminists who helped our activist sisters see the absences in the past (largely thanks to author bell hooks).*

—Corina, 22, Michigan

I am a graduate student in chemical engineering. I have always considered myself a feminist since I began to think, "How can I be a woman without being a feminist?" Of course that word means a lot of things to many people. To me it's about not letting gender limit my role in society, fighting for women's equality, and being a role model. As a young woman raised in a family of fairly well-educated people, I was obsessed with being a contributing member of society. Even in this day and age lots of people think a woman's most important contribution is raising the next generation. Of course that is important, but what I'm still dealing with is finding a place in society, carving a comfortable niche, and doing something I like and am good at.

One of the most important things for me was believing in myself and trusting my instincts. Being able to trust oneself is the most important thing to getting on the road to where you want to be. One of the things that helps is having good role models of strong women who are accomplished and happy to point the way and offer encouragement and advice and support.

Facts About Women

Women hear, "You've come a long way, baby," but this ad slogan is addressed to an infant and defines liberation as slinky clothes and smoking. We're told that this is the post-feminist era when the need for feminism is over. The facts tell a different story.

U.S.

→ Women earn an average of 73 percent of what men earn, putting the U.S. in 33rd place among 55 countries surveyed by the UN.

→ The U.S. ranks 24th of 54 western countries in the percentage of women in national legislatures, with only 10 percent of the politicians.

→ Women do better in Sweden, Norway, Finland, and Denmark, putting U.S. women in fifth place (a UN "gender-related development index"). U.S. women ranked eighth on a "gender empowerment measure" that ranks their earnings, career status, and representation in politics. (They are behind the Nordic countries, plus Canada, New Zealand, and the Netherlands.)

→ Women own only 35 percent of the income earned in the U.S.

International

❖ Women are 70 percent of the world's 1.3 billion poor people.

❖ Women are typically paid 30 to 40 percent less than men for doing the same job.

❖ Women are two-thirds (more than a billion) of the adult illiterates.

❖ Women hold only 14 percent of the world's managerial and administrative jobs.

❖ The number of women in parliaments dropped from 15 percent in 1988 to 11 percent in 1994. In one-third of governments worldwide, there are no women in the decision-making body.

- Three to four million women are battered each year. About one-third of wives in developing countries are physically abused.

- About one million children are forced into prostitution or used in pornography each year.

- Women work longer hours (an average of 12 percent more) than men in all countries except Peru, when paid work and household work are combined.

- Women and children are 80 percent of the world's refugees.

- Estimates are that 85 million to 114 million girls suffer genital mutilation each year. (As part of her initiation into womanhood, depending on the local tradition, part or all of her clitoris is removed. In some areas, the labia are also removed and the vaginal opening is sewed almost shut.)

- Only six of the 185 ambassadors to the UN were women in 1994 (UN data).

Lisa DiMona and C. Herndon, eds. *Women's Sourcebook.* Boston: Houghton Mifflin, 1994.

Women's Action Coalition. *WAC Stats: The Facts About Women.* NY: New Press, 1995.

History of Feminism

—Rebecca West, 1913

I myself have never been able to find out precisely what feminism is: I only know that people call me a feminist whenever I express sentiments that differentiate me from a doormat.

—Pat Robertson, 1992

Feminism encourages women to leave their husbands, kill their children, practice witchcraft, destroy capitalism, and become lesbians.

Feminism is the belief in the equality of the sexes. It does not mean man-hating, bra-burning, lesbianism, hairy legs, or any other stereotypes. Susan B. Anthony explained in the 19th century that her goal was "Men, their rights and nothing more; women, their rights, and nothing less." We're still working towards this kind of justice. Women generally earn less than men, even in the same field, and are rarely at the head of organizations. Although women are over half the population, they are only about 14 percent of all the elected officials. About half of the women will experience sexual harassment at school or work. A woman is raped about every minute and battered every 15 seconds. Their speech pattern is less assertive and more subordinate than men's.

The first wave of the women's rights movement began in 1848 with the drive to get the vote, finally achieved in 1919. Because the women's movement focused too much energy on a single issue, it died down after the vote was won. As a result, no additional legislation was passed for women's equality until the Equal Pay Act of 1963, the beginning of the second wave of feminism—part of the civil rights' movement, the Kennedy presidency, and protest against the war in Viet Nam.

In 1963, Betty Friedan's book *The Feminine Mystique* brought the second wave of feminism to middle class women with her message that it was natural for both women and men to want more in life than to be good housekeepers. She made people think critically about psychological definitions of women, such as Sigmund Freud's teaching that women were naturally passive, masochistic (enjoy punishment), self-centered and not interested in the world outside the home. The largest feminist organization in the world, the National Organization for Women, was founded by Ms. Friedan and others in 1966.

The high point of the second wave was in the early 1970s:

→ Title VII of the Civil Rights Act (prohibited gender discrimination in the workplace)

→ Title IX (prohibited sex discrimination in educational institutions)

→ Roe v. Wade (supreme court decision legalized abortion)

→ *Ms. magazine* (then considered so radical that some women asked that it be mailed to them in a plain brown wrapper)

→ The National Women's Political Caucus.

Then the backlash set in during President Reagan's administration and opposition to the Equal Rights Amendment. Young feminists are now organizing a third wave with their own issues and organizing style.

An anonymous person explains "How to Be a Fabulous Feminist."

Fight sexism. Do it now, say Yes to female—to justice—to freedom—love yourself, love other women. Say No! Get angry, get active. Don't agonize—organize. Fight racism—classism [discrimination against working class or poor people]—*ageism—homophobia—sizism* [discrimination against fat and small people] *and physicalism* [judging people by their bodies]. *Lower pain and isolation. Raise consciousness. Raise self-esteem. Think globally—act locally. Avoid burnout. Be woman identified. Create safety. Take risks. Take your power back. Do it now. Live equality! Thank yourself. Celebrate women survivors. Invent new herstory. Shatter myths. Pioneer—trail blaze.... Make peace with men. Be a mover and a shaker. Join a feminist political organization. Volunteer. Give love. Give money. Get powerful. Get respect. Heal yourself, heal the world. Collect fabulous memories. Do it to win. Do it now!!!*

What's in It for Men?

—Kevin, 21, Iowa

Perhaps most importantly, feminism seeks to uphold the rights of women. All men have women close to them in their lives. Our lives are hurt indirectly whenever one of our classmates, sisters, girlfriends, wives, mothers, or daughters is insulted, abused, raped, hurt, harassed, or discriminated against. Their feelings are important to us, so we should work to improve the situations in which they live and work. I myself have heard the stories of four of my close friends raped by people they trusted, and it broke my heart and severely angered me every time. I don't know if I could bear another.

My "consciousness raising" to feminist issues came as part of a larger understanding early in high school. In particular, I began to become more and more aware of the many privileges I had in this society: as white, as middle class, as mentally and physically able, and also as a man.

I began to realize that much of what made things easy for me in school had to do with my upbringing and social status. But my advantages weren't just a matter of class. I also had teachers—as well as parents and mentors—who encouraged me to be outspoken, to think critically, to be interested in science and math, to experiment with computers. The same was not always true for my female peers, who were often encouraged to think more about clothes, feelings, and eventually raising a family. Some womyn [he uses this spelling so the word isn't built around "men"] I know have even told me that as adolescents they were taught not to look "too smart" because it would make boys not like them. I have always been encouraged to engage actively with my education, and indeed even today, the classroom is the place I feel most comfortable being outspoken, assertive, and self-confident. I cannot help but think that this different socialization has had a large impact on my life and the successes in it.

All along, I have had role models very much like me—white, male, intellectual—to model my life after. I have been tested and educated primarily with regard to material formulated and written by people who think like me and have had similar life experiences. I know that womyn and minorities do not often share this privilege. Certainly, this had been a tremendous advantage in my life.

When I got to college I was exposed to feminist theory and got to know many activists not only in the feminist movement, but in environmentalism, and for human rights, etc. I started to become aware of how deeply a part of everyday life sexism and male privilege are. I learned about media images which make womyn strive to realize unrealistic body types. I learned of the problems of date rape, sexual harassment, and discrimination in the classroom. I learned the significance of sexism in language. I began to see more and more forces working against womyn, and how lucky I was to be free of such constraints.

I recognize people as being feminist whenever they recognize that womyn are wrongfully underprivileged and work towards creating a situation of equality and sorority.

Men can be active feminists, as when I helped organize these events: I was a cochair of a campus lecture committee dedicated to dealing with issues of sex and sexuality. We brought in a number of feminist and gay rights speakers, organized take back the night rallies and marches, and a self-defense class for womyn. Also I am the facilitator for a discussion group exploring what it means to be a male profeminist.

How to Organize a Young Feminist Group

NATIONAL ORGANIZATION FOR WOMEN
—Heather Haxo Phillips, 20, Massachusetts

Today's youth have a raw, unbridled energy that hasn't been seen since the days of JFK. We have an understanding of ourselves and our surroundings that is far more mature than any preceding generation, but many of us have no direction in life. There are several reasons for this. We haven't had enough contact with adults who have a sense of purpose and direction who could serve as role models. Also, many of us have lost hope and faith in this crazy world. Many of us, having grown up in the post-women's movement era and without access to women's studies, do not understand how the women's movement has changed our world. Many do not understand the need for a "third wave" of feminism.

I started the first NOW high school task force in 1992 when I was a senior at Berkeley High school in California. It started with an informal women's group composed of girls headed for Ivy League colleges who first called themselves NOW in 1990. [In 1991 **students and teacher Susan Groves set up a women's studies curriculum.**] My U.S. History teacher, Ms. Groves, was a feminist who asked me to take over. At that point I was an activist, not a feminist, but I said, "Sure."

I read a lot of women authors, took a Women's Literature class and the Women's History class. I didn't have organizational skills or understand what activism really was, but I put out the word in the bulletin and about 50 girls showed up and continued to meet weekly. At our first meeting everyone introduced themselves, then we brainstormed issues we cared about, and decided which ones we wanted to focus on.

We ran our meetings in four-week blocks. We spent three weeks discussing a particular subject and then ended the block with an action, such as a petition or a letter to a politician. For instance, one block focused on body image. We started by showing a video on how ads portray women. The next week we had a discussion about how we view our bodies and body image. And the next week we had a speaker come and talk about eating disorders. We rounded out the block by writing to different companies telling them what we were offended by or liked about their advertisements.

We became part of East Bay NOW chapter. Those adults and our advisor, Ms. Groves, taught me leadership skills. The women in my chapter showed me how to do press releases and gave me experience speaking in front of a microphone. I learned how to do civil disobedience on the front lines at clinics.

This learning was all very gradual: I never quite realized that they were teaching me anything. All of a sudden, I was speaking at school board meetings and feeling confident doing it. I found myself planning school assemblies without questioning whether I could carry it off. I was making appointments with the principal, never questioning whether I had the right to be there. I was able to do this because the women in my NOW chapter taught me how to challenge the status quo. They taught me to believe in my opinions and to see that my concerns and feelings were legitimate in others' eyes.

We became the largest and most active club on campus. Each board member took charge of one task, such as inviting speakers or taking minutes. We learned to do publicity, and we found that putting notices on the backs of bathroom stall doors is probably the most effective. We got articles in the school newspaper and local TV coverage of our projects. We organized an extremely popular school assembly for International Women's Day. We did a large survey about sexual harassment: Fifty-four percent of the girls reported they had been sexually harassed at school. The results led the administration to hire two consultants to train staff to bring the school district into compliance with state law and provide peer counseling to students.

We talked with politicians about young feminist issues. We're concerned about self-esteem, body image, date rape, abortion, sexual harassment at school, sex education, pregnancy prevention, AIDS, eating disorders, relationships with parents, ageism, and gang violence. Child care, health care, the glass ceiling at work, and job security are not pressing issues for most teens.

Now I attend Harvard-Radcliffe College in Boston and serve on the national NOW Young Feminist Committee. It was formed around 1990 and meets once a year, but we have monthly conference calls and stay in touch through e-mail and faxes.
[Heather's younger sister, Claire, went to the U.N. conference in Beijing and got interested in international feminism, but reports the high school NOW group was inactive in 1996.]

Heather Haxo Phillips. "Organizing in the Third Wave," four pamphlets available from East Bay NOW, P.O. Box 635, Berkeley, CA 94701. $2.50 donation each.

—Sara Marcus, 18, Maryland

I started our high school NOW chapter two years ago when I was in 10th grade. I went to the principal and asked my English teacher to sponsor the club. We relied on word of mouth, announcements in the bulletin, and flyers on bulletin boards.

This year we have 30 people. We've brought in speakers and videos and a self-defense workshop. We've discussed eating disorders, violence in dating, sexual harassment, single-sex classrooms, and genital mutilation of women. Before NOW, there was nowhere to discuss these topics, no support network. News spread and the NOW club was soon infamous.

I was surprised by the hostility our fledgling group elicited. Meetings were frequently interrupted by hecklers yelling antifeminist epithets; our bulletin boards were vandalized repeatedly; and the school newspaper printed several articles saying that feminism was useless and silly, or purporting that NOW club members were a dangerous bunch of radicals. All our energy went into defending our club's right to exist.

As the year progressed, we managed to accomplish some of our goals. We assembled a leaflet of sobering statistics about women's status in society, illustrating the necessity of feminism. We brought in speakers and undertook a letter-writing campaign to state legislators urging passage of stricter domestic violence ordinances. Working toward a belief that sexism will be eliminated only when men and women collaborate in the spirit of true equality, we encouraged our male friends to attend meetings.

This year our meetings have become tremendously well attended. Our debates on issues such as sexual assault and female circumcision are dynamic. We plan to attend a self-defense seminar, volunteer at a women's shelter, and organize an assembly in the middle-school to combat recent outbreaks of harassment and abuse.

The most important effect of the club lies more in its very presence than in its specific activities. Although sexism, harassment, and discrimination are still common at school, complacency is diminishing, because the perpetrators know some people are prepared to stand up to them. In addition, students distressed by sexism have an outlet, not only to share their own experiences and learn from others, but to learn how to confront sexist attitudes and behaviors constructively. When I see new 9th graders attending meetings, I think how helpful a NOW club would have been to me when I started high school, and how proud I am that these students won't have to cope alone.

—Steven Wendell, 19, Maryland

As a senior I cofounded the NOW chapter at my high school in Silver Spring with Cecily Iddings. I thought there was a need. I got in contact with other high school NOW chapters. We created a place to talk and brought in speakers. About 10 percent of the members were male. As a male cochair, I didn't get any flack from guys and got a little praise from girls. Students aren't that divided by sex, more by ideology.

I got started as an activist as a sophomore when I heard a speaker from Men Against Rape (MAR), a Washington, DC group that focuses on education through demonstrations, zap actions, and marches. I organized speakers on sexual harassment for three different high schools to get men to think more about it, since people are being hurt.

National Organization for Women (NOW)
(ask about the *Young Feminist Resource Kit*)
1000 16th St., NW, #700
Washington, DC 20036
now@now.org
http://now.org/now/

Feminist Majority

This group was started by a former president of NOW, Ellie Smeal, to focus on advocacy and research. It also has a legal wing and provides informational pamphlets and news briefings on topics including sports and media. Youth are involved as interns in offices in Washington, DC and Los Angeles and organize chapters on university campuses such as Cornell, Swarthmore, Oberlin, and University of Chicago.

—Kate McCall, 21, Ohio

I founded the Feminist Majority at Oberlin College because I had the opportunity to have an internship at the Feminist Majority in Washington, DC. For a year I commented on the lack of a feminist organization that wasn't issue bound (like students for reproductive freedom or the lesbian, gay, bisexual union). I wanted a group that could respond to affirmative action attacks, cuts in welfare, bulimia and anorexia, the lack of tenured female professors, pay inequity, and on and on. There is a community outreach part of the feminist majority so we are planning to go into high schools and hopefully there will be high school chapters as well.

From starting F.M., I learned I am good at organizing and public speaking and I am willing to stand up for what I believe in. If this means embarrassing my parents at a restaurant because the waiter said something racist and I didn't let him/her get away with it, then good.

This was a hard thing to learn. You feel nauseous, your hands sweat, your voice sounds like you are about 13 years old and you are going to cry. But it gets better and I learned that some fears can be conquered, that out of challenging some fears, one can actually build confidence and poise. I learned that some people will back down, while others will shout, and that some people believe that nothing is off limits to attack. So I have also learned to pick my fights a little more carefully.

I founded this group, so it has meant building the group from the ground up: I made all the posters, did all the postering around campus, and facilitated our first meetings and discussions. I have definitely given the group an initial direction. Because I am the only founding chair, I worry that the group is not balanced. Feminism does not have a monolithic way to think, but I worry that because it was founded with one voice, the group might lean that way.

I solved some of that problem, with the help of the group, by choosing five sub-groups (body image, political action, community outreach, discussion groups, and reproductive freedom). That way I would be a voice in one of the subgroups, rather than the main voice of the larger group. So far so good.

If there isn't an organization in your high school or your town that addresses the issues that you feel need to be addressed, start it. If you are feeling that way, most likely there are a bunch of others who feel the same way. The hardest part of being an activist is the feeling that you are fighting all of your battles alone. You need to get support. One great way to do that is to get on the Internet and find other groups which believe in what you do. Reach out to campuses, get connected. It is easy, cheap, and fast to e-mail other activists for ideas and support.

The biggest problem area to watch out for is building a group that looks like yourself. Don't just tell your friends. Don't just put posters in your neighborhood. You have to cross boundaries—gender, race, religion, ethnic, sexuality, weight, piercing—whatever. Get diversity; it's the hardest thing to do, but perhaps the most important.

Feminist Majority Foundation
1600 Wilson Blvd.
Arlington, VA 22209

National Young Girls' Coalition

Coalition members include the Girls Scouts, Girls Inc., *New Moon* Magazine, YWCA, AAUW, etc. Their first national conference was January, 1997, at the United Nations, to create a girls' platform for action. This group was organized by Andrea Johnston, leader of Girls Speak Out/Talks for Girls.

NYGC
18200 Sweetwater Springs Rd.
Guerneville, CA 95446

Riot Grrrls

A newsletter by DC Riot Grrrls tells girls,

Riot Grrrl is about change. It's about feeling comfortable with yourself, your own body, and other girls. It's about being able to talk comfortably with other girls who always listen to whatever is on your mind, without judging you. It's about being sick and tired of being treated like an inferior, and wanting to be treated like an equal. It is not about man hate, it's about girl love.

You don't have to take shit from anyone. Be who you want, do what you want. Don't be pushed to the back at shows if you want to be in the front. Don't stop doing something just because someone says you can't do it, or doesn't encourage you. Go skateboard, write a zine, form a band. Make yourself heard!

—Sara Marcus, 18, Maryland

I got involved as a junior with DC Riot Grrrls, weekly meetings. Riot Grrrls started in DC in the summer of 1991 and in Olympia, Washington, with punk girl bands like Bikini Kill and Brat Mobile. We created an all-girl space in reaction to the male-domi-nated punk scene and shared the idea with friends in other towns.

In DC we met in a punk group house. We started meetings by organizing actions, such as wheat pasting our flyers at night on poles, or creating a flyer on how to start a chapter, or painting a park pink—its swings and other equipment—as a statement of girl power. Then we shared events in our lives to get advice. Third, we discussed topics such as body hate, jealousy, or things we don't like and do like about girls.

Before, I didn't really get along with girls. I thought talking about hair, makeup, and boys wasn't very interesting. Now I connect with girls through their zines and mine, called "Out of the Vortex." The network of girl zines is our communication system: *Action Girl Newsletter* reviews our zines (handmade magazines). Other Riot Grrrls chapters come and go, only DC kept the same post office box address and meeting place. We had a list of chapters in the states, England, Australia, British Columbia, and Ontario.

Riot Grrrls was so important for me to counteract the negative things that were happening to me. For example, sexual harassment. In the 9th grade, a boy pushed me up against a wall and tried to kiss me. I felt it was my fault. I needed a reverse message. Before I felt I had to tread the middle line, to make concessions. We try to break down the walls that separate girls, to see what it's like growing up in a misogynist [woman hating] society. Riot Grrrls helped me to understand society and helped me find my voice, as when I did a zine with a friend.

Action Girl Newsletter/Sarah Dyer
P.O. Box 060380
Staten Island, NY 10306

Riot Grrrl DC chapter
P.O. Box 11002,
Washington DC, 20008

Riot Grrrl Press (distributes zines)
656 W. Aldine #3
Chicago, IL 60657

Riot Grrrl Review (of zines and music)
922 NE 17th St.
Cape Coral, FL 33909
Xastrokidx@aol.com

The Third Wave

—Amy Richards, 22, New York

I "came out" as a feminist about the same time that I was introduced to the Third Wave, the movement and the organization, when it began in 1992. Third Wave was founded in 1992 by Shannon Liss and Rebecca Walker. They wanted to fill a void in youth leadership and respond to the political climate at the time, such as the Anita Hill-Clarence Thomas Senate hearings.

Third Wave is a multicultural membership organization, with members in 30 states and three countries. It promotes and facilitates young women's activism, run by a 13-member board of directors who are already leaders in their communities. [Amy is one of the directors.]

In most instances, young women's issues—welfare, violence, access to safe and affordable birth control, to name a few—are similar to those of our older sisters, yet they affect us in different ways and sometimes to a greater extent. For instance, one in five girls is sexually abused before the age of 18; 40,000 girls drop out of high school each year because of pregnancy, and women under 30 are one-fourth of the homeless.

After its creation, Third Wave immediately came into the national spotlight through Freedom Summer '92. The voter registration drive took 120 young people to 21 cities across the U.S. in 23 days and registered more than 20,000 new voters. The bus riders came from all walks of life and ranged in age from 13 to 50. However, the majority were young women aged 18 to 26. We were inspired by the Freedom Rides of the early 1960s that traveled through the South to register African Americans and to empower people through teaching them their history. We discovered that people don't think their vote counts, although in the 1994 congressional elections, we saw that one vote does make a difference. We did a get out the vote campaign in 1996.

In addition, Third Wave distributes a quarterly newsletter by its members. See It, Tell It, Change It is used to spark an ongoing dialogue about what young women think and care about.

The Third Wave
185 Franklin St.
New York, NY 10013.

Young Women's Project

YWP was founded in 1989 as an offshoot of the Institute for Women's Policy to "develop and support young women leaders through training, technical assistance, information, and issue-focused, community-building campaigns." Issues include better access to health care, reproductive rights, and ending violence against women. The Peer Technical Assistance Project assists young women's initiatives. Membership fees are sliding scale and members receive fact sheets, a quarterly newsletters, T-shirts, and discounts on publications.

YWP is funded mainly by foundation grants and has a staff of four young women. It's governed by the 10-woman board of directors, who are mainly young women and a majority are women of color. The group assembled information in *The Young Women's Handbook: Beyond Surviving in the 90s*. With self-esteem as a major issue. Naida Moritz, Editor, reported,

If there is one common theme in these essays, it's a fear of our own expression. What it means, who it refers to and insults, who will agree, disagree. Because we are young and female...we write with many question marks. We footnote a lot, we raise questions. We are cautious, polite. We are less comfortable with our own ideas, theories, suggestions....We need to trust ourselves more....

Young Women's Project
1511 K St., Suite 428
Washington DC 20005

Feminist Resources

Barbara Findlen, ed. Listen Up: *Voices from the Next Feminist Generation*. Seattle, WA: Seal Press, 1995. (Twenty-eight writers ages 19 to 29 write about the concerns of young feminists: eating disorders, underemployment, racism in the women's movement, AIDS, marriage, and motherhood.)

Feminist political groups and Fund-raisers for Feminist Candidates:
National Women's Political Caucus
1-202-785-1100

Women's Campaign Fund
1-202-393-8164
EMILY'S List 1-202-326-1400
(for Democrats)

WISH List 1-908-747-4221
(for Republicans)

Internet Addresses for Feminist Computer Newsletters

Campus Activists' Network/ Young Feminist Network: To subscribe send to canet@pencil.cs.missouri.edu with a subject of "canet" whose body says: sub can-yfn First name Last name.

Cat's Claws: Feminist Newsletter: To subscribe, write: Listserv@Netcom. and in the body only write: subscribe Catts-Claws

sanfran@webgrrls.com
http://www.cybergrrl.com
(computer information and link to other sites for women)

Feminist Activist Resources on the Internet:
http://www.igc.org/women/
feminist.html

Feminist Majority Feminist Alert Network:
majordomo@feminist.org (subscribe fem-alert in the message body)
http://www.feminist.org

GIRL, for women 25 and younger who are feminists and/or lesbians. To subscribe, send a bio to:
girl@uci.edu

Pleiades Networks
http://www.pleiades-net.com/
(provides a guide to the Internet, directories of women's resources, and discussion groups)

PolWoman@aol.com (provides updates about legislation and resources for feminists)

REAL Girls: Rgirls@aol.com

Webgrrls: http://www.femina.com

Women Leaders Online:
http://worcester.Im.com/women/wom
en.html

Women's International Center:
http://www.wic.org

Women's Wire:
http://www.women.com

Womenspace: http://www.women-space.com (for young women and girls, information about sexuality, health, etc.)

Legal Rights in Regard to Police

It's difficult gaining respect from authorities (parents, police, school authorities). Adults often categorize all teens together, but I feel they should accept our troublemaking as an experiment in life. We are expected to act like an adult without having the freedom and respect adults get. I live my life as I want, staying in tune with myself and my morals, not for them or anyone else.

—Aiko, 15, California

Dan Macallair works at the San Francisco Center for Juvenile and Criminal Justice. He observes that "the demonization of youth" (as by negative media coverage) has resulted in increases in the number of incarcerated youth. Legislators are nervous about the arrest rates for teen murderers, which more than tripled in the last decade. Almost all the states have changed their laws, allowing more youths to be tried as adults and dumping protections like the confidentiality of juvenile court proceedings or allowing arrest records to be erased. This trend continues despite studies (i.e., in Florida and New York) that show youths tried as adults committed more serious crimes later than those incarcerated in juvenile institutions. "We are stepping down a very grim path toward eliminating childhood," in the legal system, notes Lisa Greeer of the Los Angeles County public defender's office.

Juvenile courts are handing out tougher sentences, including time in adult jails, although defense attorneys may handle more than 500 cases at a time. In some courts, youths meet their lawyers for the first time when they sit down at counsel table in detention hearings, or have no attorney at all. "The juvenile justice system is a sick patient," according to a report by the American Bar Association. Some courts establish teen courts where offenders are judged by their peers, as in Sarasota, Florida.

The U.S. probably has more children in the juvenile justice system than any other country, a costly practice, as a year in a juvenile detention center costs more (an average of $30,000 per child) than Harvard University tuition. Poor children and abused children are more likely to be in juvenile justice institutions.

Over one-half million youths are imprisoned every year, although two-thirds committed minor or nonviolent crimes. The unemployment rate and incarceration rate are higher for young black males than any other group of people. Young prisoners rarely learn marketable job skills and are too often the victims of violence in these "correctional" institutions. A RAND Corporation study, "Diverting Children from a Life of Crime," found that arrest rates for students who participate in graduation incentive programs were 70 percent lower than those without help.

The most common crimes committed by youth are theft, taking a vehicle without consent of the owner, assault (fighting, sexual fondling), burglary (entering a building with the intent to commit a crime), possession of alcohol, malicious mischief (graffiti), and trespassing.

Youth forums held in Seattle with teens and police officers talking together identified the two most frustrating situations for both groups—hanging out/loitering and traffic stops of vehicles driven by teens.

Your Rights

(Excerpted from RESPECT, a booklet written by the Seattle Youth Involvement Network and the Seattle Police)

1. If stopped and questioned by a police officer, you may be silent. You are required to show identification if you are driving a vehicle (and your license, registration, and proof of insurance) or are in a place where alcohol is served. Lawyers advise that you provide your name, age, and address.

2. If stopped, ask if you are under arrest. If not, you are free to leave, unless you are under "investigative detention." Never run from a police officer, put your hands in your pockets, or make quick movements that might make the officer think you are reaching for a weapon. To make an arrest, an officer needs a warrant or "probable cause" to believe the suspect has committed a crime.

3. Police are permitted to check you for weapons by patting the outside of your clothes. If searched beyond this level, don't resist, but you may file a complaint (your police department probably has an internal investigations section). Police may search your car without a warrant if they have reasonable suspicion or your consent. If you do not consent to a search, say so clearly. If police say they have a search warrant, ask to see it.

4. If you are suspected of drunk driving and refuse a breath test, your license can be suspended.

5. If arrested, go with the officer. You have the legal right to remain silent, except to tell your name, age, and address. You can ask to talk to a lawyer by telephone. You

can choose not to talk to the police until your lawyer is there. If you are under 18, ask that your parent or guardian be telephoned.

Miranda warnings are required if the officer has probable cause to believe the person has committed a crime and is asking questions related to the crime. The warnings the officer must repeat are

1. "You have the right to remain silent."

2. If you are under 18, "Anything you say can be used against you in a juvenile court prosecution...."

3. "You have the right at this time to talk to a lawyer. Having these rights in mind, do you wish to talk to us now?"

If a person is arrested and held in custody, the prosecutor may ask that he or she be held until charges are filed. Within 24 hours of the arrest, a judge must decide if the person can be held in custody for *probable cause*. The prosecutor must file charges within 72 hours of the arrest or the person is released. If charged, the person will be *arraigned*, formally charged with the crime in court. The judge rules whether the person will stay in custody, be released on bail, or be released on *personal recognizance* without bail. If charges are filed, the person is summoned to a court hearing where he or she is entitled to either his or her own lawyer or a free court-appointed attorney. If you feel your rights have been violated, you may want to get information from a group such as the American Civil Liberties Union.

—Navy, 19, Maryland

If you don't want to engage in breaking the law and your peers are calling you a chicken for not doing so, remember this: You're even more of a chicken if you give in to them. Think about the future, always! What are a few moments of excitement compared to the possible consequences?

—Brandon, 20, California

Growing up I got into drugs and stealing. I just needed to realize that I didn't have to do stupid things to make friends or impress them. Be yourself, don't let people push you over. Breaking the law is not worth it, believe me. Once you get caught, you'll wish you were dead or a different person.

—Lisa, 21, California

I was walking in a drug store with my mom and putting things in my jacket. At one point a security guard walked up to me and asked me to hand over the items. She then made me take her to my mom and tell my mom what I did. It was hell! I had to look my mom in the face and tell her I was shoplifting. Basically, all I can say is get a job and buy it yourself!

Legal Issues for Youth

Civil Rights Complaint Hotline
1-800-368-1019

National Juvenile Justice Clearinghouse 1-800-638-8736 (information and referrals about juvenile programs)

American Civil Liberties Union,
Children's Rights Project
132 W. 43rd St.
New York, NY 10035

Children's Defense Fund
Legal Division
1520 New Hampshire Ave., NW
Washington, DC 20036

Center for Law and Education
236 Massachusetts Ave., NE
Washington, DC 20002

National Child Labor Committee
1510 Broadway, Suite 1111
New York, NY 10036

National Juvenile Law Center
P.O. Box 14200
St. Louis, MO 63178

Student Press Law Center
1735 Eye St., NW
Washington, DC 20006

SYIN "RESPECT" Booklet
1772-20th Ave.
Seattle, WA 98122

Youth Law Center and National Center
for Youth Law
114 Sansome St., Suite 900
San Francisco, CA 94104-3820
(provides free information to youth
advocates about low-income children
and fights for them in the courts)

Kathleen Hempelman. *Teen Legal Rights: A Guide for the 90s.* Westport, CN: Greenwood Press, 1994.
(Explains your rights as a driver, at school, at home, on the job, in divorce, marriage, to an abortion and birth control, and to be safe from abuse.)

Masculism
(organizing to change the oppressive parts of the male sex role, using the model of feminism)

I asked leaders in the men's movement to discuss the impact of sex roles on teen boys (see also Chapter 6). Author Jack Kammer (*Good Will Toward Men*, St. Martin's) discusses **male options**.

Young women today have many options that they can at least dream about and hope for in their lives: full-time careers, full-time parenthood, and multiple arrangements over time. The same is generally much less true for young men. As they move into adulthood and feel the pressure to be attractive to women, they should be aware of the pressure they feel to limit their own options to maximize options for—and to be attractive to—women.

In the early days of feminism, many men were turned off by women who wanted to give up full-time homemaking to pursue equal careers. Similarly, in these early days of masculism, many women will be turned off by men who want to give up full-time money making to pursue equal parenthood. But if a young man can find a truly egalitarian woman, he is much less likely to suffer the downsides of the traditional male role, and much more likely to enjoy a healthy, balanced, happy life for himself, his wife, and his kids.

Young men interested in masculism might want to subscribe to the mailing list maintained by the National Coalition of Free Men. Join by e-mailing a request to ncfm@liii.com.

—Tom Williamson, president of National Coalition of Free Men explains the need for a **men's movement**.

What it is to be a man is not a settled question and there are a lot of mixed messages. For example, should you be the one who pays for the date? When I was in high school, most of us got our money from the allowances that our parents gave us. Some of the girls I dated came from neighborhoods that were a lot wealthier than the one I came from. It always bothered me that my dad was in effect paying for the good time of someone else's daughter who had ten times the money he did. What were these adults grooming me for?

Today more girls are paying their own way on dates, so at least that is changing, but what about other things? If a boy gives a girl unwanted looks that is called sexual harassment. But if a girl acts as a sexual tease her behavior is ignored. Why don't we hold girls responsible for their behavior?

What do men have to gain from gender equality? Think carefully about the expectations you have of others. Do you have friends who are shy around girls? If you don't have this problem, does this make you feel superior, or are you capable of empathizing with the guy who is not doing as well as you do? Do you not pay attention in class, because to do well academically is unmanly? If so, keep in mind that it is your perception of the expectations of others that is manipulating the way you act. It is not "you" who is in control.

Do you do things on a dare or do you have the character to walk away? Listen carefully the next time your peers use words like "chicken," "coward," "lacks balls," or "weenie." Watch the way these words change behavior in yourself and others. Always ask what is best for you. If you want to develop a legitimate sense of sensitivity and awareness, watch how these words can hurt other boys. Don't just think about how girls can get hurt, because they are supposed to be weaker. In the real world, sometimes girls are the stronger.

When you and other boys can begin to question these things and talk about it openly among yourselves, then men will be able to define for themselves what they want in a changing world and go after it in a respected way. Unlike for women, the serious questioning of men's roles is seen as unacceptable. There has been no supporting movement, such as the National Organization for Women, to give any guidance for how men should come to respectably question their role. "Coward" or "wimp" are words of disrespect reserved for men who have questioned their role. To insure that one's interests are formally looked after, men need organizations so they can band together in mutual support and achieve whatever it is that they want. That is the role of an organization like the National Coalition of Free Men.

Other branches of the men's movement are: Feminist Men (which includes NOMAS, National Organization of Men Against Sexism); Men's Rights (which includes NCFM); Father's Rights (child custody after divorce); the Mythopoetics (the people who gravitated to poet Robert Bly); and most recently, Religious (which includes Promise Keepers—right wing Christians; and Quakers, and Unitarian/Universalist—left wing Christians).

NCFM
P.O. Box 129
Manhasset, NY 11030
www.ncfm.org

NCFM recommends these books:

Francis Baumili. *Men Freeing Men: Exploding the Myth of the Traditional Male.* St. Louis, MO: New Atlantis Press, 1985. (out of print but can send check for $16.95 to 4 Ranch Lane, St. Louis, MO 63131)

Warren Farrell. *The Myth of Male Power.* NY: Simon and Schuster. 1993.

Herb Goldberg. *The Hazards of Being Male.* NY: New American Library, 1976.

David Thomas. *Not Guilty: The Case in Defense of Men.* NY: William Morrow, 1993.

(Other books about the male role and men's liberation are listed in Eugene August's reference book, *The New Men's Studies.* Littleton, CO: Libraries Unlimited, 1994.)

The American Men's Studies Association
329 Afton Ave.
Youngstown, OH
44512-2311
djrobins@cc.ysu.edu